Marti[illegible]

Marriage and Cohabitation
Regulating Intimacy, Affection and Care

The Family, Law & Society
Series Editor: Michael D Freeman

Titles in the Series:

Parents and Children
Andrew Bainham

Marriage and Cohabitation
Alison Diduck

The Multi-Cultural Family
Ann Laquer Estin

Domestic Violence
Michael Freeman

Resolving Family Conflicts
Jana Singer and Jane Murphy

Marriage and Cohabitation

Edited by

Alison Diduck

University College London, UK

ASHGATE

Wherever possible, these reprints are made from a copy of the original printing, but these can themselves be of very variable quality. Whilst the publisher has made every effort to ensure the quality of the reprint, some variability may inevitably remain.

Published by
Ashgate Publishing Limited
Wey Court East
Union Road
Farnham
Surrey GU9 7PT
England

Ashgate Publishing Company
Suite 420
101 Cherry Street
Burlington, VT 05401-4405
USA

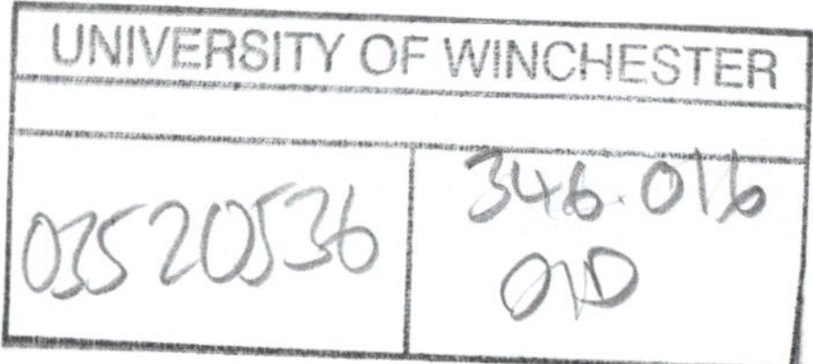

Ashgate website: http://www.ashgate.com

British Library Cataloguing in Publication Data
Marriage and cohabitation: regulating intimacy, affection and care. – (The family, law & society)
1. Marriage law 2. Unmarried couples – Legal status, laws, etc. 3. Gay couples – legal status, laws, etc.
I. Diduck, Alison
346'.016

Library of Congress Control Number: 2007941119

ISBN 978–0–7546–2680–0

Reprinted 2010

Printed and bound in Great Britain by
TJI Digital, Padstow, Cornwall

Contents

PART III WHY LEGAL REGULATION AT ALL?

PART IV LAW AND MARRIAGE

PART V LAW AND CIVIL REGISTRATION

PART VI LAW AND CONJUGAL COHABITATION

PART VII LAW AND NON-CONJUGAL RELATIONSHIPS

Acknowledgements

The editor and publishers wish to thank the following for permission to use copyright material.

Sage Publications Ltd for the essays: Elisabeth Beck-Gernsheim (1998), 'On the Way to a Post-Familial Family: From a Community of Need to Elective Affinities', *Theory, Culture & Society*, **15**, pp. 53–70. Copyright © 1998 Sage Publications Ltd; Lynn Jamieson (1999), 'Intimacy Transformed? A Critical Look at the "Pure Relationship"', *Sociology*, **33**, pp. 477–94. Copyright © 1999 Sage Publications Ltd; Sasha Roseneil and Shelley Budgeon (2004), 'Cultures of Intimacy and Care Beyond "the Family": Personal Life and Social Change in the Early 21st Century', *Current Sociology*, **52**, pp. 135–59. Copyright © 2004 Sage Publications Ltd.

Jordan Publishing Ltd for the essays: Mary Hibbs, Chris Barton and Joanne Beswick (2001), 'Why Marry? – Perceptions of the Affianced', *Family Law Journal*, **31**, pp. 197–207. Copyright © 2001 Jordan Publishing Ltd; Simon Duncan, Anne Barlow and Grace James (2005), 'Why Don't They Marry? Cohabitation, Commitment and DIY Marriage', *Child and Family Law Quarterly*, **17**, pp. 383–98. Copyright © 2005 Jordan Publishing Ltd; Brenda Hale (2004), 'Homosexual Rights', *Child and Family Law Quarterly*, **16**, pp. 125–34. Copyright © 2004 Jordan Publishing Ltd; Kenneth McK Norrie (2000), 'Marriage is for Heterosexuals – May the Rest of Us be Saved From it', *Child and Family Law Quarterly*, **12**, pp. 363–69. Copyright © 2000 Jordan Publishing Ltd; Lisa Glennon (2005), 'Displacing the "Conjugal Family" in Legal Policy – A Progressive Move?', *Child and Family Law Quarterly*, **17**, pp. 141–63. Copyright © 2005 Jordan Publishing Ltd.

The Editorial Board of the Sociological Review for the essay: Lynn Jamieson, Michael Anderson, David McCrone, Frank Bechhofer, Robert Stewart and Yaojun Li (2002), 'Cohabitation and Commitment: Partnership Plans of Young Men and Women', *Sociological Review*, **50**, pp. 356–77. Copyright © 2002 Editorial Board of the Sociological Review, published by Blackwell Publishing Ltd.

Blackwell Publishing Ltd for the essays: John Eekelaar and Mavis Maclean (2004), 'Marriage and the Moral Bases of Personal Relationships', *Journal of Law and Society*, **31**, pp. 510–38. Copyright © 2004 Blackwell Publishing Ltd; David McLellan (1996), 'Contract Marriage – The Way Forward or Dead End?', *Journal of Law and Society*, **23**, pp. 234–46. Copyright © 1996 Blackwell Publishing Ltd; Anne Barlow (2004), 'Regulation of Cohabitation, Changing Family Policies and Social Attitudes: A Discussion of Britain Within Europe', *Law & Policy*, **26**, pp. 57–86. Copyright © 2004 Blackwell Publishing Ltd; Cynthia Grant Bowman (2004), 'Legal Treatment of Cohabitation in the United States', *Law & Policy*, **26**, pp. 119–51. Copyright © 2004 Blackwell Publishing Ltd.

The UB Foundations Activities Inc. for the essay: Mavis Maclean and John Eekelaar (2005), 'The Significance of Marriage: Contrasts between White British and Ethnic Minority Groups in England', *Law &Policy*, **27**, pp. 379–98. Copyright © 2005 The UB Foundations Activities Inc. for and on behalf of the Baldy Centre for Law and Social Policy, and Blackwell Publishing Ltd.

The University of Rome for the essay: Bernadette Bawin-Legros and Anne Gauthier (2001), 'Regulation of Intimacy and Love Semantics in Couples Living Apart Together', *International Review of Sociology*, **11**, pp. 39–46. Copyright © 2001 The University of Rome 'La Sapienza', published by Taylor & Francis.

Oxford University Press for the essays: Stephen Parker (1987), 'The Marriage Act 1753: A Case Study in Family Law-Making', *International Journal of Law and the Family*, **1**, pp. 133–54. Copyright © 1987 Oxford University Press; Jane Lewis (2001), 'Debates and Issues Regarding Marriage and Cohabitation in the British and American Literature', *International Journal of Law, Policy and the Family*, **15**, pp. 159–84. Copyright © 2001 Oxford University Press; Ruth L. Deech (1980), 'The Case Against Legal Recognition of Cohabitation', *International and Comparative Law Quarterly*, **29**, pp. 480–97. Copyright © 1980 Oxford University Press; Claude Martin and Irène Théry (2001), 'The Pacs and Marriage and Cohabitation in France', *International Journal of Law, Policy and the Family*, **15**, pp. 135–58. Copyright © 2001 Oxford University Press.

Mary Lyndon Shanley for the essay: Mary Lyndon Shanley (2003), 'Just Marriage: On the Public Importance of Private Unions', *Boston Review*, **28**, pp. 1–13. Copyright © 2003 Mary Lyndon Shanley.

Wade K. Wright for the essay: Wade K. Wright (2006), 'The Tide in Favour of Equality: Same-Sex Marriage in Canada and England and Wales', *International Journal of Law, Policy and the Family*, **20**, pp. 1–37. Copyright © 2006 Wade K. Wright, published by Oxford University Press.

Virginia Law Review for the essay: Nancy D. Polikoff (1993), 'We Will Get What We Ask For: Why Legalizing Gay and Lesbian Marriage Will Not "Dismantle the Legal Structure of Gender in Every Marriage"', *Virginia Law Review*, **79**, pp. 1535–50. Copyright © 1993 Virginia Law Review.

Cambridge University Press for the essay: Sasha Roseneil (2004), 'Why We Should Care About Friends: An Argument for Queering the Care Imaginary in Social Policy', *Social Policy and Society*, **3**, pp. 409–19. Copyright © 2004 Cambridge University Press.

Every effort has been made to trace all the copyright holders, but if any have been inadvertently overlooked the publishers will be pleased to make the necessary arrangement at the first opportunity.

Series Preface

The family is a central, even an iconic, institution of society. It is the quintessentially private space said, by Christopher Lasch, to be a 'haven in a heartless world'. The meanings of 'family' are not constant, but contingent and often ambiguous. The role of the law in relation to the family also shifts; there is increasing emphasis on alternative dispute mechanisms and on finding new ways of regulation. Shifts have been detected (by Simon Roberts among others) from 'command' to 'inducement', but it is not a one-way process and 'command' may once again be in the ascendancy as the state grapples with family recalcitrance on such issues as child support and contact (visitation) arrangements. Family law once meant little more than divorce and its (largely) economic consequences. The scope of the subject has now broadened to embrace a complex of relationships. The 'family of law' now extends to the gay, the transgendered, 'beyond conjugality', perhaps towards friendship. It meets new challenges with domestic violence and child abuse. It has had to respond to new demands – from women for more equal norms, from the gay community for the right to marry, from children (or their advocates) for rights unheard of when children were conveniently parcelled as items of property. The reproduction revolution has forced family law to confront the meaning of parentage; no longer can we cling to seeing 'mother' and 'father' in unproblematic terms. Nor is family law any longer a 'discrete entity'; it now interfaces with medical law, criminal law, housing law and so on.

This series, containing volumes on marriage and other relationships (and not just cohabitation), on the parent–child relationship, on domestic violence, on methods of resolving family conflict and on pluralism within family law, reflects these tensions, conflicts and interfaces.

Each volume in the series contains leading and more out-of-the-way essays culled from a variety of sources. It is my belief, as also of the editors of individual volumes, that an understanding of family law requires us to go beyond conventional, orthodox legal literature – not that it is not relevant – and use is made of it. But to understand the context and the issues, it is necessary to reach beyond to specialist journals and to literature found in sociology, social administration, politics, philosophy, economics, psychology, history and so on. The value of these volumes lies in their coverage as they offer access to materials in a convenient form which will not necessarily be available to students of family law.

They also offer learned and insightful introductions, essays of value in their own right and focused bibliographies to assist the pursuit of further study and research. Together they constitute a library of the best contemporary family law scholarship and an opportunity to explore the highways and byways of the subject. The volumes will be valuable to scholars (and students) of a range of disciplines, not just those who confront family law within a law curriculum, and it is hoped they will stimulate further family law scholarship.

MICHAEL D. FREEMAN
University College London

Introduction

Ten, even five years ago, there probably would have been no subtitle to this book. Debate about the legal regulation of adult family affiliation in Britain centred around two options: marriage, which changed the legal status of the partners and with it the nature and extent of their rights and responsibilities to each other (and to other family members, to the state, to the market, and even to strangers or co-citizens), and conjugal cohabitation, which ascribed no legal status and attracted only ad hoc regulation. Same-sex partners and those who cared for another, loved another and/or committed themselves to another without co-residence or sexual intimacy were simply not recognized by law or family policy as 'partners' or families at all and so were left out of the debates entirely. But as we have heard repeatedly, relationships, *families*, seem to have changed in recent times, and these changes have demanded social and legal attention. Some say that families have changed to their detriment and to the detriment of society, while others say that the ways in which adults commit to each other and care for each other or `practise family' (Morgan, 1996) have always been variable (see, for example, Stephen Parker, Chapter 10 in this volume) and so the so-called changes are illusory. In any event, they would say, the so-called 'new family forms' we are living in now are not evidence so much of a breakdown in family but of an assertion of its centrality and its adaptability.

With the apparent increase in options for family living, or at least in the increased visibility of those options, have come questions about whether some or all of them ought to be subject to legal regulation and thus legitimation and, if so, what form that regulation ought to take. The subtitle to this volume, then, indicates that my intention in choosing the essays I have included is to examine those questions by providing a taste of the ways in which scholars have located marriage and cohabitation within a range of intimate affiliations in order to address them.

Marriage and Cohabitation?

Our changing family practices may be a result of changing social norms or may precede them. As Jane Lewis reminds us in Chapter 11, normative influences go both ways. Social norms interact with legal ones so that the effects of discourses of individualization, rights, equality or care can be uncovered in both. Those influences may be direct and obvious, as in the Law Commission of England and Wales's mandate (2006) to find a way to recognize legally demographic changes in cohabitation behaviour, or they may be more subtle such as the way in which the continuing social and ideological primacy of marriage is reflected in that same mandate. Indeed, to recognize, even to celebrate, different ways of organizing our intimate lives does not mean that traditional heterosexual marriage has lost either its appeal or its idealized[1] status in the public imagination or in legal and social policy.

---

1 O'Donovan (1993, p. 44) calls it a 'sacred, magical status'.

Marriage is still an aspiration for many people, straight, gay or lesbian. Indeed, Patricia Morgan (2000, p. 6) tells us that 90 per cent of young people in Britain want to marry and that having a `good marriage' as a life goal has increased in importance for young people,[2] and researchers from the (David) Morgan Centre for the Study of Relationships and Personal Life report that a large minority of their same-sex couple respondents had hoped that marriage, rather than civil partnership, would have been made available to them by law (Smart *et al.*, 2006, p. 2). Apparently, the attraction of marriage is obvious: it is associated with love and so is a romantic ideal (Mary Hibbs *et al.*, Chapter 3 in this volume; Diduck, 2003), and as a happy bonus, we are also told that marriage is good for us physically, emotionally and financially (Waite and Gallagher, 2000). Marriage is also associated with embarking upon a joint project with someone, with sharing one's life with someone, with *commitment* to that project or that person. (Mary Hibbs *et al.*, Chapter 3; John Eekelaar and Mavis Maclean, Chapter 6; Mavis Maclean and John Eekelaar, Chapter 7, all in this volume; see also Berger and Kellner, 1964; Diduck, 2003; Diduck and Kaganas, 2006). In 2003 the majority of people in England and Wales over age 16 had achieved this goal; 51.7 per cent of us were married (ONS, 2006b, p. 78) and while in 2006 there was a 4 per cent drop in marriages from the previous year in England and Wales (ONS, 2008a), that drop followed a four-year rise in the marriage rate (ONS, 2008b; ONS, 2006a, p. 71).

Marriage seems to remain popular, yet at the same time cohabitation has also increased in acceptability. Only 25 years ago unmarried cohabitation was contrasted in the academic literature with marriage; it was said to be qualitatively different from marriage and to engender different expectations (Ruth Deech, Chapter 13; see also Freeman and Lyon, 1983). Cohabitation was understood as a relationship that created and required less commitment on the part of its participants. It was thought to be frivolous, contingent or temporary, and certainly to be less stable than marriage, and thus merited the social and legal disregard, if not disapproval, it received (Ruth Deech, Chapter 13; Barlow *et al.*, 2005; Morgan, 2000). Since then, however, surveys report that cohabitation with no intent to marry is acceptable to 80 per cent of people under age 35 (Simon Duncan *et al.*, Chapter 4) and in 2004 24 per cent of non-married men and 25 per cent of non-married women aged 16–59 in Great Britain were cohabiting (Law Commission, 2006, p. 28, para. 2.6). One could be forgiven, in the light of these statistics, for suggesting that cohabitation has now emerged as the first acceptable example of those 'new family forms' of which scholars are writing, but although the family 'box' itself may look different, its contents look remarkably familiar. When cohabiting heterosexual couples were asked why they did not marry only a minority reported disapproval of marriage as an institution, or of the ideals of marriage (Lynn Jamieson, Chapter 2; Simon Duncan *et al.*, Chapter 4; John Eekelaar and Mavis Maclean, Chapter 6). Most couples approve of and desire the contents of the marriage 'box' – commitment, sharing, companionship, sexual intimacy – but they simply see the box itself as irrelevant to them. Indeed, where marriage is an option, many cohabitants just do not bother; they see themselves as being 'as good as married' (Simon Duncan *et al.*, Chapter 4).

---

2 She doesn't tell us, however, what she or these respondents mean by a 'good marriage'. Perhaps this omission is significant; perhaps it is evidence of marriage's continued iconic status – we all just 'know' what makes a good marriage.

Kiernan (2002) identifies a four-stage process as patterns of heterosexual partnership shift. The first stage is when cohabitation is viewed as an unusual habit of a small minority; the second stage is cohabitation as a prelude to marriage; the third is cohabitation as a relationship that is socially accepted as an alternative to marriage; and the fourth is cohabitation as indistinguishable from marriage in terms of commitment and parenting. Kiernan speculates that Britain is currently in between stages three and four. If this view is accurate, then the question now seems to be not how, if at all, cohabitation is to be regarded as an alternative to marriage, but how it has come to be a variety of marriage. If cohabitation has lost its early association with rebellion, transgression or alternativeness, then there seems to be no reason to distinguish between it and marriage for legal purposes (see on this Ruth Deech, Chapter 13; Stephen Parker, Chapter 10).

On the other hand, there are still conjugal cohabitants who make a conscious choice not to marry. For some, its gendered, hierarchical, heteronormative or other institutional characteristics make marriage distasteful to them personally (see, for example, Lynn Jamieson, Chapter 2; Simon Duncan *et al.*, Chapter 4; Lynn Jamieson *et al.*, Chapter 5). Others perceive marriage as an emotional or economic risk that they are not yet ready to take (Lewis, 2005; Smart and Stevens, 2000). Many lone mothers, for example, see their partners as not yet marriageworthy – for them, cohabitation represents a sensible arrangement combining independence for them and a father for their children (Smart and Stevens 2000). For these people, distinguishing legally between marriage and cohabitation makes social, emotional and financial 'sense'.

Still other cohabitants are not able legally to marry. For example, marriage is not (yet? – see Wade Wright, Chapter 17; Brenda Hale, Chapter 12) available to same-sex partners in the UK, yet many have demonstrated its appeal by choosing the alternative to marriage that became available to them in 2005. Between 5 December 2005 when the Civil Partnership Act came into force and 31 December 2006, 18,059 civil partnerships were registered in the UK (ONS, 2007). Civil partnership is only available to same-sex partners and gives couples most of the rights and responsibilities of marriage. While the government was clear that civil partnership was not marriage by another name, Smart *et al.*'s research (2006) demonstrates the strength of the marriage ideal; many of the same-sex couples in their study referred to their civil partnerships as 'marriages' and most expressed 'traditional' reasons, such as public proclamation of commitment, for entering into them.

We see thus far that marriage, civil registration and cohabitation now appear to be socially 'acceptable' lifestyle choices in Britain. Unsurprisingly, however, the choices, even if less accepted, do not end there. For many, being a part of a couple and sharing one's life with another does not require either state sanction or cohabitation. 'Living apart together' (LAT) has become a recognized sociological and demographic term (see Bernadette Bawin-Legros and Anne Gauthier, Chapter 8; Haskey, 2005) and researchers in Britain are beginning to explore its legal and social policy implications (Haskey and Lewis, 2006). According to Haskey (2005) around one in three people aged 16–59 who are neither co-residentially cohabiting nor married and living with their spouse are in a LAT relationship (see also Haskey and Lewis, 2006). Many choose to enter into these relationships and many are forced into them by employment or other circumstances, but maintaining independence while at the same time being in a 'relationship' is a common feature. Unlike cohabitation and civil partnership, both of which remain marriage-like, 'living apart together' challenges one of the markers of marriage/conjugal coupledom by disassociating it from common residence. In this way, LAT, unlike contemporary cohabitation, may be a real example of a new way to affiliate. Perhaps like cohabitants did years ago, those living in a committed, sexually exclusive, intimate yet non-co-residential relationship must learn to manage their version of autonomous intimacy with external norms of what it means to be a 'couple' (Bernadette Bawin-Legros and Anne Gauthier, Chapter 8). Perhaps, also like cohabitants, by doing so they may yet effect changes in the normative requirements of 'coupledom'.

Sasha Roseneil and Shelley Budgeon in Chapter 9 challenge the conjugal imaginary even further. They and others (see, for example, Carl Stychin, Chapter 23; Weeks, 2002) suggest that, particularly but probably not exclusively within the 'homosexual community', friends offer the 'emotional continuity, companionship, pleasure and practical assistance' (p. 152) usually characteristic of partners. This destabilizing or blurring of the friend/lover binary may be yet another way in which intimacy is being transformed. It may be intimacy and commitment between 'friends, non-monogamous lovers, ex-lovers, partners who do not live together, partners who do not have sex together ... [that come to] decentre the primary significance that is commonly granted to sexual partnerships and mount a challenge to the privileging of conjugal relationships in research on intimacy' (p. 152) and in law and policy. We must even, according to Felicity Kaganas and Christina Murray in Chapter 21, open our minds to the possibility of polygynous relationships. At least, we must be clear about the reasons for social, moral and legal disapproval of them. By disassociating intimacy, affection and care from the conjugal, co-residential couple of the marriage model, these 'non-normative intimacies' may yet transform family/partnership/marriage norms in a way that cohabitation and civil partnership have yet to do.

Theorizing the Changes

Sociology is now, or again (Smart and Neale, 1999), interested in families and relationships and may be able to provide some explanation for, or at least insight into, our changing family practices. Social and political theory is also beginning to explore the relationships among intimacies, the responsibilities they engender and their relationships with ideas of democracy and citizenship (Fudge and Cossman, 2002). Many of these approaches identify individualization as the key phenomenon at the end of the twentieth century that affected our relationships with the state and the international polity as much as it did our relationships with intimates (see, for example, Jane Lewis, Chapter 11; Smart and Neale, 1999). Beck and Beck-Gernsheim (1995), for example, identify individualization, globalization and women's liberation as primary factors in what they see as our need constantly to make and remake our biographies, our identities and relationships. To them, our biographies and the commitments and relationships we choose in relation to them are flexible, unwritten, personal works in progress and have produced 'post-familial families'. These families have moved from being communities of need to elective affinities. As Elisabeth Beck-Gernsheim puts it in Chapter 1 (p. 17):

> Since individualization also fosters a longing for the opposite world of intimacy, security and closeness ... most people will continue ... to live within a partnership or family. But such ties are not the same as before, in their scope or in their degree of obligation and permanence. ... As people make choices, negotiating and deciding the everyday details of do-it-yourself relationships, a 'normal chaos' of love, suffering and diversity is growing and developing.

Another influential perspective has come from Anthony Giddens (1992), who also sees relationships changing as individualization becomes more reflexive. He described revolutions in sex, love and gender relations as producing a 'transformation of intimacy' in which relationships last only as long as the partners continue to get something from them. Obligation and commitment in relationships become negotiable rather than remaining static and externally imposed. To him, these 'pure relationships' based upon contingent, 'confluent love' may be more fragile than traditional relationships based upon romantic love, but they are also more democratic and fulfilling. Jeffrey Weeks (2002) uses these ideas to identify 'families of choice' within the gay and lesbian communities, and speculates that these new affinities could come to define all forms of intimacy.

These theories of late modernity highlight social change, risk and disembeddedness as the conditions of the time and they postulate changes in our ways of living to cope with these conditions. These changes mean a new importance in relationships of intimacy for negotiability, individuality and the search for an authentic and fulfilled self (see Lewis, 2001). For the most part, however, these social theorists are not doomsayers; Giddens, for example, declares that the pure relationship is a more democratic family form than the traditional family and Beck-Gernsheim's post-familial family does not signal the end of family, but simply its taking on a new form.

These theorists contrast with others who see similar historical changes occurring, but see them as dangerous. Scott FitzGibbon in Chapter 14, for example, identifies a similar crisis at the end of the twentieth century in which individuality and disaffiliation became contrasted with obligation/duty, but his solution, like Regan's (1999) and Morgan's (2000), is to reassert the good of marriage and the obligation that inheres in it. Rather than acknowledge and support the post-familial family, these authors say that there are both moral and social reasons why law and policy must discourage it and encourage individuals towards marriage and the traditional family (see also Finnis, 1994; Morgan, 2000).

Yet others query whether individualization has been as dominant a trend either socially or personally as is commonly believed (Lynn Jamieson, Chapter 2; Smart, 2007). Most, however, agree on the value of continued theorizing of intimacy and family life. Theorization generates a refinement of ideas and excites innovative empirical work and recent theory, including individualization theory, for example, has injected debate and excitement into the study of families and relationships (Smart, 2007, pp. 24–25).

The Empirical Research

There is a burgeoning body of empirical research to accompany or flesh out both the demographic studies which confirm that people are exercising a broad range of choices in forming relationships and the social and theoretical research that attempts to understand what these choices mean personally and socially. Some of this research, such as that in Part II of this volume, examines and assesses the meaning for people of different forms of relationship, the functions their relationships serve for them and the importance of principles such as self-fulfilment, commitment, obligation, tradition, security, autonomy or sharing in different types of relationships. While some research, including that of Lynn Jamieson in Chapter 2 of this volume, suggests that the pure relationship is more a sociological ideal than a new type of relationship, other research suggests that individualization, globalization and changing gender norms may indeed have changed the way we form, negotiate and structure our relationships. They have not, however, so clearly affected the values we bring to them. Commitment is still important to people (Lewis, 2001), risk is still avoided (Lewis, 2005) and gender roles in partnerships continue to belie their supposed equality, democracy or confluence (Lynn Jamieson, Chapter 2).

Part II includes a selection of recent empirical studies, many of which, contrary to the 'decline of family' pessimists – those who link the perceived rise in individualism with the decline in commitment and family values – demonstrate that values such as commitment, obligation and sharing remain important for people. While marriage is for many still the 'highest' form of commitment, obligation and commitment to a shared life project remain fundamental to a good relationship. In other words, cohabitants tend to be as committed to the relationship or to a partner as married people, even though their commitment may take a slightly different form or be perceived as coming from within rather than imposed normatively (see Lewis, 2001). In Chapter 4 Simon Duncan *et al.*, for example, find that most of their cohabiting respondents felt `as good as married' (see also Lynn Jamieson *et al.*, Chapter 5); they had embarked upon, and were committed to, a shared life plan or experience and had constructed what the authors call a 'DIY marriage'. Their choices about whether to marry or not had less to do with the level of commitment, love or obligation they felt to their partners than with the personal and structural context in which they were able to express those values (see also Lewis, 2005; Smart and Stevens, 2000).[3]

This empirical research is important evidence of how social norms may indeed have changed in 'late modernity' and may be important signals for law- and policy-makers who are concerned that legal changes 'make sense' to people (John Eekelaar and Mavis Maclean, Chapter 6; Mavis Maclean and John Eekelaar, Chapter 7; Jane Lewis, Chapter 11). The research also reminds us that people make a series of different choices over the course of their lifetimes. The snapshot captured by the statistics at any point in time does not reflect the actual messiness of family practices or the myriad ways both 'rational' factors, like economic well-being, and 'irrational' ones, like love, wax, wane and interact in individual lives.

Legal Responses

Notwithstanding the range of partnering practices theorized and lived, so far legal and policy 'space' has been created only for those relationships that are 'marriage-like' (Cossman and Ryder, 2001). The Civil Partnership Act is the clearest example of legal norms responding to newly created social ones,[4] but cohabitation without registration or marriage is another. To the then newly elected Labour government in 1998, it was almost as good as marriage:

---

3 In this context, see also Gary Becker's classic pieces analysing marriage (1973) and caring between mates, polygamy, separation, divorce and remarriage (1974) from an economic perspective. He presents a model of marriage that assumes '(1) that each person tries to find a mate who maximizes his or her well-being, with well-being measured by the consumption of household produced commodities, and (2) the "marriage market" is assumed to be in equilibrium, in the sense that no person could exchange mates and be better off' (1974, p. 811).

4 But as the DTI also said, the Act was also intended to help combat homophobia by normalizing same-sex relationships.

> This Government believes that marriage provides a strong foundation for stable relationships. This does not mean trying to make people marry, or criticising or penalising people who choose not to do so. We do not believe the government should interfere in people's lives in that way. But we do share the belief of the majority of people that marriage provides the most reliable framework for raising children. (Home Office, 1998, para. 4.3)

And so, almost ten years later the UK government, belatedly perhaps compared to countries like Australia, Canada, Sweden and France, acknowledged that the increasing number of cohabitants cannot be ignored and that their relationships, or rather the breakdown of their relationships, have social and legal consequences.[5] In 2005 it asked the Law Commission to consider reform of the law governing cohabitants' property and finances when their relationships end (Law Commission 2006, p. 17, para. 1.3). The Consultation Document, published in May 2006, endorsed the 'official' incongruent view of marriage and cohabitation, and while the Commission found justification for the legal regulation of cohabitants' post-separation financial issues, it did not recommend simply extending matrimonial law to cohabitants in the way it was extended to civil partners. That solution, said the Law Commission, may not pay sufficient respect to marriage as an institution (Law Commission, 2007). Marriage (and, apparently, civil partnership) presupposes a type of partnership that is not appropriate for cohabitants (Law Commission, 2006, Overview; Law Commission, 2007).[6]

Non-conjugal homesharers, on the other hand, still befuddle the official view (Law Commission, 2002), friends are not yet a part of the 'family' picture and LATs are only beginning to appear on the policy radar (Haskey, 2005). Again, though, it may be simply a matter of time before all of these different family or partnering choices are taken seriously. Researchers in Sweden and Korea, for example, have concluded that LAT is 'not so much a stage but a different kind of partnering' (Haskey and Lewis, 2006, p. 38) and the Law Commission of Canada published a report in 2002 seeking ways in which rights and responsibilities might be allocated independently of relational status, specifically excluding conjugality as a relevant factor in the allocation (see also Lisa Glennon's discussion of this report, in Chapter 27). While none of these countries may yet be at the stage, for example, where government frames 'work–life balance policies ... in terms of the range of important personal relationships and commitments within which people live their lives, rather than narrowly with reference to family responsibilities' (Sasha Roseneil, this volume, p. 559), it will be interesting to see if changing social practices may yet effect some normative change.

Until then, marriage-like conjugality remains the focus of legal attention. Most of the research on this area in this volume is British, but the preoccupation with changing family norms and changing family practices is not only a British phenomenon. Questions about the legal regulation of changing intimacies have increased all over the world and they have not always produced coherent answers. Even within a single, albeit federal, state there may be inconsistencies of approach (Cynthia Bowman, Chapter 25; Lisa Glennon, Chapter 27).

---

[5] Until this time, it seemed to be only academic researchers and the Law Society (2001), those who worked on the 'front lines', and so saw that unmarried cohabitation had enormous financial consequences upon partners and children, who were interested in legislative reform in this area.

[6] It suggests that marriage, unlike cohabitation, creates an obligation to meet a former partner's needs (Law Commission, 2006, Overview, paras 3.62 and 3.63).

In the USA official federal government policy is to promote marriage (even to make receipt of welfare dependent upon it) yet, from state to state, there is no consistency in policy. As Cynthia Bowman explains in Chapter 25, unmarried cohabitation is recognized legally in a number of states and same-sex marriage is legal in a few, but the overall position is uneven. She describes the 'immense variety' of approaches that 'range from one extreme, where cohabitants have no rights against one another or third parties, to the other extreme, under which cohabitants are treated as though they were married for all purposes of state law' (p. 519). She describes the variability as creating legal instability, but is not overly pessimistic about what that instability might mean. While on the one hand it creates not only conflicts of law problems but also differences in treatment between same and different sex couples that are increasingly difficult to justify, on the other it may open up the possibility of change so that family law can perform successfully its two functions, which, in Bowman's view, are protecting the vulnerable and privatizing the costs of welfare (p. 544). These functions are themselves controversial and I return below to the social functions that families, and by extension family law, ought to play, but suffice it to say at this point that Bowman's review of the unstable state of US law makes another point. Her review demonstrates simultaneously the range of legal options available to normalize different partnership practices *and* the ease with which debate about them becomes polarized into one of marriage/not marriage.

Nancy Polikoff's recent work (2007) criticizes precisely that formulation of the question. She challenges those who advocate same-sex marriage in order to obtain the legal benefits of marriage. While in this work she supports same-sex marriage (cf. her earlier work, Chapter 20), she does so only on civil rights grounds while at the same time arguing that no couples should have to marry in order to obtain legal benefits. For her, as a matter of family policy, marriage is the wrong fight; there are other ways to solve the problems that same-sex couples describe – ways which would not discriminate against all other family types.

In Chapter 24 Anne Barlow describes variability in the laws across Europe, some of which move outside the stark marriage/not marriage dichotomy. Some state laws reflect the plurality of couple relationships, while others offer no response at all to changing family forms and norms (p. 489). She describes four approaches that laws could take. The first, exemplified by Italy and Ireland, is no recognition of any relationship other than the heterosexual marital one. The second is laws that regulate and recognize relationships based upon 'function plus form' and includes places like Sweden (and perhaps soon, England and Wales), which deal with relationship breakdown in those relationships that 'do family' appropriately. Thus Swedish legislation gives rights to cohabitants in relationships 'reminiscent of marriage' (p. 492) and permits same-sex couples to register their partnerships, giving them rights corresponding to marriage. Barlow's third category is the `diverse marriage model' which began in the Netherlands and may now include Spain and Germany. This model does not allocate rights or recognition according to function, but simply extends the marriage form to more people. It first applied to registered partnerships of all cohabitants and now permits same-sex marriage. The fourth model, arguably the only one to challenge the meaning of 'couple' by removing it from the marriage 'box', Barlow calls 'the new style couple registration'. She places France and Belgium in this category. The French *Pacte Civil de Solidarité* (Pacs) is perhaps the best illustration of this model.

The Pacs is an agreement signed by two people, whether living in a conjugal relationship or not but who are not related to each other or already married or 'pacsed', to determine their property relations both during and at termination of the Pacs. They must also agree to provide mutual assistance and support. Unlike marriage or civil registration, a Pacs can be ended unilaterally. The Pacs thus seems to create a whole new, if indefinable, type of relationship. As Claude Martin and Irène Théry state in Chapter 22, 'The Pacs is neither a legal union nor a simple property contract. It is neither public nor private. It is neither for couples nor for pairs of friends. It is neither a legal recognition of same-sex couples nor is it non-recognition' (p. 446). Although it was the result of strong lobbying from the 'homosexual community' in France, it is not confined to same-sex partners. The Pacs is thus a new kind of universally available relationship, but, according to Martin and Théry, it is its very universality that dilutes the equality rights of lesbian and gay couples. Despite its basis in the principle of 'republican equality', because such partners have no other way to effect a legal union, they are, in effect, accorded a weaker version of equality and dignity than in countries where marriage or registration of exclusively same-sex relationships is possible (see also Lisa Glennon, Chapter 27 and Polikoff, 2007 on this point).

Martin and Théry provide a fascinating study of the history of the Pacs and highlight the role of politics, demographics and lobbying by interest groups in its formation. Carl Stychin's study of Britain's Civil Partnership Act 2004 (CPA) in Chapter 23 provides us with a similar history, but from the perspective of queer theory. Stychin sees the CPA as founded upon and exhibiting a number of dichotomies, which, we might say, reflect the ideological, political and social struggles around all new relationships. The Act is located upon both sides of binaries such as 'marriage/not marriage; sex/no sex; status/contract; conjugality/care; love/money; responsibilities/rights' (p. 460). This placement means that registered civil partnerships may be both normative and non-normative partnerships; they are certainly an example of the compromise taken by many states in recognizing same-sex relationships.

And so, despite looking remarkably like marriage, civil registration is not the same as marriage. Marriage, Stychin reminds us, is still the ideal family form, and the government made clear the distinction between it and civil partnership when it promoted the legislation.

> The Bill does not undermine or weaken the importance of marriage and we do not propose to open civil partnership to opposite sex couples. Civil partnership is aimed at same-sex couples who cannot marry ... [W]e continue to support marriage and recognise that it is the surest foundation for opposite-sex couples raising children. (Quoted in Stychin, this volume, pp. 460–61)

Instead, the Act is justified on the basis of equality, non-discrimination and rights. A close analysis of it, however, reveals that it does more than simply provide for most of the same rights and responsibilities as marriage. Because it resides on both sides of the marriage/not marriage binary, it both raises questions about the meaning of 'couple' in the family context (the CPA requires neither conjugality nor co-residence), *and* increases the primacy of the conjugal co-resident, traditional heterosexual couple. This primacy is further confirmed when Smart *et al.* (2006) tell us that many registered partners call their partnerships 'marriage'.

Most of the authors in this volume agree that the decision to regulate relationships and the form that regulation takes have much to do with the degree to which law is perceived as being able to influence behaviour. In Chapter 24 Anne Barlow speculates that a state's response to changing relationships may depend upon its view of whether law is an effective tool for moralizing people, or at least for influencing their intimate behaviour. Others agree (for example Stephen Parker, Chapter 10; Lewis, 2001) and suggest also that the form regulation takes says something about individual citizenship and the links between political ideals and the private sphere (Claude Martin and Irène Théry, Chapter 22; Carl Stychin, Chapter 23; Cossman, 2002). This insight may explain the approach to same-sex relationships adopted in Britain, when it is compared with the French alternative. In Chapter 23 Stychin locates the Pacs within the 'French ideology of republicanism and universality. It is justified as a universally applicable contract to which all are equally entitled to participate on the basis of being members of the Republic' (p. 463). By contrast, the UK's 'multicultural ideology' resulted in the Civil Partnership Act, which is 'focused on remedying the problems of specific, targeted communities' (p. 467).

The question of whether intimacy is ever entirely governable or ungovernable, of course, flows from the question of whether it ought to be governed at all. There are those, like Ruth Deech, in Chapter 13, and Weitzman (1981), who argue that the regulation of intimacy must remain a personal matter between the partners and that they must be able to contract the terms of their partnership without interference from the state. Others, like Mary Shanley (Chapter 15) and Scott FitzGibbon (Chapter 14), suggest that the symbolic and normative roles of law are important, and if we agree, for example, that marriage is a good, then it must be promoted and privileged publicly and legally. Still others would examine the good to be promoted. We have seen that marriage seems to have become personally irrelevant to many people, even though commitment has not. People's behaviour and obligations, their *commitment to commitment*, remain strong and may now be prescribed by being in a relationship, of whatever form, rather than in a marriage. And so, even if there is an inherent 'good' in obligation, even if acceptance of obligation is what it means to be a person, is part of the human good, as Scott FitzGibbon (Chapter 14) says, we must question whether marriage or indeed any prescribed form of relationship is either a necessary or sufficient context for its acceptance (John Eekelaar and Mavis Maclean, Chapter 6). Mavis Maclean and John Eekelaar's empirical research, presented in Chapter 7, uncovers people's values and reasons for behaving the way they do and while noting that ethnic differences may exist in the routes taken to perceptions of responsibility and obligation in marriage, the end result is basically the same.

It has also been argued that other 'goods' usually located in public, civil and political relations are also important within intimate relations and that law ought to promote those. Brenda Hale (Chapter 12), Lisa Glennon (Chapter 27) and Wade Wright (Chapter 17) argue that the norms of equality, non-discrimination and rights that have come to define public or political relations ought to be applied to intimate relations as well, at least to the extent of making marriage a legitimate choice for all who desire it (see also Polikoff, 2007). In Chapter 21 Felicity Kaganas and Christina Murray also use this argument in order to re-evaluate Western opposition to polygyny. They say that recourse to simple gender equality arguments may not be a sufficient basis to outlaw these relationships without taking adequate account of the context in which these partnership choices are made.

Others argue that the relationships themselves may be enriched and democratized by public and legal statements about them (Diduck, 2008; Eekelaar, 2006). In Chapter 15 Mary Shanley accepts the feminist critique of marriage as promoting gendered roles that lead to women's economic subordination, but argues that only if marriage is regulated publicly can it reflect and incorporate public norms of equality and rights. In this way, both marriage law and other laws such as employment and child care laws can change to transform the institution of marriage. To her, the institution is important. She, like Regan (1999) believes that the marital partnership is not reducible to, or identical with, its individual components. It creates 'a right to provide … and receive care' (p. 296).

It has been suggested by others that marriage publicity or regulation simply cannot perform those functions. Nancy Polikoff (Chapter 20) and Kenneth Norrie (Chapter 19), for example, argue that the gendered and sexed nature of marriage means that making it available to same-sex partners would simply assimilate those relationships to a heterosexual norm and deny any transformative power they might otherwise have socially and potentially legally. Lisa Glennon in Chapter 27 adds another perspective to this argument when she suggests that only after same-sex marriage is achieved legally should critics begin to advocate other, more potentially transformative partnership forms (see also Polikoff, 2007). In general, however, most authors in this collection agree that beliefs about marriage and relationships (and presumably laws about marriage and relationships) help to shape our understanding of other social institutions (see, for example, Martha Fineman, Chapter 18, p. 359), especially gender and sex (Carl Stychin, Chapter 23). They differ only on the degree to which they are prepared to concede this regulation to the state.

Whereas for Mary Shanley in Chapter 15 public regulation of marriage is a means to equality in relationships, Martha Fineman in Chapter 18, like Polikoff and Norrie, believes that marriage writes too many gender scripts and she advocates abolishing it as a legal category (see also Diduck and Kaganas, 2006). Marriage has, for Fineman, been an acceptable way for the state and for individuals to manage dependency, but it has been a way which has depended upon the subordination and often exploitation of women's unpaid labour. She proposes that intimate relations require no specific laws; that the dependencies or vulnerabilities they engender can be dealt with adequately by existing laws of contract, tort, equity and so on. She does not advocate private contract as the exclusive means by which the state retreats from regulating intimacy, as this form of self-regulation has its own difficulties. These are highlighted forcefully by David McLellan in Chapter 16. Apart from the problematic assumption of equality of bargaining power and the practical difficulties involved in enforcement of marriage contracts, he raises important questions about the assumptions that a contract model of relationships makes about the nature of the individual, how she exercises her choices in the bargain, the nature of relationships and the type of society contract presupposes.

Fineman's query in Chapter 18 as to why marriage has provoked so much agitation for legislators across time and place may, in fact, be a tidy way of reframing all our questions about regulating intimacy, dependency and care. She, like many of the authors here, argues that we must be clear about the meaning we assign to marriage before we assess its value, socially or personally. 'This type of consideration forces our focus away from the nature or form of the marital relationship to the role or function we want the institution to serve in our society' (p. 356). The empirical research by Lynn Jamieson in Chapter 2 shows us that, for the individuals concerned, marriage can mean anything from a relationship of hierarchy and subordination to a means of self-fulfilment to an economic relationship to an expression of religious faith, but it has multiple meanings for society as well. Fineman recounts some of them: the imposition of order for record-keeping purposes; the domestication of unruly sexuality; providing a symbol of religious or cultural convention or a site for the reproductive and caring tasks that are essential in any society (p. 354). It is clear that these functions, both social and personal, can be and are being performed by relationships other than marriage.

It is also clear that these functions are not new, as Stephen Parker demonstrates in Chapter 10 about the movements behind the development of England's first secular law regulating marriage.

Inquiring about the functions of relationships confirms that the question about whether intimacy ought ever to be regulated depends upon what we want the relationship or its regulation to accomplish. The inquiry also confirms the importance of gender and sex to the economic and other consequences for the parties *and* for civil society and the state, of the relationship and its regulation or non-regulation (Martha Fineman, Chapter 18; Cossman, 2002; Diduck, 2005).

Conclusions

At this point I cautiously express two conclusions to readers of this volume. The first is perhaps obvious: that people's choices about their family and partnering practices do not and cannot exist outside of social or legal norms and the social and economic conditions in which they encounter them. Attempts by law or social policy to influence those choices may have some success, but it is just as likely that family practices themselves influence legal change. Preferences and choices both reflect and remake legal and social norms and partnering decisions are made and remade in these always complicated personal and social contexts.

The second conclusion is about the traditional understanding of relationships as private affairs. The essays in this volume demonstrate that our new partnership practices and legal treatment of them have in common a lack of respect for the separation of public and private. Apart from the by now accepted view that family matters are never entirely private, the research in this collection reveals the extent to which the traditional view of partnering as a private and personal matter with which law must not interfere expresses neither people's experiences nor their wishes. As feminist scholars have always argued, intimacy, or at least its consequences, *is* a matter of public concern. Forms of intimacy affect the well-being of individuals and of the state, they are expressions of personal, political and moral choices, they influence one's political engagement and citizenship and they are profound regulators of sex and gender.

These conclusions bring me back to the subtitle of this volume. Perhaps the family practices explored in this collection really *are* about marriage and cohabitation after all, or are at least about what marriage and cohabitation traditionally symbolize: legal acceptance of our relationships or legal disregard of them. Or alternatively, rather than raise questions about how relationships like civil partnership, cohabitation, living apart together or non-conjugal intimacy are given social and legal meaning similar to or distinct from marriage, they may actually raise questions about the previously taken for granted social and legal meanings of those elements of intimacy once thought exclusive to marriage, such as coupledom, commitment, caretaking or co-residence.

References

Barlow, A., Duncan, S., James, G. and Park, A. (2005), *Cohabitation, Marriage and the Law*, Oxford: Hart Publishing.
Beck, U. and Beck-Gernsheim, E. (1995), *The Normal Chaos of Love*, Cambridge: Polity.
Becker, G.S. (1973), 'A Theory of Marriage: Part I', *Journal of Political Economy*, **81**(4), pp. 813–46.
Becker G.S. (1974), 'A Theory of Marriage Part II, *Journal of Political Economy*, **82**(2), pp. S11–S26.
Berger, P.L. and Kellner, H. (1964), 'Marriage and the Construction of Reality', *Diogenes*, **46**, pp. 1–24.
Cossman, B. (2002), 'Family Feuds: Neo-Liberal and Neo-Conservative Visions of the Reprivatization Project', in J. Fudge and B. Cossman (eds), *Privatization, Law and the Challenge to Feminism*, Toronto: University of Toronto Press.
Cossman, B. and Ryder, B. (2001), 'What is Marriage-like Like? The Irrelevance of Conjugality', *Canadian Journal of Family Law*, **18**, pp. 269–326.
Diduck, Alison (2003), *Law's Families*, Cambridge: Cambridge University Press.
Diduck, Alison (2005), 'Shifting Familiarity', *Current Legal Problems*, **58**, pp. 235–54.
Diduck, Alison (2008), 'Family Law and Family Responsibility', in J. Bridgeman, C. Lind and H. Keating (eds), *Responsibility, Law and the Family*, Aldershot: Ashgate, pp. 251–68.
Diduck, A. and Kaganas, F. (2006), *Family Law, Gender and the State*, Oxford: Hart Publishing.
Eekelaar, John (2006), *Family Law and Personal Life*, Oxford: Oxford University Press.
Finnis, J. (1994), 'Law, Morality and Sexual Orientation', *Notre Dame Law Review*, **69**, pp. 1066–76.
Freeman, M.D.F. and Lyon, C.M. (1983), *Cohabitation Without Marriage*, Aldershot: Gower.
Fudge, J. and Cossman, B. (eds) (2002), *Privatization, Law and the Challenge to Feminism*, Toronto: University of Toronto Press.
General Register Office (GRO) (2006), News Release, 23 June, ONS, London.
Giddens, Anthony (1992), *The Transformation of Intimacy*, Cambridge: Polity.
Haskey, John (2005), 'Living Arrangements in Contemporary Britain: Having a Partner Who Usually Lives Elsewhere and Living Apart Together (LAT)', *Population Trends*, **122**, pp. 35–46.
Haskey, John and Lewis, J. (2006), 'Living Apart-together in Britain: Context and Meaning', *International Journal of Law in Context*, **2**(1), pp. 37–48.
Home Office (1998), *Supporting Families: A Consultation Document*, London: The Stationery Office.
Kiernan, K. (2002), 'Cohabitation in Western Europe: Trends, Issues and Implications', in A. Booth and A. Crouter, *Just Living Together: Implications of Cohabitation on Families, Children and Social Policy*, Mahwah, NJ: Lawrence Erlbaum Associates, pp. 3–31, cited in *Married or Not: Who Cohabits, When and Why?*, available at www.oneplusone.org.uk/marriedornot (accessed 15 August 2006).
Law Commission (2002), *Sharing Homes: A Discussion Paper*, Law Com. No. 278, Cm. 5666, London: The Stationery Office.
Law Commission (2006), *Cohabitation: The Financial Consequences of Relationship Breakdown*, London: Law Commission Consultation Paper No. 179.
Law Commission (2006 Overview), *Cohabitation: The Financial Consequences of Relationship Breakdown*, London: Law Commission Consultation Paper No. 179 (Overview).
Law Commission (2007), *Cohabitation: The Financial Consequences of Relationship Breakdown*, Law Com. No. 307, Executive Summary, London: Law Commission.
Law Commission of Canada (2002), *Beyond Conjugality: Recognizing and Supporting Close Personal Adult Relationships*, Ottawa: Law Commission of Canada.
Law Society (2001), *Cohabitation: The Case for Clear Law*, London: The Law Society.
Lewis, Jane (2001), *The End of Marriage? Individualism and Intimate Relationships*, Cheltenham: Edward Elgar.

Lewis, Jane (2005), 'Perceptions of Risk in Intimate Relationships: The Implications for Social Provision', *Journal of Social Policy*, **35**, pp. 39–57.

Morgan D.H.J. (1996), *Family Connections*, Cambridge: Polity.

Morgan, Patricia (2000), *Marriage-lite: The Rise of Cohabitation and its Consequences*, London: Institute for the Study of Civil Society.

O'Donovan, Katherine (1993), *Family Law Matters*, London: Pluto Press.

ONS (2006a), 'Marriages in England and Wales', *Population Trends*, **123**, pp. 71–74.

ONS (2006b), 'Marriages and Divorces during 2003, and Adoptions in 2004: England and Wales', *Population Trends*, **123**, pp. 77–84.

ONS (2007), 'Civil Partnership', UK snapshot, http://www.statistics.gov.uk.

ONS (2008a), 'Marriages', UK snapshot, http:// www.statistics.gov.uk.

ONS (2008b), 'Marriage, Divorce and Adoption Statistics', Series FM2 No. 33, Newport: ONS.

Polikoff, Nancy (2007), *Beyond (Straight and Gay) Marriage: Valuing all Families under the Law*, Boston: Beacon Press.

Regan, M.C. (1999), *Alone Together: Law and the Meanings of Marriage*, Oxford: Oxford University Press.

Smart, Carol (2007), *Personal Life*, Cambridge: Polity.

Smart, Carol (2006), Mason, J. and Shipman, B. (2006), *Gay and Lesbian "Marriage": An Exploration of the Meanings and Significance of Legitimating Same-Sex Relationships*, Manchester: Morgan Centre for the Study of Relationships and Personal Life, University of Manchester.

Smart, Carol and Neale, Bren (1999), *Family Fragments?*, Cambridge: Polity.

Smart, Carol and Stevens, Pippa (2000), *Cohabitation Breakdown*, London: Family Policy Study Centre.

Waite, Linda and Gallagher, Maggie (2000), *The Case for Marriage: Why Married People are Happier, Healthier and Better Off Financially*, New York: Doubleday.

Weeks, Jeffrey (2002), 'Elective Families: Lesbian and Gay Life Experiments', in A. Carling, S. Duncan and R. Edwards (eds), *Analysing Families: Morality and Rationality in Policy and Practice*, London: Routledge.

Weitzman, Lenore (1981), *The Marriage Contract: Spouses, Lovers and the Law*, New York: Free Press.

Part I
Changing Intimacies – The Theory

[1]

On the Way to a Post-Familial Family

From a Community of Need to Elective Affinities

Elisabeth Beck-Gernsheim

Prologue: Stages in a Controversial Debate

IN WESTERN INDUSTRIAL societies of the 1950s and 1960s, paeans were being sung to the family. In West Germany it was enshrined in the Constitution and placed under special state protection; it was the recognized model for everyday life, and the dominant sociological theory regarded it as essential to a functioning state and society. But then came the student and women's movements of the late 1960s and early 1970s, with their show of resistance to the traditional structures. The family was exposed as ideology and prison, as site of everyday violence and repression. But on the opposite side, others appeared in the arena 'in defence of the bourgeois family' (Berger and Berger, 1984) or rediscovered it as a 'haven in a heartless world' (Lasch, 1977). A 'war over the family' broke out (Berger and Berger, 1983). Suddenly it was no longer even clear who or what constituted the family. Which types of relationship should be described as a family and which should not? Which are normal, which deviant? Which ought to be encouraged by the state? Which should receive financial support?

Meanwhile, in the late 1990s, the discussion has become still more confused. Many theorists perceive massive changes, perhaps even the end of the traditional family; others criticize what they call the constant talk of crisis and argue that the future belongs with the family; while a third group, lying somewhere in between, prefer to speak of tendencies towards pluralism. What makes the debate particularly stimulating is the fact that all sides appeal to empirical data, and especially to demographic statistics.

In this article I shall first look at two positions which emphasize continuity and stability of the family. In considering these, I will show that the black-and-white alternative 'end of the family' or 'family as the future' is not appropriate. The focus should instead be on the many grey areas or, better, the many different shades in the niches inside and outside the traditional family network. The main argument here will be that these forms signal more than just pluralism and contiguity, more than just a colourful motley thrown together at random. For a basic historical trend can be discerned in all this variety, a trend towards individualization that also increasingly characterizes relations among members of the same family. A shorthand way of saying this is that a community of need is becoming an elective relationship. The family is not breaking up as a result; it is acquiring a new historical form. Paradoxically, we could say that the contours of a 'post-familial family' are taking shape (Rosenmayr, 1992).[1]

The Construction of Normalcy

On the Handling of Figures

Not long ago a respected daily paper carried a feature article under the programmatic headline 'The Family Is Not a Discontinued Model' (Bauschmid, 1994). The first sentence already makes the point: 'Sometimes it is the normal situation which amazes the observer: 85 per cent of children and young people under eighteen in the Federal Republic grow up in complete families with natural parents who are still in their first marriage.'

The statistic is indeed surprising, and it is therefore worthy of closer examination. Where does it come from? What is the basis of calculation? Three points immediately strike one. First, the cited figure takes children and young people in 'complete' families as its reference. The picture is therefore distorted in advance, because it excludes those who decide against a family. Two groups that have clearly grown in recent years are missing – men and women who do not marry in the first place, and those who remain childless.[2] Second, the author writes that the figure comes from the year 1991, but in reality it covers a period stretching from 1970 to 1987.[3] And already within that period – even more in the years since then – a clear shift has taken place towards non-traditional forms of living. Since 1970, for example, the proportion of children born out of wedlock has been constantly rising;[4] and those born within it face an ever greater risk that their parents' marriage will break up (Nauck, 1991: 427). Third, population figures that give a picture of family life say nothing about whether people live willingly or unwillingly in such relationships. Nor do they say anything about the dynamic concealed behind these statistics. It is therefore necessary to look beyond the objective data and to investigate their subjective meaning. Then it becomes relevant to consider what sociological studies of the family show:[5] namely, that in many relationships there are partly open, partly submerged conflicts over the domestic division of labour and gender life-projects, and that although traditional arrangements still largely prevail, there is increasing dissatisfaction on the part of women. In short, a considerable potential for conflict is visible beneath the surface normality.

What we find, then, is a screening-out of groups which do not fit the image of normality (single persons, the childless); a disregard for the declining trend in the traditionally normal family (more children born outside marriage, more divorces); and also a disregard for the conflict potential within so-called normal families. One thing is obviously common to these three elements: they all lead to a picture that emphasizes the aspect of continuity and systematically underestimates the aspect of change. It is not so much normality as constructions of normality that are involved.

Redefinitions and Immunization

In an essay entitled 'Family in Dissolution', the sociologist Laszlo Vascovics trenchantly criticizes those who point to radical changes in the family. He sees here just the long-familiar talk of crises: 'Over the last two centuries, crisis and breakdown of the family have again and again been "detected" or predicted' (Vascovics, 1991: 186). And he is quite clear about his own conclusions:

> The family as nuclear or conjugal family has kept its dominance up to the present day.... The 'normal chaos of love', as it has been called, continues to display quite clear and dominant patterns of the partnerships which ... in most cases lead to a quite normal family. (Vascovics, 1991: 197)

In order to assess this view of things, it is important to know how Vascovics defines the 'normal family'. In fact, practically everything goes into his definition. With or without a marriage certificate, temporarily or for life, once or a number of times – everything is indiscriminately included in the nuclear family or its precursors. Even people living alone become 'partnership-oriented' within this framework, because in Vascovics' view they do not in principle exclude a marital or non-marital partnership and even partly aspire towards one. Most non-marital partnerships are said to be 'at least geared to a medium-term perspective'. And if such couples separate, it can still be assumed 'that they will sooner or later enter into a non-marital long-term relationship with another partner'. It is true that there has been a decline in birth-rates, but this changes nothing with regard to the normal family. 'Parenthood has not ceased to be an important aim for young women and men.' Developments such as later parenthood show nothing new:

> Why should there be a difference in how late and early parenthood, shorter and longer-lasting families, are regarded? It is in the nature of things that a family will be founded at one point in the life cycle and dissolved at another. (Vascovics, 1991: 188–94)

Within this conceptual schema, Vascovics is undoubtedly right that the normal family is alive and flourishing. But the series of redefinitions that allows him to argue this mostly discards what a short time ago constituted the essence of marriage and family: legal certification, binding force, permanence and so on. If, amid massive change, all this is simply disregarded, then obviously no change will be left. It is as in the race between the hare and the tortoise: the normal family is there already. Proof to the contrary is impossible, because everything that looks or could look otherwise is simply built into the original concept. This is what theory of science knows as immunization – explanations which cannot be refuted and so are not really meaningful.

The result is that the central questions are systematically left out. For example, it is well known from the data available that most men and women do indeed say that having children is one of their aims in life. The interesting question here is why do young people *fail* to achieve this aim more often than previous ones. What are the barriers, the resistances? Or do other goals in life nowadays have greater attraction? Furthermore, it is hardly surprising that most single people do not dismiss all thought of a partnership. But far more intriguing is the question of why they *actually* live alone. What are the resistances or the rival goals? Finally, not much can be said against the statement that every family starts at some point and comes to an end at another. It is as correct as it is trivial. What is not at all trivial is when the family is founded and especially why it is ended – through death or through divorce. How many go on to found another family? How many let it all drop? How many set up several families in succession?

If such questions are not asked, if instead all forms of private life (with or without children, with or without a certificate, with or without permanence) are bunched together under the heading of the 'normal family', then all contours go by the board. Change? The perspective does not allow for it. And so it nowhere comes into view. The conclusion is fixed in advance: 'Nothing new under the sun.'

Family and Individualization: Stages in the Process of Historical Change

The emphasis on continuity of the family will now be contrasted to an approach that consciously places new elements at the centre of analysis. To draw out what is new, we shall take the discussion on individualization as our reference, focusing first on the historical changes that can be located in the lifespan of the individual. Individualization is understood as a historical process that increasingly questions and tends to break up people's traditional rhythm of life – what sociologists call the normal biography. As a result, more people than ever before are being forced to piece together their own biographies and fit in the components they need as best they can. They find themselves bereft of unquestionable assumptions, beliefs or values and are nevertheless faced with the tangle of institutional controls and constraints which make up the fibre of modern life (welfare state, labour market, educational system, etc.) (Beck and Beck-Gernsheim, 1993). To put it bluntly, the normal life-history is giving way to the do-it-yourself life-history. What does this imply about the family? How is the relationship between family and individualization to be conceived? Above all, what is new in all this?

The Obligation of Solidarity

It is advisable to start by glancing back at the preindustrial family. As many studies from social history have shown, this was essentially a relationship centred upon work and economics. Men and women, old and young people each had their own place and tasks within it. But at the same time, their activities were closely coordinated with one another and subordinated to the common goal of preserving the farm or workshop. Members of the family were thus exposed to similar experiences and pressures (seasonal rhythms, harvest, bad weather, etc.), and bound together by common efforts. It was a tightly knit community, in which little room was left for personal inclinations, feelings and motives. What counted was not the individual person but common goals and purposes. In this respect the preindustrial family may be defined as a 'community of need' held together by an 'obligation of solidarity' (Borscheid, 1988).

> Family, household and village community made productive assets out of the estate, ensured that the many efforts were not just a labour of Sisyphus, partly afforded the possibility of welfare and social prestige, and promised some security in the event of destitution, sickness and old age. Unless one was integrated into a family and a village community, one was virtually nothing, an impotent creature looked down upon by society.... In this network of dependence, it was not individual freedom but the material interests of one's own family, farm and village that were uppermost in people's minds. For better or for worse, everyone was tied to this community; it was at once their sheet anchor and their lead weight. (Borscheid, 1988: 271f)

As many historical documents testify, family members were not bound to one another only in love and affection; tension and mistrust, even hatred and violence, were not uncommon. Yet the basic experience remained one of mutual dependence, to which personal wishes and dislikes had to be subordinated in case of conflict. There was not much scope, then, for individuals to break out. To go one's own way was possible (if at all) only at a high personal cost.[6]

With individualization came the decisive historical break. The family lost its function as a working and economic unit, and started up a new relationship with the labour market. In a first phase, it was chiefly men who were involved in gainful employment outside the home. The imperatives of the performance-oriented society meant that what counted was now the individual person rather than the community. Women, however, were initially relegated to the realm of home and children, to the newly forming space of the private. (At least that was the model for the rising bourgeoisie, institutionally underpinned through the administration of justice, education, philosophy and so on.) Within this framework of relations between the sexes, which was geared in principle to a 'halved modernity' (see Beck, 1986: 179), a new form of dependence began to assert itself: the woman became dependent on the man's earnings, while he needed her everyday labour and care to be capable of functioning in the workplace. The obligation of solidarity that had characterized the preindustrial family went on existing in a modified form.

The Welfare State and the Logic of Individually Designed Lives

A new stage in the history of the family and individualization began with the gradual development of the welfare state, first around the end of the 19th century but above all in the second half of the 20th. A series of social security mechanisms (old age pension, sickness and accident cover, etc.) was introduced to give some protection against the rigours of the market, and various forms of material assistance to weaker groups (income support, education grants, housing benefit, help with buying a home, etc.) were meant to assure greater social justice. One result of such measures was that even if individuals could not function in the labour market, or could do so only to a limited extent, they still became less dependent on family, goodwill and personal favours. The beginnings of social security thus guaranteed a minimum existence beyond the family. Individual members of the family were no longer unconditionally required to fit in and to knuckle under; they could also get out in the event of conflict. The logic of individually designed lives was thus given a boost, and ties to the family were considerably loosened.

> Insofar as the state bestows its gifts upon individuals rather than the families to which they belong, it becomes more likely that young people on a grant will leave their family, that large households extending over several generations will split up, or that married couples in employment will be able to divorce. By reducing economic constraints, the state increases the scope for individual action and mobility. But it thereby also increases the probability that people's lives will move outside collective contexts. (Mayer and Müller, 1994: 291)

The Demand and Pressure for Women to Have a 'Life of their Own'

Another major break occurs with the change in women's normal life-history – something which also began towards the end of the last century but has greatly accelerated since the 1960s. Let us summarize this as concisely as possible (for a more detailed account see Beck-Gernsheim, 1983). As women move at least partly outside the family as a result of changes in education, occupation, family-cycle, legal system, etc., they can no longer rely on men as providers. Instead, in ways that are naturally often contradictory, a perspective of autonomy and self-sufficiency is held out to them.

The 'subjective correlate' of such changes is that women today increasingly develop, and must develop, expectations, wishes and life-projects which relate not only to the family but also to their own persons. At the level of economics first of all, they have to plan ahead for some security in life – if need be, without a man. They can no longer think of themselves just as an 'appendage' of the family, but must increasingly come forward as individuals with their own interests and rights, plans and choices.

The power of the family – above all, of the husband – has been correspondingly restricted. Unlike most of their forebears in previous generations, women are no longer referred to marriage as the route to economic security and social status. They can choose, perhaps not altogether freely but more than before, whether they really want to marry or to stay single, and whether to seek a divorce rather than put up with endless conflicts if the marriage does not turn out as they hoped. This means that, in women's biographies too, the logic of individual design is gradually asserting itself and the obligation of solidarity is further breaking down.

Meanwhile, feminists have analysed this development with new categories and concepts. Whereas traditional sociology always conceived the family as a unit with homogeneous interests and positions in life, there is now a contrasting focus on gender difference. Whereas 'the family' always used to occupy the whole field of vision, now men and women are becoming visible as separate individuals, each linked to the family through different expectations and interests, each experiencing different opportunities and burdens. In short, the contours of distinctively male and distinctively female lives are now becoming apparent within the family.

Individualization and the Staging of Everyday Life

As a result of historical developments, then, a trend towards individualization has made itself felt. This increasingly affects relations between family members too, setting up a special kind of dynamic. A number of examples will help us to understand what is meant by this 'staging of everyday life', as we shall call it. More and more coordination is needed to hold together biographies that tend to pull apart from one another. At a number of levels, the family thus becomes a daily 'balancing act' (Rerrich, 1988) or a permanent 'do-it-yourself' project (see Beck and Beck-Gernsheim, 1993; Hitzler and Honer, 1994). The character of everyday family life is gradually changing: people used to be able to rely upon well-functioning rules and models, but now an ever greater number of decisions are having to be taken. More and more things must be negotiated, planned, personally brought about. And not least in importance is the way in which questions of resource distribution, of fairness between members of the family, have come to the fore. Which burdens should be allocated to whom? Who should bear which costs? Which claims have priority? Whose wishes have to wait?

The Divergence of Tempos and Abodes

In preindustrial society, it was the demands of the family community centred on work and economics which directly set the course of everyday life. As the farm or workshop occupied the central place, each family member usually acted within a radius of which the others could easily keep track. And the distribution of tasks, having been practised for generations, followed a familiar rhythm that was tightly defined and coordinated.

Starkly contrasting with this is the everyday family life in highly industrialized societies. Most men are in employment outside the home, and so are an increasing number of women. The children go to school and spend more and more of their leisure in organized activities outside the home (sports club, painting class, music lessons, etc.), in the new forms of 'insulated childhood' spread right across the city (see Zeiher, 1994). Family life no longer happens in one place but is scattered between several different locations. Nor a fortiori is there a common temporal rhythm, for the family's life is structured by different social institutions: the timetable of kindergarten, school and youth organization, the working hours of the husband and wife, the opening hours of shops, the schedule of public transport and so on. Most important of all, the flexibilization of working hours directly intrudes upon family life, as it produces irregular and fluctuating tempos that do not correspond to such requirements of living together as continuity, stability and coordination.[7]

It is extremely difficult to tie together the threads of these different rhythms. The watchword is: 'Join together what is moving apart!' (see Rerrich, 1994) so that everyday family life becomes a kind of 'jigsaw' that is hard work rather than a game (Rerrich, 1991). The individual pieces have to be put together time and again, the temporal and spatial arrangements compared and collated. This is vividly shown by the results of a detailed empirical study (Jurczyk and Rerrich, 1993). The lives of individual family members, with their different rhythms, locations and demands, only rarely fit together naturally. Much more often, discrepancies appear and lead to repeated attempts to establish a balance. A harmonious everyday life is thus an 'achievement based on a great deal of preparation' (Rerrich, 1993: 311), which requires the family coordinator to be a skilful timetable-juggler. Usually it is women who perform this task which entails considerable practical and emotional effort, often with the help of a grandmother, au pair girl or child-minder. The need to plan, organize and delegate is thus growing all the time as the family becomes a kind of small business. 'Elements of rationalization and calculation are marching into private life' (Rerrich, 1993: 322). My, your, our time becomes the issue in a struggle between time of one's own and a quest for common time. And it is not uncommon for this to result in tension and competing demands – especially between men and women. Who will take responsibility for what? When and for how long? Whose need for time has priority? Who is free when?

Multicultural Families

In preindustrial society, when a man and a woman got married they nearly always shared a wide repertoire of local experiences, values and attitudes. For life-worlds were then far more closed than they are today, and marriage opportunities were greatly limited by factors ranging from class and property to ethnic origin and religion. In comparison, the everyday life-world is nowadays much more thoroughly mixed: people from different regions and social strata meet and often marry one another. The old barriers erected by the law or by the wider family have not completely disappeared, but they are much weaker than they used to be. The principle of a free choice of partner has become generally accepted, so that people who live together (with or without a marriage certificate) often come from quite different backgrounds. Or, as Berger and Kellner put it in a classic text, the modern choice of partner is characterized by the meeting of two strangers.

> Marriage in our society is a dramatic act in which two strangers come together and redefine themselves.... the term 'strangers' [does not] mean, of course, that the candidates for the marriage come from widely discrepant social backgrounds – indeed, the data indicate that the contrary is the case. The strangeness rather lies in the fact that, unlike marriage candidates in many previous societies, those in ours typically come from different face-to-face contexts. (Berger and Kellner, 1974: 160)

The marital relation thereby acquires new meaning, but also, of course, is subject to new strains. For the great opportunity of personally chosen togetherness – namely, the creation of a common world beyond the legacy of family and kin - requires that both participants make enormous contributions. Within the system of modern marriage, the partners are not only expected to construct their own form of togetherness; they *must* do so.

> Marriage and the family used to be firmly embedded in a matrix of wider community relationships.... There were few separating barriers between the world of the individual family and the wider community.... The same social life pulsated through the house, the street and the community.... In our contemporary society, by contrast, each family constitutes its own segregated sub-world.... This fact requires a much greater effort on the part of the marriage parties. Unlike in earlier situations in which the establishment of the new marriage simply added to the differentiation and complexity of an already existing social world, the marriage partners now are embarked on the often difficult task of constructing for themselves the little world in which they live. (Berger and Kellner, 1974: 162–3)

This is especially true of bi-national or bi-cultural couples, where each partner comes from a different country or culture. Such unions also existed in earlier epochs, of course, but their number has increased considerably in recent times, owing to migration of labour, political upheavals and political persecution, mass tourism and foreign travel for education or business. In Germany, every seventh couple marrying today is nationally mixed.[8] What Berger and Kellner saw as characteristic of modern marriage is here even more applicable. For in nationally mixed marriages, the strangers are 'even stranger and the differences in socialization are greater' (Hardach-Pinke, 1988: 116).

Today in every marriage, different lifestyles, values, ways of thinking and communicating, rituals and everyday routines have to be fitted together in one family world. In the case of bi-national/bi-cultural marriages, this means that both partners must achieve the 'construction of a new intercultural reality' (Hardach-Pinke, 1988: 217), build an 'intercultural life-world' (Hardach-Pinke, 1988) or a 'bi-national family culture' (Scheiber, 1992: 87ff). They act within a space that has been little structured beforehand, as two different worlds meet. In this situation, for which there is no preparation and no specific rules, the partners have to work out arrangements of their own (Scheiber, 1992: 45).

Much that used simply to happen, without any questions asked, must now be weighed up and decided upon. Where shall we live: in your country or mine, or perhaps in a third where neither has the advantage of its being home? Shall we stay here or later move to your home country? Who has which opportunities where? Who must bear which burdens where? Who will be without legal status, job protection or pension cover? Do we communicate in your language or mine, or in a third, or in whichever suits the occasion? Which festivals and holidays will we celebrate? What shall we do about family visits and all the many branches of the family? What about the division of labour at home? How are the children to be brought up: in your religion or mine, in your language or mine? What forenames will we choose, reflecting which of our origins?

To repeat: there are no models for any of these decisions. Each couple goes its own way, seeks its own forms. Whether they choose to follow one or the other cultural tradition in its entirety; whether they try to find forms combining elements from both; whether they test out several options and perhaps keep switching around (Scheiber, 1992: 44ff) – all this will depend on their previous history, actual place of residence and plans for the future, as well as on the cultural preferences and prejudices in their surroundings. Each bi-national couple lives out its own story, its own distinctive version of bi-national family culture.

The biography of each partner is far from unimportant in this process. The one who comes from a different country is 'the stranger' here. Perhaps their background was one of poverty and hunger, or perhaps of torture, persecution and escape; anyway they have gone through experiences and anxieties quite different from those of people in their new surroundings. Their life is, to a greater or lesser degree, cut off from their own cultural roots, their socialization, their language. If their mode of expression, behaviour and appearance becomes noticed, they live with the stigma of 'the other' (see Goffman, 1963). They have to face humiliating treatment and mistrust at the hands of courts and officials, landlords and employers. They live without protection, and if their legal status is insecure they can have their work permit withdrawn and perhaps even be deported. True, the native partner is not unaffected by all this, but he or she is in a comparatively secure position and can take steps in self-defence. It remains completely open what attacks from the outside will mean for the couple's relationship: in one case it may be tested to the point of breakdown, while in another it may be made all the stronger. But whatever the outcome, the structure of their relations is typically such that one partner is more exposed than the other. So, differences between their social positions establish themselves. There is an imbalance, more or less pronounced, between their respective opportunities and dangers.

Finally, a bi-national/bi-cultural marriage also makes both partners confront their own origins, with sometimes paradoxical results. Someone who looked for the attraction of 'the other' in a relationship with a foreigner suddenly discovers the 'native' element in his or her own self. 'One sees how deeply rooted is one's own value system – indeed, in many respects one sees it for the first time' (Elschenbroich, 1988: 368). Contemplating the children's future brings memories back with particular force, making it necessary to confront one's own socialization and history, values and desires – one's own identity. The question 'Who am I, what do I want?' is posed anew in the course of a bi-national marriage. And it leads on to further questions that call for a crucial decision: 'What do I want to keep?', 'What can I give up?', 'What is important to me?'

Divorce and its Consequences

The number of divorces has risen dramatically in the course of the 20th century. Every third marriage ends in divorce in the Federal Republic of Germany, every second one in the USA.[9] Children too are increasingly affected. A German study that compared children born in 1960 and in 1980 came to the following conclusion: 'During these twenty years, the risk of being affected in childhood by parental separation has risen more than threefold' (Nauck, 1991: 427).

When divorce occurs, the situations of men and women, adults and children, develop in different directions. This is true first of all in a directly geographical sense: one partner (nearly always the man) moves to another dwelling and perhaps another town (so as to make a fresh start). Women and children stay behind, but it is not uncommon for them to move too at a later date (to cheaper accommodation, closer to grandparents and so on) – which means a change in surroundings, school and neighbours. New economic situations are especially important: a drop in income usually takes place, depending on the laws of the country concerned. In the USA the standard of living sharply declines for women and children, while it not infrequently rises for men (because they often pay no maintenance) (Cherlin, 1992: 73f). In Germany money, or lack of it, is more evenly divided and most men have to contend with a reduced budget, but still the women and children generally are worse off (Lucke, 1990).

In addition, a new organization of everyday life becomes necessary after a divorce. It has to be negotiated, often fought over, between the two who used to be a couple. Who keeps the apartment, who gets which share of the household goods, which keepsakes? How much maintenance will be paid for whom? And above all, who gets the children and what are the custody rights? Man versus woman: claims and demands are raised, rights and duties redistributed. New agreements are sought, often with a great deal of argument. Instead of a common daily life and a common abode, there are now separate 'access' times for the father. When should he come, and for how long? How much is he entitled to have the child at weekends and holidays? In extreme cases, the man or woman may even try to settle things by force: the number of child kidnappings has also been increasing.

Family therapists, lawyers and judges see every day how wounding and bitterness, rage and hatred can escalate between ex-partners after a divorce. But even when the separation is calm and reasonable, it inevitably leads to a new relationship among husband, wife and children. Much more clearly than before, they confront one another as individuals eager to assert their own interests and pursuits, their own wishes and rights. The ex-partners differ in how they think not only about the future but also about their time together in the past – often too about who was to blame and how the whole thing should be seen (he always had other women, she always threw their money around).

In between are the children (on their situation see Cherlin, 1992; Furstenberg and Cherlin, 1991; Wallerstein and Berlin Kelly, 1980; Wallerstein and Blakeslee, 1989). Naturally they have wishes of their own. As various studies have shown, they usually hope that the parents will get together again. Yet the parents still go their own way regardless. The children then have to learn to live with divided loyalties. Where fights break out over who they should stay with, they are asked by the court whether they would prefer to live with the mother or the father. However carefully it is done, the child is being asked to make a statement against one or the other parent – and when little care is taken, the child directly experiences the parents' manoeuvres and attempts to gain influence. Where visiting rules are in force but the ex-partners cannot overcome their sense of hurt, the children become involved in a post-divorce battle in which they are sounded out about the lifestyle and new relationships of the former spouse, or used as carriers of information between the warring fronts. Nor is that always all. In some families, the children become split between the parents, as brothers and sisters too may divide against each other, Much more often, however, their relationship to the father rapidly tails off as he disappears from their immediate horizon. Relations with the paternal grandparents also grow weaker and more problematic, sometimes partly prevented by the mother as a way of wiping out all reference to the father (Cherlin and Furstenberg, 1986: 136ff).

What all this means for the growing child is a matter of dispute. Many studies indicate that children, being sensitive and vulnerable, often suffer lifelong disturbances when early relations are severed (see Wallerstein and Blakeslee, 1989). Others suggest that children are more flexible, robust, even thoroughly adaptable, and that although the period after a divorce is certainly a dramatic crisis, the children usually get over it and settle into the new conditions (see Cherlin, 1992; Furstenberg and Cherlin, 1991). It may be that both interpretations are not completely wrong, but also not completely right; perhaps they are both too narrow. In keeping with what has been said so far, I would therefore like to propose a third interpretation. The series of events connected with separation may, that is, involve a special kind of socialization, the essence of which is a message of, and a hard lesson in, individualism. If children manage to come to terms with changing family forms, this means that they have had to learn to sever close bonds, to cope with loss. They learn early what it means to be abandoned and to part. They see that love does not last for ever, that relationships come to an end, that separation is a normal occurrence in life.

Conjugal Succession and Elective Family Relationships

Many divorced people later remarry or cohabit with a new partner who was also married before and may also have children of their own. More and more children thus grow up with one non-biological parent. On closer examination, these step-families appear in a sense to be a variant of the bi-cultural family. According to recent findings, they are a 'curious example of an organizational merger; they join two family cultures into a single household' (Furstenberg and Cherlin, 1991: 83). Here too, values, rules and routines, different expectations and everyday practices – from table manners and pocket-money to television viewing and bedtime hours – have to be negotiated and agreed. In addition, many children move backwards and forwards between their different family worlds, between the 'everyday parent' who has custody and lives with a new partner, and the 'weekend parent' who does not have custody and may also have a new family. This may well lead to complex relationship structures that can be presented only in diagrams with many ramifications. 'Marriage and divorce chains',[10] 'conjugal succession' (Furstenberg, 1989), 'multiparent families' (Napp-Peters, 1993), 'patchwork families' – all these are concepts designed to make the new family forms easier to grasp. One key characteristic, of course, is that it is not clear who actually belongs to the family. There is no longer a single definition – that has been lost somewhere in the rhythm of separations and new relationships. Instead, each member has their own definition of who belongs to the family; everyone lives out their own version of the patchwork family.

> Let us consider the case in which a married couple with two children divorces and the wife retains custody of the children.... If we ask the divorced mother who is in her immediate family, she certainly would include her children, but she might well exclude her ex-husband, who now lives elsewhere. If we ask her children who is in their immediate family, however, we might get a different answer. If the children still see their father regularly, they would probably include both their father and their mother as part of their family. And if we ask the ex-husband who is in his immediate family, he might

> include his children, whom he continues to see, but not his ex-wife. Thus, after divorce, mother, father and children each may have a different conception of who is in their immediate family. In fact, one can no longer define 'the family' or 'the immediate family' except in relation to a particular person. (Cherlin, 1992: 81)

In this constellation it is no longer the traditional rules of ascription (descent and marriage) which determine the family bond. The key factor now is whether the social relations stemming from it persist after the divorce. Where these relations are broken or gradually fade, there is also an end to the ties of kinship. What could be seen emerging in other family constellations of modernity is here fully displayed: maintenance of the family link is no longer a matter of course but a freely chosen act. In the situation following a divorce, kinship is worked out anew in accordance with the laws of choice and personal inclination – it takes the form of 'elective affinities'. As it is no longer given as a destiny, it requires a greater personal contribution, more active care. As one study of patchwork families puts it: 'From the huge universe of potential kin, people actively create kin by establishing a relationship – by working at becoming kin. And they have wide latitude in choosing which links to activate' (Furstenberg and Cherlin, 1991: 93). Many relatives by the first marriage continue to be 'part of the family'; many by the second marriage are added to them; and others remain outside or drop out.

The outcome no longer follows a predetermined model. For where there is a choice, personal preferences more and more become the yardstick; each individual draws his or her own boundaries. Even children growing up in the same household no longer necessarily have the same definition of who belongs to the family (Furstenberg and Cherlin, 1991: 93). What all this means is that 'conjugal succession implies greater fluidity and uncertainty in kinship relations. Cultivating family ties may become more important as less can be taken for granted about the obligation of particular kin to one another' (Furstenberg, 1989: 28f). This confronts everyone involved with new questions that need to be answered; new rules of solidarity and loyalty become necessary.

> It will be extraordinarily interesting to see the relative strength of consanguinal and affinal bonds within families whose members have been multiplied by successive marriages. How will grandparents divide their inheritance among biological grandchildren whom they barely know, stepgrandchildren acquired early in life, or stepgrandchildren acquired from their own second marriage who have helped to nurse them later in life? Do biological fathers have more obligation to send their biological children, who have been raised by a stepfather, to college or their own stepchildren whom they have raised? (Furstenberg, 1989: 29)

When such networks take shape, the net result of divorce for the children is an enlargement rather than a narrowing of their kinship boundaries. The character of the ties does, however, change in the process. No longer taken for granted, they become thinner and more fragile, more dependent upon personal cooperation and also upon external circumstances (such as a change of place). This kind of bonding contains special opportunities but also special risks. On the other hand, we should not underestimate the value of bonding which, precisely because of its weakness, encompasses a wide kinship network. But on the other hand, 'this thinner form of kinship may not be an adequate substitute for the loss of relatives who had a stronger stake in the child's success' (Furstenberg and Cherlin, 1991: 95). Today, through divorce and remarriage, people are indeed related to more people than they used to be, but the obligations involved in the bond have been decreasing.

Prospects for the Future

Whereas, in preindustrial society, the family was mainly a community of need held together by an obligation of solidarity, the logic of individually designed lives has come increasingly to the fore in the contemporary world. The family is becoming more of an elective relationship, an association of individual persons, who each bring to it their own interests, experiences and plans, and who are each subjected to different controls, risks and constraints.

As the various examples from contemporary family life have shown, it is necessary to devote much more effort than in the past to the holding together of these different biographies. Whereas people could once fall back upon rules and rituals, the prospect now is of a staging of everyday life, an acrobatics of balancing and coordinating. The family bond thereby grows more fragile, and there is a greater danger of collapse if attempts to reach agreement are not successful. Since individualization also fosters a longing for the opposite world of intimacy, security and closeness (Beck and Beck-Gernsheim, 1995), most people will continue – at least for the foreseeable future – to live within a partnership or family. But such ties are not the same as before, in their scope or in their degree of obligation and permanence. Out of many different strivings, longings, efforts and mistakes, out of successful and often unsuccessful experiments, a wider spectrum of the private is taking shape. As people make choices, negotiating and deciding the everyday details of do-it-yourself relationships, a 'normal chaos' of love, suffering and diversity is growing and developing.

This does not mean that the traditional family is simply disappearing. But it is losing the monopoly it had for so long. Its quantitative significance is declining as new forms of living appear and spread – forms which (at least generally) aim not at living alone but at relationships of a different kind: for example, without a formal marriage or without children; single parenting, conjugal succession, or same-sex partnerships; part-time relationships and companionships lasting for some period in life; living between more than one home or between different towns. These in all their intermediary and secondary and floating forms represent the future of families, or what I call: the contours of the 'post-familial family'.

Notes

1. Leopold Rosenmayr (1992) speaks of a 'post-familial family'.

2. These trends are more marked in West Germany, but they are also on the increase in East Germany. As to singles, the percentage of men and women who stay single over their lifetime has been increasing continuously, in West Germany since 1930, in East Germany since 1950 (Engstler, 1997: 85). As to cohabitation, in West Germany, the number of non-married couples living together rose tenfold between 1972 and 1996, from 137,000 to 1,408,000. In East Germany, this number rose from 327,000 in 1991 to 442,000 in 1996 (Engstler, 1997: 62). As to those without children, in West Germany, of women born in 1945, 13.3 percent remained childless; of those born in 1960, approximately 23.3 percent will remain so. In East Germany, until recently the number of women remaining childless was very low, but it is now also increasing (Engstler, 1997: 96, 103).

3. The figures quoted by Elisabeth Bauschmid evidently come from Bernhard Nauck's article (1991), based on research work carried out in 1988. The forms of family in question refer to the period from 1970 to 1987.

4. In West Germany, the number of children born outside marriage rose threefold between 1965 and 1997, from 4.7 percent to 14.3 percent (Statistisches Bundesamt 1990: 116; for 1997, data from the Federal Bureau of Statistics in Wiesbaden, not yet published). In East Germany, nearly half of the children (44.1 percent) were born outside marriage in 1997 (data from the Federal Bureau of Statistics in Wiesbaden, not yet published).

5. See the survey contained in Elisabeth Beck-Gernsheim (1992).

6. See the example of an 18th-century divorce, in Bock and Duden (1997: 126).

7. For more data on the growth of flexitime working (weekend, shift, part-time work, etc.), see Gross et al., 1987, 1989.

8. According to the latest available figures, for the year 1996, from the Federal Bureau of Statistics in Wiesbaden. This points to a rapid increase in such marriages, which still only accounted for a twelfth of the total in the second half of the 1980s. See also Engstler (1997: 83).

9. For recent figures see Engstler (1997: 88, 90), and Cherlin (1992: 7, 24).

10. The concept of 'divorce chains' originated with the anthropologist Paul Bohannan and was adopted by other authors such as Cherlin (1992: 83).

References

Bauschmid, Elisabeth (1994) 'Familie ist kein Auslaufmodell', *Süddeutsche Zeitung* 4 January: 4.

Beck, Ulrich (1986) *Risikogesellschaft. Auf dem Weg in eine andere Moderne.* Frankfurt am Main: Suhrkamp.

Beck, Ulrich and Elisabeth Beck-Gernsheim (1993) 'Nicht Autonomie, sondern Bastelbiographie', *Zeitschrift für Soziologie* 3: 178–87.

Beck, Ulrich and Elisabeth Beck-Gernsheim (1995) *The Normal Chaos of Love.* Cambridge: Polity Press. (Orig. 1990.)

Beck-Gernsheim, Elisabeth (1983) 'Vom "Dasein für andere" zum Anspruch auf ein Stück "eigenes Leben" – Individualisierungsprozesse im weiblichen Lebenszusammenhang', *Soziale Welt* 3: 307–41.

Beck-Gernsheim, Elisabeth (1992) 'Arbeitsteilung, Selbstbild und Lebensentwurf. Neue Konfliktlagen in der Familie', *Kölner Zeitschrift für Soziologie und Sozialpsychologie* 2: 273–91.

Berger, Birgitte and Peter L. Berger (1983) *The War over the Family*. Garden City and New York: Anchor Press/Doubleday.

Berger, Birgitte and Peter L. Berger (1984) *In Verteidigung der bürgerlichen Familie*. Reinbek: Rowohlt.

Berger, Peter L. and Hansfried Kellner (1974) 'Marriage and the Construction of Reality', in R. L. Coser (ed.) *The Family: Its Structures and Functions*. New York.

Bock, Gisela and Barbara Duden (1977) 'Arbeit aus Liebe – Liebe als Arbeit', pp. 118–99 in *Frauen und Wissenschaft. Beiträge zur Berliner Sommeruniversität für Frauen*. Berlin.

Borscheid, Peter (1988) 'Zwischen privaten Netzen und öffentlichen Institutionen – Familienumwelten in historischer Perspektive', pp. 271–80 in Deutsches Jugendinstitut (ed.) *Wie geht's der Familie?* Munich: Kösel.

Cherlin, Andrew J. (1992) *Marriage, Divorce, Remarriage*. Cambridge, MA: Harvard University Press.

Cherlin, Andrew J. and Frank F. Furstenberg (1986) 'Grandparents and Divorce', ch. 6 in *The New American Grandparent*. New York: Basic Books.

Elschenbroich, Donata (1988) 'Eine Familie – zwei Kulturen', in Deutsches Jugendinstitut (ed.) *Wie geht's der Familie?* Munich: Kösel.

Engstler, Heribert (1997) *Die Familie im Spiegel der amtlichen Statistik. Aktualisierte und erweiterte Neuauflage 1998*, ed. Federal Ministry for Family, Senior Citizens, Women and Youth. Berlin.

Furstenberg, Frank F. (1989) 'One Hundred Years of Change in the American Family', in Harold J. Bershady (ed.) *Social Class and Democratic Leadership: Essays in Honor of E. Digby Baltzell*. Philadelphia, PA.

Furstenberg, Frank F. and Andrew J. Cherlin (1991) *Divided Families: What Happens to Children when Parents Part*. Cambridge, MA: Harvard University Press.

Goffman, Erving (1963) *Stigma: Notes on the Management of Spoiled Identity*. Englewood Cliffs, NJ.

Gross, Hermann, Ulrich Pekuhl and Cornelia Thoben (1987) 'Arbeitszeitstrukturen im Wandel', in Der Minister für Arbeit, Gesundheit und Soziales des Landes Nordrhein-Westfalen (ed.) *Arbeitszeit '87*, Part 2. Dusseldorf.

Gross, Hermann, Cornelia Thoben and Frank Bauer (1989) *Arbeitszeit '89. Ein report zu Arbeitszeiten und Arbeitszeitwünschen in der Bundesrepublik*. Cologne.

Hardach-Pinke, Irene (1988) *Interkulturelle Lebenswelten. Deutsch–japanische Ehen in Japan*. Frankfurt am Main: Campus.

Hitzler, Ronald and Anne Honer (1994) 'Bastelexistenz. Über subjektive Konsequenzen der Individualisierung', pp. 307–15 in Ulrich Beck and Elisabeth Beck-Gernsheim (eds) *Riskante Freiheiten. Individualisierung in modernen Gesellschaften*. Frankfurt: Suhrkamp.

Jurczyk, Karin and Maria S. Rerrich (eds) (1993) *Die Arbeit des Alltags*. Freiburg.

Lasch, Christopher (1977) *Haven in a Heartless World: The Family Besieged*. New York.

Lucke, Doris (1990) 'Die Ehescheidung als Kristallisationskern geschlechtspezifischer Ungleichheit', pp. 363–85 in Peter A. Berger and Stefan Hradil (eds) *Lebenslagen, Lebensläufe, Lebensstile*. Göttingen: Schwartz Verlag.

Mayer, Karl Ulrich and Walter Müller (1994) 'Lebensverläufe im Wohlfahrtsstaat', in Ulrich Beck and Elisabeth Beck-Gernsheim (eds) *Riskante Freiheiten. Individualisierung in modernen Gesellschaften*. Frankfurt: Suhrkamp.

Napp-Peters, Anneke (1993) 'Mehrelternfamilien – Psychosoziale Folgen von Trennung und Scheidung für Kinder und Jugendliche', *Neue Schriftenreihe der Arbeitsgemeinschaft füre Erziehungshilfe* 49: 12–26.

Nauck, Bernhard (1991) 'Familien und Betreuungssituationen im Lebenslauf von Kindern', pp. 389–428 in Hans Bertram (ed.) *Die Familie in Westdeutschland*. Opladen: Laske und Budrich.

Rerrich, Maria S. (1988) *Balanceakt Familie. Zwischen alten Leitbildern und neuen Lebensformen*. Freiburg: Lambertus.

Rerrich, Maria S. (1991) 'Puzzle Familienalltag: Wie passen die einzelnen Teile zusammen?' *Jugend und Gesellschaft* 5–6.

Rerrich, Maria S. (1993) 'Gemeinsame Lebensführung: Wie Berufstätige einen Alltag mit ihren Familien herstellen', in Karin Jurczyk and Maria S. Rerrich (eds) *Die Arbeit des Alltags*. Freiburg: Lambertus.

Rosenmayr, Leopold (1992) 'Showdown zwischen Alt und Jun?', *Wiener Zweitung* 26 June: 1.

Scheibler, Petra M. (1992) *Binationale Ehen*. Weinheim: Deutscher Studienverlag.

Statistisches Bundesamt (ed.) (1990) *Familien heute. Strukturen, Verläufe, Einstellungen*. Stuttgart: Metzler-Poeschel.

Vascovics, Laszlo (1991) 'Familie im Auflösungsprozess?', pp. 186–98 in Deutsches Jugendinstitut (ed.) *Jahresbericht 1990*. Munich.

Wallerstein, Judith S. and Joan Berlin Kelly (1980) *Surviving the Breakup: How Children and Parents Cope with Divorce*. New York: Basic Books.

Wallerstein, Judith S. and Sandra Blakeslee (1989) *Second Chances*. New York: Ticknor & Fields.

Zeiher, Helga (1994) 'Kindheitsträume. Zwischen Eigenständigkeit und Abhängigkeit', in Ulrich Beck and Elisabeth Beck-Gernsheim (eds) *Riskante Freiheiten. Individualisierung in modernen Gesellschaften*. Frankfurt: Suhrkamp.

Elisabeth Beck-Gernsheim teaches Sociology at Erlangen University. Her publications include *Das halbierte Leben. Männerwelt Beruf, Frauenwelt Familie* (Frankfurt: Fischer, 1980), *Die Kinderfrage. Frauen zwischen Kinderwunsch und Unabhängigkeit* (München: Beck, 1988), *Technik, Markt und Moral. Über Reproduktionsmedizin und Gentechnologie* (Frankfurt: Fischer, 1991), translated as *The Social Implications of Bioengineering* (New Jersey: Humanities Press, 1995), *Welche Gesundheit wollen wir? Dilemmata des medizintechnischen Fortschritts* (Frankfurt: Suhrkamp, 1995) and *Was kommt nach der Familie? Einblicke in neue Lebensformen* (München: Beck, 1998), the translation of which will be published by Polity Press in 1999.

[2]

INTIMACY TRANSFORMED? A CRITICAL LOOK AT THE 'PURE RELATIONSHIP'

LYNN JAMIESON

Abstract It has recently been claimed that a particular form of intimacy, 'the pure relationship' is increasingly sought in personal life. For a couple, 'the pure relationship' involves opening out to each other, enjoying each other's unique qualities and sustaining trust through mutual disclosure. Anthony Giddens (1992) postulates a transformation of intimacy in all personal relationships with radical consequences for the gender order. Popular discourse supports the view that heterosexual couples are more equal and intimate. However, stories of everyday lives told to researchers paint a very qualified picture. Much of personal life remains structured by inequalities. Gendered struggles with the gap between cultural ideals and structural inequalities result in a range of creative identity and relationship-saving strategies. More, perhaps much more, creative energy goes into sustaining a sense of intimacy *despite* inequality than into a process of transformation. Moreover, the rhetoric of 'the pure relationship' may point people in the wrong direction both personally and politically. It feeds on and into a therapeutic discourse that individualises personal problems and down-grades sociological explanations. In practice, intimacy remains multi-dimensional and for the contenders for successful heterosexual equality, acts of practical love and care have been more important than a constant dynamic of mutual exploration of each other's selves.

Key words: couples, intimacy, marriage, parents, 'pure relationship', sex.

In describing late twentieth-century processes of social change, which involve a transformation in the nature of self-identity and intimacy, Giddens talks of the ascendancy of 'confluent love' and 'the pure relationship'. Confluent love is contingent on lovers opening themselves out to each other. The 'pure relationship', like the ideal-typical dyad, has no overarching structure to sustain it. Rather, its key sustaining dynamics are mutual self-disclosure and appreciation of each other's unique qualities.

> A pure relationship is one in which external criteria have become dissolved: the relationship exists solely for whatever rewards that relationship can deliver. In the context of the pure relationship, trust can be mobilised only by a process of mutual disclosure
>
> (Giddens 1991:6)

> It [a pure relationship] refers to a situation where a social relation is entered into for its own sake, for what can be derived by each person from a sustained association with another; and which is continued only in so far as it is thought by both parties to deliver enough satisfaction for each individual to stay within it.
>
> (Giddens 1992:58)

The type of intimacy involved in 'the pure relationship' necessarily requires equality between the parties to the relationship, that is a shared sense of self-disclosure and contributing on an equal footing to the relationship.

Giddens claims that the trend towards 'the pure relationship' is paralleled by the emergence of a more responsive and creative form of sexuality which he calls 'plastic sexuality', referring to a heightened self-awareness of the plasticity of sexuality, a late twentieth-century freedom from any essential pre-given way of being sexual.

> Sexuality has then become, as Luhmann might put it, a 'communicative code' rather than a phenomenon integrated with the wider exigencies of human existence. In sexual behaviour, a distinction has always been drawn between pleasure and procreation. When the new connections between sexuality and intimacy were formed, however, sexuality became much more completely separated from procreation than before. Sexuality became doubly constituted as a medium of self-realisation and as a prime means, as well as an expression, of intimacy.
>
> (Giddens 1991:164)

While it is quite possible to have intensely intimate relationships which are not sexual and sexual relationships which are devoid of intimacy, Giddens suggests that preoccupation with the body and exploring sexual pleasure is increasingly part of both self-construction and 'the pure relationship'. For Giddens, a 'revolution in female sexual autonomy', that is in women finding sexual pleasure in ways which are not dictated by men, and 'the flourishing of homosexuality' (1992:28) are manifestations of 'plastic sexuality'. In 'confluent love' sexuality and intimacy are tied together 'as never before' (1992:84).

The underlying causal factors promoting the ascendancy of the pure relationship and plastic sexuality are the uncertainties and new social conditions created by reiterative processes of social change characteristic of late modernity. In combination they heighten the sense that individuals have of their own creativity and their own limitations in the business of producing their selves and their social world. These deep-rooted changes are detailed in Giddens's earlier work on the development of 'high modernity' (1990, 1991): globalisation, disembeddedness, enhanced sense of risk, dominance of experts and abstract systems, reflexivity. The pace of social change is such that traditions are more profoundly swept away than ever before (1994).

> Where large areas of a person's life are no longer set by pre-existing patterns and habits, the individual is continually obliged to negotiate life-style options. Moreover – and this is crucial – such choices are not just 'external' or marginal aspects of the individual's attitudes, but define who the individual 'is'. In other words, life-style choices are constitutive of the reflexive narrative of self.
>
> (Giddens 1992:75)

The phrase 'narrative of the self' emphasises the ongoing process of self-construction. In the social conditions of the late twentieth century personal relationships are the key site in which men and women find 'forms of self exploration and moral construction' (Giddens 1992:144). A successful pure relationship recreates psychological stability by resonating with the ontological security and basic trust of others which is developed in an untraumatised and successful childhood and which derives from the trust placed by children in their 'caretakers' (Giddens 1991:186). But at the same time, 'pure relationships' necessarily contain the internal tension of attempting to reconcile mutual trust and commitment with the knowledge that the relationship is voluntary and only 'good until further notice'. For Giddens such tension and consequent fragility is an inherent aspect of the more profound potential for openness and intimacy rather than a symptom of general *malaise.* In his optimism, Giddens draws selectively from psychological theory, setting aside accounts which emphasise the inevitability of inner conflict, self-discontent and disappointment in relationships (Craib 1994, 1997).

One of the tantalising aspects of Giddens's work is this optimism. He frequently suggests that a more profound equality between men and women is emerging through the transformation of intimacy. More general claims are also made concerning the potential for radical and positive social change through personal life.

> Yet the radicalising possibilities of the transformation of intimacy are very real. Some have claimed that intimacy can be oppressive, and clearly this may be so if it is regarded as a demand for constant emotional closeness. Seen, however, as a transactional negotiation of personal ties by equals, it appears in a completely different light. Intimacy implies a wholesale democratising of the interpersonal domain, in a manner fully compatible with democracy in the public sphere. There are further implications as well. The transformation of intimacy might be a subversive influence upon modern institutions as a whole. For a social world in which emotional fulfilment replaced the maximising of economic growth would be very different from that which we know at present.
>
> (Giddens 1992:3)

I wish to begin with some brief critical observations concerning his optimism about a new impetus towards gender equality and democratisation of personal life, before going on to a more detailed consideration of relevant empirical work.

Critical Issues

Giddens presents the trends he is identifying as relatively recent. Yet the idea that how personal life is conducted is more intensely intimate, individualised or personalised than ever before, is a long-running theme. For example, eighteenth-century philosophers of the Scottish Enlightenment saw intimate friendship as a 'modern' pattern emerging in their time (Silver 1997). Adam Smith believed that, prior to the development of the impersonal markets of commercial society and the impersonal administration of legal-rational bureaucracies, all friendships tended to have the character of necessity. It was only with the separation of commercial relations and personal life that friendship could become a matter of sympathy and affection devoid of calculation of interest. In more recent sociological writing about marriage and the family, the themes of growing intimacy, privacy and equality date back to at least the 1940s (Burgess and Locke 1945) and are part of the orthodox account of how the 'modern family' developed (Jamieson 1987). In the 1960s Peter Berger and Hans Kellner (1964) laid out theoretically the claim that an intense dialogue between marriage partners (or members of co-resident couples) functions to create a stable sense of the self, screening off a sense of chaos, despite the fragility of a socially constructed world. This prefigured a key strand of Giddens's argument by over twenty years. Giddens is, of course, not the only recent theorist to claim a distinctive late twentieth-century twist. Ulrich Beck (1992; Beck and Beck-Gernsheim 1995), for example, has produced a comparable account. The sociological literature of the 1950s–70s, like the more recent contributions, engaged with popular debate about the demise of the family. However, eagerness to counter simplistic negative accounts sometimes resulted in over-simplification, underplaying how continued structural inequalities shaped personal life, insufficiently unravelling causality and timing (Harris 1983), failing to distinguish the experiences of lived lives from views of how they should be lived (Coontz 1992; Finch and Summerfield 1991; Morgan 1991, 1992; Skolnick 1991). All of these issues re-emerge as problems in Giddens's account.

David Morgan (1991, 1992, 1996) has analysed how the twentieth-century story of change in family and marriage 'from institution to relationship', became an ideological simplification of social change particularly promoted by professionals with a vested interest in marital and relationship problems. As Morgan notes, ideological constructions are nevertheless consequential. However, the nature of the fit between the ideological story and everyday relationships is not simple. It is possible, for example, for the discourse of 'relationship experts' to infuse everyday talk while other factors modify the parameters of everyday practice. Such issues are not fully explored in *The Transformation of Intimacy.* Despite reference to the reflexive interrelationship between his work, popular culture and therapeutic discourse, Giddens draws relatively uncritically on therapeutic literature, as documents about and symptoms of personal and social change (Giddens 1992:86). Not surprisingly, his account of 'the pure relationship' fits well with a therapeutic discourse that assumes the value of self-disclosure in therapy and in the relationships which therapy hopes to cure.

In contrast, many academic and popular commentators express concern over individualism 'going too far' and critique the individualising tendencies of therapy for distorting recognition of social problems and mitigating against collective resistance. Giddens explicitly counters Foucault's discussion of therapy as a mechanism of extending subtle forms of regulation and control (Giddens 1992:28–34). In the process, Giddens also silently lays aside accounts such as those of Christopher Lasch (1977) and Bauman (1990) which focus on the negativity of dependency on experts for self-direction, self-creativity and unmediated social interaction. Bauman (1991:205) refers to Richard Sennett's (1977) concept of 'destructive *gemeinschaft*' in asserting that damage is caused to social cohesion by the psychological burdens of incitements to mutual disclosure. There are other earlier warnings in the sociological literature. Georg Simmel (Wolff 1950) argued that total lack of secrets could bankrupt a relationship as there was nothing left to wonder about. In claiming openness as a constructive process, Giddens interleaves his analysis of late modernity with a rather unpacked psychological theory. It is the ontological security of childhood that provides the self-resources for a subsequent creative process of self-disclosure. The starting premise is that a wide range of social circumstances in childhood, anything more caring than suffering violent, sexually abusive or highly neglectful parents, will create the necessary psychological conditions for 'generalised trust' in others and ontological security. This leaves an under-explained biographical contrast between an easily acquired secure sense of self in childhood and an adult who only just escapes doubts about self-authenticity by working hard on a narrative of the self and fragile personal relationships. Given the emphasis Giddens places on the fragility of personal life in a highly self-reflexive late modernity, the exempting of the parent–child relationship from fragility involves resort to a psychology divorced from his own sociological analysis.

The contribution of therapeutic discourse to damaging gender stereotypes is also unremarked, reflecting a more general underplaying of structures of gender inequality in *The Transformation of Intimacy*. Feminist work has documented how women carrying the burdens of systematic gender inequality have been recast by medical and therapeutic experts as pathological individuals (recent accounts are given by Busfield 1996; Dobash and Dobash 1992). Morgan has recently warned that the continued theoretical focus on the relational character of heterosexual partnerships can obscure persisting and institutionalised gender inequalities (1996:77–8). While drawing on particular pieces of feminist work, there is no sustained discussion in *The Transformation of Intimacy* of the feminist scholarship that has subjected the interrelationships between 'private' and 'public', 'personal' and 'political' to intensive theorising and empirical exploration over the last decades. Yet debate concerning the resilience of gender inequality is centrally relevant to Giddens's case. This is far from a settled matter, but many key players in the debate would declare the undermining of male privilege through transformations in heterosexual intimacy theoretically unlikely. Some would claim the postulated change in heterosexual relationships unlikely in itself; those who accept the possibility are likely to doubt that radical transformation would necessarily follow. It is not clear, for example, that change in the quality of heterosexual relationships would shatter the interconnection of gendered labour markets, gendered distributions of income and wealth, and gendered divisions of domestic labour.

Most theorists who remain committed to the term 'patriarchy' would see difficulties, although not all are as definitive as Christine Delphy and Diana Leonard in the following advice: 'It may be that the family and heterosexuality are not the place to start when trying to change gender relations' (1992:266). Moreover, it should be noted that many leading theorists of gender and power can envisage gender equality within a heterosexual personal life within and despite patriarchal arrangements. 'Further, if we see patriarchy as referring to properties of a system as a whole rather than to the individual actors who make up the system, it may be possible to find at the more individual or interpersonal level, examples of non-patriarchal [non-oppressive] yet gendered practices' (Morgan 1996:91). Theorists who prefer speaking in terms of 'doing gender' and different 'gender regimes' to deploying the concept of 'patriarchy' willingly acknowledge the possibility of gender equality in one setting without necessary transformation of another (Connell 1987, 1995). The actual impact of changes within domestic and interpersonal relations on the wider structuring of gender relationships is an empirical matter (Morgan 1996:80). There is no weighing of either theoretical or empirical states of play by Giddens and *The Transformation of Intimacy* seems strangely cut off from both the wealth of relevant feminist research and his own earlier discussions of the interrelationships of structure and action.

For obvious epistemological and methodological reasons, in examining the empirical evidence of how personal lives are conducted there is no possibility of verifying or disproving Giddens's broad-sweep account. The aim of this paper is necessarily a more modest one of looking for signs concerning the nature of intimacy as it is constructed in everyday relationships and considering how well proximities to and divergences from 'pure relationships' sit with his understanding of social change. In what follows, I mainly focus on research literature that deals with heterosexual couple relationships, as they are the most heavily researched by the key players in the argument. A more general review of personal relationships (Jamieson 1998) suggests that intimacy has more than one dimension, that diversity in the make-up of intimacy is considerable even within one category of relationship such as friendships or mother–child relationships. Moreover, personal interactions, even those of friendships, the least structured of intimate relationships, often reinforce gender, class and ethnic divisions rather than democratise personal life (Allan 1989; Griffiths 1995; Hey 1997; Thorne 1993). Personal relationships are not typically shaped in whatever way gives pleasure without the taint of practical, economic and other material circumstances. Few relationships, even friendships, are mainly simply about mutual appreciation, knowing and understanding.

Couple Relationships

Giddens intimates potential radical shifts in heterosexual practices. If 'pure relationships' are indeed becoming more common, equalisation in men and women's interest in and experience of sex and intimacy can be anticipated. Similarly the ascendancy of 'plastic sexuality' will mean greater sexual experimentation and hence an increase in the diversity of sexual practice.

There has undoubtedly been a significant shift in public discourse about sex and sexuality that appears to acknowledge gender equality and show greater tolerance of diversity in sexual practices (Weeks 1995). Greater acceptance of gender equality is typified by the shift in magazines aimed at women and girls. Where once their content retained a coy silence on sex and a strong emphasis on romance, readers now receive acceptance or encouragement of active sexuality and sexual desire (McRobbie 1991, 1994, 1996). However, as Jackson and Scott note, the messages of public discourse remain mixed, reasserting as often as challenging the boundaries of conventional femininity. Incitements to active female sexuality have not undermined the dominant view of 'real sex' as coitus ending in ejaculation. Moreover, 'women and girls are positioned as sexual carers who do the emotional work and police their own emotions to ensure that they do not place excessive demands on men' (Jackson and Scott 1997:567).

Sexual behaviours, their meanings and significance are notoriously difficult to investigate. Only partial insight can be gleaned from the behavioural measures which surveys offer, such as incidence of 'mutual orgasm'. However, relevant indicators can be found in recent large-scale surveys published in Britain and the United States (Wellings *et al.* 1994; Lauman *et al.* 1994). There is modest evidence of departures from conventional forms of sexual activity and of the more varied sexual repertoire implied by 'plastic sexuality.' The British survey found high levels of 'non-penetrative' sex and the US survey of 'oral sex', although it is not possible to know about the meanings and inter-personal dynamics behind these activities. However, there was no clear evidence of gender convergence in sexual behaviour but rather a rediscovery of patterns of gender difference, which appear to have only modestly moderated since Kinsey (1948, 1953). On all measures of sexual activity investigated, ranging from questions on thinking about sex and masturbating (asked only in the United States) to questions on number and type of partners and forms of sexual activity engaged in with them, more men are sexually active than women. The US survey revealed that men are still more likely to experience orgasm during sex than women and the British survey that men think orgasm is more essential to sexual satisfaction than women. Nevertheless, there is some evidence of gender convergence in expectations and ideas about sex. When responding to attitude questions in surveys men and women often say very similar things about the meaning and significance of sexual behaviour in a couple-relationship. For example, in the British survey, most men and women think that 'companionship and affection are more important than sex in a marriage'.

However, in-depth interview studies continue to uncover a persistent, tenacious and phallocentric view of heterosexual sex as something that men do to women. It is conclusively documented that the early sexual experiences of most young people involve neither the negotiation of mutual pleasure nor a fusion of sex and emotional intimacy (Holland *et al.* 1991, 1993, 1994, 1998; Thomson and Scott 1991; Tolman 1994; Wight 1994, 1996). Evidence of mutual sexual pleasure, equality and deep intimacy among older heterosexuals is outweighed by sex and gender trouble. In their study of long-term couples, Jean Duncombe and Dennis Marsden (1993, 1995, 1996) find women complaining about lack of intimacy and men about lack of sex. It seems that men are more emotionally withdrawn from the relationship than women and men derive more pleasure from sex in the relationship (see also Mansfield and Collard 1988; Thompson and Walker 1989). Robert Connell's (1995) biographical explorations of masculinities indicate persistent difficulties in reconciling equality, intimacy and sexuality even among 'new men' and 'gay men'.

The *Transformation of Intimacy* raises the possibility of equality and intimacy in personal life democratising gender relationships more generally. However, empirical work on heterosexual couples routinely continues to find that men exercise more power than women in the partnerships: for example, having more choice concerning opting in and out of domestic work and child care (Brannen and Moss 1991), and exercising more control of money (Morris 1990; Pahl 1989; Vogler 1994). But at the same time, research continues to find couples exhibiting such inequalities who collaboratively generate a sense of caring, intimate, equal relationships. This was eloquently demonstrated by Kathryn Backett (1982) in the 1970s and her findings continue to be echoed in much more recent work. Couples' carefully constructed sense of each other as good, mutually caring partners, despite unequal sacrifice for their common good, diverges considerably from the 'pure relationship'.

Research suggests that the ways in which couples generate a sense of themselves and their partners as mutually caring often reproduce gender inequality – the creativity and intimacy of couples is not yet typically harnessed to gender transformation. Many couples refer to gendering (i.e. underpinning gender difference) structural factors – the vagaries of employment including men and women's different earnings and prospects in the labour market, the incompatibility of combining the demands of childrearing and full-time employment – as if a traditional division of labour adopted because of such structures beyond their control were therefore exempted from any possible inequality. Many also deploy a variety of gendering but apparently gender neutral devices to maintain a counterfactual sense of equality ('she happens to be better at cooking,' 'he doesn't enjoy cooking as much').

Others continue to make explicit reference to traditional beliefs about manhood and womanhood, sometimes disavowing that this is how life should always be organised, but accepting that it works for them (for example, 'It's how I/he/she was brought up' – see other examples in Brannen and Moss 1991; Hochschild 1990; Mansfield and Collard 1988). This is not to deny the significance of a sense of equality for a sense of intimacy among many couples. There is a general taken-for-granted assumption that a good relationship will be equal and intimate. Rather it is to suggest that creative energy is deployed in disguising inequality, not in undermining it (Bittman and Lovejoy 1993).

Mutual self-disclosure is the basis of intimacy in 'the pure relationship', but empirical evidence suggests this is not the sole or necessarily the ascendant type of intimacy between couples. Love and care expressed through actions is a very different dimension of intimacy from 'knowing', the mutual disclosure of the 'pure relationship', but it continues to loom large in how many couples view their relationship. For couples who live together, the time, money and effort each devotes to their household often symbolises love and care for each other. A common traditional rhetoric which couples can and have drawn on when overlooking everyday differences in power and privilege is the visualisation of their relationship in terms of complementary gifts – the man's wage as his expression of care for his partner and his family, and the woman's matching gift of housework as expressing her tender loving care (Cheal 1988; Morgan 1991). Many dual-worker households continue to use a slightly modified version of this theme by talking down the woman's wage as supplementary rather than the main earnings and talking up the man's typically relatively limited contributions to domestic work (Brannen and Moss 1991; Hochschild 1990). Tactics also include minimising the significance of men's lack of practical involvement in the household or child care and maximising the significance of their role as an emotional support (although discontent is then the consequence when emotional support is perceived as weak). Expressions of interest, concern and reassurance, 'emotional work', can compensate for a lack of practical assistance. Visualising their relationship as rebalanced in these ways centres on an intimacy that is somewhat removed from the 'pure relationship'. Love and care as expressed by a more practical doing and giving is as much the crux of their relationship, as a process of mutually discovering and enjoying each other.

Couples who achieve a more objective equality are not necessarily any closer to a 'pure relationship'. Empirical research identifies a minority of couples who make painstaking efforts to achieve relatively equal contributions to a joint project of a household. In an Australian study, Goodnow and Bowes (1994) discuss heterosexual couples who have been recruited *because* they do things differently. However, unlike a number of other studies they are not recruited through feminist networks (Haas 1982; Kimball 1983; VanEvery 1995). For these couples, the supposedly gender neutral 'circumstances', 'competencies' and 'preferences' (Mansfield and Collard 1988) that others use to justify unequal divisions of labour were not good enough reasons if they then produce a situation in which men systematically have more privileges such as free time. Goodnow and Bowes suggest that their respondents were not of a wholly different mind set from more traditional couples but rather that they focused on the same dimensions of love and care. It was not their assumption that a loving couple would mutually care for each other in practical ways which was distinctive but their thorough analysis of the who, when, where and why of how this was done fairly. This was initiated in the name of fairness towards each other without necessarily adopting any feminist rhetoric, although women had typically prompted the process. These women had talked their way out of co-operating in an enterprise of covering over the gap between an ideal of equality and making more effort in practice to sustain their joint project. The thoroughness of establishing basic principles of fairness ruled out many of the tactics that might otherwise have justified gendered patterns. By the time of interview couples were settled into 'doing things differently', but conflict had often been the initial consequence.

The fact that researchers have identified heterosexual relationships that seem equal and unexploitative does not necessarily make these couples the vanguard of the future but even supposing they are, then something rather different is going on for them than 'the pure relationship'. The couples have applied reflexive awareness of the malleability of the world and themselves to creating a framework of rules. The dialogue that they engage in, reworking what is fair and what is not, is a practical as well as political, sociological and philosophical piece of personal engagement. Any consequent politicisation and personal empowerment has not stemmed only from a preoccupation with their own relationship but a more general engagement with the world. While starting from their own situation, their rules of fairness seek universal principles and are not tied to or derived from knowledge of each other's unique qualities. In focusing intense dialogue on practical arrangements and abstract rules, the couple creates projects that inevitably add to the institutionalised framework over and above their relationship. Hence they stand outside of the ideal-typical pure relationship which seeks to bracket off distractions from the intensity of the relationship itself.

Giddens suggests that high rates of dissolution among couples reflect the fragility of the 'pure relationships', which require the psychological balancing act of sustaining mutual trust while knowing the relationship is only 'good until further notice'. However, it seems more plausible to see the fragility of heterosexual couples as a consequence of the tension between strengthening cultural emphasis on intimacy, equality and mutuality in relationships and the structural supports of gender inequalities, which make these ideals difficult to attain. Studies such as Brannen and Moss (1991), Hochschild (1990) and Mansfield and Collard (1988) document how collaborative effort can produce a sense of being equal and intimate, in spite of inequalities. What is important is not an intense process of mutual self-disclosure and exploration but a shared repertoire of cover stories, taboos and self-dishonesty. However, inequalities and asymmetries in parenting, domestic divisions of labour and 'emotion work' sometimes breed simmering discontent which defies the desire to feel equal and intimate. Drawing on Hochschild's work, Duncombe and Marsden (1993) talk of women 'deep acting' in order to maintain a sense that their relationship is 'ever so happy', but sometimes 'deep acting' gives way to more critically aware and cynical 'shallow acting'. Diane Vaughan (1986) suggests that uncoupling begins with a secret, one partner's unspoken but nurtured feeling of discomfort with the relationship. She theorises the process of uncoupling as the converse of constructing a sense of self and shared world-view through the marriage dialogue described by Berger and Kellner (1964). Interestingly, her respondents' stories of uncoupling show that while the disaffected partner withdraws from the relationship, the other partner often has no sense of loss until the secret is dramatically announced. Couples did not seem to be seeking to inhabit 'pure relationships' in any of these studies but rather relationships which were intended to last, which couples worked to institutionalise *and* wanted to feel equal and intimate.

Same-sex couples, and particularly lesbians, are identified by Giddens as in the vanguard of developing 'pure relationships' and hence as having a high incidence of relationship breakdown. There is a body of work which suggests that same-sex couples, and particularly lesbians, tend to have and to see themselves as having more equal relationships than heterosexual couples (Dunne 1997; Kurdek 1993; Weeks, Donavan and Heaphy 1998; Weston 1991) and that, moreover, lesbian relationships are particularly characterised by high levels of intimacy and communication (Dunne 1997:201). However, the empirical evidence does not convince me that either lesbians or gay men typically have 'pure relationships', although Weeks and his colleagues sometime use the term. Some research indicates that lesbians are wary of treating their partner as the sole source of intimacy but rather carefully maintain a supportive network, a 'chosen family' of friends, ex-lovers and kin (Heaphy, Weeks and Donovan 1998; Weston 1991). Scrutiny of the 'ground rules' Christian gay couples construct reveals a range of practical devices to protect their relationship, including an understood tactical silence about casual sexual encounters outside the relationship (Yip 1997). As yet the evidence on which to assess the relative fragility of same-sex relationships is rather sparse and tends to stress similarities to heterosexuals rather than difference (Kurdek 1991). Moreover, there are reasons, other than 'the pure relationship', why same-sex relationships may be vulnerable to breakdown. It is clear that if same-sex couples do manage to securely maintain a long-term relationship they do so despite a wider social fabric, which is relatively hostile to its institutionalisation.

Couples and Parent–Child Relationships

The processes of having children and making a joint project of their upbringing create structures over and above a relationship and therefore necessarily detract from the purity of the 'pure relationship'. Giddens evades the contradiction he has set up theoretically between parenting and 'the pure relationship' through the assertion that parent–child relationships, like couple relationships, are tending towards 'the pure relationship'. However, he does not then lay claim to the full range of attributes of 'the pure relationship' in the case of parents and children. Unlike couple relationships, this apparently does not render parent–child relationships as fragile, as 'good until further notice', at least not before 'basic trust' and 'ontological security' have typically formed. The research literature suggests that having children can unbalance couples but not primarily because children detract from their pure relationship but as a consequence of gender inequalities becoming more extreme. Parenting is rarely a gender-neutral activity and often exacerbates inequalities in divisions of labour, free time, disposable income and other privileges. Mothers typically remain much more emotionally and practically involved with their children than fathers.

Unlike his discussion of couple relationships, which more strongly resonates with similar arguments elsewhere, Giddens's claims about 'pure relationships' between parents and children have had little take-up. While empirical research finds parents claiming they want to have closer relationships with their children than they had with their own parents, there is no clear evidence of a trend to democratic 'pure relationships' even among parents and teenage children. The search for a 'pure relationship' with children seems to be an unattainable ideal particularly pursued by white, middle-class mothers. Research into their mothering finds them stressing empathy, understanding and communication with older children (Brannen *et al.* 1994) and employing reasoning and pseudo-democracy with younger children (Walkerdine and Lucey 1989). Mutually intimate mother–child relationships are not necessarily the consequence, however.

Julia Brannen and her colleagues (1994) document the complex negotiations between London-based parents and their 15 and 16 year old children. While many fathers were rather shadowy figures in young men's and young women's lives, mothers typically worked hard at trying to maintain a good relationship with their children. However, what a good relationship meant varied by class and ethnicity. Mothers were generally confident that their teenage children knew they continued to love and care for them; but some talked of a 'good relationship' in terms which echoed 'the pure relationship', with particular emphasis on a deeper knowing and understanding of each other. White middle-class mothers were most likely to claim to be very close to their teenage child. They stressed empathy and understanding, being able to 'talk', having 'listened' and 'tried to understand'. However, teenagers did not necessarily experience the practice of 'knowing' in this way. Middle-class mothers were more likely to be constantly on the lookout for information that would warn them of possible trouble. In doing so they were working against their cherished desire to really *know* their child. Knowing as a means of control interfered with knowing as a dimension of intimacy. What parents consider to be a 'confiding' relationship could be experienced by the teenager as one-sided pressure to make disclosures. Mothers who were attempting to retain some control over their teenager, while being like a friend and equal, could not conceal their precarious balancing act.

Clearly the ideal of the involved and sensitive father has grown in stature in recent years, but research continues to find many men who are content to be providers and background figures (Bjornberg 1992; Brannen and O'Brien 1995; Busfield 1987; Lewis and O'Brien 1987; Russell 1983). The statistics continue to show that many non-custodial fathers lose touch with their children; research indicates that cumulatively, by the end of the second post-divorce year, about half of fathers have faded out of regular contact (Cherlin 1992; Cherlin and Furstenberg 1988). Nevertheless, the ideal of the involved father and equality in mothering and fathering can be highly consequential. For example, Bren Neale and Carol Smart (1997) have found fathers claiming their right to custody of their children following divorce on the grounds that 'everybody's talking about new age man'. Their study revealed that men's interest in custody sometimes reflects a combative approach to their wives rather than their prior relationship with their children. Moreover, men used ideas of gender equality to do their wife down, claiming that because women in general have equality then their wife should forfeit any special claim to children even if she had been a full-time wife and mother. This is a good empirical demonstration of how the ideals of equality and intimacy can feed into consequences that are a negation of 'the pure relationship'.

The significant dimension of intimacy in many parent–child relationships may not be being close by 'knowing' and talking to each other. A sense of unconditional love, trust and acceptance may be sustained with caring actions and relatively few words. Studies suggest that a good relationship between some parents and their growing-up children requires increasing silence on the part of the parents rather than an intense dialogue of mutual disclosure. Just as in couple relationships, silence need not mean an absence of care.

Conclusion

Giddens's work suggests a radical transformation of intimacy is under way with potentially profound consequences for gender politics and the wider social fabric. In order to keep faith with the argument, the much messier and less optimistic picture provided by empirical research has to be seen as the flux and confusion of an uneven transition. Indeed, some commentators seem prepared to give this benefit of the doubt (Weeks 1995). However, this is a generosity that I balk at on political and theoretical as well as empirical grounds.

Extolling the values of mutual self-disclosure and 'the pure relationship' feeds into a therapeutic discourse that has sometimes been the antithesis of empowering for women and gays. While in *The Transformation of Intimacy* women are treated as the vanguard of the new intimacy, as Stevi Jackson and Sue Scott note 'we should be wary of valorising what is symptomatic of subordination however tempting it might be to deride men's emotional incompetence'(1997:568). At the same time as treating women as the vanguard of social change, the book eschews any systematic review of feminist scholarship. It is important to note that feminist-informed work of the last few decades has not typically concluded that if sufficient men and women can live together as equals and intimates then how other institutions, work-places, the state, the street, and the like, 'do gender' will automatically radically unravel. If anything, the causal arrows point in the other direction to the ways in which efforts within personal life are constantly countered elsewhere. Giddens refers to the diffusion of change from the personal to other arenas without offering a developed sociological explanation of the intervening mechanisms. Ironically, this gives credence to the popular psychology of changing the world by transforming your inner self at the expense of more sociological accounts of social change.

Theoretically, the pure relationship seems to be a near impossibility for domestic partnerships and parent–child relationships that are necessarily embroiled in financial and material matters over and above the relationship. When adults share responsibility for physical space, money and material things, how these are managed cannot but become both symbolic of and reflexively constitutive of the relationship itself. Matters ranging from who last cleaned the toilet to how the insurance claim was spent become means of communicating care or neglect, equality or hierarchy, unity or division. Actions can speak louder than words and perhaps the important words, if men and women are to live together as equals, may be sorting out fair ways to get things done rather than purer forms of mutual self-disclosure.

The current state of play in gender politics remains a matter of debate. No theorist believes that what is happening in everyday gender play can be simply read off from the volume of talk about gender equality and heterosexual or homosexual intimacy. Ideals of equality and intimacy between men and women have been part of public discourse for decades, albeit that the themes have become louder and more diverse, for example, inciting men to become more emotionally expressive, more considerate lovers, communicative partners and sensitive fathers. Unquestionably, this barrage is consequential and must be associated with other changes that are in some sense in this direction. Yet, it is perfectly possible that widely disseminated ideals are, nevertheless, not widely or radically experienced lived realities of the present, nor will they be of the future. Although the evidence suggests most individuals now approach couple relationships with expectations which include mutual emotional support and treating each other like equals, this tells us relatively little concerning how people actually behave towards each other. Empirically, intimacy and inequality continue to coexist in many personal lives. Personal relationships remain highly gendered. Men and women routinely both invoke gender stereotypes or turn a convenient blind eye to gendering processes when making sense of themselves as lovers, partners, mothers, fathers and friends. While agreeing with Giddens's rejection of the more pessimistic account of personal life at the century's end, I note that the creative energies of many social actors are still engaged in coping with or actively sustaining old inequalities rather than transforming them.

Acknowledgements

Thank you to the three reviewers for their extremely helpful comments.

References

ALLAN, G. 1989. *Friendship: Developing a Sociological Perspective.* Hemel Hempstead, Harvester Wheatsheaf.

BACKETT, K. 1982. *Mothers and Fathers.* London, Macmillan.

BAUMAN, Z. 1990. 'Modernity and Ambivalence'. In M. Featherstone (ed.), *Global Culture: Nationalism, Globalization and Modernity.* London, Sage.

BAUMAN, Z. 1991. *Modernity and Ambivalence.* Cambridge, Polity.

BECK, U. 1992. *Risk Society: Towards a New Modernity.* London, Sage.

BECK, U. and BECK-GERNSHEIM, E. 1995. *The Normal Chaos of Love.* Cambridge, Polity.

BERGER, P. and KELLNER, H. 1964. 'Marriage and the Construction of Reality'. *Diogenes,* reprinted in M. Anderson (ed.), *The Sociology of the Family.* Hamondsworth, Penguin, 1980, pp. 302–24.

BITTMAN, M. and LOVEJOY, F. 1993. 'Domestic Power: Negotiating an Unequal Division of Labour within a Framework of Equality'. *Australian and New Zealand Journal of Sociology* 29:302–21.

BJORNBERG, U. (ed.), 1992. *European Parents in the 1990s: Contradictions and Comparisons.* New Brunswick and London, Transaction.

BRANNEN, J., DODD, K., OAKLEY, A. and STOREY, P. 1994. *Young People, Health and Family Life.* Buckingham, Open University Press.

BRANNEN, J. and MOSS, P. 1991. *Managing Mothers: Dual Earner Households after Maternity Leave.* London, Unwin Hyman.

BRANNEN, J. and O'BRIEN, M. (eds.), 1995. *Childhood and Parenthood: Proceedings of the ISA Committee for Family Research Conference 1994.* London, Institute of Education, University of London.

BURGESS, E. W. and LOCKE, H. J. 1945. *The Family: From Institution to Companionship.* New York, American Book Company.

BUSFIELD, J. 1987. 'Parenting and Parenthood'. In G. Cohen (ed.), *Social Change and the Life Course.* London, Tavistock.

BUSFIELD, J. 1996. *Men, Women and Madness: Understanding Gender and Mental Disorder.* London, Macmillan.

CHEAL, D. 1988. *The Gift Economy.* London, Routledge.

CHERLIN, A. 1992. *Marriage, Divorce, Remarriage*. Cambridge, Mass., Harvard University Press.

CHERLIN, A. and FURSTENBERG, F. 1988. 'The Changing European Family: Lessons for the American Reader'. *Journal of Family Issues* 9: 291–7.

CONNELL, R. W. 1987. *Gender and Power*. London, Allen & Unwin.

CONNELL, R. W. 1995. *Masculinities*. Cambridge, Polity Press.

COONTZ, S. 1992. *The Way We Never Were: American Families and the Nostalgia Trip*. New York, Basic Books.

CRAIB, I. 1994. *The Importance of Disappointment*. London, Routledge.

CRAIB, I. 1997. 'Social Constructionism as a Social Psychosis'. *Sociology* 31:1–15.

DELPHY, C. and LEONARD, D. 1992. *Familiar Exploitation: A New Analysis of Marriage in Contemporary Western Societies*. Cambridge, Polity Press.

DOBASH, R. E. and DOBASH, R. 1992. *Women, Violence and Social Change*. London, Routledge.

DUNCOMBE, J. and MARSDEN, D. 1993. 'Love and Intimacy: The Gender Division of Emotion and "Emotion Work"'. *Sociology* 27:221–41.

DUNCOMBE, J. and MARSDEN, D. 1995. '"Workaholics" and "Whingeing Women": Theorising Intimacy and Emotion Work: The Last Frontier of Gender Inequality?' *Sociological Review* 43:150–69.

DUNCOMBE, J. and MARSDEN, D. 1996. 'Whose Orgasm is it Anyway? "Sex Work" in Long-Term Heterosexual Couple Relationships'. In J. Weeks and J. Holland (eds.), *Sexual Cultures: Communities, Values and Intimacy*. New York, St Martin's Press.

DUNNE, G. 1997. *Lesbian Lifestyles: Women's Work and the Politics of Sexuality*. London, Macmillan.

FINCH, J. and SUMMERFIELD, P. 1991. 'Social Reconstruction and the Emergence of Companionate Marriage'. In D. Clark (ed.), *Marriage, Domestic Life and Social Change: Writings for Jacqueline Burgoyne (1944–88)*. London, Routledge.

GIDDENS, A. 1990. *The Consequences of Modernity*. Cambridge, Polity and Stanford, Calif., Stanford University Press.

GIDDENS, A. 1991. *Modernity and Self-Identity: Self and Society in the Late Modern Age*. Cambridge, Polity.

GIDDENS, A. 1992. *The Transformation of Intimacy: Sexuality, Love and Eroticism in Modern Societies*. Cambridge, Polity.

GIDDENS, A. 1994. 'Living in a Post-Traditional Society. In U. Beck, A. Giddens and S. Lasch, *Reflexive Modernization: Politics, Tradition and Aesthetics in the Modern Social Order*. Cambridge, Polity.

GOODNOW, J. and BOWES, J. 1994. *Men, Women and Household Work*. Melbourne, Oxford University Press.

GRIFFITHS, V. 1995. *Adolescent Girls and Their Friends: A Feminist Ethnography*. Aldershot, Avebury.

HAAS, L. L. 1982. 'Determinants of Role Sharing Behaviour: A Study of Egalitarian Couples'. *Sex Roles* 8:747–60.

HARRIS, C. C. 1983. *The Family and Industrial Society*. London, Allen & Unwin.

HEAPHY, B., WEEKS, J. and DONOVAN, C. 1998. '"That's Like my Life": Researching Stories of Non-heterosexual Relationships'. *Sexualities* 1:453–70.

HEY, V. 1997. *The Company She Keeps: An Ethnography of Girls' Friendships*. Buckingham, Open University Press.

HOCHSCHILD, A. 1990. *The Second Shift: Working Parents and the Revolution at Home*. London, Piatkus.

HOLLAND, J., RAMAZANOGLU, C., SCOTT, S., SHARPE, S. and THOMSON, R. 1991. *Pressure, Resistance, Empowerment: Young Women and the Negotiation of Safer Sex*. London, Tufnell Press.

HOLLAND, J., RAMAZANOGLU, C. and SHARPE, S. 1993. *Wimp or Gladiator: Contradictions in the Acquisition of Masculine Sexuality*. London, Tufnell Press.
HOLLAND, J., RAMAZANOGLU, C. and SHARPE, S. 1994. 'Power and Desire: The Embodiment of Female Sexuality'. *Feminist Review* 46:21–38.
HOLLAND, J., RAMAZANOGLU, C., SHARPE, S. and THOMSON, R. 1998. *The Male in the Head: Young People, Heterosexuality and Power*. London, The Tufnell Press.
JACKSON, S. and SCOTT, S. 1997. 'Gut Reactions to Matters of the Heart: Reflections on Rationality, Irrationality and Sexuality'. *Sociological Review* 45:551–75.
JAMIESON, L. 1987. 'Theories of Family Development and the Experience of Being Brought Up'. *Sociology* 21:591–607.
JAMIESON, L. 1998. *Intimacy: Personal Relationships in Modern Societies*. Cambridge, Polity.
KIMBALL, G. 1983. *The 50–50 Marriage*. Boston, Mass., Beacon Press.
KINSEY, A. 1948. *Sexual Behaviour in the Human Male*. Philadelphia, W. B. Saunders.
KINSEY, A. 1953. *Sexual Behaviour in the Human Female*. Philadelphia, W. B. Saunders.
KURDEK, L. 1991. 'The Dissolution of Gay and Lesbian Couples'. *Journal of Social and Personal Relationships* 8:265–78.
KURDEK, L. 1993. 'The Allocation of Household Labour in Gay, Lesbian, and Heterosexual Married Couples'. *Journal of Social Issues* 49:127–40.
LASCH, C. 1977. *Haven in a Heartless World*. New York, Basic Books.
LAUMANN, E., MICHAEL R., MICHAELS, S. and GAGNON, J. 1994. *The Social Organization of Sexuality*. Chicago, University of Chicago Press.
LEWIS, C. and O'BRIEN, M. (eds.) 1987. *Reassessing Fatherhood: New Observations on Fathers and the Modern Family*. London, Sage.
MCROBBIE, A. 1991. *Feminism and Youth Culture: From 'Jackie' to 'Just Seventeen'*. Basingstoke, Macmillan.
MCROBBIE, A. 1994. *Postmodernism and Popular Culture*. London, Routledge.
MCROBBIE, A. 1996. '*More!* New Sexualities in Girls' and Women's Magazines'. In J. Curran *et al.* (eds.), *Cultural Studies and Communication*. London, Edward Arnold.
MANSFIELD, P. and COLLARD, J. 1988. *The Beginning of the Rest of Your Life: A Portrait of Newly-Wed Marriage*. London, Macmillan.
MORGAN, D. 1991. 'Ideologies of Marriage and Family Life'. In D. Clark (ed.), *Marriage, Domestic Life and Social Change: Writings for Jacqueline Burgoyne (1944–88)*. London, Routledge.
MORGAN, D. 1992. 'Marriage and Society'. In J. Lewis, D. Clark and D. Morgan, *Whom God Hath Joined Together: The Work of Marriage Guidance*. London, Tavistock and Routledge.
MORGAN, D. 1996. *Family Connections: An Introduction to Family Studies*. Cambridge, Polity.
MORRIS, L. 1990. *The Workings of the Household*. Cambridge, Polity.
NEALE, B. and SMART, C. 1997. 'Experiments with Parenthood?'. *Sociology* 31:201–19.
PAHL, J. 1989. *Money and Marriage*. London, Macmillan.
RUSSELL, G. 1983. *The Changing Role of Fathers*. Milton Keynes, Open University Press.
SENNETT, R. 1977. 'Destructive Gemeinschaft'. In N. Birnbaum (ed.), *Beyond the Crisis*. Oxford, Oxford University Press.
SILVER, A. 1997. '"Two Different Sorts of Commerce", or, Friendship and Strangership in Civil Society'. In J. Weintraub and K. Kumar (eds.), *Public and Private in Thought and Practice: Perspectives on the Grand Dichotomy*. Chicago, University of Chicago Press.
SKOLNICK, A. 1991. *Embattled Paradise: The American Family in an Age of Uncertainty*. New York, Basic Books.

THOMPSON, L. and WALKER, A. 1989. 'Gender in Families: Women and Men in Marriage, Work, and Parenthood'. *Journal of Marriage and the Family* 51:845–71.

THOMSON, R. and SCOTT, S. 1991. *Learning about Sex: Young Women and the Social Construction of Sexual Identity*. London, Tufnell Press.

THORNE, B. 1993. *Gender Play: Girls and Boys in School*. New Brunswick, Rutgers University Press, and Milton Keynes, Open University Press.

TOLMAN, D. L. 1994. 'Doing Desire: Adolescent Girls' Struggle for/with Sexuality'. *Gender and Society* 8:324–42.

VANEVERY, J. 1995. *Heterosexual Women Changing the Family: Refusing to be a 'Wife'*. London, Taylor and Francis.

VAUGHAN, D. 1986. *Uncoupling: Turning Points in Intimate Relationships*. Oxford, Oxford University Press.

VOGLER, C. 1994. 'Money in the Household'. In M. Anderson, F. Bechhofer and J. Gershuny (eds.), *The Social and Political Economy of the Household*. Oxford, Oxford University Press.

WALKERDINE, V. and LUCEY, H. 1989. *Democracy in the Kitchen: Regulating Mothers and Socialising Daughters*. London, Virago.

WEEKS, J. 1995. *Invented Moralities: Sexual Values in an Age of Uncertainty*. Cambridge, Polity.

WEEKS, J., DONOVAN, C. and HEAPHY, B. 1998 'Everyday Experiments: Narratives of Non-heterosexual Relationships'. In E. Silva and C. Smart (eds.), *The 'New' Family?* London, Sage.

WELLINGS, K., FIELD, J., JOHNSON, A. M. and WADSWORTH, J. 1994. *Sexual Behaviour in Britain: The National Survey of Sexual Attitudes and Lifestyles*. London, Penguin.

WESTON, K. 1991. *Families We Choose: Lesbians, Gays, Kinship*. New York, Columbia University Press.

WIGHT, D. 1994. 'Boys' Thoughts and Talk about Sex in a Working-Class Locality of Glasgow'. *Sociological Review* 42:702–37.

WIGHT, D. 1996. 'Beyond the Predatory Male: The Diversity of Young Glaswegian Men's Discourses to Describe Heterosexual Relationships'. In L. Adkins and V. Merchant (eds.), *Sexualizing the Social: Power and the Organizing of Sexuality*. London, Macmillan.

WOLFF, K. H. 1950. *The Sociology of Georg Simmel*. Glencoe, The Free Press.

YIP, A. K. T. 1997. 'Gay Male Christian Couples and Sexual Exclusivity'. *Sociology* 31:289–306.

Biographical note: LYNN JAMIESON is a Reader in Sociology at the University of Edinburgh. Her recent work includes *Intimacy: Personal Relationships in Modern Societies*, Polity Press, 1998.

Address: Department of Sociology, University of Edinburgh, 18 Buccleuch Place, Edinburgh EH8 9LN; e-mail L.Jamieson@ed.ac.uk

Part II
Changing Intimacies – Empirical Research

[3]

WHY MARRY? – PERCEPTIONS OF THE AFFIANCED

MARY HIBBS Senior Lecturer in Law, PROFESSOR CHRIS BARTON Director and JOANNE BESWICK Research Associate, Centre for the Study of the Family, Law and Social Policy, Staffordshire University

Observing the general decline in the numbers of couples marrying each year (down 40% to 267,303 between 1972 and 1998) we speculated not why is cohabitation popular (it quadrupled to 31% of all single women aged 18–49 between 1979 and 1998), but why, these days, do some couples choose to marry? In the future, will couples who decide to marry be regarded as endearingly old-fashioned or will it become chic to wed? Are couples marrying because they are aware of the legal consequences of marriage? Do they like what the law offers compared with what the law offers to cohabitants? Or does the law form no part of their decision to wed? Would more couples marry if they saw marriage as legally advantageous? A related question is whether cohabiting couples should be encouraged to marry, and if so, by whom? The Government 'share the belief of the majority of people that marriage provides the most reliable framework for raising children' (Government Consultation Document *Supporting Families* (Home Office, 1998), at para 4.13) and note that 'marriage remains the choice of the majority of people in Britain. For all these reasons, it makes sense for the Government to do what it can to strengthen marriage'. How can, and should, such aims be achieved: by a publicity campaign extolling the current legal (and other) advantages of marriage or, against the tide, a change in the law which would give (even) greater benefits to married couples (and thereby add to the discrimination against cohabitants)? It should be noted, however, that the Government's avowed support for families is somewhat equivocal in its support for marriage. It says that it neither has a wish to interfere in family life nor to pressure people into one type of relationship. It does not wish to try to make people marry, or criticise or penalise those who choose not to. However, the Government is placing additional obstacles in the path of those who wish to marry. It proposed an introduction of a requirement for couples to give a minimum of 15 days' notice of their intention to marry (in fact, this has already been done, but only as a by-product of other concerns). Part IX of the Immigration and Asylum Act 1999, in force from 1 January 2001, made changes to the Marriage Act 1949, in particular in relation to time-limits for giving notice of intention to marry, and the evidence required by registrars. The existing procedures for giving notice by superintendent registrar's certificate and licence (21 days) and superintendent registrar's certificate without licence (one day) are replaced by a common 15-day notice period (Immigration and Asylum Act 1999, s 160).

Yet if such a hasty marriage should happen to succeed, or at least endure, then that is something to celebrate. If, sadly, the marriage were to fail and the couple divorce, at least they would have access to the courts' discretionary powers to make financial provision and property orders, which take into account all the circumstances of the case, and attempt a fair and reasonable solution for the parties. However, if a couple were to be deterred from marriage by the extended waiting period and opted instead to cohabit, or to continue to cohabit, then they would have no recourse to such provisions. So, if marriage provides a neater (or, at least, better than nothing) end to a relationship by way of divorce provisions, why make marriage more difficult to enter, particularly for those partnerships rightly suspected of being doomed to failure?

At the moment, the Government's preferred option in support of marriage appears to be informed choice. One proposal is a 'simple and clear guide' (see *Supporting Families*, paras 4.13, 4.14) to the rights and responsibilities of marriage, to be made available through register offices, churches and other places of worship and other bodies providing advice to married people. A similar statement for cohabitants, on the other hand, had been relegated to 'CABs, libraries etc' (para 4.15).

The questions posed above can be better answered in the light of the perceptions held by the affianced of the legal consequences of marriage and the weight they attach to those perceptions. If, as we suspected, their perceptions proved to be faulty or they attached little or no importance to any legal knowledge they had, then would a change in those legal consequences be ineffective as a means of encouraging marriage? Are social, economic and emotional factors more persuasive than legal consequences in making the decision to marry?

Note – in the interests of brevity, we have omitted the sources of all non-legal materials cited and the details of our questionnaire, etc; we are happy to supply this information on request, together with those of our findings not included here. We also wish to thank Dr Stephen Cretney for his comments on an earlier draft (and for his encouragement), and Stephen Hardy and John Sudbery for their help in drafting the questionnaire.

THE LOVEBIRDS – A PROFILE OF OUR RESPONDENTS

All of our – 172 – respondents had made arrangements for some part of their wedding. However, some of them, who had agreed to marry and even had bookings for as far ahead as 3 years, stated that they would not be 'getting engaged just yet'. Such shared confidences gave us an early warning of the misunderstandings that were to follow. Our respondents came from (gritty?) North Staffordshire and (softer?) Cheshire, and we met them in 1998 and 1999.

Wedding fairs (fayres) proved to be a good hunting ground, our 'prey' were to be found in abundance and were extremely co-operative in sharing their views, and happiness, with us. Other of our respondents came via a friendly Superintendent Registrar of Marriages (such officers are, incidentally, instructed to discourage any individuals examining their Notice Boards for purposes other than in furtherance of the Marriage Acts), hairdressers, and from media interest in our research. We should emphasise that we took whom we could find; our affianced were not 'statistically representative' – so far as we are aware – of the nation's inamorata, and it is with due humility that we report what we learnt from them.

We were intrigued and heartened by the fact that only a very small number of the affianced declined our questionnaire: the reasons given for the rejections were often interesting. One said that she 'did not wish to think about after the wedding at all'. Another said that she did 'not want to know what he thought'. Another did not wish to take a questionnaire for her partner as she 'did not want him to think too closely about the issues'. One who did respond said she did not want to think about death or divorce happening to her, and thus did not want to know the relevant law. Yet all marriages are fated to end in one or other of those circumstances: perhaps there is a natural unwillingness to confront that fact.

Sixty-four per cent of our respondents consisted of each half of a couple: we were naturally intrigued to compare their (separately supplied) answers. One couple's responses revealed they did not agree as to the place they met, whether or not they had fixed a date for the wedding nor the venue of the ceremony. Interestingly, when asked, 'when did you decide to marry?' he said 'last month', whereas her answer revealed that she had made that decision 2 years earlier: perhaps it is more surprising that all the other couples gave the same date for their own decision to marry.

We now proceed to classify them in

advance of the cross-tabulated results which follow later.

Gender

Our respondents were split 63/37 in favour of fiancées. It was not that men refused to answer the questionnaire: they were just in comparatively 'short supply' at wedding fairs. No male respondent was present at any of the fairs without an accompanying fiancée.

One Canadian study highlighted the view that wedding preparation, which often entailed up to a year of planning, was regarded primarily as women's work. This is perpetuated in part by bridal magazines. Apparently, for the Canadian respondents, the transient nature of the wedding day made them feel they were not compromising their expectations for egalitarian marital relations, despite the fact that the work of organising weddings involved an unequal division of labour.

Age

The mean age of the men was 29.7 years and that of women 25.8 years. These figures appear to reflect the national tendency for people to marry, for the first time, a little later in life than in the recent past. Between 1971 and 1997 the mean age at first marriage in England and Wales rose from 24 years to 29 years for men, and from 22 years to 27 years for women.

Parenthood

Thirty-one respondents (19% of the 167 respondents who answered the question) were parents. Sixty-three per cent of the children were from previous relationships.

Cohabitants

We were particularly interested in the motivation of the 73% of those who were converting cohabitation into marriage. In England and Wales in 1998, 71.2% of brides and bridegrooms gave identical residential addresses before marriage.

The non-cohabitants were asked 'what are your views about living together before marriage?' and 18% of them disapproved of it. However, one cohabiting respondent was so enthusiastic about the benefits of premarital cohabitation that she thought that it should be compulsory for all. Another wished he had 'done it the first time around'.

Annual income

The average annual income of Cheshire respondents was £19,900 (slightly higher than the national average). Stoke-on-Trent (Staffordshire) respondents' average annual income was £15,300. This confirmed, to a limited extent, the stereotype of a relatively affluent county and its poorer neighbour. Our low figure for Stoke-on-Trent respondents' annual income may be due to the high proportion of females in that group.

Planned venue of wedding ceremony

Sixty per cent of respondents had chosen a religious venue, 13% a register office, 13% an hotel, 7% a stately home, 6% other (for example a foreign country) and 1% had not made a decision.

Fifty-nine per cent of all weddings in the UK in 1997 were conducted with civil ceremonies. This had risen to 61% by 1998. However, more first marriages (56%) had a religious ceremony than a civil ceremony (compare figures with the 60% of our respondents who had chosen a religious venue). For second and subsequent marriages, civil ceremonies outnumbered religious ceremonies by four to one.

Couples now have a choice of wedding venues. However, the law on formalities of marriage (the primary aim of which is to provide certainty about who is married to whom) limits that choice. The Marriage Act 1994 extended the choice for those who wanted a civil ceremony. For those couples who wanted neither a religious ceremony nor a wedding in a (perceivably) bleak register office, the 1994 Act introduced the ability to contract a valid marriage in approved premises. The local authority must be satisfied that the premises will support the dignity of marriage, and have no recent or continuing connection with any religion. In 1998 in England and Wales, 17.7% of all civil marriages were in 'approved premises', which, in Staffordshire, include not only the usual hotels, golf and country clubs and stately homes, but also the Bass Brewery Museum,

Uttoxeter Racecourse and Alton Towers.

Finally, social conservatives may like to know that only 56% of our cohabiting respondents chose a religious venue as opposed to 74% of 'non-cohabitants'. Perhaps not surprisingly, 68% of our 'first-timers' also chose a place of worship in marked contrast to the 26% of those who had been divorced.

Where had they met each other?

To assist in compiling a profile of respondents we were interested not only in their planned wedding venue but also where they first met. Unsurprisingly (although we have been unable to find any comparable national study) the most popular meeting place proved to be work. Work and education accounted for 30% of female respondents (40% of male respondents), and all the rest could be classified as social networking. In the 'other' category, some had met at weddings, amateur dramatic societies, scuba diving, the gym, on a blind date and one couple had met playing rugby (on the same side). Disappointingly, no one mentioned art galleries or supermarkets as meeting places, the 'preferred' meeting places of the 'chattering classes', if we are to believe the Sunday supplements, or could it be that their natural habitat lies further south?

WHY MARRY?

Perhaps a useful comparison can be made between couples' motives for marriage in the past and reasons given by respondents in our research project. The historian Lawrence Stone wrote that during the sixteenth century in England, marriage of the rich was usually arranged rather than consensual and the emotional ties were left to develop at a later date (or not). Stone noted that by the mid-eighteenth century a marked surge in what is now called individualism occurred, which was exemplified by the growing attraction of romantic love as the basis for marriage. Yet Stone's critic, Wrightson, pointed out that the familial behaviour of the English élite was very far from representative of that of their countrymen, and that there is little reason to follow Stone in regarding the rise of the companionate marriage as a new phenomenon for the later seventeenth and eighteenth centuries.

Today, are there any good legal reasons to marry? What are the legal benefits that are not available to cohabitants: either at all or not without positive action by cohabitants, for example joint ownership, wills, cohabitation contracts, etc? A spouse, exclusively, acquires rights, for example: reasonable financial support during marriage; matrimonial home rights; transfers between spouses exempt from inheritance tax and capital gains tax; better protection from domestic violence; intestate succession; and access to financial relief on divorce, nullity and judicial separation. Of course, one spouse's right is the other's duty, although there is the view, recently expressed by Ruth Deech, that there are now virtually no duties flowing from marriage (and that there would have been even fewer had Part II of the Family Law Act 1996 been implemented).

We wished to discover whether respondents were aware of any of these legal rights and if so whether they then took them into account when deciding to marry.

Table 1 – Why decide to marry?

Reason	%
Love	30
Commitment	13
Progression	9
Together	6
Love and ...	12
Children	4
Don't know	3
Other	23

No one claimed, or admitted to, financial reasons for marriage. Love was the single highest-ranking reason given for marriage. The 'other' category included such answers as 'about time', 'felt right', 'recognition', 'social norm', 'let's do it', 'wanted a party', 'just graduated', 'spur of the moment', 'like each other's company', 'conventional thing to do', 'fiancée wanted to', 'what a funny question' and 'family bereavement' (causing a re-evaluation of priorities). One woman cited religion. Two respondents when asked 'why?' answered 'why not?'. Only one person, a woman, said 'for legal reasons'. Four women said that they did not know why they were marrying; none of the men said that. Two women said 'because he asked', no man said 'because she asked' or even 'because I thought she would have me'.

When we cross-tabulated county against reasons for marriage we discovered that 38% from 'gritty' Stoke-on-Trent gave 'love' as the single reason, compared with 13% from 'softer, lusher' Cheshire. When reasons and county/gender were compared a picture of romantic Stoke-on-Trent men emerged (or, more cynically, maybe they had less income and property to protect than their Cheshire counterparts). Specifically, 50% of Stoke men compared with 14% of Cheshire men cited 'love' as the sole reason for their impending nuptials. When considering male and female respondents from Stoke-on-Trent it could be seen that women wanted love and something more: love and children; love and respect; love and commitment; and love and progression. Two Cheshire females cited 'recognition'. The reasons given by respondents conflict with Lord Byron's pronouncements in *Don Juan*: 'Man's love is of man's life a thing apart, 'Tis woman's whole existence' – proportionally half as many again of the male respondents, compared to the females, gave 'love' as their sole reason – and 'love and marriage rarely can combine'. Respondents appear to be more in tune with Frank Sinatra's vocalisation of the view that 'love and marriage go together like a horse and carriage'.

As can be seen from Table 2 below, 38% of cohabitants and 54% of non-cohabitants included love in their reasons for marriage. Was the lower percentage figure for 'love' from cohabitants because their initial cohabitation resulted from amorous motives, and that they were now moving on? Progression was identified by more cohabitants than non-cohabitants. (Only) two cohabitants identified recognition of their relationship as the reason to marry. One depressing national statistic is that those who cohabit premaritally were less likely – compared with those who do not premaritally cohabit – to think of marriage as a lifelong commitment. It is thought (by John Haskey) that this may be due to initial doubts about the relationship rather than cohabitation itself.

LEGAL KNOWLEDGE

Here we briefly return to the current law and to respondents' perceptions of that law. Alarmingly, 41% of all respondents thought marriage would not change the legal nature of their relationship with their partner, and 37% thought it would not have legal consequences for them with regard to their present or future children. Perhaps they shared Lady Bracknell's opinion that 'a man who desires to get married should know everything or nothing'. Under her interrogation Jack, her hapless interlocutor, admitted to knowing nothing and to being 29 (coincidentally, the average age of male respondents (see above)).

Table 2 - Reasons for marriage given by cohabitants and non-cohabitants

Why decide to marry?	Cohabitant (%)	Non-cohabitant (%)
Love	26	42
Commitment	13	15
Progression	10	6
Love and ...	12	12
Together	6	3
Children	6	3
Don't know	3	0
Recognition	2	0
Other	22	19

Marriage law is *table d'hote*, rather than *à la carte*. Despite sometimes being called 'the marriage contract', its terms are standard and imposed (unlike the private ordering of their affairs available to cohabitants by way of contract et al). In 1885 His Honour Judge Hannen said that: 'The contract of marriage is a simple one, which does not require a high degree of intelligence to comprehend' (*Durham v Durham* (1885) 10 PD 80, at p 82). One hundred years later, Mick Jagger anticipated the results of our research more accurately in likening marriage to 'signing a 356-page contract without knowing what's in it'.

Cohabitation

The Cohabitation Committee of the Solicitors Family Law Association (SFLA) has recommended that the law should be reformed to protect cohabitants. In the view of the committee, legal consequences of cohabitation should obtain after 2 years' living together or immediately on a child being born to the couple. In 1999 Jane Lewis found that one group of cohabitants would like some recognition of their status, some means of acknowledging that they had responsibilities, rather than a new legal status.

The final 52 of our respondents were asked: 'Does living together have legal consequences'. Nineteen per cent said 'no' and 69% said 'yes'. Their view was that rights accrued after a certain time, generally 6 months, of living together. Some respondents (11 male, five female) stated that as a result of cohabitation a couple became 'common law' husband and wife. Another misperception was that sharing household expenses resulted in property rights. Neither marriage nor cohabitation, of course, confers a right to a 'partner's' property during the lifetime of either relationship. But there are striking differences at the end of the relationships, whether by death (see intestacy below) or separation.

Twenty-three per cent of all male respondents had moved into their future spouses' property, compared to 33% of all female respondents. Forty-three per cent of the men and women who had moved into their partner's property thought they had acquired a claim on that property (69% of respondents, both cohabiting and non-cohabiting, thought that by living together rights accrued – see below).

Fifty per cent of all male respondents and 55% of all female respondents had moved with their future spouses into a new home. Seventy-four per cent of those people said they had a claim on the property.

Prenuptial agreements

The Government is considering whether to make prenuptial agreements legally binding (*Supporting Families*, paras 4.20–4.23). For those who wish to marry for other than legal reasons the Government might be wise to offer such an inducement: to allow the parties to order their own affairs and opt out of some of the rigid terms of the 'marital contract'. Our respondents' attitudes to prenuptial agreements ranged from: 'I don't agree with them' and 'We don't need one, we're not getting divorced', to 'only for millionaires' or 'for the rich and famous'. In 1999 Jane Lewis received similar responses to questions about premarital and cohabitation contracts. Her respondents regarded such agreements as 'too cold', 'too inflexible' and generally 'too American'.

Wills

A will is revoked by the testator's marriage (Wills Act 1837, s 18; substituted with a saving by Administration of Justice Act 1982, ss 18(1) and 73(6)). However, where it appears from the will that it was made in contemplation of marriage to the person subsequently married, then the will is not revoked (Wills Act 1837, s 18(3) and (4)). In England and Wales approximately 38% of those who died in 1999 had made a will.

Thirteen per cent of all of our 172 respondents had already made a will: their average age was 32 years (the overall average age of respondents was 27 years). Respondents were relatively young and probably had other things on their minds at this point in their lives: maybe approaching three score years and ten will focus attention sufficiently for the proportion to increase to the national level. One respondent had made a will following the complications of sorting out her grandfather's estate when he died intestate.

Forty-one per cent of parents had made a will. Twenty per cent of all respondents intended to make a will before they married. Sixty-five per cent of them intended to make a will after marriage. We suspect that this latter decision resulted from a mixture of a large dose of procrastination and, to a lesser extent, cost, rather than an awareness of the legal effect of marriage on existing wills. Additionally, it is acknowledged that respondents may have been prompted into a realisation that this was something that 'should be dealt with at some point' by a series of questions about wills.

Intestacy

From the figures on wills (see above) it can be seen that, currently, approximately 62% of people die intestate. The following supplementary – and open – question was asked of the final 52 respondents.

Table 3 – If cohabitants die without making a will, what happens to their money and property?

Beneficiary on intestacy?	%
Next of kin	64
State	10
Cohabitant	4
Don't know	13
Other	9

The respondents defined next of kin variously as parents, children and blood relatives – depending on the personal circumstances of the individual. Although 69% of those who were asked thought that living together had legal consequences – they were of the view that property would be divided equally if they were to 'split up' – only one of that group thought that the deceased's estate would go to the surviving cohabitant. The illogical, yet majority, view to emerge was an equal division in life but nothing on death.

Children

About 200,000 children are currently being born annually to cohabiting, but unmarried, parents. Yet only about 11,500 non-marital fathers acquired parental responsibility (PR) in 1998 (7798 PR orders and 3763 PR agreements registered). Ros Pickford's research indicates that, nationally, many people assume that non-marital fathers have automatic PR, especially those who jointly register the birth. Presumably, many never discover their lack of status. Those who do become aware of the discrepancy between their assumptions and the legal reality often make the discovery when their child starts (or changes) school, needs medical treatment or at a time of parental discord. Recently, the Lord Chancellor's Department, *Supporting Families* and the Advisory Board on Family Law have all recommended that the signing of the birth register by both parents would be an appropriate way for a non-marital father to obtain PR. (Incidentally, we were surprised that the Board did not address the vital question of whether, as under s 4 of the Children Act 1989, the non-marital father's PR could be excised.) Writing in 2000, Smart and Stevens point out that such reform would probably only bring the law into line with people's thinking.

This supplementary question was asked of the last 52 respondents – 'do fathers, who are not married to the mothers of their children, have the same rights over their children as married fathers?'.

Table 4 – Do non-marital fathers have PR?

Do non-marital fathers have parental responsibility?	%
Yes	53
No	25
Should have	2
Depends on birth certificate	4
Don't know	16

Parents appeared to be little wiser than non-parents in this matter. Five of the nine parents (56%) to answer this question thought that non-marital fathers had automatic parental rights. Fifty-two per cent of the non-parents held the same belief.

(Legal) benefits of marriage by gender

Not wishing to attempt to teach *Family Law* readers to suck eggs, we have naturally avoided a detailed superimposing of the 'correct' answers on to our respondents' views. Here, our diffidence is further compounded: we are unsure of what the right, net, answer is, and, in any event, wiser heads than ours differ as to which gender, if either, generally has the better of the more important, non-legal, advantages of union. One hundred and eleven respondents answered the following question:

Table 5 - Who do you think does better legally out of marriage?

Who does better legally?	%
Men	1
Women	46
Same	44
Don't know	6
Other	3

Included in 'other' are 'depends', 'least wealthy' (the most accurate brief – if ungrammatical – answer to the question?) and – 'lawyers'.

Table 6 - Who do you think does better legally out of marriage (gender)?

Who does better legally?	Men think %	Women think %
Men	0	1
Women	58	38
Same	35	49
Don't know	2	9
Least wealthy	2	0
Other	3	3

One male respondent said: 'It's much better now that it is all equal. Historically, men did better'.

WEIGHT ATTACHED TO PERCEPTIONS

Engaged couples who seek information about the legal effects of their forthcoming union could expect any advice session to range over such issues as: property and how it is to be held to reflect their intentions (particular thought being required where there are previous, sometimes complex relationships, for example it is a second marriage for either of the parties, and there are children from the first marriage); wills; tax; welfare benefits; pensions; right to financial support; matrimonial home rights; children (present and future); and prenuptial agreements. All of these issues, and more, need to be addressed by cohabitants. If we are to believe (see above) that the 'average couple' spend over £13,000 on their wedding, then is this the same couple who thought that it would be too expensive to consult a lawyer for advice on the legal implications of marriage, or to make a will? As a result of the high costs of so many weddings, wedding insurance has blossomed in the last 10 years. It can cover ruined clothes and bankrupt caterers but it covers neither a later divorce nor the bride and/or groom failing to turn up on the day. (*The Times*, 2 March 1996).

Five per cent of respondents had consulted a lawyer and a further 4% intended to seek legal advice (this intention may, of course, have been prompted by the question). One couple had consulted a lawyer because they were planning to wed in another country, which required documentary evidence that they were free to marry (for a list of legal requirements for marriages overseas see www.confetti.co.uk/travel/weddings_abroad/).

One 27-year-old female pagan had consulted a lawyer. She thought that marriage 'just makes the legal situation clearer'. A managing director with an annual income of £40,000 had no intention of making a will. He thought that on marriage his wife would automatically become entitled to half his estate and that on his death she would inherit it all. He thought that he would probably be 'worse off' in relation to property on marriage but was going ahead regardless. He was aware that premarital contracts were not binding. Another respondent was of the view that legal advice was unnecessary as 'we know all we need to know'. Others expressed the view that seeking legal advice was 'rather clinical'. Another view was 'we don't want legal advice – we trust each other'. A 22-year-old thought she was too young to make a will. One respondent ventured that he would not marry anyone who had consulted a lawyer; another said he would 'feel betrayed'.

Respondents were asked how far their view of the legal consequences of marriage had influenced their decision to marry.

Table 7 – Influenced by legal consequences?

Influenced by legal consequences?	%
Influenced	3
Consideration	11
Not at all	86

Two out of the five in the 'influenced' group had consulted a lawyer, compared with two of the 18 in the 'consideration' group and four of the 141 of the 'not at all' group. (However, four of the eight of those who had consulted a lawyer were 'not at all' influenced by the legal consequences of marriage.) All of those who said that they were influenced by the legal consequences of marriage were aware that marriage changes the legal nature of the relationship between couples. However, none of the 'influenced' group had made a will. Two of the group of five said they intended to make a will before marriage; two said they would make a will after marriage. None of the 'influenced' group thought that non-marital fathers had automatic parental responsibility. It was only in the 'not at all' group that anyone (eight of the 40, ie 20%) admitted to not knowing the answer to the question. In the divorced or widowed group (either themselves or their partners) four of the 14 said they were influenced or that the legal consequences of marriage were a consideration. Yet only 17% of the 'never married' respondents were influenced or gave consideration to the legal consequences.

One 27-year-old female respondent was to be 'divorced in the next few weeks'. She was not living with her fiancé – he did not wish to cohabit before their marriage. She said she was 'not bothered about marrying – he wants to'. This respondent had 'signed all property over to her "ex-husband" to escape hassle'. She thought women did better out of marriage. She said that she was not influenced by any legal consequences of marriage, unsurprisingly, as she did not think that marriage changed the legal position of couples. She had one child from her marriage.

As can be seen below, cohabitants and non-cohabitants had exactly the same profile here.

Table 8 – Are cohabitants influenced by legal consequences of marriage?

Influenced by legal consequences?	Cohabitant %	Non-cohabitant %
Influenced	3	3
Consideration	11	11
Not at all	86	86

Table 9 – Are cohabitants influenced by legal consequences of marriage (gender)?

Influenced by legal consequences?	Male %	Female %
Influenced	2	4
Consideration	8	13
Not at all	90	83

Cheshire females appeared to attach more importance to the legal consequences of marriage than any of the respondents in the other groups. However, we suspected that many respondents' indifference to the legal consequences of marriage arose from their view that by cohabiting they already 'have it all'. Another perception was that sharing household expenses resulted in property rights. One male respondent said that his cohabitant, who had moved into his property, had acquired an interest in the property because 'until we marry she will be my common law wife. We have a daughter together. I intend to make a will before marriage, not after. A lawyer will not be necessary'.

CONCLUSIONS

The Government is urging those who are about to marry to think twice before making such a commitment (*Supporting Families*, para 4.27). One proposal was that both parties should attend the register office to give notice of marriage, thus avoiding headlines seen in local papers such as 'Surprise! It's your wedding', where the bridegroom had been 'duped into believing he was to be best man' at a family wedding, only to have the roles reversed on his arrival. However, from 1 January 2001 it is compulsory for both parties to a proposed marriage to attend at the register office in person to give notice of their intention to marry (Immigration and Asylum Act 1999, s 161). Ironically, the motive is to pre-empt bogus marriages by asylum seekers, rather than the positive pursuit of family policy.

Will only those couples who consider and reflect, and then do not anticipate a personal involvement in the divorce system be encouraged to marry? What is to happen to the couple who are a little more sanguine about the durability of their forthcoming marriage? Particularly if they have little or no disposable income (and, therefore, are seen as a likely burden on any legal aid system on divorce), will they be advised (and by whom) not to marry (because it will cost the state too much and contribute to higher divorce statistics)? Even if a marriage does end in divorce, it appears to last longer than most cohabitations. Five years after the birth of their first child, only 48% of cohabiting mothers were still living with their child's father, compared with 92% of married mothers and with the 75% of those who were initially cohabiting but later married their partner (Office for National Statistics *Population Trends* (ONS, 1999)). (Could it be that the public commitment of marriage encourages stability or is it, conversely, that couples recognise they have an enduring relationship and so decide to marry?)

> 'To ascertain the nature of the contract of marriage a man (sic) must be mentally capable of appreciating that it involves the responsibilities normally attaching to marriage. Without that degree of mentality, it cannot be said that he (sic) understands the nature of the contract.' (*In the Estate of Park* [1953] 2 All ER 1411, at p 1430)

So at the time of the marriage ceremony the parties must be able to understand the nature of the contract they are entering. This can be compared with the requirement under the Enduring Powers of Attorney Act 1985 that the donor must have had the necessary capacity (understood the nature and effect of the power) when the power was executed. However, 'one cannot expect that the donor should have been able to pass an examination on the provisions of the 1985 Act' (*Re K, Re F* [1988] 1 All ER 358, at p 363). If pre-marriage information packs or information meetings are introduced there is no suggestion, as yet, that couples should be required to pass a test to obtain a licence (ie be able to demonstrate a knowledge and understanding of the legal consequences of marriage). Although couples are not tested for their legal knowledge, computer questionnaires are available to check compatibility. In the US more than one million people have taken a 125-question multiple-choice test (*The Times*, 2 August 1997). After the results came through 10% of them decided not to marry. The test claims to predict divorce with 85% accuracy. In England some of the clergy are using the system (*Prepare*) and the results as the basis for further discussions on compatibility.

'Preparation for marriage' programmes tend to focus on such matters as, for example, how to: deal with stress; deal with anger; raise children; plan a budget; deal with in-laws/family; and keep romance alive. At the very least, tests, questionnaires, information packs and even non-enforceable (at the moment) prenuptial contracts have the effect of concentrating the mind, causing couples to look to their futures. If nothing more, such devices encourage communication between the parties about significant issues and highlight potential disputes, which can only be a benefit to all concerned.

Surely there can be no argument against providing (legal and non-legal) information to couples to assist them to make informed choices about what should be the most fulfilling area of their lives? However, using the preliminary evaluation reports of divorce information meeting pilots, Janet Walker concluded that one standard package is unlikely to meet the needs of all comers. Presumably, similar conclusions may be drawn about pre-marriage information: too little, too late, if it is to be left to registrars to distribute information. Information on the legal consequences of all types of domestic partnerships (for example engagement; cohabitation, same sex and opposite sex; and marriage) should be part of the school (or is this too much, too soon?) and college curriculum and even in induction week at university, where many relationships are likely to develop. Another information 'opportunity' may be available during, or on completion of, the divorce process, as individuals are embarking or have already embarked on new relationships. In the long term it may cost 'society' less, both financially and emotionally, for individual pre-marriage meetings to be provided, rather than paying the price of picking up the pieces later: preventive law (rather like preventive medicine). It cannot 'cure' all but it must be worth a try.

We have seen that most respondents were unaware of the legal consequences of marriage; however, that is not to suggest that they were incapable of appreciating those consequences if they were to be made aware of them. For example, one respondent found answering our questions a valuable exercise, 'we had just floated through life together – this research is good because it makes you think about your situation'.

Couples' relationships are difficult to categorise. 'Going out together' may be the initial step on a road (almost in any order and some steps may be omitted): sexual relationship; cohabitation; engagement; marriage; and parenthood. Of course, they may choose to 'stop off' at cohabitation, or one, or both, of them may even divert to other partners. Their choice of status (presuming all the options are available to them) should be informed by an understanding of the legal rights and duties that attach to each level of commitment. The Government should not use the law to coerce people into, or dissuade them from, marriage. The law is, anyway, likely to be an ineffective tool. As we have seen, our respondents had misperceptions about the law relating to marriage and cohabitation, and were anyway little concerned with the legal consequences of their decision. As far as adult relationships are concerned there should not only be a free choice of partner, but also a free and informed choice, by the parties, as to the form and status of that relationship, including the legal recognition of private ordering. Although governments should not interfere in private adult choices, we argue that they do have a duty to enable citizens to make informed decisions about their preferred status.

[4]

Why don't they marry? Cohabitation, commitment and DIY marriage

Simon Duncan, Anne Barlow and Grace James[*]

This article asks why cohabitants do not marry, when it would seem to be advantageous for them to do so. First, we examine the influence of the 'common law marriage myth', the mistaken but widespread belief that cohabitants gain marriage-like rights through living together for a certain time. Finding that this does not provide an adequate explanation for the social prevalence and acceptance of cohabitation, we then examine alternative rationalities, looking in turn at commitment in cohabiting partnerships, and how cohabitants use 'lived law' to create a DIY variety of marriage, as well as an alternative to it.

INTRODUCTION: UNMARRIED COHABITATION AS IRRATIONAL BEHAVIOUR?

Unmarried heterosexual cohabitation (henceforth 'cohabitation') is both widely practised and accepted in Britain. The 2000 British Social Attitudes (BSA) Survey[1] shows that over one-third of people under 35 who live with a partner are unmarried, and over 80 per cent of this age group view cohabitation as 'all right'. By 2004, over one-quarter of births were to cohabitants, and in 2000 around 60 per cent of this age group also thought this acceptable. While older people practise cohabitation less, the majority are still accepting of it – and even think it is a good idea before marriage. In addition, cohabitation is common for older people with new partners after divorce. Similarly, there was little difference by social class, except that it is more likely for the better off to get married when they have children. The average period spent in cohabitation is also becoming longer. Consequently, both the incidence of cohabitation, and the numbers of children with unmarried, but cohabiting parents, are expected to increase substantially over the coming decade.[2] In this way Britain seems

---

* Lecturer in Social Science and Humanities, University of Bradford; Professor in Law, Exeter University; and Lecturer in Law, Reading University, respectively.

The authors wish to thank the Nuffield Foundation for providing the funding for this research, and to Sharon Witherspoon for help and advice.

1 A. Barlow, S. Duncan, G. James, and A. Park, 'Just a Piece of Paper? Marriage and Cohabitation in Britain', in A. Park et al (eds), *British Social Attitudes: The 18th Report* (Sage Publications, 2001).

2 J. Haskey, 'Cohabitation in Great Britain: past, present and future trends – and attitudes' (2001) *Population Trends* 103, at pp 104–125.

to be moving towards a Scandinavian pattern, where cohabitation is quite normal and where marriage is more of a lifestyle choice rather than an expected part of life.[3]

At first sight all this seems like mass irrationality, as marriage in Britain gives partners substantial and automatic legal benefits which unmarried cohabitants do not possess. It is not that cohabitants do not have any legal rights, but for cohabitants the law is confusing, complex, usually inferior, and hardly ever automatic.[4] Moreover, those people – generally children and caring dependants – are particularly vulnerable as cohabiting family members, especially on death or familial breakdown.

While there are legal remedies to which cohabitants can turn in tackling some of the disadvantages of their status, the 2000 BSA survey showed that only 14 per cent of then current cohabitants had changed or made wills, just nine per cent had made property agreements, and an even lower proportion of fathers – just five per cent – had obtained parental responsibility agreements or orders. As a result, most cohabitants remain in a vulnerable legal situation.

This article asks why cohabitants do not marry, when it would seem to be advantageous for them to do so. First, we examine the influence of the 'common law marriage myth', the mistaken but widespread belief that cohabitants gain marriage-like rights through living together for a certain time. Finding that this 'myth' does not provide an adequate explanation for the social prevalence and acceptance of cohabitation, we then examine a wider set of social, moral and emotional rationalities, looking in turn at commitment in cohabiting partnerships and how cohabitation may be taken to be a variant of marriage or an alternative to it. First, however, we describe our methodology and sources.

METHODOLOGY

We adopted a 'mixed' research design, employing both 'extensive' and 'intensive' research,[5] using both quantitative and qualitative data. Extensive research, usually employing quantitative data, aims to describe overall patterns and distinguishing features, for example the social characteristics of a population of cohabitants. While helpful in providing a representative description, this design is weaker in explaining how and why these patterns have occurred. In contrast, intensive research, usually employing in-depth case study and qualitative methods, is better at answering the 'how' and 'why' questions because it accesses more directly what social agents, such as cohabitants, actually do, believe or understand in the particular situations in which they find themselves. While, therefore more powerful than extensive research in explanatory terms, intensive research is weaker in providing representative descriptive information.[6] In this way each research design has different strengths and weaknesses, and are best seen as complimentary. Mixing the two approaches enabled us to employ each research design, and use each type of data, where most appropriate and so maximise the strength of each, while compensating for their respective weaknesses.

The extensive research here used information from the BSA Survey 2000. This included answers to a 'module' of 25 questions (many were multiple questions)

---

3 K. Kiernan, 'Unmarried cohabitation and parenthood: here to stay? European perspectives' in D. Moynihan, T. Smeeding, and L. Rainwater, *The Future of the Family* (Russell Sage, 2004).

4 A. Barlow, S. Duncan, G. James, and A. Park, *Cohabitation, Marriage and the Law: Social Change and Legal Reform in 21st Century Britain* (Hart Publishing, 2005).

5 R. A. Sayer, *Method in Social Science: A Realist Approach* (Routledge, 2nd edn, 1992).

6 But see G. Payne and M. Williams, 'Generalisation in qualitative research' (2004) 39 *Sociology* 295.

specially designed for this research, together with answers to 'standard' BSA survey questions about social characteristics, such as age, class, gender and occupation. This gave us nationally representative information about overall attitudes towards cohabitation and marriage; the social characteristics of the cohabitant population in Britain; the prevalence of the 'common law marriage myth'; the nature of legal understandings; and preferences for legal reform. While most of this information is cross-sectional for 2000, comparison with previous BSA surveys does allow some longitudinal information on changing attitudes.[7]

The intensive research was based on 48 follow-up interviews with respondents living in England and Wales who took part in the BSA survey. These were semi-structured, conversational interviews, lasting about 1.5 hours, and were conducted between April and September 2001. The interviews focused on three broad areas:

- Practices and experiences of, and attitudes and values about, cohabitation and marriage.
- Belief in common law marriage.
- Views about legal reform.

Our concern was not to find a statistically representative sample of interviewees (the function of the BSA survey). Rather, small quotas of different sets of cohabitants were taken, based on expectations of differences in behaviour and/or values, as suggested by previous research including the BSA survey. An advantage was that our interview sample was based on the BSA survey respondent list, and thus we could find a range of cohabitant types, in contrast to most previous studies which have, by necessity, had to focus on particular groups of cohabitants.[8]

We interviewed cohabitants and former cohabitants with different current partnership and parental status, different lengths of cohabitation, and covering a range of social divisions by gender, age, housing tenure, occupation and class. Basing the qualitative sample on the BSA survey also gave us the advantage of access to the standard survey information already gathered.[9]

---

7 See A. Barlow, S. Duncan, G. James, and A. Park, 'Just a Piece of Paper? Marriage and Cohabitation in Britain', in A. Park et al (eds), *British Social Attitudes: The 18th Report* (Sage Publications, 2001), A. Barlow, S. Duncan, G. James, and A. Park, *Cohabitation, Marriage and the Law: Social Change and Legal Reform in 21st Century Britain* (Hart Publishing, 2005), and for the Scottish part of the survey where the legal situation is somewhat different, see A. Barlow, 'Cohabitation and Marriage in Scotland: Attitudes, Myths and the Law' in J. Curtice, D. McCrone, A. Park and L. Paterson (eds), *New Scotland; New Society?* (Edinburgh University Press, 2002).

8 For example J. Lewis, T*he End of Marriage? Individualism and Intimate Relationships* (Edward Elgar, 2001); C. Smart and P. Stevens, *Cohabitation Breakdown* (Joseph Rowntree Foundation Family Policy studies Centre, 2000); C. Lewis, A. Papacosta and J. Warin, *Cohabitation, Separation and Fatherhood* (Joseph Rowntree Foundation, 2002).

9 We also took small additional interview samples, outside the BSA sample frame, of eight British African/African-Caribbean current and former cohabitants, and 17 British Asians (most of whom had not experienced cohabitation) in order to gain additional information where these groups were not well represented in either the BSA survey or the follow-up interviews. However, we do not use this material here. Similarly, we do not extensively use here material collected in the BSA survey or in the follow-up interviews on legal understandings and preferences. See A. Barlow, S. Duncan, G. James, and A. Park, *Cohabitation, Marriage and the Law: Social Change and Legal Reform in 21st Century Britain* (Hart Publishing, 2005).

LACK OF KNOWLEDGE AND THE 'COMMON LAW MARRIAGE' MYTH

At first sight the 'common law marriage' myth provides a plausible explanation of the increasing prevalence of unmarried cohabitation. As the 2000 BSA survey demonstrates, over half of all respondents (56 per cent) believed that unmarried couples who lived together for some time definitely or probably had a 'common law marriage' and were treated equally in law. Many also believed that this could be triggered by the birth of a child to the couple. Nor was there much difference in this proportion by social class, income or educational level, although younger people were somewhat more likely to believe the myth.

According to this explanation, if people believe that marriage-like rights come automatically after a certain period of cohabitation, and/or after joint registration of a child, then they are less likely to go to the expense and practical trouble of getting married. So, for example, Diane, who had been cohabiting for just a year, and had one child, simply thought:

> 'Well, what's the point of getting married because we're classed as though we're married – we're living together and if we do split up we still do what a married couple would do – split everything, kids, responsibility and everything.'[10]

The British government seems to give this explanation some credence. For while the Civil Partnership Act 2004 provides marriage-like rights for same-sex cohabitants, this option is denied to heterosexual cohabitants. The government's argument is that while many heterosexual couples do not appreciate the true legal situation of unmarried cohabitation, they can get married if they wish. Hence the Department for Constitutional Affairs began a publicity campaign in summer 2004, 'to dispel the myth surrounding "common law marriage"'.[11] However, as soon as we examine this 'lack of knowledge' explanation further, we find that at best it can only provide a partial and superficial explanation for the increase in unmarried cohabitation. There are three major problems.

The first lies in the historical trends. For, while unmarried cohabitation is rapidly increasing, it seems unlikely that the belief in common law marriage is increasing at a commensurate rate. The evidence that can be pieced together[12] points towards the gradually decreasing practice of unmarried cohabitation from the late-eighteenth up to the mid-twentieth century. While we have no direct evidence, the spread of education, the deeper influence of mass media, and an increasing 'legalisation' of society (for example, as people are more likely to consult lawyers in buying homes, in getting divorced and so on) would arguably reduce belief in common law marriage. The alternative – to assume that people are becoming less legally aware over time, that this ignorance of the law is increasingly spreading among the well-educated and rich just as much as the ill-educated and poor, and hence belief in common law marriage is galloping apace to create the rising trend in cohabitation – is somewhat counter-intuitive.

A second major problem with the 'ignorance' explanation lies in the very longevity and enormity of this myth. For common law marriage, which did at one time legally exist, was abolished by Act of Parliament in 1753. How is it that such completely

---

10 All quotations from the interviewees use pseudonyms.

11 Department of Trade and Industry, Women and Equality Unit, *Responses to Civil Partnership: A Framework for the Legal Recognition of Same-Sex Couples* (Department of Trade and Industry, 2003), para 3.6.

12 See A. Barlow, S. Duncan, G. James, and A. Park, *Cohabitation, Marriage and the Law: Social Change and Legal Reform in 21st Century Britain* (Hart Publishing, 2005).

incorrect legal assumptions can last for more than 250 years for over half the British population? In contrast, by 2000 nearly everyone knew that homosexual relations for adults were no longer illegal – a mere 33 years since the Sexual Offences Act in 1967. Similarly, most people know that simple breakdown of a marriage with separation is sufficient grounds for divorce, just 31 years after the Divorce Reform Act 1969. It is not the case that ordinary members of the public are experts on laws about sexual behaviour or divorce law, rather they are aware of the general direction and message; certainly they are not so spectacularly and pervasively wrong as with common law marriage. We might perhaps expect that those who had not been cohabiting for very long, or who were ill-educated, might show less knowledge – but the 2000 BSA survey found that belief in common law marriage was common among all ages, social classes, and educational levels, and for single people, unmarried cohabitants (both short-term and long-term) and married spouses alike. Both the longevity and pervasiveness of the common law marriage myth, and the enormous gulf between myth and law, point to another explanation; the idea of common law marriage chimes in with people's everyday lived experience in some way. We will return to this issue in the next section.

The third problem with the 'common law marriage myth' explanation for the prevalence of cohabitation is the most telling. For the 2000 BSA Survey shows that the third of the British population in 2000 who did *not* believe that common law marriage exists, in the sense of cohabitation giving marriage-like legal rights, showed little difference in their legal behaviour. Indeed, there was no difference at all in the proportions of cohabiting 'myth believers' and 'non-believers' who had taken out parental responsibility agreements/orders, or who had made property agreements. While 15 per cent of the non-believing group had made or changed a will as a result of cohabiting, compared to nine per cent of the 'believers'; this is hardly a profound difference. This similarity between 'believers' and 'non-believers' was equally evident in the qualitative follow-up interviews where, in most cases, people's perceptions of the legal consequences, whether accurate or inaccurate, had no impact on their decision to cohabit. Significantly, this is equally apparent for those who do marry. Thus Hibbs et al[13] found that 41 per cent of their 1998/99 sample of 173 engaged respondents (three-quarters of whom were already cohabiting) thought that marriage would not change the legal nature of their relationship. As many as 37 per cent saw no legal consequences of marriage for present or future children. Indeed, in this study only one respondent cited 'legal reasons' as a cause for marriage, and only three per cent of the respondents admitted to any legal influence at all. Similarly, in 2002 Eekelaar and Maclean[14] found only one out of 39 respondents who admitted to legal considerations as a reason for marrying. Most of our respondents, like those interviewed by Hibbs et al, were likely to view questions about legal measures with surprise or even indignation; it was the private promises between the partners that were regarded as important. Duncan, a schoolteacher who had been cohabiting for five years, gives a nice summary of this consensus:

> 'there are some things that you are better off if you are married but then that's not the final reason for getting married, what's the point of getting married if it's just to save money on your income tax or your pensions or whatever else it might be ... They're not good reasons in my view ...'

---

[13] M. Hibbs, C. Barton, and J. Beswisk, 'Why marry? Perceptions of the affianced' [2001] Fam Law 197.

[14] J. Eekelaar and M. Maclean, 'Marriage and the moral bases of personal relationships' (2004) 31(4) *Journal of Law and Society* 510.

This response perhaps indicates the key to why people cohabit rather than marry; they see living together as an emotional relationship, not an economic transaction or legal contract. We turn to this issue in the next section.

COHABITATION AND COMMITMENT

In the political and media discourse, commitment to a relationship is most usually equated with marriage. Partners who are committed to one another get married, unless – and this is a more recent addition to the argument – they are misled by the common law marriage myth. In this discourse, cohabitation is viewed as a second-rate family structure, characterised as fragile, informal, and lacking commitment.[15] This assumption is supported by reference to statistical comparisons, where on average married spouses are less likely to break up, and when marriages last longer than cohabiting relationships. The legal reflection of this assumption is illustrated by the Family Law Act 1996. Cohabitation is defined as an arrangement where: 'a man and a woman who, although not married to each other, are living together as husband and wife' (s 62(1)), where judges should 'have regard to the fact that [cohabitants] have not given each other the commitment involved in marriage' (s 41).

This is a picture that many cohabitants would not recognise, still less agree with. Empirical studies, including our own, routinely record expressions of commitment by cohabitants that are little different from those of married spouses.[16] As Lewis et al point out: 'The word used by the vast majority of interviewees to describe cohabitation was "commitment"'.[17] Among our respondents, Nigel – a retired head teacher with one stepdaughter – felt that: 'my commitment to the relationship and our family is absolute'. Similarly, Susan favourably compared her current cohabiting union to a previous marriage:

> 'I don't see it as being married or not. What I do is compare my relationship, my and Mike's relationship, with the person I was with before regardless of the fact that I was married to one and not to the other, and it's how happy I am and how the relationship's working, and I think that's much more important than the fact that one was a marriage and one isn't.'

Indeed, some cohabitants claimed that the lack of a formal, legal union demanded greater commitment on their part, and more attention to their partner and the relationship. This meant that cohabitation was, for them, the more ethically sound and honest relationship. For Melanie, who had also been married before: 'At least this way you know you're together because you love each other and you want to be together'. In this way unmarried cohabitants also claim the 'moral high ground'.[18] The statistical evidence brought to support the 'marriage equals commitment' assumption seems compelling at first sight, in that it reflects what people actually do, rather than what

15 See, for example, J. Ermisch, 'Trying Again: repartnering after dissolution of a union', Working Paper of the Institute for Social and Economic Research, paper 2002-19 (University of Essex, 2000); P. Morgan, *Marriage-lite: the Rise of Cohabitation and its Consequences* (Institute for the Study of Civil Society, 1999).

16 J. Eekelaar and M. Maclean, 'Marriage and the moral bases of personal relationships' (2004) 31(4) *Journal of Law and Society* 510; L. Jamieson et al, 'Cohabitation and commitment: partnership plans of young men and women' (2002) 52(3) *Sociological Review* 354; C. Lewis, A. Papacosta, and J. Warin, *Cohabitation, Separation and Fatherhood* (Joseph Rowntree Foundation, 2002); J. Lewis, *The End of Marriage? Individualism and Intimate Relationships* (Edward Elgar, 2001).

17 C. Lewis et al, ibid, at p 10.

18 See also C. Lewis et al, ibid, and J. Lewis, op cit, n 16.

they say. The fact that cohabitants are more likely to break up, and their unions last for less time, appears to speak more about commitment than their reported happiness, aspirations or expectations, however sincerely expressed. However, this evidence often commits the statistical error of not comparing like with like, as the following two points make clear.

First, the married population is on average older than the cohabiting population; in 2000 only around 20 per cent of the married population was under 35, and just two per cent under 25. This compares with nearly 70 per cent under 35 and 20 per cent under 25 for cohabitants. The age at which partnership starts is one of the most powerful factors associated with subsequent breakdown; younger unions – whether married or not – are less stable in both emotional and structural terms.[19] Quite apart from personality and emotional issues, income, jobs and housing will be less secure and fixed.[20] If the cohabiting and married populations had the same age structures, this factor alone would substantially reduce differences in breakdown rates.

Secondly, cohabiting couples are less likely to have children, partly because of their younger age, and the presence of a child has been estimated to reduce breakdown rates by as much as 40 per cent. Indicatively, research in the USA also shows little difference in 'relationship quality' between cohabitants and married spouses who had children, or who wanted children.[21] Thirdly, cohabitation often follows marriage breakdown; this 'post-separation cohabitation' has increasingly replaced remarriage, where the remarried were always at a much higher risk of breakdown. Finally, the married population includes partners who find it difficult to separate because of external pressures, such as those of religion or family pressure.

The evidence suggests that if we compared like with like, for example young secular childless couples, or older couples in a long-term union with children, there would probably be little difference between separation rates for cohabiting and married couples. Thus 23 per cent of the BSA 2000 sample of cohabitants had been together for over 10 years.[22] It is not possible or meaningful (just because so many marriages date from a time when cohabitation was uncommon) to give an average length of marriage, but the median duration of those 40 per cent of marriages currently ending in divorce is also around 10 years. And the younger the age of spouses at marriage, the higher the rates of breakdown.[23] The example of the 'shotgun marriage' – where partners were virtually forced to marry after an unplanned pregnancy – is particularly telling. This social institution of the 1950s and 60s is now virtually extinct (in 2000 only three per cent of marriages were preceded by pre-marital conceptions, compared to almost a quarter in 1970), but were notorious for high rates of dysfunctionality and breakdown.[24]

---

19 C. Gibson, 'Changing family patterns in England' in N. Katz, J. Eekelaar, and M. Maclean (eds), *Cross Currents: Family Law and Policy in the US and England* (Oxford University Press, 2000); M. Murphy, 'Demographic and socio-economic effects on recent British marital breakdown patterns' (1985) *Population Studies* 39.

20 J. Haskey, 'Marital status and age at marriage: their influence on the chance of divorce' (1983) 32 *Population Trends* 4; B. Thornes and J. Collard, *Who Divorces?* (Routledge, 1979).

21 S. Brown and A. Booth, 'Cohabitation versus marriage: a comparison of relationship quality' (1996) 58 *Journal of Marriage and the Family* 668.

22 The cross-sectional nature of the BSA data may underestimate the number of very short unions.

23 Haskey, op cit, n 20.

24 L. Coombs and Z. Zumeta, 'Correlates of marital dissolution in a prospective fertility study: a research note' (1970) 18 *Social Problems* 92; Thornes and Collard, op cit, n 20.

If we are to compare commitment between married and unmarried cohabiting partners, we need to define what it is and what makes it up. After a wide-ranging discussion of various attempts to do this, Lewis comes back to Johnson's distinction of three dimensions to commitment.[25] These are:

- Personal commitment to the partner, summed up as wanting the relationship to continue.
- Moral–normative commitment, summed up as the feeling that the relationship ought to continue.
- Structural commitment, summed up as the feeling that a relationship has to continue because of the investments made in the relationship (such as housing, finance, job arrangements, children), and costs of ending it.

As we have discussed above, many, if not most, cohabitants display the first, more personal, dimension to commitment. There may be some types of cohabitation where partners do not feel this commitment so completely, for example following an unexpected pregnancy. Equally, there will be some marriages where this dimension will also be weak. 'Shotgun' marriages are most likely to fall into this category, as will some arranged marriages, or those made for largely economic reasons. In these cases it will be dimensions 2 and 3 that keep the partnership intact.

While structural commitment, dimension 3, is not normally felt or experienced until dimensions 1 and 2 are weak and the partnership is liable to break up, it is easy to show that most cohabitants experience this in a similar way to married spouses. For studies show that divisions of labour, leisure behaviour, the sharing of property and income, and joint responsibility for children are virtually identical for demographically and socially similar married and cohabiting couples.[26] Again, it is age, class and parenthood that are more influential. For example, Vogler found that young, 'nubile', and post-separation cohabitants were more likely than married spouses to keep separate financial accounts, but that cohabitants with a biological child together were even more likely than married spouses to maintain a traditional, breadwinner model, housekeeping allowance system. Our own follow-up interviews confirmed this general consensus, with these household practices varying much more by age than by the form of the union. Similarly, the divide was much more between men and women than between cohabiting and married partners. If lack of joint involvement in childcare and household chores is taken as an index of commitment to a relationship, then some married couples must be very uncommitted indeed!

We might expect that cohabitants would differ more from married couples on the second dimension of commitment identified above; moral–normative views that the relationship ought to continue. There is some evidence that this can be the case. For a small sample of separated cohabitants with children, Lewis et al found that some respondents saw cohabitation as offering greater freedom to monitor, re-evaluate and negotiate their relationships at any time.[27] And if people 'grew apart', relationships could more easily be ended. In comparison, these same respondents thought of

---

[25] J. Lewis, *The End of Marriage? Individualism and Intimate Relationships* (Edward Elgar, 2001); M. Johnson, 'Commitment to personal relationships' in W. Jones, and D. Perlman (eds), *Advances in Personal Relationships: a Research Annual* (Jessica Kingsley, 1991), vol 3, at pp 117–143.

[26] J. Lewis, ibid; C. Lewis, A. Papacosta, and J. Warin, *Cohabitation, Separation and Fatherhood* (Joseph Rowntree Foundation, 2002); J. Eekelaar and M. Maclean, 'Marriage and the moral bases of personal relationships' (2004) 31(4) *Journal of Law and Society* 510; C. Vogler, 'Cohabiting couples: rethinking money in the household at the beginning of the 21st century' (2005) 53 *Sociological Review* 1.

[27] C. Lewis, ibid.

marriage as putting people under pressure to stay together despite such changes – sometimes seen negatively in terms of preventing self-development and honesty, but sometimes seen as a positive feature just because of the feeling that important relationships 'ought to continue'. But this is what we might expect from a sample of separated partners. In contrast, other studies, using samples of ongoing partners (both cohabiting and separated), find that the only major difference between most cohabitants and married spouses concerned the wider presentation of their commitment. Cohabitants saw their commitment as private, whereas those who had married (often after long-term cohabitation) felt the need to make a public commitment. For the cohabitants, commitment was private in two senses – it was theirs alone and did not involve state, church, community or kin, and it eschewed any public ceremony. For the married couples, public commitment seemed to be most important for relatives and kin, especially the parents, who then knew where the relationship stood and how they should behave as a result. Younger respondents (under 50), whether married or cohabiting, mostly believed that commitment came from within – from love of the other person and their children – rather than any externally prescribed moral code. It was the fact that they had made a commitment which was the important thing, not the formal or legal form this took.[28] Our own follow-up interviewees made a similar response; marriage was basically about making commitment public – sometimes seen negatively as just showing off or keeping up with the Joneses. But the basis for partnership, married or not, was a strong private commitment to another person.

In this section we have seen that many unmarried cohabitants see themselves as being just as committed to their partners as married people and – if we compare like with like – that their behaviour seems to bear this out. While there are different types of cohabitation and marriage, and both may show a range of commitment, the evidence does not support the 'official' assumption that cohabitation necessarily means less or contingent commitment. The crucial thing for the majority is the existence of commitment, rather than whether it is manifested as marriage or unmarried cohabitation. This means, in turn, that by and large cohabiting partners do not avoid marriage because of low levels of commitment.

This conclusion returns us to the original problem, however. If it is the case – as the evidence reviewed in this section suggests – that cohabiting partners are mostly just as committed as married spouses, and if they can gain substantial legal benefits, and potential economic gains, from marriage, then why do they not do so? In fact the problem is compounded, for rather than seeing cohabiting partners as selfish or ignorant, we can now see them as committed and caring individuals who presumably would like their partners and children to have the full protection of the law. Certainly, as the 2000 BSA survey showed, a large majority thinks that the legal benefits of marriage should be extended to cohabitants. In the next two sections we will go on to explore how cohabitants themselves explain why they are not formally married.

'LIVED LAW' AND COHABITATION AS DIY MARRIAGE

A first way into the conundrum of why caring and committed cohabitants do not marry is to return to the common law marriage 'myth'. For while in a strict legal sense the description 'myth' is appropriate – there is widespread belief in the legal existence of

---

[28] J. Lewis, *The End of Marriage? Individualism and Intimate Relationships* (Edward Elgar, 2001); L. Jamieson et al, 'Cohabitation and commitment: partnership plans of young men and women' (2002) 52(3) *Sociological Review* 354; J. Eekelaar and M. Maclean, 'Marriage and the moral bases of personal relationships' (2004) 31(4) *Journal of Law and Society* 510.

common law marriage, this belief is factually incorrect, it is maintained through informal networks that use oral traditions rather than a written code[29] – in other ways this appellation is inappropriate. This is because beliefs in common law marriage, while they do not reflect the formal law, do much more closely reflect how people experience – and collectively regulate – their everyday lives. So rather than belief in common law marriage being simply myth as fantasy, it has a real basis in material, social life. This is what we call 'lived law'.

The notion of 'lived law' has been developed in development studies in researching social practices in sub-Saharan Africa. In this context everyday life is partly regulated through informal social custom and practice, drawing on but not hidebound by historically developed traditions. This 'lived law' is often more effective than the formal law of colonial and post-colonial states, even though it sometimes contradicts this.[30]

How can we see unmarried cohabitation, widely seen as 'common law marriage', as reflecting 'lived law'? A first basis relates to the rationale underlying people's belief in common law marriage. This rests upon notions of social logic, fairness and morality; 'believer' follow-up interviewees (and many 'non-believers') assumed that the law would reflect what they saw as socially logical and morally sensible in supporting families, while also being fair to individuals.[31] This moral view of what the law ought to do probably explains the particularly high rates of belief in marriage-like rights for cohabitants where children and fathering is concerned, whereas for rights over income and property, levels of belief are both lower and often time restricted. Beliefs about what the law does are conflated with beliefs about what the law *ought* to do.

This moral view of what the law ought to be fits in with how people experience cohabitation in their everyday lives. Even in the legal sphere, cohabitants do have some legal status and rights, even though these are usually inferior to those held by married spouses, and in the allocation of various state benefits and tax credits they are more equal. Here, government, and hence the law, treats unmarried cohabitants as husband and wife in applying eligibility rules about joint income and expenditures. As a result, state bodies have come up with various definitions of cohabitation, most based upon evidence of shared living arrangements, a sexual relationship, stability, financial support, the presence of children and public acknowledgement.[32] These definitions are then used to equate such couples with married couples. For example, the Inland Revenue's 2004 Child Tax Credit application form helpfully includes those who 'live with someone as if you are married ... as a couple', along with the formally married. Other institutions, such as insurance and utility companies, can also use common law marriage as a definitional category. Their treatment of customers, for example in working out premiums, may differ as a result (one of the authors regularly embarrasses himself in trying to explain – unsuccessfully – to call centre workers that this category does not exist). Such official definitions can promote a quite powerful validation of the 'myth', because many people will have day-to-day experience of this parity. Again, this as an area where periodic experience will validate the 'myth'.

Even more powerfully, the idea of common law marriage is validated by day-to-day practice in everyday life. Thus, as the 2000 BSA survey suggests, heterosexual

---

29 A. Barlow, S. Duncan, G. James, and A. Park, *Cohabitation, Marriage and the Law: Social Change and Legal Reform in 21st Century Britain* (Hart Publishing, 2005).

30 For example, D. Hodgson, 'My daughter belongs to the government now' in C. Creighton and C. K. Omori (eds), *Gender, Family and Work in Tanzania* (Ashgate, 2000); R. Odgard, 'Scrambling for land in Tanzania' (2002) 14(2) *European Journal of Development Research* 70.

31 Barlow et al, op cit, n 29.

32 C. Davies, 'The definition of cohabitation' (1999) 79 *Solicitors Family Law Association Review* 15.

cohabitants, certainly those with children and/or some length of co-residence, are commonly treated as 'man and wife'. Socially, they are usually treated as an exclusive couple, and the female partner is often referred to as 'Mrs'. Similarly, the cohabitants themselves will often present themselves in an equivalent way, even at times referring to their 'in-laws'. In maternity wards, doctors' surgeries, school meetings, work parties and social gatherings throughout the land cohabitants will receive affirmation of married status. Or, increasingly, married spouses will be treated as cohabitants by inclusion in the more universal category of 'partner'. This 'lived law' then receives further validation in that cohabitation is now so widely practised and accepted across Britain. In this sense, common law marriage is not a myth at all.

In turn, most of the cohabiting follow-up interviewees saw themselves 'as good as married'. They may have begun to live together as a 'trial' for marriage, or because of an unexpected pregnancy or housing problems, but that was some time ago and their relationship had now progressed to a long-term, committed partnership. Others became 'married' in this sense straight away. As Chris, who had been cohabiting six years and had two daughters, explained:

> 'We were just courting and decided we wanted to be more serious. Children were on the agenda straight away so we talked about it and decided to have the children straight away.'

This was no principled alternative to marriage; rather, cohabiting as if married was an alternative to remaining single. Angela, cohabiting for 13 years with one son, elaborated:

> 'We'd been together for about three years before we moved in together – I can't really remember how it came about but ... I wanted more commitment and he said right we'll live together.'

Lewis found much the same with her small sample of long-established married and unmarried partners with children, as did Jamieson et al with a sample of married and unmarried young partners between 20 and 29, with and without children.[33] In both samples, as in our follow-up interviews, most saw themselves as good as married, and could see little point in getting married now even if they did not reject marriage as an institution. Hence, as shown in the previous section, most interviewed cohabitants expressed and practised levels of commitment in the same ways as demographically similar married couples. Their union may not have been formalised by law, but for them that was a side issue. Rather, their experience of cohabitation as a variety of marriage fitted in well with what we have called 'lived law'. Everyday social and institutional practice treats longer term cohabitants, especially those with children, just like married couples. For some, this view was bolstered by belief in the existence of common law marriage.

This is what we might call 'Do-It-Yourself' marriage. More grandly, to adapt from Bordieu, this common type of cohabitation is a form of 'institutional bricolage'.[34] People have taken existing institutional forms – in this case formal marriage and the lived law of 'living together as if married' (as the Inland Revenue puts it), combined them, and developed their own variety of marriage. They have responded to change by drawing

[33] J. Lewis, *The End of Marriage? Individualism and Intimate Relationships* (Edward Elgar, 2001); L. Jamieson et al, 'Cohabitation and commitment: partnership plans of young men and women' (2002) 52(3) *Sociological Review* 354.

[34] F. Cleaver, 'Reinventing institutions; bricolage and the social embeddedness of natural resource management' (2002) 14(2) *The European Journal of Development Research* 11.

on and adapting existing norms. This is partly to conserve cognitive and social energy – it is far harder to forge completely new institutions, as the pioneers of 1970s communes can testify. In so doing, people confer the new arrangements of 'common law marriage' with the legitimacy of tradition, and this, therefore, becomes part of 'the right way of doing things'. As we have seen, this do-it-yourself marriage does not exclude formal marriage at all and partners are not opposed to legal marriage. Indeed, why should they be when they perceive themselves to be as good as married? Rather, formal marriage is often seen more as an expectation, sometimes a rather vague and ideal expectation, for some future date.

In this case, if cohabiting partners were 'as good as married', then why bother with formal marriage at all, even as a vague expectation? There seem to be several linked reasons for this, which relate to public display, rather than private commitment. The first is to secure a name change, particularly if there are children, so that all members of the family share the same name. Many of the follow-up interviewees saw having a different surname to their partner and children as the greatest disadvantage of not marrying. In fact, female name changing upon marriage is not a legal requirement, but, rather, a powerful tradition. Conversely, it is perfectly lawful for an unmarried cohabitant to take her, or his, partner's name, or to choose a combined surname for themselves and/or their children. The desire for a name change can also be linked to a feeling that this will complete the marriage-like partnership already bestowed through cohabitation.

For some respondents, especially those who did not believe in common law marriage, the ability to tidy up financial arrangements through legal marriage was also part of this desire to seal an already existing 'lived law' marriage. For example, Phillip, a 54-year-old plumber, had been cohabiting for two years. He was also a JP, which perhaps gave him more legal knowledge than most. Getting married the week after the interview, one reason he gave was that:

> 'we felt that from that practical and legal point of view it's far easier to administer as a married couple ... we also thought it would tidy up things and make it easier for us to do what we wanted for the future for our own children and grandchildren.'

The major reason for wanting marriage, however, either as a vague expectation or as a practical plan, was for public performance and display. As most cohabitants saw themselves 'as good as married', then there was no need for a cheap and easy register office marriage in order to mark their personal commitment. Rather, the respondents wanted a 'proper wedding' to show this publicly. Caroline explained:

> 'Probably somewhere in beautiful grounds, beautiful gardens, all outside, beautiful cars or horse-drawn carriage – really spend a few grand on it and have a really fantastic day for him as well as for her. We could go to the Register Office up the road tomorrow if we wanted!'

To see the wedding as public display is quite logical; after all it is a public occasion. There are, however, two crucial differences with earlier practice. One is the expense; display does not only mean marriage in public, but conspicuous consumption. Secondly, when partners often see themselves as already as good as married, marriage itself becomes reduced to the 'proper wedding'. This is reminiscent of Giddens' description of marriage as a 'shell institution' and of Beck's notion of social institutions as 'zombie categories', which are 'dead and still alive'.[35] In this view the structural reasons which support a particular institution are fatally weakened, and enormous changes have taken place in what actually happens, although the facade is seemingly unchanged. In this case marriage is no longer socially expected for partnership, sexual intimacy and childbearing, and relations within marriage are conducted in quite different ways to before, but the institution itself survives – emptied of its former social content and now used for something quite different. The wedding itself also becomes a shell institution in this way. As Wallis suggests, people often use a vague idea of tradition to impart a proper sense of gravitas to the ceremony as display, choosing an idyllic village church for instance, with very little regard for the religious or community content once centrally involved.[36]

So if a 'proper wedding' is about display, what is this display about – what is being shown to friends and relatives? We might imagine that one motive was the desire to show personal commitment through public performance. This often seemed to be linked to a desire to show social success; marriage was no longer a rite of passage into adulthood, as in the 1950s and 60s, but rather a rite of passage into the ranks of the socially successful. Many of our respondents were less circumspect and simply saw marriage as a means of showing off. Sharon, cohabiting for seven years with three children, had no thoughts of marriage and speculated:

> 'I suppose people try and outdo each other. I suppose it's keeping up with the Joneses. If your friends get married and have a big white wedding then you probably want one bigger and better.'

Philip, the JP shortly to be married, was more caustic:

> 'I feel that a young bride likes to have a big day to show off to her friends, her family and everybody else. "Look, it's me, I'm getting married, we're going to spend £15,000–£20,000" which is quite the norm now – "Look at me, look at us".'

Pamela, recently married herself but cohabiting for eight years with her husband to be before this, explained why showing off was so important, and why this meant expense to work:

> 'I think it's ever so important today because it's such a materialistic world. Everybody is trying to outdo everybody on everything. For example my wedding dress was £700 and I though that was lot of money – a friend of mine who got married the other month, her dress was £2,500 and it was beautiful and everything but it's like everybody's trying to outdo everybody.'

This is reminiscent of Boden's analysis of wedding consumer culture, where she concludes that the bridal role is infused with consumer identity.[37] However, despite (or perhaps because of) 'the bride's imagination being colonised by market forces',[38] women still extract pleasure out of the whole wedding experience.

The wedding as public display, to be effective, can therefore cost a lot of money. In other words, the commodification of marriage as another 'consumer good', albeit one

35 A. Giddens, *Runaway World: How Globalisation is Shaping Our Lives* (Profile, 1999); U. Beck, 'Zombie categories; interview with Ulrich Beck', in U. Beck and E. Beck-Gernsheim, *Individualisation* (Sage Publications, 2002), at p 203.

36 J. Walliss, 'Loved the wedding, invite me to the marriage': the secularisation of weddings in contemporary Britain' (2002) 7 *Sociological Research Online* 4.

37 S. Boden, '"Superbrides": wedding consumer culture and the construction of bridal identity' (2001) 6 *Sociological Research Online* 1.

38 Ibid, at 7.3.

which is particularly useful in establishing social status, is not without economic consequences. We found, like Eekelaar and Maclean,[39] that the fact that many people can not afford the expense, or chose not you, to be a telling factor in the minds of many respondents. Sharon, for example, was inclined to give formal marriage a miss for the following reasons:

> 'Expense is a major factor. It's not cheap to get married ... if we had the sort of money to get married I'd rather take the children on holiday personally or he'd rather have a new car ...'

Gail simply ranked marriage beneath other, more attractive, acquisitions:

> '... it's a case of we're looking now for a conservatory for the house and that's going to cost a lot more money. We want to start going on holidays and that's costing money, he says "what would you rather have?" – a new car, we got a new car last year, it's "what would you rather have, a new car or a wedding?" and now it's a conservatory.'

For these cohabitants, who saw themselves as good as married, the legal side of getting married formally – just like the legal side of not being married – remained peripheral. The church or civil registration was just another part of the ritual on which to hang the public display of a 'proper marriage'. They had no objections to marriage, felt that the same norms were applicable to both cohabitation and marriage, and even intended to formally marry eventually. This sort of cohabitation is a 'do-it-yourself' variety of marriage.

COHABITATION AS AN ALTERNATIVE TO MARRIAGE

Not all the follow-up interviewees saw themselves as practising a variety of marriage, or as always having done so while living together. Some referred to a period of 'trial marriage' in the past. Pamela, who married during the course of the research, put this most vividly:

> 'It's like going to buy a car, you don't go and buy a car without test-driving it, would you at the end of the day? That's the way I've felt. Live together, test each other out first, and you feel like you've done the hard work.'

Cohabitation has often been viewed as a simple prelude to marriage; couples would be simply trying out living together with marriage in mind, much as Pamela describes.[40] Successful unions are transformed into a legal and formal marriage; other partnerships just break up. While couples will have a commitment to one another, this would not be the same as a long-term commitment.

It is indeed the case that it is now both statistically normal, and an expected norm, that couples will start living together through unmarried cohabitation, as the 2000 BSA survey showed. However, while 10 of the 48 follow-up interviewees had been together less than two years, none currently described themselves as living together as a conscious preparation for marriage. We should be careful here to distinguish between the general, but vague, expectation that marriage might occur at some unspecified point in the future, and a more conscious trial marriage. As the BSA survey also shows, this 'trial' period is often quite a long one; the mean duration of cohabitation was six and a half years, and only 20 per cent of current cohabitants had been living

---

39 J. Eekelaar and M. Maclean, 'Marriage and the moral bases of personal relationships' (2004) 31(4) *Journal of Law and Society* 510.

40 C. Prinz, *Cohabiting, Married or Single* (Avebury, 1995).

together for less than a year (although a cross-sectional survey of this type will underestimate the number of very short unions). In other words, many cohabitants live together longer than any reasonable trial period. For partners would presumably have discovered most of each other's hidden faults after a year or so of 'test-driving'. Indeed, Pamela, quoted above expounding the benefits of cohabiting as trial marriage, had in fact been a cohabitant for eight years at the time of the interview. In such cases, cohabitation has progressed beyond a 'trial' to a committed long-term relationship. Formal marriage may remain an expectation, but is now just one part of the progression of the partnership, rather than a means of establishing and defining it.

Several of the follow-up interviewees described this evolutionary process, as a relationship progressed from initial dating to committed, long-term co-residence. Marriage was more an incidental in this progress, rather than a defining marker. By the same token, it is important to remember that the reasons for entering a relationship are not necessarily the reasons why people stay in a relationship. An initial 'trial' can develop into long-term commitment, and some interviewees gave striking retrospective accounts of the various stages through which their partnerships had progressed. Importantly, although some had considered marriage at particular, life-marking times (like buying a house or having children), it was not seen as necessary for this progression. Perhaps the idea of 'trial marriage' is more appropriate to an earlier version of cohabitation, when formal marriage – or dissolution – within a year or two was more the norm. Now, when longer term cohabitation is 'as good as married', this is no longer socially accurate – rather we should perhaps think of shorter cohabiting unions as 'trial cohabitation'.

A significant minority of the follow-up respondents (16 out of 48) did see cohabitation in a different way, as an alternative to marriage rather than a variety of it. They did not want to get married, even though they wanted to live with and commit to a partner. There were two main reasons for this. The first was a desire to avoid male control. For some of the follow-up interviewees, this reflected a long-term principle where marriage was seen as a patriarchal institution. Perhaps not surprisingly, these views were more prevalent in the small sample of separated cohabitants interviewed by Lewis et al, as compared to our wider ranging sample.[41] In their case, two-thirds of the sample described marriage in negative terms, focussing on an antipathy to control by church and state and institutionalised sexism. For them, as with our respondents in this group, cohabitation offered the better way to commit to a partner – and to end a relationship – in an egalitarian way, free of externally imposed rules. For others, being married in the past encouraged this 'political' view of marriage; their experiences had shown them marriage as a form of male control.

The second, overlapping, reason for avoiding marriage was disillusion with it as an effective institution – it was a failing or dangerous institution. There was a strong possibility of breakdown and the costs of this were high, often confirmed by close or personal experience. It is these likely costs of a quite possible breakdown that may help to explain why a high proportion of cohabitants – up to one-third according to Haskey[42] – are either divorced, or separated from spouses. Finally, we saw in the last section that marriage, in the form of a 'proper wedding', is used as a type of social status display. But this display can easily be double-edged, as breakdown will also be on display. Duncan was particularly concerned about this:

---

41 C. Lewis, A. Papacosta, and J. Warin, *Cohabitation, Separation and Fatherhood* (Joseph Rowntree Foundation, 2002).

42 J. Haskey, 'Cohabitation in Great Britain: past, present and future trends – and attitudes' (2001) *Population Trends* 103.

> 'it's the public thing so if it goes wrong there's a lot of public statements as well, sort of public failure if the marriage goes wrong which might be a background thing which is affecting the way I'm thinking.'

Respondents in this group saw marriage in negative terms, and cohabitated as an alternative to it. In this aversion to marriage they differ from the majority view of cohabitation as a variety of marriage, where a formal wedding is not ruled out and may even be expected. However, in effect this minority is still practising a variety of marriage – one which explicitly rejects legal formalisation.

CONCLUSION – VIRTUAL AND REAL FAMILIES IN POLICY MAKING

Cohabitants seem to show as much commitment to their partnerships, when we compare like with like, as married people do. Some cohabitants are less committed than others, but the same goes for married people. A dramatic spread in lack of commitment, therefore, cannot explain the increasing levels of cohabitation in Britain. Nor is ignorance of the law, in the form of widespread belief in the common law marriage myth, a satisfactory explanation for increasing cohabitation.

Rather, we find that cohabitation is often perceived as a type of do-it-yourself marriage, set within an everyday 'lived law' that contradicts formal, official law. In this way longer term cohabitation is seen as a variety of marriage – cohabitants are 'as good as married'. Even the minority who are opposed to marriage, either for reasons of principle or because of practical disillusionment, are in effect practising a variety of a marriage. Cohabitation is experienced as an adequate way of conducting committed relationships with other adults, and of bringing up children. Cohabitants are not acting irrationally, therefore, although many are left in a less secure legal position than married spouses. Nor should we forget the rapid changes occurring in formal marriage itself, where re-evaluation of the partnership is increasingly taken for granted and, consequently, where divorce has become a functional necessity, almost a part of the life course. It is perhaps more accurate to say that marriage is a variety of cohabitation. Both cohabitants and married spouses are attempting to work out how to combine personal freedom with commitment to others. In this way it is quite wrong to see the statistical decrease in marriage, and the rise in unmarried cohabitation, as leading to or reflecting the 'breakdown of the family'.

Unfortunately, the development of legal and other policies has not gone inside the black boxes; in focusing on outward distinctions in the legal form of families – on cohabitation versus marriage – this debate has neglected what families actually do. The similarities between cohabitation and marriage have thereby been missed. In this way policy has instead become fixated on attributing family dysfunctionality by form, where cohabitation is seen as the inferior partnership form. Rather, policy should focus on how partners can best exercise care and commitment towards each other and their children.

[5]

Cohabitation and commitment: partnership plans of young men and women

Lynn Jamieson, Michael Anderson, David McCrone, Frank Bechhofer, Robert Stewart and Yaojun Li

Abstract

Popular commentators on marriage and the family often interpret the increase in heterosexual couples living together without marrying as reduced willingness to create and honour life-long partnerships. Survey and in-depth interviews with samples of 20–29 year olds living in an urban area of Scotland finds little support for the postulated link between growing cohabitation and a weakened sense of commitment to long-term arrangements. Most of the cohabiting couples strongly stressed their 'commitment'. Socially acceptable vocabularies of motive undoubtedly influenced answers but interviews helped to explore deeper meanings. Many respondents' views were consistent with previous research predictions of a weakening sense of any added value of marriage. At the same time, some respondents continued to stress the social significance of the distinction between marriage and cohabitation, consistent with research interpreting cohabitation as a 'try and see' strategy part-way to the perceived full commitment of marriage. The notion that 'marriage is better for children' continued to have support among respondents. While, on average, cohabiting couples had lower incomes and poorer employment situations than married couples, only very extreme adverse circumstances were presented as making marriage 'too risky'. Pregnancy-provoked cohabitation was not always in this category. Cohabitation was maintained because marriage would 'make no difference' or because they 'had not yet got round to' marriage. Most respondents were more wary of attempting to schedule or plan in their personal life than in other domains and cohabitees' attitudes to partnership, including their generally 'committed' approach, do not explain the known greater vulnerability of this group to dissolution.

Introduction

Commentators on marriage and the family sometimes view pessimistically the increase in heterosexual couples living together without marrying as a reduction in willingness to create and honour life-long partnerships. High or rising rates of divorce and lone parenthood are seen as a similarly damning 'evidence'. However, sociological analysis has not unequivocally supported the postulated link between growing cohabitation and waning interest in life-long partnerships. As some European commentators have suggested, (Ermisch, 2000; Lewis, 1999a, 1999b, 2001; Manting, 1996; Prinz, 1995; Smart and Stevens, 2000) the empirical and theoretical basis for assuming that cohabitation without marriage means less commitment to long term couple relationships is rather equivocal.

It is worth noting that the current usage of the term 'commitment' to describe an intention to maintain a couple relationship over a long-time if not a life-time is rather historically-specific. It reflects social changes in everyday hopes for and expectations of couple relationships including a shift away from emphasis on traditional obligations as a husband/wife to emphasis on a more personally negotiated relationship. The everyday adoption of the term 'commitment' is as recent as the late twentieth century. Jane Lewis's study of couples from different generations notes: 'the notion of obligation was more readily accepted by the older generation and commitment by the younger' (1999b: 44). Many commentators argue that ideals concerning couple relationships, married or otherwise, have moved closer to what Giddens (1991, 1992) describes as the necessarily fragile 'pure relationship', the relationship that only lasts as long as it brings mutual benefit, even if the lived practical realities may be rather more complicated (Jamieson, 1998, 1999).

Christopher Prinz (1995) and Dorien Manting (1996) categorise changes in the meaning of cohabitation since the late twentieth century. Summarising change in partnership formation in the Netherlands over the decades since the 1950s, Manting suggests: 'Cohabitation started as an alternative way of living, developed into a temporary phase before marriage, and finally became a strategy for moving into a union gradually' (1996: 53). In making predictions concerning the future of cohabitation in the UK, Chris Shaw and John Haskey (1999), like Kiernan (1999) assume attitudes to cohabitation will move from 'being seen as a prelude to marriage to being an acceptable alternative to marriage' (1999: 13; Haskey, 2001). It is likely that what the authors mean here by 'alternative' is that couples will regard it as a matter of no consequence whether they get married or not as Prinz (1995) suggests, rather than 'alternative' in the stronger sense of alternative life-style used by Manting (1996). Jane Lewis has suggested that there is no longer any moral distinction between marriage and cohabitation for recent generations who believe 'true morality has to come from within . . . rather than from an externally prescribed moral code' and 'the kind of commitment a couple makes – public or private – is *their own affair*.' (2001: 145).

Social analysts sometimes present cohabitation as a bet-hedging strategy, a half-way house between full and no commitment. There is a suggestion that high hopes for 'a good relationship' encourage a process of weighing the quality of the relationship. Cohabiting allows more flexibility than marriage if one partner is not convinced that the quality is as good as s/he could hope for, and wishes to continue to weigh the relative benefits of being single, or living with another potential partner, against the experience of living with this partner (Kravdal, 1999: 66). So this is a trial not in the sense of 'Am I suited to being partnered in this way?' but 'Is this person good enough?' or 'the right one?' In this analysis, cohabitation is seen as having the advantage of easier exit, while, for its duration, search for alternatives is more or less suspended but not completely off the agenda. Ermisch's (2000) analysis of the British Household Panel Study suggests that, for this representative sample of the British population, cohabitation was mainly used as a trial marriage. He notes that most cohabitation either ended in marriage or people breaking up and trying again but the balance remains towards the former; more partners prove satisfactory than unsatisfactory. Smart and Stevens (2000) suggest that couples opt for cohabitation with little sense of any marriage prospects in circumstances, such as low incomes, poor employment prospects and unplanned parenthood, that are viewed as making marriage particularly 'risky'. (See footnote 5 for a description of income and employment in our own sample.)

The fact that there is no automatic association between cohabitation and absence of commitment has been demonstrated empirically for British cohabitants in a number of ways. Jane Lewis has conducted a qualitative study of two generations of relatively affluent long-term childrearing couples, exploring attitudes to marriage and cohabitation. She found that the meaning of cohabitation can change over time for some couples. For example, some couples in her sample had drifted into cohabitation for pragmatic reasons but by the time of interview saw their cohabitation as an expression of a private commitment to their relationship, a commitment that was, as one respondent put it, 'strong enough,' for them to decide to have children (Lewis, 1999b: 32–42). It is perhaps not surprising that commitment often grows in relationships that have survived over time. By the same token, a withering of commitment might be more common among relationships that fail. Carol Smart and Pippa Stevens conducted interviews with a small sample of parents who were ex-cohabitees in order to explore the causes of the breakdown of their relationship and the nature of their previous commitment to it. They found that even in this group a substantial proportion of cohabitees had begun their relationship with a strong sense of mutual commitment to staying together. Others always felt their commitment was contingent, usually on their relationship or their partner somehow getting better, and a few, exclusively men, had no sense of commitment but rather saw their cohabitation purely in terms of convenience.

This paper discusses the meaning of marriage, cohabitation and commitment for young adults in the age group 20–29 in the first year of the 21st century. It is possible for a couple to enter into cohabitation with different levels and understandings of commitment. They may view living together as the beginning of a permanent partnership. Alternatively they may see cohabitation as a way of testing out whether a permanent partnership is viable, bet-hedging as it has been described. Or, thirdly, they may drift into cohabitation with very little thought for the future, seeing it as a pragmatic arrangement that carries little or no burden of expectations. Each of these three ways of viewing the beginning of cohabitation, can be accompanied by positive, negative or fairly neutral views of marriage as an institution and as a possible future part of personal life. In the first two cases, cohabitation may be seen as part of a process of getting married or an equivalent path that is as-good-as-married or an alternative that is better than marriage. It is also quite possible that each member of a couple will have a somewhat different view and that however they see their partnership at the outset, their views will change over time. Without ignoring this complexity, we attempt to capture the balance of typical ideals and behaviours among our 20–29 year old respondents. Which of the various optimistic and pessimistic academic visions of the future does this balance support?

The data

Our study[1] is based on a sample of men and women aged 20–29. This is an ideal age group for an investigation of partnership practices and attitudes as it spans the modal age of cohabitation and first marriage. While this paper focuses on the coupled respondents, it draws on the single respondents to provide a more complete sense of the age group.

The sampling procedures aimed to find 200 randomly selected individuals in the age range 20–29 from within pre-specified postal districts in Fife, Scotland.[2] The sample was stratified equally between the 20–24 and 25–29 age groups and between men and women. This resulted in an initial sample of 202 respondents within the age group, 93 living in couples,[3] and 109 'singles', that is not living with a partner. Among the coupled respondents, we attempted to interview both partners and both were interviewed successfully in the majority of households. Most partners were also in the 20–29 age group.[4] The result was data on 246 20–29 year olds, 109 single people and the remaining 137 drawn from 93 couples. Respondents in couples were almost equally divided between the married and the cohabiting, with higher rates of cohabitation in the early twenties and higher rates of marriage in the late twenties.[5]

In the survey, a structured questionnaire was used to ask a series of questions of couples that are relevant to their sense of commitment to each other in the past, present and future. Questions included their reasons for setting up home together and their plans at that time, their views in the present including their attitude to cohabitation versus marriage, and their plans for the future. Where appropriate, questions were drawn from existing household surveys such as the General Household Survey and the British Household Panel Survey. When possible, both partners of a couple were surveyed simultaneously by a single interviewer. Self-completion questions were used when the possibility of partners influencing each other's answers was not desired, or when the topic might force disclosure of sensitive information or initiate disagreement between couples.

As a follow-up to the survey, intensive interviews were conducted with 16 'single' people and 25 couples. The intensive couple interviews were largely conducted with couples in their late twenties, among whom the married predominate. Couples were interviewed together but in two cases one partner was absent for all or most of the interview. 17 intensive interviews were conducted with married couples, 12 had lived together before marriage and five had not. 12 of the married couples had children at the time of interview. Eight intensive interviews were conducted with cohabiting couples, seven of whom had children.[6] All couples were interviewed by Robert Stewart. This paper draws on both the survey and these intensive interviews which are referred to by pseudonyms.[7] The paper is organised by interweaving the survey data and material from the intensive interviews.

Commitment from the beginning

In the survey, all couples were asked 'When you and your current partner first decided to set up home or move in together, did you think of it as a permanent arrangement or something that you would try and then see how it worked?' This was one of a set of self-completion question followed up by asking about why they set up home together when they did. The majority of respondents, both men and women, described their arrangement as one that they thought of as permanent. However, the evidence suggests that a minority were using cohabitation in a bet hedging way. Overall, 80% said that their partnership was a permanent arrangement from the beginning and 20% said 'try and see'. The minority describing the arrangement in terms of 'try and see' was higher (30%) among currently cohabiting respondents than among those who cohabited and then married (15%). Also it was higher among younger cohabitees (38% of those under age 25), than among older cohabitees (21% of those of age 25 and over) and higher among younger men than younger women (43% of cohabiting men age under 25 and 35% of cohabiting women aged under 25). The picture is further complicated if agreement between members of the couple is taken into account.

Table 1 shows that agreement between couples in describing the arrangement as permanent varied by partnership status. Only cases in which both partners answered are included. There were lower rates of agreement and lower proportions seeing it as a permanent arrangement among the cohabitees than among the married. The few couples who married without first living together all agreed that the arrangement was permanent. A clear majority of couples who cohabited then married agreed that it was permanent but 29% did not agree, although as individuals only 16% thought in terms of 'try and see'. Among those currently cohabiting, as individuals 33% thought of setting up home in terms of 'try and see' and the majority, two thirds, as a

Table 1 Couples giving the same and different answers to: 'When you and your current partner first decided to set up home or move in together, did you think of it as a permanent arrangement or something that you would try and then see how it worked?'[8]

	All cohabiting without marriage	Those who cohabited and then married	Married without cohabiting
Both 'Permanent'	48%	67%	100%
Both 'Try and see'	13%	4%	
Different answers	39%	29%	
N = 100%	31	24	9

permanent arrangement, but less than half the couples agreed that their arrangement was permanent. 39% did not agree and 13% agreed it was a case of 'try and see'.

The cohabiting respondents who were particularly likely to describe the beginning of their partnership in terms of 'try and see' were younger respondents with children. In combination the survey data and the intensive interviews suggest that those who set up home together very young and who experienced an unexpected pregnancy at an early stage in their relationship were particularly likely to describe the beginning of their arrangement in terms of 'try and see'. These issues are explored further in the next section.

Some of the intensive interviews indicate that not all respondents drew a clear line between a permanent arrangement and 'try and see'. Lorraine and Craig Duncan were the youngest couple among our intensive interviews, at aged 22 and 23. They had been a couple since they were at school together and began living together as teenagers, first with parents and then in their own council house. They married at ages 19 and 20. In the survey, Lorraine described the point of setting up home together in terms of 'try and see' and Craig as 'permanent'. However, in interview Craig described how 'seeing if it would work' had been involved in the gap between asking Lorraine to marry him and getting married.

Craig: Aye it wis like the year before kinda, that wisnae like after when I first asked her or anything, it was like a year before the actual wedding date that we actually picked that date. So. Didnae ken why it was that long, like, but we just left it when I first asked her. Ken I suppose just in case we did ever split up or anything so we just left it to see if things would work out.

R.S.: Were you living together then?

Craig: Aye, so that was maybe part of it, seeing if it would work.

Table 2 Percentage choosing each reason[10] for setting up home when they did, by partnership status

	Never married[11] cohabiting	Married after cohabiting	Married never cohabited
I wanted to commit myself to our relationship	72%	63%	54%
We fell in love and could not live without each other	62%	52%	79%
The time had come when I wanted to live with a sexual partner	27%	44%	17%
I/my partner was pregnant	20%	24%	17%
Rented accommodation became available	15%	35%	8%
We'd got enough money together to get a house	15%	17%	17%
I was at a suitable point in my working life	13%	9%	29%
My partner was at a suitable point in his/her working life	13%	7%	17%
Some other important factor	2%	4%	4%
[N] = 100%	60	46	24

The survey explored couples' reasons for setting up home together when they did, by offering a list of items that might have influenced them to do so and allowing respondents to choose as many as they wished. With the exception of 'the time had come when I wanted to live with a sexual partner', an answer more common among younger respondents, the pattern of responses did not vary markedly by age or gender but they did vary by partnership status. The differences are generally not sufficient to be statistically significant[9] but the overall pattern of difference is nevertheless interesting. The results are shown in Table 2, by partnership history and status.

For respondents who were cohabiting without marriage, the most chosen item was 'I wanted to commit myself to our relationship', selected by over three quarters, followed by 'We fell in love and could not live without each other' chosen by over a half. While the pattern was similar for married respondents the order was reversed and 'We fell in love' was chosen by over three quarters and 'I wanted to commit myself to our relationship' by over a half. No other items commanded such support but a series of items referring to more pragmatic decisions and practical circumstances attracted the support of more than 20% of at least one of the three groups shown in the table: 'The time had come when I wanted to live with a sexual partner', '1/my partner was pregnant', 'rented accommodation became available', 'I was at a suitable point in my working life'. Those who had cohabited and then married more often chose 'the time had come to live with a sexual partner' and 'rented accommodation became available'. This may be more to do with acceptable vocabularies of motive than differences in behaviour. Unlike 'I was at a suitable point in my working life', these are not conventional good reasons for getting married and are chosen by very few of those who married without cohabiting. However, those who have made the transition from cohabitation to marriage can acknowledge these reasons for first setting up home together without suggesting any lack of substance to their relationship now. Cohabitees might feel that selecting such explanations carry greater risk of trivialising their relationship.

Over 40% of those surveyed chose both 'love' and 'commitment' among their reasons for setting up home together when they did. This was true, for example, of Mary Hutton and Bill Noble, both of whom we interviewed at length with their respective partners, cohabitees Greg Graham and Sharon Noble. Both couples now have children.

Mary Hutton was only 16 years old when she moved in with Greg who was then aged 23. On her survey she chose 'love', 'I wanted to live with a sexual partner' and 'I wanted to commit myself'. Greg chose 'I wanted to commit myself'. Both also indicated that they saw the arrangement as permanent at the time, although living together was not the result of a longstanding plan. Mary had been going out with Greg for three months when he asked her to move in with him. Mary explained that she asked her mother's permission: 'We were gonna leave it a wee while before we moved in. And, em, my mum was like, "Well, if you are moving in, you may as well do it this weekend", eh. So, that was that.'

Sharon and Bill Noble were aged 20 and 21 when they first met. Sharon was living with but in the process of 'breaking-up with' somebody else when she met Bill. Despite housing difficulties, they more or less started to live together very soon after first meeting. In the survey Bill is one of the larger minority among younger cohabitees who described the beginning of living together as 'try and see'. This couple are also among those who do not give the same answers as Sharon spoke of a 'permanent arrangement'. However, this is not a couple in disharmony. Both Bill and Sharon chose 'love' as a reason for setting up home together when they did but Bill also chose 'I wanted to commit myself'. This couple was effusive about being in love. Bill describes them as being 'daft about each other' and 'made for each other' and Sharon said 'when I met him, I knew that was him; he was the one.' As is discussed later, this couple discussed plans to marry from an early stage in their relationship, although they still had no definite date at the time of interview.

Beginning with an unplanned pregnancy

Couples who set up home together because of an unplanned pregnancy have a distinct set of experiences that shed light on more general attitudes and approaches to cohabiting and marriage. The experience of an unplanned pregnancy focuses prospective parents on their views of the future of their relationship as a couple, bringing up children, cohabiting and marriage. About 25% of our respondents who were coupled with children reported a pregnancy as being an important influence in setting up home at that point in their life, rising to about a third among those who are still under 25. The proportions were similar for married and cohabiting respondents. We conducted intensive interviews with respondents who were at different stages in their relationship when they experienced an unplanned pregnancy. Their accounts illustrate how reactions to unplanned pregnancy vary depending on whether a couple viewed themselves as established and committed or not. Some, who did not see themselves as either, at least not prior to that point, nevertheless chose to gamble on living together in a bet-hedging 'try and see' way. For those who saw themselves as already both established and committed, responding to the pregnancy simply speeded up anticipated aspects of consolidation as a couple.

Douglas Syme and Jean Taylor were a couple who had not even started to consider their future when Jean became pregnant. Both answered 'try and see' to the survey question. Jean was several years older than Douglas. She was legally separated from but still married to the father of her two older children. Very soon after their own son was born, Douglas moved in with Jean and her children. At the time of interview they had lived together for five years. Douglas speaking to the interviewer alone, explained,

> I met my partner I'm wi' the now. I only knew her for five weeks before she fell pregnant. And I think it was just lucky that we were kinda in love, eh. And five years doon the line we're still together, so.

Douglas was keen to be a father. He stated that his commitment to Jean was reassessed as a result of his desire to be a good father. He wanted to prevent the reproduction of his own childhood feelings of being let down by an absentee father. This means staying with Jean.

> Douglas: maybe if we never had a bairn, maybe, would me and Jean still be together? . . . That's going through my mind 'cause I'm thinking, 'cause I remember saying to mysel', well I would never ever leave, split up 'cause I'd always stay wi' Jean for the child eh. Because maybe 'cause I never had that when I was young.

Our interviews also included couples who had already made a commitment to each other, in the sense of shared understanding of a long-term future together, before the accidental pregnancy. Joseph and Tracey Malcolm decided to get married when Tracey became pregnant. At that time, Tracey was aged 18 and Joseph aged 20. They had been engaged for a month and had a target wedding date in 15 months time. However, the date was brought forward a year in response to the pregnancy. At the time of interview, Tracey regretted this, not because she had any doubts about a commitment to Joseph or because she had reasons for preferring cohabitation to marriage but because she was not allowed to plan her wedding to her satisfaction. She felt that she missed out on her special day.

Tracey: If I look back on it now, I wouldn't have got married. I would've waited until after the pregnancy and got married. But because I was just young, I just went with the flow.
R.S.: Was there any pressure to do it?
Tracey: Aye. And plus we werenae paying for it, eh, it was my parents.
Joseph: There wis a lot of pressure, like, at the time, eh, but . . .
Tracey: I do wish I could have my time back again and do it our own way. Have my own say in it. My own dress, my own everything. . . . I didn't feel like I was important.

Although they themselves married, the Malcolms did not make a definitive distinction between marriage and cohabiting in terms of commitment. In the next section, examples are given of couples who were already living together and anticipating a long-term future together when they experienced an unexpected pregnancy. Such couples also did not typically emphasise a line between marriage and cohabitation in terms of less or more commitment. On the other hand, making a distinction between marriage and living together, emphasising the presumed easier exit from the latter, was important to some couples. They included some who were cautiously wishing to 'try and see' how living together worked out and some who wished to mark a transition in their relationship away from 'try and see' to a state of marriage that they defined as a more definite commitment.

Views of cohabitation and marriage

The survey included two questions about the relative advantages of marriage and cohabitation that were put to single people and cohabiting couples.[12] First we asked if respondents thought there were any advantages in living together as a couple rather than being married. The second question simply reversed the position of 'living together as a couple' and 'being married'. The data indicate that the majority did not see one as clearly better than the other. Over half, 58%, gave the same answer to both questions, that is they either thought that both living together and marriage have advantages over the other, or that neither has advantages over the other.[13] 32% were prepared to declare one

Table 3 Percentage of all single cohabiting and married respondents[15] identifying advantages of particular living arrangements

	Single	Cohabiting	Married
Yes advantages of living as a couple rather than being married	60%	34%	Not asked
No legal ties	38%	15%	N/A
Trial Marriage	28%	20%	N/A
It does not have to be a permanent commitment	26%	2%	N/A
Saves the cost of the wedding	20%	7%	N/A
A lot of marriages fail	18%	7%	N/A
Better relationship	18%	7%	N/A
Personal independence	16%	2%	N/A
Yes advantages of being married rather than living together as a couple	45%	42%	63%
Better for children	31%	27%	45%
More definite commitment	29%	20%	57%
Financial Security	27%	17%	35%
Legal status	27%	15%	26%
No Social Stigma	10%	3%	5%
Public recognition as a couple	9%	3%	17%
The occasion of the wedding	7%	10%	11%
N = 100%	97	59	65

as having advantages and not the other, with cohabitees marginally preferring marriage and single people typically choosing 'living together'.[14]

All who acknowledged advantages of either living together or marriage were then asked about what the advantages were by additional questions allowing multiple choices from lists of possible advantages. In the case of both 'living together as a couple' and 'being married' the lists of possible advantages included an item which used the word 'commitment'. 'Does not have to be a definite commitment' seems to have been treated by single people as an equivalent advantage to 'trial marriage' and 'no legal ties'. This was not the case among cohabitees, however, who almost never picked this item, despite a majority of those cohabitees who answered choosing 'trial marriage' and 'no legal ties'.

Table 3 shows the precentages of all single, cohabiting and married people who identified particular advantages with marriage. For obvious reasons, respondents who did not see any advantages in an arrangement were not asked what those advantages were. In order not to give an inflated sense of those who picked advantages, responses are shown as a percentage of all respondents rather than all who answered.

For married respondents, 'more definite commitment' was the main advantage. The difference between the 57% of married respondents and the 20% of cohabiting respondents who chose this item is statistically significant. More than half of married respondents thought that marriage had the advantage of being a more definite commitment and 45% thought it was 'better for children'. For single and cohabiting respondents the most chosen advantage of marriage was 'better for children' although this item was chosen by statistically significantly fewer cohabiting respondents than married respondents.[16] The pattern of answers suggests that the married respondents, despite the fact that the overwhelming majority of them had previously cohabited, were more likely to distinguish marriage and cohabiting in terms of degrees of commitment than cohabitees who have not married. At the same time, it is important not to overstate this as almost half of married couples do not declare that marriage involves a more definite commitment.

Among our intensive interviews, several cohabiting respondents reflect a combination of commitment to long-term partnership and lack of definite preference for marriage or cohabitation shown by a substantial group in the survey. Many loosely link cohabitation and marriage through getting engaged then living together with a more or less specific plan of marrying. As MacRae (1993) found for many of her cohabiting respondents with children, some respondents were cohabiting because they had not yet got married. In our study, there were couples who explained that marriage was an anticipated event but not a high priority. Their reasons for planning to marry were not about commitment, which was already taken for granted, but the desire for a party, a special day, and sometimes a gesture that would please others. Most assumed that marriage would make no difference to their relationship.

Sharon and Bill Noble who were 'daft about each other' from the beginning of their relationship, quickly started to discuss both having children and plans to marry. They had been living together for about three years before Sharon became pregnant. Although they were not using contraception, the pregnancy was a shock because they started trying to have a child two years previously and had come to assume fertility problems. They cancelled their wedding because Sharon would have been eight months pregnant on the chosen date. Once they had a child, marriage seemed less important.

Sharon: I think we would like to do it but then when we think about the money. I think we would just rather get something. Like we would like to get a bigger TV. I think we would take that rather than get married. . . . It doesn't matter because I think before we really wanted to get it over and done with but now that we have had [baby] we are a bit more relaxed about it now. It isn't like we are going to go anywhere noo, you know, it doesn't matter.

Similar sentiments were expressed by other cohabiting respondents who were planning to marry. Marriage is not the point at which they commit themselves to their relationship. As Neil Martin put it:

> You, you've made that commitment you know. And it's just like you're married, you know. But I think it's, that little bit more having your own, your own day, you know.

This perspective led some cohabitees to delay or abandon marriage plans because the special day could not be the way they wanted it. They couldn't afford the money or time needed or ensure relatives would co-operate with the kind of 'special day' they wanted.

Similarly, some married couples explained that the event and fact of being married was not of great importance. For example when asked about important events that have happened since leaving school Sheila Wilson said 'buying this house' and when prompted for 'anything else', suggested 'must be getting married, eh?' to which her husband Alex Wilson replied 'I don't know if that's really important'. Sheila then went on to elaborate an account of why the house was more important than the wedding:

> I mean oor wedding day was a formality. I mean we knew we wanted to be the gether [together] but it was really tae satisfy everybody else, you know. We would've just went away somewhere but I think, the most important thing as far as we, as a couple are concerned and myself, is buying the house because that's something that you've worked for and it's something that's yours and naebody can take it away frae you no matter like . . . I mean Alex had, well he was married before and, kinda lost everything he had. So, em, a' the time we were the gether he wisnae a hundred percent secure until such times as we actually got something of our own. That gave him a wee bit o' security.

On the other hand some couples who cohabited and then married did distinguish between cohabiting and marriage in terms of degrees of commitment. This is said quite clearly, for example, by Mark and Debbie Thorpe when they were asked why they did not simply continue to live together rather than getting married.

> Debbie: Dinnae feel there's the same commitment then.
> Mark: Naw. It isnae.

Debbie went on to note that her friends who lived together without being married did not make this distinction but both she and Mark reasserted that, for them, marriage was more of a commitment.

> Mark: As I say, the commitment, and you say, it's commitment, and it's finally makes it that, eh, taking vows and sticking to they vows.

> That's obviously what marriage is but they [friends who choose not to marry], they obviously dinnae see it in that, in that light.

And Debbie also raised the issue of children.

> Debbie: I feel it is a more of a stable basis for family as well, if you do have a family.

A strongly expressed reason for marriage among respondents concerns the issue of children and having a common family name. Lewis (1999) and Smart and Stevens (2000) have found this to be an issue which retains importance for many couples. Many of our respondents wanted to act on the view that marriage was better for children. Anne Whyte shared this view but an unexpected pregnancy meant that events did not unfold in this way. She and Colin Whyte had not begun to plan a future together when Anne became pregnant at age 20. Each still lived with their parents and Colin moved in to Anne's parents' house until they managed to get a council flat. After two years of living together, they decided to get married.

> Anne: 'Cause I decided for the sake o' [child] as well, I'd rather we were married for her sake, as well. Because she's got the same name as Colin whereas I wouldn't as well you know. It's a bit o' this and that. I wanted to. Colin wanted to. So there's no much point in not. It's never made any difference on us really, no changed anything, because we knew, we would be the gether anyway.

After this reassurance about how being married was no different from living together, Anne, nevertheless, added some further remarks suggesting that marriage tidies thing up with a form of completion or closure confirming a permanent arrangement.

> Anne: So we'd got our house, got car, got jobs, we had [child], we had really everything, so it was just a case of sorting oursels and just getting married. . . . We had lived the gether anyway for two years, so we ken what each other was like and everything. And if it was a case o' that we were just no gonna make it, then we wouldnae have bothered I suppose.

As noted in the introduction, whether couples enter into cohabitation as the beginning of a permanent partnership, as a way of testing out the suitability of a relationship for such a partnership, or with little thought for the future, a range of attitudes to marriage is possible. The views of marriage held by our respondents generally seem to be either neutral or positive seeing marriage as 'better for children' or a more definite commitment. The numerical balance was in the neutral camp. Opinions about marriage and cohabitation often lacked vehemence. Only one couple among the interviewed cohabitees, Stuart Sheridan and Karen Groves, had specific negative things to say about marriage. Stuart Sheridan was a self-employed tradesman who has previously been married and has recently started to see more of his child from this marriage. He and Karen lived together for six years. Both saw it as a permanent arrangement from the beginning. They had one child. The couple were in a great deal of debt, most of it generated by Stuart and much of this was a legacy of his previous marriage. This led to a defensive sense of the importance of financial independence. Karen went reluctantly back to her paid employment when their child was only ten weeks old in order to ensure that she would keep her job and her sense of independence. Marriage was viewed negatively as legally obliterating financial independence. But underlying the concern to maintain financial independence was also the unspoken assumption that their relationship might break down. What was actually said was that when things do break down then marriage makes it much worse.

Karen: After seeing and hearing, hearing about the split up with his ex-wife, financially it's easier to keep separated, in that sense of the word like.

Stuart: Aye it's easier to keep like we are rather than being married. You get married and money becomes, if you separate money becomes a right mess.

Karen: Like for example when him and his ex-wife split up he was, when I first met him he was paying thousands of pounds of debt for stuff that she had with her. And its like uhh. Just things like that ken. Best to keep it separate to a certain degree I think. We've not even got a joint bank account though and we keep to that, but we do – people say that you mustn't live together if you don't have a joint bank account but that's rubbish.

Discussion

The study reported here gives insight into attitudes to cohabiting and commitment to long-term or life-time partnering among heterosexual couples aged 20–29, a key age group in terms of ideals and practices of partnership formation. It provides new evidence that there is no simple relationship between cohabiting and 'lack of commitment'. This does not support the pessimistic view that a growth in cohabitation reflects selfish unwillingness to make significant investments in family relationships. The majority of couples in this study chose to describe how they began living together as entering a permanent arrangement. Interviews found most cohabiting couples stressing and itemising their commitment to each other. A minority described the beginning of living with a partner as a bet hedging 'try and see' strategy. For most this meant trying to see whether this relationship was going to become a permanent partnership rather than entering into an acknowledged temporary and casual arrangement. However, cohabitation did have connotations of less permanence for many in the age group but this idea was strongly repudiated by most, although not all, cohabitees.

Despite the fact that a permanent relationship is the assessment most young people give of the starting point of their cohabitation, this does not mean that setting up home together was a planned and anticipated event. The majority of our sample claimed to lack any prior plan concerning the timing of setting up home together and, among those with children, this lack of planning extends to the timing of their first child. Young people with well developed plans for employment and housing denied planning their personal life, suggesting cultural taboos against some forms of overt planning persist, making it difficult to unravel interaction between planning in other domains and personal life (Anderson *et al.*, 2002). The act of moving in together and marriage as a 'special day' or 'big day' offer very different opportunities for socially acceptable planning and expressions of spontaneous versus staged romance. While a stated intention to marry at some stage preceded living together for many, a sense of commitment was often generated in a context of no specific plans for the future of the relationship and no ceremony at the point of moving in together.

Over half of respondents demonstrate the blurring of marriage and cohabitation through their lack of strong views about the relative advantages and disadvantages of each. It seems that they did not want to make a clear distinction between the two forms of partnership. Very few cohabitees claimed that living together outside of marriage is something different to and better than marriage and the majority repudiate the notion that it is a lesser commitment. Nobody we interviewed who had been successfully cohabiting for some time explicitly talked of it as a temporary arrangement. This is a judgement that seems more likely to be passed in retrospect on past failures.

On the other hand, both the survey and the intensive interviews show that a significant minority continue to emphasise the greater commitment of marriage. A significant minority of single people, over half of married couples, and a fifth of cohabiting couples declared on the survey that they saw marriage as a greater commitment than cohabitation. However, endorsements of marriage were relatively low key. Interviewees who felt strongly that marriage is more of a commitment, acknowledged that others do things differently and do not see it this way. As Lewis (2001) has suggested, there was little sense of any clear moral distinction.

It is interesting to try and establish which respondents emphasised the easier exit of cohabitation rather than the greater commitment of marriage as a desirable distinction. In interviews, young men and those who perceived their relationships as at a high risk of breakdown made a particular point in stressing the advantages of easier exit. In the survey, a more substantial minority of younger respondents, and particularly younger men, described entering into their cohabiting relationships in terms of 'try and see'. The higher incidence of a 'try and see' approach among younger respondents may mean that acknowledging the prospect of failure and seeking easy exit is becoming more socially acceptable. This need not signal a profound change in ideals, but simply that it is more acceptable to acknowledge doubts, uncertainties and hence the need for trial and error. This interpretation is consistent with the seemingly contradictory account of the likes of Bill Noble who declared his starting point as very in-love with his partner and anticipating a long-term arrangement yet on a 'try and see' basis. Conventions of masculinity may also modify the vocabulary of young men. A persistent version of youthful masculinity that denigrates prematurely 'settling down' may encourage a 'try and see' vocabulary among younger men, albeit that explicit talk of retaining 'freedom' was only common among some single male respondents (Jamieson *et al.*, forthcoming). In-depth interviews suggest caution about the type of fit that should be assumed between public descriptions of 'try and see' and private hopes.

Sometimes the use of 'try and see' among younger respondents reflected higher than average risks. Starting a cohabiting relationship at a younger than average age and/or as a result of a pregnancy are objectively risky ventures. The statistics may not be well known, but a sense of the possibility that 'things might not work out' was clearly recognised by respondents like Douglas Syme. In other words, our findings contain examples that are entirely consistent with Smart's and Stevens' (2001) suggestion that some respondents are making rational choices when they view marriage as 'too risky'. Youthful marriage has largely been replaced by youthful cohabitation and relationships entered as teenagers remain more likely to end in separation whether they involve subsequent marriage or not. Similarly, pregnancy-provoked marriage has largely been replaced by pregnancy-provoked cohabitation. While pregnancy-provoked cohabitation can be an outcome for couples of a range of ages, the younger the couple experiencing an unplanned pregnancy, the more probable it is that the pregnancy occurred before a sense of consolidation and planned future as a couple. Understandably, those who respond to an unexpected pregnancy by living together despite no previously agreed future together are very likely to talk of setting up home together in terms of 'try and see'. While an entirely pregnancy-provoked partnership was always perceived by those experiencing it as involving risk, experience of other factors that are objectively associated with relationship breakdown, such as low income and unemployment, were rarely talked of in this way. While on average cohabiting couples are objectively more at risk than married couples, because of lower incomes and more uncertain unemployment, only exceptionally were economic circumstances seen as making marriage 'too risky'.

Unexpected pregnancy does not always mean trying to get on as a couple in circumstances of previous lack of commitment as it often occurs in a context of an established relationship. In such circumstances, the pregnancy is not a factor causing the relationship to be viewed as a risky venture and, indeed, there is no such subjective sense of risk. Yet our intensive interviews suggest that among couples who are already cohabiting and committed, an unplanned pregnancy might be more likely to delay marriage than to hasten it. With respect to the British Household Panel Survey, John Ermisch and Marco Francesconi (2000) note that once cohabiting couples have children they are just as likely to split up as childless couples and less likely to marry. One possible explanation that they suggest is that those who felt they should marry when they started a family did so before children were born. This may be true for many but not all. Our and other qualitative studies (McRae, 1993) identify consolidated couples who did expect to have a child together at some point and planned to marry first but the timing became out of sequence. Some still planned to marry but have not yet 'got round to it'. It is not clear if or why such couples should be more vulnerable to subsequent dissolution than their equivalents who implemented plans to marry in time. The main reasons cited for delay in marriage by these would-be-married cohabitees are that the wedding now competes for resources that have been made more scarce and with other needs that have been heightened by the presence of a child. It is likely that those who fail to achieve plans to marry are the least well resourced and economic insecurity is an objective risk factor known to make couples more vulnerable to dissolution.

Exceptionally, economic insecurity in itself can be a perceived as a reason for preferring cohabitation over marriage. It is possible for cohabitees, and particularly those with previous failed marriages, to feel that the legal and financial ties of marriage might bring more losses than gains. The example of Stuart and Karen is an extreme case in which prior debts and a strong sense of financial insecurity encouraged the absence of legal ties. For them cohabitation was a form of insurance against the possibility of one sucking the other down to new levels of economic insecurity. However, Stuart and Karen were unusual among cohabitees in making a virtue of the easier exit from cohabitation than marriage. More cohabitees were at pains to stress the opposite, by emphasising that marriage would make no difference to their relationship and itemising practical and material factors binding them together, running a household together, buying a house, planning a child, bringing up a child together, which, in their view, were more important than a marriage certificate.

The paper shows clearly the value of in-depth interviews if we wish to go beyond respondents' choice of acceptable vocabulary for describing their relationship to the deeper meaning of relationships for respondents. Whatever people say about the beginning of their relationship, relationships are a process and people's views of cohabitation and marriage change over time. For example, couples who described the start of their relationship in terms of 'try and see', often then planned to marry and sometimes put plans on hold, as was the case with Sharon and Bill Noble. Once established, their sense of having a long-term relationship was apparently unaltered by the objective strains of unemployment, shifts in income and the demands of an unexpected child, although getting married became less important. While asking about different time periods in a survey can give some insight into process, in-depth interviews undoubtedly offer more scope for understanding how processes unfold. Interviews allowed people to tell a story of growing or sometimes faltering commitment. Combining in-depth interviews and survey material also illustrates how responses to surveys conceal variations confounding similar and different answers. For example, although interviews typically confirmed a desire and expectation of permanence, they also picked up acknowledgements of earlier doubts among the those who declared their relationship as 'a permanent arrangement' from the beginning and desires for permanence among those who declared their arrangement as one of 'try and see' at the outset.

In earlier discussion of the literature, it was noted that a number of authors predicted a shift from cohabitation as a prelude to marriage to an alternative to marriage. Authors seem to suggest a blurring of cohabitation and marriage, a loss of any sense of significant difference between them among new generations making their first partnership decisions (Haskey, 2001; Kiernan, 1999; Lewis, 2001, 1999a, 1999b; Prinz, 1995; Shaw and Haskey, 1999). At the same time, some of this literature (see also Ermisch 2000 Kravdal 1999, Smart and Stevens, 2000) continues to stress the social significance of the distinction between marriage and cohabitation, suggesting that cohabitation has come to be seen as a half-way house, a try and see, 'bet hedging' strategy that is only part-way to the full commitment of marriage. Support is found in this study for both of these apparently contradictory views. This is possible both because of variation within the sample, neither cohabitation nor marriage meant the same thing for everybody, and because people sometimes seem to hold both these contradictory views. While many young people now think it makes little difference whether they marry or not, cohabitation is sometimes maintained as the default position, even when marriage is acknowledge as more desirable. This is because circumstances are seen as working against marriage, sometimes by making the relationship too risky but more commonly simply by creating obstacles to the ideal wedding event.

University of Edinburgh

Received 18 October 2001
Finally accepted 12 April 2002

Notes

1 The study is an Economic and Social Research Council funded project, R 000238020, 'Telling the Future', principal investigators Michael Anderson, Frank Bechhofer, David McCrone, and Lynn Jamieson, researchers Yaojun Li and Robert Stewart. The survey questionnaires were designed by the research team and the fieldwork carried out by Public Attitude Surveys (PAS). We are grateful to the Institute for Social and Economic Research (ISER) at the University of Essex, and especially Dr Heather Laurie, for helping commission and pilot the surveys, data checking and cleaning, and carrying out occupational coding. Telling the Future was

designed to complement a study of adults aged 30–70, 'Decade of Change', (conceived and designed by the principal investigators Michael Anderson, Frank Bechhofer and David McCrone, funded by an ESRC grant (R 000236922) and carried out with the help of the researchers Yaojun, Li and Robert Stewart) which was following up a sample of respondents from the ten year earlier ESRC funded 'Social Change and Economic Life Initiative'. This paper, like all those arising from this project, is the product of a collegiate form of working in which the fieldwork, the analysis and the drafts of the papers have been discussed by the entire research team throughout. The first author has been responsible for initially drafting this paper, carrying out analyses and revisions and seeing it into print; the second author has also contributed to analysis; the names of the other authors are in random order.

2 The postal districts comprised the travel to work area of Kirkcaldy district, a mainly urban area of small and medium sized towns.

3 Couples were identified as such because they were 'living with a partner'. While this approach to identifying couples theoretically could have included same-sex partners, none emerged from the sampling process.

4 Sixteen partners were older, five were younger and in one case the age was not recorded.

5 As in other studies, cohabiting respondents have higher rates of unemployment, lower average educational qualifications and lower average incomes than married respondents. In our sample, 24% of cohabiting men and 23% of cohabiting women were unemployed and an additional 12% of males and 26% of females were out of the labour force because of caring responsibilities or ill health. This compares with unemployment levels of 3% and 13% and non-employment levels of 3% and 23% among our married male and female respondents. 27% of cohabiting men and 26% of cohabiting women had at least Higher Grade/A level qualifications compared with 35% of married men and 36% of married women. There is no difference in terms of the proportion of men with no or vocational qualifications, 42%, but 50% of cohabiting women have no or vocational qualifications compared with 38% of married women. Differences in terms of household income between cohabiting and married respondents are as follows (net household income after deductions and benefits). For both cohabiting men and cohabiting women, the median lies in the £12,480–14,559 band. For both married men and women it fell in the £18,720–20,799 band.

6 Our intensive interview respondents are more socially mixed than Lewis's qualitative sample of 17 married and 12 cohabiting affluent young couples with children. They are younger and have been cohabiting for shorter periods than both Lewis's and Smart and Stevens's samples and, unlike these samples include childless couples. The majority of Lewis's sample were aged between 30 and 45 years old and had been cohabiting for over ten years and the majority of Smart and Stevens's sample had cohabited for over two years. They are also differ from Smart and Stevens sample in that this is a sample of couples who are cohabiting rather than individuals who have cohabited.

7 Details are sometimes changed slightly or made vague in order to protect confidentiality. For brevity and ease of reading, quotations are edited to remove the interviewer's encouraging utterances 'yeah' and 'right' which pepper the flow of conversation but add nothing to the meaning. Otherwise quotations are verbatim. Inaudible parts are shown (. . . ?) and omissions are indicated by three full stops. . . . Any explanatory comments added after the interview are shown in square brackets [ ].

8 This table is based on couples in which both partners were participants in the survey and includes partners who fall outside of the 20–29 age range.

9 The differences in the table that are statistically significant are generally between those who married never having cohabited and those who married after cohabitation. This is true of answers for the following: 'We fell in love . . .', 'The time had come . . .', 'Rented accommodation . . .', 'I was at a suitable point . . .'.

10 'We are interested in why you and your partner got married or set up home together when you did. Would you please tick those things which were important in influencing *the point in your life* when you first set up home together'. Only respondents and their partners aged 20–29 are included in this table; older and younger partners have been excluded.

11 Seven cases of respondents age 20–29 who were cohabiting following a previous marriage have been excluded. They have the potential to be sufficiently different to merit their own column within the table but the numbers are too small to justify the calculation of percentages.

12 Married couples were not asked whether there were advantages of living together over marriage.

13 Among single respondents 29% of men answered yes to both questions and 25% answered no to both questions; 38% of women answered yes to both questions and 23% answered no to both questions. Among cohabiting respondents 28% of men answered yes to both questions and 31% of men answered no to both questions but there was a more marked differences among women with 18% answering yes to both questions and 41% answering no to both questions.

14 23% of single people thought there were advantages of living together over marriage and not vice versa and 6% thought there were advantages of marriage over living together and not vice versa. The equivalent figures for cohabitees were 14% and 23%. Of all who were asked 10% said did not know.

15 Single include those who have previously cohabited but exclude the previously married as they have a rather different pattern of responses but numbers are too small to justify a separate column in the table. Similarly cohabiting excludes the previously married.

16 There were some gender differences in choice of advantage with women stressing 'no legal ties' as an advantage of living together rather more than men. With respect to the advantages of marriage, women stressed financial security, 'more definite commitment' and legal status more than men.

References

Anderson, M., Bechhofer, F., Jamieson, L., McCrone, D., Li, Y. and Stewart, R., (2002), 'Confidence amid Uncertainty: Ambitions and Plans in a Sample of Young Adults', *Sociological Research Online*, vol. 6, no. 4, *http://www.socresonline.org.uk/6/4/anderson.html*

Ermisch, J., (2000), 'Personal relationships and marriage expectations: evidence from the 1998 British Household Panel Study', Working Paper 2000–27, Institute for Social and Economic Research.

Ermisch, J. and Francesconi, M., (2000), 'Patterns of household and family formation', in Berthoud, R. and Gershuny, J. (eds) *Seven Years in the Lives of British Families: Evidence on the dynamics of social change from the British Household Panel Survey*, London: The Policy Press.

Giddens, Anthony, (1991), *Modernity and Self-Identity: Self and Society in the Late Modern Age*, Cambridge: Polity Press.

Giddens, Anthony, (1992), *The Transformation of Intimacy: Sexuality, Love and Eroticism in Modern Societies*, Cambridge: Polity Press.

Haskey, John, (2001), 'Cohabitation in Great Britain: past, present and future trends and attitudes', *Population Trends* 103: 4–25.

Haskey, John, (1999), 'Cohabitational and marital histories of adults in Great Britain', *Population Trends* 96: 13–23.

Jamieson, L., Stewart, R., Li, Y., Anderson, M., Bechhofer, F. and McCrone, D., (forthcoming), 'Single, twenty something and seeking?' in Allan, G. and Jones, G., *Time and the Life Course: Age, Generation and Social Change*, London: Palgrave.

Jamieson, L., (1999), 'Intimacy transformed: a critical look at the pure relationship', *Sociology*, 33: 477–494.

Jamieson, L., (1998), *Intimacy: Personal Relationships in Modern Societies*, Cambridge & Malden, MA: Polity Press.

Kiernan, Kathleen, (1999), 'Cohabitation in Western Europe', *Population Trends*, 96: 25–32.

Kravdal, Oystein, (1999), 'Does marriage require a stronger economic underpinning than informal cohabitation', *Population Studies*, 53: 63–80.

Lewis, Jane, (2001), *The End of Marriage: Individualism and Intimate*, Relations Cheltenham: Edward Elgar Publishing.

Lewis, Jane, (1999a), *Marriage, Cohabitation and the Law: Individualism and Obligation*, London: Lord Chancellor's Department, Research Series no1/99.

Lewis, Jane with Datta, Jessica and Sarre, Sophie, (1999b), *Individualism and Commitment in Marriage and Cohabitation*, London: Lord Chancellor's Department Research Series no 8/99.

Manting, Dorien, (1996), 'The changing meaning of cohabitation and marriage', *European Sociological Review*, 121: 53–65.

McRae, Susan, (1993), *Cohabiting Mothers: Changing Mothers and Motherhood?* London: Policy Studies Institute.

Prinz, Christopher, (1995), *Cohabiting, Married or Single: Portraying, Analyzing and Modeling New Living Arrangements in the Changing Societies of Europe* Aldershot: Avebury.

Shaw, Chris and Haskey, John, (1999), 'New estimates and projections of the population cohabiting in England and Wales', *Population Trends*, 95: 7–17.

Smart, Carol and Stevens, Pippa, (2000), *Cohabitation Breakdown*, London: published for the Joseph Rowntree Foundation by the Family Policy Centre.

[6]

Marriage and the Moral Bases of Personal Relationships

JOHN EEKELAAR* AND MAVIS MACLEAN**

Marriage is a legal institution. Current debates about whether it should be extended beyond its traditional heterosexual constitution, and whether many of its legal incidents should apply to couples who live together without marrying, and about the introduction of civil partnership (modelled closely on marriage) for same-sex couples, make an examination of its contemporary role particularly timely. This article is about the interplay between the institution of marriage and ideas of obligation within personal relationships. It takes as its starting point some commonly held opinions. First, that the sense of obligation which hitherto guided people's behaviour in their personal relationships has much diminished or even disappeared. Second, that this diminution is reflected in the decline in marriage. We will then examine what the evidence of an empirical study conducted by the Oxford Centre for Family Law and Policy reveals about the way people in married and unmarried relationships understand the nature of their personal obligations. In doing this it will be seen that the moral bases which underpin people's personal relationships is complex and does not correspond in a simple way with formal, external social categories.

I. THE DECLINE OF OBLIGATION[1]

Prior to formulating an argument (to which we will return) that the obligations created by marriage constitute a human good, Scott Fitzgibbon asserts that 'the twentieth century brought a crisis of obligation'.[2] He cites little evidence for

* *Pembroke College, St Aldates, Oxford OX1 1DW, England*
** *Department of Social Policy and Social Work, University of Oxford, Barnett House, 32 Wellington Square, Oxford OX1 2ER, England*

1 This has been covered at greater length in J. Eekelaar, 'Personal Obligations' in *Family Law and Family Values*, ed. M. Maclean (2003).
2 S. Fitzgibbon, 'Marriage and the Good of Obligation' (2002) 47 *Am. J. of Jurisprudence* 41–69, at 47.

this proposition,[3] but the sentiment is common enough. Gilles Lipovetsky has referred to the alleged phenomenon as '*le crépuscule du devoir*'[4] and Zygmunt Bauman has described postmodern sociality as one which 'knows not and hears not of rights, obligations, contracts or legal entitlements'.[5] The 'culprit' (if such there be) for this state of affairs is said to be the rise of 'individualism'. Thus, in 1985, Robert Bellah and colleagues[6] identified 'individualism' as 'the first language in which Americans tend to think about their lives', leading them to value 'independence' and 'self-reliance' above all else.[7] For these authors, individualism seems to denote a kind of self-centred indulgence, to be contrasted with a disposition towards 'commitment' and recognition of 'obligations'. But it is not so simple. Some writers have argued that the sense of obligation to others has been replaced by a sense of obligation to oneself to live a authentic life.[8] In a more complex analysis, Giddens in 1992[9] and Beck and Beck-Gernsheim in 1995,[10] drawing on a wide range of contemporary literature (in Giddens' case, especially psychoanalytical discourses), developed a more complex version. According to Giddens:

> Confluent love is not necessarily monogamous ... What holds the pure relationship together is the acceptance of each partner 'until further notice', that each gains sufficient benefit from the relationship to make its continuation worthwhile.[11]

3 His cites only the rise in bankruptcy filings by individuals and families in the United States of America, an assertion by Allan Bloom that American students have impoverished ideas of friendship (A. Bloom, *The Closing of the American Mind* (1987) 82–140), and the claim by Patrick Atiyah that respect for promises has declined in English life, see P.S. Atiyah, *The Rise and Fall of Freedom of Contract* (1979) 649–59.

4 G. Lipovetsky, *Le Crépuscule du Devoir* (1992).

5 Z. Bauman, *Postmodern Ethics* (1993) 130.

6 R.E. Bellah, R. Madsen, W.M. Sulian, A. Swindler, and S.M. Tipton, *Habits of the Heart: Individualism and Commitment in American Life* (1985, updated 1996).

7 id., p. viii. This was a very broad-brush analysis. Much of the discussion on values in the private sphere centres around four individuals chosen as paradigms, who speak in very general terms about their 'philosophies of life'. The authors found that they had difficulty in 'justifying the goals of a morally good life'; they were confused about defining 'the nature of success, the meaning of freedom and the requirements of justice.' Since these are issues with which philosophers and theologians have wrestled for centuries, the problems of the respondents are very understandable. Similarly, their observation that 'Americans are ... torn between love as an expression of spontaneous inner freedom, a deeply personal, but necessarily somewhat arbitrary, choice, and the image of love as a firmly planted, permanent commitment, embodying obligations' does not do other than take up an age-old theme, whether expressed in terms of conflict between individual passion and obligations to wider family, country or spouse.

8 For an excellent discussion, see H. Reece, *Divorcing Responsibly* (2003) 84–92.

9 A. Giddens, *The Transformation of Intimacy: Sexuality, Love and Eroticism in Modern Societies* (1992).

10 U. Beck and E. Beck-Gernsheim, *The Normal Chaos of Love* (1995).

11 Giddens, op. cit., n. 9, p. 63.

Central to this is the role of 'negotiation'. The rights and obligations arising from the relationship are subject to negotiation.[12] Even sexuality is a matter of negotiation, whether it be the matter of sexual exclusivity, or even the nature of the sexuality itself.[13] Beck and Beck-Gernsheim describe the same phenomenon. They call it, creating a 'do-it-yourself life history'.[14] In daily life, 'more and more things have to be negotiated, planned, personally brought about'.[15] The organization of life after divorce 'has to be negotiated, often fought over'.[16]

This new individualism is hardly a world of 'do as I please'. Autonomy may have become a newly important value, but it is restrained by the necessity of coexisting with other people who are exercising the same value. Coexistence is made possible through negotiation. But this analysis throws up new problems. What is meant by negotiation? It surely does not occur within a vacuum. How, then, is it affected by the social or moral context in which it occurs? *Is* there such a context? Janet Finch, in an important analysis of what negotiation might mean in this context, saw it not as being the equivalent to conscious bargaining, but as an *understanding* which emerged over time 'that there are certain things which they would do for each other if necessary'.[17] But Finch was clear that such 'negotiation' takes place within 'external structures'. It is these structures which create 'shared understandings' absorbed through membership of society that underlie the negotiations, for example (as Finch explains):

> most people, both sons and daughters, acknowledge some responsibility for their parents in old age; daughters are commonly thought to be the people most suited to provide nursing care, for their mothers especially; men do not give up their jobs to care for a parent.[18]

This reference acknowledges the role of 'social rules', which Finch describes as not being so much 'moral' rules 'concerned with determining how someone "ought" to behave, as common perceptions of "how the world works".'[19]

In 1999 Carol Smart and Bren Neale reported on a study of post-separation parenting involving 31 women and 29 men interviewed twice during 1994–6, at twelve and eighteen months after their separation. The purpose was to detect whether there were 'newly emergent forms of responsibilities, caring patterns and ethical codes'.[20] Smart and Neale concluded that indeed there were. These

12 id., p. 191.
13 id., pp. 63, 96.
14 U. Beck and E. Beck-Gernsheim, *Individualization* (2001).
15 id., p. 91.
16 id., p. 94.
17 J. Finch, *Family Obligations and Social Change* (1989) 181.
18 id., p. 183.
19 id.
20 C. Smart and B. Neale, *Family Fragments?* (1999) 40.

people were not acting amorally, in the sense that they reflected on their decisions and weighed up their consequences. They argued that the mothers exhibited an ethic of care, in the sense that, for them, their decisions about what 'should be done' were solutions to specific problems in which the primary guideline was the practical manifestation of 'care' for another, in this case, the children. The fathers, by contrast, tended to proclaim an 'ethic of justice', which was abstract and rights-based, and they used the rhetoric of equality.

The circumstances of post-separation parenting is of course a good context in which to examine the norms to which people have reference when determining what their personal obligations are. But it is a very special context, which arises only after shared living has finished. We still need to know more about the norms to which shared living may give rise. Jane Lewis has made an important contribution to this knowledge.[21] Lewis accepts that the advent of individualism 'does not mean that there will be no consciousness of "ought", but it is no longer imposed but has to be negotiated'.[22] To discover more about such negotiation, she interviewed 17 married couples with children and 17 unmarried couples with children, aged between 27 and 50, recruited by advertisement in nursing, teaching, and social work publications. In order to provide a generational perspective, 72 of their parents were also interviewed. This was clearly not a 'representative' sample of the general population, and was not intended to be because one of the main objectives was to explore areas 'likely to reveal the balance between attention to self, as opposed to attention to other and to the relationship',[23] and the sample was designed to further that objective. However, some further questions (but not interviews) were posed to 777 people drawn from an Omnibus Survey by the Office for National Statistics, which was representative. Lewis describes the central issue as revolving around the idea of 'commitment'. The unmarried had tended to 'drift' into long-term unmarried cohabitation. They had lived together for so long they saw little point in marrying.[24] They saw their 'commitment' as being 'private' rather than 'public'. Half of the unmarried and one-quarter of the married said they had no obligations to one another, or had not thought about them; but for the rest, they saw the obligation as coming from 'within' and not externally imposed:

> The crucial thing ... was seen to be the existence of commitment rather than its manifestation. Given that ... it is not surprising that most people in the sample also felt that it was proper to treat married and cohabiting parents the same.[25]

The picture is one of pragmatic compromise, and, although Lewis herself does not emphasize the concept, a sense of the importance of mutual *respect*.

21 J. Lewis, *The End of Marriage? Individualism and Intimate Relationships* (2001).
22 id., p. 126.
23 id., p. 128.
24 id., pp. 135–6.
25 id., p. 145.

THE GROWTH OF 'RIGHTS'?

When we consider the character of interpersonal relationships, the question arises how far, if at all, ideas of 'rights' are present or indeed appropriate. We should say, immediately, that we are not primarily referring to legal rights here. Whether A has a legal right against B is in principle, if not always in practice, a straightforward matter. The answer lies in the legal texts and legal practice. But can we also imagine that people have rights of a different kind, moral or ethical, to the way the other party to a relationship should behave?

Some people have thought that the very idea of rights in personal relationships is meaningless, or even dangerous. For example, the judge, Sir John Laws, expressed this view in a lecture in 2002.[26] For him, the content of morality was contained entirely in the realm of duties. To make a moral claim was to assert what you, or someone else, ought to do with regard to another person: in other words, to assert the existence of a duty. In contrast, this view holds that to claim a right is entirely self-centred, and therefore not a moral claim except perhaps in the trivial sense that it refers indirectly to duties of others. Others have expressed similar views.[27] By way of contrast, Giddens considered that concepts of rights and obligations were very important in postmodern 'intimate' relationships. Indeed, he writes that 'intimacy should not be seen as an interactional description but as a cluster of prerogatives and responsibilities that define agendas of practical activity' and notes that the importance of rights as a means of achieving intimacy can be seen from women's struggle to achieve equal status in marriage.[28] John Dewar and Stephen Parker have suggested that family law has progressed from a 'formal' era (from about 1857 to the 1960s), when 'there was a strong sense of spouses as rights-holders', through a functionalist era to the present 'complex' or 'chaotic' era. But complexity has not reduced the role of rights; indeed:

> there is now a greater emphasis on rights, but the rights-claims are more diverse and stem not from marriage itself ... but from other states, mainly to do with childhood or parenthood.[29]

These contrasting views do not take into account the perceptions which individuals in relationships themselves hold about rights. Even if one does

26 Sir J. Laws, 'Beyond Rights' (2003) 23 *Ox. J. of Legal Studies* 265–280. Laws argued that the language of rights was only appropriately used to refer to legal claims against the state.

27 For example: M.A. Glendon, *Rights Talk: The Impoverishment of Political Discourse* (1991); A. Etzioni, *The New Golden Rule: Community and Morality in a Democratic Society* (1996); M.C. Regan Jr., *Alone Together: Law and the Meanings of Marriage* (1999).

28 Giddens, op. cit., n. 9, p. 190.

29 J. Dewar and S. Parker, 'English Family Law since World War II: From Status to Chaos' in *Cross Currents: Family Law and Policy in the US and England*, eds. S.N. Katz, J. Eekelaar, and M. Maclean (2000) ch. 6.

not expect such individuals to have engaged in sophisticated conceptual analysis, perceptions of rights can be a powerful driver of behaviour. It seemed important to explore this issue.

A FURTHER INVESTIGATION: STRUCTURE OF THE RESEARCH

We wished to tap into that generation which experienced its childhood during the years when the 'great disruption'[30] began to first make its impact on family life. These would be people born between the late 1960s and late 1970s, who are now between their late 20s and early 40s. We wanted to include only people who were likely to have had the opportunity to experience extended relationships. We also wished to obtain a sample drawn from a fully representative base, and were fortunate in obtaining the consent of the Office of National Statistics to introduce a screening question into its Omnibus Sample on family change.[31] This question allowed us to identify respondents who were within the desired age range and who had experienced partnerships of some kind. We interviewed 39 individuals, 18 men and 21 women. Two were under 29, and the rest between 30 and 45; 26 were married, nine currently cohabiting, two were now living alone and two were 'living apart together' (in a current relationship but living in separate homes). One of the last was the only gay relationship in the sample.

Since we also wished to examine whether ethnic diversity was a significant factor in the responses, we were also able to weight our sample so as to ensure such diversity among the respondents. Sixteen respondents were from ethnic minority groups (in which we include White Irish). In presenting our data, we have followed the categories used by the ONS in indicating ethnicity. We have indicated the ethnicity of the respondents in what follows, but will explore issues of ethnicity directly in a later article. The study should be seen as a qualitative one, indicating the range of perceptions, values and behaviours relevant to personal relationships which people hold in contemporary British society. We cannot make quantitative extrapolations from our data about the extent to which any particular type of response is held in the general population.

Our questions were designed to discover how the respondents reacted to certain key events in what is often called the family life cycle, but which, in more individualist mode, might be called their personal lives, and, above all, *why* they responded as they did. The key events are forming a co-residential unit, marrying, becoming a parent, leaving a co-residential unit, experiencing

30 The expression used by Francis Fukuyama to describe the transformation in family and personal relationships described in the text: F. Fukuyama, *The Great Disruption* (1999).

31 We express our special thanks to John Haskey of the Office of National Statistics for much assistance on this.

the departure of children from home, and feeling the first effects of the dependency of elderly parents. Not every respondent will have experienced all these events.

The respondents were asked both about the effect of such events on their actual behaviour and their reasons for such behaviour. The latter questions raised certain difficulties. It was difficult to know how people would react. However, whatever people may say, they must act for a reason. We notice the proposition[32] that, while at some level we can talk about acting on one's desires (eating when hungry; sleeping when tired), this turns out to be a very limited way of accounting for behaviour. It is not simply that there are many occasions when we do not in fact act on our desires, crudely conceived. It assumes that the only way we can decide between conflicting desires is to choose the strongest desire (although the expression 'choose' seems inappropriate, for the image seems closer to the stronger desire dictating the choice). In such a scenario, you would not need to, perhaps could not, weigh up all your desires. Your action would just 'happen', flowing from the desire. But that seems a strange way to explain behaviour. While people sometimes do lose control and act on urges alone, those are generally considered to be pathological cases. You can also sometimes want things, but have no reason to have them (you already have enough, for example). In such cases acquiring them can be some form of addiction. It therefore seems more plausible to say that in the standard case the action you choose you choose for a reason.

Uncovering the reasons for action has not only an explanatory purpose. A reason must refer to something which is of value to the actor. To act for a reason which holds no value for the actor is to act for no reason at all. As Raz has put it: 'reasons are rooted in values'.[33] This is of particular importance in this context, for by reflecting on people's reasons for acting, we may access the values they hold. An important goal was to gain an insight into the values people hold in conducting their personal lives. We were initially unsure whether subjects would find it easy to articulate such reasons, and they sometimes struggled to formulate them. Our work is not one of psychoanalysis, and we do not claim to have accessed unconscious motivations. The articulated reasons nevertheless provide indicators of those values which the respondents were prepared to lay some claim to.

32 J. Raz, *Engaging Reason* (2000) 51-6. T.M. Scanlon, *What we Owe to Each other* (1998) argues that even when quenching 'brute' wants, satisfaction of the desires are not reasons for action but the future pleasures which the desires point towards (pp. 41–49). See, also, J. Dancy, *Practical Reality* (2000) 35–8.

33 Raz, id., p. 252; '. . . one can only want something because of a good one believes the thing to have' (p. 261).

THE ANALYSIS

In what follows, for reasons of space, the evidence supporting the analysis is selective. The evidence is set out in full in an Occasional Paper of the Oxford Centre for Family Law and Policy (OXFLAP). We start with an account of the reasons those respondents who had married gave for choosing to marry rather than live together without marrying. This was not an outlandish choice for these people, since most of the respondents will have been partnering during the 1980s, and, while in 1971, 97 out of every 1000 single women over 16 were married, this ratio had fallen to 56:1000 in 1987. The proportion of all women who had never married and were cohabiting outside marriage increased from 8 to 17 per cent between 1978 and 1987. 53 per cent of women who married in 1987 had lived together with their partner before marriage.[34] Clearly, the generation of people who were entering into personal partnerships during the 1980s faced a realistic choice between marriage and (continuation of) living together without marrying.

But why did the married marry? The answers should give some indication about what values they thought marrying held for them. This might further reveal what importance it had in respect to their relationships, and allow inferences to be drawn about how they viewed the relationships. But inference is not enough. We also needed to ask directly how they considered marriage, or the other life events described earlier, affected their sense of how they felt they should behave towards their partner. We did not direct our questions solely at the relationship between the partners, for we wanted to know whether the partnership (married or not) could provide a source for a sense of obligations to certain other people (in particular, to in-laws), and, if so, why that was so. We will make some reference to these responses here, but a fuller treatment will be the subject of another paper.[35] At present we will direct attention at the relationship between the partners themselves, married and unmarried.

REASONS FOR MARRYING

Of our 39 respondents, nine were currently living in a partnership but had not married their partner, and two were living singly after having cohabited. Of these, four had been married earlier. Two further respondents were in the position sometimes described as 'living-apart-together', which, for these purposes, we will include among the unmarried cohabitants. We will return to this group later, but will start by looking at both all those who were now

34 See J. Eekelaar, *Regulating Divorce* (1991) 53.

35 See M. Maclean and J. Eekelaar, 'The Obligations and Expectations of Couples within Families: Three Modes of Interaction' (2004) 26 *J. of Social Welfare and Family Law* 117–30.

married, and also those of the first group who had been married before their subsequent cohabitation. This constitutes 32 respondents.

This large group had all married at some time. We have divided their reasons for marrying into three main categories. The first are entirely *pragmatic* (three cases). Marriage was entered into to achieve some collateral objective, and not by reason of any value attaching to marriage itself. The second group of reasons we call *conventional* (18 cases). This is because the respondent refers to some social source, external to the respondent, whether it be in the form of the practice of others, or the opinions of others, which are recounted as being significant in determining his or her decision. The respondent in these cases can be seen as placing value in *conforming* to some kind of convention. The third group of reasons we term *internal* (18 cases). Here the respondent perceives the institution of marriage as allowing the respondent to realize or promote a goal which is important to himself or herself. The respondent does not seek to satisfy external demands, but his or her internal goals. Of course respondents could hold more than one reason, so some cases appear in more than one category. The overlap between cases in the conventional and internal categories is of particular interest. Two cases could not be allocated to any category.

1. Pragmatic reasons

There were three examples:

> Int. Why get married?
> R. My husband went to work in [middle eastern country] and the only way I could go out there was if we were married ... I wouldn't say it was the only reason but that is what precipitated it at that time; we were happy as we were.
> (Female, 39, Cohabiting after previous marriage ended in divorce; White British, speaking of first marriage) [13].

> Int. Why marry after living together?
> R. It just happened; we were going to emigrate and it was easier with all the papers.
> (Female, 34, Married, White Irish) [26].

> Int. Why marry at this time?
> R. Inheritance tax. My husband saw this Panorama programme on TV last October.
> (Female, 39, Afro-Caribbean) [38].

2. Conventional reasons

Curiously, the number of cases in this category (18) turned out to be the same as the number in the 'internal' category, discussed below. But there were nine cases of overlap between them, and we will give these special attention when we discuss the internal category. The conventional reasons given were: following religious prescription, following parental wishes, and following social or cultural practice.

In two cases religious prescription was cited as a sufficient reason in itself:

> Int. Why marry rather than live together?
> R. I'm a Catholic ... a practising Catholic. My wife isn't. She is C of E. My family is Catholic.
> (Male, 38, married, White British) [32].

> Int. Why marry?
> R. I'm a practising Muslim; my wife was born a Muslim but knew nothing about it ... she converted to Islam and gave me an ultimatum: live the Muslim way and marry ... after a year of the marriage I came to Islam, it took a year, studying; before we lived by society's rules, now I live as a Muslim.
> (Male, 24, Afghani, Muslim) [33].

In the second case, the religious prescription governed the wife's behaviour rather than the husband's: becoming a Muslim and marrying was the only way he could have a relationship with this woman. Nevertheless, it was the religious prescription which led to the marriage.

In three other cases, parental prescription was afforded similar status. For example:

> (We) did not live together before marriage.
> Int. What view did you take about living together before marrying?
> R. Personally I would not have had a problem with it but my father would not have countenanced it at all; there would have been no way my Dad would have allowed it.
> (Female, 43, Married, White British) [20].

Two respondents combined this with religious prescription. Here is one:

> I am a practising Catholic ... my Dad told us to get married ...
> (Female, 38, married, Black African) [35].

A number of respondents regarded the social conventions of their community as exerting a considerable force on their behaviour. But this tended to be combined with religious practice and parental wishes. For example:

> R. I think it was a cultural thing to do with it, and expectations of parents ... back home, if you start living together you get married ... we are Christians ...
> Int. Would you say part of the reason was a religious reason?
> R. It is difficult to say, isn't it ... it is both cultural and religious.
> (Male, 45, married, Black African) [19].

Another way of expressing this was to say that it was 'the thing to do at the time' (male, 39, married, White British) [14] or 'because that's what you did and maybe it's because what your parents did as well' (female, 44, married, White British) [17] or 'I was brought up you didn't do it until married' (female, 42, married, White British) [27] or 'I didn't want a baby and not to be married. It was 1980 ... still a bit of a stigma' [29].

These expressions indicate an acceptance of the prescriptions of religion, cultural practices or family expectations as sufficient reason to enter marriage. The extent to which respondents cited their desire to conform to the wishes of their parents was striking and took us somewhat by surprise. These, after all, were people who would have been marrying in the 1980s. However, it was noticeable that when cultural and family expectations were cited as relevant factors, some respondents appeared to wish to distance themselves from the appearance of treating those as exclusive determinants of their decision. For example:

> Int. There was a wish you would get married?
> R. Absolutely ...
> Int. What were your own feelings about that?
> R. Mmmm ... well, because in Ireland at the time family expectations were of a church marriage ... I would say for me it was something I owed my parents ... for my wife, she's more religious, very religious parents ... though I can't say it was just for the parents. I think we ourselves were traditional enough to believe that commitment would involve marriage.
> (Male, 41, married, White Irish, Roman Catholic) [11].

Here the respondent recognizes a duty towards both his and his wife's parents, as well as to his wife's religion, but introduces a new element which is neither expressly anchored in religion nor in filial duty: it is 'tradition'. Tradition has a compromise quality to it. Following a tradition suggests a lifestyle choice, freely entered, rather than being subject to prescriptions by reason of one's membership of a community which one may not have freely chosen. This perspective could be adopted in the absence of any, or any strong, religious motivation. Giving as a reason for marrying that one is 'old-fashioned' (female, 40, married, White British) [31] seems to be adopting a similar viewpoint.

3. *Internal reasons*

The value which marriage was seen to hold by these respondents all related to the idea of commitment. But they seemed to do so in slightly different ways, which we describe as confirmation (four cases), completion (eight cases), and construction (six cases). As we will explain, some of these cases overlapped with those in the 'conventional' category.

(a) Confirmation
Here marriage appeared to hold a purely symbolic significance for the respondent. It was important for the respondent in so far as it demonstrated, usually to the outside world, a state of affairs already reached by the parties. In itself it made no difference to the relationship as these respondents perceived it, but was seen to confirm what already existed. For example, one respondent, who, when asked why he married his cohabiting partner, said:

> It's the final thing, really, plus the legalities ... it was just the final thing to do.
> (Male, 32, married, Black British) [37].

Another:

> It makes everything in place, din't?
> (Male, 39, married, White British) [12].

In these cases, marriage appears to be no more than a single event – indeed, as one said – a 'party', with no further implications in itself, though representative of responsibilities already felt or assumed. It is perhaps not surprising that none of them overlapped with those in the 'conventional' category. The symbolic effect of the marriage was indeed a matter of value, but since it was symbolic only, these respondents did not feel that external conventions provided any reason in themselves for going through the ceremony.

(b) Completion

There were eight cases, however, where marriage seemed to play a more significant role from the internal point of view. It was more than merely a public display undertaken mostly for others, but assumed a more personal nature, and provided in itself an added impetus for, or source of, further commitment. In this sense it was a significant element in completing the sense of commitment which the parties already felt. But it is interesting that five out of the eight cases in this category overlapped with the 'conventional' category. As will be noted, the respondents who combined conventional and internal reasons were able to reconcile their individualistic aspirations with their acceptance of the external conventions. Perhaps they found the two aspects mutually reinforcing.

An example was the following:

> Cohabitation is not a full committment. My parents wouldn't be happy with us living together, but only because we wanted to.
> (Female, 31, married, Asian British) [16].

The strongest version of this attitude was where marriage had provided a catalyst, some kind of turning point; it forced the respondent (or both parties) into a decision that their relationship really was for life; that they should settle into a more permanent mode of living:

> Marriage for me is the point at which it moves from being 'This is very nice now' to 'we've got to make a life together with a view to being together for as long as you last, ultimately probably having children, etc.' In that sense it's a deeper commitment.
> (Male, 41, married, White Irish, Roman Catholic) [11].

A further case showed a strong personally held view that marriage 'completes' the personal commitment. The respondent had expressly insisted that they should enter into marriage, despite her pregnancy, but only if her partner 'wanted' it:

> [Partner] proposed when I was pregnant; he said we ought to get married. I said 'no', only if you want to get married; we had discussed having a family and agreed we wanted it ... a proper family is mum and dad and married.
> (Female, 42, married, White British) [15].

These cases all show marriage operating as an event which seals, or raises to a new level, a relationship which has been maturing over time. It is often consistent with seeing marriage as mandated by external convention. No doubt the parties believe the relationship will continue to grow after the marriage, but marriage is essentially seen as the event which has an independent effect in completing the fundamental nature of the partnership.

(c) Construction

But there is another reason for marrying, also associated with the idea of commitment, but this time it represents an earlier stage in the relationship: it sets up a framework within which the partners *work towards* the deeper commitment which, for the earlier group, marriage already signified. We see the significance of marriage here as constructing a framework within which the partners consciously strive to achieve a still deeper commitment. Usually that deeper commitment occurs on the birth of a child. As in the 'completion' cases, it was possible for respondents to combine the use of marriage as a framework for deepening their relationship with accepting conventional reasons for marrying, and three did so (cases [2], [21], and [22]).

Typical construction cases are the following:

> Int. Why marry at all?
> R. I don't know. I s'pose we just wanted to ... it was like a way of saying 'I want to be with you for ever' ... [but] when you're married, you've always got a get-out, not that you hope to divorce, but you're not bonded in the same way. The real commitment is having kids, not the marriage. Then you're connected to that person further.
> (Female, 38, married, White British) [4].

> We both wanted children and we wanted to get married first before we had any children.
> (Female, 32, married, White British) [9].

This use of marriage as a framework for deepening a commitment which was completed on the birth of a child could have operated as an additional or subsidiary reason in some cases where the primary reason seemed to be conventional. For example, the Hindu respondent who explained that he had married out of conformity to cultural traditions and parental expectations, added:

> Although you see each other during the day [before marriage] it's totally different living together ... most people have children in two years, we delayed it until five years ... I think the delay for settling down and having

> children was just to make sure that we were compatible and knew what way we were heading.
> (Male, 36, married, Asian British, Hindu) [21].

This was a respondent to whom cultural factors were important. It is possible that the very fact that such respondents were subject to strong conventional prescriptions to marry, so that the act of marriage did not necessarily fully coincide with a sense of confirmation of emotional commitment (as in the completion cases), *encouraged* the perception of the marriage being a framework within which commitment grows. Unlike the overlap cases in the completion category, where the respondents were able to synthesize their own ethical motivations with conformity to convention, these overlap cases show respondents using the convention as a resource for promoting a sense of commitment, which would normally be confirmed by a later event, typically the birth of a child.

REASONS FOR NOT MARRYING

There were ten respondents in current relationships outside marriage. Some had strong negative views of marriage:

> I would never marry again ... it's like bungee jumping ... once is enough, it was not a nice time; we're fine now and don't want to change it.
> (Female, 42, White Irish, cohabitant after marriage involving violence) [29].

In four cases, the respondent equated marriage with 'the wedding': it was no more than a one-day event, with no apparent further significance, and was therefore irrelevant. For example:

> Int. Do you see yourselves marrying in the future?
> R. That's a very difficult question. The answer is yes, but it's financial ... finances permitting. At the end of the day, we don't want to just go down to the Registry Office and do it for £10. If you want to do it properly it costs something like £15,000, especially because me and (my partner) have both got massive families ... I could always see a better way of spending £15,000 than sunnying around in a white dress, personally.
> (Male, 38, cohabitant, White British) [1].

It seems that these respondents could be considered as having a very similar approach to marriage as two who had married for pragmatic reasons ([13] and [26]).

Reasons people have for marrying, and for not marrying, are important indications of the role marriage plays in contemporary life. For many, marriage is undertaken as a matter of conformity: to parents' wishes, to religious prescription or to cultural norms. But marriage was just as widely used by people to express a personal value: this might be an achieved state of commitment or a mode of clearing the pathway towards such commitment. It is quite possible, of course, that people could see these goals as being independent of each other. That is, that marriage may be undertaken for conventional reasons, but not be seen as having any relevance to whatever internal reasons a person may have for entering a relationship. But, as we have seen, a significant number of people see the state of marriage in itself as contributing in some way to enhancing an internal attitude.

However, the internal reasons we have been examining are attitudes towards *marriage*. They do, of course, reflect, and have implications for, the respondents' attitudes towards the other partner. But we thought that issue demanded a separate inquiry. We did this by asking how various events, namely, beginning to live together, getting married and having a child, affected their sense of 'what they owed' to their partner.

PERCEPTION OF RESPONSIBILITIES BETWEEN PARTNERS

In analysing the data we will break the reasons people gave for explaining their behaviour towards their partner into three types: first, when the behaviour is ascribed to following duties which derive from a source external to the parties. We will call this the 'external-duty' approach. The second sees the source of obligations as being embedded in the relationship itself. It is seen as something that builds up over time, and is coterminous with the relationship. This idea seems to be closely related to a particularist view of ethics. The behaviour just follows from the nature of the circumstances. Being in a relationship simply *means* acting in a supportive way towards one another, and the more so the longer the relationship has lasted. We will dub this the 'evolutionary' approach. The third perception appeals more directly to certain ethical principles. We will call this the 'ethical' approach. This might seem very similar to the second group. For those respondents in the second group who cited the relationship itself, or being in a relationship, rather than making a direct appeal to an ethical principle, such as love or care, as the reason for acting supportively towards their partner, did not, of course, mean that they did not act lovingly or caringly, or did not see these as virtues. But they saw the virtues as being intrinsically tied to what one did if one had a working relationship. Those in the third group seemed to express a commitment to the ethical principle which was independent of the relationship, although, as we will see, it was possible for elements of more than one perspective to be held.

1. The external-duty approach

One might anticipate that those who undertook marriage for conventional reasons would be inclined to see the relationship as being dominated by rules or obligations set by the marriage itself. There was some indication of that. For example, a fundamentalist Christian said, in answer to the question whether he thought it was his duty to share, or whether they just wanted to do it that way:

> I am a Christian ... God say there is no man and there is no woman ... man and woman is one, not two ... so why think differently ... everything belong to me belong to her; not I must do, I think I should do ...
> (Male, 38, married, Brazilian, Christian) [24].

Although the respondent distinguished between 'I must do' (which he rejected) and 'I think I should do' (which he accepted), it seemed clear that his acceptance of the obligation derived from his Christianity-based view of marriage: 'man and woman is one, not two'. So here we have a link, which we might expect, between an external-duty approach and a strongly conventional reason for marrying.

Similarly, a Muslim respondent said:

> There are rules about marriage ... it tells you how to live together and keeps us happy.
> (Male, 24, married, Afghani, Muslim) [33].

Such respondents had a strong conventional element in their reasons for marrying. But it was not only those with a religious background who adopted the external duty approach, although for these others it seems to have played a weaker role. One, for whom concern over parental disapproval had motivated marriage, but who admitted to being 'old-fashioned' about it, had even gone to a solicitor while she was still living together with her husband to get a letter demanding he give her money (female, 40, cohabiting after divorce) [31].

2. The evolutionary approach

As explained above, these respondents see the nature of their behaviour as being inherently determined by the nature and progress of the relationship. Paradigmatically, one would be inclined to associate this primarily with unmarried cohabitants. There was certainly a strong example from that group:

> Int. Would your partner have any right [against you, now]?
> R. I wouldn't have seen it as a right ... it sounds almost contractual ... I'm trying to search for a softer word than a right ... again, obligation is quite a strong word ... it's part of being in a relationship.
> (Male, 33, cohabitant, White British) [8].

Such responses show that those adopting this approach can be reluctant to concede they are under an obligation. Yet the relationship seems to exert some kind of normative force. For example, a respondent who had married for pragmatic reasons said:

> Being together should be mutually supportive ... now people provide support in different ways depending on their personality or on their ... how they are equipped within the relationship ... so a mutual supportive role ... otherwise you are just living with a friend ... it's a developmental relationship ... I don't think I had a right to financial support ... emotional support though ... ummm ... I think you have a right for somebody to support you if you are in a long-term committed relationship.
> (Female, 39, cohabiting after previous marriage ended in divorce; White British) [13].

That respondent went as far as to see a long-term relationship as capable of giving a 'right' of some kind. This approach is found also in other categories, such as those who saw marriage as a confirmation of the relationship. Another respondent, whose partner had a teenage son, when asked whether she had any obligations towards the boy, replied:

> We have made a family, the way I want it, there is no 'ought' about taking on [son] I can't see [son] as anything other than part of the relationship with [partner] ... we are no different from married ... it all depends on the quality of the relationship, not legal status ... maybe commitment should contain the length of time together ... but that should apply to marriage too ...
> (Female, 45, cohabitant planning to marry, White British) [34].

This response introduces an important additional element to this perception. The respondent characterized her attitude towards her stepson as *an element of her relationship with her partner*. To complicate matters further, the evolutionary approach was also articulated by some who had conventional reasons for marrying. This was a respondent who married for a multiplicity of conventional reasons, including seeing it as a completion of the relationship. The obligation is expressed here in terms of the 'right' of the partner:

> I think if you're making that degree of commitment to somebody, then I think at some level they have a right to expect you to behave ... there is an implicit contract somewhere in that ... this is where an awful lot depends on the quality of the relationship because I don't think any of these things flow from a system of law ... it's a betrayal of the relationship ... so there's a right on the basis of the evolution of the relationship.
> (Male, 41, married, White Irish, Roman Catholic) [11].

We conclude that, while people who had strong conventional reasons for marrying would often see the obligations flowing from the conventions they were following as having some, sometimes strong or exclusive, force in directing their behaviour in their relationship, people marrying without such conventional reasons (but also some who *did* have such reasons) very often also saw their behaviour as being prescribed by the fact of being in the relationship itself rather than from the marriage. And of course this could be true for those who did not marry.

3. The 'ethical' approach

There were pervasive responses, spread among all 'types' of marriage, and among those who were not married, where the respondents referred to some independent ethical value in explaining the way they thought they should behave in their relationships.

(a) The golden rule

The most commonly cited 'ethical' basis for behaving towards a partner was the so-called 'golden' rule: do unto others as you would have them do unto you. This might look like a manifestation of the reciprocal or reflexive relationships which Giddens identified as being characteristic of modern intimate relationships. But there is a difference. The reflexive relationship is one in which (at least theoretically) the relationship is kept constantly under review and renegotiation so as to keep the interests of each partner in balance. There were indeed some examples of this. Here is one from a married woman, a Roman Catholic, whose relationship had clearly weakened. But even this deviates from the Giddens model because she was bringing into the calculation the effect of her behaviour on others, notably her children:

> Even when I first got married, I was never one of those to tempt fate and say that it was so fantastic that we were never going to break up. I don't like saying that because I've seen too much go wrong for other people. Long-term relationships are very difficult and it depends how much compromise you want to do. However, the flipside is how much devastation you cause if you do break up. The price of having an affair for your family is high. Basically, I've found that price too high to pay at the moment ... If I didn't have children the whole thing would be different . . , I think I'd get out of a relationship much quicker, or at least have a cooling off period, where you could find out whether you still wanted to be together or not.

This respondent had initially expressed an ethic in terms of the 'golden rule', but went on to suggest that her view had changed. Perhaps the respondent felt that she had now made more of a contribution to the family: she was not just taking, but contributing (or was in a better position to contribute). But this must also be seen in the context of the weakening relationship:

> When somebody's been supporting the whole family as long as he has, you don't feel in quite as strong a position to argue 'well, I want to do this' because you feel selfish, when somebody else has been working all these hours and [my husband's] not just going off and doing what he wants either. But now, I've changed ... I've re-educated myself and gone to university, my horizons have broadened ...
> (Female, 40, married, White British) [5].

But reciprocity was more likely to be expressed in terms that indicated the acceptance of an obligation towards the other from the fact that the other had given benefits to the respondent, or had undertaken detriments. The obligation this generated was a continuing one (though presumably not immutable):

> I think at the back of my mind I must have felt, he's working so hard, if I just stayed at home doing nothing, that would have been very unfair on him; if it had been the other way around, and I'd been working all day long, coming back, and my husband having a nap all day, I would not be very happy.
> (Female, 43, cohabiting after divorce, discussing former marriage undertaken for strong conventional reasons, Japanese) [10].

A cohabitant who expressed the 'evolutionary' paradigm strongly seemed to trace the source of his responsibilities to his partner to the fact that she had moved to his 'territory':

> Int. The reason you gave for your responsibilities ... [you indicated that] it was because she'd moved?
> R. Because previously we had been on neutral territory ... and it was shifting the balance to go one way or the other way or to stay in a neutral town, so the very fact that [she] made the move ... I expect it was a case of appreciating what she'd done ... I would do anything to support her decision to move.
> (Male, 33, cohabitant, White British) [8].

Another cohabitant, who put great weight on the birth of the child in cementing the relationship ('Now it's a very firm bond. I'm one half of a whole, whereas before there was that bit of independence'*)*, had expressed the 'golden rule' as governing his attitude to his partner's parents:

> Int. Would you help your partner's parents?
> R. Yeah
> Int. Why?
> R. To be honest, they're nice people, but more importantly ... you should do unto others as you'd have done unto yourself. They've helped me in the past and I would like to reciprocate if it was required.
> (Male, 30, cohabitant, White British) [1].

It is interesting that this open reference to the golden rule appeared more prominent in unmarried cohabitations than in married ones. It is possible that, for the married, the ethic simply became absorbed in the duties of marriage, or the conceptualization of the relationship.

(b) Trust building

Another expressed ethic drew on the idea of trust. We saw this expressed in the context of both marriage and cohabiting relationships. This could be seen as a form of reflexivity, but it is more than simply adjusting to find the maximum benefit for each partner: the goal is an ethical one of mutual confidence.

> I think [financial arrangements] was simply a more sensible way of doing things ... I suppose, in a way, in the early part it was a bit like saying, well, let's start working together and tying ourselves up more ... it's that sort of trust building; to say it's trust building sounds like there's a suspicion, but it's more a natural step that far along ... we have separate accounts as well as the joint account ... we try to keep the separateness but togetherness.
> (Male, 44, married, White British, Buddhist) [2].

> Int. If you were still living together with your new partner and got into need, would your partner have a responsibility to you?
> R. I don't know if it is a responsibility but I would probably expect something from him, some help, I don't know in what way; but if he ignores (me) I don't trust him any more.
> (Female, 43, cohabitant after divorce, Japanese, describing cohabitation relationship) [10].

In this last example, the reciprocal element is reversed, for under the golden rule the respondent's sense of obligation rests on benefits received or the other party's detriments undergone, whereas here the respondent reposes trust in the other in the expectation that it will be honoured. But it is a mutual process.

(c) Love, respect, and care

It is perhaps surprising that respondents did not mention love as a reason for their behaviour more often. This does not, of course, imply that love was absent in cases where it was not mentioned. Failure to mention it may indicate some coyness about putting what might be thought of as an emotional response up-front to an interviewer. But three male respondents had no such difficulty. It is interesting (but not necessarily significant) that all three had married according to strong conventional reasons. Here are two examples:

> Int. When you started to live together having got married, how did that change things ...?
> R. Well, I think it both started with love ... and respect to each other and if you have that then we see we have better productive if you do things together. I think the foundation was I say love then respect and you build on it: that's how I see it.
> (Male, 45, married, Black African, Christian) [19].

> Int. You think you've got responsibilities to your wife primarily because you're married to her: that would be our reason ...
> R. No ... I married her because I love her, that would be (the reason) ...
> (Male, 38, married, British Asian, Sikh) [22].

Three women ([9], [17], and [31], all White British) also mentioned love as being a reason for marrying in the first place. Two of these ([17], [31]) coupled it with strong conventional reasons. It is curious that it was only the married who referred to 'love' as a basis for behaviour. Perhaps it is because it appeared as a reason for marrying, and of course the cohabitants did not marry. Yet the cohabitants failed to refer to it as a reason which explained the way they behaved towards their partners. Jane Lewis[36] also did not refer to 'love' in discussing the way her respondents, both married and unmarried, viewed their relationship. However, 'caring' was referred to by two women as being an important feature of their relationship and a cohabiting woman, who had had a (literally) bruising experience of marriage, said simply:

> Int. What kind of support can you expect from your partner; do you have any rights?
> R. Rights don't come into it. I expect him to treat me with respect; that's all.
> (Female, 42, cohabiting after divorce, White British) [29].

36 Lewis, op. cit., n. 21.

PERCEPTIONS OF RIGHTS

Having considered the way in which respondents saw their duties or responsibilities, we now turn to consider specifically the extent to which respondents felt the language of rights was appropriate within their relationship. We recall that a number of authors have expressed scepticism about the appropriateness of using concepts of rights within personal relationships, but also that we see claims about rights as attempts to secure the application of duties by others in accordance with certain background moral principles.

1. Discomfort with ideas of rights

We found evidence that respondents indeed had discomfort about speaking in terms of rights. This was so for cohabitants and for married people.

> Int. Do you think you have a right to expect certain behaviour of your partner?
> R. I don't think 'expect' is the right word. No ... obviously I would like certain things to be done, but I'm understanding in the circumstances, how difficult it is to get things done when you have a child. So if I come home and dinner is not on the table ... that's not a problem.
> (Male, 30, cohabitant, White British) [1].

> Int. Would she have a right (to support from you)?
> R. I wouldn't have seen it as a right ... it sounds almost contractual ... I'd have thought more of a ... I'm trying to search for a softer word than right ... it's part of being in a relationship.
> (Male, 33, cohabitant, White British) [8].

> It doesn't mean you would not provide it (support), but it's different about whether it's a right ... I don't think right is a word I would use anyway ... I don't think people have a right to things ... it's about consideration.
> (Female, 39, cohabiting after divorce, White British, talking about position in her former marriage) [13].

So while, as one might expect, we can find those who adopted the 'evolutionary' approach to their sense of responsibilities to have particular reluctance to speak about rights ([8], [3], [12], and [13]), we find similar reluctance among those who were willing to acknowledge an ethical basis for *responsibilities* ([1], [2], [8], and [29]) and even one who saw duties being externally imposed ([22]).

2. Rights seen as respecting the interests of the partner

Yet there were contexts in which some respondents did find the expression appropriate. One was where the respondent expressly acknowledged an interest of the partner. This might be for personal space:

> My wife has a right to go out and visit her sisters and her friends and go out to work: I can't say, you stay in, you can't go out to work.
> (Male, 45, married, Black African, Christian) [19].

Or it might be an acknowledgement of the partner's interests to consideration:

> Ummm ... I'm quite easy going, so I'd say she has a right to be happy, that's the only thing I'd say ... it's up to me in some sort of way to make sure she is happy ... I don't feel I've got any rights from her.
> (Male, 32, cohabitant, White British) [23].

One interpreted the word as referring to her own interest in a degree of independence:

> I think I should have a right to say ... 'I'm going out' ... and then, if he's got any plans, we can sort it out, find a babysitter, whatever. He shouldn't be saying, 'no you can't go'.
> (Female, 38, married, White British) [4].

It might be significant that this was uttered in the context of what appeared to be a deteriorating relationship.

3. Association of rights with economic contributions

Interestingly, some linked this idea of rights to the fact they had made economic contributions. For example:

> Int. Do you think the right, which you say you feel you now have, is linked to any responsibilities?
> R. Because if you're earning as well, you have more power, you have more say: 'I'm going to do this because I'm contributing to the house'. But when somebody's been contributing to the whole family, you don't feel in quite as strong a position to argue: 'well, I want to do this', because you feel selfish, when somebody else has been working all these hours.
> (Female, 40, married, White British) [5].

The fact that they were making economic contributions also led some women to the thought that they had some right to support from their husbands or partners. For example, respondent [13] thought she had some right to share in his pension for that reason. Similarly, in replying to the question whether she had a right to support from her husband, a respondent said:

> We're both working: so a bit of a right, yes.
> (Female, 31, married, White British) [16].

But women were ready to concede that their husbands or partners had rights to expect support from them, when the husband was providing all the economic support. For example, a Japanese respondent attributed her feeling that her former husband had rights against her to the fact that he supported her. This was recognized even where the woman was working:

> Int. Did your partner have any right to ask you to help him out financially when you were in transitional stage (i.e. living together before marriage)?
> R. Yeah, because in effect I was living there, so I don't see why not ... we were both working, so I'd say you split things up.
> (Female, 26, married, White British) [6].

However, one male respondent cited the fact of economic contributions as a reason against his wife having rights to support:

> Int. Do you see yourself or your wife as having a right to the kind of support you talked about?
> R. It depends ... if you're both working, both looking after the children ... I don't see one has got a right over the other ... when she's not working there is an obligation on me to support her.
> (Male, 43, married, White British) [30].

4. Rights based on convention

Certain respondents saw themselves as having some kind of right flowing from the rules related to marriage. such as a right to the security of the home [17]. One woman had gone to a solicitor to have her right to support enforced while the marriage was ongoing. Those respondents for whom the conventional aspects of marriage were important were not surprisingly inclined to see rights and duties as flowing naturally from the convention. For example:

> I think it goes without saying ... both of us have a right to each other and responsibility to each other as well.
> (Male, 45, married, Black African, Christian) [19].

Another, whose marriage was in the conventional category:

> Both sides have rights, in a family, both sides have got responsibilities ... I got rights, she got rights.
> (Male, 42, married, Indian) [18].

However, this respondent seemed later to place a particular restraint on this by saying this did not 'come from the marriage' but rather from the duty towards children. Even if 'rights' were not specifically referred to, they must have been implicit in the response which stated that marriage laid down 'rules' (male, 24, married, Afghani, Muslim) [33]. But that was not an inevitable response from those who married for conventional reasons.

> Int. Would you have felt you had a right to that (knowledge about finances)?
> R. I don't know whether it's a right or not; it's always been for us ... I wouldn't say that ... had we wished to keep that personal I wouldn't say I had a right ... but we were in a partnership and, yeah, we shared everything.
> Int. So you would not have thought he had rights against you or you had rights against him ...?
> R. No ... not at all.
> (Female, 43, married, White British) [20].

However, that respondent did say 'we would expect' financial support from one another if they split up 'just because we've been married for 24 years'.

COMMUNALITY

It is sometimes said that people in unmarried cohabitation are less inclined to share resources than the married.[37] In our data, some cohabitants did seem inclined towards retaining a degree of economic independence, but this seemed to be related to the fact that the cohabitant had experienced difficulties in an earlier relationship. However, it was possible to find cohabitants who had a strong sharing ethic:

> I don't think we see it as each other's property, we see it as our property, we find it very difficult to say, that's mine, that's yours.
> (Male, 33, cohabitant, White British, first cohabitation) [8].

Another placed this approach as arising after the birth of a child, when:

> It really became a situation of 'what's mine is hers' and vice versa.
> (Male, 30, cohabitant, White British) [1].

Others, who had now married, had adopted a sharing approach from the time their pre-marital cohabitation started:

> R. We share everything.
> Int. You did that right from the beginning (i.e. when moved in together before marrying)?
> R. Yes ... money ... everything ... cars ... whatever ...
> (Male, 39, married, White British) [12].

Some married respondents also expressed a strong sharing ethic:

> I was quite surprised to see friends of ours that had separate accounts and kept them. I find that extremely strange.
> (Female, 40, married, White British) [5].

> We work together as a team ...
> (Male, 45, married, Black African) [19].

Others retained a degree of independence. In one case, where the parties kept separate accounts for their own purposes, the wife kept a secret stash because the husband was bad with money ([6]). Two other married couples had a similar arrangement ([7], [16]). In another, a full-time mum received 'an allowance' ([15]).

DISCUSSION: MARRIAGE, RELATIONSHIPS, AND THE 'GOOD' OF OBLIGATION

We referred earlier to the paper by Scott Fitzgibbon in which the author expresses the view that obligation is non-instrumentally good as an instantiation of the good of steadfastness and stability'[38] and that 'marriage

37 See L.J. Waite and M. Gallagher, *The Case for Marriage* (2000) 39.
38 Fitzgibbon, op. cit., n. 2, at p. 64.

is a drama of mutual reinforcement of obligation'.[39] The point seems to be that acknowledgment of obligation to another is a manifestation of 'steadfastness' and 'stability' (which are goods for both the person displaying these characteristics and the one towards whom they are displayed), and that marriage generates such obligation. We would not wish to dissent from the idea of steadfastness and stability as being goods. Reflecting on our data, however, we are led to wonder whether the sense of obligation can come only from an external source and therefore to doubt whether marriage is either a necessary or sufficient context for the acceptance of personal obligation.

As far as expectations of endurance of the relationship is concerned, cohabitants could express as much incomprehension at the thought of possible future separation as married people. It was so unthinkable that they could not easily contemplate how the eventuality should be dealt with:

> Int. If things went wrong, would either have any rights or a claim?
> R. I don't know ... I've never considered it ...
> Int. In terms of splitting up, would having a child make a difference?
> R. I'm sure it would, though in our case it's not something we've given any consideration at all ...
> Int. Should people think about it?
> R. Yes and no ... The probability is so low on the scale ... it's not something to consider.
> Int. You would see this relationship lasting for life?
> R. Yes.
> (Male, 33, cohabitant, White British) [8].

A respondent who was now married made it clear that he had expected the relationship to be for life from the moment pre-marital cohabitation began:

> Int. Is it your feeling that this relationship will go on for the rest of your life?
> R. Yes, I'd expect that.
> Int. From the beginning ...
> R. From the beginning of what ... marriage or when we were together?
> Int. When you were first together.
> R. Yes, you would expect that, yeah.
> (Male, 39, married, White British) [12].

One did have very low expectations:

> I tend not to live too much in the future to be honest ... yeah, I would say my expectations are less as far as the future is concerned ... a more short-term assessment.
> (Female, 39, cohabitant undergoing divorce, White British) [13].

However, this was true of some married respondents too. Here are two:

> Int. Do you imagine remaining married for life?
> R. No ... we just argue so much ... when it becomes detrimental to the children.
> (Female, 38, married, White British) [4].

39 id., at p. 66.

> Int. What of the future ... would you see yourself being married for life?
> R. Erm ... I don't know ... even when I first got married, I was never one of those to tempt fate and say it was so fantastic that we were never going to break up ... the flipside is how much devastation you cause if you do break up. The price of having an affair for our family is high. Basically, I have found that price too high to pay at the moment.
> (Female, 40, married, White British) [5].

We are not suggesting that this was characteristic of the married; on the contrary, they too could find splitting up so remote as to be out of range:

> Int. What if you and (wife) were to separate?
> R. I find this very hard to imagine ... if it did happen I would have to be not myself ... it's so hard to say ...
> (Male, 39, married, White British) [14].

Of course the above evidence shows only what the respondents' expectations were and it might be said that to identify the sense of obligation so closely with the persistence of the relationship is to rob it of prescriptive effect, because each individual is free to terminate the relationship. At most, the obligation is treated as an *instrumental* good: valuable to the extent that it is necessary to keep the relationship going (but disposable along with the relationship), rather than as a good in itself which nurtures the relationship. However, the respondents who expressed themselves in this way did also indicate an attitude which showed a desire to invest efforts in making the relationship work in event of difficulty. The relationship exercised a normative 'pull':

> I would have to ... I don't know: to struggle on the best we can [23].

> We're both difficult people. If we married it might spoil it [34].

In addition, cohabitants frequently referred to some additional factor, such as having a child, or some ethical principle, which reinforced this normative position, and would have commended steadfastness:

> R. The only thing that's ever changed our relationship has been the baby ... before the baby came along we were always independent financially, but since the baby came along that just changed instantaneously, and it really became a situation of 'what's mine is hers' and vice versa ... I think it's now a very firm bond. I'm one half of a whole, whereas before there was that bit of independence.
> (Male, 30, cohabitant, White British) [1].

> Int. Does marriage make any difference to people's responsibilities in relationships?
> R. No ... um ... no maybe people around us expect differently, but I don't think it makes much difference really.
> Int. Then what is important, if not marriage, what things are important for you?
> R. Trust and care ...
> (Female, 43, cohabitant after divorce, Japanese, describing cohabitation relationship) [10].

In any case, married people also expressed the 'evolutionary' approach (cases [6], [12], [34]), and also appealed directly to 'ethical' principles ([2], [5], [6], [10], [11], [14], [19], [22]) and having a child ([9], [15], [16], [21], [33]) as sources of obligations. So, while married people had an additional source available from which to derive their obligation, many of them referred to the same ones as the non-married. It becomes increasingly difficult to identify being married in itself as *necessarily*, or even *characteristically*, constituting a significant source of personal obligations in the eyes of the participants in such relationships. Nor can we say that we found evidence, either among the married or the unmarried, that our respondents saw their sense of obligation as primarily owed to themselves. The conventional and ethical bases of obligation are clearly inconsistent with this, and, while the 'evolutionary' approach might appear to have some similarities to that view, it was really very different because the obligations were seen to be owed to the other, albeit that they arose out of the 'situation', as 'situational' ethicists would put it. All in all, the evidence showed rich and diverse sources for perceptions of obligations, which suggests that the thrust of much of the literature reviewed at the beginning of this article should be re-evaluated.

Finally, we revert to the role of rights, and the interrelationship with perceptions of obligation. We must stress that we were not focusing on how people might perceive their rights if the relationship came to an end. The conclusion seems to be that, as far as people's perceptions of their ongoing relationships is concerned, ideas of rights are not prominent. This appears to be somewhat at odds with the Giddens view of relationships being in a continual state of renegotiation. However, while not prominent, they are not necessarily absent. They seem to be part of the conceptual means by which partners recognize the interests of the other, which is inconsistent with the perception that ideas of rights are necessarily self-centred. They also seem to be associated with two specific factors. One is where the respondent sees the marriage in strongly conventional terms. Of course such respondents will associate responsibilities with such terms as well, but it appears that in these cases they will also be conscious of their 'own' entitlements. This sits uneasily with claims that marriage pre-eminently instantiates *obligations*. Of course it does that, but can also prompt a 'rights-based' view of aspects of the relationship, whereas the unmarried cohabitants, many (but not all) of whom grounded their sense of obligations in either the normative pull of the relationship itself or in ethical values, were less inclined to think in terms of rights as protecting their self-interest. The other factor is in connection with a perception of economic contribution, either by the respondent or the partner. As far as allocation of capital on divorce is concerned, the English courts have only recently proclaimed that financial and non-financial contributions to a marriage should be seen as having equal worth,[40] and the principle is

40 *White* v. *White* [2001] 1 All E.R. 1.

still not acknowledged if the couple are not married.[41] We should not be too hasty to extrapolate from these responses to the view that partners who do not contribute financially should not have rights on separation, for, as we have said, the present context did not assume separation. Rather, it suggests to us an unwillingness in most respondents to see their role in personal relationships as one which places demands on the other. They accept obligations on themselves and these tend to be related to background moral values like recognizing what the other has done for them, care, and respect, or are seen as necessary ingredients for making a relationship work, something which held value in itself. Rights, in the sense of claims on the other, seemed to have special resonance where economic contributions may have entered the calculation.

On the whole, though, we found that being married was consistent with a range of attitudes, both to marriage itself, and also to the relationship within it. For some people, it was an important catalyst for their relationship, either as providing some kind of seal to the state of commitment they had already reached, or a framework in which an even deeper sense of commitment, usually reached by the birth of a child, would be attained, or a reinforcement of their internal goals. But it could also play other roles, such as the purely symbolic, or openly instrumental. So marriage is useful and important to many people in a number of ways. But when we examine the way people think about their relationships, we find that there are many variations between those who are married, and many similarities with those who are not. Cutting across them all, though, we find a range of values which are held in common, and which have a substantial effect on generating ideas of personal obligation.

This conclusion should lead to caution over claims that marriage is *uniquely* capable of producing certain 'goods'. The picture is more complex. Whether marriage delivers those 'goods' more successfully than when people live together without marrying[42] is also hard to substantiate. It appears to be true that, statistically, married relationships last longer than unmarried ones.[43] But it is also true that, at times when marriage was more widespread than it is now, the marriages of the young, the poor, and the remarried were at much higher risk of breaking up than those of older, more financially secure, first-time married people.[44] Those risk categories may now be being substantially filled by unmarried cohabitants,[45] so the reasons

41 *Lloyd's Bank* v. *Rosset* [1991] 1 A.C. 107.

42 Arguments of this kind have been put forward most notably by Waite and Gallagher, op. cit., n. 37.

43 This is demonstrated, and discussed fully, in M. Maclean and J. Eekelaar, *The Parental Obligation: A Study of Parenthood across Households* (2000).

44 The evidence is summarized by C. Gibson, 'Changing Family Patterns in England' and D. Ruane Morrison, 'A Century of the American Family' in Katz, Eekelaar, and Maclean, op. cit., n. 29, chs. 2 and 3.

45 This seems to be true for the United Kingdom with respect to unmarried cohabitants who have children: see Maclean and Eekelaar, op. cit., n. 43, p. 20.

why married people who were in those circumstances were more likely to separate than others probably apply disproportionately to unmarried cohabitants. Our evidence shows that married and unmarried people who are living together share many values. Indeed, the similarities in the normative determinants of their behaviour may be greater than the dissimilarities. This is a intriguing perspective on a society in which, outwardly, the form personal relationships take seems to be becoming increasingly diverse.

[7]

The Significance of Marriage: Contrasts between White British and Ethnic Minority Groups in England

MAVIS MACLEAN and JOHN EEKELAAR*

It is widely believed that the institution of marriage enhances communal wellbeing, and governments in the United States and the United Kingdom have expressly adopted policies designed to "promote" marriage. These policies, however, are little informed by evidence about how people who marry are using the institution, or how entering or not entering marriage affects people's ideas about the rights and obligations they owe within intimate partnerships. An Oxford study has sought to explore these issues. The study allowed special attention to be paid to the way individuals with differing ethnic backgrounds responded to the investigation, and the current article reveals the results. They show that marriage is used in a variety of ways, and that these uses may vary between ethnic groups. The evidence suggests that the usefulness which people find in marriage may depend on cultural and individual factors that are independent of the goals that government policies seek to promote.

It is a commonplace to observe that contemporary politicians in the United States and the United Kingdom proclaim the virtues of marriage. As Reece (2003: 106) has observed: "the predominant postliberal approach is to hold up marriage as the ideal community." Thus, Berger and Kellner (1999) claim that marriage creates a framework in which people can experience their life as making sense. Waite and Gallagher (2001) assert that "Married People are Happier, Healthier and Better Off Financially". The British government (1998: paras. 4.3–4), despite cautioning that "families do not want to be lectured about their behaviour" has nevertheless asserted that "we do share the belief of the majority of people that marriage provides the most reliable framework for raising children. We are therefore proposing measures to strengthen the institution of marriage. . . ." The Bush administration's policy of "promoting marriage" is well known. Political commitment to

* We express our thanks to John Haskey of the Office for National Statistics for much help on this article.

Address correspondence to John Eekelaar, Pembroke College, Oxford OX1 1DW, UK; E-mail: john.eekelaar@law.ox.ac.uk.

"support" marriage inhibits promotion of policies that may be represented as "undermining" (heterosexual) marriage, such as allowing same-sex marriage, or increasing legal recognition of unmarried cohabitation (Barlow & James 2004).

It is not our intention in this article to examine the veracity of such claims made on behalf of marriage. Rather, we cite them only as manifestations of idealizations of the institution, which reflect deeper ideological and/or religious positions. They are seldom grounded in empirical evidence about how people themselves think about their relationships. We have attempted to obtain some information about this in a research project undertaken at the Oxford Centre for Family Law and Policy, with the kind assistance of the Office for National Statistics (ONS). The primary purpose of the research was to obtain qualitative evidence about what individuals felt about the nature of their personal relationships when these had progressed to the point of marriage or cohabitation. We sought to discover how the respondents reacted to certain key events in what is often called the family life cycle, and, above all, *why* they responded as they did. The key events are forming a co-residential unit, marrying, becoming a parent, leaving a co-residential unit, experiencing the departure of children from home, and feeling the first effects of the dependency of elderly parents. The respondents were asked both about the effect of such events on their actual behavior, and their reasons for such behavior. By exploring the reasons, we could uncover the relevant values held by the respondents, and in particular what part marriage had in those values.

We wished to tap into that generation which experienced its childhood during the years when the "great disruption" (Fukuyama 1999) began to first make its impact on family life. These would be people born in the late 1960s, who are now between their late twenties and early forties. We also wished to obtain a sample drawn from a fully representative base, and were fortunate in obtaining the consent of the ONS to introduce a screening question into its Omnibus Sample on family change. This question allowed us to identify respondents who were within the desired age range and who had experienced partnerships of some kind. We interviewed thirty-nine individuals, eighteen men and twenty-one women. Two were under 29, and the rest between 30 and 45. Twenty-six were currently married, nine currently cohabiting, two living singly after separation, and two "living apart together" (in a current relationship but living in separate homes). Since we also wished to examine whether the responses varied according to the ethnicity of the respondents, we weighted our sample to include a sufficient proportion of respondents from minority ethnic communities to enhance the likelihood that we could detect whether such respondents were articulating perceptions that differed from those of the bulk of the sample. We used the same categories of ethnicity employed by the ONS (matching that of the Census 2001), and reported by the respondents. Sixteen respondents were from ethnic minority groups.

The main findings of the study have been published in Eekelaar and Maclean (2004). The main findings can be summarized as follows:

1. As regards marriage, it appeared that respondents married for three types of reason:

   - *pragmatic*—three cases—where marriage was entered only to fulfil some collateral, instrumental objective, and had no further significance for the respondent;
   - *conventional*—eighteen cases—where in marrying the respondent was following some prescriptive convention, usually religious or cultural, but often following parents' wishes; and
   - *internal*—eighteen cases—where marriage held internal significance for the respondent.

   Internal reasons were of three kinds:

   - *confirmation*—four cases—where the marriage symbolically confirmed that a stage in the relationship involving commitment had already been reached;
   - *completion*—eight cases—where the marriage itself provided the additional "seal" completing the commitment;
   - *construction*—six cases—where the marriage provided the framework within which the relationship would be expected to develop, often reaching the stage of commitment on the birth of a child.

2. Respondents saw their responsibilities for their partners as deriving from three types of source, some of which overlapped. One source lay in duties that were external to the relationship, and derived from the marriage (the *external-duty approach*). A second lay in the evolution of the relationship itself. The relationship itself provided a normative force: being in a relationship simply *meant* behaving in a certain way (the *evolutionary* approach). The third lay in expressly articulated ethical principles such as the "golden rule" (do unto others as you would have them do unto you), or the cultivation of trust, care, and love (the *ethical* approach). The last two sources were used by both the married and the unmarried.
3. There was some reluctance to think of rights in the context of these relationships, but there was also evidence that the concept was used as a device for conceptualizing the interests of the other party as well as of the respondent.
4. Most significantly, it was found that being married was consistent with a wide range of attitudes towards personal obligations as well as towards marriage itself, and that many of the attitudes towards relationships cut across the married and the unmarried alike. The evidence showed that married and unmarried people who are living together share many values, and that the similarities in the normative determinants of their behavior may be greater than the dissimilarities.
5. We must emphasize that we cannot make quantitative extrapolations from our data about the extent to which any particular type of response is held in the general population.

Table 1. Breakdown of Ethnic Minority Groups in the Study

Ethnic minority group	Number of respondents
Japanese	1
White Irish	3
Black Africans	2
Mixed Caribbean	1
Black British (Afro-Caribbean)	3
Afghani	1
Brazilian	1
India	1
British Asian	3

I. THE ETHNIC DIMENSION

This article examines one specific dimension of the study: that concerning ethnicity. Ethnicity is an area in which UK society is becoming increasingly diverse. By mid-2000, ethnic minorities constituted 7.1 percent of the total population of Great Britain. Kiernan and Smith (2003) report from data from the Millenium Cohort Study that the family behavior of minority groups varies between those groups, and from that of the "white British." For example, Asian groups were much more likely to be married when they have a baby than either the white or black groups (see Kiernan & Smith 2003: Table 1). Although our study is not quantitative, and its findings cannot in themselves be generalized to the whole population, the findings are consistent with those data. Our study enabled us to explore in greater depth the role that marriage played for respondents in certain ethnic groups, including the white British, and how this related to their general sense of family obligations.

As stated above, sixteen of our thirty-nine respondents were drawn from ethnic minority (EM) groups. The detailed breakdown is shown in Table 1.

We are of course aware of the invalidity of treating this category as if the individuals were homogenous in all respects, and have been careful in presenting the data to record the actual ethnicity of each respondent. But we did want to see whether, in relation to the subject matter of our study, members of these ethnic minority groups offered different types of response from those who were members of the white British (WB) majority community. We therefore grouped all individuals belonging to minority groups into a single unit, in order to enable us to explore the hypothesis that such differences might appear. The groups are thus a device for analysis, and the procedure carries no implication that their members are to be seen as a united category in other respects.

REASONS FOR MARRYING

One difference between the EM and the WB sets is that a lower proportion of the former were living together, or "living apart together", unmarried (25 percent as against 39 percent), and that many more of the WB set who were married had cohabited before marriage than had those in the EM set. The explanation lies in the strong role that conventional practices played for the some of the EM group, among whom it was common to find expression of strong conventional reasons for marrying:

Interviewer: *Why marry?*
Respondent: *I'm a practising Muslim; my wife was born a Muslim but knew nothing about it . . . she converted to Islam and gave me an ultimatum: live the Muslim way and marry . . . after a year of the marriage I came to Islam, it took a year, studying; before we lived by society's rules, now I live as a Muslim.*
(Male, 24, Afghani, Muslim) [Case 33]

Being an Asian, although I was born in this country, still, to keep Mom and Dad happy, I keep their Asian values.
(Male, 36, Married, Asian British, Hindu) [Case 21]

This respondent later referred to "parent's law rather than government's law" as being significant.

My father not happy if I not marry.
(Male, 38, Married, Brazilian, Christian) [Case 24]

One respondent combined this with religious prescription:

I am a practising Catholic . . . my Dad told us to get married. . . .
(Female, 38, Married, Black African) [Case 35]

A number of respondents regarded the social conventions of their community as exerting a considerable force on their behavior. But this tended to be combined with religious practice and parental wishes.

(My previous marriage [in Japan]) was almost like a thing you have to do, very normal, most of the people do, and I really liked my husband, and I didn't question much . . . but now I think more about relationship rather than following everybody else.
(Female, 43, Cohabiting after divorce, Japanese) [Case 10]

Respondent: *I think it was a cultural thing to do with it, and expectations of parents . . . back home, if you start living together you get married . . . we are Christians . . .*
Interviewer: *Would you say part of the reason was a religious reason?*
Respondent: *It is difficult to say, isn't it . . . it is both cultural and religious.*
(Male, 45, Married, Black African) [Case 19]

It's cultural, in terms of we're Indians, living together is not the thing; you marry and then you live together, that's the only way it is . . . expectations, family and culture.
(Male, 38, Married, Asian British, Sikh) [Case 22]

Of course, such sentiments were not confined to the EM group. For example:

I fell in love I suppose; it was the right thing to do, there was no such thing as living together when I was 18. My parents would have frowned on anything else.
(Female, 40, Cohabitant after Divorce, white British) [Case 31]

Another way of expressing this was to say that it was "the thing to do at the time" (Male, 39, Married, white British) [Case 14], or "because that's what you did and maybe it's because what your parents did as well" (Female, 44, Married, white British) [Case17], or "I was brought up you didn't do it until married", (Female, 42, Married, white British) [Case 27]. But there was a tendency among the WB group for respondents appear to "distance" themselves from the conventions they were following by characterizing themselves as "traditional." Tradition has a compromise quality to it. Following a tradition suggests a lifestyle choice, freely entered, rather than being subject to prescriptions by reason of one's membership of a community that one may not have freely chosen.

> Interviewer: *Why marry and not carry on living together?*
> Respondent: *Because it was something that I've always believed in . . . never thought of not doing it. Just a traditionalist really.*
> (Female, 30, Married, white British) [Case 7]

Giving as a reason for marrying that one is "old-fashioned" (Female, 40, Married, white British) [Case 31] seems to be adopting a similar viewpoint.

It did not follow that EM respondents did not have pragmatic reasons for marrying. Indeed, three of our four respondents who married for primarily "pragmatic" reasons were in that group. One was white Irish, two were black British (Afro-Caribbean). But, at least for the last two, the reasons were quite weighty. Compare:

> Interviewer: *Why get married?*
> Respondent: *My husband went to work in* [Middle Eastern country] *and the only way I could go out there was if we were married.*
> (Female, 39, Cohabiting after previous marriage ended in divorce, white British, speaking of first marriage) [Case 13]

And

> Interviewer: *Why marry after living together?*
> Respondent: *It just happened; we were going to emigrate and it was easier with all the papers.*
> (Female, 34, Married, white Irish) [Case 26]

With

> Interviewer: *Why marry at this time [after seven years' cohabitation]?*
> Respondent: *Inheritance tax . . . my husband saw the Panorama programme on TV last October. He got a real thing about this . . . with owning the house and everything.*
> (Female, 39, Married, black British (Afro-Caribbean)) [Case 38]

And

> Interviewer: *What triggered the marriage?*
> Respondent: *That was just a final . . . it's the final thing really, plus the legalities. Obviously a will could sort out the dying intestate, but she's almost automatically next of kin being my wife. . . .*
> (Male, 32, Married, black British (Afro-Caribbean)) [Case 37]

Although the respondent in Case 38 reports the view of her husband rather than herself, the views reported in the last two extracts show a more deeply serious attitude to legalities than the first two. This serious attitude to marriage also shows in the fact that, when looking at "internal" reasons for marrying, we found that no member of the EM group fell into the "Confirmation" category. That category refers to cases where marriage was seen entirely as a one-off event, a "party" or "celebration," symbolically important to proclaim the parties' relationship, but not perceived as being of itself valuable. As one WB respondent put it:

> *You just get out of the pool, get married, get back in the pool . . . it's just a good day; a really good party. Just a day to remember.*
> (Male, 33, Cohabitant, white British) [Case 36]

Such a view was not found in the EM group. In the "Completion" category, marriage seemed to play a more significant role from the internal point of view. It was more than merely a public display undertaken mostly for others, but assumed a more personal nature, and provided in itself an added impetus for, or source of, further commitment. We found such perceptions in both the EM and WB sets.

> *It was personal, to show our commitment.*
> (Male, 39, Married, white British) [Case 14]

> *Cohabitation is not a full commitment. My parents wouldn't be happy with us living together for them, but only because we wanted to.*
> (Female, 31, Married, Asian British) [Case 16]

> Interviewer: *So marriage made a little bit of difference, but not a lot?*
> Respondent: *I guess it's the security of knowing you're going to be married together . . . it wasn't (just) a dream. . . .*
> (Female, 44, Married, white British) [Case 17]

> *Marriage for me is the point at which it moves from being "This is very nice now" to "we've got to make a life together with a view to being together for as long as you last, ultimately probably having children, etc." In that sense it's a deeper commitment.*
> (Male, 41, Married, white Irish, Roman Catholic) [Case 11]

> Interviewer: *. . . did marriage make a difference?*
> Respondent: *Yea, it did—I still look at it as a long term commitment . . . but again it made a difference to the way I felt about (wife) protecting wise, but the actual relationship . . . it didn't make a great deal of difference, but . . . it is more my male role I imagine . . . I jumped from being a boyfriend to a husband.*
> (Male, 32, Married, black British (Afro-Caribbean)) [Case 37]

These cases all show marriage operating as an event which seals, or raises to a new level, a relationship that has been maturing over time. It is often consistent with seeing marriage as mandated by external convention. No doubt the parties believe the relationship will continue to grow after the marriage, but marriage is essentially seen as the event that has an independent effect in completing the fundamental nature of the partnership. In the final category, however, (the "Construction" cases) the marriage operates more as a framework within which the partners *work towards* the deeper commitment which, for the earlier group, marriage already signified. Usually, that deeper commitment occurs on the birth of a child. As in the Completion cases, it was possible for respondents to combine the use of marriage as a framework for deepening their relationship with accepting conventional reasons for marrying.

Typical Construction cases are the following:

Interviewer: *Why marry at all?*
Respondent: *I don't know. I s'pose we just wanted to . . . it was like a way of saying "I want to be with you for ever" . . . [but] when you're married, you've always got a get-out, not that you hope to divorce, but you're not bonded in the same way. The real commitment is having kids, not the marriage. Then you're connected to that person further.*
(Female, 38, Married, white British) [Case 4]

Respondent: *If I didn't have children the whole thing would be different . . . I think I'd get out of a relationship much quicker, or at least have a cooling off period where you could find out whether you still wanted to be together or not.*
Interviewer: *So marriage itself isn't the commitment?*
Respondent: *No, it's the children.*
(Female, 40, Married, white British) [Case 5]

This use of marriage seemed to have a particularly significant role in some cases where the primary reason seemed to be conventional. For example, the Hindu respondent, who explained that he had married out of conformity to cultural traditions and parental expectations, added:

Although you see each other during the day [before marriage] it's totally different living together . . . most people have children in two years, we delayed it until 5 years . . . I think the delay for settling down and having children was just to make sure that we were compatible and knew what way we were heading.
(Male, 36, Married, Asian British, Hindu) [Case 21]

And the Sikh respondent made a similar response:

Interviewer: *What difference did it make when your first child was born?*
Respondent: *That was probably the biggest transition in terms of responsibility . . . we were young and we loved each other, there were a lot of things we could do together . . . it was different from being single, but I wouldn't say that much difference; but when my son was born, that is when it comes that you have a responsibility for a long term . . .*
(Male, 38, Married, Asian British, Sikh) [Case 22].

It is possible that the very fact that many in the EM set were subject to strong conventional prescriptions to marry, so that the act of marriage did not necessarily fully coincide with a sense of confirmation of emotional commitment (as in the Completion cases), *encouraged* the perception of the marriage being a framework within which commitment grows.

II. PERCEPTION OF RESPONSIBILITIES BETWEEN PARTNERS

A. THE EXTERNAL-DUTY APPROACH

One might anticipate that those who undertook marriage for conventional reasons would be inclined to see the relationship as being dominated by rules or obligations set by the marriage itself. There was some indication of that. For example, a fundamentalist Christian said, in answer to the question whether he thought it was his duty to share, or whether they just wanted to do it that way:

> *I am a Christian . . . God say there is no man and there is no woman . . . man and woman is one, not two . . . so why think differently . . . everything belong to me belong to her; not I must do, I think I should do. . . .*
>
> (Male, 38, Married, Brazilian, Christian) [Case 24]

Similarly, a Muslim respondent said:

> *There are rules about marriage . . . it tells you how to live together and keeps us happy.*
>
> (Male, 24, Married, Afghani, Muslim) [Case 33]

and another Christian respondent, having mentioned mutual rights and responsibilities, replied to the question whether these came from the fact of marriage:

> *Well, this is a personal belief and I think I take seriously the religious . . . and the ceremony we went through and what it really meant and I would take it to the letter; there is the legal aspect as well . . . and also the cultural aspect . . . the expectation that . . . so I think it's not just the one factor, but it is multi-factored . . . so that you sort of know you are . . . obliged to adhere to. . . .*
>
> (Male, 45, Married, black African, Christian) [Case 19]

For a black British respondent, who had an Anglican upbringing (but was not passing this on to his children), marriage also generated independent reasons for action.

> *You're getting married; it's a bond, it keeps you together longer than you would do if you weren't.*
>
> (Male, 32, Married, black British (Afro-Caribbean)) [Case 37].

All these respondents, except for the last, had a strong conventional element in their reasons for marrying. The link between marrying for conventional reasons, and seeing obligations deriving from the marriage, is obviously strong, and, as we have seen, marrying for conventional reasons was a strong feature of the EM set. Although some in the WB set did adopt the external duty approach, for them it seems to have played a weaker role. For example, the WB respondent began to value rights and obligations created by marriage only as time went on:

> Interviewer: *Why does he owe you that security?*
> Respondent: *Because we signed a piece of paper.*
> Interviewer: *If you had not got married, it might have been different?*
> Respondent: *It would have been different . . . it's going back to the law thing . . .*
> Interviewer: *That was the important thing? It gave you security . . . ?*
> Respondent: *It wasn't important then, but now . . .*
>
> (Female, 44, Married, white British) [Case 17]

B. THE EVOLUTIONARY APPROACH

Moving to those who adopted the "evolutionary" approach to their responsibilities, paradigmatically, one would be inclined to associate this primarily with unmarried cohabitants. There were certainly strong examples from that group:

Interviewer: *If you had to make real sacrifices which might make demands upon you to . . .*
Respondent: *To look after her? Then I would, probably, yea . . .*
Interviewer: *Why? After all, you're not married, so you can't say its because you're married.*
Respondent: *No. If you've been with somebody for 17 or 18 years, that somebody is like part of you, part of your life. . . .*
(Male, 33, Cohabitant, white British) [Case 36]

But this could be found among the married as well. This was particularly so when the birth of the child was seen as completing the relationship.

(On separation) whoever had the baby the other should give for, but not for each other. (Female, 31, Married, British Asian, Muslim) [Case 16]

So even where a respondent saw obligations deriving from marriage itself, these could be seen as designed to secure the interests of children. Perhaps the strongest example was the Indian respondent who had followed cultural practice in marrying at the age of 25 and remaining in his parents' house with his siblings until his children were getting too big. The respondent struggled to express his thoughts in the English language, but an interesting analysis emerged. Early in the interview it was clear that he considered marriage imposed rights and duties:

Both sides have rights . . . both sides have responsibilities . . . if that's my duty, then I have to do it. . . .

Later, in comparing marriage with unmarried cohabitation, the following occurred:

Interviewer: *What do you think of living together without marriage?*
Respondent: *I would say as far as living together it is not a bad thing, but once children are there it is safer for children* [to marry]*. . . the most reason is, if you are married, you've got the duties to do it . . . your duties, you've got to follow it . . . if you're not married then the children are totally standing independently . . . and in the open society like here, some things I think it's OK but some I don't like. . . .*
Interviewer: *So you think the duties come from being married?*
Respondent: *It's not come from the marriage . . . it has to come from the understanding . . . if you're not married even though this is our duty, your children are there so that's your duty how you're going to keep them . . . and especially the broken families.*
(Male, 42, Married, Indian) [Case 18]

We think this respondent can be interpreted as saying that, while marriage does impose duties, the real reason for the duties is for the benefit of children. So you have duties towards your children in any case, but the duties of marriage underpin the duties towards children.

C. THE ETHICAL APPROACH

The "Ethical" approach—where the respondents referred to some independent ethical value in explaining the way they thought they should behave in their relationships—could be found among all "types" of marriage, and among those who were not married. There did, however, seem to be a variance between the EM and WB groups, again largely deriving from the prevalence of conventional reasons for marrying and the associated "External-duty" basis for obligations. The variance lay in the apparent absence of references to the "golden rule"—do unto others as you would have them do unto you—in the former group. The approach resembles the a quasi-contractual notion of reciprocity, but differs from it since there is no suggestion that one activity was undertaken in expectation of the reciprocal response. It was prominent among unmarried cohabitants and was also found in married respondents in the WB group. For example:

> Interviewer: *What obligations might you have to your husband in later life?*
> Respondent: *I suppose you should support each other on retirement . . . it's part of being a couple, being married. I don't think it's necessarily an obligation, but then on the other hand he's been looking after* [me and the kids] *for God knows how many years.*
> (Female, 26, Married, white British) [Case 6]

This respondent clearly felt that the mere fact that her husband had supported her generated an obligation to care for him. A cohabitant, when asked why he would look after his partner in adversity, said:

> *Well, why shouldn't I? I've been together with* [partner's name] *now for 17 years; if I fell ill, she'd look after me. I'd like to think she would; ummmm, that's the type of person I am. If she fell ill, I'd look after her.*
> (Male, 33, Cohabitant, white British) [Case 36]

It is interesting that this open reference to the golden rule appeared more prominent in unmarried cohabitations than in married ones. It is possible that for the married the ethic simply became absorbed in the duties of marriage, or in the conceptualization of the relationship.

Another expressed ethic drew on the idea of trust. We saw this expressed in the context of both marriage and cohabiting relationships. Among the EM group, we saw this expressed by both a Japanese, and a white Irish respondent:

> *If you begin to behave in some way which is unreasonable . . . it's a betrayal of the relationship.* (Male, 41, Married, white Irish, Roman Catholic) [Case 11]

> Interviewer: *If you were still living together with your new partner and got into need, would your partner have a responsibility to you?*
> Respondent: *I don't know if it is a responsibility but I would probably expect something from him, some help, I don't know in what way; but if he ignores* [me] *I don't trust him any more.*
> (Female, 43, Cohabitant after divorce, Japanese, describing cohabitation relationship) [Case 10]

However, references to "love" as a basis for obligation were surprisingly rare, and where found, tended to be made by members of the EM group. All were married.

> Interviewer: *When you started to live together having got married, how did that change things . . . ?*
> Respondent: *Well, I think it both started with love . . . and respect to each other and if you have that then we see we have better productive if you do things together. I think the foundation was I say love then respect and you build on it: that's how I see it.*
> (Male, 45, Married, black African, Christian) [Case 19]

> Interviewer: *You think you've got responsibilities to your wife primarily because you're married to her: that would be your reason . . . ?*
>
> Respondent: *No . . . I married her because I love her, that would be* [the reason]. . . . (Male, 38, Married, British Asian, Sikh) [Case 22]

> Interviewer: *If we were to ask again about if there were problems regarding your wife, should she get ill, needing support.*
> Respondent: *Support, I would do everything I could.*
> Interviewer: *Why do you feel that?*
> Respondent: *Because actually love her . . . deep down . . . no it wasn't even deep down really . . . it's just taken a little while to realize that.*
> (Male, 32, Married, black British (Afro-Caribbean)) [Case 37]

Three women (all WB) also mentioned love as being a reason for marrying in the first place. Two of these coupled it with strong conventional reasons. It is interesting that it was only the married, who referred to "love" as a basis for behavior, whereas "care" was referred to both by the married and cohabitants. Perhaps the respondents felt that love, on its own, would have seemed an insufficient, or inappropriate, basis for grounding responsibilities. However, where it was understood that love was underwritten by marriage, which creates an externally imposed duty, respondents felt more willing to mention it as an independent source of obligation. But where there was no marriage, or where marriage was seen as having weak normative force, respondents may have felt it necessary to find something less intangible (as it were) than love, as a source for obligations, and therefore referred to the duties inherent in making a relationship work, or sometimes to some independent ethical principle, instead.

III. WIDER KIN

We were particularly interested to discover whether respondents felt they had duties to their partner's wider family (especially their parents) and, if so, why they did. Almost all respondents accepted that they would help their "in-laws", but the degree of this commitment, and the basis for it, varied. The reasons for perceiving the duty fell into three distinct categories. The first derived primarily from the fact of the marriage; the second derived from independent ethical principles, and the third were parasitic upon the obligation to the partner.

As before, the EM set was strongly represented in the first group:

> *My mother-in-law . . . she says she is always there if the baby isn't well . . . I work such a long way away, they are family to me.*
> (Female, 31, Married, Asian British, Muslim, married to Irish father) [Case 16]

> Respondent: *It is my full duty to keep them and to do what can do the best for them*
> Interviewer: *If they fall into need?*
> Respondent: *I have to work for them . . . I.*
> (Male, 42, Married, Indian) [Case 18]

> *Yes, she comes with the baggage . . . I have when I marry her, I don't just marry her, I marry her whole tribe.* (Male, 45, Married, black African) [Case 19]

> Respondent: *As far as responsibilities go, there's the obvious fact that they're her parents, and we try to help . . . anything I can do I will do, there is no thinking twice about it. . . .*
> Interviewer: *So you would stick with them through thick and thin like friends?*
> Respondent: *Yes absolutely.*
> (Male, 38, Married, British Asian (Sikh)) [Case 22]

> *Yes, I would have to do something looking after them, because they'd do it for their parents . . . in that way it becomes something that is part of the family.*
> (Male, 32, Married, black British (Afro-Caribbean) [Case 37]

Sometimes quite elaborate rules seemed to operate:

> *If my wife's mother were to survive, because my wife's got a brother . . . normally by default it goes to the brother. . . .*
> (Male, 36, Married, British Asian, Hindu) [Case 21]

We do not suggest that a sense that such sentiments could not be found in the married respondents in the WB group. For example:

> Interviewer: *When you got married, did that effect how you related to his family?*
> Respondent: *Yes, all of a sudden . . . his sister . . . she became my younger sister and I felt an obligation to her I think.*
> (Female, 43, Married, white British) [Case 20]

But the obligation tended to be less fulsomely expressed. Indeed, many seemed to wish to deny its existence at all. For example, one woman specifically stated she would not ask her husband to support her mother: "This is *our* family", she remarked [Case 15], although she went on to admit that "if she or my Mum was in real trouble we would step in." Similarly, when asked if how she would respond to a request from her husband to support his family, a WB respondent said:

> Respondent: *If he asked, yeah.*
> Interviewer: *Why?*
> Respondent: *Because they're my family as well. It's not an obligation, it's just something I would do . . . I've been brought up like that, that your family is . . . you just do that, you go that extra mile for them.*
> (Female, 30, Married, white British) [Case 7]

Here are other examples:

Respondent: *I would have done that* [helped her mother in law in practical ways] *because at that time I was only working 4 days. . . .*
Interviewer: *Is that different from being a friend?*
Respondent: *I would probably say I was more obliged to do it for family than for a friend, but then again . . . the person that I am I would probably do it for a friend as well.*
(Female, 32, Married, white British) [Case 9]

Interviewer: *Do you help them?*
Respondent: *Not financially, but doing things for 'em.*
Interviewer: *Why?*
Respondent: *It's just the way I am . . .*
Interviewer: *Is it just the same as friends . . . ?*
Respondent: *No, not really, I mean, it's family and you make that extra effort to help them.* (Male, 39, Married, white British) [Case 12]

But I wouldn't have felt any obligation to help [her husband's mother before the marriage] *and I don't think I do now* [during the marriage] . . . *although I would. I wouldn't turn her down.* (Female, 26, Married, white British) [Case 6]

You wouldn't want to see them go through anything too awful . . . because they're family . . . but then again, you'd probably do that for friends as well.
(Female, 40, Married, white British) [Case 5]

Respondents in the EM group tended to reinforce the duty by reference to some independent value: for example, reciprocation for the fact that the in-laws looked after their own children [Case 18], or by appeal to the value of friendship. Reference to friendship could be seen as diminishing the strength of the obligation, as possibly in Case 5 just cited. But in the following response, friendship is seen as adding to the strength of an obligation already established through the marital link (even though that marriage had ended in divorce):

Respondent: *If I can I would help them but I don't think they need my help at the moment, but I like them personally very much . . . it is more like friendship.*
Interviewer: *When they get older, they would be able to count on you, and presumably their son?*
Respondent: *Yes.*
(Female, 43, Cohabiting after divorce, speaking of her former husband and his parents, Japanese) [Case 10]

The way unmarried respondents explained their sense of obligation to their partner's parents was interesting. They might rest it directly on an independent ethical principle, such as the "golden rule":

Respondent: *We put her mother up here for three months when she was having difficulties. . . .*
Interviewer: *Why . . . after all, she's not your own mother?*
Respondent: *Well, it's the sort of thing . . . you couldn't say no . . . but she'd probably put me up in the same situation. It's just the sort of thing you do.*
(Male, 33, Cohabitant, white British) [Case 36]

Interviewer: *Would you help our partner's parents?*
Respondent: *Yeah*
Interviewer: *Why?*
Respondent: *To be honest, they're nice people, but more importantly . . . you should do unto others as you'd have done unto yourself. They've helped me in the past and I would like to reciprocate if it was required.* (Male, 30, Cohabitant, white British) [Case 1]

But another approach was to see the obligation as part of, or derivative from, the obligation to the partner. Here the "golden rule" underlies the duty to the partner:

The way I look at it, considering how much I care about my mother and father, if anything happened to them, I would hope my partner would want to help me to help them, so I would do exactly the same, but then again, I like her mother and father . . . well, let's put it this way, she would be responsible and I would be behind her supporting her because she'd need that support in a difficult time and I'd like to think that if the tables were turned, if I had the pressure, I wouldn't want to have the pressure of worrying what's my partner thinking, is she going to approve.
(Male, 32, Cohabitant, white British) [Case 23]

There were fewer EM respondents who were not married, but two adopted a similar approach:

Respondent: *I do feel responsible* [for my parents] . . .
Interviewer: *How about his parents?*
Respondent: *Not so much, but I would be assisting him to execute is responsibilities.*
(Female, 35, Living Apart Together—cohabitation temporarily suspended—black British (Afro-Caribbean)) [Case 39]

Interviewer: *Would you help your partner's family?*
Respondent: *If he was to discuss it with me, and if I could help, I would help.*
Interviewer: *Why?*
Respondent: *Again, I guess it's because he's my partner . . . I would try to do as much as I could, only because it's helping him as well.*
(Male, 41, Living Apart Together, gay, mixed Caribbean) [Case 3]

IV. PERCEPTIONS OF RIGHTS

Having considered the way in which respondents saw their duties or responsibilities, we now turn to consider specifically the extent to which respondents felt the language of rights was appropriate within their relationship. We found evidence that respondents tended to feel discomfort about speaking in terms of rights. This was so for cohabitants, and for married people. Here is an example from the EM set, but it could be replicated across the sample:

No . . . I mean, I go out to work, she does most of the housework, we're never thinking on those terms that, you know, that's something special, we do share things out, and there are certain things I do; she respects that, and it goes the other way as well, so, no I don't think so.

Interviewer: *So you wouldn't think, I have a right to know, or to do something.*
Respondent: *No, no . . . if I want to do something I tell her what I want to do, we have a discussion; there's never been an issue where we agree to disagree.* (Male, 38, Married, Asian British, Sikh) [Case 22]

Yet there were contexts in which some respondents did find the expression appropriate. Those respondents for whom the conventional aspects of marriage were important were not surprisingly inclined to see rights and duties as flowing naturally from the convention. Once again, this is strongly associated with the EM group. Even if "rights" were not specifically referred to, they must have been implicit in the response that stated that marriage laid down "rules" (Male, 24, Married, Afghani, Muslim) [Case 33]. Other examples are:

> *I think it goes without saying . . . both of us have a right to each other and responsibility to each other as well.*
> (Male, 45, Married, black African, Christian) [Case 19]

Another, whose marriage was in the conventional category:

> *Both sides have rights, in a family, both sides have got responsibilities . . . I got rights, she got rights.*

However, as we noted earlier, this respondent seemed later to place a particular restraint on this by saying this did not "*come from the marriage*" but rather from the duty towards children (Male, 42, Married, Indian) [Case 18]. A third, who saw marriage as creating "a bond," was happy with the idea of rights, which he defined (interestingly) as "taken-for-granted expectations," but stressed that they were reciprocal:

> *In an underlying sort of way I suppose that's what marriage is about; that you have . . . you do have a hold over each other because you're bound . . . I suppose (the word) does pop into your head; there are expectations aren't there; so I suppose expectations do become sort of taken for granted that's how they become rights I suppose; yea, you do. . . .*
> (Male, 32, Married, black British (Afro-Caribbean)) [Case 37]

This recognition of reciprocity is important, for it shows the concept of a right as being used in a way to acknowledge an interest of the partner. This might be for personal space:

> *My wife has a right to go out and visit her sisters and her friends and go out to work: I can't say, you stay in, you can't go out to work.*
> (Male, 45, Married, black African, Christian) [Case 19]

Or to reasonable behavior:

> *I suppose in a sense we got married having made the decision to stay together, so it is a change in the degree of commitment . . . there is an implicit contract somewhere in that . . . if you behave in a way which is in some way unreasonable . . . then they certainly have the right to be angry with you. . . .*
> (Male, 41, Married, white Irish, Roman Catholic) [Case 11]

So we can see that where marriage is seen as a source of rights, this can be seen not only as a source of rights for the respondent, but also for the respondent's partner. But the unmarried could also acknowledge that their partner had a right to have their interests taken into consideration:

> *Ummm . . . I'm quite easy going, so I'd say she has a right to be happy, that's the only thing I'd say . . . it's up to me in some sort of way to make sure she is happy . . . I don't feel I've got any rights from her.*
> (Male, 32, Cohabitant, white British) [Case 23]

V. COMMUNALITY

There was some indication that cohabitants were less inclined to adopt a "sharing" ethic than the married, but this seemed related to experience of difficulties in an earlier relationship. It was also possible to find cohabitants with a strong sharing ethic in both the WB and EM groups:

> *I don't think we see it as each other's property, we see it as our property, we find it very difficult to say, that's mine, that's yours.*
> (Male, 33, Cohabitant, white British) [Case 8]

> Interviewer: *So, how do you look on things you buy, do you look on them sort of yours and hers, or ours?*
> Respondent: *Yes, there's no his and hers; everything we buy is pretty much straight down the middle actually, there's no secrets at all.*
> (Male, 33, Cohabitant, white British) [Case 36]

> *It's my partner and I feel that what's mine is his, sort of thing.*
> (Male, 41, Living Apart Together, mixed Carribean, gay)) [Case 3]

Married people from both sets also expressed a sharing ethic.

> *We have a joint bank account . . . we share everything.*
> (Female, 34, Married, white Irish) [Case 26]

> *He's a very good Dad; before we married I asked him, would it be 50/50 with the children: he said "yes" and I really feel it is.*
> (Female, 31, British Asian (Muslim, married to Irish Catholic) [Case 16]

> [Husband] *and I share looking after the children; he works nights so he can.*
> (Female, 38, Married, black African) [Case 35]

> *Everything is just one . . . man and woman is one, not two.*
> (Male, 38, Married, Brazilian (Christian)) [Case 24]

> *We have a very open and friendly atmosphere, two of us, we don't hide anything.* (Male, 42, Married, Indian) [Case 18]

> *Right from the beginning we were sharing responsibilities.*
> (Male, 36, Married, British Asian (Hindu)) [Case 21]

> *We work together as a team.* (Male, 45, Married, black African) [Case 19]

Respondent: *We share everything.*
Interviewer: *You did that right from the start i.e. when moved in together before marrying?*
Respondent: *Yes... money... everything... cars... whatever.*
(Male 39, Married, white British) [Case 12]

I was quite surprised to see friends of ours had separate accounts and kept them. I find that extremely strange. (Female, 40, Married white British) [Case 5]

There were, however, a few cases among the married where a wife kept some resources apart from the husband because he was bad with money, and in another a full-time Mum received an "allowance." We were thus not able to detect from our data any clear difference in attitudes between the EM and WB groups with respect to the ideal of communality in the relationship.

VI. CONCLUSIONS

In summarizing the contrasts in the data between the two groups, EM and WB, we must stress that, while we are able to report the reasons given by our respondents for their actions, and observe the values that underlay them, we are not making an analysis of the various cultures involved. We could surmise, for example, that a higher degree of religiosity occurs in some cultures than in others, and that this might account for certain attitudes of our respondents. But we could not assess the strength of our respondents' religious beliefs, nor how the interaction between religious belief and cultural conformity operated in their case.

Taken as a whole, our data indicate that the sense of obligation in personal obligations need not only arise from an external source, and therefore marriage is neither a necessary nor sufficient condition for the acceptance of personal obligation. Cohabitants could express as much desire to work to make the relationship succeed (the "normative pull"), and lack of comprehension at the thought of possible future separation as married people, while married respondents could express uncertainty about the future of the relationship. In addition, cohabitants frequently referred to some additional factor, such as having a child, or some ethical principle, which underlay the "normative pull" that the relationship itself generated. In any case, married people also expressed the idea that responsibilities grew as the relationship developed, and appealed directly to "ethical" principles and having a child as sources of obligations. So, while married people had an additional source (the marriage) available from which to derive their obligation, many of them referred to the same ones as the non-married. It becomes increasingly difficult to identify being married in itself as *necessarily*, or even *characteristically*, constituting a significant source of personal obligations in the eyes of the participants in such relationships.

But it appears that marriage played a more significant part for the EM than for the WB respondents. It did so in the following ways. Its members tended to cite stronger "conventional" reasons for marrying, indicating a stronger sense of feeling bound by the prescriptions mandating that long-term relationships should only be undertaken within marriage. But, while being married certainly gave rise to a sense of responsibility, this was consistent with a recognition of a later and stronger source of obligation, which arose out of the development of the relationship itself, and in particular if a child was born. It was indeed a particular feature of the EM group that marriage could be used as a framework within which it was expected that the relationship would grow towards a new stage. Interestingly, though, it is this feature (what we call the "Construction" category of marriages) that illustrates the extent of the common ground between most of our respondents, whether married or unmarried, and whether in the EM or WB set. This is that the relationship itself is seen as setting the demands to behavior. For many married people, and especially those in the EM set, the relationship is seen to be so closely integrated with the institution of marriage, that it is possible more easily to anchor responsibilities in that institution, perhaps making it easier to refer more openly to love as a driver of the relationship itself. For those who are not married, the source of obligations needs to be located elsewhere. This is often found in independent ethical principles, but mainly in the "normative pull" of the relationship itself: the idea that you need to "work" to make the relationship successful, and that being in a relationship requires you to do that work.

So, while the routes to perceptions of responsibilities may be different, the end result looks very similar. It is much the same regarding the sense of obligation to a partner's side of the family. Within the context of marriage, members of the EM group tended to articulate this sense in a fairly robust way, which many of the married in the WB group were not able to match. However, on closer examination, we wonder if the end results would be very different. Even when the initial response was to deny any obligation, the respondents tended to concede they would act to help them anyway if necessary, sometimes (as in the case of the unmarried) seeing this as part of their obligations to their partner, or on an independent ethical principle. As for perceptions of rights—and we must stress that we were not focusing on how people might perceive their rights if the relationship came to an end—the conclusion seems to be that these are not strong in the context of people's ongoing relationships. Nevertheless, they do play a stronger role for the EM group, for whom rights and duties are seen as flowing from the marriage. This could be important in promoting recognition of the couple's reciprocal interests. Yet, again, the contrast with the unmarried cohabitants may be more apparent than real, for these too could recognize the interests of the other, either as a matter of right, or as part of the responsibility for making the relationship "work." Similarly, we could find no observable differences in attitudes to communality between the married and unmarried, and between the EM and WB sets.

Our overall conclusion is that, while there are a variety of ways of achieving stability in relationships and by which people formulate their personal obligations, one cannot conclude that any one method is uniquely capable of achieving certain results. People use marriage in different ways depending on the different perceptions they have about its place with regard to their personal relationships.

These perceptions differ between cultures. It therefore seems too simple, and even futile, for policy makers to embark on general campaigns to promote marriage as referred to at the beginning of this article, because their goals and understanding of marriage may be different from the way people use it. Furthermore, when we examine the way people think about their relationships, we find that there are many variations between those who are married, and many similarities between those who are married and those who are not. Cutting across them all, though, we find a range of values which are held in common, and which have a substantial effect on generating ideas of personal obligation. Our evidence shows that married and unmarried people who are living together, and our respondents from both the EM and WB groups, share many values. Indeed, the similarities in the normative determinants of their behavior may be greater than the dissimilarities.

JOHN EEKELAAR *is Reader in Family Law, University of Oxford, and Fellow of Pembroke College, Oxford.*

MAVIS MACLEAN *is co-director of the Oxford Centre for Family Law and Policy.*

REFERENCES

Barlow, Ann, and Grace James (2004) "Regulating Marriage and Cohabitation in 21st Century Britain," *Modern Law Review* 67: 143–76.

Berger, P., and H. Kellner (1999) "Marriage and the Construction of Reality," *Diogenes* 46: 1–17.

Eekelaar, John, and Mavis Maclean (2004) "Marriage and the Moral Bases of Personal Obligations," *Journal of Law and Society* 31: 510–38.

Fukuyama, Francis (1999) *The Great Disruption*. London: Profile Books.

Kiernan, K., and K. Smith (2003) "Unmarried Parenthood: New Insights from the Millennium Cohort Study," *Population Trends* 114: 23–33.

Reece, Helen (2003) *Divorcing Responsibly*. Oxford: Hart Publishing.

United Kingdom Government (1998) *Supporting Families: A Consultation Document*: London, The Stationery Office.

Waite, Linda J., and Maggie Gallagher (2001) *The Case for Marriage*: New York: Broadway Books.

[8]

Regulation of Intimacy and Love Semantics in Couples Living Apart Together

BERNADETTE BAWIN-LEGROS AND ANNE GAUTHIER

Department of Sociology, University of Liège, Belgium

Conjugal transformations have been many over the last 30 years. They have particularly affected the domain of divorce rather than marriage. Having passed completely unseen for a long time, the residential autonomy of couples has been the particular subject of interest of family specialists. The spread of couples living together without marrying and the increase of second unions might have encouraged the development of double residences and explain the recent excitement of interest in this lifestyle commonly called 'Living Apart Together' (LAT). However, according to a study published in France by Villeneuve-Gokalp (1997) living as a couple and yet maintaining one's individual independence would appear to be a relatively common occurrence in the early stages of a relationship. Sixteen per cent of couples do not live together all the time at the beginning of their 'conjugal life'. It also seems, according to this same study, that two-thirds (66%) of members of couples claim that this separation is due to pressures external to the couple itself, usually family related or professional; 34% claim that it is in order to retain their independence.

A voluntary separation of domicile might appear to be a prudent behaviour, with both parties taking the time to verify the solidity of their relationship while maintaining their individual space. Perhaps it is a way of imposing a lifestyle that respects the individual autonomy of each party. The preference of an independent relationship is much more common in second unions, and this fact reinforces both the hypothesis of prudence and the desire for autonomy. If one of the two members of a couple has experienced at least one break up, in nearly 2 cases out of 10, cohabitation is delayed, but does eventually happen.

According to the *Institut National de Statistiques et d'Etudes Economiques* (INSEE) (Villeneuve-Gokalp, 1997) data, it would seem that few couples can withstand long-term residential separations. In fact, among couples who still consider themselves united after five years, only 12% continue in separate residences. The others have succumbed to the charm or to the necessity of a shared domicile.

Twenty years ago, couples living together without marrying was beginning to be more common; now, the two-household couple is the new style. Each, in its own time, may have served the purpose of loosening the overly rigid bonds of the traditional marriage and, then, the equally restraining ones of permanent cohabitation. Perhaps there is also a new form of love semantics, as we shall see.

40 *B. Bawin-Legros and A. Gauthier*

During the 1970s, living together was not yet an alternative to marriage, but was instead a way of delaying it. Double residences seem, at first sight, to play the same role. In our interviews the idea of cohabitation is often separated from the notion of the couple, as if the couple could be a couple from a long distance, disregarding all of the rituals that govern the most important acts of conjugal life, such as meals, the conjugal bed and shared household tasks. These couples that resemble couples begin their 'disunion' with a deritualization of daily life. In the 1980s paperless unions steadily replaced legitimate ones and births out of wedlock rose. Separate residences, if we make an exception of movie stars for whom it is a common lifestyle, constitute the most significant development of the last decade.

The questions we want to treat here are two:

(1) Why do people who claim to love each other not live together?
(2) Why do others, who are not joined by equally solid ties, claim to be couples nonetheless?

What is important is to analyse the very notion of the couple such as it is lived today. The differences between it and the traditional sociological and common-sense visions of it needs to be delineated. Even novelists open with the sentence, a couple, 'a man and a woman who live together under the same roof'. Since Durkheim's day, not one sociologist, not Burgess, Parsons, Thomans or Obson has questioned this founding principle of the couple, neolocal in nature, with or without marriage.

Four elements emerge from the eight long interviews we conducted with couples of different ages and with heterogeneous conjugal histories. These elements allow us to question both the concept of couple and the rhetoric of love.

Material Constraints and Symbolic Creation

If certain couples tend to consider LAT a specific form of union, desirable and desired at the same time, others do not hesitate to speak of their situation as a transitory phase while waiting for the 'real' thing to come along:

> On the one hand, when we met, we were still students, so living together was out of the question, and then things have developed so that now we have both finished our studies but we have decided not to live together yet. That won't last 15 years, of course, but we've decided to wait a little longer in order to take advantage, for diverse reasons. (M: female, 47, divorced)

We notice that this situation is often linked to material constraints (financial problems, the presence of a child who does not accept the new partner), and most often leads to the expression of a certain dissatisfaction:

> Let's just say that I'd like to experience something else. I'd like to live with somebody because at the present I just run all the time, I have two households . . . (M: female, 47, divorced)

> Well, it's starting to feel like it's dragging on too long. It's not easy to say goodnight and leave every evening. (L: female, 44 divorced at 24)

These are elements that do not really challenge the 'classical' ideal concept of a couple, founded on cohabitation:

> A couple? It's the union of two people who are nevertheless different, but who manage to live together, but it's all guided by love, too. (M: female, 47, divorced)

Other couples, on whom we will concentrate in the remainder of this paper, consider LAT a specific form of functioning for a couple. It is accompanied by a sort of symbolic creation which is, in turn, expressed in the redefinition of the couple.

Erosion of Thresholds

When does a couple become a couple? Is it the first time they have sexual relations? When they decide to live together? When they establish a common system to manage their daily affairs? Not only are we witnessing the decline of rites of passage, of movement between stages in the cycle of life, but the thresholds between them have become imperceptible, shifting, uncertain. To this general problem of definition of thresholds is added the fact that for each couple taken in isolation it is often difficult to say where it is in the process.

How do you define a couple?

> It's a unit in which you feel like you share something with someone that you don't share with anyone else.
>
> What a question . . . a couple? I would say that it's not especially living in fusion with someone, 24 hours a day like you might think at the beginning of a relationship; a couple; it's a sort of complimentarily, but . . .
>
> A couple? Well, it's the union of two people who maybe have something in common somewhere, but I think that it's mostly a question of principles, values. If you have the same values as someone I think it can work, although . . . It's a hard question to answer. I used to have a much more united view, the couple is looking together in the same direction, but now I think that I'm beginning to see it differently and to think that you have to enjoy the good times with the person of your choice as long as they last and when it's over, too bad. (P: male, 24, single)

Is sex of primary importance for you?

> Yes, in any case.

Would you say that the first requirement of a couple is intimacy?

> Not exclusively, but certainly. It's also doing things together, difficulties . . . ? although, when you don't live together it's more difficult because you necessarily share less, but I have realized projects while

> living with someone. It's the time we spent together that made us a couple. (L: female, 44, divorced at 24)

How do you define a couple?

> Living without third-party interference, whether it be in a closed environment like an apartment building or in nature, in great intimacy that comes, for example, from a walk in nature even if we don't talk, even if one person walks 10 meters behind the other; it's really, really deep intimacy.

It is the exclusion of outsiders?

> Yes, intimacy is the exclusion of outsiders. (JM: male, 54, divorced)

It is clear that for these individuals unity is no longer found in the components of a cell, but in an individual ordering of those components. The life of a couple no longer depends on its capacity to maintain its own existence; it depends on its capacity to preserve a certain permeability between the private sphere and the rest of the world. Thus, there must be two worlds, the love cell that protects its distinction from the surrounding world and the outside world which has little or nothing to do with the fusion of the cell. Every pair is a world in itself, and the life of a couple resides in its capacity to preserve its existence, its difference. This life is not situated in the components of the couple, nor does it lie in the relationship with the external world. It resides, rather, in the participation of each member in the maintenance of the elements that determine the identity of the couple and hinder differentiation. In other words, it resides in the 'dance' that the couple does among myths and rituals, or in the interpenetrations of the two actors into systems. The couple does not have to be geographically situated to exist. Love relationships often flourish better in the realm of the imaginary:

> . . . in order to attain happiness through liberty, you have to be two. It is impossible to attain happiness being the only one who's happy. That is my philosophy, no, rather my reality. A couple is like a tribe, you have to be two for exchanges to take place, but it's so complex that we shut ourselves up in our universe. (H: male, 33, single)

In order to better understand these new conjugal lifestyles, we must speak of the weakening of the thresholds, but first we must re-establish the analysis of life cycles. Since the lines indicating the stages (cohabitation, marriage, children, divorce) can no longer be distinguished, life goes by as if there were a loss of that which constitutes community life, essentially everyday life. Even the moments of breaking tend to become the only negative ones, as if the actors wanted to protect themselves against a possible mistake:

> I left my wife at the age of 50. I could have done it five years earlier. Why didn't I? Out of cowardice? For the children? Or maybe I was waiting for an opportunity, I mean, another woman. (JM: male, 54, divorced)

A redefinition of the thresholds should allow us to evaluate the extent and the meaning not only of the love attachment but also of 'unattachment'.

The Hopeless Search for Self, Intimacy Management and Relationship to Others

As de Singly (1996) writes, the couple or the family is no longer exclusively defined as a space where love and domestic work circulate. If the family distributes this desired and hard-to-find commodity on other markets it also produces something else—the construction of the identities of each of its members. In individualistic societies like ours, 'l'instance identitaire' serves a central purpose, that of permanently consolidating the adult's self. Children's, unfortunately, often comes in second place.

The need for an identity of self comes first from someone who is close, stable and exclusive. But individuals are like Narcissus—they like to think of themselves even if they are different from him in their need for a specific mirror, other people's eyes:

> We are told that 'it's selfish,' the way we live, because we only see the best in each other. It's true, greater attention is given to the other in the way we structure our couple because we don't have to see each other, it' s not imposed by an external force. Being at home making dinner for a companion who is going to arrive at 9:00 after she gets off work is like preparing to receive a guest. We invite each other over and that forces us to make an effort, which is the source of that impression that we only see each other at our best. For example, we never clean house in front of each other. (JM: male, 54, divorced)

In this type of relationship there is a negation of the unconditional devotion to others. Personal autonomy does not exclude the creation of emotional ties, but we exclude ourselves from the societal model in which the self is only born in a relationship with someone else:

> What I appreciate in him is that he respects my solitude, my need for silence when we walk. (I: female, 27)

The absence of limitations associated with cohabitation appears to be an advantage, validated as a basic element of sentimental autonomy. This does not mean that being single is positively viewed; rather, the interdependency associated with love on a daily basis is rejected.

> We reject the suffering of day to day love, and why not? (JM: male, 54, divorced)

Nevertheless, we find there is a necessity to re-create the little things from which ordinary love is made, almost as if we were miming them. We see a shortened version of them in the little, everyday gestures:

> There are moments when we reflect on what we are doing and we congratulate ourselves on having spent a very conjugal evening resembling

ordinary love, because that afternoon she prepared a lesson while I prepared my tax return and one of us got up to make tea for the other. We imitated that ordinary life, but it's positive because it's not our everyday life. (H: male, 33)

These non-residential couples are characterized by the fact that they safeguard their difference while at the same time demanding the interpenetration of a social existence. On one hand, they safeguard their myth and do not let norms invade. On the other, they must be acceptable to their entourage and avoid adopting a functional ideal too far outside the boundaries of the normal, without which the intimate would be threatened at its very essence. There is no intimacy without norms, as Simmel stated in the 19th century. The life of a non-residential couple depends, then, on the way in which it manages its intimacy and external norms, rendered concrete through the eyes of others:

I haven't spoken about it at all because in what constitutes a couple there is also the external onlooker. People are in couples because they have the same name, they are in the same place, they have the same children. There are identifiable signs. Nevertheless, I believe rather strongly in the role of the third party and this is perhaps the opportunity to correct some things that I said earlier that might lead you to believe that everything occurs between two people one on one. That's not true; society plays an extraordinarily powerful role and therefore, how a third person views us is extremely important. I forgot to say that being a couple is also being recognized as a couple by others. It's automatic for married people. They might not even think of themselves as a couple and still be considered a couple by society.

On the other hand, in our situation, the fact that we live separately denies society of one of its most powerful signs which is the identification of the common domicile. This means that the free couple, living in separate quarters, seeks nonetheless signs of recognition. It is satisfying for the couple that I am a part of to be recognized, when individuals invite us together, when someone sends us a postcard while on vacation; they put both names on the card ... We hang onto that moment, perhaps onto miniscule identifying signs that are expected by 'official' couples, but more significant to us. We give much more weight to all of those signs, which means that there is a certain fragility.

That's one of the disadvantages, the fact that we are not sufficiently recognized. Then there are the material inconveniences, it's the toothbrush joke, they're weak, they can be easily resolved, just put the hair drier and the tampons on one side and the razor on the other. But, in a more general way, it's the fact that when we are at the other's home we are not necessarily in our own environment. Let me give you an example. I personally need to be surrounded by books, others need to be surrounded by bottles of wine or other things, but I need books. I need to be able to get up and take a book that I recognize off a shelf. That's it. I can't pick up the book I want if I am someplace the books are not which is the case when I am at my companion's home. You mustn't underestimate the importance of that sort of difficulty. If you have a summer home you can't pick up the book you want because it's on the shelf at home. It's a minor problem.

In my case, we live in places that are geographically speaking relatively close to each other. If we had to travel 45 minutes or an hour to see one another it would be much more difficult to handle. Here the travel time is not a problem. (JM: male, 54, divorced)

Every couple exudes this intimacy/norms relationship which is its true identity, its signature, and which must be protected. Based on this hypothesis, it is possible to classify non-residential couples and to show that they progress between two poles: the intimate and the normal. The non-residential couple privileges intimacy knowing that normality is indispensable to it. The more classic couple often privileges the normal to the disadvantage of intimacy. Externally, these non-residential couples appear narcissistic and are thrown off balance by any event that perturbs their equilibrium. If we were to draw a picture of it, we would see a spinal column, representing the intimate part of the couple and an envelope of skin representing the relationship to others. There is an infinite number of couples oscillating between the spinal column and the skin.

Fidelity Without Merit or the New Order of Love

One last element seems to us to characterize both couples who live together and non-residential ones, which is the promotion of hedonistic values going much further than the sexual liberation of the 1960s and 1970s. Rendering sexuality totally autonomous, 'whenever you want, wherever you want', cannot be justified within the conventional or affective rules of morality, or ideals, but in itself as an instrument of happiness and of individual balance:

Sexual relations, it's really when we feel like it, whether that's every day or not. We show our good side. We share what's good. (I: 27, single)

Post-moralist sex (Lipovetsky, 1992) must be defined functionally, erotically and psychologically. It is not to be watched, repressed or sublimated. It acts without constraints or taboos on the one condition that it does not harm anyone. In the process of disassociating sex and morality Eros cut all ties that bound him with vice, and he acquired an intrinsically moral value owing to its importance in the equilibrium and the personal blossoming of individuals. Liberation from sexual norms does not mean the law of the jungle; the erasure of the culture of duty does not bring with it an orgiastic turn. But the non-residential couple corresponds in a certain way with a social regulation of pleasures outside of licentiousness. The obligation of returning home is gone. No more having to justify being late. Power of conformist, nonetheless? One might think so since the majority of couples interviewed claim to be moved by projects, but essentially pleasurable projects they have together. Fidelity is still expected on both sides, and if one does not return home, and does not wear a ring, the cult of the free couple loses its power of attraction. Of course, not all non-residential couples follow the same pattern; some will eventually live together, and for them it is only a temporary phase; others have already been through one marriage and do not want any more; and some see it as a lifestyle, preserving intimacy because it preserves secrecy.

This new post-moralist culture diminishes duty to oneself and to others and reinforces the requirement of individual liberty and pursuit of perfection. We are far from a drift towards hyperpermissiveness. Post-moralist-individualism produces rules that structure sexual relations and social relations, but the new chastity or virtue is anchored in love and no longer in duty. Love, here, is experienced more in semantics (Luhmann, 1990), a rhetoric of excess produced by the romantic novel. Passion, as a concept, practically excludes the duty of reporting any activity that might result from it. Often invoked in non-residential couples, passion becomes freedom of action requiring no justification, neither of itself, nor of its consequences.

Conclusion

In light of the elements of change to the forms of conjugal life detailed here, we must conclude by trying to reintegrate these conjugal lifestyles into a systematic theory. Intimate relations are social relations from which the parties involved expect to have their needs fully and entirely met. Intimate relations, however they may be experienced, stem from personal expectations and these expectations weigh on the global sense of social cohesion.

Acting out of love does not only imply that we seek to please, nor that we fulfil our own desires. What counts is finding meaning in another person's world. Since nobody's world is devoid of problems, its meaning is not either. The loving world, whether it be experienced under one roof or not, is a world of interpenetrations (Luhmann, 1990). Each partner may try to hide there. It is also in terms of interpenetrations that we must conceive what occurs when the 'lovers' concede to one another their respective worlds and refuse to make it a totality. The universality that the reference signifying love implies does not need to embrace the totality of the existence of the loved one. Only someone who is still filled with the romanesque and romantic notion of love is surprised by the idea of two people who love one another lend no importance to shared activities or to a single shared living space. The way we feel about love today is perhaps more mature than that which sociological discourse tells us about it.

References

Lipovetsky, G. (1992) *Le crépuscule du devoir*, Paris, Gallimard.
Luhmann, N. (1990) *L'Amour comme passion*, Paris, Authier.
Villeneuve-Gokalp, C. (1997) 'Vivre en couple chacun chez soi', in *Population*, INED, No. 5, Paris, pp. 1059–1082.
Singly, F. de (1996) *Le soi, le couple et la famille*, Paris, Nathen.

[9]

Cultures of Intimacy and Care Beyond 'the Family': Personal Life and Social Change in the Early 21st Century

Sasha Roseneil and Shelley Budgeon

In an era of powerful processes of individualization, issues of intimacy and care have assumed a renewed importance for sociologists. The question of how people organize their personal lives, loving and caring for each other in contexts of social, cultural and economic change which increasingly demand the pursuit of individual life strategies is central to the sociological agenda of the 21st century. In this article we argue that if we are to understand the current state, and likely future, of intimacy and care, sociologists should decentre the 'family' and the heterosexual couple in our intellectual imaginaries. We recognize that the idea of 'family' retains an almost unparalleled ability to move people, both emotionally and politically. However, much that matters to people in terms of intimacy and care increasingly takes place beyond the 'family', between partners who are not living together 'as family', and within networks of friends.[1]

The first section of the article provides a critique of family sociology and the sociology of gender for the heteronormative frameworks within which they operate. It proposes an extension of the framework within which contemporary transformations in the realm of intimacy may be analysed, and suggests that there is a need for research focusing on the cultures of intimacy and care inhabited by those living at the cutting edge of social change. In the second part of the article we draw upon our own research on the most 'individualized' sector of the population – adults who are not living with a partner. We explore contemporary cultures of intimacy and care among this group through a number of case studies, and argue that two interrelated processes characterize these cultures: centring on friendship, and decentring sexual relationships.

Thinking Beyond the Heteronormative Family

As the global distribution and mainstream success of a plethora of television series such as *Friends*, *Seinfeld*, *Ellen* and *Will and Grace* attests, popular culture is proving rather better than sociology at proffering stories which explore the burgeoning diversity of contemporary practices of intimacy and care. If we were to seek our understanding of cultures of intimacy and care solely from the sociological literature, we would be told that they are still almost solely practised under the auspices of 'family'.

There *have* been significant shifts within specific subfields of the sociologies of family and gender. For example, they have sought to meet both the empirical challenge of social changes in family and gender relations, and the theoretical challenge of anti-essentialist, postmodern, black and minority ethnic feminist, and lesbian and gay emphases on difference and diversity. They have, most notably, moved on from an early focus on the study of 'family and community',[2] which were 'yoked together like Siamese twins' (Morgan, 1996: 4), through the early phase of feminist intervention, which focused on unequal gender divisions of care and intimacy in the family,[3] to a predominant concern today with the analysis of family change – particularly through the study of divorce, repartnering and cohabitation – and recognition of family diversity.[4]

Moreover, many British and US family sociologists have engaged with the problem of the concept of 'family' in a time of increasing levels of family breakdown and re-formation. David Morgan (1996), for instance, suggests that we should use 'family' not as a noun, but as an adjective, and proposes a notion of 'family practices' to counter the reification of the concept. Others have sought to deal with social change and the challenges posed by lesbian and gay movements and theorists by pluralizing the notion of 'family', so that they now always speak of 'families'. The approach currently dominant in Anglo-American sociologies of gender and family emphasizes the diversity of family forms and experiences, and how the membership of families changes over time, as they break down and reform. Certainly, in its more liberal-minded incarnations, this approach welcomes lesbian and gay 'families of choice' into the 'family tent' (Stacey, 2002).

This shift has been an important one. It acts as a counter to the explicitly anti-gay and anti-feminist political discourse of 'family values', which developed in the US and UK during the 1980s and 1990s.[5] However, these moves to pluralize notions of 'family', even when they embrace the study of lesbian and gay families, are insufficient to the task of understanding the contemporary and likely future experience of intimacy and care, for two reasons. First, they leave unchanged the heteronormativity of the sociological imaginary; and second, they are grounded in an inadequate analysis of contemporary social change.

Lauren Berlant and Michael Warner have recently argued that heteronormative public culture in the US constructs belonging to society through the 'love plot of intimacy and familialism', restricting 'a historical relation to futurity . . . to generational narrative and reproduction' (Berlant and Warner, 2000: 318). Their argument is a powerful one. However, it is not just US public culture that finds it hard to see those who are not heteronormatively coupled as centrally part of the social formation, and to think of the future outside a generational mindset. Sociology continues to marginalize the study of love, intimacy, care and sociality beyond the 'family', even though it has expanded the scope covered by this term to include a wider range of 'families of choice'.[6]

The sociologies of family and gender, in which the study of intimacy and care is largely conducted, are undergirded by heteronormative assumptions; in other words by 'institutions, structures of understanding, and practical orientations that make heterosexuality seem not only coherent – that is, organized as a sexuality – but also privileged' (Berlant and Warner, 2000: 312). In other words, sociologists in these fields continue to produce analyses which are overwhelmingly focused on monogamous, dyadic, co-residential (and primarily hetero) sexual relationships, particularly those which have produced children, and on changes within these relationships. Jo van Every's (1999) systematic survey of British sociological research and writing on families and households published in 1993 found 'an overwhelming focus on the "modern nuclear family" ' consisting of married couples who lived together in households only with their children. She argues convincingly that 'despite all the sociological talk about the difficulty of defining families and the plurality and diversity of family forms in contemporary (postmodern?) societies, sociologists were helping to construct a "normal" family which looked remarkably similar to that which an earlier generation of sociologists felt confident to define' (van Every, 1999: 167).

The 'non-standard intimacies' (Berlant and Warner, 2000) created by those living non-normative sexualities pose a particular challenge to a discipline which has studied intimacy and care primarily through the study of families. Some lesbians and gay men refer to their emotional networks quite consciously – often with a knowing irony – as 'family'.[7] However, when writers such as Kath Weston (1991), Jeffrey Weeks et al. (2001) and Judith Stacey (this issue, pp. 181–97) adopt the term 'families of choice' to refer to lesbian and gay relationships and friendship networks, this may actually direct attention away from the extra-familial, radically counter-heteronormative nature of many of these relationships.

Considerable evidence from sociological and anthropological research suggests that friendship, as both a practice and an ethic, is particularly important in the lives of lesbians and gay men.[8] Networks of friends, which often include ex-lovers, form the context within which lesbians and gay men lead their personal lives, offering emotional continuity, companionship, pleasure and practical assistance. Sometimes rejected, problematized and marginalized by their families of origin, lesbians and gay men build and maintain lives outside the framework of the heterosexual nuclear family, grounding their emotional security and daily lives in their friendship groups. Weeks et al. (2001) and Roseneil (2000a) draw attention to the blurring of the boundaries, and movement between, friendship and sexual relationships which often characterizes contemporary lesbian and gay intimacies. Friends become lovers, lovers become friends, and many have multiple sexual partners of varying degrees of commitment (and none). Moreover, an individual's 'significant other' may not be someone with whom she or he has a sexual relationship:

> It has finally come into our vocabulary that Tom is my significant other. After eight years, we have finally acknowledged what to others has probably been self-apparent all along.
>
> Tom cares for me virtually every day, and when he cannot be with me himself, he arranges for others to help. He buys my groceries and keeps his Tupperwared lunches in my refrigerator. He knows which underwear I want to put on any given morning, and which drawer he'll find it in.
>
> Tom's significance is more than logistical. He is my medical and legal power of attorney, the who if and when it comes time, will decide what measures should be taken to let me live or die. He will plan my funeral. He is the sole beneficiary of my will.
>
> Although he has spent many nights in my apartment, we have never had sex. . . . But to call us merely best friends denies the depth of who we are to each other. (Preston with Lowenthal, 1996: 1)

Practices such as these within non-normative intimacies – between friends, non-monogamous lovers, ex-lovers, partners who do not live together, partners who do not have sex together, those which do not easily fit the 'friend'/ 'lover' binary classification system – and the networks of relationships within which these intimacies are sustained (or not) have the following significance: they decentre the primary significance that is commonly granted to sexual partnerships and mount a challenge to the privileging of conjugal relationships in research on intimacy. These practices, relationships and networks largely fail to be registered in a sociological literature which retains an imaginary which, without ever explicitly acknowledging it, sees the heterosexual couple as the heart of the social formation, as that which pumps the life-blood of social reproduction.

In fact, little has changed since Beth Hess pointed out in 1979 that there is 'no large corpus called the "sociology of friendship" '[9] to provide an alternative archive for the study of intimacy and care beyond the family. But it is not just the heteronormativity of the discipline which has rendered friendship largely invisible. Equally important is the fact that the sociological tradition, from the founding fathers onwards – Tönnies' distinction between

Gemeinschaft and *Gesellschaft*, Marx's work on alienation, Durkheim on forms of social solidarity, Weber on bureaucratization, the Chicago School on urbanization – has assumed that the development of modernity renders social relationships increasingly impersonal, and affective bonding is seen as increasingly marginal.[10] The result is that the discipline has never granted as much importance to the study of informal, private and sociable relationships as it has to matters of public, economic and political organization.[11]

Friendship lies in the realm of the pleasurable, emotional and affective, areas which have been relatively neglected by serious-minded order-seeking sociologists concerned with issues of structure, regulation and institutionalization. There have been exceptions, as in the work of Simmel (1950), in the ethnographic work of Whyte (1943) on 'street corner society', of Litwak and Szelenyi (1969) on 'primary groups' of kin and friends, and in the 1950s and 1960s, in the British tradition of community studies. More recently, there have been a small number of studies of friendship,[12] and there is a growing field of research on new forms of sociability facilitated by new technologies,[13] but there is no subfield of the discipline devoted to the study of friendship comparable to the well-established sociology of family and kinship. It is time for this to change, time for more research which focuses on friendship, 'non-conventional' forms of sexual/love relationships, and the interconnections between the two.

Personal Life and Social Change – Expanding our Understanding of the Transformation of Intimacy

A substantial body of literature takes as its starting point the belief that we are living through a period of intense and profound social change in the sphere of intimacy. For example, in the context of a wider argument about the undoing of patriarchalism, Manuel Castells (1997) suggests that the patriarchal family is under intense challenge, and that lesbian, gay and feminist movements around the world are key to understanding this challenge.[14] Anthony Giddens's (1992) argument about the 'transformation of intimacy' and Ulrich Beck and Elisabeth Beck-Gernsheim's (1995, 2002) work on the changing meanings and practices of love and family relationships suggest that in the contemporary world processes of individualization and detraditionalization and increased self-reflexivity are opening up new possibilities and expectations in heterosexual relationships.[15]

With a (rather cursory) nod in the direction of feminist scholarship and activism, such work recognizes the significance of the shifts in gender relations mainly due to the changed consciousness and identities which women have developed in the wake of the women's liberation movement. Giddens considers that the transformation of intimacy currently in train is of 'great, and generalizable, importance' (Giddens, 1992: 2). He charts changes in the nature of marriage such as the emergence of the 'pure relationship' characterized by 'confluent love', a relationship of sexual and emotional equality between men and women. He links this with the development of 'plastic sexuality' freed from 'the needs of reproduction' (Giddens, 1992: 2). He identifies lesbians and gay men as 'pioneers' in the pure relationship and plastic sexuality, and hence at the forefront of processes of individualization and detraditionalization.[16] Beck and Beck-Gernsheim (2002: 22) argue that 'the ethic of individual self-fulfilment and achievement is the most powerful current in modern society'. They believe the desire to be 'a deciding, shaping human being who aspires to be the author of his/her life' is giving rise to unprecedented changes in the shape of family life. Family membership shifts from being a given, to a matter of choice. As social ties become reflexive, and individualization increasingly characterizes relations among members of the same family, we are moving into a world of the 'post-familial family' (Beck-Gernsheim, 1999).

While this body of work perhaps overstates the degree of change, and underplays the continuance of gender inequalities and class differences in intimate life (e.g. Jamieson, 1998), it maps the theoretical terrain from which investigations of the future of intimacy and care must proceed, and has proved extremely influential on those conducting empirical research on family change. However, that literature does not exhaust the resources for theoretical analysis of contemporary social change on which those seeking to understand cultures of intimacy and care should draw. Following Roseneil (2000b), we propose an extension of this analysis to consider how the wider sexual organization of the social is undergoing transformation. Roseneil (2000b) argues that we are currently witnessing a significant destabilization of the homosexual/heterosexual binary which has characterized the modern sexual order. She suggests that there are a number of 'queer tendencies'[17] at work in the contemporary world, which are contributing to this fracturing of the binary. For example, there a trend towards the 'normalization' of the homosexual (Bech, 1999) in most western nations, as there are progressive moves towards the equalization of legal and social conditions for lesbians and gay men.[18] Most significantly for our argument, there is a tendency towards the decentring of heterorelations, both socially and at the level of the individual.

The heterosexual couple, and particularly the married, co-resident heterosexual couple with children, no longer occupies the centre-ground of western societies, and cannot be taken for granted as the basic unit in society. This is a result of the dramatic rise in divorce rates over the past 30 years, the increase in the number of births outside marriage (and to a lesser extent outside any lasting heterosexual relationship – births to mothers who are 'single by choice'), the rise in the proportion of children being brought up by a lone parent, the growing proportion of households that are composed of one person, and the increasing proportion of women who are not having children. Individuals are being released from traditional heterosexual scripts and the patterns of heterorelationality which accompany them. By 2000, only 23 percent of all households in the UK comprised a married couple with dependent children (National Statistics, 2001), and broadly similar patterns are observable across Europe, North America and Australia.[19]

Postmodern living arrangements are diverse, fluid and unresolved, constantly chosen and rechosen, and heterorelations are no longer as hegemonic as once they were. We are experiencing the 'queering of the family' (Stacey, 1996), as meanings of family undergo radical challenge, and more and more kinship groups have to come to terms with the diverse sexual practices and living arrangements chosen by their own family members. At the start of the 21st century there can be few families which do not include at least some members who diverge from traditional, normative heterorelational practice, whether as divorcees, unmarried mothers and fathers, lesbians, gay men or bisexuals. At the level of individual experience, as heterorelations are decentred, friendship networks become more important in people's everyday lives, and the degree of significance and emotional investment placed in romantic coupling comes to be re-evaluated.

This queering of the social calls into question the normativity and naturalness of both heterosexuality and heterorelationality.[20] It increasingly means that ways of life that might previously have been regarded as distinctively 'homosexual' are becoming more widespread.[21] Giddens's rather throw-away remark that lesbians and gay men are forging new paths for heterosexuals as well as for themselves is picked up by Jeffrey Weeks, Brian Heaphy and Catherine Donovan, who suggest that 'one of the most remarkable features of domestic change over recent years is . . . the emergence of common patterns in both homosexual and heterosexual ways of life as a result of these long-term shifts in relationship patterns' (Weeks et al., 1999: 85). They see both homosexuals and heterosexuals increasingly yearning for a 'pure relationship', experiencing love as contingent, and confluent, and seeking to live their sexual relationships in terms of a friendship ethic (Weeks et al., 2001).

Alongside the need for more research exploring the impact of individualization and reflexive modernization on people's intimate lives, there is a need for empirical investigation of the extent to which the destabilization of the homosexual/heterosexual binary, as posited by Weeks, Heaphy and Donovan and by Roseneil, is taking place. Our research therefore sets out to explore both the individualization thesis and the queering of the social thesis, by examining the extent to which, across the spectrum of sexualities, there might be:

- A decentring of sexual/love relationships within individuals' life narratives;
- An increased importance placed on friendship in people's affective lives;
- A diversification in the forms of sexual/love relationships, and the more widespread embracing of forms, such as those discussed earlier, which are less conventionally heteronormative, and more commonly associated with lesbians and gay men.

Methodology and Sample

We carried out in-depth narrative interviews, lasting between one-and-a-half and two-and-a-half hours, with 53 people aged between 25 and 60, living in three localities in Yorkshire, UK. These localities were chosen as being representative of differing gender and family cultures, drawing on Simon Duncan and Darren Smith's (2002) work on the geography of family formations in Britain, which mapped spatial differences of gender and family cultures according to four indices – a Motherhood Employment Effect, a Family Conventionality Effect, a Traditional Household Index and a Family Restructuring Index.[22] Our localities compare:

1 A deindustrialized ex-mining town which is more conventional in terms of gender and family relations and traditional in terms of household form;
2 A small town in which alternative middle-class, 'down-shifted' lifestyles and sexual non-conformity are common; and
3 A multiethnic, inner-city area, characterized by a diversity of gender and family practices, a higher than average proportion of women in the labour force, and a large number of single-person and non-couple households.

Beyond this, the sample was drawn purposively to include (as far as was possible within the localities selected) diversity of age, gender, sexuality, relationship status, living arrangements and 'race' (see Table 1).

Because we wanted to explore the impact of individualization on intimacy and care, we decided to interview people who did not live with a partner, on the basis that cohabitation – resulting from the decision to share a home with a partner – tends to mark the most significant moment when individuals become 'couples', and is more significant than marriage, for instance. In attending to the narratives of individuals we wanted:

- To gain an understanding of how and to what extent people are living in non-conventional cultures of intimacy;
- To study the practices of intimacy and care in which they are engaged; and
- To understand the values that underpin these practices.

Table 1 Description of Sample Characteristics ($N = 53$)

Locality	*Gender*	*Sexuality*	*Age*	*Race*	*Relationship status*	*Living arrangements*
Inner city $n = 32$	Women $n = 30$	Hetero $n = 38$	25–34 $n = 19$	White $n = 48$	Single $n = 34$	Lone $n = 32$
Deindustrialized town $n = 11$	Men $n = 23$	Homo $n = 15$	35–44 $n = 22$	African Caribbean $n = 5$	Relationship $n = 19$	Shared $n = 21$
'Alternative' small town $n = 10$			45–55 $n = 12$			

Our aim was to give the people we interviewed the opportunity to tell us what was important to them, and to allow, as much as possible, their own ways of valuing their relationships to emerge. Influenced by Wendy Hollway and Tony Jefferson's (2000) work on the free association narrative interview method, we did this through the use of very broad questions which allow interviewees time and space to construct their own stories, within which meaning and values gradually unfold.

Our questions allowed people to talk in a broad context about their lives, and were phrased thus: 'Can you tell me about the people who are most important in your life?', 'Can you tell me about a time when you have cared for/ been cared for by a friend?', 'Can you tell me what it's like to be single?' and so on. We relied upon the fundamental premise of the narrative method, which is that people make sense of their lives and communicate this understanding through telling stories about things that are important to them.

Case Studies of Intimacy and Care Beyond 'the Family'

We now consider four case studies from among our interviewees. Their narratives are distinctly situated within the specificity of their individual biographies, but they also illustrate some of the highly reflexive and non-conventional cultures of intimacy and care which our research found.[23] Following Jennifer Platt (1988: 9), and for the purposes of the argument in this article, the value in studying these cases is that each 'case may show the effects of a social context which is the object of interest': in this instance, how intimacy and care are practised beyond 'the family'. Each individual's story is interesting in its uniqueness, but these stories are not exceptional; they speak of patterns of transformation in personal life that we found more generally across our sample. Our data consist of narratives that vary in content and form as well as by age, life course, gender, locality and so forth. However, the pattern that exists within or behind their diversity is made visible in discussing these cases. In particular, they tell us what care and intimacy mean in terms of practices and ways of everyday life in a context where processes of individualization have affected how people construct their personal lives.

The Individuals

Karen is 35, heterosexual, single and has two daughters aged seven and 13. She works in the film industry as a hair and make-up artist. Three years ago her 13-year long cohabiting relationship with the father of her children broke down when he had an affair. Since then her life has undergone a significant reorientation and transformation.

Polly, one of Karen's closest friends, is 36 years old, heterosexual, single and currently running her own business with a friend in arts administration. Three years ago, Polly, who was not in a long-term relationship, decided that she wanted to have a child, and that she did not want to do this within the context of a conventional heterosexual relationship. Due to fertility problems and ineligibility for IVF treatment as a single woman, she decided to adopt a child, and was matched with Alice, a seven-year-old girl of mixed-race parentage. Polly and Alice have been together for two years.

At the time of their interviews, the decision that Karen and Polly had made 18 months earlier to buy a derelict house, do it up and raise their daughters together in the house was central to their narratives. Karen explained that they decided this at a time when both of them had hit 'rock bottom'. Karen had just split up with her long term-partner and for Polly the process of adopting her daughter was becoming complicated, uncertain and stressful. They had been close friends for many years and had relied upon each other through many times of difficulty, but out of this particular set of circumstances came the idea to rely upon each other in a more concrete sense – that is to pool their (rather limited) resources and create a home for themselves and their children. Although Karen's and Polly's lives had been very different before this time, with Karen settled in a long-term relationship from her early twenties, and Polly living a nomadic life working in the theatre, at this particular juncture their needs and goals were coalescing in important ways.

Dale is 49, a heterosexual man who describes himself as 'single' although he has a lover whom he has been with for two-and-a-half years. He is now living in her flat, but they are clear that they do not live together, as she is working and has been living in another part of the country for at least a year. Dale works part-time as a teacher and also runs his own business as a mechanic. He has never been married but has previously been in two long-term relationships and has three children with these two women. He maintains close contact with these ex-partners as well as several of his other ex-lovers. These partners constitute, along with his friends, his sister, who is a lesbian, her partner and ex-partner, his children and several neighbours, what he calls his 'kinship network'. Dale was articulate about his emotions and relationships and thoughtful and reflexive about his friendships.

Eleanor is a 48-year-old single lesbian who lives with a friend who used to be her brother's partner. At the time of the interview, Eleanor was just coming out of what had been a very difficult period of her life. Over the past six years she had experienced the death of her brother, the death of her father, the ongoing illness of her mother and her own diagnosis of and treatment for cancer. She explained how having cancer, from which she has recovered, marked a turning point in her life. Where once her priorities were 'job, partner, house, settling down', they are now about living life less conventionally, travelling more and seeking out new experiences. Eleanor is not currently in paid employment but volunteers for a local charity.

The biographies narrated by these four individuals speak of significant transformations in cultures of intimacy and care. Each of the interviewees is consciously and reflexively engaged in an individual 'life project', and was explicit about seeking to create a particular set of conditions and a particular way of life for themselves which would meet their particular needs for connection with others.[24] Key to understanding their life projects are the interrelated processes of *centring on friendship* and *decentring sexual relationships*. A strong emphasis on the value of friendship, and on choosing to surround themselves with a network of friends, went hand-in-hand with a deliberate de-emphasizing of the importance of conjugal relationships.

Centring on Friendship

Across a range of lifestyles and sexualities, we found that friendship occupied a central place in the personal lives of our interviewees. There was a high degree of reliance on friends, as opposed to biological kin and sexual partners, particularly for the provision of care and support in everyday life, to the extent that it could be said that friendship operated as an ethical practice for many.

Giving and Receiving Care and Support

Karen and Polly each have a wide network of geographically dispersed friends who figure centrally in their narratives, but they are also embedded locally in a network of friendships held together by a conscious mutual commitment to provide support and care. Many of these friends have chosen to live in the same area of this northern inner city in order to be close to one another. Karen and Polly's three daughters are close to these friends, and Karen says these friends provide another 'anchor' for her children. Prior to the break-up of Karen's relationship, she had been living several hours away from Polly and this circle, but after the break-up she returned to this city because of her friendships there.

Seeing Karen in a bad emotional state, this group of friends gathered together and physically moved her and her children back to the city, actively putting in place the things she would need upon her return. Contacts in the film industry found her a job, a house was rented and decorated for her and a school was found for the children. Similarly, Jenny, a good friend of Polly's who was living a considerable distance away, had also been having a difficult time recently, and so Polly took it upon herself to oversee the purchase and renovation of a house on the street where she and Karen live for Jenny to move to with her children. It is Polly's 'project' to bring the people in her network closer to her when she sees them struggling in their lives. As she reported saying to the people who have moved to be near: 'you're too far away from me but I can bring you here and I know that your lives are gonna improve because I can introduce you to these people, and they're fabulous'.

One of the strongest motivations behind Polly and Karen's decision to buy the house together was to provide a safe and stable environment for the children, in which, as two single parents, they could help each other with childcare. As close friends they felt that they could give each other a commitment and provide support to each other and their children in a way that would be significantly more secure than if they attempted to pursue this in the context of a love relationship with a man. In effect they co-parent the children, and share the management of the household. For example, when Karen had to go away for three months to work on a film in Africa Polly took over running the house and caring for the children. The stability that this situation affords them is also bolstered by the wider context of the friendship network within which they are living. They are reworking the notion of 'stability' often associated with conventional family forms by refusing to invest in a sexual relationship as the basis for security, and replacing this with a reliance upon friendships.

In Dale's narrative, the significance of friendships in providing care and support also emerged as a key theme. When he was in his early twenties, he had an extremely serious motor bike accident and was hospitalized for the better part of two years. Many of the friends he has today were instrumental in providing care and support to him during this time and in the period following this release from hospital. This care extended to his mother, who, while Dale was hospitalized, required assistance in moving house. One of Dale's closest friends took it upon himself to look after her move.

> John, he's a very interesting man. He doesn't make friends easily but he's extremely loyal with the friends he does have. He's been an enormous support to me during harder times in my life. For instance, when I smashed myself up and I was in hospital, my mother decided that she was moving out of the family home that we'd shared, that I'd been brought up in and moving to somewhere smaller quite a distance away and you know, John virtually took it upon himself to just . . . You know, I was in bloody traction in Cambridge. He got a van, went down, helped my mother move her stuff, moved my stuff back up to Yorkshire for me, picked my wrecked bike up in Cambridge and took that back up to Yorkshire, generally looked after my interest. He also – two days after I got out of hospital in Cambridge – rolled up on a motor bike at the flat where I was staying and virtually dragged me physically down the stairs, sat me on the back of this bike and drove me very fast for an hour or two just to get this out of my system, 'there's nothing to be scared of', for which I thank him very much.

Care is central to Eleanor's narrative: the giving and receiving of care is interwoven throughout the dynamics of her intricate set of personal relationships. Her story is both about the care she has extended to others and the care she herself has received. A couple of years prior to the interview Eleanor was diagnosed with cancer. Existing networks of personal relationships often tend to operate in a 'heightened' mode during times of crisis. In Eleanor's case, this meant that friends provided for a range of needs. They went to the hospital with her when she had to undergo numerous tests. They read to her while she was having scans done. At one point, Eleanor explains how frightened she was and how one of her friends helped her prepare a list of questions to ask a specialist so that she might gain some control over the situation. This friend then accompanied her on this visit. To care for Eleanor at home during her illness a sleep-over rota and cooking rota were set up to share collectively in the needed provision of care.

Friendship as an ethic is apparent here. In Eleanor's narrative, there emerges a sense of obligation to give what is needed on the basis of friendship. Eleanor is living with a friend whom she considers to be family. Ian was the partner of Eleanor's brother, who died several years ago. It was during Ian's relationship with her brother and particularly throughout the time that Ian cared for Eleanor's brother during his illness that he and Eleanor became close friends. After his death, Ian's life spiralled out of control through addiction to drugs. Eleanor spoke of how one day Ian rang up and asked her to come and get him. Eleanor says she never thought twice about it. She brought him to her home to stay, he enrolled in a drug treatment project and at the time of the interview he had been off drugs for a year.

> His whole life was going down the pan and every time I went to London I'd try and go visit him and kept seeing him getting worse and worse and worse, and it was just like this unfinished thing that I had to somehow help him out with really. And I kept saying to him 'you know you have to leave this flat', and I was glad that he actually thought, 'well I will go to Eleanor' because he's got family. But he came here, and I suppose it was not long after my cancer stuff as well.

In Eleanor's narrative, the relationship between care and living space emerges as a focal theme. Friendship, and the practices of care and support which are central to its meaning to her, occur within a 'private' space of the home, which is not preserved for the conventional family.

Reconfiguring Domestic Space

For Karen and Polly, Eleanor and Dale the *where* of practices of intimacy and care was a matter of considerable importance. Without explicit prompting, each of them chose to talk in considerable detail about issues of domestic space, and how they were choosing to open up this space to others who are not part of their conventionally defined 'family'. Their narratives reveal that the physical space within which their life projects were designed and lived out is very significant.

As we have already seen, the decision to live with, or close to, others is often related to immediate practical concerns about the provision and receipt of care. For Dale, thinking about reconfiguring domestic space was more of an idealistic, future-orientated project, driven by an understanding that those living individualized lives outside conventional relationships need to look to each other for support. He explained how he and his circle of close friends, his 'kinship group', were beginning to formulate a communal retirement plan which would involve buying some land together and custom-building houses that would address their various needs. As he has been involved in housing cooperatives in the past, he is beginning to research the possibilities of pursuing such a project.

> I know a fairly large kind of kinship group around here who are all people who don't have partners, or don't wish to have partners, who are engaged in some kind of very individualistic 'this is how I make my way in the world . . .', and it is a constant source of discussion about how do we look to each other. We're currently still reasonably young and healthy, and there are various ideas being floated about and various sort of lifestyles being practised towards reaching that which I feel a great sense of affinity for – it's a kind of, it's a tribalist model, I suppose. And this guy Harry is an architect. He is pushing quite hard to kind of get groups set up to actually look at housing provision for people in that situation. A lot of single parents whose children have now left home who've got houses that are too big for them – where would they want to move to next? And so it's quite a currency of discussion amongst this group of people about putting some kind of co-housing project together, actually purpose-building housing that's kind of an estate of the like-minded, buying the land, custom-building the houses, probably with a very kind of heavy eco slant on it, communal areas, collectively held areas of property where friends and relations can come and stay, but your own living space because that's what you're accustomed to, a door you can shut. This isn't just like a room, and work space within that, because they're all people who are kind of quite active or quite creative. Garden space, you get a lot of people who are into that sort of stuff. We say watch this space.

In the here and now, Karen and Polly's decision to share a home was about meeting their need for mutual support in raising their children, but it also involved opening up their domestic space to others. They each separately talked about the constant flow of people through their house and they jokingly referred to it as 'The Hilton' because they have 'hundreds of people coming to stay all the time'. The choice to live with Polly was, for Karen, also about deciding to live in a particular place – being part of a neighbourhood that is ethnically and culturally diverse. Karen wants stability for her children but she also wants to expose them to a wide range of different ways of living so they will grow up with an awareness of the wider world. She implicitly wants them to see that there are many ways to live one's life and so part of her project is the self-conscious undermining of what she referred to as taken-for-granted 'white, middle-class' values, which she does through choosing to live in an inner-city area rich in diversity.

The flow of different people through domestic space was also a theme of Eleanor's narrative. When Eleanor spoke about her network of friends and ex-lovers, it became apparent that she had lived with most of her friends at one time or another. She has opened her home to a range of different people when they have needed a place to stay; for example, one friend came to her after her relationship had ended, another while he was going through a bereavement following the death of his father. However, it was not only at times of heightened need that Eleanor welcomed others into her home. Like Karen and Polly's house, her house was a central place for her friends to meet and spend time together. All three tended to have 'an open door' policy, and the space of their homes was collectively inhabited.

> My normal style is to entertain and I always have parties and barbies and murder mysteries and things like that which I really enjoy and I get loads out of. And this place is, you know, I've had parties in the garden, and everyone considers it as their garden.

The flow of friends through spaces traditionally occupied by conjugal couples and nuclear families points to one of the ways in which the individualized lives of those living without co-resident partners destabilize heteronormativity. In many of the narratives relayed by our interviewees, there was a refusal to organize their daily lives around a distinction that divided physical space along the lines of family/friend dichotomy. This is not just indicative of a blurring of the category of 'friend' and 'family' often cited in the 'families of choice' literature, but a blurring of the boundaries, and the transformation of the meaning of physical space as well. Space normatively constructed as 'private' and heterosexual is reconfigured as collective.

Decentring Sexual Relationships

Each of the four interviewees told a story of choosing to emphasize friends over lovers, at this particular point in their lives, while also acknowledging that there had often been a considerable degree of fluidity and movement between the categories of friend and lover in their lives. Their clear prioritizing of friendship over and above sexual partnerships, however, also paradoxically served to re-establish the distinctiveness of these categories.

For Polly, the categories of lover and friend have often blurred, but it is only as friends that those who are also lovers become central to her life. In some cases, the sexual interaction continues to be an aspect of the friendship, but to her these relationships are primarily meaningful as friendships which provide an ongoing source of support. Indeed, one of Polly's and Karen's closest friends, who has bought a house nearby, is an ex-lover of both of them.

Karen says that her relationship with Polly is rather like being married, and that it has become a different kind of relationship for them since making the commitment to buy the house together. Recognizing that it is neither a conventional friendship nor a conventional partnership, both women spoke about how their relationship causes confusion because it does not easily fit into a predefined category. In attempting to make sense of the situation people often assume that they are in a lesbian relationship, which triggers heteroreflexivity (Roseneil, 2000b) for both Karen and Polly, as they encounter the heteronormativity of the neighbours and social institutions, such as schools, with whom they come into contact. The house-sharing dyad of Karen and Polly, and the network of friends, lovers, ex-lovers and biological kin within which it is embedded, is an example of how a mode of living intimacy and care pioneered in the 'life experiments', or 'families of choice', of lesbians and gay men (Weeks et al., 2001; Weston, 1991) is being practised by two individuals who do not identify themselves as homosexual.

For Karen and Polly, the decision to decentre sexual relationships is first and foremost about providing security for their children.[25] Karen has not been in a committed relationship for the past three years, although she has been involved in a number of brief relationships during this time. She says she fears commitment and considering everything she already has in her life – the house, her children, her career and close friends – she doesn't need a man. Indeed, for Karen relationships have proven 'risky'. The end of her relationship with her daughters' father has had a profound effect on her life and her girls' lives. As a result of these experiences, Karen's life has been significantly reoriented and for the time being sexual relationships are not a priority. The risk of becoming a couple for Karen outweighs the benefits, and maintaining friendships and her children as priorities, she is happy to manage her involvement with men through short-term attachments, avoiding commitment in such a way as to limit their impact on her daily life.

> I was in a long relationship for 13 years. We've been separated for three years now so I've been on and off single. I've had a variety of boyfriends and it's been fantastic . . . I don't want to tie myself up totally to anybody, but last year I did have somebody who came into my life who was very special, but that was so terrifying . . . I said you know, it can wait, it doesn't have to happen now. This is more important here – my security for my girls. You know, I'd lived with someone for 13 years. I don't need to go diving back into anything like that, for a long time. So it's not a major part for me. . . . No, I'm really enjoying this moment and I enjoy finding somebody new that comes along for a short term but I don't involve them or try not to involve them too much with what's here.

Dale's decentring of sexual relationships is an established, conscious life choice. His personal history has long been unconventional; his two long-term committed relationships with the women with whom he had children also did not involve living together. Although he is in a relationship that has lasted two-and-a-half years and is currently living in this lover's flat, he has never lived *with* her and does not intend to. At the time of the interview, the two of them were living at a significant geographical distance. One of the reasons he would not relocate to be with his partner is because his 'main friendship network' is in the city where he lives, and he also admits that he is frightened that living together will 'knacker the relationship'. Dale's 'people', as he calls them, tend to remain in each other's lives as friends, despite the movement in and out of various roles and dynamics. One of his ex-partners, Marie, had a relationship with his closest friend, John, which didn't work out, but they are all still friends.

> John had an absolutely disastrous affair with Marie after we split up which I could have told him was going to be a disaster, and I did tell him was going to be a disaster, and sure enough it was, because they're both very, very – what's the word? – kind of acerbic people. They're very cutting edge people. But we survived all that and remained extremely good friends. So yeah, we've been through quite a bit of stuff together.

In Eleanor's narrative, the categories of lover and friend interchange constantly. It is striking the extent to which people move in and out of particular positions yet remain central to her. Friends become lovers, ex-lovers become friends, friends' ex-lovers become lovers, and so forth. For example, she explained how Judith, who is now one of her closest friends, was the partner of Eleanor's first girlfriend in Leeds. She explained that at the time, 'I stole [Judith's] girlfriend from her and then we all stuck together and lived together. The three of us.' When Eleanor's relationship with this woman ended, Judith then started seeing her again. This relationship, however, did not last, and Judith then moved back in with Eleanor. Eleanor's narrative illustrates the intricacies of intimate dynamics which are often in such a state of flux that the relevance and meaning of categories are constantly under negotiation.

Eleanor was also sceptical about the value of sexual partnerships. She complained about friends who had become 'joined at the hip', and expressed dissatisfaction with friends of hers who act too much like 'a couple' because they need to do everything together and ask permission to do things separately. A further problem she cited is that when people become involved in a relationship they tend to drop friends. Eleanor herself has been single for the past eight years. During this time one of her ex-partners has become a very significant friend to her and it is clearly friendship networks that are central to her life. Forecasting the future, Eleanor remarked:

> If you can manage to stay out of relationships you can have a great time with your friends. I like it when I hear about older people that aren't in relationships but are absolutely having a great time and I have this view of myself, I've had this since I was a kid, this idea of myself lying on a chaise longue at some point in the future and having this room full of interesting things all partying and talking and that's kind of how I've developed my life and my house, it's been a meeting place and an exchange and I love that.

Imagining Personal Lives Beyond 'the Family': An Agenda for Future Research

The case studies reported in this article offer a glimpse of the consciously constructed life projects which are emerging among those who are living and loving without a cohabiting partner. To sum up, we found that some of those leading the most individualized existences are choosing to centre their personal lives around friendship, and to decentre sexual partnerships, in ways which challenge the heterorelational social order. As part of this process,

- Care and support flow between individuals with no biological, legal or social recognized ties to each other;
- Domestic space is reconfigured, and its association with the conjugal couple and the nuclear family is challenged;
- Non-normative cultures of intimacy and care are brought into being, as lifestyles which were once a politicized strategy pursued by those within alternative and feminist communities in the 1970s and 1980s are extending to those who do not think of themselves as activists or radicals.

In discussing the twin themes of centring on friendships/decentring conjugal relationships and showing how these themes operate within practices of everyday life we have sought to highlight the significance of casting a different lens on the study of intimacy and care, a lens which focuses on those living at the cutting edge of social change. We have not been concerned with asking about the extent to which the narratives in our study are representative of the population as a whole, but rather we would like to point to the possibilities that that these cases present. Jennifer Platt's (1988: 11) defence of the use of case studies suggests that if these practices are possible in these cases, they may exist in other cases, and that they must be taken into account in the formulation of general propositions about intimate life. Thus, these case studies have implications for the research agenda of all sociologists interested in the organization of personal life at the start of the 21st century. In particular, they suggest that if the study of intimacy and care remains within the frame of 'the family' and the heterorelational then much of what matters to people in their personal lives will be missed.

In the context of individualization, increased reflexivity, detraditionalization and the destabilization of the homosexual/heterosexual binary, practices of intimacy and care can no longer – if indeed they ever could – be understood solely through a focus on families and kin. We believe that an exploration of *networks and flows of intimacy and care*, the extent and pattern of such networks, the viscosity and velocity of such flows, and the implications of their absence, is likely to prove much more fruitful for future research than attempts to interpret contemporary personal lives through redefinitions of the concept of 'family'.[26] Focusing the sociological gaze on intimacies and practices of care wherever they take place – in domestic spaces, public spaces, work spaces, virtual spaces – between friends, sexual partners, family, neighbours, work colleagues, civil acquaintances – will bring to light practices of intimacy and care, and ethical cultures associated with these practices, that have rarely been studied by sociologists of the family. A new sociology of affective life is needed which can register a fuller range of practices of intimacy and care.

Notes

The research on which this article is based was carried out as part of the Friendship and Non-Conventional Partnership Project under the auspices of the ESRC Research Group for the Study of Care, Values and the Future of Welfare (CAVA) (award M564281001) at the University of Leeds (www.leeds.ac.uk/cava). An earlier version of the article was presented at the World Congress of Sociology in Brisbane, July 2002. Many thanks to Lorne Tepperman, and colleagues in CAVA, particularly Simon Duncan.

1 It is probably the case that far more of people's affective lives has always taken place outside 'family' than has been recognized by sociologists.
2 See Young and Willmott (1957)and Frankenberg (1966).
3 See Graham (1987), Duncombe and Marsden (1993) and Finch (1989).
4 See Smart and Neale (1999), Stacey (1996) and Silva and Smart (1999).
5 See, for example, Roseneil and Mann (1996), Stacey (1996), Weeks (1995) and Jaggar and Wright (1999).
6 Ingraham (1996) argues that feminist sociology and the sociology of gender, and their studies of marriage, family and sexual violence, in particular, depend on a heterosexual imaginary, and argues for a shift from the study of gender to the study of heterogender.
7 See Weston (1991), Nardi (1992, 1999), Preston with Lowenthal (1996) and Weeks et al. (2001). Weeks et al. (2001) discuss the differences between their interviewees in relation to the adoption of the term 'family' to describe their intimate relationships, and acknowledge that many reject the term.
8 See, for example, Altman (1982), Weston (1991), Nardi (1992, 1999), Weeks (1995), Preston with Lowenthal (1996), Roseneil (2000a) and Weeks et al. (2001).
9 Quoted in Jerrome (1984: 699).
10 More recently, Sennett (1977) has argued that there has been a historic shift towards a 'culture of personality', in which impersonality and the public sphere are in decline. Misztal (2000) discusses the balance between formality and informality in the contemporary world.
11 This argument is made by one of the few sociologists to have made the study of friendship their central field of research interest, Graham Allan (see Allan, 1979; 1989; Adams and Allan, 1998).

12 See Booth and Hess (1974), Fischer et al. (1977), Fischer (1982a, 1982b), Allan (1979), Hess (1972, 1979), Jerrome (1984), O'Connor (1992), Hey (1997) and the contributors to Adams and Allan (1998), Nardi (1999) and Pahl (2000).
13 See, for example, Rheingold (1993), Shields (1996) and Wakeford (1998).
14 Castells (1997) also sees the rise of the global informational economy and the technological transformation of biology and reproduction as central explanatory forces in the undermining of the patriarchal family.
15 The research of Finch (1989) and Finch and Mason (1993) on family obligations suggests that family ties are now understood less in terms of obligations constituted by fixed ties of blood, and more in terms of negotiated commitments, which are less clearly differentiated from other relationships.
16 In this acknowledgement of non-heterosexual identities and practices, Giddens's work differs from that of Beck and Beck-Gernsheim, whose discussion fails to acknowledge its exclusive concern with heterosexuality.
17 The word 'tendency' is used deliberately to suggest the still provisional nature of these shifts, and with the existence of countervailing tendencies in mind. The use of the term is indebted to Sedgwick (1994).
18 Adam (2002). On US exceptionalism, see Adam (2003).
19 We acknowledge that the majority of births outside marriage are to cohabiting couples, and in general, we acknowledge the increase in the prevalence (Ermisch and Francesconi, 2000; Lewis, 2001) and the social acceptability of cohabitation among heterosexual couples (Barlow et al., 2001). This does not, however, diminish our argument about the significance of the social decentring of, first, the married heterosexual couple, and second, the heterosexual couple, per se.
20 Watney (1988) and Fuss (1991) made early suggestions that such a process was underway.
21 Bech (1997, 1999) makes a similar argument, but pushes it further arguing that in continental northwestern Europe, we are seeing 'the disappearance of the homosexual'.
22 For a detailed explanation of the construction of these indices, and their application to 1991 census data, see Duncan and Smith's (2002) paper. For a discussion of the selection of the localities which are studied by the CAVA Research Group, see Duncan (2000a, 2000b, 2000c).
23 Although this research is based upon 53 interviews, we have chosen to use a case study approach here so as to preserve the composite whole of the narratives which is central to the gestalt principle underlying narrative analysis (see Hollway and Jefferson, 2000). In this analysis it is our goal to 'approach the understanding of lives in context rather than through a prefigured and narrowing lens' (Josselson, 1995: 2).
24 Reflexivity is a key aspect of the narratives in our data. Those individuals who exhibited a greater reflexivity in their narratives were more likely to question taken-for-granted assumptions and normative expectations surrounding the organizations of their personal relationships. Not all the individuals in our sample did so however. For example, some individuals were arguably more embedded in cultures of intimacy where blood ties were privileged without question. This also tended to vary by locality thus supporting the logic underpinning the sampling

strategy – processes of individualization, family conventionality and gender cultures are not uniformly distributed but are spatialized.

25 This echoes Beck and Beck-Gernsheim's (1995) argument that as relationships are increasingly unstable, children become the primary love object in parents' lives.

26 See Urry (2000) for a powerful exposition of the value of metaphors of mobility and flow for the understanding of the contemporary social world.

Bibliography

ADAM, B. (2002) 'Families without Heterosexuality: Challenges of Same-sex Partnership Recognition', CAVA International Seminar Paper, at: www.leeds.ac.uk/cava/papers/interseminar3adam.htm

ADAM, B. (2003) 'The "Defence of Marriage Act" and American Exceptionalism', *Journal of the History of Sexuality*, 12(2): 259–76.

ADAMS, R. G. and ALLAN, G., eds (1998) *Placing Friendship in Context.* Cambridge: Cambridge University Press.

ALLAN, G. (1979) *A Sociology of Friendship and Kinship.* London: George Allen and Unwin.

ALLAN, G. (1989) *Friendship: Developing a Sociological Perspective.* Hemel Hempstead: Harvester Wheatsheaf.

ALLAN, G. (1998) 'Friendship, Sociology and Social Structure', *Journal of Social and Personal Relationships* 15(5): 685–702.

ALTMAN, D. (1982) *The Homosexualization of America.* New York: St Martin's Press.

BARLOW, A., DUNCAN, S., EVANS, G. and PARK, A. (2001) 'Just a Piece of Paper? Marriage and Cohabitation in Britain', in A. Park, J. Curtice, K. Thomson, L. Jarvis and C. Bromley (eds) *British Social Attitudes: The 18th Report.* London: Sage.

BECH, H. (1997) 'Real Deconstructions: The Disappearance of the Modern Homosexual and the Queer', paper presented at the 14th World Congress of Sociology, Montreal, 26 July–1 August.

BECH, H. (1999) 'After the Closet', *Sexualities* 2(3): 343–9.

BECK, U. and BECK-GERNSHEIM, E. (1995) *The Normal Chaos of Love.* Cambridge: Polity Press.

BECK, U. and BECK-GERNSHEIM, E. (2002) *Individualization.* London: Sage.

BECK, U., GIDDENS, A. and LASH, S. (1994) *Reflexive Modernization: Politics, Tradition and Aesthetics in the Modern Social Order.* Cambridge: Polity Press.

BECK-GERNSHEIM, E. (1998) 'On the Way to a Post-Familial Family: From a Community of Needs to Elective Affinities', *Theory, Culture and Society* 15(3–4): 53–70.

BERLANT, L. and WARNER, M. (2000) 'Sex in Public', in L. Berlant (ed.) *Intimacy.* Chicago, IL: Chicago University Press.

BOOTH, A. and HESS, E. (1974) 'Cross Sexual Friendships', *Journal of Marriage and the Family* 36: 38–47.

CASTELLS, M. (1997) *The Power of Identity.* Oxford: Blackwell.

DUNCAN, S. (2000a) 'The Use and Abuse of Locality Research', CAVA Workshop Paper No. 17a, at www.leeds.ac.uk/cava/papers/workshoppapers.htm

DUNCAN, S. (2000b) 'Choosing Case Study Areas for Strand 3 Research – Localities and Neighbourhoods', CAVA Workshop Paper No. 17b, at: www.leeds.ac.uk/cava/papers/workshoppapers.htm

DUNCAN, S. (2000c) 'Variations in Parenting and Partnering at the Local Level', CAVA Workshop Paper No. 17c, at: www.leeds.ac.uk/cava/papers/workshoppapers.htm

DUNCAN, S. and SMITH, D. (2002) 'Geographies of Family Formations: Spatial Differences and Gender Cultures in Britain', *Transactions* 27: 471–93.

DUNCOMBE, J. and MARSDEN, D. (1993) 'Love and Intimacy: The Gender Division of Emotion and Emotion Work', *Sociology* 27: 221–41.

ERMISCH, J. and FRANCESCONI, M. (2000) 'Cohabitation in Great Britain: Not for Long, But Here to Stay', *Journal of the Royal Statistical Society* Series A 163(2): 153–71.

FINCH, J. (1989) *Family Obligations and Social Change.* Cambridge: Polity Press.

FINCH, J. and MASON, J. (1993) *Negotiating Family Responsibilities.* London: Routledge.

FISCHER, C. (1982a) 'What Do We Mean by "Friend"?: An Inductive Study', *Social Networks* 3: 287–306.

FISCHER, C. (1982b) *To Dwell among Friends.* Berkeley: University of California Press.

FISCHER, C., JACKSON, R. M., STUEVE, C. A., GERSON, K., MCCALLISTER-JONES, L. with BALDASSARE, M. (1977) *Networks and Places.* New York: Free Press.

FRANKENBERG, R. (1966) *Communities in Britain: Social Life in Town and Country.* Harmondsworth: Penguin.

FUSS, D. (1991) *Inside/Out: Lesbian Theories, Gay Theories.* New York: Routledge.

GIDDENS, A. (1992) *The Transformation of Intimacy: Sexuality, Love and Eroticism in Modern Societies.* Cambridge: Polity Press.

GRAHAM, H. (1987) 'Women's Poverty and Caring', in C. Glendinning and J. Millar (eds) *Women and Poverty in Britain.* Brighton: Wheatsheaf.

HESS, B. (1972) 'Friendship', in M. W. Riley, M. Johnson and A. Foner (eds) *Aging and Society*, Vol. 3. New York: Russell Sage Foundation.

HESS, B. (1979) 'Sex Roles, Friendship and the Life Course', *Research on Ageing* 1: 494–515.

HEY, V. (1997) *The Company She Keeps: An Ethnography of Girls' Friendships.* Buckingham: Open University Press.

HOLLWAY, W. and JEFFERSON, T. (2000) *Doing Qualitative Research Differently.* London: Sage.

INGRAHAM, C. (1996) 'The Heterosexual Imaginary: Feminist Sociology and Theories of Gender', in S. Seidman (ed.) *Queer Theory/Sociology*, pp. 168–93. Oxford: Blackwell.

JAGGAR, G. and WRIGHT, C., eds (1999) *Changing Family Values.* London: Routledge.

JAMIESON, L. (1998) *Intimacy: Personal Relationships in Modern Societies.* Cambridge: Polity Press.

JERROME, D., ed. (1983) *Ageing in a Modern Society, Contemporary Approaches.* Kent and Australia: Croom Helm.

JERROME, D. (1984) 'Good Company: The Sociological Implications of Friendship', *Sociological Review* 32(4): 606–715.

JERROME, D. (1992) *Good Company: An Anthropological Study of Old People in Groups.* Edinburgh: Edinburgh University Press.

JOSSELSON, R. (1995) 'Imaging the Real', in R. Josselson and A. Lieblich (eds) *Interpreting Experience: The Narrative Study of Lives.* Thousand Oaks, CA: Sage.

LEWIS, J. (2001) *The End of Marriage? Individualism and Intimate Relations.* Cheltenham: Edward Elgar.

LITWAK, E. and SZELENYI, I. (1969) 'Primary Group Structures and their Functions: Kin, Neighbours and Friends', *American Sociological Review* 34: 465–81.

MISZTAL, B. (2000) *Informality: Social Theory and Contemporary Practice.* London: Routledge.

MORGAN, D. H. J. (1996) *Family Connections.* Cambridge: Polity Press.

NARDI, P. (1992) 'That's What Friends Are For: Friends as Family in the Gay and Lesbian Community', in K. Plummer (ed.) *Modern Homosexualities: Fragments of Lesbian and Gay Experience.* London: Routledge.

NARDI, P. (1999) *Gay Men's Friendships: Invincible Communities.* Chicago, IL: Chicago University Press.

NATIONAL STATISTICS (2001) *Social Trends 2001*, London: Office for National Statistics.

O'CONNOR, P. (1992) *Friendships between Women: A Critical Review.* Hemel Hempstead: Harvester Wheatsheaf.

PAHL, R. (1998) 'Friendship: The Social Glue of Contemporary Society?', in J. Franklin (ed.) *The Politics of Risk Society*, pp. 99–119. Cambridge: Polity Press.

PAHL, R. (2000) *On Friendship.* Cambridge: Polity Press.

PLATT, Jennifer (1988) 'What Can Case Studies Do?', in R. G. Burgess (ed.) *Studies in Qualitative Methodology. A Research Annual*, Vol. 1, pp. 1–23. London: JAI Press.

PRESTON, J. with LOWENTHAL, M., eds (1996) *Friends and Lovers: Gay Men Write about the Families They Create.* New York: Plume.

RHEINGOLD, H. (1993) *The Virtual Community: Homesteading on the Electronic Frontier.* Menlo Park, CA: Addison-Wesley.

ROSENEIL, S. (2000a) *Common Women, Uncommon Practices: The Queer Feminisms of Greenham.* London: Cassell.

ROSENEIL, S. (2000b) 'Queer Frameworks and Queer Tendencies: Towards an Understanding of Postmodern Transformations of Sexuality', *Sociological Research Online* 5(3); at :www.socresonline.org.uk/5/3/roseneil.html

ROSENEIL, S. and MANN, K. (1996) 'Backlash, Moral Panics and the Lone Mother', in E. Silva (ed.) *Good Enough Mothering? Feminist Perspectives on Lone Motherhood.* London: Routledge.

RUSTIN, M. (2000) 'Reflections on the Biographical Turn in Social Science', in P. Chamberlayne, J. Bornat and T. Wengraf (eds) *The Turn to Biographical Methods in Social Science*, pp. 33–52. London: Routledge.

SEDGWICK, E. K. (1994) *Tendencies.* London: Routledge.

SENNETT, R. (1977) *The Fall of Public Man.* New York: Alfred Knopf.

SHIELDS, R., ed. (1996) *Cultures of Internet: Virtual Spaces, Real Histories, Living Bodies.* London: Sage.

SILVA, E. B., ed. (1996) *Good Enough Mothering? Feminist Perspectives on Lone Mothering.* London: Routledge.

SILVA, E. and SMART, C., eds (1999) *The New Family?* London: Sage.

SIMMEL, G. (1950) *The Sociology of Georg Simmel*, trans. and ed. K. H. Wolff and R. Bendix. New York: Free Press.

SMART, C. and NEALE, B. (1999) *Family Fragments.* Cambridge: Polity Press.

STACEY, J. (1996) *In the Name of the Family: Rethinking Family Values in the Post-modern Age.* Boston, MA: Beacon Press.

STACEY, J. (2002) 'Fellow Families? Genres of Gay Male Intimacy and Kinship in a Global Metropolis', CAVA International Seminar Paper at: www.leeds.ac.uk/cava/papers/intseminar3stacey.htm

URRY, J. (2000) *Sociology beyond Societies: Mobilities for the Twenty-First Century.* London: Routledge.

VAN EVERY, J. (1999) 'From Modern Nuclear Family Households to Postmodern Diversity? The Sociological Construction of "Families" ', in G. Jagger and C. Wright (eds) *Changing Family Values*, pp. 165–84. London: Routledge.

WAKEFORD, N. (1998) 'Urban Culture for Virtual Bodies: Comments on Lesbian Identity and Community in San Francisco Bay Area Cyberspace', in R. Ainley (ed.) *New Frontiers of Space, Bodies and Gender*, pp. 176–90. London: Routledge.

WATNEY, S. (1988) 'AIDS, "Moral Panic" Theory and Homophobia', in P. Aggleton and H. Homans (eds) *Social Aspects of AIDS*, pp. 52–64. London: Falmer.

WEEKS, J. (1995) *Invented Moralities: Sexual Values in an Age of Uncertainty.* Cambridge: Polity Press.

WEEKS, J., DONOVAN, C. and HEAPHY, B. (1999) 'Everyday Experiments: Narratives of Non-Heterosexual Relationships', in E. Silva and C. Smart (eds) *The 'New' Family?* London: Sage.

WEEKS, J., HEAPHY, B. and DONOVAN, C. (2001) *Same Sex Intimacies: Families of Choice and Other Life Experiments.* London: Routledge.

WESTON, K. (1991) *Families We Choose: Lesbians, Gay Men and Kinship.* New York: Columbia University Press.

WHYTE, W. H. (1943) *Street Corner Society.* Chicago, IL: Chicago University Press.

WILLMOTT, P. (1986) *Social Networks, Informal Care and Public Policy.* London: Policy Studies Institute.

WILLMOTT, P. (1987) *Friendship Networks and Social Support.* London: Policy Studies Institute.

WILLMOTT, P. and YOUNG, M. (1967) *Family and Class in a London Suburb.* London: Nel Mentor.

YOUNG, M. and WILLMOTT, P. (1957) *Family and Kinship in East London.* London: Routledge and Kegan Paul.

Part III
Why Legal Regulation At All?

[10]

THE MARRIAGE ACT 1753: A CASE STUDY IN FAMILY LAW-MAKING

STEPHEN PARKER*

ABSTRACT

The main purpose of this article is to suggest that modern unmarried cohabitation and the legal responses to it can be seen as part of an historical process whereby the relationship between legal and social definitions of marriage is readjusted. It is argued that there are functional similarities between informal marriage in mid-eighteenth century England and Wales and cohabitation today. Both are the results of popular attempts to create a living arrangement which maximizes the benefits and minimizes the costs of economic and social realities. Lord Hardwicke's Marriage Act 1753 swept away any legal validity that informal marriage may have had and created the largest gap that has existed in English history between legal and social definitions of marriage. Since then the gap has closed, largely as a result of the law assimilating popular practices. The assimilation process which has been observed in modern English law whereby cohabitation is increasingly accorded the consequences of formal marriage is, therefore, simply part of an historical process.

A subsidiary purpose of the article is to argue that family lawyers should pay more attention to the way that laws come about because emergence studies can illuminate in ways that static analyses cannot.

I.

The 1980s has seen almost a plethora of literature on unmarried cohabitation in England and Wales. There are expository law texts aimed at practising lawyers (Parker, 1981) and social workers (Parry, 1981) and there are more general handbooks with varying degrees of legal content (Rights of Women, 1981; Clayton, 1981 and Dyer and Berlins, 1982). There is a specialist book on cohabitation contracts (Barton, 1985) and a wide-ranging socio-legal study (Freeman and Lyon, 1983). The latter work deals extensively with policy considerations concerning legal recognition of cohabitation and takes what is emerging as the majority view; to deplore the creeping assimilation between cohabitation and legal marriage. I have argued elsewhere

* *Lecturer in Law, University College, Cardiff, UK.*

that this analysis tends to overstate the assimilation thesis (Parker, 1984) but it does appear to be fashionable to speak in forthright terms (see, for example, Deech, 1980). My purpose here is to suggest that the debate might be enriched if the issues are placed in their historical context. If this is done, then the focus tends to shift away from cohabitation and towards what is meant by marriage.

Although there is no exhaustive definition of legal marriage in English law, its meaning is not generally thought of as in doubt. Procedural requirements are laid down principally in the Marriage Acts 1949 to 1986 and an indirect definition can be found in the law of nullity[1] which, by telling us what is void and voidable, tells us what may be valid. In the background is the classic statement of Lord Penzance in *Hyde v Hyde*[2] that marriage is the union for life of one man and one woman to the exclusion of all others, although much of this has been superseded or qualified (Poulter, 1979). My speculation is that these provisions constitute a notion of marriage which is historically, and perhaps culturally, specific and that there have always been social definitions of marriage as well as legal ones. Sometimes these definitions coincide, but quite frequently they do not. The relationship between them is best seen as a dialectical or interactive one so that legal rules concerning marriage may affect social definitions whilst changing social behaviour can give rise to changes in the legal rules.

I am by no means the first to question whether one can clearly demarcate marriage and non-marriage; see for example Weyrauch's writing on informal and common law marriage (Weyrauch, 1960 and 1980), Glendon's cross-cultural discussion of marriage-like institutions (Glendon, 1977: 81), O'Donovan's account of private ordering (O'Donovan, 1985: 44–50) and Freeman and Lyon's acknowledgement that the line between marriage and cohabitation was not as clearly drawn as it is today (Freeman and Lyon, 1983: 8). As far as I know, however, there is no sustained treatment of the process whereby certain relationships have been categorized as legal marriage and others excluded. This article is drawn from wider research where I have charted the emergence of marriage legislation between 1753 and 1907 and the growth of cohabitation law since 1945 (Parker, 1985). I concentrate here on the Marriage Act 1753, more commonly known as Lord Hardwicke's Act, and the law of marriage that immediately preceded it. My main purpose is to suggest that what we are witnessing today may simply be a continuation of the process whereby legal and social definitions of marriage are re-adjusted. A subsidiary purpose is to submit that our understanding of family law might be deepened if we pay more attention to the way that it comes about rather than concentrating solely on its formal and ideological content.

The detailed provisions of Lord Hardwicke's Act do not concern us here. Briefly, it was provided that, with the exception of marriages by the Royal Family, Quakers and Jews, the only method of contracting a valid marriage in England and Wales was through a ceremony in a Church or public chapel in the presence of two witnesses apart from the celebrating minister. Parental consent was required to the marriage of a party under twenty-one and there were detailed rules concerning publicity of proposed marriages through the reading of Banns in church upon three preceding Sundays or by giving notice of the impending grant of a licence. Anyone knowingly and wilfully attempting to solemnize a marriage without publication of Banns or a licence was liable to transportation for fourteen years. There were detailed rules concerning the maintenance of registers of all marriages and Banns. The penalty for intentionally taking part in any irregularity concerning the register, the publication of Banns or the issue of a licence was death as a felon without benefit of clergy. I am more concerned with the economic and social conditions which gave rise to popular marriage practices and the factors which brought about such a radical change in the law. To do this, I spend a little time setting the scene.

II. SOCIETY, MARRIAGE AND THE FAMILY IN 1750

England at this time, although no longer feudal, was still a highly stratified society with vast disparities of power and wealth. In order to understand the social context within which Lord Hardwicke's Act must be situated, it is necessary to describe separately the circumstances of the propertyless and the propertied.

The country can best be seen as a patchwork of distinctive local communities, each with its own traditions and heritages (Porter, 1982: 17). It was overwhelmingly rural in character, the rural population comprising about 70 per cent of its inhabitants. Despite some long-distance population mobility (Clark, 1979) most migration was over short distances (Horn, 1980: 14; Butlin, 1982: 28). In the absence of regular transport systems, those who left their family of origin might effectively sever links with their kin and loyalties be transferred to the local community. Malcolmson has argued that social customs are most deeply entrenched in communities where geographical and social mobility is limited (1981: 93) and much of the social life of ordinary people at this time was liberally interlaced with communal feast days, rituals and ceremonies. The customs and practices concerning marriage which we look at below should be seen as ways in which people routinely re-affirmed their identity with their local environment and traditions.

The ordinary family in the mid-eighteenth century was in the critical moment of transition from a unit of production to a unit of consumption brought about by the increase in wage labour. It was, however, exceptional for there to be only one source of income for a family. Rather, its members were engaged in a range of remunerative employments, some within and some outside the home, which would vary according to the season and the market. So, spinning, weaving, knitting, glove-making, metal-working and the like would be undertaken to supplement the livelihood gained from agricultural wages, a small-holding or common rights (Rose, 1981: 267). The skilful combination of these employments, the ability to complement the talents of husband and wife and make optimum use of children and other relatives were crucial to sustaining a regular income for the household. Marriage remained just as much an economic partnership as it had been in a time when the family more directly owned the means of production. It is, therefore, wrong to see the family as suddenly dislocated from the workplace – the much-vaunted separation of work and home – because the process was more subtle (Rowbotham, 1973: 27). Industrialization preceded the growth of factories and much industry took place within village communities (Anderson, 1980: 30). 'Putting out' of tasks to home-workers was quite common. Wage-labour was, however, increasing and its effect upon power relations between husband and wife has been much discussed (see, for example, O'Donovan, 1985: 35). Less commonly observed is the change that it caused in the balance of power between the generations (Gillis, 1974). As we will see later, wage labour boosted the financial independence of the young and enabled them to marry against the wishes of their parents.

The family in the propertied classes was also in transition, although in a different way. Until the eighteenth century, the means of production (in the sense of property which could produce wealth) was predominantly land. The law of real property was therefore an integral part of the economic substructure and, in the words of Christopher Hill, 'the law of marriage is almost the groundwork of the law of property' (Hill, 1961: 253). It is true that England, more than any other European country, had a long tradition of alienability of freehold land, a fact which Macfarlane regards as the most tangible origin of English individualism (Macfarlane, 1978), but marriage and death nevertheless remained the significant events upon which freehold lands changed hands. Primogeniture, the rule of law whereby in the absence of a lifetime or testamentary disposition the eldest male in the same degree succeeded to his ancestor's land, was crucial politically for patriarchy. The exclusion of daughters from the land, buttressed by the common law rule that on marriage control of the wife's realty passed to her husband, was 'an indispensable means for keeping the patrimony in the lineage' (Goody, 1976: 18). Allied to primogeniture were subsidiary customs and common law requirements providing for other members of the family; widow's dower and portions for younger sons and daughters. The legal focus for marriage amongst the propertied classes was not, therefore, the ceremony itself but the drawing up of the settlement. This device could continue the entail whilst providing for the wife and unborn (non-inheriting) children.

Fundamental economic changes which, in the form of proletarianization, were giving rise to new forms of family structure amongst the lower orders, were also altering the nature of marriage amongst the ruling classes. In particular, with the emergence of national markets, merchant and industrial capital was beginning to challenge real property as the major form of wealth so that by 1760 durable assets (other than land) already amounted to slightly less than a third of the national capital of Great Britain (Feinstein, 1981: 128). This growth of commercial capital had profound effects on the marriage practices of the wealthy. Marriage was starting to become a crucial alliance in a new sense; an alliance of different types of capital. As Porter graphically says (Porter, 1982: 66):

> 'The alliance of a gentleman's son with a merchant's daughter, the landed embracing the loaded, was marriage a la mode.'

The effect of this was that each child, through his or her marriage potential, was more strategically useful than had previously been the case. Younger sons could attract merchant's daughters who were valuable because primogeniture was not strictly applicable to the new form of wealth. If few daughters of top businessmen married into the aristocracy, many married into gentry families (Clark, 1985: 71). In consequence, wealthy parents felt a greater need to police all their children to ensure wise marriages accompanied by the appropriate settlements. Contradictory forces were, however, at work to make this policing more difficult. The fiction-reading young were becoming intoxicated with the idea of marriage based on romantic love and personal compatibility. So, at the time when parents wished to have greater control over their children, those children had a greater wish to be free of it. There was, therefore, inter-generational conflict amongst the propertied classes, as well as the propertyless. This conflict was played out through a moral panic over clandestine marriage and led to the enactment of Lord Hardwicke's Act. But before we can turn to this drama we must look at the pre-existing methods of marriage contraction.

III. THE LAW OF MARRIAGE PRIOR TO LORD HARDWICKE'S ACT 1753

The law of marriage at this time can be stated simply. The church reluctantly recognized promises in the present tense ('sponsalia per verba de praesenti') and promises for the future followed by consummation ('sponsalia per verba de futuro') as creating valid marriages. There was no ecclesiastical insistence on a celebration of the contract in or at the door of the church ('in facie ecclesiae') and these non-church marriages were variously known as common law, irregular or formless marriages or 'precontracts' (based on the assumption that a church marriage would follow). The common law courts, whilst accepting in theory the church's right to decide on the validity of marriage, in practice insisted that if consequences for real property were to follow then the exchange of consents to marriage had to be 'in facie ecclesiae' after the necessary formalities.

In England, the attack on irregular marriage had begun in 1540 when an ineffectual Act was passed declaring that a precontract was not an impediment to a later marriage unless followed by sexual intercourse. In the nature of things, however, intercourse did usually follow swiftly and the Act had little bite. Its Preamble condemned the canonical doctrine of precontracts on the grounds that it brought 'many just marriages' into doubt, disinherited 'lawful heirs' (sic) and contributed to the general uncertainty regarding the status of marriage. In 1604, new legislation stipulated that a church wedding must take place between the hours of 8.00 am and noon in the church at the place of residence of one of the pair after Banns had been read for three weeks running. This Act, too, was ineffective because a marriage in contravention of the canons was still valid, although the minister was liable to penalties. For a brief period during the Interregnum of the Seventeenth century, clandestine marriages of minors became void. Under the Civil Marriage Act 1653, parental consent was required to all marriages in which one of the parties was under twenty-one. Heavy penalties were imposed for the abduction or fraudulent marriage of minors. On the Restoration this Act became void. The intention behind all these measures was clear. Patriarchy required control over the marriages of the young in order to ensure the orderly transmission of the means of production. The reason why effective legislation had not yet been passed was probably because the threat to that control was not yet perceived as great. Irregular marriage was not accorded full consequences in property law and so the worst that it could do was occasionally take out of the formal marriage market a potential heir (because any subsequent marriage was void as bigamous[3]).

As the rules of formal marriage were, in effect, adjuncts to the rules of property law, those with little property were, not surprisingly, less concerned with their observance. The evidence that we have indicates that in many localities the church and state rules for marriage were only dimly perceived and often ignored and there was at work a quite separate normative order from church teaching and state law. Estimates of the extent of irregular marriage in the first half of the eighteenth century vary. Some historians have settled for a figure of one-fifth (Gillis, 1980) whilst others have put it as high as one half (Stone, 1979: 31). Research into litigation in the ecclesiastical courts to determine the validity of marriages in earlier periods suggest that formal marriage was actually a minority practice (Helmholtz, 1974; Ingram, 1980; Goody, 1983: 147). Because irregular marriages were peculiar to certain areas, it is likely that any average figure would mask the fact that in some regions these customs were prevalent whilst in others they were less so.

Probably the best-known secular custom is the broomstick wedding or 'besom marriage'. A birch besom was placed across the doorway of a house and the couple would then jump over it in the presence of witnesses. One still hears of broomstick weddings and living over the brush in parts of England and Wales today to describe irregular unions. Regional methods of marriage contraction seem often to have had a material function linked to local considerations and they are best seen as examples of what Menefee has called 'informal institutions'. His ethnographic study of wife-selling is an important contribution to our understanding of popular ideologies and beliefs. He argues that 'in almost every case each institution represents an unique solution to some human condition or problem' (Menefee, 1981: 7) and we look at some of the problems to which customary marriage provided a response.

Ensuring Support

One of the most pressing local concerns was to ensure a male provider for dependent women and children and one response to this was what we might call processual marriage; in other words where the formation of the marriage was regarded as a process rather than a clearly defined rite of passage. Recent evidence suggests that in many cases consent to intercourse and consent to marriage were not separated analytically, and perhaps were blurred deliberately in some communities in order to ensure support obligations. Quaife, for example, in his study of sexual behaviour in an earlier period in Somerset notes that:

> In effect, for the peasant community there was very little pre-marital sex. Most of the acts seen as such by Church and state were interpreted by the village as activities within marriage – a marriage begun with the promise and irreversibly confirmed by pregnancy (Quaife, 1979: 61).

In other words, marriage, may have been imposed *ex post facto* and in some places this may have had the support or connivance of the local clergy. In Newman's study of the east Kent parish of Ash-Next-Sandwich we find that 'the priest's attitude to stable unions was unpredictable' and are told of one case where a couple had six bastards (sic) but four of them were registered as legitimate (Newman, 1980: 146). E. A. Wrigley's work on the parish registers of Tetbury in Gloucestershire for the 1690s discloses how there was a separate category of marriage entry where the groom's name alone was entered and no date mentioned. It seems that certain priests were doing their best to register what the *community* regarded as marriages even though the relevant statutes (in this case the Marriage Act 1695) made no provision for such entries (Wrigley, 1973: 15).

Lack of Divorce

Another major problem in the life of ordinary people at this time was the practical absence of legal divorce. The only form of divorce permitting remarriage entailed petitioning Parliament for a Bill of Divorce. The cost of this varied from about £700 to several thousand pounds, depending on the length of the litigation, (Manchester, 1980: 374) and this made it inaccessible to the vast majority of people. A second remedy for an unsuccessful marriage was to petition for a decree of nullity on the ground of some antecedent defect which rendered the marriage void *ab initio* or voidable at the request of one of the parties. It may be that many marriages could have been impugned on the basis that the parties were too closely related by blood (Goody, 1983: 142) even if consanguinity had nothing to do with the breakdown of the relationship, but it is likely that ignorance and poverty meant that nullity petitions were relatively rare. In practice, it seems that ordinary people adopted their own measures and there are indications that customary forms of divorce co-existed with customary forms of marriage. Leaving aside desertion, which for centuries had been known as 'poor man's divorce' and regarded as morally dissolving the marriage (Stone, 1979: 35), the most common institution was probably that of wife-selling; a practice which has recently caught the imagination of a number of historians (Menefee, 1981; Thompson, 1978 and Malcolmson, 1981: 103). This procedure was highly ritualized and was almost certainly believed to have legal effect by those taking part. There is evidence that many, if not most, wife-sales took place with the wife's consent, or at least acquiescence, and in one case all three parties to the contract reduced its terms to writing and signed it (Gillis, 1980: 15). On the other hand, having a halter placed around one's neck hardly promotes cool reflection and we know of no institution of husband-selling.

Many customary marriage forms had some provision for divorce built into them. Jumping the broom, for example, worked both ways so that in Wales it was possible for the couple to jump backwards over the broom in the presence of witnesses (Gwyn, 1928: 156). Menefee quotes one nineteenth century song which goes (Menefee, 1981: 20):

> 'So let us be married by Mary,
> If ever dislike be our lot,
> We jump'd o'er the broom, then an airy,
> Jump back shall unfasten the knot.'

In remote areas, especially in the Scottish border country, Wales and the extreme South-West of England, 'handfasting' was common. This involved an exchange of promises before witnesses with the man and woman joining hands. The couple lived together for a year and a day and, if pleased with the arrangement, could extend it for life (Baker, 1977: 32). Irregular marriages, by having some claim to legality (and accepting that many people either took a rather robust interpretation of the law or were simply plain wrong about it) and were an important safety valve in what was, formally, a divorceless society (Mueller, 1957). And the law should not be regarded as irrelevant in most people's minds. It seems that wife-selling began to die out largely because an extensive campaign in the newspapers, perhaps prompted by judicial remarks in bigamy trials, was undertaken to demonstrate the legal ineffectiveness of the practice.

Ensuring Fertility

Continuing the theme that customary practices can often be seen to have clear links with local economic conditions we can see how practical forms of divorce, recognized by the community, were essential where marriage was an economic partnership requiring an efficient combination of skills. If the couple were incompatible, in whatever sense, then the risk of pauperism increased. One particular difficulty requiring specific mention is the inability to have children. The actual value attached to children in English society at this time has recently been questioned by Macfarlane (1986). His analysis proceeds at a high level of abstraction and generality and it still seems clear that in some rural communities, children were an economic necessity because they could be productive at an early age. With the advent of industrialization and the increase in out-working, children were useful in assisting cottage workers and, of course, when factory production gradually took over from cottage industry, the children's wage earnings were an important supplement to the family income. In the longer term, the prospect of having several adult children when the parents grew old was an important insurance for the future.

The ability to produce children, then, may have been an essential attribute for both partners to a prospective marriage, and high local rates of child mortality would put a premium on fecundity. Customary marriage practices seem to have been important devices in ensuring fertility before the parties were irretrievably committed; in other words they enabled trial marriage. This was achieved in two senses. First, in some areas the relationship might not be properly regarded as a marriage until the woman was pregnant. Second, as we have seen, some marriages were regarded as dissoluble within a specific period and this period may have been linked to the time in which it was reasonable to expect conception to take place. Evidence of the existence of deliberate trial marriage has only recently been appreciated through the re-evaluation of conventional accounts of illegitimacy statistics; in particular those of the Cambridge Group for the History of Population and Social Structure

(Laslett, 1980: xiv and 134 and Meteyard, 1980). In other words, what appear to be registrations of illegitimate births might be births in stable families where the parents were regarded by the community as validly married to each other. In fact, trial marriage has been alluded to in the past but its significance has not properly been appreciated. Thomas Hardy's fantasy *The Wellbeloved*, published in 1897, is set on the fictional Island of Slingers which had a closed community with restricted resources and customs going back to pagan times. It was an island custom that the marriage ceremony only took place when the bride became pregnant and the plot centres around a conflict between this tradition and the 'new education' of Victorian morality. The Island of Slingers was meant to represent the Isle of Portland, off Dorset, and we know from other sources that the custom of trial marriage was prevalent amongst quarrymen there in the mid-eighteenth century (Baker, 1977: 23; Horn, 1980). In what ways did the flexible laws on marriage formation facilitate deliberate trial marriage? It seems that the idea that mere consent was the basis of a valid marriage was sufficient to permit local communities to elaborate by developing notions of conditional and revocable consent. The clergy were, apparently, prepared to go along with this in many cases by entering the children's births as legitimate even if the parents' marriage escaped the register.

Conflict-handling

Irregular marriage was an important way in which conflict within the community might be defused by enabling couples to evade social and parental pressures and present the world with a fait accompli. Widows or widowers marrying 'too soon' after the death of a spouse or against the wishes of their family; couples disparate in age, social status or religion; bigamists and bankrupts all had reasons to seek privacy (Outhwaite, 1973: 64–7). The main constituency was, however, the young. In areas where land was both the primary means of production and in short supply it was important to regulate the size of the population which would be depending upon it. One main way of doing this was to control entry into marriage; partly through simple community pressure and partly through the requirement of parental consent. Poster suggests that the decision about marriage between young people was often one for the community as a whole to make (Poster, 1978: 186) and Levine, supporting this, argues that (Levine, 1977: 148):

> the people of the village community enforced the strategies of family formation they had themselves created to promote a form of stability, an optimisation of the demo-economic balance so far as the group was concerned.

(Arensberg's works on the family in the west of Ireland in the 1930s show how a similar communal involvement in marriage formation survived there for a further two centuries; see, for example, Arensberg, 1937: ch 3)

It seems that the mid-eighteenth century saw an increase in inter-generational conflict over entry into marriage. The reason appears to lie in the gradual break-up of traditional family patterns due to the increase in wage labour (Medick, 1976: 303; Alderman, 1986: 3). Wage labour increased the financial independent of the young but the emerging towns and cities did not yet have the abundant factory employment to enable them to migrate. Instead their wages continued to come mainly from the land and their social practices governed by the force of tradition. One can speculate that this contradiction between the opportunities of the new and the restraints of the old heightened inter-generational strain.

Couples who did not wish to announce their impending marriage for fear of parental and social pressure would often avoid formal marriage (which required publication of Banns in church for three consecutive weeks). On the other hand, they might not be content to rely upon a purely private contract and might prefer their vows to be publicly notarized in some way. Sometimes the clergy were prepared to ignore the requirement of Banns, particularly those clergy without benefice, preferring to risk their employer's sanctions than the loss of income (Wynne, 1955: 8) but otherwise prominent local people, such as the barber or blacksmith were often willing to officiate.

Conscientious Objection

A final constituency attracted by informal marriage might be described as conscientious objectors. Atheists, religious dissenters and Catholics objected to the Anglican forms of ceremony and clearly benefited from the fact that exchange of consents was sufficient to create a marriage, albeit a second class one, in the eyes of the common law. Objections to the English language might have been a strong ground for opposition in Wales where a large proportion of the population were Welsh monoglots. Any insistence on the ceremony being conducted in English (the policy on this being left to the Bishop) would make the marriage incomprehensible to the participants (Pryce, 1978: 5 and 26). Women with property also objected to formal marriage because it entailed the vesting of their personality in their husbands and the loss of control over their realty. Common law marriage was believed (partly correctly) to preserve the separate civil identity of the wife. One particular custom was that of the smock wedding where the woman was married wearing only her smock. It was thought that this meant that her financial obligations and assets remained entirely separate from those of her husband. Baker cites an example where the bride took this custom one step further and went to the altar 'like Mother Eve' (Baker, 1977: 46).

Informal marriage amonst ordinary people prior to Lord Hardwicke's Act should be viewed as the product of a dialectical relationship between economic forces, popular ideology and superior normative orders. People engaged with laws handed down from church and state, in this case the basic requirements for legal marriage, and complied with them, adapted them or flouted them according to local conditions. To put it another way, we can observe local legal systems operating relatively autonomously, but not totally dislocated, from formal and general legal rules. The danger in suggesting a 'fit' between social practice and wider forces is that one slips into an undesirable sort of functionalist analysis whereby description is confused with explanation and intention attributed to people when none existed. It may be that historical research will tell us more about the subjective meanings with which people endowed their world but it is likely that much will be left to inference. We are, after all, dealing with lives that went largely unchronicled. The literature that we do have, however, suggests that people of all classes in pre-industrial England and Wales did understand the nature of marriage in social life. The propertyless, drawing on a long tradition of marginal subsistence living, did understand that the household needs a sufficient number of hands to sustain an income which would support each of them whilst, on the other hand, too many mouths to feed would push them all into destitution. And if one understands that England at that time resembled a quilted patchwork of insular, chauvinist communities one can believe that these basic perceptions were turned into conventional social wisdom that would be enforced by local normative orders. The practice of trial marriage, for example, made such obvious economic sense that one can only assume it was deliberately created and perpetuated.

A related danger of functionalist analysis is that an over-romanticized antiquarian impression is given of an equitable and stable system functioning smoothly. Anderson points out that 'there certainly is evidence that not all strategies were equally effective in the long run . . ., of individuals lonely and starving, of women forced to adopt solutions involving prostitution' (Anderson, 1980; 82). The historical oppression of women is being increasingly well documented and no doubt customary responses to unjust conditions, such as wife sales in a divorceless society, were in themselves oppressive. The only claim made here is that popular customs were attempts – sometimes successful, sometimes not – to negotiate with hostile forces. In Menefee's words, they were attempts to solve some human condition or problem.

It is doubtful whether the uncertainty caused by the marriage rules could have lasted into the nineteenth century. The formation of a central state organized on bureaucratic lines entailed more detailed regulation of social behaviour. Furthermore, as we shall see, popular customs of all kinds increasingly came under attack by a ruling class fearful of their public order consequence and keen to control the emerging proletariat. In fact, it was alarm over a problem virtually exclusive to the upper classes which triggered legislative intervention.

IV. CLANDESTINE MARRIAGE

It would be hard to find a better description of patriarchy's view of clandestine marriage than that provided by the early nineteenth century novelist and historian Tobias Smollett (Smollett, 1830: 100):

'The practice of solemnizing clandestine marriages, so prejudicial to the peace of families and so often productive of misery to the parties themselves thus united, was an evil that prevailed to such a degree as claimed the attention of the legislature. The sons and daughters of great and opulent familes, before they had acquired knowledge and experience, or attained to the years of discretion, were every day seduced in their affections, and inveigled into matches big with infamy and ruin: and these were greatly facilitated by the opportunities that occurred of being united instantaneously by the ceremony of marriage, in the first transport of passion, before the destined victim had time to cool or deliberate on the subject.'

But whilst, on paper, moralists might condemn such practices, there is no doubt that the idea of secrecy and elopement caught the imagination of genteel society which was increasingly accustomed to the idea of romantic marriage. Popular fiction abounded with references to secret weddings. Trevelyan suggests that a sham marriage enters into the plot of half the novels of the period (Trevelyan, 1881: 13):

'Numerous were the cases in which boys of rank had become the prey of infamous harpies, and girls with money or beauty had found that the services of a clergyman were employed as a cloak for plunder and seduction.'

Matters were brought to a head by the notorious practice of 'Fleet Marriages'. The Fleet was the prison in which prisoners for debt were confined. Because accommodation was insufficient, those prisoners who could give security for their appearance, when summoned, were permitted to take lodgings nearby. Those who officiated over Fleet Marriages were usually, but not always, clergymen deprived of their benefices for misconduct (Howard, 1904: 438). According to Lecky (1883: 490):

'Almost every tavern or brandy shop in the neighbourhood had a Fleet parson in its pay. Notices were placed in the windows, and agents went out in every direction to solicit the passers-by. A more pretentious and perhaps more popular establishment was the Chapel in Curzon Street, where the Rev Alexander Keith officiated. He was said to have made a very 'bishopric of revenue' by clandestine marriages, and the expression can hardly be exaggerated if it be true, as was asserted in Parliament, that he had married on an average 6,000 couples every year.'

The level of concern over clandestine marriage can best be appreciated if we remind ourselves of the change in function of upper class marriage at this time. It had become even more important as a device for capital accumulation and thus had to be controlled more tightly. The existence of merchant wealth not tied to primogeniture increased the potential value, both to parents and seducers, of children other than the first born. The reasons why the legislative reform took the form it did and why no attempt was made to restrict its application to those for whom it had importance can only be explained by looking at class relations at this time and, in particular, the law-makers.

V. THE LAW-MAKERS

If Lord Hardwicke had a likeable side to his character, it has been firmly hidden from history. Born Philip Yorke, the son of a Dover attorney, he rapidly rose to public office as a lawyer. He became Solicitor-General at the age of twenty-nine and eventually, by way of the offices of Attorney-General and Lord Chief Justice, the Lord Chancellor. He has been described as the 'quintessence of Whiggism' (Thompson, 1977: 208) and 'the old spider of the law' (Plucknett, 1940: 623). His disgust for the poor is well-documented. In 1737, he was complaining that 'the people are always jealous of those in power, and mighty apt to believe every piece of scandal or reproach that is thrown upon them'.[4] He was the architect of numerous capital statutes passed during the 1730s, attributing their necessity to the 'degeneracy of human nature', and in his judicial capacity he added subtle refinements to his inventions by, for example, ordering a Cornish rioter's body to hang in chains (an order he only respited when told that insurrection would follow) (Hay, 1977: 5 and 120). But Hardwicke was not alone in his view of the common people. He simply personified the new breed of ruler. Patricians grew increasingly snooty about the 'vulgar world', with popular customs and festivities coming in for particular obloquy and the concept of 'hegemony', in its specifically Marxist sense, can assist in understanding why.

Deriving particularly from the work of the Italian marxist Antonio Gramsci (1891–1937), the term 'hegemony' has come to mean more than simple political preponderance by one class over another. Rather, it implies the ability to impose a whole 'world-view' on the subject. The rulers' *culture* is accepted as well as their political and economic institutions. Williams suggests that the ability to impose 'ways of seeing' is crucial in societies where government depends, in the last resort, on consent rather than coercion (Williams, 1976: 118 and 1980: 37–40). And Whig rule in an England without a police force or flexible militia depended upon popular consent; albeit a consent manipulated through the majesty, mercy and (occasional) justice of the criminal law (Hay, 1977). Popular customs stood in the path of hegemony at various levels. Ideologically, the superstitions and beliefs underlying many of them conflicted with the 'rationalism' of the new political economy. Popular festivities, wakes, church-ales and fairs were seen as silly and troublesome

(Porter, 1982: 80) and potential threats to public order (Slack, 1984; Golby and Purdue, 1984). They hindered the establishment of new norms of work and social conduct and, because they were frequently based on a notion of a 'moral economy', they challenged the emerging logic of the market (Thompson, 1971).

Against this background, we can understand why those who objected to the Bill on the basis of its effect on the poor were swept aside. Some of those objections did, in any event, sound particularly disingenuous. Henry Fox was the main opponent and his opposition may not have been untinged by his own experiences. When Secretary at War he had fallen in love with the daughter of the Duke and Duchess of Richmond, Lady Caroline Lennox. The Duke refused his daughter's hand and so, in 1744, the couple wed secretly and, by all accounts, enjoyed a happy marriage. Fox claimed that the Act would discourage marriage amongst the poor for a number of reasons. First, it would make marriage more expensive because the clergyman would have to be paid. Second, the compulsory period of notice, in effect four weeks, would give time for a change of mind and allow the ardour to cool. Third, the compulsory register would deter those who were illiterate.[5] Fears over the discouragement to marriage were not born, however, out of concern for the emotional development of the poor. Rather, they stemmed from worry that the population might fall. According to Fox:[6]

> 'Without a continual supply of industrious and laborious poor, no nation can long exist, which supply can only be got by promoting marriage amonst such people.'

Perhaps the only remark which can be viewed without excessive cynicism is that by Henry Nugent concerning local customs of processual marriage. Nugent correctly saw that the removal of legal backing from these customs would be dangerous to the woman (and the rate-payer):[7]

> 'A young woman is but too apt by nature to trust to the honour of the man she loves, and to admit him to her bed upon a solemn promise to marry her. Surely the moral obligation is as binding as if they have been actually married: but you are by this Bill to declare it null and void.'

Other points of opposition had little to do with ordinary people. There was some concern that the Bill was an aristocratic plot to prevent commoners from marrying into their ranks. Charles Townshend asked 'are new shackles to be forged to keep young men of abilities from rising to the level of their elder brothers?'[8] This alludes to primogeniture and suggests a belief that seduction was the alternative open to younger sons, such as himself, incidentally. (In any event, Mahon remarks wryly that 'the Bill proved no such obstruction in the way of Townshend's own career. Only a year afterwards he espoused a wealthy dowager from the House of Buccleuch – the Countess of Dalkeith' (Mahon, 1858: 27).) It may be that there were sound reasons for suspecting the motives of the aristocracy.

Lasch argues that the agrarian revolution, which was eradicating feudal traditions, abolishing feudal tenures and commercializing agriculture had led to a resurgence of aristocratic power; temporarily halting the ascendance of the middle class (Lasch, 1974: 102). It is quite likely, then, that some commoners were suspicious of the measure.

The Bill was passed with a comfortable majority. There was only the faintest opposition in the House of Lords but its passage there was predictable. Most of the previous attempts to regulate clandestine marriage (1677, 1685, 1689, 1691, 1711 and 1735) had passed in the Lords but failed in the Commons (Trumbach, 1978: 102). Those now objecting in the Commons were greatly outnumbered by those such as John Bond who found it astonishing that anyone should oppose such an 'eminently sensible measure'.[9]

VI. THE AFTERMATH

We do not know how often the Act was enforced but we do know that when a case came to court its provisions were interpreted strictly. Any misdescription of the parties might invalidate the marriage (Manchester, 1980: 365). For example, in *Pouget v Tomkins*[10] the omission of one christian name invalidated the publication of the Banns and hence the marriage. For the first few years the Act was seen by its promoters as a success and we are told that it practically drove the Fleet Chaplains out of business 'except in the bogs of Ireland' (Arnold, 1950: 488). Nevertheless, interaction between the people and the law continued. Stone suggests that 'up to a third of all marriages between 1753 and 1836 were illegal and void' (Stone, 1977: 31) whilst Newman in her study speculates that 'a proportion of up to 15 per cent for non-church unions might be reasonable at this time' because 'common law marriage was a deep-rooted tradition amongst a section of the population' (Newman, 1980: 151). So it seems that alternative practices continued and developed, now without any claim to formal legal validity. Others adopted evasive practices such as the Gretna Green marriage. Because Lord Hardwicke's Act did not extend to Scotland, couples could cross the border and engage in a civil contract. As religious dissent grew, so did the attraction of these marriages. Olive Anderson suggests that 'when the Newcastle and Carlisle, and then the Caledonian railway lines were opened, the practice became almost universal among working people' (Anderson, 1975: 69). For those who desired privacy but who did not live near the border and could not afford to travel, it was common to establish residence in another district. We know that around Exeter the tradition was to come to town on three consecutive Saturday nights and sleep in lodgings. This meant that the Banns could be read where the couple were unknown.

Eventually, a combination of pressure from dissenters, the state's need for a centralized system for registering births, deaths and marriages and a desire to restore legitimacy to the marriage laws led to the introduction of civil marriage in 1836. With the Marriage Act 1836 the state seemed temporarily to restore its position of catering for the overwhelming majority of marriage preferences. But that is another story.

VII. CONCLUSION

It can be argued that the past is a different country and what happened over two centuries ago does little to illuminate the present. After all, the age of consent has now been reduced to sixteen and there is capacity to marry at eighteen even without parental consent. As far as statute law is concerned there is universal suffrage and Parliament is regularly advised by a highly skilled and fair-minded Law Commission on family law matters. We are told that any attempt to regulate the conduct of married life has been abandoned (Hoggett, 1982: 399) and that family law in the west is now neutral (Glendon, 1981). Furthermore, Lord Denning, as influential a figure as any in the reconstruction of family law since 1945, has announced that women have become equal (Denning, 1980).

I suggest that the episode of Lord Hardwicke's Act is significant for at least three reasons. First, it marks a clear beginning to the civil state's intervention into the family, albeit indirectly by requiring a religious ceremony (Weeks, 1981: 83). It was not uncommon for the Church and parish to be used as instruments of regulation prior to the evolution of a secular bureaucracy. The licensing of physicians, surgeons and mid-wives was originally conducted by Bishops. O'Donovan notes that a 'centralised bureaucratic state could not tolerate the ambiguities of the pre-Hardwicke era' and that 'Patriarchy was secured to work with the state in regulating the family' (O'Donovan, 1984: 48). Her periodization may, however, be a little premature. State formation was still in its early stages and it is interesting to note that a proposal for a national Census was roundly defeated in 1753 but accepted in 1800. The Civil Marriage Act 1836 was more obviously a bureaucratic measure in the Weberian sense as it was passed with the Births and Deaths Registration Act and was seen as part of a programme which embraced the Poor Law Amendment Act 1834. Lord Hardwicke's Act could, however, be seen as a by-product of the process of state formation in that it reflected a growing desire for certainty in legal relations within civil society.

Secondly, this account of the Act's introduction invites comparison between informal marriage in the past and modern cohabitation. There is relatively little research into the motives of heterosexual couples who live together in the same household without benefit of clergy or registrar (see Oliver, 1982; Chappel, 1982; Dyer and Berlins, 1982; Freeman and Lyon, 1983: ch. 3). My preliminary view is that an explanation which goes behind the subjective intentions of the cohabitees themselves lies in the effect that commodity capitalism and relative affluence has had on family formation (Parker, 1985: ch. 6). These have led to an increased emphasis on personal fulfilment through relationships and have probably decreased marital stability. At any rate, they have encouraged those who are unhappy in their marriages to do something about it, so increasing legal divorce. It may be that some of those who have been through the trauma of divorce prefer to live with a future partner, either as a prelude or an alternative to marriage. Another constituency attracted by cohabitation may be young mobile middle class people dislocated from their family of origin by higher education or job opportunities. Tending, as they do, to defer having children, some of this group regard the risks and costs of marriage as outweighing the advantages. When they do have children, some of them marry whilst the remainder are unpersuaded of the need. In other words, some people today are negotiating with the economic and social forces that bear on them and are attempting to carve out a living arrangement which maximizes the benefits and minimizes the costs. How different is this behaviour from informal marriage customs in the eighteenth century? What is now happening should not be seen so much as a challenge to marriage because this assumes that there is such a fixed institution. Rather, it may simply be a resurgence of private ordering of relationships; of other marriages.

When further empirical work has been carried out into cohabitation it would be interesting to see the participants broken down into ethnic origin. We know from anthropological literature that some third world societies have various categories of marriage (Smith, 1956: ch. VIII, Smith, 1962) and, if the above analysis of eighteenth century customs has value, then it may also be of use in illuminating these different forms. It may be that immigration has brought with its forms of marriage appropriate to less developed economies which co-exist here with modern forms prompted by new conditions.

The response to cohabitation by law-makers is a complex one. In outline, the assimilation process which has been observed whereby marriage-like behaviour is increasingly accorded the consequences of legal marriage (Parker, 1981: ch. 12; Freeman and Lyon, 1983) is in my submission an attempt to preserve a form of family which by and large suits the dominant class, and in particular men. How different is this process from the abandonment in 1836 of the strict definition of marriage entry introduced by Lord Hardwicke's Act in order to draw dissenters into the net of legal marriage?

Thirdly, I suggest that this account may show the usefulness of emergence studies in family law. The last fifteen years have seen a refreshing expansion of family law literature beyond traditional black-letter texts. Attempts have been made to assess family law against perceived 'social policy' objectives; see, for example, some of John Eekelaar's work (Eekelaar, 1971; 1978 and 1984) and Freeman and Lyon (1983). Allied to this nascent socio-legal interest has been the publication of a number of empirical studies on family laws in action. For example, we now have published research on the operation of child custody proceedings (Eekelaar and Clive, 1977) and alleged bias towards mothers (Maidment, 1981 and 1984). We also have information on the actual application of family property law by divorce court registrars (Barrington Baker, 1977), out of court bargaining (Mnookin, 1979), the role of divorce court welfare officers (Murch, 1980), the economic impact of divorce (Maclean and Eekelaar, 1983 and Eekelaar and Maclean, 1986) and care proceedings (Dingwall et al., 1983). Less prominent, but increasing, is an interest in theoretical concerns; see, for example, Freeman's study of violence in the home (Freeman, 1979) and his overview of family law (Freeman, 1981), O'Donovan's examination of the public/private distinction (O'Donovan, 1985) and Alcock's discussion of ideology and family law (Alcock, 1979). Non-lawyers, too, have made exciting contributions (see Barker, 1979 and Smart, 1984). What is surprising, however, is the relative absence of attention to the ways that family laws come about. Of course, many works begin with an historical introduction but these tend to fall far short of contextualized case studies.

Family law is not alone in this. Even within the sociology of law there has been a tendency to take a very positivistic view of law which reifies it rather than sees it as a social product which cannot be understood independently of social processes (Tomasic, 1985: 101; Dixon, 1980: 101). The result is that we have little in the way of processual analyses of family law, as opposed to static ones. There are, it is true, some fascinating accounts of particular legislative episodes written by historians (Stetson, 1982; Holcombe, 1983) but these tend to be written without a general knowledge of the corpus of family law and sometimes connections are lost which a family lawyer might have been able to make (Parker, 1984). I hope that this case-study suggests one way in which a family law can be analysed and the use to which the analysis can be put.

NOTES

1 Matrimonial Causes Act 1973, ss11–13.
2 (1866) LR 1 P & D 130.
3 See, for example, Wigmore's Case (1706) 2 Salk 437.
4 Cobbett's Parliamentary History, Vol IX, Col 1295.
5 ibid, Vol XV, p 70.
6 ibid.
7 ibid, 17.
8 ibid, 69.
9 ibid, 3.
10 2 Hag Con 142.

REFERENCES

Alcock, P. (1979), *Legal Ideology, The Family and the Position of Women*, Paper presented to the 1979 British Sociological Association Conference at Warwick University.

Alderman, G. (1986), *Modern Britain 1700–1983: A Domestic History*, London, Croom Helm.

Anderson, M. (1980), *Approaches to the History of the Western Family 1500–1914*, London, Macmillan.

Anderson, O. (1975), *The Incidence of Civil Marriage in Victorian England and Wales*, 69 *Past and Present* 50–87.

Arensberg, C. M. (1937), *The Irish Countryman*, London, MacMillan.

Arnold, J. C. (1950), 'The Marriage Law of England'. *Quarterly Review*, Vol 288, 486–9.

Baker, M. (1977), *Wedding Customs and Folklore*, Newton Abbott, David and Charles.

Barker, D. L. (1979), 'The Legal Regulation of Marriage: Repressive Benevolence', in Littlejohn, G. (et al.) *Power and the State*, London, Croom Helm, 239–66.

Barrington Baker, W., Eekelaar, J., Gibson, C. and Raikes, S. (1977), *The Matrimonial Jurisdiction of Registrars*, Oxford, SSRC.

Barton, C. (1985), *Cohabitation Contracts*, Hants, Gower.

Butlin, R. A. (1982), *The Transformation of Rural England c1580–1800*, Oxford, Oxford University Press.

Chappell, H. (1982), 'Not the Marrying Kind?', *New Society*, p 295.

Clark, J. C. D. (1985), *English Society 1688–1832*, Cambridge, Cambridge University Press.

Clarke, P. (1979), 'Migration in England during the late 17th and early 18th centuries', 83 *Past and Present* 57–90.

Clayton, P. (1981), *The Cohabitation Guide*, London, Wildwood.

Deech, R. (1980), 'The Case Against Legal Recognition of Cohabitation', in Eekelaar, J. M. and Katz, S. N., *Marriage and Cohabitation in Contemporary Societies*, Toronto, Butterworth.

Denning, Lord (1980), *The Due Process of Law*, London, Butterworths.

Dingwall, R., Eekelaar, J. M. and Murray, T. (1983), *The Protection of Children: State Intervention and Family Life*, Oxford, Blackwell.

Dixon, D. (1980), '"Class Law": The Street Betting Act of 1906', *Int Jo of Sociology of Law*, Vol 8, 101–28.

Dyer, C. and Berlin, M. (1982), *Living Together*, London, Hamlyn.

Eekelaar, J. M. (1971), *Family Security and Family Breakdown*, Harmondsworth, Penguin.

Eekelaar, J. M. (1977), *Family Law and Social Policy*, (1st Ed) London, Weidenfeld and Nicolson.

Eekelaar, J. M. (1984), *Family Law and Social Policy*, (2nd Ed) London, Weidenfeld and Nicolson.

Eekelaar, J. M. and Clive, E. (1977), *Custody after Divorce*, Oxford, SSRC.

Eekelaar, J. M. and Maclean, M. (1986), *Maintenance after Divorce*, Oxford, Clarendon Press.

Feinstein, C. H. (1981), 'Capital Accumulation and the Industrial Revolution?, in Floud, R. and McCloskey, D. (eds), *The Economic History of Britain since 1700*, Cambridge, Cambridge University Press.

Freeman, M. D. A. (1979), *Violence in the Home*, Farnborough, Saxon House.

Freeman, M. D. A. (1981), 'The State, The Family and Law in the Eighties', *Kingston Law Review*, Vol 11, 129–72.

Freeman, M. D. A. and Lyon, C. (1983), *Cohabitation without Marriage*, Hants, Gower.

Gillis, J. R. (1974), *Youth and History-Traditions and Changes in European Age Relations 1770–Present*, London, Academic Press.

Gillis, J. R. (1980), 'Resort to Common Law Marriage in England and Wales 1700–1850', unpublished paper presented to the 1980 Past and Present Society Conference on Law and Human Relations.

Glendon, M. A. (1977), *State, Law and Family*, Oxford, North Holland.

Glendon, M. A. (1981), *The New Family and the New Property*, Toronto, Butterworth.

Golby, J. M. and Purdue, A. W. (1984), *The Civilization of the Crowd: Popular Culture in England 1750–1900*, London, Batsford.

Goody, J. (et al.) (1976), *Family and Inheritance: Rural Society in Western Europe 1200–1800*, Cambridge, Cambridge University Press.

Goody, J. (1983), *The Development of the Family and Marriage in Europe*, Cambridge, Cambridge University Press.

Gwyn, G. (1928), *Folklore*.

Hay, D. (1977), 'Property, Authority and the Criminal Law' in Hay, D. (et al.), *Albion's Fatal Tree*, London, Peregrine.

Helmholz, R. M. (1974), *Marriage Litigation in Medieval England*, Cambridge, Cambridge University Press.

Hill, C. (1961), *Century of Revolution*, Harmondsworth, Pelican.

Hoggett, B. (1982), 'Families and the Law', in Rapaport, R. N. (ed), *Families in Britain*, London, Routledge and Kegan Paul, 399–415.

Holcombe. L, (1983), *Wives and Property: Reform of the Married Women's Property Law in Nineteenth Century England*, Oxford, Blackwell.
Horn, P. (1980), *The Rural World 1780–1850*, London, Hutchinson.
Howard, G. E. (1904), *A History of Matrimonial Institutions*, University of Chicago Press.
Ingram, M. (1980), 'Spousals Litigation in the English Ecclesiastical Courts c1350–c1640', in Outhwaite R. B. (ed) 1980, *Marriage and Society: Studies in the Social History of Marriage*, London, Europa.
Lasch, C. (1974), 'The Suppression of Clandestine Marriage in England; The Marriage Act of 1753', *Salmagundi*, 90–109.
Lecky, W. (1883), *History of England in the Eighteenth Century*, London.
Levine, D. (1977), *Family Formation in an Age of Nascent Capitalism*, London, Academic Press.
Macfarlane, A. (1978), *The Origins of English Individualism*, Oxford, Blackwell.
Macfarlane, A. (1986), *Love and Marriage in England 1300–1840*, Oxford, Blackwell.
Maclean, M. and Eekelaar, J. M. (1983), *Children and Divorce: Economic Factors*, Oxford SSRC Centre for Socio-Legal Studies.
Mahon, Lord (1858), *The History of England 1713–1780*, London.
Malcolmson, R. W. (1981), *Life and Labour in England 1700–1780*, London, Hutchinson.
Maidment, S. (1981), *Child Custody: What Chance for Fathers?*, London, National Council for One Parent Families.
Maidment, S. (1984), *Child Custody and Divorce*, London, Croom Helm.
Manchester, A. H. (1980), *Modern Legal History*, London, Butterworth.
Medick, H. (1976), 'The Proto-Industrial Family Economy: The Structural Function of Household and Family during the Transition from Peasant Society to Industrial Capitalism', 3 *Social History*, 291–315.
Menefee, S. P. (1981), *Wives for Sale*, Oxford, Blackwell.
Meteyard, B. (1980), 'Illegitimacy in Marriage in Eighteenth Century England', *Jo of Interdisciplinary History*, Vol 3, 479–9.
Mnookin, R. (1979), *Bargaining in the Shadow of the Law: The Case of Divorce*, Oxford, SSRC Centre for Socio-Legal Studies.
Mueller, G. O. W. (1957), 'Inquiry into the State of a Divorceless Society', *University of Pittsburgh Law Review*, Vol 18, 545–78.
Murch, M. (1980), *Justice and Welfare in Divorce*, London, Sweet and Maxwell.
Newman, A. (1980), 'An evaluation of bastardy recordings in an East Kent Parish', in Laslett, P. (et al.), *Bastardy and its Comparative History*, London, Edward Arnold.
O'Donovan, K. (1985), *Sexual Divisions in the Law*, London, Weidenfeld and Nicolson.
Oliver, D. (1982), 'Why Do People Live Together?' *Jo of Social Welfare Law*, 209–22.
Outhwaite, R. B. (1973), 'Age at Marriage in England from the late Seventeenth to the late Nineteenth Centuries', *Transactions of the Royal Historical Society*, Vol XVII, 64–7.
Parker, S. J. (1981), *Cohabitees*, Chichester, Barry Rose.
Parker, S. J. (1984), 'History of Family Law', *Jo. of Law and Society*, Vol 11, 120–4.
Parker, S. J. (1984), 'Unmarried Cohabitation: A Threat to the Patriarchal Family? A Review Essay', *Contemporary Crises*, Vol 8, 175–80.
Parker, S. J. (1985), *Legal Responses to Informal Marriage and Cohabitation in England and Wales since 1750*, Ph.D. Thesis, University of Wales (forthcoming, Macmillan).
Parry, M. (1981), *Cohabitation*, London, Sweet and Maxwell.
Plucknett, T. F. T. (1940), *A Concise History of the Common Law*, London, Butterworth.
Porter, R. (1982), *English Society in the Eighteenth Century*, Harmondsworth, Penguin.
Poster, M. (1978), *Critical Theory of the Family*, London, Pluto Press.
Poulter, S. (1979), 'The Definition of Marriage in English Law', *Modern Law Review*, Vol 42, 409–29.
Pryce, W. T. R. (1978), 'Welsh and English in Wales 1750–1971: A Spatial Analysis Based on the Linguistic Affiliation of Parochial Communities', (1978–80) *Board of Celtic Studies Bulletin*, Vol 28.
Quaife, G. R. (1979), *Wanton Wives and Wayward Wenches: Peasants and Illicit Sex in early Seventeenth Century England*, London, Croom Helm.
'Rights of Women', 1981, *The Cohabitation Handbook*, London, Pluto Press.
Rose, M. E. (1981), 'Social Change and the Industrial Revolution', in Floud, R. and McCloskey, D. *The Economic History of Britain since 1750*, Cambridge, Cambridge University Press.
Rowbotham, S. (1977), *Hidden from History*, London, Pluto Press.
Slack, P. (ed) (1984), *Rebellion, Popular Protest and the Social Order in Early Modern England*, Cambridge, Cambridge University Press.
Smart, C. (1984), *The Ties that Bind*, London, Routledge and Kegan Paul.

Smith, M. G. (1962), *West Indian Family Structure*, Washington, Washington University Press.
Smith, R. T. (1956), *The Negro Family in British Guiana*, London, Routledge and Kegan Paul.
Smollett, T. (1830), *The History of England*, London (1830) Vol III.
Stetson, D. M. (1982), *A Woman's Issue, The Politics of Family Law Reform in England*, London, Greenwood Press.
Stone, L. (1979), *The Family, Sex and Marriage in England 1500–1800*, Harmondsworth, Penguin.
Stone, O. M. (1977), *Family Law*, London, MacMillan.
Thompson, E. P. (1971), 'The Moral Economy of the English Crowd in the Eighteenth Century', 50 *Past and Present*, 76–136.
Thompson, E. P. (1977), *Whigs and Hunters*, London, Peregrine.
Thompson, E. P. (1978), 'Folklore, Anthropology and Social History', *Indian Historical Review*, Vol III, 247–66.
Tomasic, R. (1985), *The Sociology of Law*, London, Sage.
Trumbach, R. (1978), *The Rise of the Egalitarian Family*, London, Academic Press.
Weeks, J. (1981), *Sex, Politics and Society*, London, Longman.
Weyrauch, W. (1960), 'Informal and Formal Marriage', *University of Chicago Law Rev.* Vol 28, 88.
Weyrauch, W. (1980), 'Metamorphoses of Marriage: Formal and Informal Marriage in the United States', in Eekelaar J. M. and Katz S. N., *Marriage and Cohabitation in Contemporary Societies*, Toronto, Butterworth, Ch. 27.
Williams, R. (1976), *Keywords*, London, Fontana.
Williams, R. (1980), *Problems in Materialism and Culture*, London, Verso.
Wrigley, E. A. (1973), 'Clandestine Marriage in Tetbury in the late Seventeenth Century', *London Population Studies*, 15–21.
Wynne, J. (1955) 'A Report into the Deanry of Penllyn and Edeirnian by Rev. J. Wynne, 1730', *The Merioneth Miscellany*, 8.

[11]

DEBATES AND ISSUES REGARDING MARRIAGE AND COHABITATION IN THE BRITISH AND AMERICAN LITERATURE

JANE LEWIS*

ABSTRACT

The issue of family change has aroused considerable fear in the English-speaking countries, among both academic commentators and politicians. The most pervasive explanation of the changes has focused on an increase in an individualism that is selfish. Many have tended to read off a growth in individualism from the dramatic changes in the statistics of family change, and then to link it either to changes in individual behaviour, such as women's increased attachment to the labour market, or to changes in mentalities, such as prioritizing personal growth. In particular, it is assumed that cohabitation, a major driver of family change, involves the spread of an individualistic outlook on intimate relations. However, the meaning of both marriage and cohabitation are far from clear. Finally, the article considers some of the implications of the debate for family law and family policy, in terms of self-regulation (by the couple) and the possibility of further contractualism. It concludes that there is evidence that people want to make commitments as well as pursue their own projects, and the role of family policies in reconciling these desires is particularly important.

The issue of family change has tended to arouse much stronger fears in the English-speaking world than in continental European countries. The punitive attitudes towards lone mothers over the past decade on the part of politicians and the media have been viewed with a measure of astonishment by the UK's European neighbours (Lewis, 1997). Mentalities in the English-speaking world are usually characterized as more individualistic, but feelings about the importance of the traditional, two-parent, married, male breadwinner family model are also strongly held, and the debate about the causes of the trend towards cohabitation and away from marriage reflect this central tension. Indeed, the problematization of family change has much to do with the fear that cohabitation is symptomatic of a more individualistic orientation to family life. While there has been considerable amount of empirical investi-

* Department of Applied Social Studies and Social Research, Wellington Square, Oxford OX1 2ER.

gation to show who cohabitants are in the UK, the political and policy debates show little sensitivity to the range of cohabiting behaviour, tending rather to be caught in the same central concern about the fate of the traditional family in the face of profound change, which is in turn linked to much greater caution regarding the legal recognition of new family forms. This is reinforced by the historical tendency in both the UK and the US to regard family arrangements in general as outside the purview of the state, in contrast to the continental European countries (Hantrais and Letablier, 1996).

Family change has been accompanied by, and to a large extent preceded by, the erosion of major 'prescriptive frameworks' in the form of both the male breadwinner model family, which dictated the division of labour between married couples, and of the strict external moral code that encompassed traditional gendered patterns of behaviour in the family and underpinned family law, particularly in relation to divorce. There is therefore additional debate over the nature of the response that the state should make to family change. Should it accept the idea of increasing individualization and the privatization of decision-making about intimate relationships, or should it seek to give greater support more traditional family forms? The rapid pace of family change is a real issue, regardless of how far we accept the diagnoses that have been offered as to cause and effect. Furthermore, it raises the urgent question of what we can expect of family law and of family policies.

1. THE DEBATE ABOUT THE CAUSES OF THE TRENDS IN MARRIAGE AND COHABITATION IN THE ENGLISH-SPEAKING LITERATURE

The pace of family change has been dramatic in the last twenty-five years, such that in the UK it has become tempting to write of the 'rise and fall' of marriage in the twentieth century. Doubtless such a temptation should be resisted, but for the most part, academic commentators have decided that what has happened to the family during the last quarter of the century is problematic. In large measure, late twentieth century pessimism about the family has been a reaction to the scale and rapidity of the changes in the demographic statistics, which have produced a rethink of divorce and unmarried motherhood. During the 1950s and 1960s, British and American psychological, sociological and medical research concluded that marital conflict was as bad for a child as divorce (Goode, 1956), and that divorce might actually be better for children than living with unhappy parents who were effectively 'emotionally divorced' (eg Nye, 1957). These views were accompanied by optimistic accounts stressing the fundamental stability of marriage and the family, after all, divorce rates were low and the vast majority of births took place inside marriage, regardless of where they were conceived (Fletcher, 1966; Young and Willmott, 1973; Bane, 1976). But by the 1980s, research findings were drawing much more pessimistic conclusions against the backdrop of rapid increase in both the divorce rate and the extra-marital birth rate. American research began to emphasize the bad effects of divorce on children, launched by the work of Hetherington, Cox and Cox (1978) and Wallerstein and Kelly (1980), and the problems experienced by lone mothers more generally (McLanahan and Sandfur, 1994). The policy debate seemed disposed to overturn the long-held stress on the importance of the mother/child dyad (see especially Goldstein, Freud and Solnit, 1973) in favour of 'bringing fathers back in'. As James Davidson Hunter (1991) has commented, the debate over the family has in large measure been a debate over what constitutes the family. British empirical research followed the American in providing evidence of the detrimental impact of divorce and unmarried motherhood on the educational achievement, poverty levels, employment and personal relationships of children and young adults (eg Richards and Dyson, 1982; Maclean and Wadsworth, 1988; Kiernan, 1992). Some American writers have been more circumspect in their judgements (eg Furstenburg and Cherlin, 1991), but writing in the *Journal of Family Issues* in 1987, Norval Glenn, a respected sociologist of the family, observed that leading American writers were much less sanguine regarding the prospects of the American family in the mid-1980s than had been the case a decade before. There is no doubt that the climate of opinion has shifted radically over the course of a quarter of century on both sides of the Atlantic.

Most empirical work and most concern has been expressed about the *effects* of family change, particularly on children. The institution of marriage has long been viewed as the basic unit and bedrock of society, imposing rational bonds on irrational sexual urges, which is why relaxation of the divorce laws has proved so controversial and difficult right through the twentieth century. The married couple has been viewed as the *polis* in miniature. If they could not reach an accommodation, then what chance was there for the wider society? In this view, marriage is a discipline and an order, which also means that it is necessarily a matter of public interest and not just a private relationship. Indeed, the notion of the family, rather than the individual, as the fundamental building block has been central to most western countries, which have assumed the existence of a 'male-headed household' and a 'male-breadwinner-female-carer family'.

Early twentieth century commentators were as convinced as the functionalist sociologist Talcott Parsons in the 1950s and Fukuyama in the 1990s that the stable, traditional, two-parent family provides the best setting for raising children. Recent accounts have stressed the way in which the traditional family fosters the acquisition of 'social capital'

(Coleman, 1988), the informal values and norms that permit a group of people to work together. In the context of the family, social capital consists of the relationship between the parents and the children, which gives the child access to the parents' resources, intellectual, material and emotional. Older analyses of the importance of the family to the child, such as that of Talcott Parsons, emphasized the mediating role played by the family between the individual and the wider society, and the way in which the traditional two-parent family, with its clearly assigned roles for adult men and women, successfully 'socialized' the child. The main focus for those stressing the importance of the stability of marriage and the family concerns the benefits that are derived by children and thus the wider society, although Waite (1995) has argued strongly that the adults involved also benefit in terms of their health and material welfare and Marris (1991) has argued the primacy of need for attachment and the way in which marriage in particular protects against depression. This is more controversial, for feminist analysis has long held that traditional marriage works to the advantage of men and the disadvantage of women (Bernard, 1976; Delphy and Leonard, 1992).

Concern about the effects of family change have spread out from the implications for children to the wider society, and as McLanahan and Booth (1989) have observed, has acted as a touchstone for issues that are in and of themselves major sources of anxiety, for example, gender roles, class, race and the role of the state. Thus George Akerloff (1998), an economist, has contended that changes in marriage patterns are a more potent cause of social pathology in the form of criminal behaviour and drug abuse than unemployment or 'welfare dependency'. For Francis Fukuyama (1999), family change is part of the 'great disruption' in social norms and values that began in the 1960s and manifested itself in rising crime rates and a decline in trust, as well as in family breakdown. In Britain, Dennis and Erdos (1992) sought to trace the rise of the 'obnoxious Englishman' to family breakdown. Their chief concern was the effect of lone motherhood on the behaviour patterns of young men. Lone motherhood was in their view responsible for at best irresponsible and at worst criminal behaviour in the next male generation. But the possible link between absent fathers and rising crime rates has not been tested for any large-scale British sample. Indeed, the debates over marriage and the family are fraught because cause and effect are so difficult to establish. One of the most recent contributions to the literature on the effects of divorce on children shows that this issue, which that has been subjected to careful empirical research, is still far from resolved. Rodgers and Pryor's (1998) make it clear how difficult it is to be sure that the outcomes are directly attributable to parental separation, rather than to a range of factors that impinge on families before, during and after separation. The effects of family change are hard to establish, and in a sense it is the uncertainty about where the move away from the traditional married, two-parent family and the stability associated with it, might lead that is the problem.

While most attention has been directed at the possible effects of family change, it is not surprising that there has been considerable reflection as to what might be happening in society to *cause* it. The most pervasive explanation has focused on an increase in individualism in terms of both ideas and behaviour. Glenn warned that if a good marriage was to be judged only by hedonistic standards, then marriage might become 'so insecure that no rational person will invest a great deal of time, energy, money and forgone opportunities to make a particular marriage satisfactory' (Glenn, 1987, 351). His concern, and that of many others, is about the kind of thinking and behaviour that causes the lack of permanence and stability.

There has been widespread academic support for the idea of increased individualism as the major explanation for family change. Demographers have pointed out the degree to which demographic change has been accompanied by more individualistic values (Lesthaeghe and Surkym, 1988). Thus Van de Kaa's (1987) theory of a second demographic transition beginning in the 1960s with the separation of sex and marriage and followed by the emergence of cohabitation, stressed the importance of the accompanying belief in the rights of the individual, especially in respect of personal and career fulfilment. But the degree to which individualism is also selfish and the way in which it is manifested is a matter of debate.

The economics literature has provided the most influential theoretical underpinnings for the idea of the importance of individual rational choice and has applied it to the workings of the family. Neo-classical economists have suggested that as women's capacity to support themselves has increased, so they have been less willing to put up with unsatisfactory marriages (Becker, Landes and Michael, 1977). Gary Becker's (1981) Nobel Prize-winning work on a 'new home economics' argued that people marry when the utility expected from marriage is greater than it is if they remain single. Given that women desire children, they will look for a good male breadwinner. Men will look for a good housekeeper and carer. Thus men and women make complementary investments in marriage that result in higher joint gains. Becker's model assumes that gains are shared equally between husbands and wives (ignoring the possibility of a basic tension between an egalitarian, companionate ideal and the reality of unequal roles (Bernard, 1976; Skolnick, 1991). In Becker's analysis, women's earning power disrupts the balance in the exchange of labour between husbands and wives and causes instability. Economic bargaining models (eg Lundberg and Pollak, 1996) do not assume that resources are shared equally. Marital investment and exchanges must offer both husbands and wives more than they obtain outside the marriage. According to these theories, a rise in women's employment, or an increase in their wages will threaten the stability of marriage, for it will no longer offer women unequivocal gains. The point about these kinds of analysis is that they rely on the idea of individuals making rational choices to maximize their rewards and minimize their costs. However, much more complicated ideas involving desert and reputation (akin to what Offer, 1996, has termed the 'economy of regard') may be involved. Finch and Mason's (1993) study of family obligations has stressed that while Becker was right in perceiving the essence of commitment to reside in the fact that at some point it becomes too expensive to withdraw, the nature of the expense is not necessarily material.

Sociologists have focused much more on mentalities and the search for personal growth and development. Norval Glenn stressed the dangers of hedonism and self-gratification. Robert Bellah *et al*'s (1985) influential study of 'middle America' argued that the individual is realized only through the wider community and reached very similar, pessimistic conclusions to those of Glenn in regard to the family: 'if love and marriage are seen primarily in terms of psychological gratification, they may fail to fulfil their older social function of providing people with stable, committed relationships that tie them into the larger society' (85).

Bellah *et al.* opened their account of middle American life with a statement as to their concern that 'individualism may have grown cancerous' (vii). They identified two forms of individualism: first the utilitarian, which amounted to the traditional American desire to 'get ahead' and to be self-reliant, and second, the expressive, which emphasized self-expression and the sharing of feelings rather than material acquisition. In respect of the first, they argued that the values of the public sphere—'the coolly manipulative style' (48) that is required to 'get-ahead'—were invading the private world of the family. In Bellah *et al*'s view, the contractual nature of commercial and bureaucratic life threatened to become an ideology for personal life. Such an anxiety has a long history. The ideology of separate spheres, whereby the ruthless competition that was thought necessary for the successful operation of the market was balanced by the haven of the family, where women would care for the male worker and also for those too weak to engage in the public sphere, was central to turn of the century classical liberalism (Lewis, 1984).

In respect of expressive individualism, the 'therapeutic attitude' threatened to replace notions of obligation and commitment by an ideology of full, open and honest communication between 'self-actualizing individuals'. Bellah *et al.* were particularly concerned about the way in which Maslow's (1987) idea of a hierarchy of needs, in which satisfaction of higher needs (eg love rather than shelter) brings greater satisfaction, had been popularized by the human potential movement and non-directive counselling. Inglehart's (1997) comparative data for economically prosperous countries showed a clear shift from materialist values, emphasizing economic and physical security above all, to 'post-materialist' priorities, especially self-expression and the quality of life. But critics have argued that the healthy self became the self-in-process, with a constantly shifting identity (Kilpatrick, 1975). As Taylor (1989) has pointed out, in this set of ideas self realization becomes the end point and meaning comes to consist only of how we feel. Yankelovich's (1981) work on US survey data confirmed the shift to more 'me-centred' concerns. It seemed that the 'duty to self' was becoming primary.

Not all academic sociologists subscribing to the importance of individualism as an explanation of family change are pessimistic. Giddens (1992) also argued that late twentieth century relationships amount to a 'pure relationship', that is, it is 'entered into for [its] own sake, for what can be derived by each person from a sustained association with another; and which is continued only in so far as it thought by both parties to deliver enough satisfactions for each individual to stay within it' (35). However, unlike Bellah *et al.*, Giddens does not consider such relationships to be inherently selfish, indeed, he believes that they have served to democratize the family. But they are 'contingent' and if a particular relationship does not provide one of the partners with what they seek, then they will move on.

When it comes to polemicists and politicians, there has been a tendency to start from the dramatic statistics, and to assume that they provide a sufficient demonstration of selfish individualism at work. Love requires trust and it is certainly possible to suggest that the risk of trusting and investing emotionally has become greater as economic alternatives have opened up (Seligman, 1997), especially for women, and as the stigma attaching to divorce, unmarried motherhood and cohabitation has been eroded, making it easier for men as much or more than women to 'move on'. But, the way in which the idea has been taken up and popularized more often rests on assertion and does not hesitate to allocate blame. The American sociologist, David Popenoe (1993), has read off motivation from the aggregate statistics and argued that the data show that 'people have become less willing to invest time, money and energy in family life, turning instead to investment in themselves'. David Blankenhorn (1990), founder and president of the Institute for American Values, believes, like Fukuyama, that the statistics indicate a decline in values. Much of the debate about the family in the late twentieth century has in fact been a struggle over the meaning of the statistics (Hunter, 1991), with little attempt to refer to the admittedly limited research on the changes that have actually taken place inside family relationships, or to investigate them further. However, simple assertions as to the power of selfish individualism have had a significant effect on policy making on both sides of the Atlantic. For example, in the course of the parliamentary debates on the 1996 Family Law Act, Baroness Young said that 'for one party simply to decide to go off with another person. . . . reflects the growing *self-first disease* which is debasing our society' (*Hansard*, Lords, 29 February 1996, c 1638, my emphasis).

The selfish individualistic behaviour that is held to have resulted in the erosion of the traditional two-parent family is said to have manifested itself in a variety of ways. Both men and women have been blamed by politicians and polemicists. The most frequently cited cause of family change is the increase in women's employment.

As Oppenheimer (1994) has pointed out, the idea that women's increased economic independence has an effect on their marital behaviour is widespread, possibly because people with very different politics can buy into it. Thus feminists have been as likely to endorse a theory that stresses the importance of women's economic independence as right-wing polemicists, but they have stressed women's right and/or need to work. From a rather different political perspective George Gilder (1987) in the US and Geoff Dench (1994) in Britain have seen the increase in women's labour force participation and attachment as something that has stripped men of their traditional breadwinning role with the family, and they blame women for pursuing self-fulfilment in the form of a career at the expense of their families. Dench (1994, 16–17) argued strongly that family responsibilities are an indispensable civilizing influence on men:

> If women go too far in pressing for symmetry, and in trying to change the rules of the game, men will simply decide not to play. . . . The family may be a myth, but it is a myth that works to make men tolerably useful.

In this interpretation, as much blame is attributed to women for undermining the traditional male role of breadwinner as to men themselves. The influential journalist Melanie Phillips (1997) has also concluded that it is the erosion of the male role that has created 'yobbish men'.

Nevertheless, not since the early part of the century has as much attention been paid to the behaviour of men in families. By the early 1990s the political debate was dominated by those who stressed the selfishness and irresponsibility of men as well as women. Akerloff (1998) pointed out that the proportion of US men aged twenty-five to thirty-four in families declined from 66 to 40 per cent over the period of 1968. Either they were leaving their families or not joining in the first place. Feminists expressing anxiety about 'male flight from commitment' (Ehrenreich, 1983), alongside Conservative politicians railing against male irresponsibility. Michael Howard, then British Home Secretary, said in a speech to the Conservative Political Centre in 1993:

If the state will house and pay for their children the duty on [young men] to get involved may seem removed from their shoulders.... And since the State is educating, housing and feeding their children the nature of parental responsibility may seem less immediate (Howard, 1993).

The father's duty to maintain was argued not only on the grounds of the importance of the role model it provided for children, but also in terms of fairness to the taxpayer. According to an Editorial in *The Economist* (9 September 1995): 'A Father who can afford to support only one family ought to have only one'.

Commentators have in addition expressed the view that the state has exacerbated the situation by permitting and even encouraging selfish, individualistic behaviour on the part of men and women. Thus the reform of family law, particularly the relaxation of the divorce laws, is widely believed to have allowed men to follow their 'natural' inclinations, behave opportunistically and abandon their wives, usually in favour of younger women (Cohen, 1987; Posner, 1992). Social policies (in Britain and the US) are also believed to have helped cause the rise in the number of lone mother families by allowing unmarried and divorced women to draw welfare benefits (Murray, 1984; Popenoe, 1988); while tax policies have simultaneously disadvantaged the two parent, married family by eroding the married man's allowance and introducing independent taxation for husbands and wives, which in turn provides incentives to women to enter the labour market (Morgan, 1999).

The underlying anxiety about increasing individualism, whether expressed in the value-neutral language of the neo-classical economist, the value-conscious language of the sociologist, or in terms of the practical anxieties of the politician and the polemicist, centres on its implications for the sources of moral commitments. The atomized individual is unlikely to engage fully in either family or community, which results in an 'emptying out' of these fundamental building blocks of society. As Elias (1991, 204) has commented: 'The greater impermanence of we-relationships, which at earlier stages often had the lifelong inescapable character of an external constraint, puts all the more emphasis on the I, one's own person, as the only permanent factor, the only person with whom one must live one's whole life'.

Bellah *et al.* suggested that the therapeutic attitude begins with the self rather than an external set of obligations and that love between 'therapeutically self-actualized persons' is incompatible with self-sacrifice. Agnes Heller (1979) has argued that feeling was linked to morality until the late nineteenth century, it is only as it has become 'psychologized' that is has also been separated from both morality and reason. The strong belief in the freedom of what is assumed to be the rational individual actor to choose unfettered by regulation that characterized the long period of Conservative government in the closing decades of the twentieth century also played a major part in this process of 'emptying out'. Reflecting on the politics of Thatcherism, Marilyn Strathern (1992) identified the emergence of a 'hyper-individualism'. Morality, like everything else, became a matter of individual choice and preference. Morality was to come from within, 'but the interior has itself no structure' (159). As Sandel (1982) had already suggested, a person without constitutive attachments is a person wholly without character. Strathern severely questioned the effect of fetishizing individual choice on the person, arguing that individuality becomes fragmented in the face of such a consumerist ideology (see also Gergen, 1991).The difficulty of exercising choice in a moral and social vacuum has become an increasingly dominant theme in the literature.

This compelling and frightening picture of a world in which there is no picture of the common good and in which rampant individualism was in the process of destroying the very foundations—the family and the community—on which the market and modern liberal democracies depended has been widely echoed. While polemicists railed against what they perceived as selfish behaviour, philosophers began to try and find ways to talk about the importance of 'social glue'. Thus Coleman (1988) used the concept of social capital as a way of challenging the rational individual action paradigm. Social capital as a set of informal values and norms permit co-operation and foster trust (Coleman, 1988; Fukuyama, 1999). Trust and co-operation are thus learned in the private sphere of the family (and in civil society: Putnam, 1993) and pass into the public sphere of politics and the market. Feminists have long insisted upon the importance of connection and the relational self to women's moral sense (Gilligan, 1982; Held, 1993; Griffiths, 1995). The new-found attention to social capital represents a wider appreciation of the extent to which no one is an 'unencumbered self' (Sandel, 1996), and stresses interdependence and hence the obligations people have towards one another.

Thus the discussion of individualism as a cause of family change and the nature of the concern it evokes is diffuse, focusing on changing mentalities and behaviours at the individual level. Changing behaviour in the form of greater female labour market participation, or male 'flight' from the family is taken as a manifestation of selfish individualism. But the meanings of such behaviour need closer scrutiny and they need to be understood in a wider context of social change that includes structures, institutions, norms and values. Not only are there important links between mentalities and patterns of behaviour at the individual level to be considered, but changes in norms and values, and in structures and institutions at the collective level also need to be brought in.

As a result of my own research on these issues, I am convinced that we should pay more attention to the vexed issue of 'culture' (Lewis,

1999; Lewis *et al*, 1999). To summarize: it seems to me to be important to consider the complex interplay between mentalities and behaviour at the level of the family, and also to locate decision-making at the micro-level in the wider context of structural and normative change. The concept of 'individualization', developed in the main by Beck and Beck Gernsheim (1995, see also Beck Gernsheim, 1999), which examines the way in which the family as 'a community of need' has become 'an 'elective relationship', calls attention to the importance of structural change and yet again to the changes in the gendered division of labour in families, but does not read these off as expressions of individual*ism*. Rather, it signals the way in which profound changes in what Pfau Effinger (1998) has called the 'gender order'—the labour market and the law—can produce changes in norms. I would suggest first, that the decline of the male breadwinner model (such that it has been replaced by something approaching a one and a half earner model in most western countries) has produced different expectations of marriage; and second, that the abandonment of the external moral code provided by a family law that rested on fault-based divorce has also proved crucial in terms of eroding the major 'prescriptive frameworks' that have served to 'hold' the tensions inherent in modern marriage. Sugden (1998) has analysed the way in which conventional practices can generate 'normative expectations', which are in turn significant for the stability of conventions. Changes in such expectations are as important as changes in behaviour. The erosion of the 'traditional' expectations of intimate relationships that were embedded both in family policies based on the assumption of a male breadwinner model and in family law based on ideas about the permanence of marriage and notions of fault-based divorce has left something of vacuum. Théry (1994) has coined the concept of 'demarriage' in order to capture the way in which marriage has become largely disengaged from wider social structures such that it is a personal choice. It is now up to the couple to negotiate the ways in which their relationship will work, with the state increasingly prepared to enforce their responsibilities in this respect.

Many of those convinced as to the importance of the growth of individualism have tended in the main to read it off from the dramatic changes in the statistics of family change, and then to link it either to changes in individual behaviour, such as women's increased attachment to the labour market, or to changes in mentalities, such as prioritizing personal growth. However change at the individual level will necessarily be affected by what is going on outside the family, for example in the law and the labour market. But the relationship may not be direct, and may rather be mediated by changes in expectations about behaviour.

2. THE MEANING OF MARRIAGE AND COHABITATION

We are all aware that it is important to interrogate a category such as 'part-time work', which can mean very different things—in terms of hours worked and the nature of the jobs involved from country to country. So it is with cohabitation. Much of the American literature on cohabitation continues to focus mainly on what Kiernan and Estaugh (1993) called 'nubile cohabitation'. Undoubtedly this form still accounts for the majority of cohabitants in Britain, but there are increasing numbers of cohabitants with children and also of people who cohabit after a divorce. Indeed, as John Haskey (1995) has shown, people's lives look increasingly messy in terms of the pattern of cohabitations, marriages and divorces that may occur within a single individual's life cycle.

Cohabitation has been a strong driver of family change. Marriage has become a discretionary adult role, whereas it used to be compulsory if certain other things were to be achieved—a home of one's own and children. It may be the case that the period of courtship and engagement has been effectively replaced by 'nubile cohabitation'. In Britain we know that the majority of cohabiting couples *with children* is disproportionately poor (Kiernan and Estaugh, 1993; McRae, 1993). Smart and Stevens (2000) recent work on breakdown with a sample from this subset of cohabitants has suggested that given a choice between becoming a lone mother or marrying a man whom they are not sure they can rely on, it is rational for these women to decide to cohabit. In the past, many of them may have had 'shot-gun marriages' and subsequently divorced. In other words, we may merely be seeing new ways of dealing with rather old dilemmas; what Kath Kiernan has referred to as the issue of 'relabelling' (Kiernan, Land and Lewis, 1998).

Nevertheless, the English-speaking literature has tended to conclude that cohabitants come closest to the 'pure relationships' described by Giddens, in which the partners are committed only for as long as they feel that they benefit personally from the relationship (Hall, 1996). Early American research stressed that cohabitants made a different kind of commitment to each other. Newcomb (1981) found that cohabitants saw fewer barriers to ending their relationship than did married people, and Lauer and Lauer (1986) concluded from their study of 351 married couples in the US that commitment in marriage is 'qualitatively different'. They argued not only that marriage promoted attachment, but that contractual obligation to the institution of marriage provided a context for the resolution of problems in a way that cohabitation could not. The strong theme running through these contributions is that cohabitation amounts only to the sum of two individuals, whereas at its best, marriage is more than this. In his work on trust, Hollis (1998, 138) has written about the possibility of married couples being committed to doing what is collectively best for both partners, as opposed to merely engaging in 'mutual backscratching' where reciprocity is bilateral ('if you scratch my back, I'll scratch yours'), which is how a self-regarding version of Gidden's pure relationship might operate. The conclusion seems to be that a public declaration of commitment is a stronger form and makes for a more lasting relationship.

However, the research confined to cohabitation is rather mixed in terms of its findings. Rindfus and VandenHeuvel's study of young cohabitants (1990) argued that increasing individualism and secularization have produced higher rates of cohabitation, which threatens subsequent marital commitment. Similarly Cherlin (1981, 15–16), who is considerably less pessimistic regarding the family than many contemporary American commentators, argues that cohabitation is a relationship that the parties believe should be ended if it fails to provide satisfaction, and that people take these attitudes into marriage:

> cohabitation comes with the ethic that a relationship should be ended if either partner is dissatisfied, this after all is part of the reason why people live together rather than marrying.

Consequently the spread of cohabitation involves the spread of an individualistic outlook on intimate relations. Rindfus and VandenHeuvel (1990) found that their young cohabitants were more like never-married people, and that cohabitation was seen as a way of securing intimacy without making any long-term commitment. The findings of Schoen (1992) and Clarkberg *et al* (1995) were similar. On the basis of data from the US National Survey of Families and Households, Nock (1995) concluded that cohabitants have lower levels of commitment and lower levels of happiness. Nevertheless, Brown and Booth (1996) concluded on the basis of a national sample survey of US households and families that the relationship quality of cohabitants with children was similar to their married counterparts. All that seems clear from this literature is that it is crucial to differentiate between the different populations of cohabitants, which not very many studies do.

Nor can the meaning of marriage necessarily be assumed at the end of the century. There is, in comparison with cohabitation, an enormous English-speaking literature on marriage, but most of it is American and relies on quantitative methods. Most of the quantitative studies have looked at various aspects of relationships: particularly the division of labour, communication between the partners, and measures of power and satisfaction. As Gottman (1994) has observed, the focus has been on the relationship between particular behavioural variables, rather than on the *processes* and *mechanisms* that are crucial for understanding meanings, which can only be revealed by qualitative research. Commentators who have expressed profound anxieties about the fate of marriage and the family have painted a relatively simple picture of ever increasing attention to personal growth and development. However, the empirical research on what happens inside relationships suggests a much more complex balancing act between attention to self and to others, eg Lawson's (1988) study of adultery and Askham's (1984) attention to the tension between the search for identity and for stability. Prevalent post-war notions of marriage as a 'partnership' that was becoming 'joint' (Bott, 1957) and that would become more 'symmetrical' (Young and Willmott, 1973), collapsed in the face of mainly feminist research in the 1980s and 1990s, which emphasized continuing inequalities and new sources of tension, particularly in respect of the unequal division of paid and unpaid work (Hochschild, 1990).

We know too little about why people do make the decision to marry at the beginning of the twenty-first century. Marriage is still an institution as well as a relationship, and it does still involve the participation of family and friends in a way that a decision to cohabit rarely does. To this extent, as with the nature of the commitment that is made, marriage remains 'public'. The *British Social Attitudes Survey* of 1994 showed that 64 per cent of respondents thought that it was all right for a couple to live together without intending to get married, but 57 per cent still thought that couples intending to have children should marry first (Newman and Smith, 1997). Whether this is because of anxieties about stability, stigma or something else entirely is unclear. Attitudes have obviously changed and, perhaps most importantly in respect of policy, there is clear British and European evidence (from the Eurobarometer Survey) that people are very reluctant to prescribe how others should live in respect of their personal relationships (Reynolds and Mansfield, 1999; *Observer*/ICM poll, 28 October 1998). The *decision* to marry or to cohabit is regarded as private. Indeed, many commentators have questioned whether marriage has any remaining legal utility (Clive, 1980; Dewar and Parker, 1992). If not, this pushes us back to the emotional and possibly sacramental meanings of marriage.

3. SOME IMPLICATIONS FOR FAMILY LAW AND FAMILY POLICY

Legal reform in twentieth century Britain, up to and including the 1996 Family Law Act, has been characterized by a retreat from the attempt to impose an external moral code. Many recent commentators believe that this has resulted in a legal 'vacuum', what Glendon (1981) termed the 'deregulation' of family law. As many have observed, it is now easier to divorce someone than to fire them (Sandel, 1996), and that it is easier to renounce a marriage than a mortgage (Wilson, 1993).

From a perspective sympathetic to right-wing, neo-classical economics, Posner (1992) argued that the growing autonomy of women in terms of the material dimensions of fertility control and more especially economic independence created conditions which made it impossible for the state to impose duties (or confer rights) on couples. He favoured an outright move towards 'contractual cohabitation', the terms of which would be determined by the couple. Some feminists, particularly in the US, have also argued that the law should take account of women's increased autonomy, and that explicit pre-nuptial, marital and cohabitation contracts are the best way of so doing (eg Schultz, 1982; Scott, 1990; Kingdom, 1988, 1990). In this interpretation, the logic of increasing individualization in the private sphere leads not just to new thinking about intimate relationships, but new legal forms.

Interestingly, A. V. Dicey's enormously influential lectures on the relationship between law and opinion, delivered at the end of the nineteenth century, also suggested that individualism in the sense of democratic opinion involved marriage being seen as a contract, which in turn would make divorce easier (Dicey, 1948). But Dicey believed that this had already taken effect with the passing of the 1857 Divorce Act, which created a court for divorce and established the grounds for procedure. For Dicey, the 1857 legislation was a triumph of liberal individualism and he believed that this was being increasingly threatened by socialist or collectivist opinion, which was inclined to see marriage as a benefit to the state. While Dicey's view shows that the idea of a relationship between individualism and the relaxation of the law of marriage and divorce is far from new, it also serves to indicate longstanding confusion about the precise nature of the law of marriage and divorce and of legal change.

Legal commentators have long argued about the extent to which marriage can be conceptualized as a contract or a status, and about the extent to which it remains sacramental. O'Donovan (1993, 76) has suggested that marriage has a 'sacred, magical status'. It may have contractual and institutional elements, but it is difficult neatly to categorize it. The whole idea of fault-based divorce implied an idea of contractual obligations (Atkins and Hoggett, 1984), but it is the state rather than the parties to this implied contract that controls both entry to it and its ending. Henry Maine (1861, 170) had argued that the progress of the law was from status, derived from 'the powers and privileges anciently residing in the Family', to contract, which emerged from private transactions between individuals. The irony was that it appeared to be in respect of intimate relationships in the family that the law was very slow to change. In other areas, as Dicey perceived, the state began, from the late nineteenth century to limit the freedom of contract and to offer alternative forms of collective welfare provision in recognition of the fact that the parties to the contract between capital and labour were profoundly unequal in terms of economic strength. It is noteworthy that in the case of marriage, many, including some feminists, have argued *against* the recognition of increasing individualization by the more explicit adoption of contract, pointing out that men and women remain unequal in terms of their access to income, wealth and resources of all kinds (notwithstanding their increased economic independence), and the concomitant obligation of the state to continue to regulate the marital relation in the interests of the weaker party (Okin, 1989; Wax, 1998; Baier, 1986).

The fact that private contract continues to be proposed as a solution to the problems of the private law of the family shows that deregulation in the sense of the complete withdrawal of the state is in fact far from complete. Indeed, most legal commentators have recognized that marriage defies simple characterization in terms of status or contract. Cohen (1933) pointed out that while contractarians held that obligation should ideally arise only out of the will of the individual who freely entered into contract, with minimalist intervention by the state, feelings of security depended on the protection of government. Thus in the case of marriage, while the act of getting married was voluntary, the legal consequences were not contractual but were rather imposed 'from without' in the public interest. Later arguments also stressed the extent to which the voluntary agreement to marry established a status that in the case of women was subordinate (Rehbinder, 1971). The so-called marriage contract was, as Weitzman (1981) was to point out later still, an implicit contract, involving sexual services and care on the part of the woman and financial support on the part of the man.

However, the debate among legal commentators as to the *nature* of the law governing marriage and divorce may not be as important as the shift in the *understanding* of marriage that is signified by legal reform. Historically the law of marriage and divorce had sought to uphold the idea of the 'unity' of husband and wife and the permanence of marriage (Wolfram, 1987). In the nineteenth century, married women had no legal personality and hence no capacity to enter into contracts in the marketplace. The legal doctrine of *couveture*, which stated that husband and wife were as one and that one was the husband, was described clearly in Sir William Blackstone's famous eighteenth-century *Commentaries on the Laws of England*: 'The very being or legal existence of the wife is suspended during the marriage or at least incorporated and consolidated into that of the husband under whose wing, protection and cover she performs everything'. The shift towards women's individualization in English law took place gradually, beginning with the married women's property laws at the end of the nineteenth century, the equalization of grounds for divorce in 1923, and continuing into the 1990s with the introduction of separate taxation and the recognition of possibility of rape in marriage. But it is still far from complete. The determination of social security benefits in particular continues to rest on the concept of a household rather than individual income.

The relationship between law and behaviour is far from clear. Law facilitates and legitimates certain kinds of behaviour, as well as following behavioural change. Weitzman (1981) has suggested that the obligations imposed by the law of divorce will affect ideas about marriage. This in turn may be what serves to legitimate certain kinds of behaviour. But it is also reasonable to suppose that changing ideas about the nature of marriage will have an effect on the law.

The reform of family law in the twentieth century has been characterized by a movement towards what might be termed 'self-regulation' (by the couple), in other words the 'privatization' of decision-making about the ending of a marriage, which is in line with changing ideas about the source of sexual morality (from within rather than without). But this movement is not necessarily equivalent to deregulation. Increasingly couples have been encouraged to take responsibility for sorting out their own affairs on breakdown. The shift away from public intervention in intimate relationships has been profound. Towards the end of the twentieth century, several observers have noted that the law has had less and less to say about the adult partners to an intimate relationship, but that it continues to regulate their relations as parents (eg Dewar and Parker, 1992; Lewis and Maclean, 1997). To tell couples wishing to part that they must seek to reach accommodation about their children is a form of regulation.

However, the fear of many policymakers at the end of the century is that the steady march of legal reform away from the imposition of external rules has encouraged the growth of selfish individualism. In particular it is feared that no-fault divorce has increased the divorce rate, although the balance of opinion on this is more negative in the US than Britain, and that it has adversely affected the economic position of women after divorce (Rowthorn, 1999 provides a review). This in turn makes for reluctance to do anything about major outstanding issues such as how to treat cohabitation, for fear that it might provide additional reinforcement of the changes in ideas and behaviour that has already taken place.

A difficult balancing act has been required of governments in respect of family law and family policy during the late twentieth century. Governments may regard the pace and nature of change with anxiety, something that is not so unreasonable in respect of the family in the last quarter of the twentieth century. In common with many academics they may worry about the extent to which self-interested individualism is overtaking a sense of obligation and/or commitment. But what is to be done about it? If people have become uneasy about the explicit prescription of norms and values, can governments seek to impose them? Is it feasible for governments to seek to 'put the clock back', or should they seek to recognize and work with the kinds of family change that have occurred? It has been suggested by some that a more decisive move towards treating intimate relationships—married and cohabiting—under the regime of contract would be more successful in addressing the changes that have taken place. Others would prefer to see steps taken to privilege marriage. The concerns of policy makers in the 1980s and 1990s have been focused primarily on the high levels of relationship breakdown, with the major anxiety for governments being the welfare of children. But this also involves the welfare of their carers, with the debate revolving around how far the issue of support for children should be met individually (by fathers) or collectively via the tax/benefit system and the provision of social services.

4. CONSERVATIVE AND LABOUR GOVERNMENTS AND THE FAMILY IN THE 1980S AND 1990S

The Conservatives were divided between a more libertarian and a more authoritarian approach in the 1980s and early 1990s (King, 1986). Ferdinand Mount (1983), Mrs Thatcher's family policy adviser in the early 1980s, defended the autonomy of the family and described it as being in 'permanent revolution' against the state. However, when families demonstrated manifest signs of failure, the state did not hesitate to step in. In the face of the cost of family change arising from the increasing number of lone mother families, the third Thatcher administration began to talk much more firmly about enforcing personal responsibility. As Jeffries (1996) has noted, for Conservatives, individual freedom is underpinned by the stable moral order of the family. Personal responsibility was defined primarily in terms of the duties of parents towards their children. Mrs Thatcher (1995, 630) recalled in her memoirs that she 'was appalled by the way in which men fathered a child and then absconded, leaving the single mother—and the tax payer—to foot the bill for their irresponsibility and condemning the child to a lower standard of living'. The 1991 Child Support Act was the result of her thinking. It attempted to make unmarried and divorced fathers pay maintenance for all their biological children. In effect, this legislation tried to enforce the traditional responsibilities associated with marriage—of men to maintain and of women to care—where marriage had ended and where it had never taken place, but it did not seek explicitly to turn back the clock in respect of family change. The 1996 Family Law Act sought to enforce the obligations of mothers and fathers, rather than husbands and wives in its provisions regarding conciliation, as well as attempting to bolster marriage in its efforts to resuscitate 'marriage saving'. Both pieces of legislation demonstrated the Conservatives' deep regard for the traditional obligations that had been part of the male breadwinner model family, but in addition, the Family Law Act made it clear that the Government was not content merely to try and devise means of dealing with the results of family change. Rather, it wanted to try and reverse it by promoting marriage.

The Labour Government, elected in 1997, has pursued a less coherent policy in respect of the family. This may be, as Baldock (1999) has suggested, because it is determined to take into account the often demonstrably contradictory state of public opinion on different issues to do with the family. The 1998 Consultative Paper, *Supporting Families*, stated firmly: 'Neither a "back to basics" fundamentalism, trying to turn back the clock, nor an "anything goes" liberalism which denies the fact that how families behave affects us all, is credible any more.' (Home Office, 1998, 5, para 11). As Harding (1999) has observed, the document repeatedly made the point that the Government did not want to lecture, to preach or to nag. It acknowledged family change and that many lone parents and 'unmarried couples' raise their children successfully, but also stated that 'marriage is still the surest foundation for raising children' (ibid, 4, para 8). The document said that marriage is best, but promised no direct incentives, for example in the form of restoring the value of the married couples' tax allowance, which was abolished in April 2000. Rather it discussed the possibility of providing guidance on responsibilities and rights to those intending to marry or cohabit, and floated the possibility of pre-nuptial agreements. On the other hand, the state of the law regarding cohabitation was ignored. And, in 2000, that part of the Family Law Act dealing with the final step towards no-fault divorce was abandoned. This was because of difficulties in implementation, but also it seems that the Government feared that it would smack of the 'nanny state', while not necessarily having the desired effect of promoting reconciliation. Certainly Paul Boateng, a Minister in the new Government, had spoken strongly while in Opposition in favour of saving marriage, urging that the new legislation 'should not be simply a vehicle for the dissolution of marriage, but a means by which marriage might be supported' (House of Commons, Standing Cttee E, 25 April 1996, col 4)

Like the Conservative Party, the Labour Government's main concern has been not the unity of the couple nor even the permanence of relationships, but the need to secure stable arrangements for children. This has led to a continued emphasis on parenting beyond the bounds of marriage and on the importance of individual parental responsibility, which as Smart and Neale (1999) have commented, has not involved much attention to the quality of relationships. In keeping with the desire to enforce the obligations of biological fatherhood, in 1998 the Lord Chancellor proposed giving unmarried fathers who register on the birth certificate automatic parental responsibility for their children. This was first raised by the Law Commission in 1979, but rejected in large measure because of the problem of the 'unmeritorious father'. Cohabitants continue to be treated differently from married people in important respects when their relationships breakdown. Family law gives them no rights of occupation of the family home or entitlement to maintenance; these are issues that the idea of 'registered partnerships' is designed to address. So far, the Solicitors Family Law Association (1999) has come out in favour of these, but the Government made no mention of such a possibility in its 1998 Consultative Paper on the family. For younger couples, marriage and cohabitation represent two equally viable options. Given this, it may be that the older assumption that married and cohabiting people expect to be treated differently (eg Deech, 1980) is breaking down, among married as well as cohabiting couples. In which case, the Government's caution in taking explicit steps to privilege marriage is well-founded, however, its reluctance to address the issue of cohabitation may be less well-founded.

However, Labour has also put considerable stress on the importance of family policies to support parents. This is a new departure in the UK, where historically parents have been left to work out their own affairs (most obviously in respect of reconciling work and family responsibilities), unless there have been any gross manifestations of inadequate care. *Supporting Families* put better services and support for parents first, referring mainly to education and advice to be delivered via a National Family and Parenting Institute, a helpline and health visitors, but also through a funded initiative to provide childcare, family support, primary health care, early learning and play for young children (the Sure Start programme.) The announcement of a National Child Care Strategy and the pledge to remove child poverty within twenty years have also signalled a much wider commitment to investment in children and support in the form of cash and services for families.

What is certain is that because of the unequal gender division of labour, and particularly of unpaid work, it is not easy to deal with children separately from their carers. As Cretney (1996) and Fineman (1993) have commented, there has been a complete absence of principles regarding the maintenance of spouses, and yet the care of children depends in large measure on the welfare and support of their carers. Traditionalists have favoured a return to fault-based divorce in an effort to secure the male obligation to maintain (eg Rowthorne, 1999), even though there is no evidence that this was secured in practice (Eekelaar and Maclean, 1986). Some feminists have continued to favour the idea of treating the married couple as a partnership, but of expanding the concept of property to include, for example, the human capital represented by the degrees earned by the husband, which may have been made possible by wage-earning on the part of the wife (Weitzman, 1981). Others have favoured the equal sharing of income after divorce for a specified number of years. Still others favour a model by which a female spouse is compensated to the degree that her standard of living after caregiving falls short of what she might have expected had the marriage broken down without caregiving having taken place (Eekelaar and Maclean, 1986; Ellman, 1997). This links spousal support to child support (Eekelaar, 1991). The story of family law from in the UK from 1969 to 1996 showed how difficult it is to square the desire to treat adult relationships as involving two equal individuals on the one hand, with the desire to provide properly for children on the other. This problem is almost certainly beyond the capacity of family law alone to solve, and a substantially more active family policy may therefore be necessary.

This point is important in relation to the increasing support from many commentators on family law for a more explicit recognition of individualization in the shape of a move to a more contractual view of intimate relationships. Proponents of contracts seek to recognize what they see as the greater autonomy and growing equality of the parties involved and, by shifting the emphasis to private ordering, to provide a new means of securing obligations at a time when family law is perceived to have been engaged in a process of deregulation. In the UK, Elizabeth Kingdom (1988, 1990) has argued strongly from a feminist perspective in favour of cohabitation contracts from a feminist point of view as a means of providing an additional option and as recognition for cohabitation as a distinct status. However Michele Adams (1998) has suggested that cohabitation is 'psychologically friendly' to women because it is 'high on individuation and low on institutionalization'. Any move to institutionalize it may therefore be to the detriment of women.

It is striking that even the well-informed, for example, law students, have the capacity to separate their knowledge about marriage in general from their hopes for their own marriages (Baker and Emry, 1993). Popular reaction to the idea of explicit marriage and cohabitation contracts is often negative. The feeling that personal relationships are about more than rational calculation and negotiation translates into the view that their chemistry is too intimate to make it possible for the intentions of the parties to be known (eg Dalton, 1985); that they threaten the trust on which intimate relations are built (Andersen, 1993); or that they run counter to the ethic of care that ideally pervades family relationships (Baier, 1986; Held, 1993). De Singly (1996) argued that love can not be contractual because both partners must believe that they are motivated by feelings other than self-interest. Beck and Beck Gernsheim (1995) have also suggested that contracts would result in the secular religion of love losing its mythology and becoming a mixture of market forces and personal impulses.

Certainly in the 1990s acute difficulties have been experienced in formalizing the previously informal in the public sphere as contract has been introduced into public sector services. In particular, it has proved difficult to subsume the associational world of the voluntary sector to the rule of contract, which suggests that Karst (1980) and Bellah *et al.*

(1985) may be right in questioning its effects on the world of intimate association. A private contract model for personal relations may serve to widen the gap between the social reality of personal relationships and the legal assumptions. It may also rest on false assumptions regarding the degree of equality that has been reached between the partners (Jamieson, 1998).

Family law seeks solutions at the level of the individual, and while the obligations of individuals as parents and partners cannot be ignored, collectivist solutions to help ensure the care and support of children, and to address the fundamental problem of reconciling paid work and family responsibilities in respect of the former must also play a part. Creighton (1999) has suggested that shorter working hours is the only way to address the issue of care, certainly it is the one major solution that has not been tried. The logic of the problem of obligation in personal relationships demands both individual and collective support for children. But the implementation of child support legislation in the UK has been a disaster, and given the degree of inequality in wealth and income it is not clear how many fathers with two families to support will pay even the reduced amounts currently being proposed. The trebling in the number of children in poverty between 1979 and 1991 (Bradshaw, 1997) also testifies to the lack of collective support in the UK. This does not mean that family law reform is irrelevant, but only that its limitations must be recognized. It is difficult to see how the need for more attention first, to relationship and parenting education, and second, to the kind of investment in children that in the continental European countries plays a major part in raising expectations and delaying motherhood (whether married or unmarried) can be denied.

Family law and family policy have tended increasingly to treat men and women as if they are fully individualized, the former in terms of assuming that they will be able to negotiate as equal individuals in case of breakdown, the latter in terms of assuming that both will be in the labour market. The legal and economic models of family behaviour that sustained traditional patterns of dependency have largely disappeared, but the erosion of normative prescription has outrun the social reality. Most women do not want to be dependent on men, but the gendered inequalities in access to income cannot be ignored. If the problems that arise as a result of the needs of children for care are to be addressed alongside the desire of adults for self fulfilment, then there must be a role for collective provision in the form of family policy. It is not possible to put the clock back and return to the male breadwinner model and the imposition of an external moral code. To that extent, individualization is inevitable. There is evidence that people want to make commitments as well as pursue their self-interest. Family policies offer a better hope of helping to reconcile these twin desires in this respect than the extension of more individualist mechanisms such as contract.

REFERENCES

Adams, M. A. (1998) 'How does marriage matter? Individuation and Institutionalisation in the Trajectory of Gendered Relationships', unpublished paper, ASA conference, 21–5 August, San Fransisco.

Akerloff, G. A. (1998) 'Men without children', 108 *Economic Journal* (March) 287–309.

Anderson, E. (1993) *Value in Ethics and Economics*, Cambridge, MA: Harvard University Press.

Askham, J. (1984) *Identity and Stability in Marriage*, Cambridge: Cambridge University Press.

Atkins, S. and Hoggett, B. (1984) *Women and the Law*, Oxford: Blackwell.

Baier, A. (1986) 'Trust and anti-trust', 1 *Ethics* 1, 231–60.

Baker and Emery (1993) 'When every relationship is above average. perceptions and expectations of divorce at the time of marriage', 17 *Law and Human Behaviour* 4, 439–50.

Baldock, J. (1999) 'Culture: the missing variable in understanding social policy?', 33 *Social Policy and Administration* 4, 458–73.

Bane, M. J. (1976) *Here to Stay. American Families in the Twentieth Century*, New York: Basic Books.

Beck Gernsheim, E. (1999) 'On the way to a post-familial family. from a community of need to elective affinities', 15 *Theory, Culture and Society* 3–4, 53–70.

Beck, U. and Beck Gernsheim, E. (1995) *The Normal Chaos of Love*, Cambridge: Policy Press.

Becker G. (1981) *A Treatise on the Family*, Cambridge, MA: Harvard University Press.

Becker, G., Landes, E. M., and Michael, R. T. (1977) 'An economic analysis of marital instability', 85 *Journal of Political Economy* 61, 1141–87.

Bellah, R., Madsen, R., Sullivan, W., Swidler, A. and Tipton, S. M. (1985) *Habits of the Heart, Middle America Observed*, Berkeley: University of California Press.

Bernard, J. (1976) *The Future of Marriage*, Harmondsworth: Penguin.

Blakenhorn, D., Bayme, S., and Elstain, J. B. (eds, 1990) *Rebuilding the Nest. A New Commitment to the American Family*, Milwaukee: Family Service America.

Bott, E. (1971) *Family and Social Network: Roles, Norms and External Relationships in Ordinary Urban Families*, London: Tavistock, 1st edn 1957.

Bradshaw, J. (1997) 'Child welfare in the UK: rising poverty, falling priorities for children' in C. A. Cornia and S. Danziger (eds) *Child Poverty and Deprivation in the Industrialized Countries, 1945–95*, Oxford: Clarendon Press.

Brown, S. L. and Booth, A. (1996) 'Cohabitation versus marriage: a comparison of relationship quality', 58 *Journal of Marriage and the Family* (August) 668–78.

Cherlin, A. (1981) *Marriage, Divorce and Remarriage*, Cambridge, MA: Harvard University Press.

Clarkberg, M.. Stolzenberg, R. M. and Waite, L. J. (1995) 'Attitudes values and entrance into cohabitation versus marital union', 74 *Asocial Forces* 2, 609–34.

Clive, E. M. (1980) 'Marriage: an unnecessary legal concept?' in J. M. Eekelaar and S. N. Katz (eds) *Marriage and Cohabitation in Contemporary Societies. Areas of Legal, Social and Ethical Change*, Toronto: Butterworths.

Cohen, M. R. (1933) 'The basis of contract', XLVI Harvard Law Review 4, 553–92.

Cohen, L. (1987) 'Marriage, divorce and quasi rents; or "I gave him the best years of my life"', XVI *Journal of Legal Studies* 2, 267–304.

Coleman, J. S. (1988) 'Social capital in the creation of human capital', 94 *American Journal of Sociology* (Suppl) S95–S120.

Creighton, C. (1999) 'The rise and decline of the "male breadwinner family" in Britain', 23 *Cambridge Journal of Economics* 519–41.

Cretney, S. (1996) 'Divorce reform in England: humbug and hypocrisy or a smooth transition?' in M. Freeman (ed) *Divorce where Next?*

Dalton, C. (1985) 'An essay in the deconstruction of contract doctrine', 94 *Yale Law Journal* 5, 997–1114.

Davidson Hunter, J. (1991) *Culture Wars. The Struggle to Define America*, New York: Basic Books.

Deech, R. (1980) 'The case against legal recognition of cohabitation' in J. M. Eekelaar and S. N. Katz (eds) *Marriage and Cohabitation in Contemporary Societies*, Toronto: Butterworths.

Delphi, C. and Leonard, C. (1992) *Familiar Exploitation. A New Analysis of marriage in Contemporary Western Society*, Cambridge: Polity Press.

Dench, G. (1994) *The Frog, the Prince and the Problem of Men*, London: Neanderthal Books.

Dennis, N. and Erdos, G. (1992) *Families without Fatherhood*, London: IEA.

De Singly (1996) *Modern Marriage and its Loss to Women. A Sociological Look at Marriage in France*, London: Associated University Press.

Dewar, J. and Parker, S. (1992) *Law and the Family*, London: Butterworths.

Dicey, A. V. (1948) *Lectures on the Relation between Law and Public Opinion in England during the . Nineteenth Century*, London: Macmillan, 2nd edn.
Eekelaar, J. M. (1991) *Regulating Divorce*, Oxford: Clarendon.
Eekelaar, J. M. and Maclean, M. (1986) *Maintenance after Divorce*, Oxford: Clarendon.
Ehrenreich, B, (1983) *The Hearts of Men: American Dreams and the Flight from Commitment*, London: Pluto Press.
Elias N. (1991) *The Society of Individuals*, Oxford: Blackwell.
Ellman, I. M. (1997) 'The misguided movement to revive fault divorce', 11 *IJLPF* 216–45.
Finch, J. and Mason, J. (1993) *Negotiating Family Responsibilities*, London: Tavistock/Routledge.
Fineman, M. A. (1993) 'Our sacred institution: the ideal of the family in American law and society', 2 *Utah Law Review* 387–405.
Fletcher, R. (1966) *The Family and Marriage in Britain:*, Harmondsworth: Penguin.
Furstenburg, F. F. and Cherlin, A. J. (1991) *Divided Families, What Happens to Children when Parents Part*, Cambridge, MA: Harvard University Press.
Fukuyama, F. (1999) *The Great Disruption. Human Nature and the Reconstitution of Social Order*, London: Profile Books.
Gergen, K. J. (1991) *The Saturated Self. Dilemmas of Identity in Contemporary Life*, New York: Basic Books.
Giddens, A. (1992) *The Transformation of Intimacy, Sexuality, love and Eroticism in Modern Societies*, Cambridge: Polity Press.
Gilder, G. (1987) 'The collapse of the American family', *The Public Interest* (Fall) 20–5.
Gilligan, C. (1982) *In a Different Voice*, Cambridge, MA: Harvard University Press.
Glendon, M. A. (1981) *The New Family and the New Property*, Toronto: Butterworths.
Glenn, N. D. (1987) 'Continuity versus change, sanguineness versus concern. views of the American family in the late 1980s', 8 *Journal of Family Issues* 4, 348–54.
Goldstein, J.; Freud, A. and Solnit, A. (1973) *Beyond the Best Interests of the Child*, New York: Free Press.
Goode, W. (1956) *After Divorce*, Glencoe, IL: Free Press.
Gottman, J. M. (1994) *What Predicts Divorce? The Relationship between marital Processes and Marital Outcomes*, Hillsdale, NJ: Lawrence Erlbaum Associates.
Griffiths, M. (1995) *Feminisms and the Self. The Web of Identity*, London: Routledge.
Hall, D. R. (1996) 'Marriage as a pure relationship: exploring the link between pre-marital cohabitation and divorce in Canada', XXVII *Journal of Comparative Family Studies* 1, 1–12.
Harding, L. M. (1999) 'Family insecurity and family support. an analysis of Labour's *Supporting Families* 1998'. Paper given to the Social Policy Association Annual Conference.
Haskey, J. (1995) 'Trends in marriage and cohabitation: the decline in marriage and the changing pattern of living in partnerships', *Population Trends* 80.
Held, V. (1993) *Feminist Morality. Transforming Culture, Society and Politics*, Chicago: University of Chicago Press.
Heller, A. (1979) *A Theory of Feelings*, The Netherlands: Van Gorcum Assen.
Hetherington, E., Cox, M., and Cox, R. (1978) 'The aftermath of divorce' in J. Stevens and M. Matthews (eds) *Mother-Child, Father-Child Relations*, Washington, DC: National Association for the Education of Young Children.
Hochschild, A. (1990) *The Second Shift*, London: Piatkus, 1st edn 1989.
Hollis, M. (1998) *Trust Within Reason*, Cambridge: Cambridge University Press.
Home Office (1998) *Supporting Families*, London: Stationery Office.
Inglehart, R. (1997) *Culture Shift in Advanced Industrial Society*, Princeton: Princeton University Press.
Jamieson, L. (1998) *Intimacy: Personal Relationships in Modern Society*, Cambridge: Policy Press.
Jefferies, A. (1996) 'British conservatism: individualism and gender', 1 *Journal of Political Ideologies* 1, 33–52.
Karst, K. L. (1980) 'The freedom of intimate association', 89 *Yale Law Journal* 1, 624–92.
Kiernan, K. (1992) 'The impact of family disruption in childhood on transitions made in young adult life', 46 *Population Studies* 213–34.
Kiernan, K. and Estaugh V. (1993) *Cohabitation. Extra-Marital Childbearing and Social Policy*, London: Family Policy Studies Centre.
Kiernan, K., Land, H. and Lewis, J. (1998) *Lone Mother Families in Twentieth Century Britain*, Oxford: OUP.
Kilpatrick, W. (1975) *Identity and Intimacy*, New York: Delacorte Press.
King, D. (1986) *The New Right: Politics, Markets and Citizenship*, Basingstoke: Macmillan.

Kingdom, E. (1988) 'Cohabitation contracts: a socialist-feminist issue', 15 *Journal of Law and Society* 1, 77–89.

Kingdom, E. (1990) 'Cohabitation contracts and equality', 18 *International Journal of the Sociology of Law* 287–98.

Kymlicka, W. (1991) 'Rethinking the family', 30 *Philosophy and Public Affairs* 1, 77–97.

Lauer, J. C. and Lauer, R. H. (1986) *Till Death Do Us Part, How Couples Stay Together*, New York: Haworth Press.

Lawson, A. (1988) *Adultery. An Analysis of Love and Betrayal*, Oxford: Blackwell.

Lewis, J. (1984) *Women in England, 1870–1945*, Brighton: Harvester Wheatsheaf.

Lewis, J. (1999) *Marriage and Cohabitation and the Law: Individualism and Commitment*, London: Lord Chancellor's Department.

Lewis, J., Datta, J. and Sarre, S. (1999) *Individualism and Commitment in Marriage and Cohabitation*, London: Lord Chancellor's Department.

Lewis, J. and Maclean M. (1997) 'Recent developments in family policy in the UK: the case of the 1996 Family Law Act' in M. May, E. Brunsdon and G. Craig (eds) *Social Policy Review* 9, London: Social Policy Association.

Lesthaeghe, R. and Surkyn, J. (1988) 'Cultural dynamics and economic theories of fertility change', 14 *Population and Development Review* 1, 1–45.

Lundberg, S. and Pollak, R. A. (1996) 'Bargaining and distribution in marriage' in I. Persson and C. Jonung (eds) *Economics of the Family and Family Policies*, London: Routledge.

Maclean, M. and Eekelaar, J. M. (1997) *The Parental Obligation. A Study of Parenthood across Households*, Oxford: Hart.

Maclean, M. and Wadsworth, M. E. J. (1988) 'The interests of children after parental divorce: a long-term perspective', 2 *IJLF* 155–66.

Marris, P. (1991) *Attachment across the Life Cycle*, London: Routledge.

Maslow, A. (1987) *Motivation and Personality*, 3rd edn, New York: Harper and Row, 1st edn, 1954.

McLanahan, S. and Booth, K. (1989) 'Mother-only families: problems, prospects and politics', 51 *Journal of Marriage and the Family* (Aug) 557–80.

McLanahan, S. and Sandfur, G. (1994) *Growing up with a Single Parent*, Cambridge, MA: Harvard University Press.

McRae, S. (1993) *Cohabiting Mothers: Changing Mothers and Motherhood?* London: Policy Studies Institute.

Morgan, D. H. J. (1999) 'Risk and family practices: accounting for change and fluidity in family life' in E. B Silva and C. Smart (eds) *The New Family*, London: Sage.

Mount, F. (1983) *The Subversive Family*, London: Allen and Unwin.

Murray, C. (1984) *Losing Ground: American Social Policy 1950–80*, New York: Basic Books.

Newcomb, M. D. (1981) 'Heterosexual cohabitation relationships' in S. Duck and R. Gilmour (eds) *Personal Relationships: Studying Personal Relationships*, London: Academic Press.

Newman, P. and Smith, A. (1997) *Social Focus on Families*, London: Stationery Office

Nock, S. L. (1995) 'A comparison of marriages and cohabiting relationships', 16 *Journal of Family Issues* 1, 53–76.

Nye, I. F. (1957) 'Child adjustment in broken and in unhappy unbroken homes', 19 *Journal of Marriage and Family Living* 356–61.

O'Donovan, K. (1993) *Family Law Matters*, London: Pluto Press.

Offer, A. (1996) 'Between the gift and the market: the economy of regard', *Discussion Papers in Economic and Social History* no 3.

Oppenheimer, V. K. (1994) 'Women's rising employment and the future of the family in industrialised societies', 20 *Population and Development Review* 2, 293–342.

Pateman, C. (1989) *The Disorder of Women*, Cambridge: Polity Press.

Pfau-Effinger, B. (1998) 'Gender cultures and the gender arrangement—a theoretical framework for cross-national gender research', 11 *Innovation* 2, 147–66.

Phillips, M. (1997) *The Sex Change State*, London: Social Market Foundation.

Popenoe, D. (1988) *Disturbing the Nest, Family Change and Decline in Modern Societies*, New York: Aldine de Gruyter.

Popenoe, D. (1993) 'American family decline, 1960–90: a review and appraisal', 55 *Journal of Marriage and the Family* (August) 527–55.

Posner, R. (1992) *Sex and Reason*, Cambridge: Harvard University Press.

Putnam, R. D. (1993) *Making Democracy Work: Civic Traditions in Modern Italy*, Princeton: Princeton University Press.

Rehbinder, M. (1971) 'Status contract and the welfare state', 23 *Stanford Law Review* 941–55.

Reynolds, J. and Mansfield, P. (1999) 'The effect of changing attitudes to marriage on its stability', in J. Simons (ed) *High Divorce Rates: The State of the Evidence on Reasons and Remedies*, London: Lord Chancellor's Department Research Series, 2.99.

Richards, M. P. M. and Dyson, M. (1982) *Separation, Divorce and the Development of Children: A Review*, London: DHSS.

Rindfus, R. R. and VandenHeuvel, A. (1990) 'Cohabitation: a precursor to marriage to an alternative to being single? 16 *Population and Development Review* 4, 703–26.

Rodgers, B. and Pryor, J. (1998) *Divorce and Separation. The Outcomes for Children*, York: Joseph Rowntree Foundation.

Rodgers, H. (1999) 'Cohabitation Committee Report to the National Committee', 79 *Solicitors Family Law Association Review* (June) 3–9.

Rowthorn, R. (1999) 'Marriage and trust: some lessons from economics', 23 *Cambridge Journal of Economics* 661–91.

Sandel, M. (1982) *Liberalism and the Limits of Justice*, Cambridge: Cambridge University Press.

Sandel, M. (1996) *Democracy's Discontent: America in Search of a Public Philosophy*, Cambridge, MA: Belknap Press of Harvard University Press.

Sandel, M. (1996) *Democracy's Discontent. America's Search for a Public Philosophy*, Cambridge, MA: Belknap Press of the Harvard University Press.

Schoen, R. (1992) 'First unions and the stability of first marriage', 54 *Journal of Marriage and the Family* (May) 281–4.

Schultz, M. (1982) 'Contractual ordering of marriage: a new model for state policy', 70 *California Law Review* 2, 204–334.

Scott, E. S. (1990) 'Rational decision-making about divorce', 76 *Virginia Law Review* 1, 9–91.

Seligman, A. B. (1997) *The Problem of Trust*, Princeton: Princeton University Press.

Skolnick, A. (1991) *Embattled Paradise. The American Family in an Age of Uncertainty*, New York: Basic Books.

Smart, C. and Neale, B. (1999) *Family Fragments*, Cambridge: Policy.

Smart, C. and Stevens, P. (2000) *Cohabitation Breakdown*, York: Joseph Rowntree Foundation.

Strathern, M. (1992) *After Nature: English Kinship in the late Twentieth Century*, Cambridge: Cambridge University Press.

Taylor, C. (1989) *Sources of the Self. The Making of the Modern Identity*, Cambridge: Cambridge University Press.

Thatcher, M. (1995) *The Downing Street Years*, London: HarperCollins.

Théry, I. (1994) *Le Demariage*, Paris: Editions Odile Jacob.

Van de Kaa (1987) 'Europe's second demographic transition', 42 *Population Bulletin* 1–59.

Waite, L. (1995) 'Does marriage matter?' 32 *Demography* 4, 483–507.

Wallerstein, J. S. and Kelly, J. B. (1980) *Surviving the Breakup. How Children and Parents Cope with Divorce*, London: Grant McIntyre.

Wax, A. (1989) 'Bargaining in the shadow of the market: is there a future for egalitarian marriage?' 84 *Virginia Law Review* 4, 509–672.

Weitzman, L. J. (1981) *The Marriage Contract. Spouses, Lovers and the Law*, New York: Free Press

Weitzman, L. J. (1985) *The Divorce Revolution*, New York: Free Press.

Wilson, J. Q. (1993) *The Moral Sense*, New York: Free Press.

Wolfram, S. (1987) *In-laws and Out-laws: Kinship and Marriage in England*, New York: St Martin's Press.

Yankelovich, D. (1981) *New Rules. Searching for Self-Fulfillment in a World Turned Upside Down*, New York: Random House.

Young, M. and Willmott, P. (1973) *The Symmetrical Family*, London: Routledge and Kegan Paul.

[12]

Homosexual rights

Brenda Hale, House of Lords

A discussion of progress in English law towards removing discrimination against gay and lesbian people, with particular reference to family law, registered partnerships and equal treatment with heterosexual relationships, both married and unmarried.

It is a fair hypothesis, advanced by Kees Waaldijk, that 'most countries, at different times and different paces, go through a standard sequence of legislative steps recognising homosexuality'.[1] The first steps are taken by the criminal law: permitting homosexual acts between male adults and then removing age and other distinctions between same- and opposite-sex sexual activity. The next steps are taken by the civil law: prohibiting discrimination against homosexuals in employment, and in the provision of goods, education, housing and other services. The final steps are taken by family law, extending laws applicable to unmarried heterosexual couples to homosexual couples, recognising the parental relationship between homosexual parents and their own, their partners' or even other people's children, providing for registered civil partnerships, and finally providing for civil marriage.

Decriminalisation of homosexual acts between male adults has now been achieved throughout the existing membership of the EU and the other Council of Europe member states. For most countries in western Europe, this had been done long before the landmark decision of the European Court of Human Rights (European Court) in *Dudgeon v United Kingdom (No 2)*,[2] which meant that the newer members of the Council of Europe had to follow suit. Progress in removing all discrimination in the criminal law between homosexual and heterosexual acts has been more uneven but the removal of age discrimination is now almost complete within the EU and Council of Europe. The UK, as usual, has not been in the vanguard: the Sexual Offences Act 2000, removing age discrimination, came into force in January 2001.

Prohibition of discrimination in employment has either arrived or is in progress in all member states of the EU, the latecomers impelled by Council Directive 2000/78/EC providing for equal treatment in employment and occupation.[3] Prohibition of discrimination in other fields had already arrived for many, but is not yet even in progress in Italy, Portugal and Greece. Among the other members of the Council of Europe only Iceland, Norway and Slovenia have prohibited discrimination in both fields, although some others have gone part of the way. Others have not even begun. Once again, the UK is making slow progress. Rather than enacting comprehensive new equality legislation, the government has chosen to use the procedure for implementing EU legislation by delegated legislation. This means that it has done only that which it considers to be required by the Council Directive and no more.[4]

Progress in family law is much more uneven. Only the Netherlands and Belgium have admitted same-sex couples to the institution of marriage, but Denmark, Sweden and Norway have taken all the other three steps and several other European countries have some form of registered partnership.[5] Characteristically, the UK is still at the 'in progress' stage, although we

---

1 'Chronological overview of the main legislative steps in the process of legal recognition of homosexuality in European countries', appendix to 'Taking same-sex partnerships seriously: European experiences as British perspectives', The Fifth Stonewall Lecture, 2002 [2003] IFL 84–95. The following summary is taken from the information in that appendix, last updated in April 2003, but the author disarmingly admits that it 'will contain inaccuracies, and may have missed recent developments'.

2 (1982) 4 EHRR 149.

3 Council Directive 2000/78/EC of 27 November 2000 establishing a general framework for equal treatment in employment and occupation (2000) OJ L 303/16.

4 Employment Equality (Sexual Orientation) Regulations 2003 (SI 2003/1661).

5 Registered partnerships are also provided for in some jurisdictions in the US, Canada and Australia.

have already legislated for what many might think the most dramatic step of all, adoption by unmarried same-sex couples and are about to legislate for civil partnership.[6]

It is also a fair hypothesis that there is some correlation between the distance a country is prepared to go in these matters and the religious and moral attitudes of its population. But this is much harder to prove. The *European Values Study*[7] shows that the countries which have made most progress towards treating homosexuals equally in the law also have high rates of acceptance of homosexuality and homosexual neighbours and comparatively low rates of belief in God and in sin. It also shows that the countries making the least progress have lower rates of acceptance of homosexuality and homosexual neighbours and higher rates of belief in God and in sin. But there are also countries, such as Finland and Spain, which have comparatively high rates of belief in God, but have nevertheless made considerable progress towards equality. And there are countries, such as Great Britain, which have lower rates of belief in God but where progress has so far been slower (for this purpose, the survey wisely separates Great Britain from Northern Ireland, where rates of belief in sin are the highest in the EU).

The turmoil within the Church of England, with its well-known anxiety to accommodate a wide range of apparently incompatible beliefs, may be one explanation. One side is exemplified by the sermon in Southwark cathedral on Christmas Day, which provoked a rare round of applause for the following (among other things):

> 'The nomination and forced withdrawal of our much loved Canon Jeffrey John as Bishop of Reading means we have the inestimable benefit of his ministry for longer but it is also a grave loss to the Church of his greater ministry. It was a symptom of the deep malaise at the heart of the Anglican communion masquerading as a concern for the purity and unity of the Church but in reality self-righteousness, prejudice and exclusiveness ... When was the Church pure or united? Certainly not in our Lord's time. We celebrate today the birth of the founder of our church in a place which was unclean, among the unrespectable. We read of the disciples' personal ambition, everyone's prejudice towards Samaritans and Lepers, Jesus' ministry embracing anyone that everyone else hated, the blind, the sick, the mad, women menstruating, prostitutes, convicts on the cross and all the rest ... Jesus worked with them all, Jesus transformed them all, Jesus conferred responsibility upon them all ... One of the hallmarks of the Church of England, as the established Church of this country since the Reformation, has been that it is here for everyone.'

On the other hand are the responses to the government's consultation on the Employment Equality Regulations, cited by Anthony Lester in his recent Stonewall lecture,[8] which included the following:

> 'The document ... is greatly flawed in respect of Christian teaching and morals, as no Christian Church or Organisation that holds to biblical principles and teaching would even consider employing a homosexual or lesbian in any position whatsoever.'

The result of that and other responses was an exception, in regulation 7(3), of employment 'for the purposes of an organised religion', which allows the employer to impose a requirement relating to a person's sexual orientation either:

> '(i) so as to comply with the doctrines of the religion, or

[6] Adoption and Children Act 2002, s 49(1)(a) allows an adoption application to be made by 'a couple', defined by s 144(4) as 'two people (whether of different sexes or the same sex) living together as partners in an enduring family relationship'.

[7] L. Halman, *The European Values Study: A Third Wave. Sourcebook of the 1999/2000 European Values Study Surveys* (Tilburg University, 2001).

[8] 'New Labour's Equality Laws: Some are More Equal than Others' (The Sixth Stonewall Lecture, 22 October 2003).

(ii) because of the nature of the employment and the context in which it is carried out, so as to avoid conflicting with the strongly held religious convictions of a significant number of the religion's followers.'

Anthony Lester comments:

> 'On its face, regulation 7(3) applies not only to senior appointments but to any employment, provided that the other conditions are satisfied. It applies not only where religious doctrine requires such discrimination, but also to comply with strongly held religious convictions of a significant number – including a bigoted minority – of the religion's followers.'

I want to concentrate on family law, partly because it is the area I know most about, partly because it is the least well advanced and the most controversial, and not least because Anthony Lester has already covered the discrimination legislation in his trenchant and memorable lecture.

As he points out, the present Government committed itself to removing unjustified discrimination wherever it exists. The Deputy Minister for Women and Equality, in her Foreword to the Government's Consultation Paper on *Civil Partnership*,[9] declared that:

> 'I believe there will be a day when same-sex couples don't have to struggle to have their partnerships and their families recognised.'

Even without such declarations of government belief, legal policy is tending strongly towards the goal of equal treatment of same-sex relationships in almost everything up to the recognition of same-sex marriage. Article 8 of the European Convention for the Protection of Human Rights and Fundamental Freedoms 1950 (European Convention) guarantees to everyone the right to respect for their private and family life, their home and their correspondence. Article 14 requires that there shall be no unjustified discrimination in the enjoyment of the Convention rights. Homosexual relationships are undoubtedly an aspect of private life. This long ago enabled the European Court to rule against the criminalisation of homosexual acts between consenting adults in private: see *Dudgeon v United Kingdom (No 2)*.[10] Sexual activity is, as the court said, 'a most intimate aspect of private life'. But to regard homosexual relationships as a narrow privacy issue is to deny to them the full enjoyment which other relationships take for granted. Opposite-sex couples can walk hand in hand or arm in arm or even engage in closer intimacies in public: until recently same-sex couples could not. Albie Sachs put the argument thus in the South African Constitutional Court:

> 'There is no good reason why the concept of privacy should ... be restricted simply to sealing off from State control what happens in the bedroom, with the doleful subtext that you may behave as bizarrely and shamefully as you like, on the understanding that you do so in private. It has become a judicial cliché to say that privacy protects people, not places ... Just as liberty must be viewed not merely "negatively or selfishly as a mere absence of restraint but positively and socially as an adjustment of restraints to the end of freedom of opportunity", so must privacy be regarded as suggesting at least some responsibility on the State to promote conditions in which personal self-realisation can take place ... autonomy must mean far more than the right to occupy an envelope of space in which a socially detached individual can act free from interference by the State. What is crucial is the nature of the activity, not its site. While recognising the unique worth of each person, the Constitution does not presuppose that a holder of rights is an isolated, lonely and abstract figure possessing a disembodied and socially disconnected self. It acknowledges

9 DTI Women and Equality Unit, *Civil Partnership: A framework for the legal recognition of same-sex couples* (June 2003).

10 See n 2 above.

that people live in their bodies, their communities, their cultures, their places and their times. The expression of sexuality requires a partner, real or imagined.'[11]

The more interesting question, therefore, is whether homosexual couples and their children will be regarded as having a 'family life' together which is also to be respected under Article 8. If Article 8 is about the capacity of an individual to formulate his own perception of himself and his identity, then it could also be about the capacity of those who live and see themselves as couples and families like any others to present themselves to the world in this way. There are old decisions by the European Commission on Human Rights which have been seen as denying the protection of 'family life' to stable same-sex relationships: see *S v United Kingdom*;[12] *B v United Kingdom*;[13] *X v United Kingdom*.[14] But there are also cases recognising that there is a family relationship between homosexual parents and their children; and that to discriminate against homosexual parents in respect of this relationship can be a breach of Article 14 taken with Article 8: see *Salgueiro da Silva Mouta v Portugal*.[15] In that case, concerning custody of the applicant's daughter, the European Court held that a difference in treatment based on sexual orientation was 'undoubtedly covered' by Article 14, although sexual orientation is not expressly listed there.

The European Convention sets the minimum standards and it is open to individual member states to set higher standards than those required by the European Court. The House of Lords has already recognised that same-sex partners can be members of one another's 'family' for the purpose of the statutory right to succeed to a tenancy of their home:[16] see *Fitzpatrick v Sterling Housing Association Ltd*.[17] This might be thought a bold decision: not only would Parliament not have contemplated such an interpretation when the relevant provision was first enacted in 1922, but also, even if the legislation is 'always speaking', at the time of their Lordships' decision there was still a provision on the statute book referring to homosexual relationships as 'pretended family relationships'.[18] However, the House of Lords stopped short of recognising the surviving same-sex partner as 'a person who was living with the original tenant as his or her wife or husband', which would have given him better protection than that given to a member of the family.[19]

Since the coming into force of the Human Rights Act 1998, the Court of Appeal has taken that further step: see *Ghaidan v Godin-Mendoza* [2002] EWCA Civ 1533.[20] It remains to be seen whether their decision will survive the appeal to the House of Lords which is due to be heard in April. Their reasoning was as follows. Article 14 imposes a positive obligation upon the state to secure the enjoyment of the Convention rights without unjustified discrimination. Article 8 is engaged by the issue of statutory succession to residential tenancies, not because it protects family life (the other partner having died) but because it protects the home. Hence the question became whether the undoubted discrimination between unmarried heterosexual and homosexual relationships with otherwise identical marriage-like characteristics could objectively be justified. The suggested justifications were preserving flexibility in the use of housing stock and protection of the traditional family unit. Having rejected the former, Buxton LJ said this of the latter, at paragraph [21]:

---

11 *National Coalition for Gay and Lesbian Equality and Another v Minister of Justice and Others* (1999) (1) SA 6, at paras 116 and 117.

12 (1986) 47 DR 274.

13 (1990) 64 DR 278.

14 (1983) 32 DR 220.

15 (2001) 31 EHRR 47.

16 Under Rent Act 1977, Sch 1, para 3.

17 [2001] 1 AC 27.

18 Local Government Act 1988, s 28, eventually repealed by the Local Government Act 2003.

19 Under Rent Act 1977, Sch 1, para 2

20 [2003] Ch 380.

'so far as protection of the family is concerned, it is quite unclear how heterosexual family life (which includes unmarried partnerships) is promoted by handicapping persons who are constitutionally unable, or strongly unwilling, to enter into family relationships so defined. Second, if deterrence is really the objective, the means used to that end are singularly unimpressive.'

Keene LJ reinforced this at paragraph [42]:

'[Counsel for the landlord] sought to identify the "legitimate aim" of this difference in treatment as being the protection of the "family", or as he was constrained to put it "a unit deriving from a heterosexual couple". Nothing put before us demonstrates that this was the aim and, since it is difficult to see how such an aim would be achieved by the difference in treatment, there must be doubt as to whether that is indeed the aim of the statutory distinction. It has not been suggested that heterosexual couples, whether married or unmarried, are more likely to live together or to do so for longer because homosexual couples are denied the equivalent right of succession under the Rent Act.'

Buxton LJ also discussed the suggestion that *S v United Kingdom* had held that homosexual partners did not have a 'family life' together. In his view, the Commission's distinction between 'families' and 'other stable relationships' had been a statement about the policy of UK domestic law, not a statement about the content of the Convention rights. As such it could no longer be justified after *Sterling*. Insofar as the European Court of Justice, in *Grant v South-West Trains Ltd*[21] had relied upon *S v United Kingdom* in holding that Article 119 of the European Community Treaty dealt only with equal pay between the sexes rather than between those of differing sexual orientation it was similarly mistaken. Neither case came 'anywhere near' to deciding that discrimination on grounds of sexual orientation was justified under Article 14 of the European Convention.

The court considered that the potential incompatibility between the legislation and the survivor's Convention rights could be cured by the application of section 3(1) of the Human Rights Act 1998:

'So far as it is possible to do so, primary legislation and subordinate legislation must be read and given effect in a way which is compatible with the Convention rights.'

That could be done by reading the words 'as his or her wife or husband' to mean 'as if they were his or her wife or husband'.

Since then, the European Court, in *Karner v Austria*,[22] has employed virtually identical reasoning to arrive at the conclusion that it was a breach of the applicant's rights under Article 14 taken with Article 8 to deny a surviving homosexual partner the right to succeed to a tenancy as 'lebensgefahrte' of the deceased tenant. The court did not find it necessary to determine the notions of 'private life' or 'family life' because the complaint related to the enjoyment of the applicant's right to respect for his home.[23] It accepted[24] that 'protection of the family in the traditional sense is, in principle, a weighty and legitimate reason which might justify a difference in treatment', but the principle of proportionality required that the difference in treatment was necessary in order to achieve that aim. The government had not advanced any arguments which would allow of such a conclusion.[25]

Whatever the eventual outcome of the *Mendoza* case, if UK law already recognises that stable homosexual partners, even without children, can be members of the same 'family' then it may already be committed to according that family unit the same respect as other family units,

---

21 [1998] ECR I-621.

22 (Application No 40016/98) [2003] 2 FLR 623.

23 Ibid, at para 33.

24 Ibid, at para 40.

25 Ibid, at para 41.

unless the difference can be objectively justified. The *Mendoza* and *Karner* cases have shown how difficult it is to justify excluding homosexual couples by reference to the need to protect traditional families. Non-traditional families of many kinds are so common that it is difficult to argue that a proper way to protect the traditional family is to deny all recognition to other kinds of relationship.

There are two non-discrimination issues for UK family law:

(1) Insofar as the law provides for heterosexual couples to contract into the special status of marriage, bringing with it numerous rights and obligations not only as against one another but also as against the State and third parties, should that same or an equivalent status be extended to homosexual couples?
(2) Insofar as the law extends to unmarried heterosexual couples' rights and obligations connected with their homes and family life similar or equivalent to those extended to married couples, should those same rights and obligations be extended to unmarried homosexual couples?

Those discrimination issues have to be seen against the wider debate, which has been going on for many years now, about the law's treatment of unmarried couples generally. The facts are that marriage rates are falling and cohabitation rates are rising: in Great Britain, cohabitation increased from 11% of non-married women under 50 in 1979 to 30% in 2000/2001[26] (even in Northern Ireland, it rose from 2% of those aged 16–59 in 1986 to 10% in 1998/1999). Forty per cent of all children born in the UK are born outside marriage, although the majority are born to parents living at the same address. The great majority of these cohabiting heterosexual couples could marry if they chose to do so. Why do they not?

The Law Society[27] suggests that cohabiting couples fall into four different categories:

(1) The informed cohabitants

> 'Both parties are fully aware of the limited rights that they may have and have come to a conscious and informed decision that they wish to live together without marriage and without entering into financial responsibility for each other.'

Research evidence is clear that there are some who deliberately reject marriage. Among the reasons for cohabiting found in a recent qualitative study[28] were: (1) the desire to avoid what were seen as the gender stereotypical roles assigned by marriage; and (2) a fear of divorce and the wish to avoid it. The other reasons given did not indicate rejection of marriage as such. These were: (3) a trial of marriage; (4) the modern equivalent of a shotgun marriage – cohabitation following an unplanned pregnancy; and (5) the expense of a wedding. The study also revealed idealised views of marriage and fears that they would not be able to live up to it: an odd reason for choosing to live together instead.

But there is little evidence that even those who deliberately reject marriage have much knowledge of the different legal consequences. In the large-scale national survey that was part of the same project, only 14% of current cohabitants had made a will and only 10% had a written agreement about ownership shares in the family home. Along with this lack of evidence of knowledge, there is also positive evidence of ignorance or misconception about the law. The researchers found that in most cases, perceptions of the legal consequences have little or no impact upon the parties' decision.

---

26 *Social Trends 2003* (No 33) (National Statistics, 2003), at pp 45–46. It is not clear whether these figures include female homosexual cohabitation. By definition they do not include male homosexuals. But in 2000/2001 more than one quarter of all non-married adults aged 16–59 were cohabiting, including same-sex cohabitation: *General Household Survey 2001* (National Statistics, 2001).

27 *Cohabitation: The case for clear law: Proposals for Reform* (The Law Society, July 2002).

28 A. Barlow, S. Duncan, S. James and A. Park, 'Just a Piece of Paper? Marriage and Cohabitation in Britain', in A. Park et al (eds), *British Social Attitudes: The 18th Report* (Sage Publications, 2001).

(2) The uninformed cohabitants

> 'The parties do not think they need to get married ... neither have given the matter much thought and probably have common misconceptions about what their legal position may or may not be.'

The national survey showed that 59% of cohabiting people think that cohabiting will give rise to a legally recognised 'common law marriage'. They thought that it began after a period of time, varying from six months to six years. This is not a surprising belief: the Department for Work and Pensions treats marriage and heterosexual cohabitation alike for the purpose of denying couples the benefits available to two single persons, so they may well think that they become correspondingly entitled to the benefits to which married people are entitled. The qualitative study found that most cohabitants either thought that married and cohabiting couples had the same legal rights or were unsure. Similar results have emerged from a small qualitative study of unmarried fathers (for example, the unmarried father who somehow thought that the family home which he owned would descend to his partner even though he had made a pre-cohabitation will leaving everything to his parents).

Those planning to marry are only a little better informed. A recent study of engaged couples[29] found that 41% thought that getting married would not change the legal nature of their relationship.

(3) The reluctant cohabitants

> 'One party wishes to marry but the other does not. It could be that this relationship started out as one of the above two and that one party (possibly the one with the economic disadvantage such as the partner who has given up work to look after the children) begins to recognise their lack of rights. It may be that one of the parties is naïve or uninformed and their partner makes use of that. However, the other party does not wish to marry perhaps because they are fully aware of the obligations they are taking on.'

Ever since the divorce law and associated reforms which came into force in 1971, most rational women in England and Wales ought to regard the financial and proprietary remedies available on marriage breakdown as very good reasons to marry. Only women who are richer or more successful than their husbands (admittedly a growing proportion), *and* who can be confident that this will not change even if they have children, should prefer to cohabit. For the same reason, most rational men ought to regard them as very good reasons not to marry. Furthermore, now that an unmarried man has the same recognition as a father, the traditional genealogical reason for men to marry has also gone. Now that section 111 of the Adoption and Children Act 2002 is in force, a man will be able to gain full fatherhood status and relationships without being married, either by being registered as father or by adopting. Although, as we have seen, the association between rational behaviour and intimate relationships is not strong (whoever thought it would be?), there is some evidence that men are beginning to realise how things stand.

(4) The no-choice cohabitants

These are people who are unable to marry. This covers opposite-sex partners where one or both are still married to someone else: given the ready availability of divorce these days, this formerly common reason for cohabitation should now be of limited duration. A few heterosexual couples may be within the prohibited degrees of consanguinity or more probably affinity. But the great majority of 'no-choice' cohabitants will be same-sex couples where marriage is not an option.

These findings suggest that we should deal both with the non-discrimination issues identified earlier and with the situation of cohabitants generally; and that although provision must be

[29] M. Hibbs, C. Barton and J. Beswick, 'Why Marry? Perceptions of the Affianced' [2001] Fam Law 197.

made for those who wish to contract into a special status to do so, the position of those who do not contract in must also be considered.

CONTRACTING IN

Recent groundbreaking decisions in Massachusetts and Ontario have held it unconstitutional to deny same-sex couples the right to marry.[30] Thus far, however, the same view has not been taken of the international instruments on this matter. The UN Human Rights Committee has opined that the exclusion of same-sex couples from marriage does not violate Article 23 of the International Covenant on Civil and Political Rights 1976, which provides that 'the family is the natural and fundamental group unit of society and is entitled to protection by society and the state' and that 'the right of men and women of marriageable age to marry and found a family shall, be recognised'. Similarly, while Article 8 of the European Convention protects the right to respect for 'family life', Article 12 provides that 'men and women of marriageable age have the right to marry and to found a family, according to the national laws governing the exercise of this right'. The European Court has recently changed its views on the recognition of post-operative transsexuals in their new gender. In *Sheffield and Horsham v United Kingdom*,[31] the United Kingdom was permitted to deny them the right to marry in their new gender, although the pace of change was so rapid that the position should be kept under review. In *Goodwin v United Kingdom*,[32] however, the court could find 'no justification for barring the transsexual from enjoying the right to marry under any circumstances'.[33] Hence the House of Lords, in *Bellinger v Bellinger* [2003] UKHL 21,[34] made a declaration that our legislation on capacity to marry was incompatible. In this area, the government has chosen to legislate more comprehensively. The Gender Recognition Bill is currently before Parliament but not enjoying the smoothest of passages.

Permitting transsexuals to marry in their reassigned gender is of course quite different from permitting same-sex marriage. One problem with the current Bill is that it will require a transsexual who is married in his or her birth gender to have that marriage annulled or dissolved before a full gender recognition certificate can be issued.[35]

The government 'has no plans to introduce same-sex marriage'.[36] But it does propose to introduce registered partnerships for same-sex couples.[37] These will have all the essential features of marriage: it will be an exclusive union between two people not within the prohibited degrees for marriage; it will be formally registered in much the same way as a civil marriage is today; it will only be dissolved by a court, on almost identical grounds to those for dissolving a marriage; the legal consequences, both during and after the marriage, will be virtually identical to those of marriage. Certainly, as provided for in the Civil Partnership Bill, it will be marriage in almost all but name. This has been welcomed by Stonewall, the main campaigning group on behalf of gay and lesbian people.

Of course, if we legislate for civil partnerships for same-sex couples, the question will arise whether it is justifiable to deny that opportunity to opposite-sex couples. Anthony Lester's Civil Partnerships Bill, introduced and withdrawn on the faith of the government's assurances in 2002, provided for both. The main answer to this argument is that they have marriage available to them. Those heterosexual couples who cannot at present marry, either because they are already married to someone else or because they are within the prohibited degrees, would not be able to register a civil partnership under these proposals. Those who do not marry at

30 *Halpern v Attorney General of Canada*, 10 June 2003, ONCA C39172; *Goodridge v Department of Public Health*, 798 NE 2d 941 (Mass 2003).

31 (Application Nos 22985/93 and 23390/94) (1998) 27 EHRR 163.

32 (Application No 28957/95) (2002) 35 EHRR 447.

33 Ibid, at para 103.

34 [2003] 2 AC 467.

35 Gender Recognition Bill, session 2003/2004, HL Bill 4, cl 4(3) and (4) and Sch 2.

36 Op cit, n 7, at para 1.3.

37 Civil Partnership Bill, session 2003/2004, HL Bill 53.

present because they do not want to would not want to enter into this form of civil partnership either.

Insofar as their objections to marriage are misconceived, based upon assumptions about its legal and social consequences which have not held good since at least the 1960s, then there is no reason for the law to pander to them. Insofar as their objections are to the legal consequences themselves, then this would argue for some lesser form of civil partnership, bringing with it some but not all of the consequences of marriage. The question whether there should be such a 'second class marriage' or 'second class partnership' open to both same- and opposite-sex couples is quite separate from the question whether we should try to remove the present discrimination against same-sex relationships. We should not allow the one to cloud the other, especially as all the evidence suggests that the heterosexuals' problem is not with those who would like to opt in but do not, but with those who think that there is no need to opt in at all.

EXTENDING THE CONSEQUENCES CURRENTLY APPLICABLE TO UNMARRIED OPPOSITE-SEX COUPLES TO UNMARRIED SAME-SEX COUPLES

In typical British (or at least English) 'salami slicing' ways, some of the legal consequences of marriage have been extended to unmarried couples. One example is succession to certain types of tenancy, as discussed earlier. Others are claims against third party wrongdoers under the Fatal Accidents Act 1976 or against the estate of the deceased former cohabitant under the Inheritance (Provision for Families and Dependants) Act 1975. Most of the property and financial consequences of marriage do not apply between unmarried couples, but there are exceptions, including the court's powers under the Family Law Act 1996 to transfer secure tenancies from one to the other and to protect the occupation of the family home. These are most often used in cases of domestic violence and abuse, where again there are remedies available to present and former unmarried cohabitants. There is no reason in principle why these should not be extended to same-sex cohabitants.

One dilemma arising from the Court of Appeal's decision in *Mendoza* is how far it will be possible to use that same technique in cases where the legal case is identical but the wording of the relevant statute is not: the Family Law Act 1996, for example, defines 'cohabitant' as 'a man and a woman who, although not married to each other, are living together as husband and wife' (section 62(1)(a)). It is harder to read 'a man and a woman' to include persons of the same sex than it is to read 'a person' to include persons of either sex. Could this be an interesting example of an apparently arbitrary result produced by the incorporation technique chosen for the Human Rights Act 1998? Fortunately, the Domestic Violence, Crimes and Victims Bill will amend the 1996 Act definition to include same-sex cohabitants.

The process of assimilating same- and opposite-sex couples has gone furthest in relation to children. It is already possible for unmarried couples to share parental responsibility for one another's children or, indeed, for unrelated children who are living with them: the courts are able to make residence orders and have for some time been prepared to do this to enable, for example, a lesbian couple to share responsibility for all the children in their household.[38] Lesbian partners often have children from earlier heterosexual marriages or other relationships, but they are also able to have children by donor insemination or other forms of assisted reproduction offered by licensed clinics. A residence order gives parental responsibility but is not the same as becoming the child's legal parent; but under the Adoption and Children Act 2002 unmarried couples, both opposite and same sex, will be able to adopt unrelated children; further, a married or unmarried partner will be able to adopt the other partner's child, giving one the status of adoptive parent while the other retains the status of birth parent.[39]

Cohabitation also brings disadvantages, stemming from the state's view that those to whom marriage is available should not be treated more favourably by the benefits system than those who are married. Thus heterosexual cohabitants can only claim the same allowance as a married couple and not the total of two single person's allowances. Once registered partnership

[38] *Re C (A Minor) (Residence Order: Lesbian Co-parents)* [1994] Fam Law 468.

[39] Adoption and Children Act 2002, ss 51(2) and 144(7).

becomes available to same-sex couples, the government is considering applying the same principle to unregistered same-sex cohabitants. Stonewall has stoically accepted the logic of this.

Once again, it is a separate question whether the rights and remedies currently available to unmarried or unregistered cohabitants, both heterosexual and homosexual, should be improved. Many think that they should be, precisely because so few people understand or think about their legal situation when they embark upon intimate relationships. Yet there can be few intimate relationships, particularly if they last for any length of time or involve having or rearing children together, which do not affect the parties' economic positions in ways which are usually much more detrimental to one than to the other. That is the rationale for laws which allow some compensation for the adverse economic consequences of the relationship when it ends.

The Adoption Law Review in 1992 saw the absence of such responsibility between the adults as a good reason for refusing to allow unmarried couples to adopt: bringing a child into the family has such profound consequences, not only for the child but also for the adults involved, that the adults should be prepared to take on responsibility for one another, as well as for the child, in the interests of them all. Otherwise a rational adoptive parent would be reluctant to reduce or give up work in order to devote herself or himself to meeting the often very complex needs of the new member of the family. Once again, however, as in most areas of family law, it is necessary to catch up with the way in which people actually behave. Adoption by one person is already possible and increasingly that person is, in fact, in a long-term stable relationship where both parties will be equally important in the child's life. Refusing to recognise that fact does more harm to the child whose interests are the law's primary concern.

Thus it is that we have already reached the stage of recognising same-sex relationships for what many will think the most important purpose of regulating family relationships: providing for the care and upbringing of the next generation. It is difficult to see an objective necessity to continue to treat such relationships differently in other ways.

Part IV
Law and Marriage

[13]

THE CASE AGAINST LEGAL RECOGNITION OF COHABITATION

By

RUTH L. DEECH *

BY judicial interpretation and by outright statutory enactment, cohabitation is gradually being accorded legal status in English and in foreign law.[1] At no stage in this development has the whole question of the desirability of the recognition of cohabitation been considered. It has been treated pragmatically and fragmentarily. It is not yet too late to put the case against the legal recognition of cohabitation, whether such recognition is achieved by extending marital law to cohabitants as a general principle, or by enacting special laws for them, or by allowing the fact of cohabitation to give rise to legal situations that would not have been found if the two persons involved had never lived together. The case for the opposition is based partly on practical grounds and partly on ideological ones and the ideology (which may be dignified by the appellation " individualism ") has a facet which the writer has supported previously in relation to the economic rights of married persons: the assertion that women do not need and ought not to require to be kept by men after the conjugal relationship between them has come to an end.[2] Individualism generally is a theory upholding and protecting the rights of a single person rather than groups or categories. The basic ideas of individualism have been described as, first, the dignity of the individual; secondly, autonomy, or self-direction; thirdly, privacy, or a sphere of thought and action that should be free from public interference; and, fourthly, self-development.[3] It will be argued that each of these ideas is well reflected by legislative non-intervention in the field of cohabitation. Sir Henry Maine traced " the emergence of the self-determining, separate individual from the network of family and group ties." [4] Maine however limited his illustration of the move from status to contract to the position of women *before* marriage. Now it may be possible to apply

* Fellow of St. Anne's College, Oxford. This article is based on a paper delivered at the Third World Conference of the International Society on Family Law, held in Uppsala in June 1979. The author is greatly indebted to Mr. John Eekelaar, Fellow of Pembroke College, Oxford, for his critical comments.

1 For a survey of the relevant law, see D. Pearl, " The Legal Implications of a Relationship Outside Marriage " [1978] C.L.J. 252.

2 " The Principles of Maintenance " (1977) 7 *Family Law* 229.

3 Lukes, *Individualism* (1973).

4 C. K. Allen, Introduction to Maine, *Ancient Law* (1959) at xxvi and Maine, *ibid.*, p. 140: " The movement of the progressive societies has been uniform in one respect. Through all its course it has been distinguished by the gradual dissolution of family dependency and the growth of individual obligation in its place."

Maine's analysis to women living with men, as well as to spinsters. Individualism lends itself well to the achievement of the equality of women: it requires the treatment of the family as a collection of individuals with separate and independent rights and avoids treating the family as a unit, a treatment which is bound to suppress the personal needs of the less prominent members, usually the women, and focus on the head of household.

The opposition to the legal recognition of cohabitation here maintained originated with the reading of the dissent of Clark J. in the *Marvin* [5] case and hardened during the period of mass media publicity given to the hearing of the merits of the *Marvin* case: the televised interviews with the plaintiff, the allegations in court concerning her liaisons with men other than Lee Marvin, the question of her pregnancy and the estimate given by Marvin of the strength of his affection for her during the time that they lived together. The case and public reaction to it have influenced the nature of the arguments used to support the writer's position.

For reasons that will appear later, a few examples are given here of enactments which as a matter of general principle extend marital laws to cohabitants. In South Australia, the Family Relationships Act 1975 [6] creates the category of " putative spouse " for persons who have cohabited for a period of five years or who are parents.[7] For the purposes of claiming support, the definition of " spouse " in the Family Law Reform Act of Ontario [8] includes a cohabitant of five years' standing or one who is a parent in a relationship of " some permanence." One year's cohabitation suffices in Nova Scotia for a support claim [9] but in neighbouring Newfoundland the one year must be accompanied by parenthood,[10] as it must in Manitoba,[11] whereas in British Columbia two years of living together transform a mistress into a spouse.[12] There will be no attempt here to describe the nature or the length of cohabitation considered necessary to entitle a partner to a claim; it is sufficient for present purposes to draw attention to the lack of agreement, even within the confines of one country, as to the " qualifying period," a disagreement which reveals differences concerning the rationale for these support claims. Whatever the definition of legally recognised cohabitation, there would be some unions that would not fall within its compass. Just as there is now a feeling that certain cohabiting partnerships ought to be treated as beneficially

[5] 557 P. 2d 106 (S.C., Cal.) (1976).
[6] No. 115 of 1975.
[7] s. 11.
[8] Chap. 2 of 1978, s. 14.
[9] Wives' and Children's Maintenance Act, R.S.N.S. 1967, Chap. 341, s. 1 (1) (d).
[10] The Maintenance Act, R.S.N. 1970, Chap. 223, s. 10A, added by the Maintenance (Amendment) Act, No. 119 of 1973, s. 5.
[11] Family Maintenance Act, S.M. 1978, Chap. 25, s. 11 (1).
[12] Family Relations Act 1972, Chap. 20, s. 15 (e) (iii). In New Hampshire, persons who cohabit for three years are deemed legally married: N.H.R.S.A. 457:39.

as marriage, so there would then be a demand for justice to those unions that did not fall within the new definition of cohabitation. If, for example, cohabitation were to be legally established after one year's living together, the rejected partner of the nine-month union would feel harshly treated. It may be that one can never satisfactorily and exhaustively define cohabitation.

The cohabitant will share with the widow in the estate of the deceased under the succession laws of, for example, South Australia [13] and Ontario.[14] Her succession rights appear incidentally in the English legislation, the Inheritance (Provision for Family and Dependants) Act 1975.[15] Another example of the English method of dealing, as and when they appear, with alleged injustices arising from the termination of cohabitation is the provision of section 1 (2) of the Domestic Violence and Matrimonial Proceedings Act 1976 permitting a cohabitant to seek a court order excluding her partner from their home. As soon as the Act came into force, unforeseen and complicated problems arose from the application to cohabitants of marital law, enacted as it was without regard to their particular legal situation. The grant of occupation rights to a cohabitant raises more problems than it solves, because there is no mechanism to balance her rights against those of third parties, nor has any decision been reached as to the length of protection that should be made available to her.[16]

THE DIFFERENT EXPECTATIONS OF COHABITANTS AND SPOUSES

The first main argument against the legal recognition of cohabitation stems from the assertion that married couples and cohabitants have different expectations and intentions and that these should be met; indeed it is time that the expectations of a man entering an unmarried relationship should be recognised to be as deserving of consideration as those of the woman. The reason for establishing cohabitation is not relevant, but the reason why the cohabitants have not married is significant. If cohabitants are dissatisfied with their legal position and believe that they suffer injustice, the question must be asked, " Why don't they marry? " Perhaps by the time the alleged injustice is perceived, the relationship has terminated, so that there is no longer any question of marriage, but there is a new situation of demand from one side, looking back to a situation that no longer exists.

It is assumed here that the majority of today's cohabitants have freely chosen not to marry. This may be to attribute to them a deliberation that is absent from their actions but at least it may be argued that easier divorce, world-wide, and the relaxation of the prohibited

13 Administration and Probate Act 1919–1975, s. 4.
14 Succession Law Reform Act 1977, Chap. 40, s. 64 (*b*): support.
15 s. 1 (1) (*e*).
16 *Davis* v. *Johnson* [1979] A.C. 264 (H.L.); Practice Note [1978] 2 All E.R. 1056.

degrees of marriage have had the effect that nearly everyone can free himself or herself to marry or to remarry as the case may be. Why, then, do people choose cohabitation in preference to marriage, and what are their expectations? Some cohabitants wish for a trial period of living together before marriage. There need be no concern for them, if the relationship does lead to marriage. If it does not, is it not evidently unfair to impose the penalties of a failed marriage on persons who were experimenting precisely in order to avoid that sort of outcome? Some persons do not marry because they wish to retain benefits that would be terminated by entering marriage, for example, maintenance from a first husband or social security benefits available only to single persons. These persons are well aware of the situation in which they have placed themselves and would be surprised to find that the benefits that they wished to keep could in fact have been exchanged for support from the new partner. It would, however, also appear unjust in this situation that there should be a right to support from a second source, such as the ex-husband or the State, as well as from the cohabiting partner. It may be argued then that cohabitation should operate to end benefits wherever marriage would do so: this would be felt by cohabitants to be penal and would necessitate inquiry into the habits of the recipient.[17]

Other cohabitants reject the legal incidents of marriage, such as community of property, as well as the very ceremony itself. The traditional laws seem unsuitable or unattractive to them. There ought to be a corner of freedom for such couples to which they can escape and avoid family law. Cohabitation today carries little, if any, social stigma, and therefore people may freely choose between types of relationships and select one from which they may, they believe, easily withdraw, with the minimum disruption and without legal formalities. This choice has been recognised by at least one English judge.[18] Women in particular may wish to avoid what they see as a male-dominated legal institution and to preserve their mobility for a career and as much independence and freedom as possible. There are those who consciously opt for this type of relationship, as did the couple in *Dwyer* v. *Love*,[19] and spell out their wish to be free. The woman in *Dwyer* v. *Love* denied, at the start of the relationship, that there would be any ties and this was the belief of Mr. Love, as it was of Mr. Dove in *Richards* v. *Dove*.[20] In these situations, everything points to the fulfilment of legitimate expectations and the desirability of a clean break

17 This already occurs in England to some extent and is resented: Supplementary Benefits Act 1976, Sched. 1, para. 3 (1) (*b*) as amended by Social Security (Miscellaneous Provisions) Act 1977, s. 14 (7).

18 Stamp L.J. in *Helby* v. *Rafferty* [1979] 1 W.L.R. 13 (C.A.).

19 58 D.L.R. (3d) 735 (S.C., P.E.I.) (1975).

20 [1974] 1 All E.R. 888.

without demands, analogous to the situation selected for the termination of an engagement to marry by the English Law Commission in its Report on Breach of Promise of Marriage.[21] The loss should lie where it falls, concluded the report; pressure to continue an unworkable relationship should be avoided and so should " gold-digging."

Some cohabitants pretend to be married and give the appearance to third parties of a lawful union, but it is not to be concluded that their expectations are any different from those of the open cohabitants: they are equally aware of their illicit status. The distinction drawn in existing English law between those persons who undergo a ceremony of marriage, but whose marriage is void, and those who cohabit may be defended here as logical. In the former case expectations have been created on the part of the " spouses " and before the world: they have elected to take on themselves as far as possible the legal consequences of marriage even though they may not in fact have been free to marry. In the latter case they have not. A unique commitment is made by those who marry and not, as they are well aware, by those who refrain from marrying, and no amount of emphasis on the similarities between spouses and cohabitants can obscure the difference, one of the most fundamental in human existence. This is not an argument for the superiority of marriage or even its centrality, but rather for the preservation of the freedom to try alternative forms of relationship, a freedom which is at present being eroded by the increased tendency of the law to impose on the formerly cohabiting couple the status and structure of traditional marriage, after they have ended the relationship and therefore at the most inappropriate time. In effect the law is converting the relationship into marriage *ex post facto*. Does this not contravene the spirit and possibly the provisions of the European Convention on Human Rights? [22] Those who favour the application of family law to cohabitants may be accused of being insufficiently tolerant of the relationship and of preventing its development into an alternative to marriage, free of the existing defective family laws and possibly contributing to their improvement. Those proponents are also laying themselves open to the risk of the accusation that lawyers will foment legal difficulties between cohabitants in order to benefit themselves professionally, especially at a time when the administration of easier divorce law has ceased to provide divorce lawyers with as profitable a career as it once did.

Cohabitation could only be assimilated to marriage if the legal

[21] *Law Com.* No. 26 (1969), especially paras. 17, 42.

[22] Art. 8 (1) lays down that " everyone has the right to respect for his private and family life, his home and his correspondence." Art. 23 (3) of the International Covenant on Civil and Political Rights reads as follows: " No marriage shall be entered into without the free and full consent of the intending spouses." Art. 23 (4) is also of interest: " States Parties to the present Covenant shall take appropriate steps to ensure equality of rights and responsibilities of spouses as to marriage, during marriage and at its dissolution."

incidents of marriage itself were reduced (which would be no bad thing). The case will be made later for the application of ordinary laws to cohabitants—contract rather than status—and this too would be desirable in marriage. In other words, marriage should become more like cohabitation and not the other way around.

Once the clear commitment of marriage is absent, there is no logical reason for differentiating between the legal effects of brother and sister partnerships, heterosexual and homosexual unions; indeed there are already indications that former homosexual partners would like to be able to claim support on the same legal footing as cohabitants of opposite sexes. If cohabitation is to be a legally recognised status, is it to include couples who would be forbidden by law to marry—incestuous unions, unions within the prohibited degrees? Is it to include polygynous or polyandrous groups? To single out heterosexual unions for the compensation of the "weaker" partner is to reveal a most important basis for monetary rewards to women: domestic and sexual services rendered. To allow claims by female cohabitants is in effect to treat cohabitation as long-term prostitution, with delayed payment subject to arbitration. The only other reason for selection of the heterosexual union for special treatment is its reproductive possibilities. If the presence of children is the only good reason for cohabitation laws [23] then all unions, unlawful or not, where children are present, should be similarly treated.

THE UNEQUAL TREATMENT OF WOMEN COHABITANTS

Another ground for opposing the extension of family law to cohabitants is that the rules that have been applied are not in keeping with the notions of equality of women and of marital partnership. Underlying premises of a financial award to a woman cohabitant are that she was the weaker partner and needs the protection of the court against exploitation; that, once having cohabited, she is unable to be self-supporting again or at best her capacity for self-support has been harmed; and that she has earned a share of the man's wealth, for he could not have accumulated as much without her help.

It is anomalous that at a time when most women are establishing social and economic independence, a few should try to capitalise on the myth of the weak woman.

What do women want from family law? Unfortunately, even though the time may have arrived when they will be given what they want, they are not unanimous, and the split in opinion retards the realisation of any set of aims. The women's movement in relation to family law speaks with two voices. One argues that treatment in the past has been

[23] See, *infra*, p. 493.

bad and that today's easy divorce laws fail to recognise the extent of women's non-monetary contribution to the maintenance of the family unit; women are exploited, their position in society is inferior to men's and there should be greater recompense for this, namely, a share of family assets on divorce and maintenance to the full from the ex-husband, to offset the wife's handicaps in the labour market and in recognition of her valuable home-making and child-rearing services. An analogy has even been drawn between the position of American slaves immediately after their emancipation in the nineteenth century and that of women today and from this alleged historical parallel has been drawn the conclusion that a group that has suffered from years of exploitation, slavery, lack of opportunity and choice of life-style cannot, immediately after emancipation, be expected to fend for itself economically in a society the majority of whose members were the oppressors and enjoyed a head start of experience. So the extreme wing of this branch of the women's movement would require, not only compensation for their services in money, but also positive discrimination in favour of women in education and in employment.

The other voice of the women's movement claims simply equal treatment and equal opportunity for women, and it challenges the notion that in general women are weaker and that they have been exploited. It rejects the analogy with slavery, for women have had for a long time the choice of work or housewifery or both—nor were they forced into marriage and denied basic education. The conclusion of this wing is that the status of women in the labour market and in family law reinforce each other. As long as it is the law and the general expectation that women are dependants, to be kept, then this will be an obstacle to full acceptance in the world of work. Equal opportunity and equal treatment at work must mean equal responsibilities and standing for the men and women partners to a union. Maintenance and property awards to former cohabiting partners are not simply payment for the freedom to leave one woman for another, but would also reinforce the outmoded view, upheld by the law, of the man as the head of the household and the woman under obligation to provide domestic services and child care, a view which is too unsatisfactory in its application to married persons to permit of its extension to the unmarried.

The notion that housework is unpaid labour ought not to be sustained. Valuable as it may be, housework should not be thought of as the preserve of one sex. Moreover, even if it is the woman partner alone who undertakes it, is housework not carried out in large measure for her own purposes? A woman living alone would have to do her own housework or pay someone else to do it, so that only a proportion of the work performed in the joint household is attributable to the needs of the man. Where the man is sufficiently wealthy to attract a claim by his former cohabiting partner, the likelihood of housework having amounted to hard work is correspondingly reduced, so that the greater the amount of the woman's claim the less work she is actually likely to have done. The alleged unpaid domestic services were in reality the maintenance of a way of life and one undertaken to a great extent for her own satisfaction. Even if it were to be accepted that the performance of housework is a type of exploitation or slavery, the remedy for this would surely not be just to give the victim rights to maintenance and a share in the oppressor's property if he dispenses with her. The real remedy is a redistribution of work in the home. Is the position of the housewife really so much worse than that of the single woman? Surely " some women do less work in the home than they would if they were employed and live at a higher standard of living than they would if they were employed." [24] The housewife is in fact a privileged person, without the constraints of fixed working hours and with the opportunity, if she takes it, to continue her education or pursue her hobbies.

What of the alleged damage to the career of the female cohabitant? The argument that she has had to, or has, at the request of the man, abandoned a promising career that would have provided her with a secure future, may prove false on closer examination and should not be taken for granted. The career may or may not have become successful; it may have been taken up partly with the aim of meeting or attracting the male cohabitant; it may have been abandoned with relief for the more agreeable pastime of keeping house. Whatever its value, the sacrifice of a career is not a reasonably necessary precondition to cohabitation and it is not imposed. To argue that one job has been exchanged for another in commencing cohabitation and to claim money as a type of redundancy payment is to treat the relationship as one of master and servant. If this view were to prevail, it would follow that the quality of the " service " had to be examined and this is what has happened in cohabitation claims. Whether based on contract or *quantum meruit*, restitution or marital-type support, they have involved detailed investigation into the conduct of the claimant, reminiscent of the most offensive traits of the old fault-divorce system. The sexual fidelity of the claimant becomes relevant, and a searching inquiry into the nature of the cohabitants' relationship occurred in *Omer* v. *Omer*,[25] *Marvin* v. *Marvin* [26] and in *Becker* v. *Pettkus*.[27]

The need to evaluate in monetary terms the domestic services

[24] E. M. Clive, " Marriage: An Unnecessary Legal Concept ": paper delivered at the Third World Conference of the International Society on Family Law, Uppsala, 1979.

[25] 523 P. 2d 957 (C.A., Wash.) (1974).

[26] *Supra*, n. 5.

[27] 5 R.F.L. (2d) 344, (C.A.;Ont.) (1978).

rendered by the cohabitant arises from the recognition of a bargain between the parties. As Clark J. pointed out in his dissent in *Marvin*,[28] compensation for household services would place a cohabitant in a better position than a wife. This in itself is not an argument against compensation for such services, and perhaps both women should be similarly rewarded; but there remains the master-servant element of such a bargain and the complication resulting from the fact that the cost of the woman's support and the benefits, such as holidays, clothing, transport, gifts and entertainment, received during cohabitation would have to be deducted. She has chosen to present herself as a dismissed or redundant employee; thus the support received during cohabitation amounted to part of her salary and she should not be paid twice. It may also be necessary to determine who did the household chores: in so far as they were carried out by the man, has she failed to perform her side of the bargain?

Has a woman then perhaps earned a share in the man's assets because she supported him in his career? The extent of this assistance could be determined only by comparing the progress of the male cohabitant with another man in the same career who lived without a female's services. Many single professional men do in fact avail themselves of female assistance. The housekeeper does the same work as the cohabitant but is not treated as his business partner. A female cohabitant may in a sense free a man to work (or compel him) but so does his car and so does his secretary, and it has not yet been suggested by family lawyers that a secretary should be entitled in law to a half-share of her employer's assets. The secretary receives a salary, but so does the cohabitant in terms of support during the relationship. There is presumably no sexual relationship with the secretary, but cohabitation as defined in English law does not necessarily involve a sexual relationship.[29] In terms of assistance to career, the only case for not rewarding the secretary in a fashion similar to the cohabitant would be the difference in their respective expectations. The cohabitant may consider herself to be the business partner of the man but she should then be as ready to shoulder half the possible losses incurred by her partner as she is to share in the profits. The real contribution of the cohabitant, like the wife, to her male partner's career is likely to be limited to moral and social support, and if this is so, it would not be acceptable for the law to reinforce the notion that every woman must provide support for her man's career, but that similar services are not to be expected of him towards her career.

[28] *Supra*, n. 5.

[29] According to Lord Goddard in *Thomas* v. *Thomas* [1948] 2 K.B. 294 at p. 297: "Cohabitation consists in the husband acting as a husband towards the wife and the wife acting as a wife towards the husband, the wife rendering housewifely duties to the husband and the husband cherishing and supporting his wife as a husband should."

If the arguments of the "cohabitation lobby" are taken to the extreme, there emerges a situation of one-half of the population being entitled to lifelong support from the other half simply in return for living with them. Is it not more true to say that cohabitation (and marriage), far from being a situation of detriment, benefits women and men, and is chosen freely, is far more pleasant and rewarding financially than the single life, and needs no restoration of lost opportunities at its termination?

The Irreconcilability of Wife's and Cohabitant's Claims against a Man

Discussion of cohabitation assumes too readily that there is a straight choice between marriage and cohabitation. It is quite as likely to be the case that marriage and cohabitation exist simultaneously, that is, one or both of the cohabitants is, has been or will be married to a third person. There may also exist successive periods of cohabitation with different partners.

The extension of property rights to cohabitants will bring the female claimant into direct conflict with the male cohabitant's wife, if he has one. This situation of conflict was less likely formerly, when divorce maintenance was constricted by fault and wives were entitled only to the property that they had purchased. But now that maintenance, whether before or after the termination of the marriage, is commonly based on need,[30] and now that so many jurisdictions require a husband to share his property with his wife in some form of community at the end of the marriage,[31] a man cannot avoid his primary obligation to his wife, for it exists regardless of the fact that she may have left him to live with another man or that he is proposing to remarry. This law severely affects the fortunes of a man who marries more than once (and whose second wife must receive less on divorce), but it cannot sensibly be applied at all if it is to require simultaneous sharing of property and income with wife and cohabitant. Society in general, and men in particular, cannot support two types of marital status. In the California case of *Cary* v. *Cary* [32] the court awarded an equal share in the community property to the cohabitant. What if there had been a wife's claim also as the result of a broken marriage?

The Law Commission in England has proposed co-ownership of the matrimonial home.[33] The suggested definition of matrimonial home is wide enough to include a home once occupied by the spouses but

[30] Matrimonial Causes Act 1973, s. 25 (1); Domestic Proceedings and Magistrates' Courts Act 1978, s. 3 (1); Ontario Family Law Reform Act 1978, s. 15.

[31] Matrimonial Causes Act 1973, s. 24; Ontario Family Law Reform Act 1978, s. 4; California Civil Code § 4800.

[32] 34 Cal.App. 3d 345 (1973).

[33] *Law Com.* No. 86 (1978), *Third Report on Family Property: The Matrimonial Home (Co-ownership and Occupation Rights) and Household Goods.*

which has been vacated by the wife and subsequently occupied by the female cohabitant. Which of the two women is to be entitled to ownership where such rights extend equally to cohabitants?

Occupation rights in the matrimonial home also present problems where equal protection is given to the mistress and the wife. In *Tanner* v. *Tanner*,[34] for example, a cohabitant was awarded a sum for loss of occupation rights expressed to be in the form of a licence, and a mistress was held to have a licence in the man's home in *Chandler* v. *Kerley*.[35] This reasoning can be reconciled with the wife's right to stay in occupation or to re-enter the home if evicted in English law [36] or in Ontario law,[37] because the one receives monetary compensation for loss of her cohabitant's licence and the other has actual rights of occupation. But if the cohabitant were to be given the same right as the wife,[38] that of remaining in possession, as provided for example in the English Domestic Violence and Matrimonial Proceedings Act 1976, two women are given identical but irreconcilable rights in the same property. It is also possible that a female cohabitant may benefit doubly by exercising her rights to a share in her former husband's property and her rights in her male cohabitant's property. Some jurisdictions give the court a discretion in the award of property and occupation rights [39] but others do not.[40] In the former, the court will have to weigh the relative claims of wife and mistress; in the latter the claims are irreconcilable. In a society where earnings and housing are generally designed for the support of one family at the most, a choice has ultimately to be made between the claims of cohabitants and those of wives. Both cannot be afforded, any more than can polygamy.

There are additional conveyancing complexities for third parties in any system giving the cohabitant rights similar to those of the wife. Problems of notification of a wife's interest in a home tend to be resolved by registration.[41] At the time of writing it has been held in England that a purchaser may be bound by the interest of a wife in occupation of the home, where she has a property right arising from contribution to the acquisition of the home, and that her interest is one which entitles her to remain in the property.[42] It may be argued that this decision will impose too great a burden on a purchaser and his solicitor and certainly the difficulties are increased if cohabitants' rights, whether arising from contribution to the purchase price or

34 [1975] 1 W.L.R. 1346 (C.A.).

35 [1978] 1 W.L.R. 693 (C.A.).

36 Matrimonial Homes Act 1967.

37 Family Law Reform Act 1978, s. 40.

38 Proposed by Masson, "The Mistress's Limited Rights of Occupancy" [1979] Conv. 184.

39 *e.g.* Matrimonial Causes Act 1973, s. 24 and Matrimonial Homes Act 1967.

40 *e.g.* California, *supra*, n. 31.

41 *e.g.* Matrimonial Homes Act 1967, s. 2; *Caunce* v. *Caunce* [1969] 1 W.L.R. 286; Ontario Family Law Reform Act 1978, ss. 41, 48.

42 *Williams and Glyn's Bank* v. *Boland* [1979] 2 W.L.R. 550 (C.A.).

from status, are to bind purchasers even without actual notice. These issues, which have important consequences for parties other than the cohabitants, demand clarification before introducing cohabitants' rights into the law. The problem has already been revealed by the lack of categorisation of cohabitants' rights under the English Domestic Violence and Matrimonial Proceedings Act 1976.[43]

WIDESPREAD CONSEQUENTIAL AMENDMENTS TO GENERAL LAW

It is not only in family law proper that problems are created by special treatment of cohabiting couples. Wives and husbands enjoy certain testimonial privileges, based on the belief that they would not want to incriminate each other and that family harmony would be threatened if they were forced to. These privileges too ought to be accorded to cohabitants under the prevailing trend of assimilation, as should all the welfare benefits at present given by the State to spouses. The right to sue for injury or death would also be extended, and pensions and insurance premiums would have to be reassessed if the coverage were to extend to cohabitants as well as to wives. Tax laws would have to give to cohabitants reliefs that are now confined to one beneficiary per payer, and clearly the costs would be high. It can be seen that to regard any relationship other than that of marriage as one of intimacy and dependency is comparable to the throwing of a stone into a lake. The circle of logical claimants is ever-widening and their number cannot be ascertained in advance by the giver of benefits. It has been argued already that extension of family law to cohabitants must logically entail similar treatment of persons of the same sex living conjugally, and the additional inclusion of this category into the dependency claims and status described above would create a situation of uncertainty. One begins to question why the existing entitlement to State benefits should depend at all on the recipient's having lived with another person. Why is the elderly widow or cohabitant more deserving of support than the elderly spinster? Surely poverty should be treated as an individual rather than a family need. If every adult, married or not, had independent social security rights, many existing legal difficulties, as well as the hypothetical ones described above, could be solved.

A NEED FOR PROTECTION AND READJUSTMENT?

The strongest argument put forward to justify the legal embrace of cohabitation is that of protection. It is alleged that the need for protection and readjustment exists whether the breakdown is of a marriage or mere cohabitation: the parties have the same needs and the same

[43] *Supra*, n. 16.

moral claims as spouses, and principles of humanity demand that the cohabitant be treated as fairly as the wife, for she has behaved similarly and has been equally affected by the consequences of conjugal life. It may be replied that the application of family law does not ensure stability. Existing family law has not proved remarkably successful in its declared aims and we should be shy of extending it to new situations. The argument that cohabitants need family law is often based on the premise that women are weaker, and it may be rejected on the basis that cohabitation ought not to cripple a potential wage-earner, but that, if it does, this may be a burden that society generally should shoulder rather than the wage-earning partner, whose expectations of an unfettered relationship are equally deserving of consideration.

Is it unduly harsh or materialistic to expect former cohabitants to keep themselves? It has been demonstrated by Reich [44] that the most prized and secure wealth of today consists of the pension, status and insurance benefits attached to a job. It would not be right to accept woman's exclusion from those benefits or to pretend that rights to assets and maintenance from a former partner can ever be as reliable or as valuable as a place in the genuine economy. To secure the real welfare of women, legislators should not wait until they have become economically equal with men before dropping their protected status in family law, for the day of equality is highly unlikely to dawn until stimulated by changes in family law that presuppose equality. The vicious circle of reduced work opportunity because a woman is a dependant, followed by protective maintenance laws because she cannot be self-sufficient, has to be broken at some stage. To reward women through family law alone is to distance them from the far more valuable largesse dispensed by government, which for many citizens has taken the place of traditional forms of wealth and private property. Reich's impressive list of the benefits that flow from the holding of a job, especially a government one, overshadows in its quality and quantity the rather paltry cash benefits a displaced housewife can expect from her man.. A system that ties women to men they have lived with for their security retards their access to the " new property " and forces them to depend on more fragile support mechanisms. As the right to a job, expressed in England by the law of unfair dismissal, has grown in strength in recent years, so has there been a corresponding decline in the right to remain a spouse, subject to good behaviour, formerly expressed in fault-based divorce law. The guarantees of security necessary to those who face old age, illness and unemployment are linked increasingly to their position in the labour force and less in theory and in practice to their family status. The

[44] C. Reich, " The New Property " (1964) 73 Yale L.J. 733.

need now is for family law and social security law to endorse the idea of the woman as self-supporting.

Assuming that women are not simply tossed around by events, but are to some extent in control of their lives, any foreseeable injury resulting from cohabitation ought to be fairly attributable to the payer of compensation. This means dealing with the problems, which, as described above, are believed to be exaggerated, on the basis of contract between the cohabitants and by the application of ordinary principles of law.

If cohabitation fulfils functions considered important by the State, then it should be the State that pays for the harmful consequences, if any, of performance. It is in the State's interests that children should be well cared for, but only a cynic would argue that, in times of high unemployment, it is useful to the State to have a number of women withdrawn from the labour market because they have found men to support them.

The real justification for the application of law may in fact lie in sympathy for the plight of the children of the cohabitants' union, such sympathy leading to support of the mother to supplement and atone for the inadequacies of the affiliation payments system. This rationale obviously underlies the New Zealand law [45] providing that a putative father may be ordered to support the mother for five years if she cannot support herself. The status of illegitimate children in law, though not the mechanism for ensuring their monetary support, has been improved in many countries, in recognition of the unfairness and futility of discrimination. It does not follow that the position of the cohabitant, mother or not, must also be improved. There is no disputing the innocence, vulnerability and lack of choice on the part of the child or the fact that there is universal recognition of the duty of a parent, mother or father, to support it. The child is not to be equated with the cohabitant, who has a choice as to her position and who may not be willing to accept increased paternal rights over the child in return for support. The proposed changes in the law of cohabitation are not limited to support of mothers, but even if they were, it could still be queried whether the obligation of the father should rightly extend beyond support for the child, especially if the mother had agreed to assume responsibility for contraception. Nor should male cohabitants necessarily bear the entire burden consequent on society's failure to appreciate the importance of, and the need for, day nurseries. It would be more logical to reform the law relating to support of children than to create new laws for all cohabitants to achieve the same end.

But if one is to find anywhere a rationale for support of female

[45] Domestic Proceedings Act 1968, s. 53.

cohabitants and for differentiating between heterosexual and homosexual unions, it is surely in the need to support an adult in the role of parent. Mothers (or fathers) who are staying at home with their children, offspring of a cohabitation, or whose careers are impeded by child care, may deserve support from the other parent or from the State. Two situations may be distinguished in this context: support for the mother who is at home with her young children, easily justifiable; and support for the mother whose children have grown up, but who claims entitlement to maintenance because of the earlier disruption to her career.

It is assumed here for the sake of argument that it may be better for a parent to remain at home with his or her young child rather than continue to work and make other arrangements for the care of the children. The social and political [46] arguments for and against mothers remaining at home are beyond the scope of this article. If this is the best approach to child care, and if the former cohabiting father is to support the mother, then the privilege accorded to this mother is one that he, the father, will probably not be able to afford to extend to a subsequent partner and mother of his children, for only a fairly wealthy man will be able to support two women during full-time child care, and thereafter, on the ground that their job prospects have been irremediably impaired by the period of full-time child care.

It may be argued that a mother should have a choice between full-time child care and continuing her job. Such a choice may be desirable, but it is one that will not be available to the father's second partner; nor to the man. Moreover, the choice by one mother to stay at home means that another working mother is paying taxes that will go to support the full-time mother, or partially support her, if the man is unable to meet the full cost of her support after the end of the relationship.

EQUALITY UNDER THE LAW

Nothing stated hitherto is intended to deny that during or at the end of a period of cohabitation there may have been created legal relationships between the parties or that there may be a cause of action under the existing law: of course, it is not here proposed that the courts be closed to cohabitants. If it is accepted that they should not have special treatment or the questionable benefit of special laws, then, like all other citizens, they will be regulated by contracts that they have made and by the other ordinary principles of law. This is an argument for the application of contractual principles rather than fixed status in

[46] *e.g.* Lord Spens on cures for unemployment, 400 H.L. Deb., col. 973 (1979). It is of note that the stay-at-home mother who devotes herself to child care is a relatively recent phenomenon: see Oakley, *Housewife* (1974).

cohabitants' relationships, and the argument is, incidentally, equally relevant to spouses. Formerly it was argued that contracts between cohabitants were void and unenforceable as tainted with immorality. It is unlikely that this would still be public policy today, especially when putative fathers have been given statutory rights,[47] and there is no valid reason why parents or other cohabitants should not be able legally to agree on their financial and other relations. In *Tanner* v. *Tanner*,[48] the female cohabitant was party to a contractual licence and public policy was not used as an argument to render the contract invalid. The majority judgment in *Marvin* v. *Marvin*[49] accepted the validity of contracts unless expressly founded on the provision of sexual services. This is to be welcomed but the judgment of Tobriner J. unfortunately did not simply recognise the freedom of two individuals who happen to cohabit to make an express contract. He went on to hold that, in the absence of an express contract, the court should enquire into the conduct of the parties to see if it demonstrated an implied contract and that if there were no grounds for finding one, resort should be had to equitable principles such as *quantum meruit*, constructive or resulting trusts. This determination to apply what are in practice special family-based laws, or to force on the couple a legal framework when they have expressly rejected one and there is no express contract, is regrettable. How would a cohabiting couple know that unless they made a contract, the court would impose one on them, as seemed reasonable to the court? Given the context and lack of precedent, it would be difficult as well as arbitrary to find an implied contract for the sharing of property; the ambiguities of *quantum meruit* in the recompense of housework have already been investigated.

Constructive and resulting trusts are not objectionable in themselves, being ordinary principles of law. To establish a share by way of constructive trust, the female cohabitant needs to prove that she has been led to act to her detriment in the belief that the man intended that she should acquire an interest in the property and also that, as her part of the bargain, she contributed towards the acquisition of the property.[50] It would be anomalous to find a constructive trust in favour of the female cohabitant, simply because she came to live with the owner, hardly a detriment.[51] To avoid court-imposed solutions, the couple should be encouraged to make a contract, as in the Ontario Family Law Reform Act 1978, s. 52 of which provides that the cohabiting

47 Children Act 1975, s. 107 (1) and the Guardianship of Minors Act 1971, s. 9.

48 *Supra*, n. 34.

49 *Supra*, n. 5.

50 *Cooke* v. *Head* [1972] 1 W.L.R. 518 (C.A.); *Eves* v. *Eves* [1975] 1 W.L.R. 1338 (C.A.).

51 *Tanner* v. *Tanner* [1975] 1 W.L.R. 1346 *per* Brightman J. at p. 1351; also *Richards* v. *Dove* [1974] 1 All E.R. 888; and see *Pascoe* v. *Turner* [1979] 1 W.L.R. 431 (C.A.) for an outstanding example of judicial generosity towards a cohabitant who had made no contribution at all to the acquisition of the home.

couple may by agreement regulate their rights during or at the end of cohabitation or on death, in respect of the ownership of property, support, the training (but not the custody) of children and any other matter.

Given the desirability of regulation by freely made contract and the likelihood of its validity, why is it argued [52] that courts should not automatically uphold a cohabitation contract made years earlier, because the parties' economic situation may have changed, because children are now involved, because circumstances generally have changed? It has also been argued that cohabitation contracts should be held void because there is not equality of bargaining power. That argument may easily be dismissed: it cannot be a general principle of contract law that women are not to be held to their bargains because of their weaker bargaining power or because they may become a burden on the State.[53] The " weakness " of the woman's position is a term much used. What does it mean when it is so applied? Fragile or comfortable? Weak in relation to a man's physique or intellect? Is the weakness self-induced or unavoidable?

It is agreed that the maintenance and custody of children should be a separate matter. One is left with the argument that changed circumstances justify the overturning of a freely made contract. This must be rejected as paternalistic and unjust to the party who enters the relationship and plans his future on the basis of the contract and in the belief that its provisions will govern. Moreover the bearing of children and changes in fortune of the parties can hardly be unexpected by cohabitants, especially not by those who make a contract. To apply such a doctrine to cohabitants, but to reject it in the case of other individuals' contracts where the more severe doctrine of frustration applies, is discriminatory.

The other " ordinary " legal principles that have been and should continue to be applied to cohabitants are those of property, of torts and of trusts. The traditional separate property approach is particularly suitable as it does not distinguish between married and unmarried persons, men and women. The trusts doctrine, which mitigates the alleged rigours of separate property, also achieves equality and has developed in recent years to reflect all types of contribution made to the acquisition and improvement of another's property. Trusts doctrines achieved a just outcome in the Canadian cases of *Smith* v. *Ahone* [54] and *Becker* v. *Pettkus*,[55] and also in the English cases of *Cooke* v. *Head*,[56]

[52] Eekelaar, *Family Law and Social Policy* (1978), p. 53.

[53] This is in effect what underlies the inability of a married woman to agree never to seek financial support: *Hyman* v. *Hyman* [1929] A.C. 601 (H.L.).

[54] 56 D.L.R. (3d) 454 (S.C., B.C.) (1975).

[55] *Supra*, n. 27.

[56] [1972] 1 W.L.R. 518 (C.A.).

Paul v. *Constance* [57] and *Eves* v. *Eves*.[58] The result of *Eves* was possibly over-generous and there is a recent tendency to use the doctrine of constructive trusts to achieve an equity based on female dependency and not on genuine contribution.

The settlement of cohabitants' disputes by existing legal principles is fair and workable. The creation of special laws for cohabitants or the extension of marital laws to them retards the emancipation of women, degrades the relationship and is too expensive for society in general and men in particular.

It is not being argued here that recognition of cohabitation would undermine the status of marriage. In the first place, if marriage *were* undermined, this would not be relevant, for marriage should not be shored up independently of its utility and desirability. But marriage will not be undermined by the recognition of cohabitation, because cohabitation will be made as expensive and legalistic as marriage and therefore no more attractive. Failure to accord legal recognition to cohabitation probably does render it more attractive than formal marriage.

Ultimately the question to be considered in the legal control of cohabitation and its consequences is, do we legislate for the past, to correct defects first perceived decades ago? Or should we legislate, or refrain from legislating, for a better future? Do we legislate to reinforce existing weaknesses in society, or do we try to eradicate them? One conclusion may be that the weaknesses of existing family laws are such that we should hesitate long before applying them to cohabitation, and then only consider laws for those cases where a partner is caring for young children of the union.

57 [1977] 1 W.L.R. 527 (C.A.).
58 [1975] 1 W.L.R. 1338 (C.A.).

[14]

MARRIAGE AND THE GOOD OF OBLIGATION

SCOTT FITZGIBBON*

"[I]t seems to bind me with mighty cables."[1]

PART ONE: INTRODUCTION

I. THE SCOPE AND DIRECTION OF THIS ARTICLE

Marriage is obligatory. This is not to say, of course, that bachelorhood must be avoided or that everyone ought to get married. The point, rather, is that those who do wed form a relationship which embraces obligation as a fundamental component ("commitment norms," as Professor Elizabeth Scott has put it).[2] This article aims to show why this is a good thing, and fundamentally so.

Marriage and other affiliations, it seems, may involve obligation in two basic ways. The first way is instrumentally. The projects of married life require long-term commitment and fixity of purpose: raising children and paying off the mortgage take a long time and a steady hand. This article is not aimed primarily at establishing this obvious point.

The second kind of involvement is not instrumental: commitment, steadiness, loyalty, and fidelity to obligation are good in a basic way and a part of the basic good of marriage. This may be controversial and is the major thesis of this article. Obligation, it is here maintained, is sometimes a final

---

* My thanks for their helpful comments to James Gordley, Shannon Cecil Turner Professor of Jurisprudence, University of California at Berkeley, to Professor Frank Herrmann, S.J., of Boston College Law School, and to Professor Catharine Wells of Boston College Law School. A version of this paper was presented at a faculty symposium at Boston College Law School: thanks to those who attended for their comments: Professors Sharon Beckman, Mary Bilder, Robert Bloom, George Brown, Phyllis Goldfarb, Ruth-Arlene Howe, Renee Jones, Sanford Katz, Joseph Liu, Ray Madoff, Judith McMorrow, James Repetti, and Aviam Soifer. Further thanks, for diligent and helpful research assistance, to Jason Giannetti of Boston College Law School Class of 2003. Thanks, for generous financial assistance, to Darald and Juliet Libby.

1. Sullivan Ballou to his wife Sarah, 14 July, 1861, *Wing to Wing, Oar to Oar: Readings on Courting and Marrying (the Ethics of Everyday Life)*, Amy A. Kass and Leon R. Kass, eds., (Notre Dame, Ind.: University of Notre Dame Press, 2000), 564, 565 ("Sarah, my love for you is deathless, it seems to bind me with mighty cables that nothing but Omnipotence could break. . . .").

2. Elizabeth Scott, "Symposium: The Legal Construction of Norms: Social Norms and the Legal Regulation of Marriage," *Virginia Law Review* 86 (2000) 1901.

good. Precepts such as those mandating sexual fidelity, requiring commitment to the raising of children, and enforcing a scrupulous commemoration of birthdays and anniversaries are fundamental to marriage. Marriage would not be fully marriage without obligation. Marriage comes into its own as man and wife embrace obligation to one another. Marriage seeks obligation, fosters it, and even rejoices in it. Marriage involves obligation just as fundamentally as it involves respect, mutual knowledge, and love. It is the purpose of this article to explain and defend this thesis (and to shed some light on related subjects such as the cultural deterioration of close affiliation).

This article approaches the matter from the point of view of secular philosophy, with special attention to Aristotle. It does not proceed on the basis of the extensive Catholic moral theology of marriage (brilliantly expounded by Professor Germain Grisez in his book *Living a Christian Life*).[3]

Odysseus' fidelity to Penelope illustrates several points, as does her loyalty to him. The *Odyssey* is the great epic of marital loyalty and is referred to from time to time herein.

II. Some Basic Features of Obligation

Obligation has much to do with the good and the right. Not so, perhaps, with positive obligation and customary obligation, but this article is not focused on them (it is not primarily concerned with obligations which the law or public opinion attribute to marriage). How obligation aims at or expresses the good or the right is the major question discussed in Part Three.

An obligation is not only a good, but also has to do with how a good involves itself with or attaches itself to the person. No obligation is implied for me by a good which is disconnected from me and has no bearing on my actions—the goods and evils of situations in other galaxies, perhaps. If I deny that I have any obligation in some respect I assert this sort of disconnection: I deny, not that there is anything at stake by way of good and bad, but that the situation is any of my concern. If I accept that I have an obligation I mean that not only is some end or course of conduct good but that its goodness bears in a special way on my life. The Latin root of "obligation" is *obligatio*, a binding up; so to have an obligation is to be tied.

Further: to have an obligation is to be tied tight, not loose; with rope, not with rubber. Obligation involves duty; it is not supererogatory; it involves

3. (Quincy, Ill.: Franciscan Press, 1992), Chapter Nine. See Patrick McKinley Brennan, "Of Marriage and Monks, Community and Dialogue," *Emory Law Journal* 48 (1999) 689, 703 (since the Second Vatican Council, "the marital union is no longer understood to be exclusively instrumental. The bond itself is now believed to be among the discovered purposes of marriage.").

requirement or strong demand, not just suggestion or recommendation. In marriage, sexual fidelity is an obligation; entertaining conversation and a good income are merely desiderata. In the political community, to avoid supporting the enemy in wartime is an obligation; to pay taxes is an obligation; to get well informed and send intelligent letters to the editor on political issues is an "extra." This fits in with the bifurcation which many ethical thinkers depict between a strict core of ethical requirements and a supererogatory penumbra.[4] Common sense and common usage of the term "obligation" support this understanding. We have an obligation to support our families; whereas sacrificial giving to the poor is not obligatory but is a good thing to do.

Another point is that obligation in its fullest form is social: it involves commitment to some specific person or group. There is some person or association "at the other end of the rope." The word usually has a transitive quality: "I have an obligation to my wife"; "I must not buy that boat because of my financial obligations to my children."[5]

Further, obligation often has the quality of perdurance: of persistence across time and circumstance. Obligation—anyway, of the kind discussed in this article—is not just a matter of one-off hits. Rather, it lasts and lasts, endures and perdures, in sickness and in health. And obligation may have a juristic character, taking the form of rules and principles and operating along the lines of general precepts.[6]

Finally, obligation seems to have a strong "personalist" element. As with a rope, so with an obligation: it, so to speak, pulls on *you*, and it may damage you if you try to pull away. And it change you, much for the better, if you accept and fulfill it. To be obliged is a part of what it means to be a person. Obligation is a component of the human good.

You can find many of these elements in Odysseus' obligations. They involved important goods (marital friendship and civil order); they were goods *for him*—involving him in a special way; pursuing them was not optional or

4. For discussion of the supererogatory compared to other moral categories, see David Heyd, *Supererogation: Its Status in Ethical Theory* (Cambridge: Cambridge University Press, 1982); Gregory Mellema, *Beyond the Call of Duty: Supererogation, Obligation, and Offence* (Albany: State University of New York Press, 1991) and works cited.

5. The elements of obligation introduced in this and the succeeding two paragraphs go beyond the meaning assigned that term in much of the scholarly literature. See, e.g., Roderick M. Chisolm, "Supererogation and Offence: A Conceptual Scheme for Ethics," *Ratio* 5 (1963) 1, 3 (adopting a usage in which the supererogatory is "that which it is good, but not obligatory, to do."). Common usage as well often implies a broader meaning for the term obligatory than that here proposed.

6. An obligation binds "as by a law." G. E. M. Anscombe, "Modern Moral Philosophy," in *Virtue Ethics*, Roger Crisp and Michael Slote, eds. (Oxford: Oxford University Press, 1997), 26, 31.

supererogatory, but rather firmly his duty; and his ends were specified and directed to a particular person and political group: they were not duties "to serve the goods of marital friendship and civil order," but rather were to Penelope and to Ithaca. He could not have been fully himself if he had neglected them. Odysseus would not have been what he became had he languished in the arms of the goddess Calypso or if upon his return to Ithaca he had wimped out and left Penelope in the hands of the suitors. He would never have become the great historic Odysseus who emerges as the epic draws to its conclusion.

III. YOU CANNOT BOIL IT ALL DOWN TO PROMISE AND CONTRACT

Some writers indicate that obligation is entirely a matter of promise or contract.[7] Many writers have said that about political obligation; Chicago School legal scholars say that about fiduciary obligation;[8] and many modern authorities have taken the same approach to marriage.[9]

---

7. Some theorists ("voluntarists") may insist that there can be no other ground for obligation. For a repudiation of this view, see Samuel Scheffler, "Relationships and Responsibilities," *Philosophy and Public Affairs* 26 (1997) 189, 201 ("[T]he existence of a relationship that one has reason to value is itself the source of special responsibilities and those responsibilities arise whether or not the participants actually value [or have agreed to] the relationship.").

8. See, e.g., Frank H. Easterbrook and Daniel R. Fischel, "Contract and Fiduciary Duty," *Journal of Law and Economics* 36 (1993) 425, 427:

> "Scholars of a non- or antieconomic bent have had trouble coming up with a unifying approach to fiduciary duties because they are looking for the wrong things. They are looking for something special about fiduciary relations. There is nothing special to find. There are only distinctive and independently interesting questions about particular consensual *(and thus contractual)* relations. . . . In short, there is no subject here, and efforts to unify it on a ground that presumes its distinctiveness are doomed."

(emphasis added). See Frank H. Easterbrook and Daniel R. Fischel, "Corporate Control Transactions," *Yale Law Journal* 91 (1982) 698, 702 ("[T]he fiduciary principle is fundamentally a standard term in a contract."); John H. Langbein, "The Contractarian Basis of the Law of Trusts," *Yale Law Journal* 105 (1995) 625, 629 ("despite decades of pulpit-thumping rhetoric about the sanctity of fiduciary obligations, fiduciary duties in trust law are unambiguously contractarian. The rules of trust fiduciary law mean to capture the likely understanding of the parties to the trust deal. . . .); Roberta Romano, "Comment on Easterbrook and Fischel, 'Contract and Fiduciary Duty,'" *Journal of Law and Economics* 36 (1993) 447. Judge Posner is also an advocate of this set of doctrines. See his dissent in *Jordan v. Duff and Phelps, Inc.*, 815 F.2d 429, 444-52 (7th Cir., 1987). But see Victor Brudney, "Contract and Fiduciary Duty in Corporate Law," *Boston College Law Review* 38 (1997) 595; Victor Brudney, "Corporate Governance, Agency Costs, and the Rhetoric of Contract," *Columbia Law Review* 85 (1985) 1403; Tamar Frankel, "Fiduciary Duties as Default Rules," *Oregon Law Review* 74 (1995) 1209, 1242-51; Scott FitzGibbon, "Fiduciary Relationships Are Not Contracts," *Marquette Law Review* 82 (1999) 303.

9. E.g., Gary S. Becker, *A Treatise on the Family* (Cambridge, Mass.: Harvard University

There is more than a grain of truth in all of this because obligations are often initiated by promise, obligation-bearing affiliations are often formed by mutual consent, and marriages commence with an impressive exchange of vows. Someone might therefore be tempted to say "well there you are: the good of obligation and of marital obligation is that it keeps a promise and honors a contract." But really this cannot be the entire story; certainly not in any narrow "commercial agreements" understanding of the term "contract." Many marital obligations are not even mentioned in the wedding vows—for example, the groom does not usually swear to live with his spouse in the same dwelling or to support her materially or to help with the babies. Many obligations have an open-ended character unfamiliar to the world of business agreements. Many go unspoken and many do not emerge until later in the course of the relationship. Even those that are specified at the outset seem to have a deeper, subpromissory basis. No one would think he had an excuse for adultery if he could reread his wedding vows in some future year and discover that they had omitted the part about "forsaking all others."[10]

Such attributes have led several scholars to propose broader affiliative words than "contract." Professor Sanford Katz uses the term "partnership":

> "[M]arriage *** is a contract *** It is also a partnership in that it is a fiduciary relationship of two individuals who love each other, and who share in and expect to reach mutual aspirations. Marital partners lead their lives with the hope that their conjugal and financial partnership will last. To that end each makes his or her contribution. . . . But the modern marriage partnership deviates from the commercial partnership in that . . . one of the partners may have to make certain sacrifices, such as abandoning a career entirely . . . ."[11]

Professor Margaret Brinig uses the term "covenant."[12]

Press, 1991), 43 ("marriage" is "the term for a written, oral, or customary long-term contract between a man and a woman to produce children, food, and other commodities in a common household."). See John Witte, Jr., *From Sacrament to Contract: Marriage, Religion and Law in the Western Tradition* (Louisville: Westminster John Knox Press, 1997), 194-215, and authorities cited.

10. As a thought experiment, imagine a couple whose wedding was the illusionary trick of some Genie. If this couple lives and thinks successfully as though man and wife for many years, only now to discover the illusory nature of their vows, have they significant ties to one another? You may with good reason deny that they are fully married, but if you think they have some such ties, then you believe that contract and promise are not the entire story.

11. Sanford N. Katz, "Marriage as Partnership," *Notre Dame Law Review* 73 (1998) 1251, 1270.

12. Margaret F. Brinig, *From Contract to Covenant: Beyond the Law and Economics of the Family* (Cambridge, Mass.: Harvard University Press, 2000) ("In this book I argue that covenant is a preferable concept for describing families that are well under way . . . for, in brief, the covenant implies unconditional love and permanence."). See generally Ira Ellman, "Contract

Such approaches are more promising than the narrowly contractual one and it is not the purpose of this article to reject them, but they do not bring us all the way down to the ethical foundation. Looking deeper, we need to inquire *why* there is an ethically binding character to any of these arrangements: what is the basis of the ethical obligation to keep a promise or honor a contract (Kantians have one approach, utilitarians another); and, similarly, what is the basis of the obligation you have to your partners or to those with whom you have a covenant. Similarly, we need to inquire into the reasons which support entering into such arrangements and adopting their obligations in the first place; and we may ask why married couples embrace many further obligations to one another as their relationship matures. Why do married people promise exclusive fidelity? Why do relationships develop a set of settled understandings about child care? This article is aimed at providing a portion of the answer to these questions.

PART TWO: THE ACHILLES SYNDROME: THE CULTURAL CRISIS OF AFFILIATION AND OBLIGATION[13]

Pope John Paul II has written that the twentieth century brought us into a crisis of solidarity.[14] It brought us to a crisis of all sorts of affiliations—marriage, family, friendship, and citizenship. It was as though man were losing his capacity to be a political animal (as Aristotle called

Thinking Was *Marvin's* Fatal Flaw," at *Social Science Research Network*, http://papers.ssrn.com/sol3/papers.cfm?cfid=676281&cftoken=92662125&abstract_id=265067 (article posted April 1, 2001).

13. Much of the material in this Part Two, as well as some of the materials on Karol Wojtyla's work further on in this article, appeared in an earlier version in Scott FitzGibbon, "Wojtylan Insight into Love and Friendship: Shared Consciousness and the Breakdown of Solidarity," in Luke Gormally, ed., *Culture of Life, Culture of Death: Proceedings of an International Conference on 'The Great Jubilee and the Culture of Life'* (London: Linacre Centre, 2002).

14. "*Instrumentum Laboris* for the Synod Of Bishops—Second Special Assembly for Europe, in *L'Osservatore Romano*, Weekly Edition in English, November 18, 1999. See John Paul II, Message to Prof. Sergio Zaninalli, Rector Magnificent of the Catholic University of the Sacred Heart, May 5, 2000, in *L'Osservatore Romano*, Weekly Edition in English, May 24, 2000 at 9 ("The value of solidarity is in crisis, perhaps mainly because there is a crisis in the only experience which could guarantee its objective and universal value: that communion between persons and peoples which the believing conscience traces back to the fact that we are all children of the one Father, the God who 'is love'. . . .").

him)[15] and his capacity to be—as Aristotle also called him—a partnership-forming creature and a "household-maintaining animal."[16]

Further, the twentieth century brought a crisis of obligation. A deterioration of the sense of being obliged to one another, or under duties to one another, or bound together by special ties. A dimming in the appreciation of the *good* of duty. A wave of impatience with and even hostility towards this aspect of life, as though the human person were some solitary deity who ought not to be tied up in any way. A distortion of our understanding of and respect for obligation: political obligation, contractual obligation[17] and the obligations between friends,[18] as well as marital obligation and the obligations

15. *Politics* 1253a.2-9. (Here and throughout this article, except where indicated, the translation of the *Politics* quoted is the Jowett translation in J. Barnes, ed., Volume II. *The Complete Works of Aristotle* (Princeton: Princeton University Press 1984), 1986-2129). Aristotle also identifies man as *politikon* in *Politics* 1278b 19-21, in *Nicomachean Ethics* 1097b 12, 1162a 17-19, and 1169b 17-19, and in *History of Animals* 488a 8-10. (Here and throughout this article the translation of the *Ethics* quoted is that by W. D. Ross (revised by J.O. Urmson) in J. Barnes, ed., Volume II. *The Complete Works of Aristotle*, 1729-1867.)

16. *"koinonikon anthropos"* and *"oikonomikon zoon."* Aristotle, *Eudemian Ethics* 1242a 22-24 ("[M]an is not merely a political but also a household-maintaining animal, and his unions are not, like those of the other animals, confined to certain times, and formed with any chance partner, whether male or female, but . . . man has a tendency to partnership with those to whom he is by nature akin.") (elision in the text as quoted; note omitted). (Here and throughout this article the translation of the *Eudemian Ethics* quoted is that by J. Solomon in J. Barnes, ed., Volume II, *The Complete Works of Aristotle*, 1921-1979.)

A related phenomenon is the decline of trust and of participation in civic institutions. See Robert D. Putnam, *Bowling Alone: The Collapse and Revival of American Community* (New York: Simon and Schuster, 2000). Compare Everett Carll Ladd, *The Ladd Report* (New York: Simon and Schuster, 1999), which optimistically notes that American are still active joiners of many community-improvement groups but inquires hardly at all into the question of what sorts of groups and what degree of bonding. Marriage is ignored and families are hardly mentioned. (Cf. the endorsement of the term "amoral familialism" to characterize family loyalty in Southern Italy (p. 15).)

17. See P. S. Atiyah, *The Rise and Fall of Freedom of Contract* (Clarendon Press: Oxford, 1979), 649-59 (noting the "decline of principles" and of respect for the "sanctity of promises" in English life). In America recently, a related phenomenon is the explosive growth in bankruptcy filings by individuals and families. The statistics are set forth in Todd J. Zywicki, "Bankruptcy Law as Social Legislation," *Texas Review of Law and Politics* 5 (2001) 393, 399-400 (reporting 1.3 million individual bankruptcies each year and that "[s]ome seven to ten percent of these individuals make more than the national median income and could repay a substantial portion of their debts with minimal hardship. . . .").

18. A sad depiction of the impoverished condition of friendship among students is presented in Allan Bloom, *The Closing of the American Mind* (New York: Simon and Schuster, 1987), 82-140 (e.g. at 109: "The young want to make commitments. . . . This is what they talk about, but they are haunted by the awareness that the talk does not mean very much and that commitments are lighter than air.").

within families. It was as though something in man had changed—as though man were experiencing an altered state anthropologically as well as ethically—so that he had ceased to understand himself as an obligation-bearing, "bonded" creature.

The Homeric exemplar is not Odysseus of course: rather, it is Achilles. Achilles became wildly destabilized as a result of his feud with his commander Agamemnon. "As his racing spirit veered back and forth" he set out to kill Agamemnon,[19] but instead, restrained by the goddesses Hera and Athena, cut himself off from the Greek army. Though the son of a god, he fell for days into a frenzy like that of a beast. He ceased to display human traits. He ceased to eat. He said: "I have no taste for food—what I really crave is slaughter and blood and the choking groans of men!"[20] He is compared to an "inhuman fire raging on through the mountain gorges," a "huge fireball . . . chaos of fire,"[21] and to a dolphin,[22] an eagle,[23] and "some lion, going his own barbaric way."[24] He is also described as "godlike"[25] and compared to a "frenzied god."[26]

Dr. Jonathan Shay, in his study of combat veterans *Achilles in Vietnam*,[27] makes Achilles the type of the infantry fighter who, traumatized by combat and a sense of betrayal, suffered a loss of "responsiveness to the claims of any bonds, ideals or loyalties outside tiny circle of immediate comrades"[28] and, in extreme cases (the "berserkers"), fell into a constant, murderous rage.

Achilles is the extreme case of the *disaffiliated* man,[29] and he resembles the isolated individual characterized by Homer: "Lost to the clan, lost to the hearth, lost to the old ways, that one who lusts for all the horrors of war with

---

19. *Iliad*, Book 1, line 227. Here and throughout, this article uses the Robert Fagles translation (New York: Penguin Books, 1990) and the line numbering is that of the translation rather than the Greek except where otherwise indicated.

20. Ibid., Book 19, lines 254-56 (and see lines 249-50: "[N]either food nor drink will travel down my throat, not with my friend dead. . . . ").

21. Ibid., Book 20, lines 545-57.

22. Ibid., Book 21, line 25.

23. Ibid., Book 21, line 285.

24. Ibid., Book 24, lines 48-49 (by Apollo).

25. Ibid., Book 24, line 570 (by Priam).

26. Ibid., Book 20, line 558 and Book 21, line 21.

27. *Achilles in Vietnam: Combat Trauma and the Undoing of Character* (New York: Simon and Schuster, 1994).

28. Ibid., 23.

29. "To emphasize Achilles' social detachment, Homer . . . [uses] a dramatic device much like the cinematic trick of cutting off the sound track: The Greek army vanishes, leaving Achilles alone with the Trojan soldiers that he slaughters. All cooperation and coordination with his own men fall away." Ibid., 86.

his own people."[30] This passage is quoted by Aristotle in the *Politics* when he makes the point that man is a *politikon* animal and contrasts the "[t]ribeless, lawless, hearthless"[31] person who loves war. "He who is by nature [not *politikon*] is either a bad man or above humanity."[32] "[H]e who is unable to live in society, or who has no need because he is sufficient for himself, must be either a beast or a god."[33] Achilles is the extreme case of the obligation-less, obligation-ignoring man. "Don't talk to me of pacts," he says to Hector. "There are no binding oaths between men and lions—wolves and lambs enjoy no meeting of the minds."[34]

Somewhat similar post-traumatic stress symptoms are reported in survivors of war and the Holocaust by Dr. Judith Herman in her book *Trauma and Recovery*.[35] She reports that "[t]raumatic events ... shatter the sense of connection between individual and community, creating a crisis of faith"[36] and that victims are less likely to marry, more likely to experience marital problems if they do, and more likely to divorce.[37]

The Western persona generally can be diagnosed as having the a version of the Achilles Syndrome: as suffering post-traumatic stress disorder caused by war, fascism, communism, and the collapse of the *ancien regime*. A kind of allergy to the obligatory has set in, rather as a wounded or infected arm ceases to tolerate the touch of the rope. Modern men, or some of us, have become affilitionally destabilized, inconstant, "*liga-phobic*."

---

30. *Iliad*, Book 9, lines 73-75.

31. *Politics* 1253a 4.

32. Ibid., 1253a 3.

33. Ibid., 1253a 28-29.

34. *Iliad*, Book 22, lines 309-311.

35. Judith Lewis Herman, *Trauma and Recovery: The Aftermath of Violence—From Domestic Abuse to Political Terror* (New York: Perseus Books, 1992).

What are the basic mechanisms by which trauma diminishes the capacity for obligation? Several possibilities suggest themselves. First, trauma may produce fearfulness and a diminution of trust: trauma produces risk-aversion whereas obligation often involves risk. Second, trauma may diminish the victim's awareness of other people, even his intimate friends. A third possibility—the most fundamental and directly ethical—is that trauma alters the victim's beliefs in and ability to comprehend the good of others.

36. Ibid., 55. See *Achilles in Vietnam*, 86: the Vietnam berserker is "cut off from all human community. . . . No living human has any claim on him, not even the claim of being noticed and remembered."

37. *Trauma and Recovery*, 63.

PART THREE: OBLIGATION—ESPECIALLY MARITAL OBLIGATION—AS A MATTER OF ETHICAL THEORY

I. THE DISTINCTION BETWEEN INSTRUMENTAL AND FINAL GOODS; WHY WE CAN SUSPECT THAT MARITAL OBLIGATIONS ARE NOT PURELY INSTRUMENTAL

It seems that obligation might be good in either of two basic ways: one obvious, the other little noticed and likely to be disbelieved-in. First, obligation can apply for another good. Second, obligation might under some circumstances itself *be* a good independent of its usefulness.

Obligation can be—sometimes is—a good instrumentally only: you must be at work on time *to* earn money *to* buy groceries. A good is instrumental to some other end when we "choose it for the sake of something else."[38] Something which is good in only this limited way is dispensable. If your job is of instrumental good only (that may not be true for the artist or for the person who works for Mother Teresa's sisters, but it is true for most employees), then you will quit if you inherit wealth. An instrumental project is malleable according to what conduces to the achievement of final good, and is not loveable for its own sake, nor ever likely to be the subject of intense devotion or of fine poetry and music.

The second possibility is that obligation might sometimes be a good noninstrumentally; "finally"; something "which we desire for its own sake."[39] We can suspect that a good is noninstrumental when we would not readily

38. This paraphrases the portion of the *Nicomachean Ethics* quoted in the next footnote.

39. Thus, in a famous passage (not addressed to obligation), the *Nicomachean Ethics* states (at 1094a 18-22):

> If, then, there is some end of the things we do, which we desire for its own sake (everything else being desired for the sake of this), and if we do not choose everything for the sake of something else (for at that rate the process would go on to infinity, so that our desire would be empty and vain), clearly this must be the good and the chief good.

For a similar distinction, see Robin Attfield, *A Theory of Value and Obligation* (London: Croom Helm, 1987), 25:

> Literally, what is of intrinsic value is what is of value in itself, rather than of value instrumentally. If something is valued simply as a means to a further state of affairs beyond itself, it is being regarded as of instrumental value only. But not everything which is of value . . . can be so only instrumentally. Some things are of value in themselves and for no reason beyond themselves . . . . And whenever this is so the state of affairs in question will supply a reason for action which is independent of other desirable end-states or values, and which derives from nothing but itself. Thus intrinsically valuable states of affairs will be ones which there are nonderivative reasons for fostering, desiring or cherishing.

forfeit or truncate it as circumstances varied; when it seems to "mean a lot" to the people who seek and possess it—when they love it for its own sake; and when it appears as the subject of devotion, ceremony, poetry, and art. We can suspect that a good is more than instrumental when people continue to pursue and make much of it even after the disappearance of whatever consequences might seem to have justified it on instrumental grounds. We can suspect that a good is "final" when people who have forfeited it make much of their loss (and not just of the ensuing deprivations).

Marital obligation displays characteristics which imply that it is more than instrumentally good. It often persists beyond the loss of its utility, as in the instance of sexual loyalty even when "what she doesn't know won't hurt her" and when, owing to old age, philandering would carry no risk of illegitimate offspring. (It may even persist when the spouse has died, as in those cultures which have commended the widow who remains celibate.)[40] Couples make much of obligation, craft it, further develop it, and sense it to be central to the relationship.

Obligation, and especially marital obligation, is celebrated in poetry and song, from the *Psalms* and the *Odyssey* to *Fidelio* and *Guys and Dolls*. Its violation in divorce can inflict trauma lasting years and far exceeding the instrumental damage. The words of the oath: "For richer for poorer; in sickness and in health; forsaking all others; 'til death do us part . . . '"—the drumbeat, the great *chamade* of the marriage rite—amount to no less than a formal renunciation of instrumentalist thought.

II. Some Counterpositions: Repudiating Obligation; Making it Instrumental to Utilitarian Goods

A. Rejecting Obligation: Romanticism and Other Antinomian Approaches —The literature and biography of the nineteenth and twentieth centuries is littered with narratives of romantic relationships in which the man and woman freed themselves, as they thought, from the bonds of convention, attached themselves to one another, as they hoped, by forces of a more vehement character, and descended to a relational condition, as they discovered in the course of its demise, characterized by misery and shame.

A fearsome example is afforded by the life of Harvard University's pioneer in nonbehavioral psychology, Professor Henry A. Murray, and his lover,

40. See Susan Treggiare, *Roman Marriage:* Iusti Coniuges *from the Time of Cicero to the Time of Ulpian* (Oxford: Clarendon Press, 1991), 233-34 and 501-502 (for a widow to remarry was socially acceptable and even sometimes encouraged, but for her to refrain from remarriage was commended in literature and carried the right, not held by those who remarried, to sacrifice to the goddess Pudicitia).

Christiana Morgan. Their relationship extended for more than forty years (1925 to 1967) and exhibited all the basic characteristics: the repudiation of conventional morality ("the Church" and its "damn rules"),[41] the adoption of an alternative ethic ("erotic adoration is the most natural religion"[42]—their relationship will "transform the world"[43]—"[t]he whole spiritual course of man will pivot on you"[44]), and its unpleasant demise. (After the death of his wife in 1962, Henry refused to marry Christiana and she took to drink and drowned herself.)[45] Someone should write an entire slim volume about the effects of various psychological movements on marital relationships during the course of these past centuries.

Professor Gilbert Meilaender gives another example:

> I had occasion recently to ponder the service folder from a wedding. . . . There in the folder was the now almost obligatory candle ceremony, a reading from Kahlil Gibran's *The Prophet*, ... [and] on the last page was a passage from Lord Byron . . . addressed here by the bride to her groom:
>
> Is there anything on earth or heaven
> that would have made me so happy
> As to have made you mine long ago? . . .
> You know that I would with pleasure give up
> All here and beyond the grave for you. . . .
> I was and am yours freely and most entirely,
> To obey, to honor, to love
> And fly with you when, where, and how
> You yourself might and may determine.
>
> What caught my attention immediately was how obviously pagan such a sentiment is. To give up—with pleasure—"All here and beyond the grave" for another human must be idolatrous. * * *

41. Behind "the sacrament and the state of marriage," Professor Murray wrote, "was the Church and the great bulk of respectable men and women with their damn rules, customs, formalities, manners, fads, proprieties, pretensions, rites, rituals, decrees, ordinances, laws, taboos, sentiments, beliefs, principles, Catechisms, creeds, and categorical negations." This is Henry Murray characterizing the attitude of Herman Melville, quoted, apparently from an unpublished manuscript, in Forrest G. Robinson, *Love's Story Told: A Life of Henry A. Murray* (Cambridge, Mass.: Harvard University Press, 1992), 241. Robinson observes that Murray agreed.

42. Henry A. Murray, quoted in ibid., 381. The quotation in the text omits a comma which appears after the word "adoration."

43. Ibid., 170.

44. Ibid.

45. Probably but not certainly on purpose. He told her she was disgusting and took a nap; when he awoke he found her drowned in two feet of water.

> [The poem] comes from the postscript to a letter written by Byron, probably in August 1812, to Lady Caroline Lamb. When she and Byron met in 1812 she was married to William Lamb. . . . Their affair lasted about three months, though Lady Caroline continued to pursue Byron's attention and affection after the affair had ended. Indeed, explaining why he no longer was attracted to her as he had been, Byron went so far as to write to her (in November 1812) that 'our affections are not in our own power'—which is true enough, of course, and is precisely the reason that the marital vow exists to bind us even as our affections come and go. . . .
>
> To what point have we come—how greatly have we failed—when a Christian bride thinks it appropriate to express her love for her husband in these terms? They come not from the Church's tradition or sacred books, nor even from the wisdom of acknowledged Christian thinkers. Yet they appealed to an uninstructed mind, who perhaps thought of the marriage rite not as the Church's but as her own. If the day comes that devotion in such a marriage flags, or if love—as is its wont—is urgently drawn towards a new beloved, it is unlikely that the Church will be in a position to say much. If it is 'our' marriage, founded on our own fleeting emotions and attachments, we will do with it pretty much as we please.[46]

So: a Romantic understanding of marriage, which, while purporting to emphasize its depth and strength, removes it from its basis in ethics, morality, and moral theology and ultimately destabilizes the relationship and weakens its bonds.

B. An Approach Which Doubts the Value of Obligation in Close Affiliations—Daniel DeNicola has written:

> Acts of love, friendship, fellow-feeling, affection, and a sense of community, are beyond our basic moral duties. To carry them out dutifully is to treat the people involved impersonally, as 'other persons' in the abstract. Acts done from duty reveal only that we are dutiful and moral in a narrow house-rules sense. There are other worthy virtues, of course, and these can be evinced in action that is gratuitous.[47]

A major purpose of this article is to dispute this thesis and to show that obligation is a part of close affiliation and has a personalist character.

C. *Utilitarian Instrumentalism*—Action can be justified, from a utilitarian point of view, only on the basis that it maximizes pleasure or the satisfaction of preferences.[48] That leaves little space for obligation in the sense in which

46. "The Mess That Is Marriage," in *First Things*, February 2002, page 18.

47. "Supererogation: Artistry in Conduct," in *Foundations of Ethics*, Leroy S. Rouner, ed. (Notre Dame, Ind.: University of Notre Dame Press, 1983), 149, 161-62.

48. Pleasure-based utilitarianism "holds that actions are right in proportion as they tend to promote happiness; wrong as they tend to produce the reverse of happiness. By happiness is intended pleasure, and the absence of pain; by unhappiness, pain, and the privation of

that term is used here. Utilitarians are consequentialists and so look primarily to the future rather than to the bonds of the past, and they make their decisions act-by-act, relegating precepts, principles, and other generalities to the status of rules of thumb, always subject to being set aside when circumstances dictate.[49] Further, utilitarianism provides little basis for gradations of norms and so makes little room for the differentiation between the mandatory and the supererogatory.[50] And utilitarians tend to have a primitive and mechanistic understanding of human nature and a similarly primitive view of human relations which would preclude their crediting the character-based foundations for obligation discussed in this article below.

Marriage should be conducted, according to utilitarianism, only as a project for the maximization of pleasure or the satisfaction of preferences.[51] Classic utilitarianism implies that marital obligations—the obligation of sexual fidelity; the obligation to return home from the Trojan War; the obligation to punish the suitors and restore peace to Ithaca—apply only when, if, and insofar as they indicate the course of action which best maximizes pleasure or preferences. More pleasure and less pain somewhere else indicate abandoning those projects. Thus, classic utilitarianism mandates marital instability—less so than Byronic romanticism, but still, to a marked degree.[52]

---

pleasure. . . ." John Stuart Mill, *Utilitarianism*, Roger Crisp, ed. (Oxford: Oxford University Press, 1998), 55 (a reprint of the Fourth Edition (1871); the quoted passage is from Chapter Two, lines 3-5). There are many varieties of pleasure-based and similar experience-based utilitarianism; an entree into the literature which identifies some of them is afforded at pages 33-35 of the introduction to the Crisp edition, supra. The present article discusses the theory in its act-utilitarian, not its rule-utilitarian, version.

For discussions of preference-based utilitarianism, see Martin Hollis and Robert Sugden, "Rationality in Action," *Mind* 102 (1993) 1, 5-7 and Amartya Sen, "The Formulation of Rational Choice," *American Economic Review* 84 (1994) 385.

49. Thus, the utilitarian sheriff would frame and hang the innocent man when doing so was the only way to avert a riot, setting aside the moral principle forbidding direct killing of the innocent which applies to all people and the more specific rules which define the obligations of an officer of the law. See John Finnis, *Fundamentals of Ethics* (Washington, D.C.: Georgetown University Press, 1983), 95 et seq. for a review of consequentialists' responses to this classic hypothetical and for decisive rejoinders.

50. A discussion of this point is in Attfield, *A Theory of Value and Obligation*, 116 et seq. The point is also briefly made and extended in Terrance C. McConnell, "Utilitarianism and Supererogatory Acts," *Ratio* 22 (1980) 36.

51. For a historical discussion of utilitarianism and marriage, see Chapter Five of Witte, *From Sacrament to Contract: Marriage, Religion and Law in the Western Tradition*.

52. A similar point is made in Robert N. Bellah, Richard Madsen, William M. Sullivan, Ann Swidler and Steven M. Tipton, *Habits of the Heart: Individualism and Commitment in American Life* (New York: Harper and Row, 1985) discussing relationships founded on the "therapeutic attitude."). For people who believe that the point of their lives is to have feelings and to express them, "love means the full exchange of feelings between authentic selves, not

Fidelity—sticking to one person, sticking to one line of approach towards one person and one's life with her—do find some foothold on the utilitarian foundation on grounds of expertise and reliance. Because you know her well, you can be more efficiently benevolent towards your spouse than towards someone new; because she knows she can count on you, she can efficiently rely on your help. These factors introduce some ballast into utilitarian affiliations but only to a limited extent. They do not seem to cut much ice for Odysseus and Penelope, after all those years of separation. Had Odysseus been a utilitarian, he would not have acted as he did. He would have included the pains and pleasures *of the suitors* in the balance and counted them as reasons against returning to Ithaca. The suitors were having a fine time, feasting and dreaming about going to bed with Penelope; so their feelings would have to be registered with quite a lot of weight, especially since there were so many of them: young guys with strong, intense passions, who were not likely to enjoy being shot through with arrows.

You should set aside loyalty to a spouse when the aggregate of pleasure or preference-satisfaction in the world is best maximized by some other affiliational modality. Pushed along to its natural conclusions, utilitarianism is inconsistent with obligation in the fullest sense, and a bunch of people who stick to utilitarianism for guidance become, not wild animals, but a semi-socialized herd, among whom affiliation perdures only in a shallow way.

The instability of the utilitarian life derives largely from the inconstancy of pleasures and preferences. Someone who makes pleasures the center of his thinking will find himself blowing in the wind of adventitious circumstances and the ebb and flow of appetites and impulses, often ones in conflict with one another.[53] His will and reason—his character generally—will fall under the sway of his passions.

These inconstancy-producing attributes undermine the credibility of utilitarian ethics. In some groups, in friendship, and in marriage, inconstancy is generally apprehended to be a bad not a good thing: a successful marriage is one which endures, not one which is efficiently wound up in a timely fashion when circumstances change. In the individual life and the individual character, similarly, we apprehend that the good for a person surely must involve consistency and coherence. As Aristotle wrote, "no one would choose to live with the mind of a child throughout his life, however much he were pleased at the things that children are pleased at . . . ."[54] The good for

enduring commitment resting on binding obligations." Ibid., 102.

53. As Aristotle says of "most men": "their pleasures are in conflict with one another." *Nicomachean Ethics* 1099a 12.

54. Ibid. 1174a 1-3 (but departing from the translation in Barnes, supra). The sentence continues: "nor to get enjoyment by doing some most disgraceful deed, though he were never

man involves steadiness, *gravitas*, and a constancy of life unfathomable to a child.

III. AN ACCOUNT OF MARITAL OBLIGATION BASED ON THE GOODS OF KNOWLEDGE AND BENEVOLENCE?

What, then, about an account which rests on some final goods other than pleasure? A great turn in ethical theory over the last few decades, prefigured by Philippa Foot and led by Professors John Finnis and Germain Grisez, proposes a set of goods worthy to be pursued in themselves, even when they may not be instrumental to other benefits. The goods of knowledge and benevolence are likely instances and this section considers them alone (not in this respect purporting to replicate the Finnis and Grisez view, which is far richer). One seeks wisdom and knowledge; seeks things to know; thinks and rethinks about what one knows and deepens one's understanding, aspiring for more occasions to do these things, not for the instrumentalist reasons that one might seek a bus to the library or the grocery store, but because such activities—and the possession of the traits which make them possible—are what it is to flourish as a human being.

Affiliations instantiate the final goods of knowledge and benevolence. Aristotle describes friendship this way:[55] it involves "mutual recogni[tion] as bearing goodwill and wishing well to each other[56] and involves "sharing in discussion and thought."[57] Common sense supports this conclusion. You cannot be friends unless you know one another and the more your friendship develops the deeper grows the understanding. You surely are not friendly towards one another unless you aim at one anothers' good; helping one

to feel any pain in consequence. And there are many things we should be keen about even if they brought no pleasure, e.g. seeing, remembering, knowing, possessing the excellences."

55. For an entree into the literature on friendship in Aristotle, see David Konstan, "Altruism," in *Transactions of the American Philological Association* 130 (2000) 1. See generally Suzanne Stern-Gillett, *Aristotle's Philosophy of Friendship* (Albany: State University of New York Press, 1995); A. W. Price, *Love and Friendship in Plato and Aristotle* (Oxford: Clarendon Press, 1989).

56. *Nicomachean Ethics* 1156a 3-5. And friends know one anothers' feelings: "[f]or many people have goodwill to those whom they have not seen but judge to be good or useful . . . but how could one call them friends when they do not know their mutual feelings?" Ibid., 1156a 1-3. See ibid. 1167a 23-24. And friends, anyway full friends, know one anothers' choices and think and know together as a part of choosing together. Full friendship involves "reciprocal choice of the good and pleasant" (*Eudemian Ethics* 1237a 31-32) and in order to choose together ("reciprocally") they must, it seems, think and know together since "[c]hoice arises out of deliberate opinion." Ibid. 1226a 8-9. Thus, as part of choosing, reciprocal reasoning and judging.

57. *Nicomachean Ethics* 1170b 11-12.

another in the projects of life is close to the heart of what it means to be a friend.

Marriage is a kind of friendship, and it involves knowledge and benevolence in special ways. Marriage is, you might say, a "field" for knowledge. That might sound a little dry. Marriage is not a study group, after all. But Pope John Paul II shows how interesting it really can be when he tells the story of Teresa and Andrew in his play *The Jeweler's Shop*[58] and shows how knowledge is involved in marriage in a distinctive way. Teresa and Andrew, a young couple recently engaged, encounter one another as though by chance in a city street. Andrew says:

> "I met Teresa when she had just paused
> in front of a large window . . .
> I stopped by her quietly and unexpectedly—
> and suddenly we were together
> on both sides of the big transparent sheet
> filled with glowing light.
> And we saw our reflections together,
> because behind the widow display
> is a great, immense mirror
>
> . . . [W]e found ourselves all of a sudden
> on both sides of the great mirror
> —here alive and real, there reflected . . . ."[59]

Soon Teresa and Andrew find themselves standing in front of a jeweler's shop. Again, in front of a window—Teresa and Andrew are looking at wedding rings. This time the window *becomes* a mirror. Teresa says:

> ". . . [T]he window has turned into a mirror of our future ;
> it reflects its shape."
> "I already saw, as in a mirror,
> myself, in a white wedding dress, kneeling with Andrew . . . ."[60]

(Later Andrew says that the mirror was "not an ordinary flat mirror but a lens absorbing its object. We were not only reflected but absorbed."[61]).

58. K. Wojtyla, *The Jeweler's Shop* in *The Collected Plays and Writings on Theater* (Berkeley and Los Angeles: University of California Press, 1987), 278-322 (B.Taborski, trans.). The play is subtitled "A Meditation on the Sacrament of Matrimony, Passing on Occasion into a Drama."

59. Ibid., 285.

60. Ibid., 288 and 287. In the original these two phases appear in the reverse order.

61. Ibid., 292. The next sentence is: "I had an impression of being seen and recognized by someone hiding inside the shop window."

The mirror—a recurrent image in Wojtylan writings[62]—is a metaphor for consciousness, which is an aspect of knowledge. A wide mirror displays not only the observer but also the scene around her and the objects behind the place where she stands,[63] and a Wojtylan mirror not only receives and reflects: it retains and records.[64] Teresa observes: "The window absorbed my person at various moments and in different situations . . . . I am also convinced that our reflection in that mirror has remained forever, and cannot be extracted or removed. A little while later we concluded that we had been present in the mirror from the beginning . . . ."[65] Consciousness in Wojtylan thought is the

62. See, e.g., Karol Wojtyla, *The Samaritan Woman Meditates*, in *Easter Vigil and Other Poems* (New York: Random House, 1979), 13 (J. Peterkiewicz, trans.)("I—yes, I —conscious then of my awakening/ as a man in a stream, aware of his image,/ is suddenly raised from the mirror and brought/ to himself, holding his breath in amazement,/swaying over his light.").

63. See Karol Wojtyla, *The Acting Person* ("Dordrecht: D. Reidel Publishing Co., 1979), 31 (A. Potocki, trans.; A.-T. Tymieniecka, ed.) (Consciousness is . . . the reflection, or rather the mirroring, of everything that man meets with in an external relation by means of any and all of his doings . . . ."). *The Acting Person* is the English edition of Karol Wojtyla, *Osoba i Czyn* (Krakow: Polskie Towarzystwo Teologiczne, 1969). There has been controversy concerning whether *The Acting Person* is faithful to *Osoba i Czyn* and to Wojtyla's thought. See, e.g., K. Schmitz, *At the Center of the Human Drama: The Philosophical Anthropology of Karol Wojtyla/Pope John Paul II* (Washington, D.C.: Catholic University Press, 1993), 60, n. 6 ("gravely misleading in important passages, and, . . . because of an unstable rendering of important technical terms, simply muddled."); see also the discussion on page 59 and page 155, n. 48. But then, *The Acting Person* is not just a translation: it is endorsed by Wojtyla in the preface as an "improved presentation" (page ix). (And see page xiv: "I thank the editor, Professor A.-T. Tymieniecka, who, guided by her excellent knowledge of the philosophical environment of the West, gave to my text its final shape. . . although the basic concept of the work has remained unaltered."). Some say that the revision process was hijacked by Tymieniecka once Wojtyla had become too busy to keep involved. This view seems to be embraced, accompanied by insider's familiarity, in George Weigel, *Witness to Hope: The Biography of Pope John Paul II* (New York: HarperCollins Publishers, 1999), 174-75, n. 8. But apparently some of the revisions, at least, came from the pen of Wojtyla. See S. Gregg, *Challenging the Modern World: Karol Wojtyla/John Paul II and the Development of Catholic Social Teaching* (Lanham, Md: Lexington Books, 1999), 56, n. 26 (noting that "there is little question that Wojtyla revised parts of AP throughout the 1970's in anticipation of its English publication.").

Doubts about *The Acting Person* do not undermine the conclusions of this article, since the relevant passages of that book are consistent with *Osoba i Czyn*. Under the guidance of Professor Mark F. O'Connor, the Director of the Arts and Sciences Honors Program at Boston College, correspondences are identified in some of the footnotes, infra. The portion of *The Acting Person* quoted in this footnote closely follows *Osoba i Czyn* at 36.

64. See *The Acting Person*, 31 ("once the action is accomplished consciousness still continues to reflect it."). This closely follows *Osoby i Czyn*.

65. *The Jeweler's Shop*, 292.

repository and reflector of what has been encountered or comprehended,[66] and the medium upon which those things which we experience or understand are preserved, "penetrated," "illuminated,"[67] and reflected back to the inner self.[68] Consciousness is, Wojtyla says at one point, "understanding."[69] Andrew and Teresa grow in awareness, each of how the other experiences the world, each coming to see things from the other's perspective; each coming to see how the other is conscious of herself.[70]

Another special feature of knowledge within friendship is the attribute of "doubling." Andrew can be conscious of how Teresa's consciousness of himself is structured. Andrew can become conscious of himself *in the way that* she is conscious of him. Because he knows her well, he can see how he looks to her. As Aristotle states: "[t]o perceive a friend must be in a way to perceive one's self and to know a friend to know one's self."[71] These help

---

66. *The Acting Person*, 31-32, closely following *Osoba i Czyn*, 35-36.

67. *The Acting Person*, 33: "[W]e attribute to consciousness the specific quality of penetrating and illuminating whatever becomes in any way man's cognitive possession." (This closely follows *Osoba i Czyn*, 35.) Compare A. Damasio, *The Feeling of What Happens: Body and Emotion in the Making of Consciousness* (New York: Harcourt, Brace and Company, 1999), 315:

> It all begins modestly, with the barest of senses of our living being related to some simple thing inside or outside the boundary of our bodies. Then the intensity of the light increases and as it gets brighter, more of the universe is illuminated. . . . Under the growing light of consciousness, more gets to be known each day, more finely, and at the same time.

68. *The Acting Person*, 36 ("consciousness can mirror actions and their relations to the ego."). (This closely follows *Osoba i Czyn*, 39.)

69. *The Acting Person*, 32: "Consciousness is, so to speak, the understanding of what has been constituted and comprehended."

70. Andrew's consciousness of Teresa embeds even awareness of her suffering: "that discreet suffering [he calls it] which at the time I did not want to know, and today am willing to regard as our common good." *The Jeweler's Shop*, Act I, Scene 1.

71. *Nicomachean Ethics* 1245a 35-36. The phrase could instead be translated, "to perceive one's self in a certain manner." Price, *Love and Friendship in Plato and Aristotle*, 121.

Self-perception through the mirror of friendship has a unique character, since it is "from the outside." When you act directly, you focus on the object of your action—your goal and the things that lead to it. When your friend acts, you can also focus on him, the actor. You always see other people that way; and when you see a friend that way you are enabled (since a friend is "another self") to take the important step of seeing yourself that way as well. See Price, *Love and Friendship in Plato and Aristotle*, 121-22:

> [I]n perception we become transparent to what we are perceiving, so that perceiving it and perceiving ourselves are the same mental act (something like seeing outside and seeing through a window). . . . [But if] I see a friend looking into my eyes, his looking is to me not transparent (as it is to him) but opaque, so that I see him looking into my eyes without thereby seeing them myself. . . . It is from him that I can learn most easily to distinguish the perceiver from the perceived; I then generalize to my own case. . . .

explain and support the numerous findings in recent studies emphasizing the importance of good communication and self-revelation within marriage.[72]

The other basic element of affiliation—benevolence—also finds a special field within marriage. Marriage is a long-term project of wishing well to the other and doing well for the other. And it seems that marriage and other friendships can "double" benevolence in much the way they double knowledge. Helping Andrew is also a good for Teresa; helping Teresa is a good for Andrew. Helping Teresa by making himself available for *her* to help *him* is a good for Andrew and a good for her. Allowing himself to be seen and understood by her in all his vulnerability is a way of helping her to achieve the good of helping him.

But what about obligation? Unless somehow supplemented, the theory can generate only this answer: obligation in marriage is a means to knowledge and benevolence. How could it be otherwise? The theory specifies for only two final goods of marriage and cannot fit obligation in except as their instrument.

And indeed obligations are often instrumental in just that way. Honoring commitments promotes reliance and so facilitates beneficence; learning to know someone well takes a long time and a lot of patience. Thus "Ted," in *Habits of the Heart*:

> When he is asked why one should not go from one relationship to another if one is tired of one's spouse or finds someone else more exciting, he begins . . . with a statement of his preferences, but moves rapidly to a discussion of the virtues of sharing: "It [shifting relationships] is just not something that interests me. I have seen us get from a good relationship in terms of sharing with each other and so on to one that's much, much deeper. . . ." This "deeper" sharing in turn suggests the value of a shared life, a sense of historical continuity, a community of memory. Ted continues, "You can't develop a deeper relationship over a brief period of time, and also I think it is probably harder to develop with somebody new at this stage in your life. Your having grown through the

---

> [The] analogue with choice and action shared with a friend of similar character yields a richer self-awareness: in my own person, my projects are (to extend the metaphor) transparent on to their objects, so that my focus is upon the objects, not my pursuit of them; but joining in those projects with a friend I become conscious of his pursuing them, and so conscious in a new way of pursuing them myself (for we are pursuing them together). I thus become explicitly aware of myself not just abstractly as an agent, but as an agent with a certain character, thereby achieving not a bare self-consciousness but a real self-knowledge.

See generally Stern-Gillett, *Aristotle's Philosophy of Friendship*; John M. Cooper, "Aristotle on the Forms of Friendship," *Review of Metaphysics* 30 (1977) 619.

72. Described and extensively cited in Milton C. Regan, Jr., *Alone Together: Law and the Meaning of Marriage* (Oxford: Oxford University Press, 1999), 22.

twenties with someone is good. Having first children and doing all those things, you could never do it again with somebody else." He concludes by moving from the notion that life is more enjoyable when shared with one person to the idea that only a shared history makes life meaningful. "I get satisfaction in growth with Debby in proceeding through all these stages of life together. . . . It makes life meaningful and gives me the opportunity to share with somebody, have an anchor, if you will, and understand where I am. That, for me, is a real relationship."[73]

As Ted's comments imply, obligation is instrumental to the "doubling" of knowledge: it is the basis for developing shared experiences, and for establishing a condition of reciprocal mirroring and the reflection of long passages of one anothers' lives.

Where does all of this take us as regards fidelity: sticking to one person, sticking to one line of approach towards one person and one's life with her? Fidelity, permanence, exclusivity, and related conditions do find a much firmer foothold on the foundation of benevolence and knowledge than they can plant on utilitarian grounds. There is an "economy of benevolence," as Dean John Garvey calls it, which precludes spreading oneself too thin;[74] and there is, similarly, an "economy of sharing of discussion and thought." Some of Ted's comments imply this, as does Aristotle when he states in the *Ethics* that "for friends . . . there is a fixed number—perhaps the largest number with whom one can live together . . . one cannot live with many people and divide oneself up among them . . . ."[75] These considerations take us some distance but not all the way. Benevolence and knowledge may sometimes be amplified by *breaking* commitment—by shifting over to another partner—when one's spouse is boring and insensitive and when another partner stands in greater need of one's benevolent attentions.

IV. A Noninstrumental Account of Marital Obligation

A. *A Noninstumentalist Account of Obligation in General*—It seems, then, that obligation may be a part of final good. The Homeric epics illustrate this

73. Bellah, Madsen, Sullivan, Swidler and Tipton, *Habits of the Heart: Individualism and Commitment in American Life*, 105. (The material between brackets appears, bracketed, in the original.).

74. John H. Garvey, *What Are Freedoms For?* (Cambridge, Mass.: Harvard University Press, 1996), 34-35.

75. *Nicomachean Ethics* 1171a 1-9. The passage continues: "Further, they too must be friends of one another, if they are all to spend their days together; and it is a hard business for this condition to be fulfilled with a large number. It is found difficult, too, to rejoice and to grieve in an intimate way with many people, for it may likely happen that one has at once to be merry with one friend and to mourn with another."

conclusion. They often use the term *empedos*, which means "steadfast"—literally, "rooted in the earth": firmly standing, fixed, safe, secure, and certain.[76] This virtue is a key to the character of Odysseus. On his visit to the underworld, he remains *empedos* awaiting the opportunity to speak with his mother and with the fallen warriors of earlier days.[77] As his ship passes the island of the Sirens, he has himself bound *empedos* to the mast.[78] Stringing his great bow as his battle with the suitors approaches, he rejoices to find his strength still *empedon*.[79] Slammed on the back with a footstool he withstands the attack, as firm—*empedon*—as a rock.[80] (Paris, by way of contrast, lacks this quality: Paris, the seducer of Helen, the pleasure-seeker and romantic, is characterized by Helen herself at one point as lacking *empedos* of mind.)[81]

Steadfastness, in Homer, is central to the human character. It distinguishes mankind here on earth from the beasts, the gods, and the dead.[82] Beasts cannot fully achieve it since, after all, it is a quality of *mind*. Gods, the poets may have felt, did not need to achieve it since in the Homeric world the major function of the *empodos* attribute was to buttress mortals against fear of death and to steady those who grieved for fallen friends. Old people, in Homer, have lost much of their steadfastness, and the dead have lost it all. Only the fully human have it in full. A man needs steadfastness in order to take what the gods dish out.

In Aristotle, a similar trait can be found not far under the surface of the system of virtues in the *Ethics*. Behind any good deed—if it is fully good and a component of excellence of life—must lie the right state of character. It is not enough just to do what is right. Plainly "some people who do just acts are not necessarily just"[83]—not those, for example, who act only out of fear or

76. Much of the material about this characteristic herein is from Froma I. Zeitlin, "Figuring Fidelity in Homer's *Odyssey*," in Beth Cohen, ed., *The Distaff Side: Representing the Female in Homer's* Odyssey (Oxford: Oxford University Press, 1995), 117.

77. *Odyssey*, Book 11, lines 173 and 719 (lines 152 and 628 of the Greek). Here and throughout, this article uses the Robert Fagles translation (New York: Penguin Books, 1990) and the line numbering is that of the translation rather than the Greek except where otherwise indicated.

78. Ibid., Book 12, line 175 (line 161 of the Greek).

79. Ibid., Book 21, line 475 (line 426 of the Greek).

80. Ibid., Book 17, line 512 (line 464 of the Greek).

81. *Iliad*, Book VI, lines 414-18 ("I wish I had been the wife of a better man. . . . This one has no steadiness in his spirit, not now, he never will . . . .").

82. See *Odyssey*, Book 11, line 446 (line 393-94 of the Greeek)(the shade of Agamemnon is no longer *empedos*) and Book 10, lines 542-45 (lines 493-95 of the Greek)(among the dead only Teiresias has been granted the gift of a steadfast mind; "the rest of the dead are empty, flitting shades.").

83. *Nicomachean Ethics* 1144a 14-15.

ignorance.[84] Looking deeper, we find that fully good deeds are only those which are performed "as a result of choice and for the sake of the actions themselves."[85] Choice involves balanced and mature assessment. Choice involves "consideration and deliberation . . . [and] arises out of deliberate opinion."[86] Choice, consideration, and deliberation can only arise from a steady character:

> [T]he case of the arts and that of the excellences are not similar; for the products of the arts have their goodness in themselves, so that it is enough that they should have a certain character, but if the acts that are in accordance with the excellences have themselves a certain character it does not follow that they are done justly or temperately. The agent must also be in a certain condition when he does them; in the first place he must have knowledge, secondly he must choose the acts, and choose them for their own sakes, and thirdly *his action must proceed from a firm and unchangeable character.*[87]

Here, then, is one component of the major thesis of this article: firmness, stability, and steadiness of character are a major part of the good for man; and again not only because of their obvious instrumental value but also because to be unstable and unsteady is to be less than a fully developed person. Only the steady, firm person, steadily reflecting and firmly choosing, "is at one mind with himself" when he acts and so to speak puts his entire self behind each action.[88] Only the steady man acts "with an eye to [his] life in its entirety[89] and so embeds his action in a "complete life."[90] Only the steady man with a consistency of mind and purpose across the years can fully display and instantiate his virtuous character in all its temporal fullness.[91]

A man will lack these qualities if he makes pleasure his sole aim. Inevitably, since the currents of pleasurable opportunity flow, now this direction, now that. But so also may even a man lack this quality who on some occasions pursues justice or learning. He is not fully virtuous unless he

---

84. Ibid., 1144a 14-16.

85. Ibid., 1144a 19-20.

86. *Eudemian Ethics* 1226b 8-9.

87. *Nicomachean Ethics* 1105a-26 through 1105b-1 (emphasis added).

88. Not so the wicked, who are "at variance with themselves" (*Nicomachean Ethics* 1166b 6-7) and "rent by faction" (ibid. 1166b 19). For a discussion of the unity of the self in Aristotle, see Stern-Gillet, *Aristotle's Philosophy of Friendship*.

89. A.W. Price, "Aristotle's Ethical Holism," *Mind, New Series* 89 No. 355 (July, 1980) 338, 342.

90. That a "complete life" is a condition of *eudaimonia* is stated in *Nicomachean Ethics* 1098a 18 and 1100a 5.

91. Cf. Price, "Aristotle's Ethical Holism," 342 ("it must take a lifetime to display ['firm and unchangeable character'] fully.").

is also fully self-governing, possessed of solidity of character, and thus stable in his consideration and deliberation. And similarly the person who pursues benevolence, but only episodically and without sustained insight or self-governance, "practicing random acts of kindness" as the bumper sticker suggests. Children, for example, and young teenagers often experience strong and pure beneficent impulses. But who would become a child again—still less an early adolescent—in order to exercise the beneficence of the young? In this uncertain and fluctuating world, pursuit of the good will produce a degree of instability of commitment except for the man who recognizes that stability of commitment is itself a part of final good.

Obligation is noninstrumenally good as an instantiation of the good of steadfastness and stability. To recognize obligation and to fulfill it even under adverse conditions is to be steadfast: to manifest steadfastness, to exercise it, and to strengthen it. To recognize obligation, to embrace it, and to develop it, and as part of this line of development to identify and develop rules of conduct for life and to act on principle: to embrace what might be called the "juristic attitude."

In the *Summa Theologica*, Thomas Aquinas makes this point, or something like it, in his discussion of vows. Why take a vow? What good may there be in taking a vow and carrying it out, over and above the good of the action you promise to take? Would it not be just as meritorious to do the good thing without the vow? No: the vow adds something important. Vowing "strengthens the will."[92]

> [A] vow fixes the will on the good immovably and to do anything of a will that is fixed on the good belongs to the perfection of virtue according to the Philosopher. . . .[93]

Of course, vows are a special, limited case of obligatory circumstances (Thomas uses the term to mean promises to God). But Thomas may imply a similar point about promises generally.[94] And surely the same could be said about all obligations, whether or not initiated by vowing or promising. To

92. Fathers of the English Dominican Province, trans, 1947, II-II question 88, article 6, reply to objection 2: "According to the Philosopher, necessity of coercion, in so far as it is opposed to the will, causes sorrow. But the necessity resulting from a vow, in those who are well disposed, in so far as it strengthens the will, causes joy."

93. Ibid. II-II question 88, article 5, corpus. The passage continues: "just as to sin with an obstinate mind aggravates the sin, and is called a sin against the Holy Ghost . . . ."

94. See John Finnis, *Aquinas: Moral, Political, and Legal Theory* (Oxford: Oxford University Press, 1998), 198 and note 58 (in a promise, an intention is affirmed in the sense of "asserted" but also in the sense of "made firm") (and note his use of the phrase "exercises of self-mastery" to characterize promissory obligations on page 199).

shoulder long-term projects, to undertake lasting responsibilities, to develop rules and principles for life and to stick to them[95]—these courses of conduct also involve fixing and strengthening the will.

B. A Noninstrumental Account of Obligation in Affiliations, Especially Marriage—Someone might exercise and develop his steadfastness of character in individual, isolated projects: through lonely pilgrimages, for example, or in his work as a solitary craftsman. But fidelity usually means steadfastness of loyalty to a person or group. Odysseus' steadfastness culminates in his reunion with Penelope; and Penelope's with Odysseus.[96] Odysseus' and Penelope's marriage bed is an emblem of the *empedos* marriage. One of its posts was the trunk of a living olive tree; on his return, Odysseus hopes that "the bed . . . still stand[s] planted firm [*empedon*]."[97]

Steadfastness and fidelity are the more radically committed when the commitment is to a person rather than a journey, for example, or a craft, because only there—at the other end of the rope —is a human life, in all its variability and complexity. Steadfastness and fidelity are the more personalist when a person is at the other end of the rope: you can commit more of yourself—your "heart."

Steadfastness and fidelity are "doubled" within a close affiliation: the ropes run both ways. The doubling of knowledge and benevolence within close affiliations has been discussed above:[98] because I can see myself through her eyes, what she knows of the world and what she knows of me are added to my knowledge. Now we can add that constancy and steadfastness are doubled as well. I can steady myself from her steadfastness of character. The point is vividly illustrated in a poem by John Donne which compares the couple to the two arms of a draftsman's compass:

95. Thomas notes that vows can be made by thought and need not involve pronouncements. Thomas Aquinas, *Summa Theologica* II-II question 88, article 1, corpus: vowing involves promising, but whereas "a promise between man and man can only be expressed in words or any other outward signs . . . . A promise can be made to God by the mere inward thought . . . ."

96. Here is how she herself characterizes her great alternatives: "Either to remain beside her child and keep everything *empeda*, her possessions, maidservants, and high roofed house, respecting the bed of her husband and the opinion of the people—or to follow after that one, the best of the [Suitors] who is wooing her in the halls and offering her gifts." (*Odyssey* Book 16, lines 74-77 in the Greek; the translation is from Zeitlin, "Figuring Fidelity in Homer's *Odyssey*," 125.). See generally Marilyn A. Katz, *Penelope's Renown: Meaning and Indeterminacy in the* Odyssey (Princeton: Princeton University Press, 1991), 93 et seq.

97. *Odyssey*, Book 23, line 228 (line 203 in the Greek).

98. In Part Three, Section III.

> Thy firmness draws my circle just
> and makes me end where I begun.[99]

I can steady myself with her help and she with mine. She can instantiate and fulfill her obligations to me by making calls on my obligations to her.

The special features of affiliational knowledge reinforce obligation. I can know my own steadfastness better as I see it reflected in the mirror of her consciousness; and knowing it better, I can develop it further and apply it more effectively. Something similar applies with respect to the special features of affiliational benevolence: he confers more good when the giver donates, so to speak, not only the gift but the giver himself. Thomas says this about the good of vowing: "he gives more who gives the tree with its fruit, than he that gives the fruit only."[100] The same can be said, more generally, about the good of shouldering obligation. Someone gives more to his wife who gives not only his services but also his commitment to serve: not only support but also commitment to support. Marriage is a drama of mutual reinforcement of obligation.

C. What Obligations?—If the thesis of this article is correct, it make sense for a couple to emphasize obligations with certain characteristics: ones well integrated into the other purposes of married life: mutually known, and mutually beneficient. Here are two types:

Romantic and sexual fidelity—This obligation—in its strongest form, a lifetime commitment to "forsaking all others"—is eminently eligible to be embraced as part of noninstrumental good, as it persists across time, it is "personal," it reflects benevolence (depth of love, unwillingness to hurt), it is difficult, and indeed it involves an arduous conquest of the wildest and most unsteady part of the psyche, Eros. Scholarship, song, and story throughout history celebrate the taming by marriage of the unruly male spirit. Thus Durkheim:

> By forcing a man to attach himself forever to the same woman, marriage assigns a strictly definite object to the need for love, and closes the horizon. This determination is what forms the state of moral equilibrium from which the husband benefits. Being unable to seek other satisfactions than those permitted, without transgressing his duty, he restricts his desires to them. The salutary

---

99. John Donne, "A Valediction Forbidding Mourning," quoted in Garvey, *What Are Freedoms For?*, 35.

100. *Summa Theologica* II-II question 88, article 6, corpus. Thomas is speaking here not of giving to man but to God: "he that vows something and does it, subjects himself to God more than he that only does it; for he subjects himself to God not only as to the act, but also as to the power . . . ."

> discipline to which he is subjected makes it his duty to find his happiness in his lot, and by so doing supplies him with the means.[101]

More than just a good idea, marital fidelity is necessary to the final good of firmness. Without it, whatever other projects the couple undertake together will be unsteadily committed.

Household chores—Chores, of course, are not essential. Rich couples may avoid them entirely. Some couples might undertake them for instrumental reasons only. Many husbands and wives, however, may find that cooperating in the practical tasks of keeping a household running is part of the warp and woof of their relationship. Household chores are eligible—like marital fidelity but not so pronouncedly—to instantiate the noninstrumental good of obligation. Getting the place spiffy for her return from her business trips, cooking dinner for him even when you are tired, are also recurrent across time, personal, beneficent, and conducive to self-discipline.

D. Noninstrumentalism in Practice?—If the thesis of this article extends beyond theory into belief and practice, we should be able to detect respect for marital obligation to a greater extent than would be predicted by the instrumentalist, and to detect distributions of obligations according to different patterns than he might foresee. Further, we should observe a correlation between obligation and happiness and between obligation and firmness of character. There is some evidence to support these predictions:

Fidelity—Classic utilitarianism seems to justify and predict adultery—and even to recommend it—when you won't be detected and won't beget a child (and sometimes even when you may); other forms of instrumentalism do not seem to rule it out either. But public opinion does not concur: studies show that large majorities disapprove of extramarital sex and that large majorities of spouses have avoided committing it even once.[102]

Classic utilitarianism and other forms of instrumentalism seem to justify and predict divorce when the result for both parties will be an affiliational deal sufficiently improved to cover the transaction cost. Professor Gary Becker's leading treatise predicts divorce when each spouse's predicted

101. Emile Durkheim, *Suicide: A Study in Sociology* (New York: Free Press, 1951), 270-71 (John A. Spaulding and George Simpson, trans.), quoted in Steven L. Nock, *Marriage in Men's Lives* (Oxford: Oxford University Press, 1998), 11-12.

102. See Nock, *Marriage in Men's Lives*, 22-23 (77% say that extramarital sex is "always wrong" and "among those whose marriages are intact, 15% of men and 5% of women admit to having had an extramarital relationship. When those whose marriages are no longer intact are included, these percentages rise only slightly, to 25% for men and 10% for women."); Anthony Peter Thompson, "Emotional and Sexual Components of Extramarital Relations," *Journal of Marriage and the Family*)(February, 1984) 35 (about 43% report ever, even once, having had a relationship outside marriage which included either sex or love).

"commodity wealth" will rise.[103] But although the divorce rate, notoriously, rocketed upwards during the 1960s and 1970s,[104] it still stands at a level far lower than what such analyses would predict. That fifty percent last a lifetime could not be predicted of truly instrumental affiliations such as those between commercial transactors or even social friends. Studies ranking the causes of divorce report high ranks for personality factors and components of bad personal relations; low rank for economic concerns; and no signficant rankings for "better deals elsewhere" of either an economic or a social nature.[105]

Chores—Instrumentalism predicts a pattern of allocating household duties which maximizes output, and this implies a lot of flexibility as changes occur in skill and marketability, in-home compared to outside-the-home (and it predicts that the spouse who can earn less will do more chores). But Sarah Berk's book *The Gender Factory* finds that task allocation tends to be stable not flexible, and studies indicate that the man may not increase his load when he begins to work less at a job or his wife more.[106] Gender roles help explain this, but so does the noninstrumental good of stable obligations discussed in this article. The man who keeps on doing the yardwork and repairs even when he is under major pressure from a second job may be implicitly saying, not simply "I am a real man" but, more basically, "I am *your* man and sticking by these tasks shows that nothing in my work situation can change that." The woman who continues to cook for her husband when he has been laid off—rather than saying to him, "you're unemployed, *you* do the cooking"—may be emphasizing her fidelity at a juncture where it counts for a lot.

A Harvest of Happiness and Steadiness of Character? Instrumentalism might predict that married couples would be less happy than cohabiting couples, since married couples have shut themselves out of the marketplace whereas cohabitors can look forward to trading up. Studies show that married

103. *A Treatise on the Family*, 331-32 (stating that a couple (a "risk-neutral" couple) will consent to divorce if the "expected commodity wealth" of each is higher after divorce than without divorce). "Commodity" is given a fairly broad meaning and is not limited to things that could move in commerce.

104. Stacy J. Rogers and Paul R. Amato, "Have Changes in Gender Relations Affected Marital Quality?" *Social Forces* 79 (2000) 731.

105. See Gary C. Kitson and William M. Holmes, *Portrait of Divorce: Adjustment to Marital Breakdown* (New York: Guilford Press, 1992), Chapter 5.

106. Sarah Fenstermaker Berk, *The Gender Factory: The Apportionment of Work in American Households*, 197-98 (New York: Plenum Press, 1985). For recent findings, see Suzanne M. Bianchi, Melissa A. Milkie, Liana C. Sayer and John P. Robinson, "Is Anyone Doing the Housework? Trends in the Gender Division of Household Labor," *Social Forces* 79 (2000) 191; Rogers and Amato, "Have Changes in Gender Relations Affected Marital Quality?" 731.

couples are happier and healthier.[107] This makes sense to the noninstrumentalist, who understand that obligation is a part of well-being and that life without it is impoverished and deprived. Instrumentalism might predict that married people would be worse employees because of their heavy duties at home. But studies show that married men are better workers;[108] a conclusion which may be explained by their steadier characters.

If this article is correct, we can use it as a basis for understanding the concluding episode of Professor June Carbone's recent book *From Partners to Parents*:

> Shortly after the birth of my first child, a friend . . . asked me if I felt more "mature." With the stress of childbirth and sleepless nights still fresh in my mind, I answered an emphatic "no." Three years later, during a walk in the park with what had by then become two children, I understood what she meant. A large dog approached us and began to bark. I have always been terrified of dogs, but this time I quickly gathered the one-year-old into my arms, held my three-year-old close to me, and confronted the intruder. The amazing thing to me was that I felt almost no fear. I no longer had the luxury: I was a parent.[109]

Parenthood, like marriage, is obligatory; and obligation involves steadiness and courage. Odysseus would have done no less.

107. The literature on the differences between married and cohabiting couples is cited in Margaret F. Brinig, "Unmarried Partners and the Legacy of *Marvin v. Marvin:* The Influence of *Marvin v. Marvin* on Housework During Marriage," *Notre Dame Law Review* 76 (2001) 1311, 1316-17. See Linda J. Waite and Maggie Gallagher, *The Case for Marriage: Why Married People are Happier, Healthier, and Better Off Financially* (New York: Doubleday, 2000).

108. Brinig, "Unmarried Partners and the Legacy of *Marvin v. Marvin:* The Influence of *Marvin v. Marvin* on Housework During Marriage."

109. June Carbone, *From Partners to Parents: The Second Revolution in Family Law* (New York: Columbia University Press, 2000), 241.

[15]

Just Marriage

On the public importance of private unions

Mary Lyndon Shanley

American conservatives pride themselves on moral clarity. And that clarity is nowhere greater than on the topic of marriage and family. The essentials of marriage are, they say, well-defined: it unites a man and a woman; it provides the foundation for a family that may include biological or adopted children; it assigns different roles to men and women; and it is a union for life, indissoluble except for the most grievous offenses. These essentials are, according to conservatives, not a product of the vagaries of social convention or contingent cultural choices but are instead given by nature, scripture, or tradition. Moreover, preserving them is intrinsically good for individuals and has great public benefits: marriage is the foundation of society, and a strong foundation will protect against society's ills, from crime to poverty.

For the past decade conservatives have worked energetically to implement this vision—more precisely, to restore it in the face of the demographic, economic, and cultural changes of the past 40 years. They have defended two-parent marriage by requiring (in the 1996 Welfare Reform Act) that single parents who receive welfare must work outside the home for wages, while allowing one parent in a two-parent family that receives welfare to stay home to take care of children. They supported President George W. Bush's "marriage initiative," which allocates federal funds to programs aimed at persuading unwed parents to marry, by rewarding, for example, a single mother who marries her child's father. And they have opposed efforts to legalize same-sex marriage in individual states and praised the federal Defense of Marriage Act (DOMA), which exempts states from recognizing same-sex marriages entered into in other states. The Catholic bishops of Massachusetts, for example, have recently been pressing the state legislature to pass a constitutional amendment against same-sex marriage: such marriages will, they say, have "devastating consequences." And Ken Connor, president of the conservative Family Research Council, has promised to make a "big, big issue in 2004" out of the idea that "marriage is a sacred covenant, limited to a man and a woman."

Critics argue that these efforts to shore up the traditional family represent an assault on 30 years of sensible reforms of marriage and divorce law that have helped to free women and men from stultifying or abusive relationships; that they threaten to reimpose oppressive gender roles; that they stigmatize and disadvantage unwed mothers and their children; and that they condemn gay men and lesbians to second-class citizenship. In short, the conservative program is characterized as the enemy of equality and a threat to personal liberty.

But these critics have been less clear about their own constructive moral and political vision. One response to the conservative project has been to concentrate on efforts to legalize gay and lesbian marriage by reforming state marriage laws. This strategy is attractive and shows some promise in a few states, but even if it succeeds it leaves other elements of the conservative project untouched. It does nothing to address the concerns of those who regard marriage itself as oppressive, to remedy the poverty that deters some people from marrying, or to support single parents and their children.

A second, more comprehensive proposal—put forward by, among others, Lenore Weitzman in *The Marriage Contract* and Martha Fineman in *The Neutered Mother*—is to abolish state-defined marriage altogether and replace it with individual contracts drawn up by each couple wishing to marry. A regime of individual contract would allow spouses to decide for themselves how to arrange their lives, and it would enable people of the same sex, or more than two persons, to marry. On this view, which I will call contractualism, the best way to treat citizens as free and equal adults is to stop treating marriage as a special public status, and permit the parties themselves to define its terms and conditions.

Contractualism has considerable force, but it suffers from two deficiencies. First, the contract model treats persons as rational and bounded individuals while paying insufficient attention to the mutual need and dependence that arise in marriage and other close relationships. It thus rests on an incomplete view of the person and fails to take account of the ideal of marriage as a relationship that transcends the individual lives of the partners. That ideal has deep cultural resonance, and contractualism unnecessarily concedes this ground to conservatives. Second, while emphasizing the need for liberty in the choice of partners, contractualism fails to give sufficient weight to positive state action to enhance equality and equal opportunity along with liberty and freedom of association. It thus is founded on too narrow a conception of justice.

A third line of response, then, would preserve the idea that a married couple is something more than its separate members, and that spouses can make claims in the name of their relationship that are not identical to claims that each could make as individuals. But it would also open up marriage so that both women and men, regardless of race, class, or sexual orientation, can, as equals, assume the responsibilities and reap the rewards of family life. I will call this the equal status view. Its defining aspiration is to preserve the idea that marriage is a special bond and public status while rejecting—as incompatible with liberty and equality—important elements of the traditional view of the purpose and proper ordering of marriage.

Can marriage be reformed to serve as a public status that promotes equality and liberty? Is the happy combination of justice and committed intimacy and love suggested by the equal status view a real possibility?

I. From Fixed Status to No-Fault

The traditional view of marriage in the United States has roots in Christian religious views and church law. The English common law, which provided the basis for the marriage laws of most U.S. states, reflected the tenets of marriage promulgated by the Anglican (and before it the Catholic) Church. When jurisdiction over marriage and children was transferred from

Marriage and Cohabitation 3

church to common-law courts, for the most part public law simply incorporated aspects of church doctrine.[1]

The Traditional View

In the Church's view marriage was first and foremost a covenant, like God's covenant with the Jews and Christ's covenant with the church (the community of the faithful). Christian marriage was thus an unbreakable bond (for Catholics, a sacrament). Marriage was to be lifelong and marital faithfulness was to include monogamy.

Marriage was also regarded as a hierarchical relationship in which husband and wife played complementary roles. The man was given authority as head of household. Blackstone, the 18th-century legal authority, explained that since Genesis declared husband and wife to be "one flesh" in the eyes of God, they were to be "one person" in the eyes of the law, and that person was represented by the husband. This suspension of the wife's legal personality was known as the doctrine of spousal unity or "coverture." Under coverture a married woman could not sue or be sued unless her husband was party to the suit, could not sign contracts unless her husband joined her, and could not make a valid will unless he consented to its provisions. As a correlate to these powers and his role as head of the family, a husband was obligated to support his wife and children. And since he would be held responsible for her actions, a husband had a right to correct his wife physically and to determine how and where their children would be raised. As late as 1945 a New Jersey court wrote:

> The plaintiff [husband] is the master of his household. He is the managing head, with control and power to preserve the family relation, to protect its members and to guide their conduct. He has the obligation and responsibility of supporting, maintaining and protecting the family and the correlative right to exclude intruders and unwanted visitors from the home despite the whims of the wife.[2]

Marriage was to be a structure in which the roles of the spouses were distinct and complementary: the wage earner and the housewife, the protector and the protected, the independent and the dependent.

The husband was expected to govern his household with neither interference nor help from the state. By and large, police turned a blind eye to violence between spouses. In most jurisdictions wives could not prosecute their husbands for marital rape because the law assumed that by marrying, spouses gave blanket consent to sexual relations (they were, after all, "one body" and "one person" in law). And judges enforced obligations of support only if spouses separated, not in an ongoing marriage.

When people married, then, they consented to enter a relationship whose terms were set by the state. Of course, consent was necessary to enter the married state, but the agreement to marry brought with it rights and duties that were not set by the partners but were treated as intrinsic to the status of being married.

The First Wave of Reform

The unequal provisions of marriage law became the object of reform efforts in the mid-19th century. Reformers were critical, for example, of the fact that many states granted divorce only for a wife's adultery and not a husband's. Moreover, adultery was in many states the *only* grounds for divorce, and some men and women began to insist that other wrongs, particularly physical cruelty and domestic violence, were significant offenses against the marriage that justified dissolving the marital bond. To forbid divorce in such instances, they said, was to make the home a "prison" for unhappy and wronged spouses, depriving them of essential personal liberty.

Feminist reformers also challenged coverture by invoking equality. They organized campaigns in a series of states to pass laws which would allow wives to hold property, sue and be sued, and enter contracts in their own names. By the end of the 19th century, many states had passed married women's property statutes, freeing married women from many of the legal effects of coverture.

While this first wave of marriage-law reform increased both the freedom to leave unsatisfactory marriages and equality between husbands and wives, dissatisfaction with marriage law remained. The grounds for divorce remained restrictive: thus, several states granted divorce only for adultery. And law still treated married men and women differently: for example, many states imposed alimony only on husbands, a stipulation that assumed, and perhaps helped to perpetuate, women's exclusion from the paid labor force. The age at which females could marry without their parents' consent was often younger than that for males, suggesting that boys needed to stay in school or learn a trade before marrying and that girls did not. Custody laws varied widely, but often contained a preference for mother's custody, again assuming that the mother was and would in the future be the better caregiver.

The Second Wave of Reform

In the mid-20th century a variety of factors (which I can only briefly allude to here) converged to spark a second wave of marriage-law reform. Demographic changes after 1900 were dramatic. Life expectancy for women was 51 years in 1900 and 74 in 1960; increased life expectancy meant that most parents had years together in an "empty nest" after their children had left home; at mid-century women began childbearing at a later age and bore fewer children than in 1900. In addition, economic changes in the decades following World War II led women, including married women and women with children, into the paid labor force in unprecedented numbers. This drew women out of the home for part of the day and gave them greater economic independence. The introduction of the birth control pill in the 1960s gave women more control over pregnancy, and the ability to plan the timing of their children encouraged women to work outside the home and to think of "careers" rather than temporary jobs.

These and related changes provoked a dramatic transformation of divorce law between 1965 and 1974. Herbert Jacob has called the adoption of no-fault divorce the "silent revolution": revolution because it involved a series of "radical changes in legal expectations about family life;" silent because the changes resulted from "routine" policy processes that never became the focus of media and public attention.

In the mid-1960s, lawyers in California began the push for no-fault divorce in large part to get rid of the subterfuge in many divorce proceedings that took place when couples tailored their stories to make them fit the legal requirements for divorce. Although California courts were lenient in granting divorce, in order to obtain a divorce a husband or wife had to prove that the other had committed an offense such as adultery, cruelty, willful neglect, habitual intemperance, or desertion. In most cases the wife was the plaintiff, and she usually charged her husband with "cruelty," which could range from disparaging remarks to physical violence. The charges were often fabricated and the testimony rehearsed, the couple having decided to end the marriage. The dishonesty, even perjury, that pervaded some divorce proceedings prompted activists to press the legislature to adopt a no-fault divorce law, which enabled a spouse to obtain a divorce without proving wrongdoing by the other.

No-fault divorce emerged prior to modern feminism, and its proponents did not aim to promote greater equality for women or greater choice among alternative family forms. Nor did they intend or anticipate the demographic watershed in U.S. families that resulted from no-fault divorce. In the wake of no-fault legislation the divorce rate rose dramatically, from 2.2 per thousand population in 1960 to 4.8 per thousand population in 1975. And by the last quarter of the 20th century only one-fourth of U.S. households fit the supposed "norm" of a wage-earning husband and homemaker wife living with children.

Alongside its dramatic demographic consequences, no-fault divorce prompted a sea change in conventional understandings of marriage. The idea that marriage partners themselves could simply decide to end their marriage was revolutionary; it affected thinking about the very nature of marriage and its permanence. The observation by 19th-century legal historian Henry Maine that the movement of the law in the 19th century was "a movement from status to contract" was finally coming to be true of marriage.

Although no-fault divorce preceded the resurgence of feminism, the idea that individuals should be able to extricate themselves from unhappy marriages resonated with feminist ideas about women's liberty and equality—and later with the movement by gays and lesbians to end legal discrimination against homosexuals and the ban on same-sex marriage. The conjunction of no-fault divorce, renewed attention to equality, and gay liberation, as Nancy Cott observed, sparked proposals to "reinvent marriage" by "extend[ing] its founding principle of consent between the couple to all the terms of the relationship, allowing the contractual side of the hybrid institution to bloom." If personal choice suffices to end a marriage, why, the contractualist asks, shouldn't personal choice define the terms of marriage right from the outset?

II. A Third Wave of Reform?

Marriage and Liberty

Liberty, the first foundational value of a liberal polity, is central to the question of who is allowed to marry. When the law stipulates who may and may not marry, it restricts the freedom of those excluded from marriage. Some exclusions are relatively uncontroversial, such as prohibiting marriage below a certain age, with a close relative, or while in prison (although each of these has been attacked as an unjustifiable limitation on individual freedom). Other restrictions are more contentious. Law precluded slaves from marrying. And only in 1967, in the case of *Loving v. Virginia,* did the Supreme Court decide that anti-miscegenation laws were unconstitutional.

Advocates of contract marriage favor legal recognition of same-sex marriage, a position consistent with their dedication to individual liberty. When marriage is a public status, they say, law inevitably draws a line separating those who may marry and those who may not. The repeated refusal by states to formalize unions of same-sex couples represents, according to the contractualists, a failure to take pluralism, privacy, and personal choice seriously. States, of course, may enforce agreements between marriage partners, just as states enforce other contracts; and they may prohibit marriages below a certain age, as they impose age restrictions on other contracts. But states may not legitimately decide who may marry whom or how spouses should order the personal and material aspects of their relationship.

I might be tempted to become a contractarian if contract marriage were the only way to achieve legal recognition for same-sex marriage, but—as current political initiatives at the state level underscore—it is not. Marriage for same-sex couples can be achieved by either legislation or court decisions that change the content of marriage law; it does not require us to replace a regime of marriage law with a regime of private contract. The fact that many municipalities have adopted "domestic partnerships" and that Vermont has recognized "civil unions" may be a harbinger of legislative victories to come. And courts may someday decide that there is a constitutionally protected right to marry that encompasses same-sex couples. The ground was laid in *Loving v. Virginia* when the Supreme Court declared "The freedom to marry has long been recognized as one of the vital personal rights essential to the orderly pursuit of happiness by free men. Marriage is one of the basic civil rights of man, fundamental to our very existence and survival." If marriage is a fundamental liberty protected by the 14th Amendment's due-process clause, then any restriction on marriage must be tailored to advance a compelling state interest. And while some religious views may condemn homosexual unions, no state interest rises to a sufficiently compelling level to justify prohibiting same-sex marriage.

The debate here is not for and against same-sex marriage, but between contractualists who would provide legal recognition of same-sex marriage by abolishing marriage law and those who would instead alter marriage law itself. Is there any reason to prefer the latter? I think there is.

The individualism and emphasis on rational bargaining that are at the heart of contracts rest on misleading models of the person and of the marriage relationship. Marriage partners are not only autonomous decision-makers; they are fundamentally social beings who will inevitably experience need, change, and dependency in the course of their lives. The prenuptial agreements that set forth how economic assets each partner brings to the marriage are to be held and distributed recognize the individuality of the partners, although they strike some people as unromantic. But the question of who should have a claim to property obtained by either spouse during the course of the marriage is more problematic, because when people marry they become part of an entity that is not always reducible to its individual components. Some states hold all such property to be held in common (community property), reflecting the notion that marriage creates a single entity and a shared fate (and hence shared resources) for marriage partners. Other states give title to the person who earned or otherwise obtained the property, but allow title to be overridden in the interests of a fair distribution at the time of divorce, reflecting a belief that marriage creates claims growing out of a shared life. The relational entity is also reflected in common language when spouses say they are doing something "for the sake of the marriage," such as choosing a place to live that would be neither partner's first choice if single. It is reflected in legal practice when one spouse is prohibited from testifying against the other in certain proceedings because the law wants to express the notion that the marriage relationship itself should be protected.

Married life is not only deeply relational, but it is also unpredictable. Not all of what spouses may properly expect of one another can be stipulated in advance. Contracts are useful devices for facilitating communication about each partner's expectations and aspirations. But contracts create obligations by volition and agreement; they do not account well for the obligations that may arise from unforeseen circumstances, including illness or disability of an aging parent, a spouse, or a child.

Finally, contract suggests that each marriage is a particular agreement between individuals, not a relationship in which the public has a legitimate interest. But the public does have an interest in the terms of marriage. It has, as the equal status view argues, an interest in promoting equality of husband and wife, both as spouses and as citizens, and in securing what Martha Nussbaum calls the social bases of liberty and self-respect for all family members.[3] And it has an interest in sustaining marital and other family relationships in the face of poverty or illness.

One way to think about the differences in these two approaches is to consider whether polygamy should be legalized in the United States. As *Boston Globe* columnist Jeff Jacoby asks, "If the state has no right to deny a marriage license to would-be spouses of the same sex, on what reasonable grounds could it deny a marriage to would-be spouses . . . who happen to number three or four instead of two?" Would a continuation of the ban on plural marriage simply shift the boundary between who's in and who's out?

For contractualists, the case for a right to plural marriage is straightforward: it expresses individuals' rights to form affective and sexual relationships free from state interference. Martha Fineman said in 2001 that "if no form of sexual affiliation is state preferred, subsidized, and protected, none could or should be prohibited. Same-sex partners and others forming a variety of other sexual arrangements would simply be viewed as equivalent forms of privately preferred sexual connection." The law would have to be gender-neutral, allowing marriages with plural husbands as well as plural wives. But as long as protections against coercion, fraud, and other abuses that invalidate any contract were enforced, people could choose multiple marriage partners.

Proponents of the equal status conception fall on both sides of the question. Laurence Tribe, supporting legal recognition of polygamy, asks rhetorically in *American Constitutional Law* whether the goal of preserving monogamous marriage is "sufficiently compelling, and the refusal to exempt Mormons sufficiently crucial to the goal's attainment, to warrant the resulting burden on religious conscience." Peggy Cooper Davis condemns in *Neglected Stories* the "cultural myopia" that led the Supreme Court to outlaw Mormon polygamy in *Reynolds v. United States* in 1879, and argues that a principled objection to polygamy in a multicultural society would require more than "a political majority's wish to define and freeze the moral character of the polity." But the flaws in the *Reynolds* decision do not mean polygamy should be legalized. Many people are convinced that polygamy is profoundly patriarchal. The "larger cultural context of female subordination" is too deeply rooted and strong even for gender-neutral principles that allow both women and men to have more than one spouse to overcome its effects. In this view, plural marriage reinforces female subordination and is unacceptable on grounds of equality.

The answer to the question, "If we legalize same-sex marriage, won't we have to legalize plural marriage?" is not, then, an obvious "yes." Equality as well as liberty is implicated in marriage law and policy. In assuming the equal agency of the parties to the contract, the contract model leaves aside the question of whether choices themselves may lead to subordination. In order to decide whether plural marriage should be legalized, one must address the question of whether polygamy can be reformed along egalitarian lines. Equality must be a central attribute of any marital regime based on considerations of justice.

Marriage and Equality

Most people today endorse "equality" as a general cultural value, but there is deep disagreement about what kind of *spousal* equality we want and how best to achieve it. Advocates of gay and lesbian marriage who are concerned principally with restrictive rules about who may marry whom typically do not engage this issue. But a vision of the proper relationship between spouses is central to the conservative project; a compelling alternative to it will require its own core vision.

Under 19th-century marriage law the fact that a wife's legal personality was subsumed in that of her husband, that she was not able to vote, and that she was excluded from many occupations was regarded by many not as inequality but as complementary difference. Today some traditionalists contend that although men and women, husbands and wives should enjoy equal rights both in marriage and as citizens, they have different roles to play in family and civil society. For example, Chad Brand explains the Southern Baptist Convention's position that "while the Bible teaches equality, it does not affirm egalitarianism or interchangeability in all things." He contends that "male-female equality and male headship may seem paradoxical, but they are both taught in Scripture, much like a thread of two strands."[4] In a secular vein William Kristol asserts that women and men must be taught "to grasp the following three points: the necessity of marriage, the importance of good morals, and the necessity of inequality within marriage."[5] Because the nation needs strong and even aggressive men to flourish, the price women pay for marriage and morals is submission to the husband as leader within the family.

Angered by the endorsement of male dominance in these views, advocates of contract marriage such as Martha Fineman argue that "abolishing marriage as a legal category is a step necessary for gender equality." Marriage by contract replaces the gender stereotyping and protectionism of traditional marriage law with the recognition of the individuality and equal agency of the partners. Marriage partners should be treated as rational actors capable of knowing and articulating their interests. Contract reflects autonomy and self-direction in general, and marriage partners are individuals who, according to the American Law Institute's *Principles of the Law of Family Dissolution*, need to "accommodate their particular needs and circumstances by contractually altering or confirming the legal rights and obligations that would otherwise arise."[6]

Supporters of contract marriage are right to reject male dominance and state protectionism. But as Carole Pateman argued in *The Sexual Contract*, while contract may be the enemy of status it alone is not adequate to defeat the legacy of patriarchy. The contract model is an insufficient foundation for spousal equality. Ensuring conditions of fair contracts is not in itself enough to establish this kind of equality in marriage and in civic life. Instead, marriage law and public policy must work to ensure that neither partner is precluded from participating in social and political life or rendered unable to provide care to family members. Vigorous state action is needed to promote spousal equality, and one important justification for such action is provided by vision of marriage as a relationship between equals that enriches both their individual and joint lives. While marriage and divorce laws themselves are now usually drafted in gender-neutral terms, cultural norms and employment practices perpetuate a division of labor at work and at home that results in a system of gender and racial hierarchy. So even if reforms are animated by concerns about joining domestic equality with special respect for marital bonds, those reforms will need to focus on the labor market as much as the domestic arena.

Most jobs, whether professional or nonprofessional, still assume the model of what Joan Williams in *Unbending Gender* calls the "ideal worker," a full-time, paid employee married to an at-home caregiver. Employment practices in the United States developed around the sexual division of labor. Jobs were designated "male" or "female," and men's jobs tended to pay higher wages than women's. Different pay scales applied to men and women doing the same work (men being presumed to be the family provider, women to be working for "pin money"). Health, unemployment, and other benefits were tied to full-time work. The workday and workweek were based on the assumption that someone else was cleaning, cooking, and caring for family members. The ideal worker model had enormous influence on both the economic resources and caregiving skills of men and women.

Although discrimination against women in the workplace has diminished, the ideal worker model continues to affect both decisions to marry and the dynamics within marriage. As Susan Okin argues in *Justice, Gender, and the Family*, the difference in wage earning capacity between men and women gives men more resources with which to deal with the world, and this in turn affects dynamics within the family. The disparity still remains despite a narrowing wage differential between men and women of all races: while women in 1979 earned 62.5 cents for every dollar men earned, in 1998 they earned 76 cents. Because uninterrupted time in the work force increases one's potential earning power, wives who stay out of the paid labor force for a number of years fall behind. This diminishes their decision-making authority within marriage and their options to leave an unsatisfactory union.

The arrangement of the workplace also affects decisions about caregiving, for children as well as elderly or sick relatives. Because benefits such as health insurance may depend on full-time work, and because the pay scale is often higher for full-time work, one partner may have to work full-time. Because many jobs are sex-segregated and wages for men's jobs are higher than those for women's, it will make economic sense in some families for the husband to work full-time and his wife to do the caregiving. The division between "workers" and "caregivers" not only harms women in the workplace but makes it less likely that men will develop interpersonal and caregiving skills.

In the Supreme Court's recent decision upholding the right of a man denied family leave to take care of his sick wife to sue the State of Nevada under the Family and Medical Leave Act, Justice Rehnquist noted the effects on both home and workplace of the assumption that women caregivers free men to be ideal workers.

> Because employers continued to regard the family as the women's domain, they often denied men similar accommodations or discouraged them from taking leave. These mutually reinforcing

> stereotypes created a self-fulfilling cycle of discrimination that forced women to continue to assume the role of primary caregiver, and fostered employers' stereotypical views about women's commitment to work and their value as employees. [*Nevada Department of Human Resources v. Hibbs*, No. 01-1368, decided May 27, 2003.]

Congress acted reasonably, Justice Rehnquist ruled, in mandating a family leave that would be help to break these stereotypes about male and female social roles.The tight linkage between work and family is influenced not only by gender but also by race and class.

Racial prejudice meant that historically fewer Black than white families had an "ideal worker" and stay-at-home caregiver. The economic need created by racial discrimination meant that the labor force participation of married Black women was always higher than that of white women. Black men were relegated disproportionately to agricultural and other low-paid labor, Black women to domestic and other service jobs. Since the last decade of the 20th century the high unemployment rate among Black males has had an additional impact on family life, as marriage rates have fallen: William Julius Wilson, Orlando Patterson, and others have argued that some people won't marry when they have no reasonable hope of being able to support a family.[7]

As to social class, the increasing number of never-married mothers living in poverty led authors of the Welfare Reform Act of 1996 (the Personal Responsibility and Work Opportunity Act) to insert a provision requiring mothers who receive welfare to identify the biological fathers of their children. The state could then go after the father for child support, and if he did not provide enough money to lift mother and child out of poverty, the mother was required to work outside the home. Sponsors hoped that if the woman identified the father the state might induce them to marry. Even if they did not marry, the man and not the government would support the child. Many women eligible for welfare, however, did not want to identify the fathers of their children, some because they preferred to parent with someone else or alone, some because they feared abuse from the father, and some because they knew the father had no money (and often no job).

Marriage is not an effective anti-poverty program, nor is it appropriate to use it as such. Unemployment rates are high because the number of jobs that pay a living wage are far below the number of unemployed seeking work. The wages available to many men who can find work are inadequate to support a family, and adding a wife's wages is of little help unless affordable childcare is available. Addressing women's poverty by attaching them to men who can support them reproduces inequality and vulnerability within marriage. Inducing women to marry men may expose them and their children to domestic violence while failing to provide them with either the personal or community resources to extricate themselves from intolerable living conditions.

The understanding of marriage as a contract does not by itself generate the reforms necessary to alter family and workplace structures, welfare, and social services in ways necessary to give both men and women the opportunity to engage in both public and caregiving work. The next phase of the struggle to achieve sexual and spousal equality must entail a public commitment to liberty and equality and tackle not only marriage law but economic circumstances as well.

A number of reforms would move society toward greater justice in marriage. One such reform would be to ensure that people can find jobs that pay a living wage. There must be equal pay for equal work, whether performed by full- or part-time employees. Benefits must be extended to all workers, not just those who meet the ideal worker model (and basic health benefits should not be tied to employment status). Work must also be restructured in such a way that it accommodates caregiving, through a shorter workweek and more flexible scheduling, for example. If caregivers are not to be marginalized, quality, affordable childcare must be part of any comprehensive family policy, as must the kind of child allowance common in European countries. Paid parental leave for both men and women would create an incentive for men to participate in child care, particularly if a father could not transfer his leave time to someone else but had to use it or forego the benefit. In the event of divorce the wages of both a primary wage earner and a primary caregiver should be treated as joint property, reflecting the commonality of marriage, particularly if there are children or other dependents.

These measures certainly do not exhaust the possibilities. They make the point that in order to meet the principle of spousal equality men and women alike must be able to perform the tasks necessary to both the public and the private realm, to shoulder the responsibilities of workers outside the home as well as family caregivers.

III. Public Status or Individual Contract?

The contractual image has much to be said for it. It captures what Milton Regan, Jr., in *Alone Together* calls the "external stance" toward marriage, which focuses on the ways in which marriage serves the interests of distinct individuals. Contract represents well the role that choice and negotiation play in any marriage. Drafting a marriage contract is a useful exercise for a couple because it encourages potential partners to asses their individual needs and sources of personal satisfaction, make their expectations explicit, and identify areas of both agreement and conflict. Legal notions of spousal unity and the sentimentalization of a woman's role as "the angel in the house" have often served to undercut married women's agency and autonomy. The external stance provides an important antidote.

Contract does less well in capturing what Regan calls the "internal stance" toward marriage, which regards it from within the relationship and focuses on shared experience rather than lives lived in parallel association. The internal stance reflects the fact that when people marry they become part of an entity that is not reducible to or identical with its individual components. Historically this concept of a marital entity distinct from either spouse was oppressive to women. The doctrine that husband and wife were "one" and formed a new "person" in the eyes of the law deprived married women of their independent right to hold property and enter into contracts in their own name until the latter half of the 19th century. Prior to the advent of no-fault divorce in the late 1960s a court had to find that one of the spouses had committed an offense "against the marriage" before granting a divorce. "Incompatibility" was not a valid ground for divorce even when both partners wanted to end their marriage. Even in our own day police may ignore complaints of domestic violence because they do not want to "intrude" on the private realm of the married couple.

Despite this dismal history, the notion that marriage creates an entity that is not reducible to the individual spouses captures a truth about significant human relationships and could be used to reshape social and economic institutions in desirable ways. This understanding of the marriage relationship as something distinct from the individuals could be used in the future not to subordinate women but to press for marriage partners' rights to social and economic supports that sustain family relationships and enable spouses to provide care to one another.

Such a right to provide care to and receive care from a spouse is not the same as an individual's right to health care or social services. Nor does public protection and support for associational and affective ties need to be limited to marriage partners and parents and children. Rather, recognition of the inevitability of dependency and the importance of caregiving should lead people to ask what other relationships deserve public support.

Marriage suggests, as contract does not, the role of committed relationships in shaping the self. The promise to love someone else, in a marriage or in a friendship or in a community, binds a person to act in ways that will fulfill that obligation. Contract also does not express the notion of unconditional commitment, both to the other person and to the relationship. Contract in lieu of marriage rests upon a notion of quid pro quo, in which each party offers something and agrees on the terms of any exchange as a rational bargainer. But the marriage commitment is unpredictable and open-ended, and the obligations it gives rise to cannot be fully stated in advance. What love attuned to the well-being of another may require is by its nature unpredictable.

With so much of our public discourse reducing individuals primarily to consumers in the market, it is especially important to insist on the social and relational sides of our lives. The contractual model for marriage that presents marriage, as Hendrik Hartog says in *Man and Wife in America*, as "nothing more than a private choice and as a collection of private practices" is insufficient to the tasks of reconfiguring marriage. Marriage entails respect for individuals and for their relationships. It is a particularly striking instance of a practice founded on both individuality and "a shared purpose that transcends the self" (Regan). If such a commitment is a valuable aspiration and one that our political community wants to facilitate, then we need to examine and remove impediments to such relationships. Those impediments are legion, especially among the poor. Removing them thus confronts us with a formidable agenda—reforms of the workplace, of welfare, and of caregiving. But with notions of the public good and collective responsibility under constant assault, withdrawing the state from the pursuit of justice in marriage and family moves in the wrong direction. We need to insist instead that marriage and family law can and must be made to conform to the principles of justice that affirm the equality and equal liberty of all citizens.

Mary Lyndon Shanley is Margaret Stiles Halleck Professor of Political Science at Vassar College. She is author of *Making Babies, Making Families: What Matters Most in an Age of Reproductive Technologies; Surrogacy, Adoption, and Same-Sex and Unwed Parents' Rights*; and *Feminism, Marriage, and the Law in Victorian England 1850–1895*.

Notes

1. In Jewish law, marriage involved a contract (ketubah) in which a man accepted a woman as his wife in exchange for a bride price, and pledged a specific amount of money to her if he divorced her. Divorce was only available to the man. The blessings of the wedding ceremony invoked a more covenantal relationship, but the contract was essential to marriage. The Jewish contractual law of marriage was different both from Christian law, which by-and-large did not permit divorce, and views of secular contractualists that I examine here.
2. *Chapman v. Mitchell*, 223 N.J. Misc. 358 at 359-60, 44 A. 2d 392 at 393, quoted in Herbert Jacob, *Silent Revolution: The Transformation of Divorce Law in the United States* (Univ. of Chicago Press, 1988), 6.

3. Martha C. Nussbaum, "The Future of Feminist Liberalism," in Eva Feder Kittay and Ellen K. Feder, eds., *The Subject of Care* (Rowman & Littlefield, 2002), 192.
4. Chad Brand, "Christ-Centered Marriages: Husbands and Wives Complementing One Another," September 1998, www. baptist2baptist.net /sbclifearticles/sept%5F98/sept%5F98.html (visited 6 June 2003).
5. Quoted in June Carbone, "Is the Gender Divide Unbridgeable? The Implications for Social Equality," *Iowa Journal of Gender, Race & Justice*, 5:31 (Fall 2001), 73.
6. Quoted in Martha Albertson Fineman, "Marriage and Meaning," in Anita Bernstein, ed., *For and Against Marriage: Strategies to Critique, Reform, Defend, and Appraise a Venerable Legal Category* (forthcoming). Fineman has written extensively on contract marriage, including *The Neutered Mother, the Sexual Family and Other Twentieth Century Tragedies* (Routledge, 1995).
7. Wilson is right to assert that ending unemployment is imperative, but decent-paying jobs for men alone will not foster spousal equality in either Black or white families. Unless jobs are available for women as well, and unless *both* men and women are provided with the means to combine wage labor and family caregiving, spousal relations will continue to be hierarchical and unequal. Orlando Patterson writes in *The Ordeal of Integration* about conflicts between Black men and women that have caused the marriage rate among Black Americans to decline.

Originally published in the Summer 2003 issue of *Boston Review*

[16]

Contract Marriage – The Way Forward or Dead End?

DAVID MCLELLAN*

This essay aims to analyse contractarian theories of marriage and considers how advisable it is that the law concerning marriage should be reformed to make it conform more closely to contractarian principles. The theories in question are at their most articulate in the United States of America, as one would expect, but the problems raised are relevant to the United Kingdom. For although no one would argue that the version of marriage established in the United Kingdom is contractarian, the contract model is colonizing more and more areas of contemporary life and marriage may not be immune. Indeed, the current policy debates surrounding the Family Law Bill's provisions on divorce have implications for the nature of marital obligations. In arguing against the contract theorists of marriage, I start with some historical background before outlining the (admittedly powerful) arguments that they can and do deploy. I then maintain that the proponents of contract are incapable of addressing the fundamental problem of the imbalance of power in contemporary marriage and rely on a conceptualization of the public/private divide inimical to the very freedom and equality that contractarian ideas claim to advance.

HISTORICAL BACKGROUND

In general, the Victorian feminist movement attacked the common law doctrine of coverture by demanding that the same principles which underlay public law should also apply to domestic law. They insisted on individual rights and equality before the law for women as well as men.[1] In this area they achieved substantial success. The disappointing Divorce Act 1857 did at least concede the possibility of civil action for divorce on the egregious grounds of incest, bigamy, or gross physical cruelty – though it confirmed the double standard that only a wife's (and not a husband's) adultery justified the severing of a marriage.[2] More importantly, the Married Women's Property Act of 1870 removed some of a wife's property from her husband's

* *Department of Politics and International Relations, University of Kent, Canterbury CT2 7NX, England*

control, though only by a fictional trust which adopted the protective language of equity: the loss of independent legal personality on marriage was left untouched. The Married Women's Property Act 1883 gave women control over property brought into a marriage, but still refused to treat married women on an equal footing with those unmarried, by granting them *femme sole* status with respect to their property and contracts.

John Stuart Mill and Victorian feminists in general paid more attention to married women's lack of economic and contractual rights and less to considering the disempowering effects of the economic dependency of most wives on their husbands. In so doing, they were, in effect, carrying the liberal tradition as founded by Hobbes and Locke to its most progressive limit.[3] As the twentieth century has advanced, approximate legal equality in marriage has been achieved with easy divorce, legal access to jobs, and control by both men and women separately or together, of their fertility. Yet the practical division of labour in the household and the grossly disproportionate share falling on women when both partners work full-time,[4] the continuing effective inequality of jobs and wages available to women, the unfairness of divorce settlements,[5] and so on, indicates that something more is needed. One reaction is to say that the individualistic side of Mill's agenda needs to be pushed further:

> . . . although we are more receptive to the ideal, we are nowhere achieving in practice the kind of equality between the sexes that Mill looks forward to. It will be a good day when *The Subjection of Women* is outdated, but it is not yet.[6]

Another approach is to say that the fault lies precisely in Mill's individualistic conceptual approach: his nineteenth-century liberalism was adequate to the first wave of feminist demands, but now what is needed is the abolition of the sex-bound stereotypes in marriage and that this is impossible within a classical liberal framework, though some who follow this line generously allow that there are aspects of Mill's thought which put it beyond a simple demand for the equal entry of women into male offices and privileges.[7] In the contemporary world, these radically different approaches come into sharp focus in the debate about the contractualization of marriage.

Those who wish to push the liberal individualistic aspects of Mill (and Locke) argue that marriage should become a contractual relationship like any other. At the present time it is clear that marriage is a peculiar form of contract. It is true that marriage has been a contractual relationship since at least the fourteenth century – though usually as a vehicle for family control over property arrangements. And Blackstone declared that 'our law considers marriage in no other light than as a civil contract'.[8] But, following Locke, it is still taken by most liberal theory to be inappropriate to apply to marriage the general principles of liberty and equality that are held to operate in political and legal institutions. In other forms of contract, the substantive decisions about the relationship are left to the parties.[9] But in the marriage contract, no such bargaining is possible and those involved in it will find they cannot vary its terms: agreement about, for example, inter-spousal payments or planning for the termination of marriage will be unenforceable. Not being a written contract, something which the parties could read and on which they could seek legal independent advice, it is difficult to see how those involved could be said genuinely to consent. This is in conflict with the standard liberal legal principle that a contract may be void unless the parties have read it (or had it read to them) before signing, because the free and informed consent of the parties is a necessary condition for the contract's validity.[10] Unlike contracts about property, the marriage contract is easy to make, but comparatively difficult to dissolve. Moreover, there are restrictions on the capacity to form a marriage which are uncharacteristic of other types of contract: the parties must be of the opposite sex, not already married, and not closely related to each other. And until recently,[11] it was held, with marital immunity from rape, that the marriage contract involved the relinquishing of the right to self-protection by one party. It would thus seem that marriage is not a contract in the ordinary sense of the word, but a status-contract: it is a contract grounded in and maintaining status or ascription. Individuals deciding to marry may have the same freedom of choice that governs other contractual relations; but once entered into, the terms and conditions of the contractual relationship are dictated by the State.

THE ARGUMENT FOR CONTRACT MARRIAGE

This state of affairs is widely regarded as unsatisfactory: the marital partners have lost those principles associated with status, while not gaining the freedom associated with contract. The continued existence of the traditional marriage contract tends to treat the family as a unit and thus allows vital decisions about names, domicile, and finance to be made by the husband. One proposed solution is the full contractualization of marriage.[12] In the formulation of one of its leading exponents, the proposal is that:

> . . . the state could leave most substantive marital rights and obligations to be defined privately, but make the legal system available to resolve disputes arising under the privately created 'legislation'.[13]

It is argued, first, that such a reform is in line with the way in which society is moving. There is a growing emphasis on individual happiness and fulfilment in marriage which mirrors the emphasis on pluralism and private choice in society at large. More specifically, recent practice has been to encourage the control of certain divorce terms by private agreement, following mediation and the consent of the parties, a trend which has influenced the proposed Parts I and II of the proposed Family Law Bill. In many areas of the law – tax, criminal, property, tort, and evidence – marital partners are increasingly treated as separate individuals with distinct aims, interests, and intentions. The possibility of the contractual ordering of non-marital relationships, highlighted in the United States of America by the *Marvin* case,[14] is being greatly strengthened.[15] The lessening of the differentiation between married and unmarried couples, the almost complete removal of sex discrimination from family law, and the ease with which marriage can be contracted – all these factors, it is said, mean that the contractualization of marriage would be going with the grain of social development. This is not to suggest that the contract view of marriage is as yet the dominant one – even in the United States, let alone the United Kingdom. But given the recent rise in the popularity of the idea of freedom of contract its application to marriage is worth considering.[16]

As well as being in tune with the *Zeitgeist*, it is also argued that the contractualization of marriage would bring with it clear advantages to the parties. First, it would facilitate communication between them, would identify potential conflicts in advance, encourage the sort of planning that is increasingly necessary in an era of disposable relationships, and even – paradoxically – give couples a greater sense of security. Second, it would allow couples to escape from an outmoded legal tradition through an agreement especially tailored to fit their needs, thus respecting the values of privacy and freedom in the ordering of personal relationships; it would give added authority to an anti-patriarchal and egalitarian stance; and it could be used to confer legitimation and structure on other forms of relationships – homosexual, polygamous, and so on. This accommodation of diversity, together with the clarification of expectations offered by prenuptial contracting, the advance identification of problems, the creation of a normative blue-print by which to resolve conflicts in an ongoing relationship would, it is claimed, offer increased security and predictability and thus enhance the stability of sexual relationships.[17] It is not, of course, being suggested that *all* aspects of such relationships are patient of contractual regulation: even its most ardent supporters concede that contracts to respect, honour, and love would be difficult to specify as to performance and breach.[18] And, clearly, contractualization would be wise to begin at least with the most economic aspects of marriage. Moreover, contracting would not be imposed on couples, but simply be an option that they could choose: a standard package of marital obligations could be laid down by statute with model contracts developed by various groups, publications, or individuals. But the main point insisted on by the proponents of contracting in marriage is that contract here would be filling an increasingly empty space since there has been a withdrawal of public policy and state control over marriage. Furthermore, social institutions such as church, extended family, and community, which used to play an important part in defining and supporting marital norms, have declined in influence. As Mary Ann Glendon writes:

> . . . the lack of firm and fixed ideas about what marriage is and should be is but an aspect of the alienation of modern man. And in this respect the law seems truly to reflect the fact that in modern society more and more is expected of human relationships while at the same time social conditions have rendered these relationships increasingly fragile.[19]

Without the introduction of any easily cognizable private contract, a certain 'lawlessness' will ensue. The state should therefore allow marital partners to define and plan their relationships with the character, content, duration, and structure that they wish and afford legal enforcement to their contractual provisions.

THE ARGUMENT AGAINST CONTRACT MARRIAGE

It is difficult to deny some validity to the above arguments. But a little reflection indicates that there are powerful theoretical, practical, and ethical problems involved. Most of the objections considered by the proponents of the contractualization of marriage are relatively superficial and easily answered. On the psychological level it is not difficult to argue against the view that the contractualization of marriage would undermine its emotional basis, foster negative attitudes, destroy trust, import the morals of the market place, create impoverished consent, and foster instability.[20] But at a more profound level, the demand that marriage should become, in John Stuart Mill's words, a 'true contract'[21] reveals difficulties that are not so easily answered.

Inevitably, there is the whole question of the status of contract. As Durkheim remarked, the scope of contract and its very meaning is controlled by implicit social understandings:

> . . . everything in the contract is not contractual . . . wherever a contract exists, it is submitted to regulation which is the work of society and not that of individuals.[22]

If there are as many types of contract as there are societies, our focus should be on the type of society we want rather than on contract itself. For to concentrate on contract can be seen as constraining the scope of our imagining possible relations with others – a large issue to which I will return in my conclusion. More specifically, there is widespread disagreement over the concept of contract: is it to do with form or substance? Is it subjective or objective? The proposals to contractualize marriage seem to rely on the will theory of contract which dominated nineteenth-century discussion and maintained the view that contract was a private matter. But the realist critique of this theory claims that the public aspects of contract dominate the private aspects. In the words of one of its most trenchant critics:

> . . . the law of contract may be viewed as a subsidiary branch of public law, as a body of rules according to which the sovereign power of the state will be exercised as between the parties to a more or less voluntary transaction.[23]

Or again:

> . . . in enforcing contracts, the government does not merely allow two individuals to do what they have found pleasant in their eyes – enforcement, in fact, puts the machinery of the law in the service of one party against the other. When that is worthwhile and how that should be done are important questions of public policy.[24]

Thus, questions of public policy loom large and public policy limitations on contractual freedom has expanded dramatically in recent decades, including limits to do with good faith and unconscionability. Contract is extremely indeterminate in that the range of intention-based or policy-based arguments makes virtually any decision possible.[25] In a slightly different vein, it is not so long since the imminent 'death' of contract was proclaimed.[26] Developments in, for example, labour law or commercial law mean that contract law is in danger of dissolving into a series of discrete bodies of law which diminish the substance of contract by moving it towards a subsidiary role within a set of relationships which are essentially ones of status involving packages of rights and duties.[27]

Even if we abstract from the above conceptual uncertainties, the proposals for the contractualization of marriage still involve difficulties of a much more empirical nature which cast doubt on whether contract can ever be the royal road to freedom and equality. Indeed, its proponents have not taken to heart the warning of the patriarchal Fitzjames Stephen in his reply to Mill:

> . . . submission and protection are correlative; withdraw the one and the other is lost, and force will assert itself a hundred times more harshly through the law of contract than it ever did through the law of status.[28]

In a society where power is systematically distributed asymmetrically, contract is likely simply to reinforce such an asymmetry. After all, the thoroughly egalitarian principles of such avatars of the liberal contractarian approach as Hobbes and Locke end up by justifying absolutist rule and a landed oligarchy respectively. The problems encountered by women in domestic relationships are inadequate child support, a weak position in the labour market, and male violence. The position of many women in society makes the possession of equal rights virtually meaningless or even counterproductive. Consider the case of a battered wife who, for economic reasons, is disinclined to press criminal charges and have her husband sent to jail and is blamed for allowing herself to be a victim. Although it is only too obvious a point, it cannot be repeated too often that inequality of bargaining power means that the construction and enforcement of contracts are liable to be symptoms of such inequality rather than its remedy. And this repetition is justified when we look at the attitude to such considerations in the work of the proponents of the contractualization of marriage. Weitzman, for example, considers the idea that:

> . . . men who typically have more power, will use that power to impose a contract that is even more unfavourable than traditional legal marriage.[29]

In reply, all she can offer is the:

> assumption that even though men have more power, they nevertheless share an egalitarian ideology and will not think it 'fair' or 'just' to try to impose an exploitative contract on the women they love.[30]

And she refuses to countenance the kind of restrictions on freedom of contract that operate in other areas to protect weaker parties such as consumers or tenants on the grounds that:

> . . . it seems appropriate to assume that the type of overreaching that is profitable in the market sector would be neither profitable nor possible in an intimate contract. This is because parties to an intimate contract are much more likely to begin with norms of fairness and a genuine concern for the welfare of the other party.[31]

And when she does explicitly discuss social policy issues, this whole vital area is dealt with under the rubric of 'concern for the weak-minded woman in love'. It is not weak-mindedness that is the enemy of equality in marriage; it is actual or threatened economic deprivation. Again, Marjorie Schultz, at the very end of her long and detailed article advocating the contractual ordering of marriage, raises the question of 'wrong' choices arising from 'the tendency of private ordering to reflect and reinforce power disparities in existing relationships'.[32] This does indeed go to the heart of the matter. But her reply simply sidesteps the issue:

> . . . any system which attempted to impose standardised rules, even where those rules reflected more modern and desirable goals, like sexual equality, would not sufficiently respect the pluralism and privacy of intimate values nor allow for the planning and self-definition of goals posited by this Article as vital to an effective system of marriage regulation. The essential point is that in intimacy no-one can say what is 'right' except the parties involved.[33]

This is woefully inadequate. For one thing, the 'parties involved' are many. Marriages result in children and their upbringing is, properly, the concern of others: neighbour, society, the State, and so on. Further, at the beginning of her article, Schultz had stressed that such ideas as reciprocity, party capacity, equality, and consent were all necessary conditions for the validity of her proposals.[34] Finally, take Will Kymlicka's sharp article on 'Re-thinking the Family': in discussing what he calls 'reproductive contract', he airily confines to a mere bracket the words 'assuming the parties are fully informed, have equal bargaining power and so on'.[35] Under current social and economic arrangements, such an assumption is utopian. There is indeed scope for utopian thinking (compare Oscar Wilde) but we should be aware that it is precisely that.

A note of realism may be injected into discussion of the contractualization of marriage by the results of liberalization at the other end of the process – divorce. This is, of course, a complex phenomenon, but it is clear that men have been in a better position than women to recover from the effects of a broken marriage. Men's earning power typically increases during marriage, while a woman's remains constant, or decreases. On divorce, according to Weitzman's well-known findings in California, men's income rises by about 70 per cent while women's decreases by about 40 per cent.[36] The much-discussed feminization of 'poverty',[37] or at least the higher visibility of female poverty, is undoubtedly connected with the increase in divorce. The pioneering reforms in Geneva involving no-fault divorces with the parties writing their own settlements, have been much criticized for their inequality of outcome – as have the recent innovations in this country concerning the role of mediators in favouring the stronger party.[38] Even the concepts evolved by contract law to protect the vulnerable, such as duress and unconscionability, would be extremely hard to specify in intimate relations, subject to widely differing interpretations, and thus likely to be ignored by the courts as not following the traditional rubrics.

Even such a clear and incisive thinker as Okin is ambivalent, not to say ambiguous, about the role of contract. As a liberal, she is obviously in favour of contract, but remains in the abstract realm of Rawlsian social contract theory. Although individual contracts might be appropriate for her 'genderless' society, she does not confront the problems involved in present society by the realities of the inequality of bargaining power. These ambiguities are not accidental: as Kymlicka says: 'Liberals believe in freedom of contract within the constraint of justice' and presuppose universal 'equality of opportunity'.[39] But a moment's thought about the kind of measures that would need to be implemented to ensure *real* equality of opportunity shows that all present thought about private contracting should be postponed until that profound transformation of society which is its necessary precondition has been accomplished. Until then, it should be realized that the 'contract marriage' as a means for women to negotiate a mutually advantageous relationship with men is open only to a few well-educated and economically independent women – such as the writers of many of the above pieces. For the majority, fairness is more likely to be improved by current proposals for splitting pensions after divorce or the reforms of the property rights of non-married cohabitants now being considered by the Law Commission along the lines of, for example, the New South Wales De Facto Relationships Act 1984.

CONTRACT MARRIAGE AND THE PUBLIC/PRIVATE DIVIDE

In addition to ignoring what Marx called 'the dull compulsion of economic life', contract marriage can be seen as perpetuating a certain type of thinking about the public/private split in society. In the seventeenth century, politics and the family were discussed together and the similarities between the two were used to justify claims about legitimate authority.[40] With the rise of the 'sentimental' family in the eighteenth and nineteenth centuries, traditional ideas about marriage law have excluded it from the realm of politics either on the Burkean grounds that marriage is too venerable and well-tried an institution to be meddled with by law, or that marriage is (or should be) a religious sacrament and thus outside the realm of political decision, or that marriage is a matter of love and trust and thus inappropriate for legal intervention. Thus what marriage law there is tends to be piecemeal in that:

> English practice . . . has been to refrain from formulating general principles as to how families should be managed. It has preferred to wait until something has gone wrong and then to provide some form of remedy for the aggrieved party.[41]

The functioning family has been seen as a private 'haven' in the face of a public 'heartless' world.[42] The entrance to this haven is policed by public authority and its perimeter guarded, but the interior remains private. This traditional view is obviously open to the criticism, not only that it leaves many women isolated in a sphere divorced from the legal order and effectively sanctions the activities of the men who control their lives, but also that law's absence from the domestic scene indicates that women and their functions are not sufficiently important to merit legal attention.[43] The response of contract marriage to this is to deprivatize marriage as a sphere immune to outside influence by pushing it into that area which is still 'private' in relation to the state (in the sense of 'private' enterprise) but is not private in the sense of a 'haven' against the harsh and only too public realities of this private enterprise. In other words, it aims to reintroduce the kind of homology between state and family which characterized the seventeenth-century approaches such as those of Hobbes and Locke mentioned above. The hope is that just as the private/public market will promote freedom and equality, so will the 'privatization' (in the current economic sense) of the family. This involves collapsing the last two elements in Roberto Unger's liberal Hegelian triptych of a democratic ideal for the state, the private communities of family and friendship, and the contracting world of work and exchange.[44] The family is dissolved into Hegel's civil society. Thus the family is depoliticized and put out of the public (equals political) realm and into an area of individual initiative where the stronger still rule, but by less overt means. Thus, the personal is indeed not political in that it is a matter of private contract with the role of the state confined to enforcing these contracts. On the other hand, it is deeply political, both because of the encouragement of a market model in society is itself a political process and because of the continuous appeal to 'family' values reiterated by those very politicians responsible for introducing the measures that inevitably corrode these values.

But any attempt to appeal from society to the family is hopeless. As Okin remarks:

> . . . law and public opinion have always regulated and influenced what goes on and who dominates whom in the private sphere.[45]

And, more importantly, law and public opinion are themselves social constructs. It is thus not only the case that, given the reality of the inequality of bargaining power, the benefits of contract are likely to prove illusory. The proposals for the contractualization of marriage embody fundamental presuppositions about the nature of the individual and of society. For contractualism in the law is closely connected with the political doctrine of minimal government and the Adam Smithian optimism that some hidden hand will promote universal well-being through the pursuit by each of economic self-interest. The principal remedy in contract is money damages which, in marriage, would be difficult to estimate and often seen as inappropriate. Nevertheless, marriage, on this view, lags behind the market and should be made to catch up.[46] It is true that tort law is beginning to put a monetary value on domestic labour; and that there have been attempts to colonize the whole area of law by economic analysis.[47] Gary Becker, for example, declares that 'the economic approach provides a valuable unified framework for understanding *all* human behaviour' and that:

> . . . likes or unlikes mate when that maximises total household commodity output over all marriages regardless of whether the trait is financial (like wage rates and property income) or genetical (like height and intelligence), or psychological (like aggressiveness and passiveness).[48]

This is indeed to enter the cold world of contract that Francis Fukayama has declared to be the inevitable fate of the modern world.[49] But not only is this a one-dimensional view of society which necessarily lacks any profundity. The idea of universal commodification is self-defeating. It involves the dissolution of elements of marriage into prostitution and, more importantly, the idea that society could consist of contract all the way down is incoherent. As Hegel, the most profound critic of contract theory, has shown, the idea that contracts must be kept presupposes something other than contract, that is, trust and fidelity.[50] Moreover, it seems plausible to suggest that, since the very idea of contract is the product of a male-dominated society, it must, itself, be gendered. Is not the idea of the individual as the owner of property in his person inherently masculine? It is most noticeable that even such a left-liberal proponent of contract theory as Rawls starts with a disembodied self-interested individual – and that such a sympathetic commentator on him as Okin is forced to introduce the ideal of empathy to make sense of Rawls. This is because the very language of contract may well prove to be alienating, given the different patterns of thinking between men and women.[51]

CONCLUSION

The contractualization of marriage is obviously open to practical objections such as that it is likely to lead to a proliferation of domestic litigation and place increased strain on already overburdened courts or, perhaps more importantly, that it fails to make allowance for unforeseen changes in circumstances: although fair at the time they were made, contracts may well not be so later and enforcing such agreements will prove unjust. But such difficulties can, in principle at least, be overcome. More fundamentally, however, the above arguments suggest that mapping marriage on to the market is not the way forward. It is bound up with the concept of rights which is a very double-edged sword where women and the family are concerned.[52] Indeed, this mapping is the sign of a society that is morally bankrupt. How shall one evaluate a society in which everything is a bargain and the very idea of something's being a gift is impossible? Consider Richard Titmuss's classic argument that human blood was not something to be allocated through the market since the very experience of donation fostered altruism and increased our sense of community.[53] Even John Stuart Mill, so ardent an advocate of contract, equal rights, and equal opportunity in marriage, looked beyond these to the hope of friendship in marriage.[54] For all the deconstruction to which it has been subject, marriage remains in most people's eyes something which is sacred, an institution whose resonances are deeply informed by timeless memory and myth.[55] Rather than attempting (fruitlessly) to demolish these resonances, they may help us to find a better way forward. However narrow and restrictive the traditional family may have been and still is, there are aspects of family life – mutuality, reciprocity, and respect for individuality – which can offer a progressive critique of the market. And if, as Okin has powerfully argued, the family is the school of justice, then perhaps it can become more than a mere haven in a heartless world. But it is important here not to revert to outmoded ideas of status. Recent lines of cases in Canada and Australia have given cohabiting women on the break-up of the relationship more than their strict economic contributions to the household would justify.[56] Although undoubtedly fair in these cases, the rationale of the decisions is based on ascribing a status to the women concerned. And it is open to question whether a relationship of status is more egalitarian than one which is based on exchange. But exchange as a monetary bargain can undermine personal identity if it goes as far as considering personal relationships and moral commitments as being monetizeable and therefore alienable.[57] It is difficult, but not impossible, to imagine a society built on ideas of parent-child relationships rather than those of contract.[58] But it is precisely this questioning of some of the presuppositions of our dominant model of society that is necessary. The articulate struggle between *Gemeinschaft* and *Gesellschaft* is more than a century old. It is being conducted today in arguments between communitarians and libertarians.[59] What is important is to realize that the assumptions of *Gesellschaft*, contract, and libertarianism which we have inherited from Hobbes, Locke, and Mill are not inevitable and still less natural. The concept of the individual that they deploy is inextricably male-orientated – as any consideration of their historical genesis demonstrates. The dichotomies private/public, woman/individual, natural/civil, and sex/gender are ripe for deconstruction. Thinking about marriage and family is a good place to start.

NOTES AND REFERENCES

1 F. Olsen, 'The Family and the Market: A Study of Ideology and Legal Reform' (1983) 90 *Harvard Law Rev.* 1518 ff.

2 See, further, K. Thomas, 'The Double Standard' (1959) 20 *J. of the History of Ideas* 341 ff.; U. Vogel, 'Whose Property? The Double Standard of Adultery in Nineteenth Century

Law' in *Regulating Womanhood: Historical Essays on Marriage, Motherhood and Sexuality*, ed. C. Smart (1991).

3 See C. Pateman, *The Sexual Contract* (1988), particularly chs. 4 and 6.

4 See, further, B. Bergmann, *The Economic Emergence of Women* (1986), particularly pp. 263 ff.

5 See L. Weitzman, *The Divorce Revolution* (1985) ch. 10.

6 J. Annas, 'Mill and the Subjection of Women' (1977) 52 *Philosophy* 179.

7 See, for example, M. Shanley, 'Marital Slavery and Friendship: John Stuart Mill's The Subjection of Women' in *Feminist Interpretations and Political Theory*, eds. M. Shanley and C. Pateman (1991).

8 Quoted in C. Pateman, 'The Shame of the Marriage Contract' in *Women's View of the Political World of Men*, ed. J. Stiehm (1984) 77.

9 I am leaving out of the discussion here the idea that marriage is effectively a contract between the couple involved and the state. See, further, M. Shultz, 'Contractual Ordering of Marriage: A New Model for State Policy' (1982) 70 *California Law Rev.* 227 ff.

10 For a strong view that such consent is not possible under present circumstances, see Pateman, op. cit., n. 8, pp. 76 ff.

11 That is, until the House of Lords' decision in *R.*v.*R.* [1991] 3 W.L.R. 767.

12 See, for example, L. Weitzman, *The Marriage Contract: Spouses, Lovers and the Law* (1981); Shultz, op. cit., n. 9.

13 Shultz, id., p. 212.

14 18 Cal. 3d 660.

15 And see, in the United Kingdom, Teresa Gorman's proposed 1991 Bill arguing for the introduction of cohabitation contracts.

16 For other conceptualizations of marriage see K. O'Donovan, *Family Law Matters* (1993) ch. 4. And for a cautious application to the United Kingdom scene of the more robust American approach, see H. Conway, 'Prenuptial Contracts' (1995) 142 *New Law J.* 1290 ff.

17 For an elaboration of these points, see L. Weitzman, 'Marriage Contracts' (1974) 62 *California Law Rev.* 1236 ff.

18 See Shultz, op. cit., n. 9, pp. 260, 323 ff.

19 M.A. Glendon, *State, Law and Family* (1977).

20 See Weitzman, op. cit., n. 12, pp. 239 ff.

21 J.S. Mill, 'The Subjection of Women' in *On Liberty and Other Essays*, ed. J. Gray (1991) 573.

22 E. Durkheim, *The Division of Labour in Society* (1960) 135.

23 M. Cohen, 'The Basis of Contract' (1933) 46 *Harvard Law Rev.* 586.

24 id., p. 562.

25 For a reinforcement of this point by reference to Derridean deconstructive approaches, see C. Dalton, 'An Essay in the Deconstruction of Contract Doctrine' (1985) 94 *Yale Law Rev.* 1007 ff.

26 See G. Gilmore, *The Death of Contract* (1974).

27 See P. Atiyah, *The Rise and Fall of Freedom of Contract* (1979) 716 ff.

28 Quoted in A. Bottomley, 'Women, Family and Property: British Songs of Innocence and Experience' in *Families, Politics and the Law*, eds. M. MacLean and J. Kurczewski (1994) 263.

29 Weitzman, op. cit., n. 12, p. 242.

30 id.

31 id.

32 Shultz, op. cit., n. 9, p. 332.

33 id., p. 333.

34 id., pp. 218 ff.

35 W. Kymlicka, 'Rethinking the Family' (1991) 20 *Philosophy and Public Affairs* 15. The same bracket is repeated on p. 18.

36 Weitzman, op. cit., n. 5, pp. 323 ff.
37 See the original article by D. Pearce, 'The Feminization of Poverty: Women, Work and Welfare' in *Urban and Social Change Rev.*, February 1978, and, for the United Kingdom, C. Glendinning and J. Miller (eds.), *Women and Poverty in Great Britain* (1987) where it is argued that, while poverty is indeed 'female', this is not a new thing and that there is no strong evidence for poverty becoming more gendered, just that in the past no one had thought to consider it in this way.
38 Compare S. Roberts, 'A Blueprint for Family Conciliation?' (1990) 53 *Modern Law Rev.* 88 ff.
39 Kymlicka, op. cit., n. 35, p. 11.
40 See M. Shanley, 'Marriage Contract and Social Contract in Seventeenth Century English Political Thought' (1979) 32 *Western Political Q.*
41 J. Eekelaar, *Family Security and Family Breakdown* (1971) 76.
42 Compare C. Lasch, *Haven in a Heartless World: The Family Besieged* (1977).
43 Compare D. Barker, 'The Regulation of Marriage: Repressive Benevolence' in *Power and the State*, eds. G. Littlejohn et al. (1978) 254 ff.
44 For commentary on similar slippage in a different context, see the last section of G. Moffat, 'Pension Funds: A Fragmentation of Trust Law?' (1993) 56 *Modern Law Rev.* 471 ff.
45 S. Okin, 'Afterword 1992' to *Women in Western Political Thought* (1992) 314.
46 For an elaboration and critique of this view, see F. Olsen, 'The Family and the Market' (1983) 96 *Harvard Law Rev.* 1513 ff.
47 See R. Posner, *The Economic Analysis of Law* (1986).
48 G. Becker, *An Economic Approach to Human Behaviour* (1976) 14 and 217.
49 Compare F. Fukayama, *The End of History and the Last Man* (1992) 325 ff.
50 See G.W.F. Hegel, *Philosophy of Right*, ed. A. Wood (1991) 108 ff.
51 See, further, Bottomley, op. cit., n. 28, p. 273.
52 See C. Smart, *Feminism and the Power of Law* (1989) 144 ff.
53 See R. Titmuss, *The Gift Relationship: From Human Blood to Social Policy* (1971).
54 See Shanley, op. cit., n. 7.
55 See O'Donovan, op. cit., n. 16, pp. 57 ff.
56 See the leading Australian case of *Baumgartner v. Baumgartner* (1987) 164 C.L.R. 137, and the commentary in S. Gardner, 'Rethinking Family Property' (1993) 109 *Law Q. Rev.* 263 ff.
57 See, further, M. Radin, 'Market-Inalienability' (1987) 100 *Harvard Law Rev.* 1849 ff.
58 See, for example, V. Held, 'Non-Contractual Society: A Feminist View' in *Science, Morality and Feminist Theory*, eds. M. Hanen and K. Nielsen (1987).
59 See, for example, S. Avineri, and A. de-Shalit (eds.), *Communitarianism and Individualism* (1992), and S. Mulhall and A. Swift (eds.), *Liberals and Communitarians* (1992).

[17]

THE TIDE IN FAVOUR OF EQUALITY: SAME-SEX MARRIAGE IN CANADA AND ENGLAND AND WALES

WADE K. WRIGHT*

ABSTRACT

The tide in favour of legal equality for gay and lesbian individuals and couples continues to roll forward on both sides of the Atlantic. In Canada, the federal Parliament recently passed legislation (the Civil Marriage Act) (CMA) that extends the legal capacity to marry for civil purposes to same-sex couples throughout the country. This change in the law was driven not by the executive and legislative branches of government but by the courts, interpreting and applying the Canadian Charter of Rights and Freedoms (the Charter). On the other side of the Atlantic, in England and Wales, the Westminster Parliament in 2004 passed legislation (the Civil Partnership Act) (CPA) that will enable same-sex couples to obtain legal recognition of their relationships, and to access most of the legal rights and responsibilities offered to married couples. However, unlike the Canadian legislation, civil marriages between same-sex couples will still not be legally recognized. This article considers whether the English courts will also facilitate the legal recognition of same-sex civil marriage, like their Canadian counterparts. The author concludes that, in light of recent case law, there is an increasingly strong argument that the opposite-sex marriage requirement in England and Wales violates Article 14 (the equality provision) of the European Convention on Human Rights (ECHR), which is incorporated into UK law by the Human Rights Act, 1998. However, the author also concludes that there are a number of reasons to be cautious that a positive result would flow, *at this point*, from a domestic court challenge to the opposite-sex marriage requirement.

INTRODUCTION

In 1997, Ward LJ wrote that 'the tide in favour of equality (for gays and lesbians) rolls relentlessly forward and shows no signs of ebbing'.[1] In

* Associate lawyer, Blake, Cassels and Graydon LLP, Toronto, Canada. This article is an appended version of an article that was written in partial fulfilment of the requirements of the degree of Master of Laws, University of Cambridge, 2004–2005. The author would like to thank Professor Mika Oldham for the assistance provided in its preparation.

Canada, the effect of this 'tide in favour of equality' was recently illustrated by the CMA, which confers on same-sex couples throughout Canada the legal capacity to enter into civil marriage.[2] This dramatic change was driven, not by the executive or legislative branches of government, but rather by the courts, interpreting and applying the Canadian Charter of Rights and Freedoms.[3] Before the CMA was conceived, two provincial appellate courts and one lower court struck down, as unconstitutional, the opposite-sex definition of marriage.[4] The courts ruled that, in restricting marriage to unions between a man and a woman, the definition of marriage discriminated against same-sex couples on the basis of sexual orientation, contrary to section 15(1) of the Charter.[5] In each case, the courts redefined marriage as the union of *two persons* to the exclusion of all others, but the Ontario Court of Appeal was the first court to order that the new definition be given immediate effect.[6] A string of provincial lower courts followed suit, and as a result, by mid-2005, same-sex marriages were legally recognized (due to judicial, not political, action) in nine of thirteen Canadian jurisdictions.[7] The federal government abandoned its defence of the opposite-sex definition of marriage in July 2003, and responded to these court challenges by referring a draft of the CMA to the Supreme Court for its opinion on the proposed legislation's constitutionality. In December 2004, the Supreme Court of Canada provided weighty support to the federal government's proposed legislation when it confirmed that the legislation was consistent with the Charter, answering claims that the legislation impaired, and discriminated on the basis of, religious freedom.[8] In July 2005, the CMA received Royal Assent,[9] giving same-sex marriage legal recognition in the four remaining jurisdictions.[10] In Canada, 'the tide in favour of equality' indeed 'rolls relentlessly forward and shows no signs of ebbing'.

In England and Wales, the effect of this 'tide in favour of equality' was illustrated recently by the Civil Partnership Act, which received Royal Assent on 18 November 2004 and entered into force on 5 December 2005.[11] The CPA allows same-sex couples in England and Wales to obtain legal recognition of their relationships, and upon doing so, to access most of the legal rights and responsibilities offered to married (heterosexual) couples.[12] However, unlike the CMA, the CPA does not give legal recognition to same-sex civil *marriage*, and the Blair government has clearly indicated that '(it) has no plans to allow same-sex couples to marry.'[13] In England and Wales, the 'tide in favour of equality' shows signs of ebbing, at least temporarily.

The purpose of this article is to determine whether the domestic courts, applying the rights 'brought home' by the Human Rights Act, 1998,[14] will drive the legal recognition of same-sex civil marriage, as the courts have done in Canada. This discussion is topical for a number of reasons. First, same-sex civil marriage has recently been recognized, not only in Canada, but also in Belgium, the Netherlands, Spain, and one American jurisdiction (Massachusetts), will soon be recognized in South Africa,[15] and may soon be recognized in Sweden. This trend has stimulated discussion about whether same-sex civil marriage should, and will, be legally recognized in England and Wales. Second, in its first five years,[16] the Human Rights Act 1998 has had a tremendous impact on family law in England and Wales. In light of the success of recent legal challenges in Canada, the question arises whether a similar challenge to the opposite-sex definition of marriage would succeed in England and Wales under the Human Rights Act 1998.[17] Third, the family laws of many countries, including England and Wales, now treat same-sex and opposite-sex couples equally, or almost equally. This raises questions about the justifiability of the separate-'but-equal' regime established by the CPA.

This article is organized in four parts. In Part 1, I outline the law relating to the (non)recognition of same-sex civil marriage in England and Wales and in Canada. In Part 2, the legal developments that facilitated the legal recognition of same-sex civil marriage in Canada are briefly described. In Part 3, I describe the purpose and effect of the CPA, and outline an argument that the bar on same-sex civil marriage in England and Wales violates Article 14 of the ECHR,[18] which is incorporated into English law by the Human Rights Act 1998.[19] Finally, in Part 4, I set out a number of reasons to be cautious about the likely success of such an argument.

Two key assumptions inform the discussion in this paper. First, I am concerned about same-sex *civil* marriage,[20] because, in my view, any attempt to *compel* religious officials to solemnize same-sex marriages would be a violation of religious freedom.[21] Second, I assume that same-sex civil marriage *should* be recognized in England and Wales. The literature supporting the recognition of same-sex civil marriage is vast and comprehensive, and for that reason, I will not re-rehearse the arguments again in this article.[22]

1. THE LAW OF (CIVIL) MARRIAGE AND SAME-SEX COUPLES

In England and Wales, it is clear that a marriage between two people of the same sex will not be legally recognized. In *Hyde* v *Hyde*,[23] marriage was defined, at common law, as the union of 'one man and one woman to the exclusion of all others'.[24] In addition, under section 11(c) of the Matrimonial Causes Act 1973, a marriage between two people who are not respectively male and female is void *ab initio*.[25]

In Canada, the law relating to marriage is complicated by Canada's federal structure.[26] Legislative jurisdiction in Canada is divided between the federal Parliament and the provincial legislatures, and federal and provincial jurisdiction frequently overlaps, particularly in the area of marriage. Under the Constitution Act 1867,[27] the federal Parliament is given jurisdiction over 'marriage and divorce' (section 91(26)), and the provincial legislatures are given jurisdiction over 'the solemnization of marriage in the province' (section 92(12)). According to judicial interpretation of these powers, section 91(26) confers on the federal Parliament legislative competence to regulate the legal capacity to marry ('essential validity'), whereas section 92(12) confers on the provincial legislatures legislative competence to regulate the formal ceremonial or evidentiary requirements ('formal validity').[28] The result is a patchwork of federal and provincial marriage legislation, and couples that want to marry must satisfy both the federal requirements and the local requirements of the province or territory where they intend to marry.

Until recently, the federal Parliament rarely exercised its jurisdiction over 'essential validity',[29] and as a result there was no federal statutory requirement that the parties to a marriage be of the opposite sex.[30] Nevertheless, at common law, a marriage between two persons of the same sex was null and void, marriage being, by definition, the union of one man and one woman. In Canada, the authority for this definition was, as in England and Wales, the formulation in *Hyde* v *Hyde*.[31]

In the last five years, however, two legislative provisions (one provincial and one federal) were enacted that explicitly affirmed the common law definition of marriage. First, in 2000, the Alberta Legislature amended the Alberta Marriage Act [32] to define marriage as 'a marriage between a man and a woman'.[33] Second, also in 2000, the federal Parliament enacted the Modernization of Benefits and Obligations Act (MBOA),[34] legislation that extended most conjugal rights and responsibilities to same-sex couples. The MBOA included a provision affirming that it did not alter the common law definition of marriage.[35]

2. SAME-SEX CIVIL MARRIAGE IN CANADA: THE TIDE OF EQUALITY ROLLS FORWARD

The right to equal treatment without discrimination set out in section 15(1) of the Charter came into force on 17 April 1985.[36] Since that time, section 15(1) has provided a powerful tool for challenging the denial of legal equality to gay and lesbian individuals and couples.[37] Laws that discriminate on the basis of sexual orientation have mostly been struck down as unconstitutional,[38] and legislators have been forced (often begrudgingly) to amend their laws to provide legal equality.[39] In this part, I will describe: a) the structure of a legal challenge under section 15(1) of the Charter; b) the key court decision striking down the opposite-sex marriage requirement; and c) the governmental response to that judicial decision.

A. Section 15(1) Charter Challenges

In *Law* v *Canada*,[40] the Supreme Court outlined three steps to be followed in determining whether section 15(1) has been breached.[41] First, the claimant must prove that there is differential treatment, which is assessed by asking whether the impugned government action draws a distinction on the basis of a personal characteristic (formal inequality), or fails to take account of the claimant's already disadvantaged position within Canadian society (substantive inequality). Second, the claimant must prove that the differential treatment is based on an enumerated or analogous ground of discrimination.[42] Third, the claimant must prove that the differential treatment is *substantively* discriminatory, which is assessed by asking whether the impugned provision impairs human dignity.

Once the claimant proves a violation of section 15(1), the burden shifts to the government to prove that the infringement is 'reasonable' and 'demonstrably justified,' in accordance with section 1 of the Charter. There is a two-part test for determining whether infringements are justified under section 1.[43] First, the government must prove that the objective of the law is pressing and substantial. Second, the government must prove that the means chosen to achieve the objective are reasonable and demonstrably justifiable in a free and democratic society. This requires: the rights violation to be rationally connected to the objective of the law; the impugned law to impair the right minimally; and proportionality between the deleterious effects of the infringement and the benefits of attaining the objective.

B. The Same-Sex Marriage Decisions

In the interests of brevity, I will describe only the decision of the Ontario Court of Appeal in *Halpern* v *Canada (Attorney General)*,[44] which was released in June 2003. This decision remains the most important, because it was the first to reformulate the opposite-sex definition, *and* to order that same-sex couples be permitted to marry, *with immediate effect*. It is important to note, however, that prior to the release of this decision, a total of eight judges, in four courts (including one other provincial appellate court), in two other provinces (BC and Québec) were asked to consider whether the definition of marriage violated the Charter.[45] All eight judges concluded that section 15(1) was infringed, and seven judges, in three of the four courts, concluded that the infringement was unjustifiable under section 1.[46] All three of those courts reformulated the definition of marriage to be the union of two persons to the exclusion of all others, but unlike the Ontario Court of Appeal, those courts suspended the application of the reformulated definition, in order to give the federal government time to respond.

The *Halpern* case arose from two separate applications. The first, brought by eight same-sex couples, was based on discrimination in relation to sexual orientation (section 15(1) of the Charter). The second, brought by the Metropolitan Community Church of Toronto (MCCT), a Christian church that solemnized same-sex unions as marriages,[47] was based on a violation of freedom of religion (section 2(a) of the Charter), and on discrimination in relation to sexual orientation and religion (section 15(1) of the Charter).

At first instance, the two applications were heard (jointly) by a three-judge panel of the Ontario Divisional Court.[48] In a judgment issued in 2002, the Court unanimously dismissed MCCT's application, but allowed the application of the couples, finding that the opposite-sex definition of marriage violated section 15(1), and that the violation could not be justified under section 1. Although the members of the Court were unanimous in declaring the common law opposite-sex definition unconstitutional, they split on the issue of remedy. La Forme J (now of the Ontario Court of Appeal) favoured an immediate reformulation of the common law definition, and an order compelling the issuance of marriage licences. Smith ACJSC felt that Parliament should be permitted 24 months to determine the appropriate remedy, failing which the parties could return to the court to seek a remedy. Blair RSJ took the middle-ground: he felt that Parliament should be given 24 months to amend the common law rule, failing which the remedy proposed by La Forme J would be triggered automatically. Blair RSJ's approach was reflected in the Court's final order.

The disagreement over remedy stemmed from a more fundamental disagreement about the constitutionality of alternative partnership regimes. Although Blair RSJ expressed doubts, unlike LaForme J, both he and Smith ACJSC were unwilling to rule out the possibility that an alternative partnership regime for same-sex couples (like that adopted in England and Wales) would be sufficient to remedy the Charter breach. Accordingly, both felt it appropriate to suspend the declaration, to give the federal executive and Parliament time to consider the feasibility and constitutional implications of such a regime.[49]

The Attorney General of Canada appealed the lower court decision on the equality rights (section 15(1)) violation to the Ontario Court of Appeal. The couples and MCCT cross-appealed the decision on remedy, and MCCT cross-appealed the decision on freedom of religion (section 2(a)) and religious discrimination (section 15(1)). In a *per curiam* decision released in 2003, the Court dismissed the appeal and held unanimously that the common law definition of marriage, limiting marriage to opposite-sex couples, unjustifiably violated the couples' equality rights. In addition, the Court dismissed MCCT's cross-appeal on freedom of religion and religious discrimination.

With respect to section 15(1), the Ontario Court of Appeal held, first, that a distinction was drawn between opposite-sex couples (who were permitted to marry) and same-sex couples (who were not permitted to marry). Second, the Court noted that the distinction was based on an analogous ground of discrimination – sexual orientation. Third, the Court held that the distinction was discriminatory. The Attorney General's argument that opposite-sex and same-sex couples were now afforded equal treatment under the law was rejected. Same-sex couples were often required to cohabit for a specified period of time before they could enjoy the legal benefits that opposite-sex couples enjoy automatically when they marry. In addition, not all of the benefits and obligations available to married couples were extended to opposite-sex and same-sex unmarried couples. Moreover, and most fundamentally, same-sex couples were excluded from a fundamental societal institution – civil marriage.

With respect to section 1, the Ontario Court of Appeal rejected the 'promotion of unassisted procreation' justification, pointing out that, in order to marry, opposite-sex couples were not required to procreate, or to demonstrate an intention or ability to procreate. In addition, the Court rejected the 'uniting the opposite-sexes' justification on the basis that a justification that favours opposite-sex couples demeans the dignity of same-sex couples, by suggesting that uniting two persons of the opposite-sex is more important than uniting two persons of the same-sex. Finally, the Court rejected the 'companionship' objective, on the basis that 'encouraging companionship between only persons of the opposite sex perpetuates the view that persons in same-sex relationships are not equally capable of providing companionship and forming lasting and loving relationships'.[50]

The most important (and most controversial) aspect of the Ontario Court of Appeal's ruling was the remedy. Like all previous courts, the Court reformulated the common law definition of marriage, as the voluntary union of *two persons* to the exclusion of all others. However, unlike all previous courts, it did not suspend the application of its declaration; rather, it ordered that the reformulated definition take effect immediately, and that the authorities begin licensing and registering same-sex civil marriages. As a result, legally recognized same-sex civil marriage ceremonies were being performed in Ontario within hours of the Court's decision.[51] By late 2004, courts in seven other Canadian jurisdictions[52] had issued similar orders, and a lower court in New Brunswick followed suit in June 2005, just two weeks before the CMA received Royal Assent.[53] As a result, even before the CMA was passed, mandating the legal recognition of same-sex marriages throughout Canada, same-sex marriages were already legally recognized in nine of 13 Canadian jurisdictions.[54]

C. Governmental and Legislative Responses

The federal government responded quickly to *Halpern*. Within two days of the release of the Court's decision, the Parliamentary Committee that had been holding hearings on same-sex relationships voted to recommend to the federal executive that it not appeal the decision. Within one week, (then) Prime Minister Jean Chrétien announced that the federal executive would not appeal the Ontario Court of Appeal's decision to the Supreme Court; would draft legislation that would recognize same-sex civil marriage; and would refer that legislation to the Supreme Court for an opinion[55] on its constitutional validity.[56]

D. Draft Legislation

In July 2003, the federal government released the draft legislation promised by Prime Minister Chrétien. The legislation contained just two sections. Following the court decisions, the first section reformulated the definition of marriage, so as to read: '(m)arriage, for civil purposes, is the lawful union of two persons to the exclusion of all others'. In an attempt to allay the concerns of religious celebrants opposed to same-sex marriage, section 2 provided as follows: '(n)othing in this Act affects the freedom of officials of religious groups to refuse to perform marriages that are not in accordance with their religious beliefs'.

E. The Same-Sex Marriage Reference

In July 2003, the federal executive also referred its draft legislation to the Supreme Court of Canada, and asked the Court to address three questions:

(i) Is the Proposed Civil Marriage Bill within the exclusive legislative authority of the federal Parliament?
(ii) If so, is section 1 of the Proposed Civil Marriage Bill, which extends the capacity to marry to persons of the same-sex, consistent with the Charter? and
(iii) Does freedom of religion, as guaranteed by section 2(a) of the Charter, protect religious officials from being compelled, contrary to their religious beliefs, to perform same-sex marriages?[57]

The executive did not ask the Supreme Court to consider two important issues: first, did the bar on same-sex marriage violate section 15(1) of the Charter; and second, was an alternative partnership regime a valid alternative to same-sex civil marriage? In short, it did not ask whether same-sex civil marriage was a constitutional imperative. However, following a change of Prime Minister in late 2003,[58] the federal executive invited the Supreme Court to address this issue, by adding a fourth question:

(iv) Is the opposite-sex requirement for marriage for civil purposes consistent with the Charter?[59]

The Supreme Court of Canada heard arguments from the Attorney General of Canada and an unprecedented 28 interveners, both pro- and anti-same-sex civil marriage, over a two-day period in October 2004. The Supreme Court released its *per curiam* opinion just two months later, in December 2004.[60]

With respect to question (i), the Supreme Court held that section 1 of the Proposed Civil Marriage Bill, extending civil marriage to same-sex couples, fell within the jurisdiction of the federal Parliament. It explicitly rejected the argument that the opposite-sex definition of marriage was constitutionally entrenched, with the result that it could be changed only by amending the Constitution. In the view of the Court, while same-sex marriage would have been unthinkable in 1867 when the Constitution was drafted, the Constitution was a 'living tree' that could (and must) adapt to new social conditions and ideas, including same-sex civil marriages. Question (i) was, therefore, answered affirmatively: the federal Parliament had the jurisdiction to extend civil marriage to same-sex couples.

With respect to question (ii), the Supreme Court held that section 1 of the Proposed Civil Marriage Bill, extending civil marriage to same-sex couples, was consistent with (and indeed flowed from) the Charter. In particular, section 1 was consistent with section 15(1) (right to equality): the mere recognition of the equality rights of one group (same-sex couples) could not, in itself, constitute a violation of the equality rights of another group (opposite-sex married couples and religious groups opposed to same-sex marriage). In addition, section 1 was not inconsistent with section 2(a) (freedom of religion): although the legislation may give rise to conflicts with the right to religious freedom, it would generally be possible to resolve such conflicts within the ambit of the Charter, by way of internal balancing and delineation. Question (ii) was, therefore, also answered affirmatively: section 1 of the Proposed Civil Marriage Bill, extending marriage to same-sex couples, was consistent with the Charter.

With respect to question (iii), the Supreme Court held that the section 2(a) guarantee of religious freedom was broad enough to protect religious officials from being compelled by the state to perform civil or religious same-sex marriages, contrary to their religious beliefs. Question (iii) was, therefore, also answered affirmatively.

Finally, the Supreme Court exercised its rarely used discretion not to answer the fourth question. According to the Court, an answer would serve no purpose, in light of the federal executive's clear intention to introduce legislation to legalize same-sex marriage.

The Supreme Court's decision provided weighty judicial support to the federal executive's proposed legislation. The Court did not explicitly state that the opposite-sex definition of marriage was unconstitutional, but it did drop some 'broad hints that it agreed with the lower court decisions that the opposite-sex requirement for marriage was discriminatory and contrary to the Charter'.[61] In addition, the Court did not explicitly state that a civil union regime would be insufficient to satisfy the Charter, but it did express doubts about the feasibility of such a regime.

F. The Civil Marriage Act

The federal executive pledged to respond 'quickly and decisively' to the Supreme Court's opinion, by introducing legislation that, like the legislation referred to the Court, would extend civil marriage to same-sex couples, while respecting the religious freedom of those who oppose solemnizing same-sex marriages.[62] In February 2005, just two months later, the federal executive tabled the CMA in the House of Commons.

The CMA contains three operative provisions, followed by a series of consequential amendments to federal legislation. As in the original draft legislation, section 2 provides that '(m)arriage, for civil purposes, is the lawful union of two persons to the exclusion of all others', and section 4 provides that '(f)or greater certainty, a marriage is not void or voidable by reason only that the spouses are of the same sex'. Similarly, as in the original draft legislation, section 3 confirms, with slightly different wording, that '(i)t is recognized that officials of religious groups are free to refuse to perform marriages that are not in accordance with their religious beliefs'.

Not surprisingly, the CMA ignited a veritable firestorm of controversy, both in Parliament and in certain segments of Canadian society. Considerable effort was invested in defeating the legislation.[63] However, the CMA passed a 'free vote'[64] in the House of Commons and received Royal Assent on 20 July 2005.

3. SAME-SEX CIVIL MARRIAGE IN ENGLAND AND WALES: THE TIDE OF EQUALITY ROLLS FORWARD?

In this part of the article, I will outline the core features of the Human Rights Act 1998, describe the purpose and effect of the CPA, and sketch an argument that the prohibition on same-sex civil marriage, maintained by the CPA, is inconsistent with Article 14 of the ECHR.

A. The Human Rights Act

The Human Rights Act 1998 incorporates into UK law most of the rights in the ECHR, and authorizes UK courts to enforce these 'Convention rights'. It does so in three ways.[65] First, it obliges courts to decide all cases before them compatibly with 'Convention rights', unless prevented from doing so by primary legislation, or by provisions made under primary legislation which cannot be read compatibly with the ECHR (sections 6(1) to (3)). Second, it places an obligation on courts to interpret existing and future legislation in conformity with the ECHR, wherever possible (section 3). Finally, it requires national courts in the UK to take the case law of the ECtHR and ECmHR into account in all cases, insofar as it is relevant (section 2(1)).

The key feature of the Human Rights Act 1998 is the section 3 obligation 'to read and to give effect to' existing and future legislation, if possible, in conformity with Convention rights. The Human Rights Act 1998 does not permit UK courts to strike down or invalidate the legislation if it is not possible to interpret the legislation in conformity with Convention rights, as Canadian courts are permitted to do under the Charter. Rather, in such cases, Higher Courts (see section 4(5)) can make a 'declaration of incompatibility' (section 4), which has no legal effect on the legislation (section 4(6)), but is intended to put pressure on the UK executive and Parliament to amend the legislation, by invoking a special 'fast-track' amendment procedure (see section 10).

B. *The Civil Partnership Act*

The purpose of the CPA is 'to enable same-sex couples to obtain legal recognition of their relationship by forming a civil partnership', and 'to set out the legal consequences of forming a civil partnership, including the rights and responsibilities of civil partners'.[66] The CPA purports to achieve this goal in three ways. First, it recognizes same-sex relationships for legal purposes, by establishing a new legal relationship (a civil partnership) which is available only to same-sex couples. According to the Joint Committee on Human Rights:

> by granting legal recognition to same-sex relationships, the (Act) was designed both to acknowledge the legitimacy of the claim of those in same-sex relationships to be accorded equal respect with heterosexual relationships . . . , and to remove the practical difficulties faced by same-sex couples as a result of the lack of legal recognition of their relationship.[67]

Second, the CPA sets out the legal requirements to enter into this new legal relationship. Two people will be permitted to register as civil partners provided they are: (a) of the same sex; (b) not already in an existing civil partnership or lawfully married; (c) not within the prohibited degrees of relationship; and (d) both over the age of 16 and have given the relevant consent (section 3(1)). Third, upon entering a civil partnership, the Act extends a host of rights and responsibilities to same-sex couples that are largely (although not entirely) similar to those already available to married couples.

The CPA has received surprisingly little discussion from commentators, and the little that has been written has been almost entirely commendatory. This praise is partly justified. By providing some measure of legal recognition and making various legal rights and obligations available to same-sex couples the CPA clearly improves the law. In addition, the CPA may eventually pave the way for the legal recognition of same-sex civil marriage, by facilitating a cultural shift in social attitudes toward same-sex couples.

There are, however, also serious issues with the CPA. First, it fails to provide *all* of the rights and obligations available to opposite-sex couples to same-sex couples and thus does not provide full legal equality to same-sex couples. For example, under the CPA, registration of a civil partnership occurs independently of any ceremony (section 2(1)); thus, unlike opposite-sex couples who choose to participate in a civil marriage ceremony, same-sex couples cannot register their partnership and participate in a ceremony on the same occasion. Similarly, the CPA provides that a civil partnership is void if entered into by a person who is already in a civil partnership (section 49), but there is no corresponding proposal to ensure that a marriage is void if entered into by a person who is already in a civil partnership. Second, as will be discussed below, creating a separate-'but-equal' legal regime for same-sex couples is unjustifiably discriminatory. One can only hope, therefore, that it is indeed an intermediate step on the road to same-sex civil marriage, rather than a veiled attempt to avoid same-sex civil marriage altogether. Third, the government has used its refusal to extend civil marriage to same-sex couples to justify creating this separate regime.[68] It is, in my view, entirely unacceptable to use one discriminatory policy to justify another discriminatory policy. Fourth, by failing to permit opposite-sex couples to enter civil partnerships, the CPA has contra-posed one form of discrimination (refusal to recognize same-sex civil marriage) with another form of discrimination (refusal to permit opposite-sex couples who do not wish to marry to enter a civil partnership). Finally, as discussed below, the CPA will have unpredictable, but potentially adverse, effects on any challenge under the Human Rights Act 1998 to the legal bar on same-sex civil marriage.

C. A claim under the Human Rights Act 1998 for same-sex civil marriage?

Several commentators have considered the possibility that a legal challenge to the opposite-sex requirement of marriage could now be brought under the Human Rights Act 1998, claiming a violation of all, or some of, Article 8 (right to respect for private and family life), Article 12 (right to marry), and Article 14 (right to equal enjoyment of Convention rights without discrimination) of the ECHR. Overwhelmingly, these commentators have concluded that it is unlikely (even 'unrealistic') that such a claim would be successful (Bailey-Harris, 1999; Probert, 2003; Murphy, 2004),[69] a view that was recently confirmed, albeit implicitly, by the Joint Committee on Human Rights.[70]

In the section that follows this claim will be reconsidered in light of recent legislative initiatives (particularly the CPA) and case law (particularly the decision of the House of Lords in *Ghaidan* v *Mendoza*[71]). The discussion will be focused on a potential violation of Article 14, read together with both Article 8 and Article 12 because, for the reasons outlined below, I believe that such an argument has the greatest chance of success.[72] However, two caveats should first be noted. First, because it is inherently difficult to predict how a court will deal with a sensitive issue like same-sex civil marriage, the following section should not read as the final word on what a court would decide. Second, because of space limitations, the analysis in this section is limited to a discussion of the *key* arguments and issues.

The domestic courts have generally adopted a two-stage approach to claims brought under the Human Rights Act 1998. At the first stage, the courts ask whether a Convention right set out in Schedule 1 of the Human Rights Act 1998 has been infringed and, if so, whether the infringement can be justified. At the second stage, if the infringement cannot be justified, the courts consider whether a Convention-consistent interpretation is possible, under section 3(1), or whether a section 4 declaration of incompatibility should be issued.

D. *Has a Convention Right Been Infringed? Article 14*

The domestic courts will consider five questions in determining whether Article 14 of the ECHR has been infringed.[73]

(i) *Do the facts fall within the ambit of a Convention right?*

Unlike section 15(1) of the Charter, Article 14 does not provide a 'free-standing' prohibition on discrimination; rather, it provides that only the 'the rights and freedoms set forth in (the) Convention' must be secured without discrimination.[74] According to the Strasbourg case law, Article 14 is engaged when the facts of the case fall 'within the ambit' of another Convention right, not merely when Article 14 is actually *breached*.[75] Wintemute (2004) has suggested that there are two ways in which the facts of the case may fall 'within the ambit' of another Convention right. First, 'the *opportunity* (right, freedom, interest, benefit or burden) that is denied to one individual but available to other individuals may fall 'within the ambit' of another Convention right' (the opportunity approach). Second, and this point is more controversial, and not *explicitly* supported in the case law, 'the *ground* on which the decision to deny the opportunity was directly or indirectly based may fall 'within the ambit' of another Convention right' (the ground approach).

There is a strong argument that the decision to deny same-sex couples the opportunity to enter civil marriages falls 'within the ambit' of three different Convention rights. First, it is arguable that this decision affects the private life of same-sex couples, and thus falls within the ambit of the Article 8 right to respect for private life, under both the 'opportunity approach' and the 'ground approach.'

An argument using the opportunity approach would attempt to place the opportunity to marry 'within the ambit' of the right to respect for private life, and might be structured as follows. Although a comprehensive definition of private life has not been provided, the courts have clearly established that the right to respect for private life includes not just the traditional right to be let alone, but also the right to establish and to develop intimate relationships.[76] Civil marriage, while not itself called for by Article 8, nonetheless falls within the ambit of this right, because it promotes ('respects') private life, by fostering the establishment and development of intimate personal relationships. In so doing it demonstrates the state's respect for private life, and thus engages Article 14. Strasbourg and domestic case law does not directly support this argument, but it does support this *type* of argument by implication. In *Petrovic* v *Austria*, for example, the ECtHR held that a parental leave allowance, which was not itself required by Article 8, fell within the ambit of Article 8, because it was intended to promote family life. It did so by enabling one parent to look after the children at home, which demonstrated the state's respect for family life; thus, Article 14 was engaged.[77]

An argument using the 'ground approach' would attempt to place sexual orientation, the ground on which same-sex couples are denied the choice to marry, within the ambit of the right to respect for private life. Unlike the previous argument, Strasbourg[78] and domestic case law[79] does *explicitly* support the argument that sexual orientation falls within the ambit of the right to respect for private life. Wintemute (2004: 371) has drawn on this case law, and has argued that *all* discrimination against a person on the basis of sexual orientation falls 'within the ambit' of Article 8, because whenever a person is forced to choose between a specific opportunity and their sexual orientation, there is a coercive effect on their freedom to make decisions about their sexual orientation, a most intimate aspect of private life.

Second, it is also arguable that the decision to deny same-sex couples the opportunity to enter civil marriages affects the family life of same-sex couples and their children, and thus falls 'within the ambit' of the Article 8 right to respect for family life. It was once fairly clear that the Strasbourg courts would find only opposite-sex couples and their children to have a 'family life,' within the meaning of Article 8.[80] However, in keeping with the interpretation of the ECHR as a 'living instrument,' this restrictive approach to 'family life' appears to be changing.[81] The ECtHR recently recognized, for the first time, that gay and lesbian parents have a 'family life' *with their children*.[82] In addition, the domestic courts (but not the ECtHR) have recently accepted that same-sex couples *themselves* have a 'family life.' In *Ghaidan*, in the context of a claim based on a violation of the Article 8 right to respect for home, Baroness Hale stated, in language reminiscent of the *M. v H.* decision, that 'homosexual relationships can have exactly the same qualities of intimacy, stability, and interdependence (as) heterosexual relationships'.[83] Picking up on this language, the Court of Appeal recently accepted, by a 2–1 majority, that a same-sex couple living together in a stable, committed relationship have a 'family life,' within the ambit of Article 8.[84] Drawing on this decision, a same-sex couple might argue that civil marriage, while not itself called for by Article 8, falls within the ambit of this right, because it promotes ('respects') family life, by contributing to the development of stable, committed family relationships. Same-sex couples living in stable relationships have been held to have a 'family life,' within the meaning of Article 8, and accordingly, the denial of marriage to same-sex couples engages Article 14.

Third, and perhaps most obviously, it is arguable that the decision to deny same-sex couples the opportunity to enter civil marriages falls 'within the ambit' of Article 12. Article 12 guarantees 'men and women of marriageable age . . . the right to marry and found a family'. The right to marry is not absolute, but is subject to relatively far-reaching limitations in domestic law. The state cannot, however, impose limitations that destroy the essence of the right to marry.[85]

There are two possible interpretations of Article 12. First, Article 12 might be interpreted to confer only a right on men to marry women of marriageable age, and vice versa. On this interpretation, only traditional, opposite-sex marriages and families are covered by Article 12. Second, Article 12 might be interpreted to confer a general (non-sex-specific) right on men and women of marriageable age to marry. On this interpretation, same-sex marriages and families are also covered by Article 12. No same-sex couple has yet asserted before the Strasbourg or the domestic courts that the refusal to permit them to marry violates Article 12 (either alone or in conjunction with Article 14). However, until recently, it was nonetheless clear that the ECtHR preferred the first (traditional) interpretation of Article 12. In *Rees* v *UK*, the ECtHR held that 'the right to marry guaranteed by Article 12 refers to traditional marriage between persons of the opposite biological sex'.[86] Accordingly, Article 12 was not infringed where the applicant, a post-operative male to female transsexual, was not permitted to marry a man. The ECtHR confirmed this ruling in two subsequent cases.[87] However, in 2002, in *Goodwin* v *UK*, the ECtHR resiled from this position on facts similar to those in *Rees*.[88] Significantly, the Court did not reference its earlier opposite-sex definition of marriage, and it suggested that the inability of a couple to procreate could no longer be regarded as removing the right to marry.

Much of the language used in *Goodwin* leaves the door open to an interpretation of Article 12 that guarantees the right of opposite-sex *and same-sex* couples to marry. For that reason, a claimant may wish to argue that the opposite-sex marriage requirement breaches Article 12. However, in my view, a claimant would be better served arguing that the opposite-sex requirement breaches Article 14, read together with Article 12, because such an argument would highlight the discriminatory nature of the rule. In making this argument, a claimant would no longer need to prove a *breach* of Article 12, but would still need to demonstrate that same-sex marriage falls 'within the ambit' of Article 12. There is, as noted, textual support for, and signs of increasing judicial willingness to accept, this interpretation.[89] It remains difficult to predict with any certainty whether the domestic courts will ultimately find that same-sex marriages fall 'within the ambit' of Article 12. Thus, it would be prudent for claimants to put forward the other two routes to satisfy the 'within the ambit' principle in order to engage Article 14.

(ii) *Is there a difference in treatment in respect of that right between the complainant and the others put forward for comparison?*

The legal rules establishing the opposite-sex marriage requirement distinguish between unmarried opposite-sex couples and same-sex couples. Unmarried opposite-sex couples have the right to marry if they so choose; same-sex couples have no such right. Thus, there is a clear difference in treatment.

The government may raise two arguments in response. It may argue that the law does not distinguish between opposite-sex and same-sex couples, but merely replicates a distinction that already exists in society. This argument, which is premised on the assumption that marriage 'is a *descriptor* of a unique opposite-sex bond that is common across different times, cultures and religions,' was forcefully rejected by the Ontario Court of Appeal in *Halpern*.[90] According to the Court this type of argument must be rejected for two reasons. First, it makes little difference whether the law creates a distinction or merely replicates a pre-existing distinction. The important point is that the state chose to provide legal recognition to an institution that distinguishes between opposite-sex and same-sex couples, and this choice must now be justified. Second, the reasoning is tautological; it side-steps the entire issue, by presenting the problem (the opposite-sex requirement) as the answer (the opposite-sex requirement exists because marriage 'just is', by definition, heterosexual).[91]

It may also argue that, following the CPA, the law no longer treats opposite-sex and same-sex couples differently. As noted above, the Act establishes a legal partnership regime for same-sex couples and extends to same-sex couples who choose to access the regime, the vast majority of the legal rights and responsibilities available to opposite-sex couples. The government may (almost certainly will) draw on the CPA to argue that there is no relevant difference in treatment, because same-sex couples can now access a regime that is, but for certain minor consequential differences, identical to the regime available to opposite-sex couples (marriage).[92] This argument should also be rejected for two reasons. First, as noted above, same-sex couples that choose to register a civil partnership will not thereby gain access to *all* of the tangible rights and responsibilities available to opposite-sex couples that choose to marry. Thus, differences in treatment remain. Second, and most fundamentally, civil partnerships do not, and cannot, provide the same intangible (symbolic) benefits that flow from marriage, benefits that include social recognition, respect, cachet and honour, all of which attach to marriage, but not (at least in equal measure) to civil partnerships. Thus, again, differences in treatment remain.

Appellate courts in both Canada and the US have noted this distinction between the tangible and intangible benefits of marriage in rejecting arguments that differences in treatment no longer remain after same-sex couples are accorded all (or most) of the tangible rights and responsibilities available to opposite-sex couples. In Canada, the symbolic (as opposed to economic) value of being treated as a couple was emphasized by L'Heureux-Dubé J (dissenting):

> (o)fficial state recognition of the legitimacy and acceptance in society of a particular type of status or relationship may be of greater value and importance to those affected than any pecuniary gain flowing from that recognition.[93]

In *Halpern*, the Ontario Court of Appeal drew on this distinction, in rejecting the federal government's argument that it no longer distinguished between opposite-sex and same-sex couples, even though same-sex couples were not permitted to marry, because same-sex couples enjoyed virtually all of the federal benefits that flow from marriage. According to the Court, 'the benefits of marriage cannot be viewed in purely economic terms. The societal significance surrounding *the institution of marriage* cannot be overemphasised.'[94] Similarly, in the US, the majority of the Supreme Judicial Court of Massachusetts recently noted the intangible benefits flowing from marriage in support of their decision to reject the Massachusetts Senate's proposal to prohibit same-sex couples from marrying, while allowing them to form civil unions, with *all* of the rights and responsibilities of marriage.[95] There is, therefore, a strong argument, supported by weighty judicial authority, that notwithstanding the CPA, the law in England and Wales still treats opposite-sex and same-sex couples differently, by refusing to permit same-sex couples to marry.[96]

(iii) *Is the chosen comparator group in an analogous or relevantly similar situation to the complainant group?*

This requirement raises two separate questions. The first asks: what is the 'chosen comparator' group? The proper comparator group here is 'unmarried opposite-sex couples.' Unmarried opposite-sex couples (who can legally marry if they so choose) should be compared with 'same-sex couples' (who cannot legally marry even if they so choose).

The second question asks whether the chosen comparator group (unmarried opposite-sex couples) and the complainant group (same-sex couples) are in an 'analogous or relevantly similar situation.' There is weighty authority, from both the Strasbourg and domestic courts, supporting the proposition that unmarried opposite-sex and same-sex couples are similarly situated. In *Karner* v *Austria*, the ECtHR recently accepted that same-sex couples and unmarried opposite-sex couples are similarly situated, and held that gay couples are equally capable of being 'life companions' for the purposes of succession to a statutory tenancy.[97] The House of Lords followed *Karner* in *Ghaidan*, and held that unmarried opposite-sex and same-sex couples are equally capable of 'living together as husband and wife,' also for the purposes of succession to a statutory tenancy. In that case, Lord Nicholls noted that 'a homosexual couple, as much as a heterosexual couple, share each other's life and make their home together. They have an equivalent relationship'.[98]

It is essential that a complainant compare the position of unmarried opposite-sex couples (who have the choice to marry) and same-sex couples (who do not), because it is clear that married and unmarried couples (whether same-sex or opposite-sex) are not generally seen to be in a comparable position. The ECtHR has confirmed this position in several cases,[99] and in *Ghaidan*, the House of Lords expressly acknowledged that the result might have been different if the legislation had given rights only to married partners.[100]

(iv) *Is the difference in treatment based on one of the grounds proscribed, whether expressly or by inference, in Article 14?*

The difference in treatment here is based on sexual orientation: opposite-sex couples can marry while same-sex couples cannot marry, because of their sexual orientation. As with section 15(1) of the Charter, discrimination on the basis of sexual orientation is not expressly proscribed in Article 14. However, the ECtHR[101] and the domestic courts[102] have clearly held that discrimination on the basis of sexual orientation is not permissible under Article 14, and that where sexual orientation is the ground for differential treatment, particularly convincing and weighty reasons will be required to justify that different treatment.

(v) *Does the difference in treatment have 'a reasonable and objective justification'?*

The domestic courts will consider the following questions when determining whether a difference in treatment has 'a reasonable and objective justification':

(a) Does the difference in treatment have a legitimate aim (or aims) that is sufficiently important to justify limiting a fundamental right?, and
(b) If so, (a) are the measures designed to meet the aim rationally connected to it?; and (b) are the means used to impair the right no more than is necessary to accomplish the aim?[103]

According to both Strasbourg and domestic precedents, it is not the measure itself, but rather the difference in treatment (the exclusion) that must be justified.[104] Thus, in this case, what must be justified is not the objective of providing legal recognition to civil marriage, but rather the objective of excluding same-sex couples from civil marriage.

It is difficult to predict with any degree of certainty the objectives the government would advance to justify its decision to deny civil marriage to same-sex couples. However, in light of the arguments made by the Canadian government in the Canadian cases and the statements made by UK government representatives during the deliberations about the CPA, it seems likely that the government would posit one or more of these three objectives:

(i) preventing offence to those who hold, for religious reasons, a traditional, opposite-sex view of marriage (the offence justification) (Herring, 48);
(ii) encouraging procreation (the procreation justification); and
(iii) protecting the traditional, opposite-sex family, in accordance with the government's policy that marriage is the best framework for stable family relationships for opposite-sex couples (the traditional family justification).

The first of these justifications, the offence justification, would be the easiest to answer. There is ample authority rejecting the proposition that preventing offence to others is sufficiently important to justify an infringement of a fundamental right. For example, in *Dudgeon*, the ECtHR wrote as follows about a criminal statute criminalizing private male/male sexual activities:

> although members of the public . . . may be *shocked, offended or disturbed* by the commission . . . of private homosexual acts, this cannot on its own warrant the application of penal sanctions[105] [emphasis added].

The ECtHR recently extended the application of this idea in *Smith* and *Lustig-Prean*, the 'gays in the military' cases.[106] In both cases, the

ECtHR rejected the UK government's argument that the attitude of others (the heterosexual soldiers) about homosexuality was sufficiently important to justify limiting a fundamental right (Article 8). The reasoning in these cases applies equally to same-sex marriage. Hence, the 'offence to others' justification would likely fall at the first stage of the analysis (legitimate aim), on the basis that the aim (preventing offence to those who oppose same-sex marriage for religious reasons) is not sufficient to justify limiting a fundamental right (Article 14).

One potential complicating factor is section 13(1) of the Human Rights Act 1998, which requires a court to have particular regard to the importance of the Convention right to freedom of religion (Article 9) when determining any question which might affect the exercise of the right by a religious organization. Section 13(1) might be used to ground an argument that the opposite-sex marriage requirement is justified because recognition of same-sex marriage would engage the right to religious freedom of those who oppose same-sex marriage for religious reasons. In my view, this argument should be rejected for three reasons. First, as noted above, the argument here is about *civil* marriage, not religious marriage; religious organizations and officials would not, and almost certainly could not, be compelled to marry same-sex couples, and thus the right to religious freedom is not engaged. Second, by its very wording, the section applies only where a court's determination might affect the exercise of the right to religious freedom of a 'religious organization'; it does not apply to individual complaints that freedom of religion is affected. Finally, as the Supreme Court of Canada recently noted in the Same-Sex Marriage Reference, even if the right is engaged, it is difficult to understand how the mere recognition of the equality rights of one group can violate the rights of another.[107]

The second justification, the procreation justification, also arguably fails at the first stage of the analysis (legitimate aim), not because encouraging procreation is not a laudable goal, but because it is not now (if it ever was) the primary objective of 'maintaining marriage as an exclusively heterosexual institution'.[108] This justification was canvassed thoroughly, and rejected, by all (but one, later overruled) of the Canadian courts in the same-sex marriage cases. The responses given boil down to the following four points:

(i) There is a dearth of judicial authority establishing that procreation is the primary objective of marriage or the opposite-sex marriage requirement; indeed, most judicial authority demonstrates that procreation is *not* an essential element of marriage;[109]

(ii) The state does not require opposite-sex couples to procreate, or to demonstrate an intention or ability to procreate, in order to marry; this belies the assertion that procreation is the primary objective of the opposite-sex marriage requirement;[110]

(iii) Same-sex couples can and do have children, by adoption, surrogacy arrangements and donor insemination; this also belies the assertion that procreation is the primary objective of the *opposite-sex* marriage requirement;[111]

(iv) There is simply no evidence that opposite-sex couples would have children less, or not at all, if same-sex couples were provided equal access to civil marriage.[112]

There is ample judicial authority to suggest that domestic courts in England and Wales would accept these arguments. First, in *Goodwin*,[113] the ECtHR held that the inability of a transsexual to procreate could no longer justify the denial of the right to marry. This argument would likely now apply to same-sex couples as well.

Second, in 1948, in *Baxter* v *Baxter*, the House of Lords denied that 'procreation is the principal end of marriage'.[114] More recently, in *Bellinger* v *Bellinger*, Lord Nicholls noted that although 'the Church of England Book of Common Prayer of 1662 declared that the first cause for which matrimony was ordained was "the procreation of children", . . . for a long time now the emphasis has been different'.[115] In light of these and other similar statements, there is a strong argument that procreation is not *now* (if indeed it ever was) the primary objective of the opposite-sex marriage requirement.

Third, judicial notice has also been taken of the fact that opposite-sex couples are not required to procreate, or to demonstrate an intention or ability to procreate, in order to marry. For example, Baroness Hale, writing extra-judicially, has stated that '(procreation) has never been the sole purpose of marriage in English law: if it had been so, the inability to bear children would have been a disqualification'.[116]

Fourth, there is also evidence that judges are increasingly unwilling to treat the ability to procreate *naturally* as a justification for differential treatment. For example, in *Ghaidan*, Baroness Hale stated:

> The relevant difference which has been urged upon us is that a heterosexual couple may have children together whereas a homosexual couple cannot. But this too cannot be a relevant difference . . . Both married and unmarried couples, both homosexual and heterosexual, may bring up children together. One or both may have children from another relationship: this is not at all uncommon in lesbian relationships and the court may grant them a shared residence order so that they may share parental responsibility. A lesbian couple may have children by donor insemination who are brought up as the children of them both: it is not uncommon for each of them to bear a child in this way. A gay or lesbian couple may foster other people's children. When the relevant sections of the Adoption and Children Act 2002 are brought into force, they will be able to adopt: this means that they will indeed have a child together in the eyes of the law.[117]

Finally, there is evidence that English judges are no longer willing to accept that treating same-sex and opposite-sex couples equally will have a detrimental effect on opposite-sex couples. For example, in *Ghaidan*, Baroness Hale noted with approval Buxton LJ's suggestion that 'it is difficult to see how heterosexuals will be encouraged to form and maintain such marriage-like relationships by the knowledge that the equivalent benefit is being denied to homosexuals'.[118] Taken together, these statements signal strongly that, if asked, the courts will reject that the procreation justification is sufficiently important to justify overriding Article 14.[119]

The final justification, the 'traditional family justification', would be the most difficult to answer, and would, no doubt for that reason, likely be the focus of the government's response to a challenge to the opposite-sex marriage requirement. Unlike the previous two justifications, it is fairly clear that the objective of protecting the traditional, opposite-sex family would be held to be sufficiently important to justify a difference in treatment on the basis of sexual orientation. The ECtHR recently affirmed its earlier statements to this effect in *Karner*, in a passage that was subsequently adopted by the House of Lords in *Ghaidan*.[120]

However, there is still a strong argument that the justification should fall at the final stage of the analysis – minimal impairment or necessity. In *Karner*, after indicating that protection of the traditional family is capable, in principle, of being a legitimate aim, the ECtHR emphasized, in a passage later cited by the House of Lords, that it still must be shown, with 'particularly serious reasons', that it was *necessary* to exclude same-sex partners in order to achieve that aim. In the absence of any such justification, Article 14 would be violated.[121] In the context of a claim about same-sex marriage, the government would be required to demonstrate that it is necessary to bar same-sex couples from marrying in order to protect the traditional family. In my view, there are (at least) four answers to the claim that the opposite-sex marriage requirement is necessary to protect the traditional family.

First, it is difficult to follow the logic of the government's claim that 'marriage is the surest foundation for opposite-sex couples (and their) children',[122] but not, by implication, for same-sex couples and their children. What possible reason is there to justify the proposition that marriage is appropriate for opposite-sex couples and their children, but not for same-sex couples and their children? In light of the government's recent decision to extend full parental and adoption rights to same-sex parents, surely it would not attempt to argue that same-sex parents are bad parents. The only answer would seem to be that permitting same-sex couples to marry would somehow have a harmful impact on *opposite*-sex married couples and their children.

Second, following from the first point, courts elsewhere that have considered this issue recently have rejected the claim that recognizing same-sex relationships in general, and same-sex marriage in particular, will have a detrimental impact on opposite-sex married couples and their children. This issue has been canvassed extensively in Canada. In *Egan*, Iacobucci J. wrote, 'it eludes me how according same-sex couples the benefits flowing to opposite-sex couples in any way inhibits, dissuades or impedes the formation of heterosexual unions. Where is the threat?'[123] This view was shared by the Ontario Court of Appeal in *Halpern*. Before the Court, the Attorney General of Canada argued that changing the definition of marriage would destabilize marriage and the family. Unable to provide uncontradicted evidence to support this claim, the Attorney General pointed to the alleged unforeseen destabilizing influence of divorce on the family as proof that tampering with another of the core features of marriage, its opposite-sex nature, may also have unexpected and unintended results. The Court rejected this proposition 'as speculative,' and wrote that '(a)llowing same-sex couples to marry does not result in a corresponding deprivation to opposite-sex couples'.[124] Earlier, the Court also indicated that '(h)eterosexual married couples do not stop having or raising children because same-sex couples are permitted to marry'.[125] This issue has also been canvassed in the US, most recently, by the Supreme Judicial Court of Massachusetts. In response to the government's claim 'that broadening civil marriage to include same-sex couples (would) . . . destroy the institution of marriage', the majority of the Court wrote, 'recognizing the right of an individual to marry a person of the same sex will not diminish the validity or dignity of opposite-sex marriage'.[126] Although the issue has yet to be addressed by the English courts in the context of marriage, there is some evidence that judges here are also wary of the claim that recognizing same-sex relationships will harm opposite-sex couples and their children (see *Ghaidan*, per Baroness Hale, cited above).[127]

Third, contrary to the view that permitting same-sex couples to marry would have a detrimental impact on opposite-sex married couples and their children, there is every reason to believe that extending marriage would have a positive, not a negative impact. This point was accepted by the Canadian courts and by the majority of the Supreme Judicial Court of Massachusetts, which wrote as follows: '(r)ecognizing the right of an individual to marry a person of the same sex will not diminish the validity or dignity of opposite-sex marriage, . . . (i)f anything, (it) reinforces the importance of marriage to individuals and communities'.[128]

Finally, even if a court accepts the argument that barring same-sex couples from marrying is somehow necessary to protect traditional opposite-sex families, the impairment of Article 14 is arguably not minimal. Although the CPA confers most legal rights and responsibilities on same-sex couples that choose to register a civil partnership, it does not (and cannot) confer the same *intangible* (symbolic) benefits on same-sex couples that marriage confers on opposite-sex couples. As noted by the Supreme Judicial Court of Massachusetts, in the context of a discussion of a bill that was almost identical to the CPA:

> The dissimilitude between the terms 'civil marriage' and 'civil union' is not innocuous; it is a considered choice of language that reflects a demonstrable assigning of same-sex . . . couples to second-class status. . . . no amount of tinkering will eradicate (the) stain. The bill will have the effect of maintaining and fostering a stigma of exclusion . . . It would deny to same-sex 'spouses' a status that is specially recognized in society and has significant social and other advantages. . . . (This amounts to) invidious discrimination, no matter how well intentioned.[129]

Indeed, by reducing the legal distinction between opposite-sex and same-sex couples, the CPA arguably actually accentuates, rather than minimizes, the impairment of Article 14 arising from the opposite-sex marriage requirement (Pickel, 2002: 52).

In light of the foregoing, there is a strong argument that, notwithstanding the changes introduced by the CPA, the refusal to permit same-sex couples to marry unjustifiably violates Article 14 read together with Article 8 and Article 12.

E. Interpretation (Section 3) or Declaration of Incompatibility (Section 4)?

If a domestic court finds that the refusal to permit same-sex couples to marry violates the ECHR, the court is almost certain to issue a declaration of incompatibility, rather than attempting to give the applicable common law rule (in *Hyde*) and statutory rule (in section 11(c) of the Matrimonial Causes Act) a Convention-consistent interpretation. In *Bellinger* v *Bellinger*, the House of Lords found that it was not 'possible' to interpret the word 'female' in section 11(c) of the Matrimonial Causes Act to include a post-operative male-to-female transsexual, because 'that would necessitate giving the words 'male' and 'female' a novel, extended meaning,' and 'would represent a major change in the law, having far-reaching ramifications'.[130] The courts would almost certainly apply similar reasoning to the question of same-sex marriage, particularly because such an interpretation would, in essence, negate the express words of the statutory and common law rules. In the result, therefore, the court would likely issue a section 4 declaration of incompatibility and the determination of how to respond would be left to Parliament.

4. SAME-SEX CIVIL MARRIAGE IN ENGLAND AND WALES: THE FORWARD ROLL OF THE TIDE OF EQUALITY: A CAUTIONARY NOTE

Although there is a strong argument that the opposite-sex marriage requirement violates Article 14 of the ECHR, read together with Article 8 and 12, there are, in my view, several reasons to be cautious (perhaps even sceptical) that a positive result would flow from a legal challenge at this time.

The first reason for caution stems from the structure of Article 14. As noted above, unlike the equality guarantee in the Charter, Article 14 is not independent; it applies only where the facts of the case fall 'within the ambit' of one or more other Convention rights. Unfortunately, difficulties arise when attempting to fit a claim relating to civil marriage for same-sex couples 'within the ambit' of each of the Convention rights discussed above.

There are two difficulties with attempting to fit such a claim 'within the ambit' of the right to respect for private life (Article 8). First, as Murphy (2004) has noted, there is 'something ironic about framing a claim for formal, public recognition of a relationship in terms of privacy'. The act of marriage is, at once, both intensely private and inherently public.[131] In England and Wales, the public aspect of marriage is reflected in a number of legal requirements, most notably, in the legal requirement that the marriage ceremony take place 'with open doors'.[132] A court, drawing on this type of distinction, may find that the opposite-sex marriage requirement does not fall within the ambit of the Article 8 right to respect for private life, because the private aspect of the relationship has not been affected (eg same-sex couples have not been denied the right to live together, to operate as a couple in society, or indeed to celebrate a commitment ceremony),[133] but what has been affected is the public aspect of the relationship (eg same-sex couples have been denied legal recognition of their commitment). Second, when faced with claims from same-sex couples, as opposed to gay or lesbian individuals, the ECtHR has preferred to deal with such claims under the home or family life branch, not the private life branch of Article 8 (Murphy, 2004).

There are also difficulties with attempting to fit a claim for same-sex civil marriage 'within the ambit' of the right to respect for family life (Article 8). First, until recently, 'family life' had been held to include only opposite-sex couples and their children. Although, as noted above, courts have recently accepted that same-sex couples have a 'family life' with their children[134] and each other,[135] the case law in this area is new and limited and should, for that reason, be used cautiously, and with the knowledge that there is earlier case law to the contrary. Second, the ECtHR has held that the right to respect for family life presupposes the existence of a family and does not safeguard the desire to found a family.[136] The application of this idea to marriage is unclear, particularly in those cases where the couple has not established family ties, for example, by living together, sharing household expenses, and so on.

There are also difficulties with attempting to fit a claim for same-sex civil marriage 'within the ambit' of the right to marry (Article 12).

First, there is case law clearly indicating that the right to marry refers to the traditional marriage between two persons of the opposite sex (eg *Rees*). Although there was a tangible softening in this position in *Goodwin*, no court, in Strasbourg or the UK, has yet explicitly departed from the existing case law, by holding that Article 12 also confers a right to marry on same-sex couples. Second, while there are statements to the contrary, most notably from Baroness Hale, who has referred to same-sex relationships as 'marriage-like', there is also evidence of some judicial sympathy, domestically, for the traditional, opposite-sex view of marriage.[137] For example, in *Ghaidan*, Lord Millett (dissenting) referred to the civil partnership regime as 'a rational and sensible scheme which does not involve pretending that couples of the same-sex can marry'.[138]

The second reason for caution is that, unlike in Canada, where courts were able to draw on almost twenty years of section 15(1) jurisprudence dealing with sexual orientation discrimination, English case law dealing with sexual orientation discrimination is still in the developmental stage. Thus, while it was fairly clear that Canadian courts would find the opposite-sex marriage requirement to violate section 15(1) of the Charter, it is difficult to predict how courts in England and Wales would respond to such a legal challenge.

Similarly, whereas the interpretation of section 15(1) itself was fairly well settled, there are at least two issues with the interpretation of Article 14. First, it is unclear when the facts of the case can properly be said to fall 'within the ambit' of Article 14.[139] Second, it is unclear when the chosen comparator group is truly in an 'analogous or relevantly similar situation'.[140] It is difficult to predict how these two issues would play out in a case challenging the opposite-sex marriage requirement. If a court finds that the facts of the case merely need a 'tenuous link'[141] with another Convention right to engage Article 14, there is a particularly strong argument that the opposite-sex marriage requirement engages, at worst, Article 8, and at best, both Article 8 and Article 12. However, if a court applies a more stringent standard, the chances of success are far less certain. Similarly, if a court agrees that the proper comparison is between opposite-sex unmarried couples and same-sex couples (as I have argued above, with support from the House of Lords), the chances of success are significantly increased. However, if a court feels that the proper comparison is between gay couples and lesbian couples, as it has in the past,[142] the chances of success are significantly reduced, because neither gay nor lesbian couples can marry, and thus there would be no difference in treatment.

The third reason for caution is the CPA, which may negatively impact a legal challenge to the opposite-sex marriage requirement in at least three ways. First, as noted above, a court may be convinced (improperly, as I have argued) that there is no longer any relevant difference in treatment between opposite-sex and same-sex couples, because legal recognition has been extended to opposite-sex relationships (through marriage) *and* same-sex relationships (through civil partnerships), and both now enjoy virtually identical legal rights and responsibilities. Second, as noted above, even if a court finds that Article 14 has been infringed, it may find the infringement to be justified (incorrectly, as I have argued), because the Act appears to minimize the distinctions drawn between opposite-sex and same-sex couples. Finally, the Act is likely to influence the general, overall tenor of any challenge. There is an argument that the issue of same-sex civil marriage is trivial, particularly now that all that is withheld is the 'marriage label'. This view is reflected in the opinion of one of the dissenting judges in the Massachusetts case, who questioned 'what is in a name?'[143] There is also a (stronger, in my view) argument that the issue is not now, nor was it ever, trivial. This contrary view is reflected in the opinion of the majority in the Massachusetts cases: 'The denomination of this difference . . . as merely a "squabble over the name to be used" so clearly misses the point that further discussion appears to be useless'.[144] However, the view taken on this key issue, an issue brought into stark relief by the CPA, is likely to have a profound effect on the outcome of any future challenge to the opposite-sex marriage requirement.

The fourth reason for caution is that a court asked to deal with this issue may decide to defer (or give a 'discretionary area of judgment'[145]) to Parliament, on the basis that the decision to extend civil marriage to same-sex couples is an important and controversial policy decision that should be left to Parliament, not the courts. The question of the extent to which judges should defer to Parliament when deciding cases under the Human Rights Act, 1998 has been controversial, both in academic[146] and judicial circles.[147] It is difficult to predict how this controversy would play out in a challenge to the opposite-sex marriage requirement (although it is fairly certain that the notion of deference would be invoked, if at all, at the justification (proportionality) and/or remedy (sections 3(1) or 4) stage of the analysis). On the one hand, a judge may be convinced to defer to Parliament, as were the dissenting judges in the Massachusetts case, because 'the issue presented is a profound one, deeply rooted in social policy, that must, for now, be the subject of legislative, not judicial action'.[148] In support of such a conclusion, a judge may cite the fact that an Act of Parliament is involved; that the issue appears to require a balance to be struck between equality (for same-sex couples) and freedom of religion (for religious opponents); that only Parliament has the institutional competence to examine the complicated and delicate issues surrounding the regulation of the family; and that same-sex civil marriage has been recently considered, but rejected, by Parliament, in the deliberations surrounding the CPA.[149] On the other hand, a judge may be convinced that deference is inappropriate, as were the judges in the Canadian cases and the majority of the judges in the Massachusetts case, because what is at stake is the right to non-discrimination, an issue which lies squarely within the constitutional responsibility of the judiciary.[150]

In the recent domestic case law, there is evidence that both approaches have been applied in cases touching on sexual orientation discrimination. There is evidence of the first approach (greater deference) in *Bellinger*, where Lord Hope, for example, felt that it was inappropriate to apply a section 3(1) interpretation, because 'problems of great complexity would be involved if recognition were to be given to same-sex marriages. (Such changes) must be left to Parliament'.[151] Conversely, there is also evidence of the second approach (less deference) in *Ghaidan*, where Lord Nicholls, for example, rejected the argument that the House of Lords should defer to Parliament in determining whether a violation of Article 14 was justified. On his view, deference would be inappropriate, even though the case dealt with housing policy, an area where Parliament was required to balance competing social and economic policy objectives, because discrimination was an issue that required 'intense scrutiny' from the courts.[152] Certainly, it is possible to distinguish these cases, on the basis that deference was (arguably) appropriate in *Bellinger*, because the House of Lords was merely being asked to defer to Parliament's assessment of the suitable remedy, after finding an inconsistency with Article 14, but was inappropriate in *Ghaidan*, because the House of Lords was being asked to refrain altogether from finding an unjustified violation of Article 14. However, the key point for the purposes of this article is that it is difficult to predict how the notion of deference would impact a challenge to the opposite-sex marriage requirement, and for that reason, it is another reason to be cautious about the likelihood of a successful result.

The fifth (and final) reason for caution is that, even if a court finds the opposite-sex marriage requirement to be inconsistent with Article 14 and issues a declaration of incompatibility to that effect, neither Parliament nor the executive has a legal obligation under the Human Rights Act 1998 to remedy the inconsistency. In England and Wales, the government can reply to a declaration of incompatibility by:

(a) introducing remedial legislation;
(b) ignoring the declaration of incompatibility; or
(c) appealing the decision, if appropriate.

If the government decided to ignore the decision (situation b), the impugned legislative provision would still be enforced, in accordance with section 4(6) of the Human Rights Act 1998, even though that provision would have been found to violate, unjustifiably, a Convention right. If the government decided to introduce remedial legislation (situation a), it is still possible that the legislative provision that was found to violate a Convention right would be left in force, if the remedial legislation failed to receive the necessary parliamentary support at any stage of the legislative process set out in section 10 of the Human Rights Act 1998. Unfortunately, in light of the inevitable controversy surrounding same-sex marriage, there is a very real possibility that situation (a) or (b) might occur, were a court to issue a declaration of invalidity. As noted, if either situation occurred, the status quo (denial of civil marriage rights to same-sex couples) would be maintained. In Canada, the result would be different: the offending legislation would be remedied by the court, and a new Charter–consistent status quo (extension of civil marriage to same-sex couples) would result.

5. CONCLUSION

The tide of legal equality for gay and lesbian individuals and couples continues to roll relentlessly forward on both sides of the Atlantic. In Canada, the federal Parliament recently passed legislation (the CMA) that extends legal capacity to marry for civil purposes to same-sex couples throughout the country. This change in the law was driven, not by the executive and legislative branches of government, but by the courts, interpreting and applying the Charter. On the other side of the Atlantic, in England and Wales, the Westminster Parliament recently passed legislation (the CPA) that will enable same-sex couples to obtain legal recognition of their relationships, and to access most of the legal rights and responsibilities offered to married couples. However, unlike in Canada, civil marriages between same-sex couples will still not be legally recognized.

The question that has been considered in this paper is whether, in light of the success of the recent court challenges in Canada, the courts in England and Wales, interpreting and applying the rights 'brought home' by the Human Rights Act 1998 will also facilitate the legal recognition of same-sex civil marriage. I conclude that there is an increasingly strong argument that the opposite-sex marriage requirement violates Article 14 read together with Article 8 and Article 12. However, there are also a number of reasons to be cautious that a positive result would flow, *at this point,* from a domestic court challenge to the opposite-sex marriage requirement. Due to the large margin of appreciation given to Member States and the lack of a sufficient European consensus about same-sex civil marriage, the result is unlikely to be different in Strasbourg in the immediate future.

However, while the tide of equality may have ebbed in England and Wales, there are strong signs that the ebb is merely temporary. First, as noted at the outset, same-sex couples are now permitted to marry in Belgium, Canada, the Netherlands, Spain and one American jurisdiction

(Massachusetts) and will soon be permitted to marry in South Africa, and Sweden is currently considering legislation that would extend civil marriage to same-sex couples. This ever-increasing acceptance of civil marriage for same-sex couples may have some impact on the interpretation of Convention rights domestically, and may lead the government to extend civil marriage to same-sex couples, without a court challenge. Second, it is foreseeable that the civil partnership regime established by the CPA will eventually drive the recognition of same-sex civil marriage, by facilitating a cultural shift in society's acceptance of same-sex relationships. Third, there are signs that domestic judges are increasingly unwilling to tolerate discrimination on the basis of sexual orientation. Finally, courts in other countries are increasingly being asked to consider this issue, and if more courts continue to find, like their Canadian counterparts, that the opposite-sex marriage requirement is unjustifiably discriminatory, this may encourage legislators or the courts to comply with an evolving Western consensus. It seems likely, for these reasons, that the tide of equality will roll forward, eventually bringing same-sex civil marriage to England and Wales. What remains to be seen, however, is when and how (by judicial or political action) the change will occur.

POSTSCRIPT

In the recent Canadian election, the right-of-centre Conservative Party of Canada secured a minority government, taking power from the left-of-centre Liberal Party. The Conservatives, led by Stephen Harper, have indicated their intention to revisit the same-sex marriage issue, by holding a free vote on the issue in the House of Commons. It is currently unclear what the Conservatives propose to do if (and this seems unlikely) the majority of Parliamentarians vote to repeal the CMA. However, this much is clear: any Parliamentary attempt once again to preclude same-sex couples from marrying is certain to be the subject of a court challenge. The Supreme Court has not yet considered whether the opposite-sex marriage requirement is constitutional (it has only determined that same-sex marriage is not unconstitutional), but it signalled quite clearly in the Same-Sex Marriage Reference that it would uphold the lower court decisions finding the opposite-sex marriage requirement to be unconstitutional. At most, then, the Conservatives may secure a temporary 'victory', but the victory will be short-lived.

NOTES

[1] *Fitzpatrick* v *Sterling Housing Association Ltd.* [1998] 4 All ER 991 (CA).

[2] An Act respecting certain aspects of legal capacity for marriage for civil purposes, SC 2005 c 33 (Civil Marriage Act).

[3] Canadian Charter of Rights and Freedoms, Part I of the Constitution Act 1982, being Schedule B to the Canada Act 1982 (UK), 1982 c. 11 (Charter).

[4] British Columbia (BC): *EGALE Canada Inc.* v *Canada (Attorney General)* (2003) 225 DLR (4th) 472 (BC CA), rev'g (2001) 95 BCLR (3d) 122 (BC Sup Ct); Ontario: *Halpern* v *Canada (Attorney General)* (2003) 65 OR (3d) 161 (Ont CA), rev'g on other grounds *Halpern* v *Canada (Attorney General)* (2002) 215 DLR (4th) 223 (Ont Div Ct); Quebec: *Hendricks* v *Québec (Procureur Général)* [2002] RJQ No. 3816 (Que CS) (QL).

[5] Section 15(1) of the Charter provides: 'Every individual is equal before and under the law and has the right to the equal protection and equal benefit of the law without discrimination and, in particular, without discrimination based on race, national or ethnic origin, colour, religion, sex, age or mental or physical disability'.

[6] The BC Court of Appeal and the Québec Superior Court decisions were released before the Ontario Court of Appeal decision. Both decisions suspended the application of the new definition. However, following the Ontario Court of Appeal decision, the BC Court of Appeal amended its order, giving immediate effect to the change and requiring the BC government to immediately begin issuing marriage licenses to same-sex couples: *EGALE Canada Inc.* v *Canada (Attorney General)* [2003] BCJ No. 1582 (BC CA) (QL).

[7] The following decisions were released in 2004. Manitoba: *Vogel* v *Canada (Attorney General)* [2004] MJ No. 418 (Man QB) (QL); Nova Scotia: *Boutilier* v *Nova Scotia (Attorney General)* [2004] NSJ No. 357 (NS Sup Ct) (QL); Quebec: *Catholic Civil Rights League* v *Hendricks* [2004] RQJ No. 2593 (Que CA) (QL), aff'g on other grounds *Hendricks* v *Québec (Procureur Général)* [2002] RJQ No. 3816 (Que CS) (QL); Saskatchewan: *N.W.* v *Canada (Attorney General)* [2004] SJ No. 669 (Sask QB) (QL); Yukon: *Dunbar* v *Yukon* [2004] YJ No. 61 (YK Sup Ct) (QL). The judgment of Justice Green of the Newfoundland and Labrador Supreme Court – Trial Division, issued on 21 December 2004, is not published.

New Brunswick was a late-comer. Same-sex marriages were not legally recognized in that province until 4 July 2005, just 15 days before the federal legislation received Royal Assent, mandating the change. See *Harrison* v *Canada (Attorney General)* [2005] NBJ No. 257 (NB QB) (QL).

[8] *Reference re Same-Sex Marriage* [2004] SCC 79 (Sup Ct Can) (Same-Sex Marriage Reference).

[9] The Civil Marriage Act received Royal Assent on 20 July 2005. It was assented to by Chief Justice Beverley McLachlin, acting in her role as Deputy Governor General.

[10] The remaining jurisdictions were Alberta, Nunavut, the Northwest Territories, and Prince Edward Island.

[11] Civil Partnership Act 2004, c. 33 (Civil Partnership Act).

[12] Explanatory Notes, Civil Partnership Act 2004.

[13] Women and Equality Unit, Department for Trade and Industry, *Civil Partnership: A framework for the legal recognition of same-sex couples* (June 2003) at 13 (available online); Women and Equality Unit, Department for Trade and Industry, *Responses to Civil Partnership: A framework for the legal recognition of same-sex couples* (November 2003) at para. 3.4 (available online).

[14] Human Rights Act 1998, c. 42 (Human Rights Act).

[15] The South African Constitutional Court recently found that the opposite-sex marriage requirement in that country unjustifiably violated the equality guarantee in the South African Constitution. The government was given 12 months to correct the defect: see *Minister of Home Affairs* v *Fourie and Bonthuys; Lesbian and Gay Equality Project* v *Minister of Home Affairs*, Case CCT 60/04 (1 December 2005) (available online).

[16] The Human Rights Act 1998 was proclaimed in force on 1 October 2000.

[17] A lesbian couple recently filed an application in the Family Division of the High Court asking that their Canadian marriage be recognized by the Court. The case is scheduled to be heard this year.

[18] European Convention for the Protection of Human Rights and Fundamental Freedoms (4 November 1950) (ECHR).

[19] Article 14 of the ECHR provides as follows: 'The enjoyment of the rights and freedoms set forth in this Convention shall be secured without discrimination on any ground such as sex, race, colour, language, religion, political or other opinion, national or social origin, association with a national minority, property, birth or other status'.

[20] There are four main types of marriage in English law: (a) marriage according to the rites of the Church of England; (b) marriage according to the rites of a religious affiliation other than the Church of England; (c) Quaker and Jewish marriages; and (d) civil marriage: Cretney, S. M., Masson, J. M. and Bailey-Harris, R. (2003) 8th edn. *Principles of Family Law*, London: Sweet and Maxwell. I am concerned only with the fourth type of marriage – civil marriage.

[21] In Canada, this was recently confirmed by the Supreme Court: Same-Sex Marriage Reference, see n 8 above at 55–70. However, in my view, the UK Parliament should reconsider the law relating to religious marriage, to *permit* religious officials to marry same-sex couples, if they decide that same-sex marriage is consistent with their religious beliefs. In Canada, this is the result under the Civil Marriage Act: see s 3 Civil Marriage Act; see also s 13(1), Human Rights Act, 1998.

[22] For sources *supporting* same-sex civil marriage, see Eskridge (1996); Wintemute and Andenaes, (2001); Sullivan (1997); Wolfson (2004); MacDougall (2001); Casswell (2001).

For sources *opposing* same-sex civil marriage, see Bradley (2000); Finnis (1997); Wardell (1998).

[23] *Hyde* v *Hyde and Woodmansee* (1866) LR 1 PandD 130 (HL).

[24] Ibid, at 133, aff'd in *Corbett* v *Corbett* [1970] 2 All ER 33 (PDA); and *S-T (formerly J)* v *J.* [1998] Family Law 239 (CA) per Ward and Potter LLJ.

[25] Matrimonial Causes Act 1973, c. 18, s 11(c). Such marriages were also void before the Act: see, eg *Talbot* v *Talbot* [1967] 111 SJ 213 (Ormrod J).

[26] See generally Hogg (1996).

[27] Constitution Act, 1867, 30 and 31 Victoria c. 3 (UK).

[28] See n 8 above at 13–39.

[29] But see the Marriage (Prohibited Degrees) Act, SC 1990 c. 46 (amending the common law prohibited degrees of consanguinity).

[30] But see Article 365 (para 2) of the Civil Code of Québec, LQ/SQ 1991, c. 64 (explicitly limiting marriage to opposite-sex couples), affirmed for federal purposes by section 5 of the Federal Law–Civil Law Harmonization Act, No. 1, SC 2001 c. 4, s 5 ('Marriage requires the free and enlightened consent of a man and women to be the spouse of the other.') This federal provision applied only in Québec (see section 4).

On 6 September 2002, the Québec Superior Court declared that both sections infringed section 15(1) of the Charter, but suspended the remedy for 2 years: *Hendricks* v *Québec (PG)*, see n 4 above. Article 365 (para 2) had already been repealed by an *Act instituting civil unions and establishing new rules of filiation*, SQ 2002 c. 6, s 22. A party other than the Attorney General of Canada appealed that decision, but that appeal was struck as moot: Catholic Civil Rights League, see n 7 above.

[31] *Iantsis* v *Papatheodorou* [1971] 1 OR 245 at 248 (Ont CA); *North* v *Matheson* (1974) 20 RFL 112 (Man Co Ct); *Layland* v *Ontario* (1993) 14 OR (3d) 658 (Ont Div Ct); *Keddie* v *Currie* (1991) 60 BCLR (2d) (BC CA).

[32] Marriage Act, RSA 1980 c. M-6.

[33] Ibid, s 1 (c.1) (definition of 'marriage'), as amended by Marriage Amendment Act, 2000, SA 2000 c 3, s 4.

[34] Modernization of Benefits and Obligations Act, SC 2000 c. 12 (MBOA).

[35] Section 1.1 of the MBOA provided as follows: 'For greater certainty, the amendments made by this Act do not affect the meaning of the word 'marriage,' that is, the lawful union of one man and one woman to the exclusion of all others'.

[36] Section 15(1) came into force three years after the rest of the Charter, to allow the federal and provincial governments time to bring their legislation into line with equality: s 32(2), Charter.

[37] See generally Caswell (1996); Lahey (1999). For expressions of doubt about the effectiveness of the Charter in achieving equality for gay and lesbian individuals and couples, see Cossman (2002).

[38] See, in particular: *Egan* v *Canada* [1995] 2 SCR 513 (Sup Ct Can) (finding that sexual orientation was an analogous, and thus prohibited, ground of discrimination under s 15(1) of the Charter); *Vriend* v *Alberta* [1998] 1 SCR 493 (Sup Ct Can) (finding the failure to include sexual orientation in the provincial human rights legislation to be an unjustifiable violation of s 15(1) of the Charter); and *M.* v *H.* [1999] 2 SCR 3 (Sup Ct Can) (finding the exclusion of same-sex couples from the provincial spousal support legislation to be an unjustifiable violation of s 15(1) of the Charter).

[39] Section 52 of the Constitution Act, 1982, see n 3 above, provides that any law that is inconsistent with the Constitution of Canada is of no force or effect. The Supreme Court has interpreted this provision as enabling courts to strike down or to amend unconstitutional legislation, by adding words to ('reading in') or deleting words from ('reading out') the legislation as enacted: *Schachter* v *Canada* [1992] 2 SCR 679 (Sup Ct Can).

[40] [1999] 1 SCR 497 (Sup Ct Can) ('Law').

[41] Ibid, at 39, 88.

[42] In *Andrews* v *Law Society of BC* [1989] 1 SCR 143 (Sup Ct Can), the Supreme Court held that section 15(1) afforded protection against discrimination on the basis of the grounds that are

enumerated in, and analogous to those enumerated in, the section. Although sexual orientation is not an enumerated ground of discrimination, in 1995 the Supreme Court held (unanimously on this point) that it is an analogous ground of discrimination: *Egan*, see n 38 above.

[43] *R.* v *Oakes* [1986] 1 SCR 103 at 138-139 (Sup Ct Can).

[44] (2003) 65 OR (3d) 161 (CA).

[45] For a detailed account of these decisions, see Wintemute (2004).

[46] Finding a violation of section 15(1) that *could* be justified under section 1: *EGALE* v *Canada (Attorney General)* (2001) 95 BCLR (3d) 122 (BC Sup Ct) per Pitfield J. Finding a violation of section 15(1) that *could not* be justified under section 1: *Hendricks* v *Québec (Procureur Général)* [2002] RJQ No. 3816 (Que CS); *Halpern* v *Canada (Attorney General)* (2002) 215 DLR (4th) 223 (Ont Div Ct); *EGALE* v *Canada (Attorney General)* (2003) 225 DLR (4th) 472 (BC CA), rev'g (2001) 95 BCLR (3d) 122 (BC Sup Ct).

[47] The marriages were performed under a provision of the Ontario Marriage Act that allows marriage by the ancient tradition of publishing the banns. Under this provision, couples do not need to acquire a marriage licence, if their intention to marry is announced in church during a service on three consecutive Sundays: see Marriage Act, RSO 1990 c. M.3, s 5(1).

[48] The couples and MCCT filed their applications separately, but their applications were consolidated for a joint hearing: *Halpern v Toronto (City) Clerk* [2000] OJ No. 3212 (Sup Ct Jus) (QL).

[49] The federal executive took up the invitation. In early 2003, the executive asked the Standing Committee for Justice and Human Rights, a committee of the House of Commons, to investigate the issues surrounding same-sex marriage. The Committee based its deliberations on a Department of Justice discussion paper: *Marriage and Legal Recognition of Same-Sex Unions: A Discussion Paper* (Ottawa, November 2002). The Committee heard from a variety of individuals and groups, some of whom opposed same-sex marriage (166), but the majority of whom favoured same-sex marriage (274). The decisions of the BC Court of Appeal and the Ontario Court of Appeal were released before the Committee had completed its report, and before Parliament had considered its deliberations. J Hiebert (Oct 2003).

[50] *Halpern*, see n 4 above at 124.

[51] 'Ontario men wed following court ruling' CBC News (13 June 2003).

[52] BC, Manitoba, Newfoundland, Nova Scotia, Québec, Saskatchewan and the Yukon.

[53] See the discussion in nn 4 and 7 above.

[54] Same-sex marriages were not legally recognized in Alberta, Nunavut, the Northwest Territories and Prince Edward Island until the Civil Marriage Act received Royal Assent. In essence, therefore, the Civil Marriage Act had a practical effect in only 4 of 13 Canadian jurisdictions.

[55] In Canada, the federal executive has the authority to refer important factual or legal (often constitutional) questions to the Supreme Court of Canada, in order to ask for its (non-binding) opinion: see Supreme Court Act, RSC 1985 c. S-26, s 53(1).

[56] Ministry of Justice, Government of Canada, *Reference to the Supreme Court of Canada: Backgrounder* (17 July 2003) (available online: http://canada.justice.gc.ca.).

[57] Order in Council PC 2003-1005 (16 July 2003), *Annexed Proposal for an Act respecting aspects of legal capacity for civil marriage purposes* (the 'Proposed Civil Marriage Bill').

[58] Prime Minister Jean Chrétien retired and was replaced by his Liberal Party colleague, Paul Martin, on 12 December 2003.

[59] Order in Council PC 2004-28 (26 January 2004), *Annexed Proposal for an Act respecting aspects of legal capacity for civil marriage purposes.*

[60] Same-Sex Marriage Reference, see n 8 above. For a more detailed account of the Supreme Court's decision, see Gee and Webber (2005).

[61] See Hogg (2004).

[62] Ministry of Justice, Government of Canada, Civil Marriage and the Legal Recognition of Same-Sex Unions: Decision of the Supreme Court of Canada, Backgrounder (9 December 2004).

[63] For an up-to-date web-based account of the controversy, see: www.samesexmarriage.ca.

[64] The governing Liberals indicated that they would allow a free vote on the legislation. However, because the Civil Marriage Act was government legislation, it required all cabinet ministers to vote in favour.

[65] This summary is gleaned from Wadham, Mountfield and Edmundson (2003).

[66] Explanatory Notes, see n 12 above at 1. For further detail about the Civil Partnership Act, see House of Commons, *The Civil Partnership Bill (HL): Background and Debate, Research Paper 04/64* (7 September 2004); and House of Commons, *The Civil Partnership Bill (H.L.): the Detail and Legal Implications*, Research Paper 04/65 (8 September 2004).

[67] Joint Committee on Human Rights, *Civil Partnership Bill* 15th Report (7 July 2004).

[68] Letter from the Rt Hon Jacqui Smith MP, Minister of State for Industry and the Regions and Deputy Minister for Women and Equality, Department for Trade and Industry, Appendix 1 to Joint Committee on Human Rights, *Civil Partnership Bill*, 20th Report (November 2004).

[69] See, eg, Bailey-Harris (1999); Wintemute (2000); see also Probert (2003); and Murphy (2004).

[70] Joint Committee on Human Rights, see n 67 at 6.

[71] House of Lords [2004] UKHL 30 (HL) ('*Ghaidan*').

[72] I will consider only the substantive, and not the procedural, aspects of such a claim. In addition, I have assumed that the challenge would focus on the statutory prohibition; note, however, that the common law prohibition may raise unique issues under the regime set out in the Human Rights Act, 1998.

[73] *Wandsworth LBC* v *Michalak* (2002) EWCA Civ 271 at [20] per Brooke LJ (CA), cited in *Ghaidan*, see n 71 above at 133-4; *A.* v *Secretary of State for the Home Department* [2004] UKHL 56 at 50 (HL); *R. (Carson)* v *Secretary of State for Work and Pensions* [2002] EWHC Admin 978 at 52 (CA); *R.(S)* v *Chief Constable of the South Yorkshire Police* [2004] UKHL 39 at 42 (HL).

Since this paper was written, the House of Lords has distanced itself from this categorical approach: see *R (on the application of Carson)* v *Secretary of State for Work and Pensions; R (on the application of Reynolds)* v *Secretary of State for Work and Pensions* (2005) 4 All ER 545 (HL).

[74] See Wildhaber (2002). The Council of Europe has now drawn up a new protocol, Protocol 12, which contains a free-standing prohibition on discrimination. Protocol 12 was opened for signature in 2000, but has not yet received the 10 signatures required to enter into force. The UK has not ratified the Protocol, and it appears to have no intention to do so: see Choudhury (2003).

[75] *Belgian Linguistics Case (No. 2)* (1968) 1 EHRR 252 at 283. The circumstances in which Article 14 will apply is unclear, partly because the ECtHR has used inconsistent language to describe the requirement. It has, for example, stated that Article 14 applies when the subject matter of the disadvantage 'constitutes one of the modalities of the exercise of a right', or whenever the measures complained of are 'linked' to the exercise of a guaranteed right: *Petrovic* v *Austria* (1998) 4 BHRC 232 at 236–7; see also *Ghaidan*, see n 71 above at 11.

[76] See, eg *Niemetz* v *Germany* (1993) 16 EHRR 97 at 29.

[77] *Petrovic*, see n 75 above.

[78] ECtHR: *Laskey* v *UK* (1997) 24 EHRR 39 at 36 (noting that 'sexual orientation . . . concern(s) an intimate aspect of private life'), conf'd in *Smith and Grady* (2000) 29 EHRR 548 at 90 and *Lustig-Prean and Beckett* v *UK* (2000) 29 EHRR 548 at 83; ECmHR: *Kerkhoven* v *The Netherlands* No. 15666/89 (1992) (noting that 'the relationship of a homosexual couple constitutes a matter affecting their private life').

[79] *Secretary of State for Work and Pensions* v *M.; Langley* v *Bradford Metropolitan District* [2004] EWCA Civ 1343 (CA) per Neuberger LJ at 50. The House of Lords heard an appeal in this case on 5/6 December 2005. A judgment in the case has not yet been released.

In addition, Baroness Hale, writing extra-judicially, has suggested that 'homosexual relationships are undoubtedly an aspect of private life': Hale (2004) 'Homosexual Rights' 16 CFLQ, 2.

[80] ECtHR: *Estevez* v *Spain* No. 56501/00 (2001); *S.* v *UK* (1986) 47 DR 274; and *X* v *UK* (1997) 24 EHRR 143; not foll'd in *Ghaidan*, see n 72 at 18. ECmHR: *X and Y* v *UK* (1983) 32 DR 220; *Simpson* v *UK* (1986) 47 DR 227; *C and LM* v *UK* No. 14753/89 (1989); *WJ and DP* v *UK* No. 12513/86 (1986).

[81] *Tyrer* v *United Kingdom* (1978) 2 EHRR 1 at 31. On the evolution of 'family,' see Liddy (1998).

[82] *Salgueiro da Silva Mouta* v *Portugal* (2001) 31 EHRR 47.

[83] See n 71 above at 139. This point appears to be conceded by the government: 'Today there are thousands of same-sex couples living in stable and committed partnerships. These relationships span many years with couples looking after each other, caring for their loved ones and actively participating in society; in fact, *living in exactly the same way as any other family*': *Civil Partnership*, see n 13 above at foreword [emphasis added].

[84] *Langley*, see n 79 above, per Sedley LJ at 49 and Neuberger LJ at 120.

[85] *Hamer* v *UK* (1979) 24 DR 5 (law that provided that prisoners could not marry inside prison violated Article 12); *R. (Crown Prosecution Service)* v *Registrar-General of Births, Deaths and Marriages* [2002] EWCA Div 1661 (no power to prevent person charged with offence from marrying prosecution witness).

[86] *Rees* v *UK* (1986) EHRR 56.

[87] *Cossey* v *UK* (1990) 13 EHRR 622; *Sheffield and Horsham* v *UK* (1998) 27 EHRR 163.

[88] (2002) 35 EHRR 18, foll'd in *Bellinger* v *Bellinger* [2003] UKHL 21 (HL); see Gender Recognition Act 2004, c 7, implementing the changes required by these decisions.

[89] In the domestic context, see *Ghaidan*, see n 71 above at 138–42 per Baroness Hale; but see, *contra*, 78–97 per Lord Millett.

[90] *Halpern*, see n 4 above at 66–71.

[91] 'The argument that, by definition, marriage can involve only a man and a woman, because it has always included only opposite sex couples, is tautological and reminiscent of anti-miscegenation laws. The fact that marriage has not included same sex couples in the past does not explain why that cannot be so now anymore than anti-miscegenation laws that prevented interracial couples from marrying justified continuation of those laws' Allen (1996).

[92] See Letter from Rt Hon Jacqui Smith MP, see n 68 above: 'There will be *no substantive difference* of treatment suffered by unmarried opposite-sex couples as compared with their same-sex counterparts, that is, same-sex couples who do not form civil partnerships.'

[93] *Egan*, see n 38 above at 565–6.

[94] *Halpern*, see n 4 above at 136 [emphasis added].

[95] *Opinion of the Justices to the Senate* 802 NE 2d 565 (2004); see also *Goodridge* v *Department of Public Health* 798 NE 2d 941 (2003) (finding the opposite-sex marriage requirement in violation of Article 1 (equality guarantee) of the Massachusetts Declaration of Rights).

[96] Baroness Hale, writing extra-judicially, has written as follows about the intangible benefits that flow from marriage: 'Sometimes it is said that it is weddings, rather than the marital relationship they create, which are so popular . . . *But it is far more significant than that; couples want a rite of passage, a public mark of their commitment to one another, and a symbol of the uniting of their two family trees . . . These symbolic functions could be just as important to gay couples*': (1996) *From the Test Tube to the Coffin: Choice and Regulation in Private Life*, London: Sweet and Mawell 83–4 [emphasis added].

[97] *Karner* v *Austria* [2003] 2 FLR 623.

[98] *Ghaidan*, see n 71 above at 17; see also at 142 per Baroness Hale.

[99] See, eg *Shackell* v *UK* No. 45851/99.

[100] *Ghaidan*, see n 71 above at 16 and 138; see, for the situation in Canada, *Walsh* v *Nova Scotia (Attorney General)* [2002] 4 SCR 325; but see *Miron* v *Trudel* [1995] 2 SCR 418.

[101] *Karner*, see n 97 above at 37; *Frette* v *France* (2003) 2 FLR 9 at 32.

[102] *Ghaidan*, see n 71 above at 9 per Lord Nicholls and 136 per Baroness Hale.

[103] *de Freitas* v *Permanent Secretary of Ministry of Agriculture, Fisheries, Land and Housing* [1999] 1 AC 69 (PC) per Lord Clyde, adopted by Lord Steyn in *R. (Daly)* v *Secretary of State for the Home Department* [2001] UKHL 26 at 27 (HL).

[104] *Belgian Linguistics Case*, see n 75 above ; *A.* v *Secretary of State*, see n 73 above at 54. This is the approach in Canada as well: see *M.* v *H.*, see n 38 above at 62; 100-1.

[105] *Dudgeon* v *UK* (1982) 4 EHRR 149 at 60 [emphasis added]; see also *Norris* v. *Ireland* (1988) 13 EHRR 186.

[106] *Smith and Grady/Lustig-Prean*, see n 78 above.

[107] *Same-Sex Marriage Reference*, see n 8 above at 46.

[108] *Halpern*, see n 4 above at 121.

[109] *Halpern (Div. Ct.)*, see n 4 above at 238–42.

[110] *Halpern*, see n 4 above at 121.

[111] Ibid, at 121–2.

[112] Ibid.

[113] See n 88 above.

[114] [1948] AC 274 at 286.

[115] *Bellinger*, see n 88 above at 46.

[116] Hale, see n 79 above at 83.

[117] *Ghaidan*, see n 71 above at 141.

[118] Ibid, at 143.

[119] Note also the following statement of the government: 'It is already the case that many children are brought up by same-sex couples. The Government considers it appropriate that same-sex couples who register a civil partnership should have access to those benefits and duties that help to support stable families. Many married couples do not have children but their access to the rights and responsibilities of marriage are not limited because they do not raise a family. There is no justification for limiting same-sex couples' rights and responsibilities if they do not have children': *Responses to Civil Partnership*, see n 13 at 40. In light of this statement, it would be completely disingenuous for the government to advance the procreation justification in court.

[120] *Karner*, see n 97 above at 40; *Ghaidan*, see n 71 above at 16; 138.

[121] Ibid.

[122] Letter from Rt Hon Jacqui Smith MP, see n 68 above.

[123] *Egan*, see n 38 above at 616.

[124] *Halpern*, see n 4 above at 137.

[125] Ibid, at 121. When the Attorney General later submitted written arguments to the Supreme Court of Canada supporting the government's proposed legislation, he resiled from his earlier position: '(n)o evidence suggests that providing equal access to marriage for civil purposes to same-sex couples would adversely affect the institution of marriage for opposite-sex couples, or that opposite-sex marriages would no longer take place if the opposite-sex requirement for marriage were not retained': *Supplementary Factum of the Attorney General of Canada* Court File No. 29866 (30 March 2004) at 9.

[126] *Goodridge,* see n 95 above at 965.

[127] See *Ghaidan,* see n 71 above at 143 per Baroness Hale.

[128] *Goodridge,* see n 95 above at 965.

[129] *Opinion of the Justices,* see n 95 above at 10–11.

[130] *Bellinger,* see n 88 above at 36–7.

[131] The public aspect of marriage was emphasized by the Ontario Court of Appeal in *Halpern:* 'Through the institution of marriage, individuals can publicly express their love and commitment to each other. Through this institution, society publicly recognizes expressions of love and commitment between individuals, granting them respect and legitimacy as a couple': *Halpern,* see n 4 above at 5.

[132] Marriage Act 1949, s 45.

[133] For a possible answer, see the judgment of Justice Albie Sachs of the South African Constitutional Court in *National Coalition for Gay and Lesbian Equality* v *Minister of Justice* (1999) 1 SA 6 at 116–7.

[134] *Mouta,* see n 82 above.

[135] *Langley,* see n 79 above per Sedley LJ at 49 and Neuberger LJ at 120.

[136] *Marckx* v *Belgium* (1979) 2 EHRR 330 at 14–15; *Abdulaziz, Cabales and Balkandali* v *UK* (1985) 7 EHRR 471 at 62.

[137] *Ghaidan,* see n 71 above at 143–4.

[138] Ibid, at 97.

[139] Ibid, at 10–11 per Lord Nicholls, discussing the uncertainty surrounding the application of the 'within the ambit' principle, and explicitly putting off resolving it.

[140] See, eg *Wandsworth LBC* v *Michalak* [2002] EWCA Civ 271.

[141] 'Even the most tenuous link will suffice for Article 14 to enter into play'. Grosz, S., Beatson, J. and Duffy, P. (2000) *Human Rights: The 1998 Act and the European Convention* at C14–10.

[142] *X, Y and Z* v *UK* (1997) 24 EHRR 143 at 602 (refusing to compare a gay couple and a heterosexual couple, finding that the gay couple could only compare themselves with a lesbian couple).

[143] *Opinion of the Justices,* see n 95 above at 572 per Sosman J.

[144] Ibid, at 570.

[145] *Brown* v *Stott* [2003] 1 AC 681 at 703 per Lord Bingham.

[146] See eg Jowell (2003) 'Judicial deference: servility, civility or institutional capacity', *PL* 580; R Clayton (2004) 'Judicial Deference and "Democratic Dialogue": The Legitimacy of Judicial Intervention Under the Human Rights Act 1998', *PL* 33.

[147] See the sources cited in Clayton, Ibid, at 36–9.

[148] *Goodridge,* see n 95 above at 395.

[149] This discussion is based on the four factors to guide judicial deliberations set out by Laws LJ in *International Transport Roth GmbH* v *Secretary of State for the Home Department* [2002] EWCA Civ 158.

[150] The statement of Iacobucci J. in *Vriend,* see n 38 above at 122 is apposite: '. . . groups that have historically been the target of discrimination cannot be expected to wait patiently for the protection of their human dignity and equal rights while governments move toward reform one step at a time. If the infringement of the rights and freedoms of these groups is permitted to persist while governments fail to pursue equality diligently, then the guarantees of the Charter will be reduced to little more than empty words'.

[151] *Bellinger,* see n 88 above at 69; see also 46–9 per Lord Nicholls.

[152] *Ghaidan,* see n 71 above at 18–19.

REFERENCES

Allen, B. A. (1996) 'Same-sex marriage: A conflict of laws analysis for Oregon', 32 *Willamette Law Review* 619.

Bailey-Harris, R (1999) 'Lesbian and gay family values and the law', *Family Law* 560.

Bradley, G. V. (2000) 'Same-sex marriage: Our final answer?', 14 *Notre Dame Journal of Law Ethics and Public Policy* 14.
Casswell, D. G. (1996) *Lesbians, Gay Men and Canadian Law,* Toronto: Emond Montgomery.
Casswell, D. G. (2001) 'Moving toward same-sex marriage', 80 *Canadian Bar Review* 810.
Choudhury, T. (2003) 'Interpreting the Right to Equality', *EHRLR* 24.
Clayton, R. (2004) 'Judicial deference and "democratic dialogue": The legitimacy of judicial intervention under the Human Rights Act, 1998' *PL* 33.
Cossman, B. (2002) 'Lesbians, gay men, and the Canadian Charter of Rights and Freedoms', 40 *Osgoode Hall Law Journal* 223.
Eskridge, W. N. Jr (1996) *The Case for Same-Sex Marriage: From Sexual Liberty to Civilised Commitment,* New York: Free Press.
Finnis, J. (1997) 'The good of marriage and the morality of sexual relations: Some philosophical and historical observations', 42 *American Journal of Juris* 42.
Gee, G. and Webber, G. C. N. (2005) 'Same-sex marriage in Canada: Contributions from the courts, the executive and Parliament', *KCLJ* 132.
Hale, B (1996) *From the Test Tube to the Coffin: Choice and Regulation in Private Life,* London: Sweet and Maxwell.
Hale, B. (2004) 'Homosexual rights' 16 *CFLQ* 2.
Herring, J. (2004) 2nd edn *Family Law,* London: Longman.
Hiebert, J. (2003) 'From equality rights to same-sex marriage', *Policy Options,* 14.
Hogg, P. W. (1996) *Constitutional Law of Canada,* Toronto: Carswell.
Hogg, P. W. (2004) 'So, where do we go from here?', *Globe and Mail* 15 December.
House of Commons (2004) *The Civil Partnership Bill (HL): Background and Debate,* Research Paper 04/64, 7 September.
House of Commons (2004) *The Civil Partnership Bill (HL): the Detail and Legal Implications,* Research Paper 04/65, 8 September.
Jowell, J. (2003) 'Judicial deference: Servility, civility or institutional capacity', *PL* 580.
Lahey, K. A. (1999) *Are We 'Persons' Yet?: Law and Sexuality in Canada,* Toronto: UTP.
Liddy, J. (1998) 'The concept of family under the European Convention on Human Rights', *EHRLR* 15.
MacDougall, B. (2001) 'The celebration of same-sex marriage', 32 *Ottawa Law Review* 235.
Murphy, J. (2004) 'Same-sex marriage in England: A role for human rights?' 16 *CFLQ* 245.
Pickel, J. A. (2002) 'Judicial analysis frozen in time', 65 *Saskatchewan Law Review* 243.
Probert, R. (2003) 'The right to marry and the impact of the Human Rights Act, 1998', 29 *IFLJ*.
Sullivan, A. (1997) (ed) *Same-Sex Marriage: Pro and Con: A Reader,* New York: Random House.
Wadham, J., Mountfield, H. and Edmundson, A. (2003) *Blackstone's Guide to the Human Rights Act 1998,* Oxford: OUP.
Wardell, L. (1998) 'Same-sex marriage and the limits of legal pluralism' in J. Eekelaar and T. Nhlapo (ed), *The Changing Family: International Perspectives on the Family and Family Law,* Oxford: Hart Publishing.
Wildhaber, L. (2002) 'Protection against discrimination under the European Convention on Human Rights: A Second-Class Guarantee?', 2 *BYIL* 71.
Wintemute, R. and Andenaes, M. (2001) (ed) *Legal Recognition of Same-Sex Partnerships,* Oxford: Hart Publishing.
Wintemute, R. (2000) 'Lesbian and gay inequality 2000', 6 *EHRLR* 603.
Wintemute, R. (2004) 'Sexual orientation and the Charter', 49 *McGill Law Journal* 1143.
Wintemute, R. (2004) 'Within the ambit': How big is the "gap" in Article 14 of the European Convention on Human Rights?: Part 1', *EHRLR* 4.
Wolfson, E. (2004) *Why Marriage Matters: America, Equality, and Gay People's Right to Marry,* New York: Simon and Schuster.
Women and Equality Unit, Department for Trade and Industry (2003) *Civil partnership: A framework for the legal recognition of same-sex couples* (June) (available online).
Women and Equality Unit, Department for Trade and Industry (2003) *Responses to Civil Partnership: A framework for the legal recognition of same-sex couples* (November) (available online).

[18]

WHY MARRIAGE?

Martha Albertson Fineman*

INTRODUCTION

In 1974, when I was a law student in a class called Injunctions, we often struggled through the factual and legal complexities of an opinion determining whether an injunction should issue. My professor, Owen Fiss, was fond of reminding us after each such session that the object of this entire struggle—the injunction—was "only a piece of paper." His point was that it takes more than the issuance of some form or document to make things happen, to transform the status quo. Words are, after all, only words. Standing alone, they often are not worth much more than the paper upon which they are written. Instead, it is the interpretation and implementation that really matter—not the issuance of the document, but what comes next, that confers content and meaning.

I cannot help but reflect upon this bit of practical-injunction-realism when confronted with the many questions that emerge in response to contemporary policy discussions about the need for laws to strengthen the institution of marriage.[1] Like an injunction, marriage is reducible to a piece of paper—the marriage license. This piece of paper distinguishes one on-going relationship from others, not officially designated marital in nature. Yet what

---

* Dorothea S. Clarke Professor of Feminist Jurisprudence and Director of the Feminism and Legal Theory Project, Cornell Law School.

1 Martha Albertson Fineman, The Neutered Mother, The Sexual Family, and Other Twentieth Century Tragedies 15 (1995) ("Policy on the national and state levels, for the most part, attempts to revitalize and replicate idealized traditional modes of intimate connection symbolized by the nuclear family. This failure of creative imagination on the part of law and legal institutions has resulted in an impoverished approach to the dilemmas of poverty for mothers and children in our society").

meaning does marriage have beyond this fragile manifestation?

This question asks us to consider what we imagine to be the content, purpose, and function of the institution we call marriage. This consideration raises two additional questions of relevance. First, what does the word "marriage" convey to us as individuals? In addressing this question, we look at marriage from a personal perspective—as a cultural and social practice in which we engage. Second, what does marriage convey to us collectively—as a society? From this perspective we look at the functions marriage performs on political, ideological, and structural levels—its construction in law and policy.[2]

Clearly, to both individuals and society, marriage constitutes a legal relationship. Through law, the state defines who may marry and the consequences of marriage at dissolution of the relationship, be it by death or divorce. In this regard, all marriages within a jurisdiction are standardized. Law may establish uniform standards, specifying who may marry whom and what formalities must be observed. Law may also define what economic and other consequences attend the dissolution of the marriage relationship. The ultimate content and conduct of marriage from an individual perspective is, however, far from clear. This is because of the way that society and law have given existing marriage relationships "privacy," thereby shielding them from supervision. For on-going marriages the norms are non-intervention and minimal regulation.[3] In some

---

2 Other questions we might ask include: Is it possible to have one societal definition of marriage in a diverse, pluralistic and secular society such as ours? Is marriage about behavior and functioning or is it about legality and form? What does the legal designation of marriage foster, reform, facilitate, support, preserve, or protect?

3 There are exceptions to this norm of family privacy, most of them recent, as in the case of abuse and neglect. Others are trivial from the perspective of this paper, such as the rules that preclude spousal testimony in criminal cases. See Frances E. Olsen, The Family and The Market: A Study of Ideology and Legal Reform, 96 Harv. L. Rev. 1497, 1504-05 (1983).

other on-going formal and legal relationships that are embodied in pieces of paper—the relationship between shareholder and corporation, for example—there is no expectation of privacy. Rights and obligations are defined, limited, and structured so that the range and nature of interactions are predictable and potentially publicly enforceable. By contrast, the issuance of a marriage certificate does not determine the conduct of any specific marriage, what it means to its participants, or how those participants will function within the relationship. The laws governing marriage leave the day-to-day implementation of marriage to the individuals. The conduct of the parties defines their marriage, giving it content and meaning. Marriages are individualized, idiosyncratic arrangements; even external articulations of what constitutes "ideal" relationships may influence them. The law recognizes and reinforces this individualized characteristic of marriage through the doctrine of marital privacy. Except in extreme situations, there are no legal enforcement mechanisms to ensure compliance with standards of conduct imposed generally across marriages.[4] The result might be characterized as creating a vacuum of legally mandated meaning for marriage—a vacuum that is to be filled with various non-legal, sometimes conflicting, individual aspirations, expectations, fears, and longings.

Reflection on the prospect of varied, individualized possibilities for the meaning of marriage suggests, that in order to answer the question "why marriage?" we must first consider "what marriage?" or more succinctly, "what is marriage?" Questioning what marriage actually is calls attention to the institution's individualized and malleable nature. By contrast, a focus on "why marriage" highlights the societal function and rationale for the institution. I will

4 Two exceptions, only recently (and imperfectly) considered "extreme," are domestic violence and marital rape. Even when there are general legal standards, such as the common law obligation of a husband to support his wife, the doctrine of marital privacy mandated the relationship end before the right could be realized in court. Martha Albertson Fineman, What Place for Family Privacy? 67 Geo. Wash. L. Rev. 1207, 1214 (1999).

discuss each question—the "what" as well as the "why" of marriage.

Marriage has various meanings to individuals entering into it. Marriage can be experienced as: a legal tie, a symbol of commitment, a privileged sexual affiliation, a relationship of hierarchy and subordination, a means of self-fulfillment, a societal construct, a cultural phenomenon, a religious mandate, an economic relationship, a preferred reproductive unit, a way to ensure against poverty and dependency, a romantic ideal, a natural or divined connection, a stand-in for morality, a status, or a contractual relationship.[5]

Marriage also has multiple potential meanings to the society that constructs and contains it. From the state's perspective, marriage may mean the imposition of order—necessary for record-keeping purposes (e.g., to facilitate property transfers at death). Marriage may also be viewed to provide order in a different context. It has been argued that marriage is the preferred method of containing and harnessing [male] sexuality in the interests of the larger society.[6] Marriage can reflect the moral or religious convention of a society—a symbolic function. Marriage can also be the site where essential reproductive tasks are preformed for society. Society must reproduce itself both through the production of children and the educating and disciplining of those children into workers, voters, and productive citizens—tasks traditionally undertaken by the marital family.[7] In this way, marriage can also be seen as

5 This is not meant to be an exhaustive list. There are additional meanings to marriage for individuals, perhaps as many meanings as there are individuals entering (or not entering) the relationship.

6 See Lloyd R. Cohen, Rhetoric, the Unnatural Family, and Women's Work, 81 Va. L. Rev. 2275, 2287 (1995).

7 The state interest in this societal function has been urged as giving the state regulatory interests in the marital family. I use this interest to develop an argument that the state has an obligation to restructure other societal institutions to accommodate and subsidize this reproductive function. In doing so, I focus not on marriage, but on the relationship of caretaker and dependent. See generally Fineman, supra note 4.

serving society by taking care of the dependency and vulnerability of some members of the marital family. Finally, marriage can be the mechanism through which society distributes and delivers social goods to its citizens.[8]

We should be clear about which of the many ways of thinking about marriage are informing the arguments that we make and the policy that we propose. If we remain clear about the role or function of marriage to which we subscribe—how we are filling the marriage-meaning-void–our own answer to the question, "why marriage?" may be revealed. In advocating for marriage, it may be the case that we are inappropriately substituting an individualized meaning for a societal rationale for the institution. Only societal-based rationales make legitimate societal regulation and control of marriage. Further, some of the historically societal based rationales for marriage may no longer seem appropriate in our changing world. For example, a couple may want to marry because marriage has a certain societal meaning: access to state subsidy in the form of economic and social benefits not available to other forms of sexual affiliation.[9] The couple may also want to marry because of the institution's individual meaning: a symbolic manifestation of their relationship that will affirm their commitment to each other. If, however, the couple is a same-sex couple, some religious leaders and politicians will oppose such a marriage because they regard marriage as a natural, divinely ordained relationship (an individualized, religious meaning), traditionally and appropriately confined to heterosexual couples (moral or tradition-based societal meaning).[10] In a secular society such as ours, however, only

---

8 This stands in contrast to individualized systems such as in Scandinavia where the individual is the unit of subsidy and policy.

9 Examples of these benefits include, among other things, health insurance and parenting/custody rights recognized if a partner dies or a relationship ends.

10 Some of the critics of civil unions in Vermont where it is now legal cite religious belief. See Julie Deardorff, Vermont Is Front Line of Gay Marriage Fight, Chi. Trib., Apr. 3, 2000, at 1. The use of history and tradition is more common. See, e.g., Bowers v. Hardwick, 478 U.S. 186 (1986). Other state court decisions in the 1970's also limited marriages

the second reason warrants consideration. The issue then becomes whether the societal function of marriage as the mechanism to provide economic benefits and protection is appropriately limited by the moral or traditional meanings of marriage.[11] The questions we would confront in this type of balance would include: when should history and tradition give way to new patterns of behavior; when should law reflect a moral position, particularly when there is no societal consensus that certain conduct is moral or immoral?

As illustrated in this example, the question "why marriage?" might become more complicated and difficult to answer if we must first reveal the meaning (or meanings) we assign to the institution of marriage. This type of consideration forces our focus away from nature or form of the marital relationship to the role or function we want the institution to serve in our society. It also reveals that we are making certain assumptions about the capabilities and capacities of marriage as distinguished from other relationships in society—assumptions about its unique ability to accomplish certain societal functions.

The concept of marriage, and the assumptions it carries with it, limit development of family policy and distort our ideology. The availability of marriage precludes consideration of other solutions to social problems. As the various (and by no means exhaustive) meanings of marriage listed above indicate, marriage is expected to do a lot of work in our society. Children must be cared for and nurtured, dependency must be addressed, and individual

---

to heterosexuals, often assuming that marriage was by definition a relationship between a man and a woman. See Martha Chamallas, Introduction to Feminist Legal Theory 265-66 (1999) (citing Jones v. Hallahan, 501 S.W.2d 588 (Ky. 1973), Baker v. Nelson, 191 N.W.2d 185 (Minn. 1971), and Singer v. Hara, 522 P.2d 1187 (Wash. App. 1974)).

11 This was the line of reasoning used in Hawaii and Vermont. See Baker v. State, 744 A.2d 864 (Vt. 1999); see also, Baehr v. Lewin, 74 Haw. 530 (1993).

happiness is of general concern.[12] The first question we should be asking is whether the existence of a marriage is, in and of itself, essential to accomplishing any of the societal goals or objectives we assign to it.[13]

I argue that for all relevant and appropriate societal purposes we do not need marriage, *per se*, at all. To state that we do not need marriage to accomplish many societal objectives is not the same thing as saying that we do not need a family to do so for some. However, family as a social category should not be dependent on having marriage as its core relationship. Nor is family synonymous with marriage.[14] Although both of these things might historically have been true, things have changed substantially in the past several decades. Marriage does not have the same relevance as a societal institution as it did even fifty years ago, when it was the primary means of protecting and providing for the legal and structurally devised dependency of wives.

The pressing problems today do not revolve around the marriage connection, but the caretaker-dependent relationship. In a world in which wives are equal partners and participants in the market sphere, and in which the consensus is that bad marriages should end, women do not need the special protection of legal marriage. Rather than marriage, we should view the parent-child relationship as the quintessential or core family connection, and focus on how policy can strengthen this tie.[15] Thus, in a responsive

---

[12] See generally The Neutered Mother, supra note 1.

[13] The second question is whether social goal or meaning is (still) a valid one.

[14] Martha L. A. Fineman, Masking Dependency: The Political Role of Family Rhetoric, 81 Va. L. Rev. 2181, 2190-91 (1995) ("Family affiliations are expressed in different kinds of affiliational acts. Some are sexually based, as with marriage. Some are forged biologically, as through parenthood. Others are more relational, such as those based on nurturing or caretaking or those developed through affection and acceptance of interdependence").

[15] See The Neutered Mother, supra note 1, at 15 (discussing the parent-child dyad).

society, one could have a marriage [or other long-term sexual affiliations] without necessarily constituting a "family" entitled to special protection and benefits under law. Correspondingly, one might have dependents, thereby creating a family and gaining protection and benefits, without having a marriage.

If this suggestion seems extreme and radical, it only serves to demonstrate the extent to which marriage continues to be uncritically central to our thinking about the family. What is bizarre is that it remains central in spite of the fact that the traditional marital family has become a statistical minority of family units in our society.[16] The tenacity of marriage as a concept explains the relatively unsophisticated and uninformed policy debates. Marriage, as the preferred societal solution, has become the problem. The very existence of this institution eclipses discussion and debate about the problems of dependency and allows us to avoid confronting the difficulty of making the transformations necessary to address these problems.[17]

I. MAN AND WIFE—FROM PROTECTED TO PARTNERED

Feminist family theorists have pointed out that marriage is a public institution.[18] It has a public function and the law has historically regulated entry into it as well as exit from it.[19] One of the public functions of marriage is

16 The latest census figures show traditional arrangement in less than a quarter of households. Single person households, cohabiting adults, and childless couples, for example, are now seen in larger numbers. See Eric Schmitt, For First Time, Nuclear Families Drop Below 25% of Households, New York Times, Late Edition, May 15, 2001, at A1 (reporting on the 2000 U.S. Census data).

17 Marriage often creates a state-sanctioned unit for dependencies, i.e., for childcare and elder care, which society then does not have to address in the public sphere.

18 See Olsen, supra note 3, at 1505.

19 Marriage is public because the state regulates who may marry, how they may divorce, who may take the products of that marriage (children, assets, etc.) regulated by government for tax purposes.

that it plays an important ideological role—our beliefs about marriage help to shape our understandings of other societal institutions. In this regard, marriage has been referred to as a foundational institution.[20]

Marriage has had particular relevance in the construction of gender. Given the importance of gender in virtually all aspects of society, our beliefs about marriage and the tasks it performs should produce an explicit consideration in the development of legal and social theory. One must remember that marriage has not been a neutral social, cultural, or legal institution.[21] It has shaped the aspirations and experiences of women and men in ways that have historically disadvantaged women.[22]

The history of marriage as reflected in the common law centers on dependency and duty. Family roles were gendered in complementary and interdependent ways. Wives owed husbands their sexual and domestic services and, in exchange, their husbands were required to provide for them economically.[23] For that reason, I imagine that since women first banded together under the label

---

[20] See Masking Dependency, supra note 14, at 2189 n.21 (observing that Bork eulogized the foundational role of marriage in Franz v. United States, 712 F.2d 1428, 1438 (D.C. Cir. 1983) (Bork, J., concurring in part and dissenting in part) by stating, "The reason for protecting the family and the institution of marriage is not merely that they are fundamental to our society but that our entire tradition is to encourage, support, and respect them").

[21] Id. at 2182 ("A traditional family is typically imagined: a husband and wife - formally married and living together - with their biological children. The husband performs as the head of the household, providing economic support and discipline for the dependent wife and children, who correspondingly owe him duties of obedience and respect").

[22] Marriage has shaped women's dependency responsibilities. Their caretaking responsibilities often prevent them from being able to take advantage of opportunities in the workplace. See id. at 2188 (noting that traditionally, "the uncompensated tasks of caretaking are placed with women while men pursue careers that provide economically for the family but also enhance their individual career or work prospects").

[23] See generally Mary Ann Glendon, The New Family and the New Property (1981).

"feminist," at least some of us have been concerned with marriage, the institution of the family, and the content of family law. Over decades, concern has generated calls for reform. These calls have been heeded, and the transformation in laws with respect to husbands and wives reflects a more significant and far reaching transformation in the marital relationship itself.

Feminists have considered family law reform necessary for two primary reasons—one internal and one external to the institution of the family. The first reason involves the unequal nature of historical family arrangements and interactions.[24] There were real injustices within the hierarchical and patriarchal family, exemplified by the economic inequities that emerged with divorce reform and the prevalence of physical and psychological abuse of women.[25] The second impetus for reform within the family has been generated by looking outside of the family and assessing the effects that women's family responsibilities have had on their position in the larger society.[26] Feminists realized that equality in education, politics, and the workplace could not be fully realized if there were not corresponding changes in family roles and responsibilities.[27]

Feminists from all disciplines asserted that women, in and outside of the family, were primarily defined by

---

[24] Id.

[25] See generally June Carbone & Margaret Brinig, Rethinking Marriage: Feminist Ideology, Economic Change and Divorce Reform, 65 Tulane L. Rev. 953 (1991).

[26] See Martha Albertson Fineman, Cracking the Foundational Myths: Independence, Autonomy, and Self-Sufficiency, 8 Am. U. J. Gender Soc. Pol'y & L. 13, 20 (2000) [hereinafter Cracking Foundational Myths] (noting that "[c]aretaking labor saps energy and efforts from investment in career or market activities, those things that produce economic rewards").

[27] See generally The Neutered Mother, supra note 1; see also generally Twila L. Perry, Caretakers, Entitlement, and Diversity, 8 Am. U. J. Gender Soc. P'ly & L. 153 (2000).

their family roles of wife, mother, and daughter.[28] These roles assumed economic dependency, self-sacrifice, and subservience. Furthermore, these family roles displaced other aspirations or occupations on an ideological level, with concrete implications for opportunities provided in or aspirations cultivated for educational or workplace settings.[29] Expectations governing the family (private) sphere correspondingly defined aspirations and possibilities for women in the workplace (public) sphere.[30]

The story of twentieth century family law in the United States has certainly been the transformation of this hierarchically organized relationship of man and wife into a regime of marital partnership, where spouses are conceived in gender-neutral terminology and each is equally responsible for himself or herself, as well as for his or her spouse.[31] As well established as these changes are, we have not yet fully incorporated their implications. We retain unaltered assumptions about marriage, even in the face of this move from dependency to partnership, in regard to women's relationships with their husbands.[32] Part of the "blame" for this failure can be laid at the feet of feminists, because they too under-theorized the family as an institution, although the market and public side of the ledger generated an extraordinary amount of critique and comment.

---

[28] For a representative selection of essays, see The State, the Law and the Family: Critical Perspectives (Michael D.A. Freeman ed., 1984).

[29] See Cracking Foundational Myths, supra note 26, at 20.

[30] The feminist legal theorist's story is similar to that of non-legal feminists. Barrie Thorne asserts that in the so-called "first wave" of feminism patriarchal laws such as those that gave husbands control over wives' bodies and property occasioned outrage and generated calls for reform. In the second wave (which occurred in mid Twentieth Century), feminists explicitly analyzed the family as a site of oppression and inequality. The family under such consideration was identified as both an idealized household arrangement and an ideology. Barrie Thorne, Feminist Rethinking of the Family: An Overview, *in* Rethinking the Family: Some Feminist Questions 7 (Barrie Thorne & Marilyn Yalom, eds. 1982).

[31] See The Neutered Mother, supra note 1, at 158.

[32] See Masking Dependency, supra note 14, at 2181.

This is not to say that the family was forgotten. Family law scholars generally embraced the feminist notion that there was an intertwined relationship between the "public" and the "private."[33] They only focused on half of the equation for change, however, accepting and expanding upon the idea that it was necessary to transform the family in order for women to act as full citizens in the public sphere. The debate about the concepts of public and private proceeded along the lines that the "private" institution of the family was in need of "public" reform, and attention was primarily directed toward how internal family relationships were structured and expressed in law. Family law scholars, however, typically left critical examinations of non-family institutions—those in the "public" sphere—to others.[34] When focusing solely on the changes made in regard to individual expectations about relationships within marriage, it seems clear that reform was successful. Family law scholars opened marriage up to scrutiny and made powerful and effective arguments that altered the way we think about gendered violence,[35] reproductive rights,[36] and the legal relationship between husband and wife,[37] as well as the construction of gendered roles within the family.[38] In a recent survey of feminism's effect on family law, Dean

[33] See, e.g., Thorne, supra note 30.

[34] For the most part, those who were busy looking at institutions and structures in the public sphere ignored the family. This was true of many feminists who also assumed some version of the family as a backdrop to their theorizing. Scholarship in that field was to a large extent divided among those who: (1) using a domination or subordination model focused attention on issues concerning sexual violence and/or reproductive rights; (2) those who worked with a discrimination model confronting issues such as arose in the workplace; and (3) those who concentrated on the family who imported notions of equality and gender-neutrality into the historically most gendered institution in society.

[35] See Elizabeth M. Schneider, The Violence of Privacy, 23 Conn. L. Rev. 973, 985-89 (1991).

[36] See Roe v. Wade, 410 U.S. 113 (1973).

[37] This has been the focus of much of my work. See generally Martha Albertson Fineman, The Illusion of Equality: The Rhetoric and Reality of Divorce Reform (1991).

[38] See The Neutered Mother, supra note 1, at 15.

Katharine Bartlett suggests that feminism's principal contribution to the law of the family "has been to open up that institution to critical scrutiny and question the justice of a legal regime that has permitted, even reinforced, the subordination of some family members to others."[39] This rendition defines the task of feminism as confronting inequality and subordination, and effecting reforms.[40] Feminism ignored the historical privacy obstacle and pulled our attention to the inner workings of marriage and the marital family.

Dean Bartlett casts the contributions of feminist family law scholars and practitioners in this manner largely as a success story. Feminists challenged the public-private divide, making abuses within the family visible.[41] They generated instability in, and subsequent reform of, "traditional" patriarchal family law. Feminist engagement with and employment of powerful legal concepts such as "equality" led to recasting marriage as a relationship between equal partners. Divorce rules have changed to reflect the perception that wages and income are the product of family labor, not only of individual efforts.[42] The legal relationship between husband and wife has been completely rewritten in gender-neutral, equality aspiring terms.[43] So-called "domestic" violence is now subjected to criminal and civil sanctions, and "marital rape" is no longer considered an oxymoron.[44] Most women, whether they identify themselves as feminist or not, benefit from and generally approve of such manifestations of gender equality.

---

39 Katharine T. Bartlett, Feminism and Family Law, 33 Fam. L.Q. 475, 475 (1999).

40 Id.

41 See generally Martha Albertson Fineman & Roxanne Mykitiuk, The Public Nature of Private Violence (1994).

42 See Fineman, supra note 37, at 46-48.

43 See Fineman & Mykitiuk, supra note 41, at xiv.

44 Id.

Given the widespread acceptance of such changes in the way gender equality is understood today, it is worth exploring what Dean Bartlett means when she concludes that the most "divisive issues" for feminists, as well as for the larger society, "have been those that concern the preservation, or elimination, of traditional gender roles" in family or family-related areas of the law.[45] Her discussion of division implies that these roles still exist. What are the implications of her assertion that [f]amily-related issues concerning gender roles have generated the most backlash against feminism in the popular culture?[46] It seems unlikely that she accurately describes the current response to new norms of gender equality that govern the relationship between husband and wife.

Dean Bartlett's remarks most likely reflect the fact that, for the most part, feminist family law has had a limited focus. It has been relentless in an exploration of internal inequities and injustices in the family but has failed to step back and consider the institution of the family in its societal context. It has also neglected to address the very questions about meaning raised in the beginning of this essay. Undertaking such an exploration from a feminist perspective moves us away from concern about family roles and gender equality (at least initially) and directs our attention to the place and meaning of marriage and the marital family in our cultural, social, and ideological system.

Until we undertake this kind of exploration it will be impossible for us to consider what kinds of reforms are likely to make things better (more equal and just) within marriage, the marital families, or society in general. Real reform cannot proceed (or even be adequately theorized)

---

45 Bartlett, supra note 39, at 500 ("The least divisive issues in family law, such as domestic violence, have been those that have been resolved by reference to familiar principles outside of family law. By the same token, the most visible conflicts outside family law, such as the debate among feminists over maternity leave, have related to family and gender roles").

46 Id.

until we understand and appreciate the way changes in the structuring and functioning of marriage and the marital family challenge and threaten other societal institutions. The backlash to which Dean Bartlett alludes is generated in response to these threats and challenges.

This is a plea for feminist family law scholars not to repeat the same sort of theoretical mistake that mars discussions in other areas of law and policy. We cannot assume that other societal institutions will simply conform in accordance with our arguments about what would be an ideal family form or function. An explicit examination of the marital family as an institution and its relationship to policy and law may not be part of economic or philosophical theory, but discussions of the constraints inherent in the "realities" of the market or the limits of existing theories of justice must be central to feminist reform. We cannot just look to the internal aspects of marital family, focusing on the gendered nature of relationships. We must also look to what work the idea of a marital family does in society, and the ways in which public and private institutions rely on that work getting done.

Dean Bartlett limits her essay to an exploration of three areas of family law that exemplify the gendered nature of family relationships between the adult marital (or heterosexual) couple: It is the relationship between women and men that is hammered out in reforms addressing divorce, sex and reproduction, and domestic violence.[47] Because of "space limitations," she omits other "relevant" areas of inquiry, including two that directly bring children and dependency into the picture—work-family regulation

---

[47] See id. at 475. Bartlett addresses the tensions within feminism in regard to the areas she does discuss. In doing so, she by necessity touches on marriage and the child support system (the privatized solution for economic dependency and therefore tied to any discussion of welfare). Perhaps this demonstrates how difficult it is to address any one area of central concern in family law without bumping into others because they are related conceptually and politically as well as in practice.

and the state welfare system.[48] This selection of family topics reflects a broad and persistent feminist preoccupation with the relationship between women and men.

These male-female relation issues are the "easy" areas for contemporary feminism. They are easy because they focus on internal and intimate relations, and because they are areas in which disagreement among feminists, as well as between feminism and the larger society are no longer so pronounced. Laws governing divorce, sex and reproduction, and domestic violence address areas in which there is equilibrium, perhaps even close to a societal consensus, forged in part through feminist sensibilities.

In making this claim about equilibrium or relative consensus, I am not forgetting about the religious right or ignoring the fact that within communities of support nuanced debates still exist, such as those concerning late-term abortion in pro-choice feminist circles. My assertions are merely that the majority of American society (feminist and not):

1. seem to be relatively settled on policies that allow relatively liberal divorce laws coupled with a partnership model for doing economic justice between spouses;

2. have settled into a "live-and-let-live" approach to sex complemented by recognition of a woman's right to "choose"; and

[48] Id.

3. believe perpetrators of domestic violence should be censored and punished whereas society should provide support and protection for their victims.

Perhaps what is at the heart of Dean Bartlett's observations about division within (as contrasted with backlash to) feminism is her unstated realization that feminist perception of what social arrangements constitute "gender issues" has (or should have) evolved. Concern with women's position *vis-à-vis* men has been displaced by concern over the tenacity of women's historic socially and culturally assigned role as caretaker or nurturer. In this regard, legal feminists seem to have a much more ambiguous response than that generated in response to the traditional roles of husband and wife.

What are we feminists to do with motherhood as both a practice and an ideological structure? In the family arena it is not what we want for women as "wife" but what we aspire to for "mother" that divides us and provokes dissention and debate in and outside of feminist communities. This realization that motherhood is the real "gender issue" also frames a conceptual and theoretical challenge in family law for contemporary legal feminism. It seems apparent that the solutions to the dilemma of dependency and caretaking cannot be found in the family; we must begin to look beyond that institution, making demands for transformation in the workplace and the state.

Returning to the areas omitted from Dean Bartlett's essay, policies surrounding marriage, work-family, and welfare, it seems clear these are among the most contentious issues in society today. They are divisive and controversial within feminism because they confront us with the failure of equality and gender-neutrality initiatives to transform the practice in many families that continues to reflect traditional, gendered patterns. Focusing on work-family conflicts, particularly welfare, brings into focus the inconsistency between what we (still) aspire to as mothers and what we (now) aspire to as equals to men in the workplace. How do we think about and argue for reform in light of the realization that the role of mother, in spite of decades of attempts to equalize family responsibility and draft gender-neutral, equality-enhancing rules, continues to exact costs to women?

Feminist legal theorists anticipated that as women became more active in the workplace, men would become more involved in the family. Within the family, however, the quest for equality and gender-neutrality has not produced the same sort of "progress" in affecting the actual practices of mothers and fathers as it did for women and men in the market. Generations after the formal articulation of gender-neutral parenting principles, the assumption of responsibilities for children and other dependents continues to be gender-skewed. The implications of motherhood are very different from those of fatherhood. Within individual families we may of course see struggles over the sharing of responsibility. Some men are actually attempting to redefine their own behavior and society's expectations for fathers.[49] Studies show that when they do, they suffer some of the same disadvantages and negative economic consequences as mothers.

Perhaps more striking is the difficulty women and men experience in trying to equalize their behavior as mothers and fathers. When contrasting the persistent gendered divisions of family responsibility against those that demonstrate the successful re-configuration of women's relationship to the workforce, it becomes apparent that norms of equality are not only firmly entrenched, they are also reflected in the expectations and behavior of men and women, wives and husbands (so long as they are not mothers and fathers). What does this continued inequality mean for feminism—or more specifically, for feminists

---

49 See Arlie Russell Hochschild, The Time Bind: When Work Becomes Home and Home Becomes Work, 117-21 (1997) (finding that men who asked for parental leave were seen as not dedicated to their career); see also Gene Koretz, Hazardous to Your Career: The Risks of Taking Unpaid Leaves, Bus. Wk., Jan. 17, 2000, at 26.

concerned with the family and with family law? For one thing, it is clear that society has some interesting (and potentially divisive) issues in need of feminist consideration. The need to define the concepts and vocabulary to be employed in addressing the dependency and resulting inequality inherent in the parent-child relationship is fundamental.[50] The task of developing a vocabulary will undoubtedly be divisive. The language of legal feminism, developed while looking at women compared to men, was framed by the quest for equality, juxtaposing ideas of domination with anti-subordination, victimhood with agency, and special treatment with equality. These are concepts developed to address the legal and structural burdens imposed on women in their roles as wives in relation to men as husbands, and do not adequately capture the dilemmas confronting women in their roles as mothers.[51]

II. THE FUTURE OF FAMILY REFORM?

The absence of feminist concepts to address the dilemmas of motherhood within the egalitarian family has not meant that other disciplines have failed to try to fill the rhetorical vacuum. Borrowing from a potential colonizer, I bring in economics, as it seems ready to supply the rhetoric and concepts to fill any void. In his new reader, "Foundations of the Economic Approach to Law," Avery Katz devotes the last section to "an application on the

[50] The lack of unequal worth and unequal ability are very difficult to discuss in non-condescending or patronizing ways. See Barbara Bennett Woodhouse, The Dark Side of Family Privacy, 67 Geo. Wash. L. Rev. 1247, 1250 n.21 (1999) (advocating use of the "stewardship" model and the "notion of children's 'need-based rights'").

[51] These concepts helped to make it clear that the historic legal treatment of women in the contexts of divorce, reproduction, and family violence was unequal and unjust. These contexts are also areas in which we are clear(er) about our aspirations for society and its institutions in regard to women's quest for equality. Victor R. Fuchs, Women's Quest for Economic Equality 72 (1988) (noting that despite equality, children are still predominantly the concern of women).

frontier: family law." Professor Katz asserts: "economic analysis can shed light on any sphere of human interaction in which individuals pursue their goals subject to constraint."[52] He describes family relations as:

> [E]xternalities imposed by individual families on the rest of society and by individual family members on others in the household; incentives to invest in the family's material assets and in the human assets of its individual members; strategic behavior arising from family members' efforts to influence each others' conduct; insurance against the financial and emotional risks of disability, unemployment, and household dissolution; and the effects of limited information and bounded rationality on such crucial personal decisions as family formation and career choice.[53]

Professor Katz speculates that among the reasons to date for economics enjoying "relatively less influence" in family law than in other doctrinal fields is the persistence of thinking of market and family as separate realms.[54] Of equal significance, and of particular relevance to feminists, is his additional identification of the difficulty associated with the "fundamental issues of liberalism" raised by the "recurring need" (inherent in the whole idea of family) for some family members to make decisions for others incapable of protecting their own interests.[55] Professor Katz thus labels the family "the archetypal paternalist institution."[56] An economic model, which posits

---

52 See Foundations of the Economic Approach to Law 410 (Avery Wiener Katz ed. 1998).

53 Id at 410-11.

54 Id. at 411.

55 Id.

56 Id. Professor Katz states that some scholars, due to the complexity inherent in the family context, see economic modeling as inappropriate. In this regard, he recognizes that there are "competing disciplines,"

independent, rational individuals not only interacting with each other, but also seeking to maximize their own utility in that interaction, does not reflect what is assumed about family relationships.[57]

This "recurring need" for a "paternalist" family does not only present a dilemma for the imperial discipline of economics. It also creates a dilemma for feminists. The feminist version of the dilemma arises because this need and the inequality it reflects cannot readily be resolved by a reference to the principles of equality and gender-neutrality that have defined the feminist family law projected thus far. Need and dependency mandate paternalism (or maternalism) in some form, but only for some relationships.

A. The Contractual Affiliation: The End of Marriage as Status

Largely through the law and economics movement, the concept of contract has made headway in legal approaches to family relationships. The idea of contract is useful once it has been adapted to allow us to move beyond a law and economics-individualistic model of contracting. Economic theory tends to accept existing structures as givens, but the idea of contract can be appropriated for consideration of the relationships within the institution of the family. Contract need not only be about the creation of relationships between individuals; it can reflect societal arrangements—interlocking structural and ideological relationships among institutions, or between the state and individuals. In that sense, we do talk about something called the "social contract."[58]

---

specifically psychology and biology, that address the issue. He does not mention feminism as a competing discipline.

57 This does not mean that economists have not used their model to predict and explain family behavior or to argue for policy. Id. at 410-39.

58 See generally Martha Albertson Fineman, Contract and Care, 76

Economics did not, however, invent the association between contract and marriage. Contract has long served as an accepted metaphor for the marriage arrangement. In traditional practice, however, the whole notion of private ordering exemplified by contracting was historically viewed as inappropriate for forging relationships of intimacy. Although some of the traditional doctrinal language associated with contract found its way into family law, marriage and sexuality were by in large considered appropriately regulated by the state.

The problem is that the idea of marriage as contract has never been taken seriously enough. Although we may discuss "consent" and "consideration" in ascertaining whether a marriage "contract" has been formed, or affix "reliance" and "expectation" in making judgments about the economic or other consequences of divorce, few scholars even today consider marriage an entirely flexible legal institution, susceptible to manipulation and the generation of individualized voluntary (but enforceable) terms. Even in areas where contracting is encouraged, such as settlement agreements, or at least tolerated, such as antenuptial agreements, courts scrutinize terms for fairness and worry about overreaching and bargaining position in ways that would be unacceptable in enforcement proceedings for other types of contracts. Conceptually, although one may have "choice" when entering marriage, when it comes to the terms and consequences of that status, there is no free marketplace in which private ordering is the rule.

What would happen if we were to take the idea of contract as a substitute for traditional, state-defined marriage seriously? If we used the idea of contract to move beyond marriage-as-we-know-it? This would present an interesting "thought experiment." Freed from the mandate of proposing a practical suggestion for social policy, we could begin to confront the reality of marriage as an ideology and mechanism for ordering relationships and

---

Chi.-Kent L. Rev. 1403 (2001).

intimacy in ways that obfuscate the dimensions of the social crisis of dependency.[59]

In *The Neutered Mother*, I urge the abolition of marriage as a legal category and, with it, the demise of the entire set of special rules attached to it, doing away with the laws of marriage and divorce as well as altering those areas in which "spouse" is a consequential category such as tax law or probate and estate rules.[60]

It is possible to view this call for the abolition of marriage as a demand for private ordering. Areas of private law—contract, torts, criminal law, property, equality, and so on—would have to do the conceptual and structural work that marriage currently does as a "status," mandating special legal consideration and consequences. The financial implications of sexual affiliates (formerly labeled husband and wife) would be regulated by private, individualized agreement—by contract—with no special rules governing fairness or unique review and monitoring of the negotiation process.[61]

A proposal for the abolition of marriage as a legal category, however, involves much more than just a "simple" preference for "privatization" of potential economic consequences. In the absence of a contract to govern a specific intimate situation, there may be a need for default rules. General regulatory rules such as those found in equity (e.g., unjust enrichment or constructive trust), partnership, and labor law could provide the bases for

59 I do not mean the type of "crisis" associated with welfare reform's casting of dependency as pathology. Rather, I am concerned with the crisis generated because inevitable dependency has been delegated to the family.

60 The Neutered Mother, supra note 1, at 228-30. I anticipate that there would still exist cultural or religious marriages. However, these unions would have no independent legal significance. Any legal consequences that would accrue to them would be provided by legal rules generally applicable across the population.

61 This is common with antenuptial agreements and doctrinally required (even if not typically practiced) with settlement agreements.

decisions in disputes involving sexual affiliates. Constitutional and civil rights laws might also offer some suggestive parameters for exploring what economic consequences should attach to joint endeavors undertaken by formerly exempt family members.[62]

In other words, in addition to contract rules, ameliorating doctrines would fill the void left by the abolition of marriage law. In fact, it seems apparent that a lot more regulation (protection) would occur once the interactions of men and women were removed from behind the veil of privacy that now shields them when they act in their family roles as husbands and wives. Without the immunity or special relationship defense provided by marriage, for example, there would be no justification for failing to apply the "normal" rules of tort and criminal law to sexual affiliates.

Feminists have pointed out for over a century that the institution of marriage is the location of a lot of abuse and violence. The institution is based on an unequal and hierarchical social arrangement in which men are considered the heads of households, owed domestic and sexual services by wives and obedience and deference by all family members. Once the institutional protection afforded to marriage is removed, behavior would be judged by standards established to regulate interactions among all members of society.

What would be the practical implications of this suggested "reform"? Marriage, no longer available, would no longer stand as a defense to rape. Conceptually bracketing off some assaults as "domestic violence," rendering them somehow less serious than the non-domestic variety, would be problematic.[63] Perhaps we

[62] I am uncommitted to any particular set of principles for these default rules at this time. The only requirement would be that they be rules of general application and apply to all types of transaction between legally competent adults. Specific categories of affiliation would not be separated out for special treatment.

[63] In the past, certain types of domestic violence were not even

would even begin to develop theories of tort to compensate sexual affiliates for conduct endemic to family interactions but considered unacceptable among strangers. A tort for intentional infliction of emotional or psychological harm might emerge, for example.[64] Norms that prohibit harassment (including stalking), verbal assault, and emotional abuse among strangers would be applied in defining appropriate conduct between sexual intimates.[65]

On a whole different vein, the end of marriage as a state regulated and defined institution undermines, and perhaps entirely erodes, the state interest in controlling and regulating sexual affiliations. If no form of sexual affiliation is state preferred, subsidized, and protected, none could or should be prohibited. Same-sex partners and others forming a variety of other sexual arrangements would simply be viewed as equivalent forms of privately preferred sexual connection. Such unions might even be celebrated in religious or cultural ceremonies, but the state would have no regulatory interest.[66] If there is no marriage, the substantial economic and other societal benefits currently afforded to certain heterosexual units would no longer be justified, nor would punishment of "deviant" sexual connections any longer be permitted.

In addition, some other types of non-sexually based family formation currently interpreted through norms of heterosexual marriage would also "open-up" with the

considered criminal behavior. Husbands had not only a right, but also a duty to chastise and punish wives and children. Physical chastisement was considered appropriate as long as it did not exceed certain limits. See The Neutered Mother, supra note 1, at 156.

[64] There has been some push to do this in the context of divorce already. See Ruprecht v. Ruprecht, 599 A.2d 604, 607 (N.J. Super. Ct. Ch. Div. 1991) (allowing for suit for intentional infliction of emotional harm without physical injury in the context of a divorce); see also Hakkila v. Hakkila, 812 P.2d 1320, 1326-27 (N.M. Ct. App. 1991).

[65] Other areas of law that would substitute for (or be supplemented by) the abolition of marriage and divorce rules would include bankruptcy, fiduciary responsibility, equity, and ethics.

[66] The exceptions to this general principle should be obvious—rape and child molestation would still be prohibited and punished by law.

abolition of marriage. Single motherhood in particular would become unregulated. Without marriage, motherhood would not be modified by the presence or absence of a legal relationship between heterosexual partners. There would be neither "single mothers" nor "married mothers"—only "mothers." Women would be free to become pregnant without fear of censure or penalty. Paternity proceedings would be neither automatic nor mandatory—inflicted against the wishes and in disregard for the privacy of mothers simply so the state can fill in the blank under "father's name" on a birth certificate and thus ensure male economic responsibility for a child. Sperm banks and specialists in reproductive technologies, including artificial insemination and fertility treatments, would not feel that the marital status of their patients was an ethical or professional concern.[67]

In addition to freeing women from the heterosexual marriage paradigm in their reproductive lives, the abolition of marriage as a legal category would have other implications. As earlier discussed, contract language is often used in referring to the family, though the rules seem more anchored in concepts of status.[68] Interestingly, from the perspective of contract as a metaphor for bargaining, human activities in which women might be considered to have either a "natural" monopoly or to possess more on the "supply" than "demand" side of the equation have been written out of contract.[69]

Sex and reproduction (certainly significant areas of barter and exchange) are not subject to contract. We do not

---

67 This method of reproduction might be preferred once such restraints were removed. It avoids any questions about "consent" vis-à-vis the sperm donor because he would have alienated his interest in his contribution of reproductive material in his donation to the sperm bank.

68 This is particularly true in modern family law jurisprudence where marriage is referred to as a "partnership" and some of the economic consequences may be tailored to individual preferences through pre-nuptial contracts and/or separation agreements.

69 More specifically, these areas were set aside and governed by special rules regulating marriage. See Fineman, supra note 58.

allow individualized bargaining, but refer sexual interactions into the extralegal (the modern position) or apply regulatory generalized coercive rules to them. Traditionally, sexual affiliation has been regulated by the marriage contract and by the many rules, both criminal and civil, which bolster and reinforce the institution of marriage by penalizing or prohibiting other sexual affiliations.[70]

There is no obvious reason why sex should be excluded from some contractual schemes (e.g., private bargaining) while it has been an explicit part of another contractual scheme (e.g., the services requirement in the marital contract).[71] Another question might therefore ask what would happen if sexual affiliation, like other

---

[70] These rules are not only the law of marriage and divorce, but large areas of criminal and civil law that bolster the institution of marriage and penalize sexual affiliations that do not conform to the marriage model. For instance, laws against prostitution, fornication, adultery, and cohabitation as well as inheritance and probate laws, property rules, and tax law treat economic exchanges between marital partners differently than those that occur between other members of society. See Martha Albertson Fineman, Law and Changing Patterns of Behavior: Sanctions on Non-Marital Cohabitation, Wisc. L. Rev. 275, 282-83, 316 (1981).

[71] Kant struggled with the idea of rights to persons as akin to rights to things—describing marital or family status entailing rights "neither to a thing nor merely a right against a person but also possession of a person." Kant further describes the three objects of acquisition: a man acquires a wife, a couple acquires children, and a family acquires servants. We are also told that "whatever is acquired in this way is also inalienable and the right of possessors of these objects is the more personal of all rights." One outgrowth of the (obviously patriarchal) assertion that what is acquired in marriage is a woman (wife) by a possessor (husband or man) was the common law rule that marriage was a defense to rape. See Immanuel Kant, The Metaphysics of Morals 61 (Mary Gregor trans. & ed., 1996); see also Jeremy Waldron, When Justice Replaces Affection: The Need for Rights, *in* Liberal Rights: Collected Papers, 1981-1991 376 (Cambridge Univ. Press, 1996).
Justice Lord Hale expressed the opinion that consent to marriage was consent to provide sexual services on demand. Fortunately, the system of obligations and entitlements built upon this view of the world has been undermined. This would seem to require a reexamination of other basic principles and assumptions. See 1 Hale P.C. 629, *as quoted in* Warren v. State, 336 S.E.2d 221 (1985).

significant areas of social interaction, were not treated differently—if there were no special category of rules regulating consensual, adult sex exchanges and all were subject to contract.[72]

There are a number of interesting legal process questions raised by this set of speculations about abolishing marriage as a legal category and relying on other areas of law to address the problems that might arise between sexual affiliates. These questions involve the mechanisms transforming law, and the ways in which doctrine can adapt to and accommodate new patterns of behavior. Ideological as well as structural forces would have to be considered. Certainly pouring sexual affiliates into the arenas of contract, tort, and criminal law would not leave those doctrines untransformed. How would the content of contract, tort, and criminal law change? Would ideas about bargaining, consideration, and unconscionability be altered? The prospect presents exciting possibilities for reexamining entire areas of substantive law, where assumptions about interactions between independent, equal, and autonomous individuals govern terms and consequences.

Of course, if we take the relationship of husband and wife out of regulation, the obvious question becomes, "What will happen to the children who are left behind?" Although we may comfortably assume in contemporary America that women can be expected to function as equals and make their own bargains, the contract paradigm does not fit so neatly with the recognized need for protection when we speak of children or others who may be dependent and in need of assistance and care.[73]

---

[72] The laws punishing prostitution would certainly fall and women would be able to charge for gestational and other reproductive services.

[73] These relationships may not function according to an equality model. They may be hierarchical and unequal. This does not mean, however, that the people are of unequal value, just that they are of unequal ability, however temporarily. See Woodhouse, supra note 50, at 1253, 1255. I am struggling here with the idea of solidarity in

Current American mythology assumes that the marital family serves the essential function of managing dependency.[74] This function has ideological and structural dimensions that shape political and policy discourse and influence law.[75] But the family imagined in this discourse and policy no longer exists; it has changed. Divorce is common and fewer people are forming relationships that conform to the traditional model.[76] Women's aspirations for themselves and expectations of their partners are substantially altered. Yet we insist on assigning primary, almost exclusive, responsibility for dependency to the marital family. Something must give way – family or work. Some women will let go of their aspirations for an equalitarian marriage, whereas others will find they have no choice but to compromise care standards or forgo having children altogether because of the incompatibility of work with caretaking. The point is that continued adherence to an inappropriate image of the marital family will have significant implications for those operating within those families.[77]

Under the marital-family-as-a-repository-of dependency-model, the costs of caretaking are born by the family and, within the family, primarily by women and children. The consequences to women often are not

---

contrast to equality as the way to understand the caretaker/dependent relationship. Others use different concepts, such as "stewardship." See id. at 1256-57.

[74] See The Neutered Mother, supra note 1, at 161-64.

[75] Id.

[76] Id. See also footnote 16.

[77] Further, one important historic role that marriage plays in defining other family relationships and responsibilities has been substantially altered in the waning years of the Twentieth Century. Other family relationships are no longer defined by marriage. Unmarried fathers have rights to and responsibilities for their children that were not part of the common law scheme. Non-marital children are entitled to benefits historically reserved for their marital counterparts. Equitable or contractual principles result in allocations of property or other economic adjustments at the termination of a non-marital cohabitation relationship in ways similar to the rules that apply at divorce in many states.

revealed until the family dissolves, by death or divorce, and the caretakers cannot manage to take on the full-time and unassisted role of primary breadwinner, while continuing to caretake. Consequences, both to the individual and to society, may also become apparent when the marital family (or enough marital families) fails in its assigned societal role and children are left on their own without adequate arrangements for care.

B. The Dependency Affiliation: The Beginning of Modern Family Law

Feminist family theorists must open up the debates and insist on a rethinking of the position assigned to the family in the larger society. We can begin with a consideration of the historic role of marital family in society. Changes in patterns of behavior are moving us toward a post-traditional, marital-family model. What role or function can and should our new families (ones that may not be marital in form) be asked to serve? Which functions must be shared with other societal institutions, such as the market and the state? How should the substantial changes in marriage affect the construction of law and policy concerning the family? Finally, how do we protect and provide for children fairly and justly?

Marriage has historically served as the "natural" repository for dependencies.[78] The family is the institution to which children, the elderly, and the ill are referred; it is the way that the state has effectively "privatized" dependencies that otherwise might become the responsibility of the collective unit or state.[79] Yet dependency is of concern well beyond the family. Dependency work is of benefit to the entire society. In this

---

[78] I distinguish between what I refer to as "inevitable" dependency—a biological category of physical dependency that may also have economic, psychological, and other social implications—and "derivative" dependency, which is the dependency created in the caretaker for resources in order to accomplish the caretaking task. See The Neutered Mother, supra note 1, at 161-62.

[79] Id.

regard, it is not fair or just that the costs associated with dependency are not more evenly distributed.

In considering these assertions, one must first understand that dependency is a human phenomenon. In earlier work, I attempted to complicate the concept of dependency.[80] This move responded in part to the derisive and pejorative characterizations of dependency that accompanied welfare "reform" and the rhetoric of individual responsibility, as well as much of the discussion surrounding the suggestion that marriage was the solution to most (if not all) social problems concerning children and poverty.[81]

Dependency is "inevitable." Far from being a "pathological" condition associated with human failure, it is an inevitable part of the human condition. It is universal—a developmental and shared experience. All of us were dependent as children, and many of us will become dependent as we age, fall ill, or are disabled.[82] In this regard, "inevitable" dependency can be viewed as a biological category.[83]

There is, however, another important dimension to the discussion about dependency. If dependency in its biological manifestations is universal and inevitable, then we all need caretakers to provide for us during segments of our lives. The simple (but entirely obvious, even if often overlooked) realization is that caretakers of inevitable dependents are themselves dependent on resources in order

---

80 During this century (at least until recently) inevitable dependency in this and all other industrialized democracies was the object of progressive social welfare policies—inevitable dependents constituting the "deserving poor" exemplified by innocent children entitled to protection by the state and entitled to collective resources for education and welfare. See Masking Dependency, supra note 14.

81 Id.

82 Id.

83 Economic and psychological dependencies are not included in this category. Although they may accompany inevitable dependencies, they are better understood in structural or ideological terms.

to provide that care. I label this type of dependency "derivative dependency." [84]

To whom should society assign the responsibility for inevitable dependency (thereby constructing the derivative dependent), and under what conditions should those so designated be expected to fulfill the delegated caretaking roles? In considering these questions one must remember that caretaking requires the sacrifice of autonomy and entails compromises that negatively affect economic and market possibilities. Caretaking has substantial costs that are borne by the family in the first instance and, within those families, by the person who is assigned the duties of caretaker.

Professor Katz got it only half-right when he stated that the family must be "paternalistic."[85] The reality is that the family must be both paternal and maternal. Children and other dependents need both the "paternal" provider and the "maternal" caretaker, but it is difficult to find an all-encompassing "parental" figure who can accomplish both roles in our society under its current organization, where dependency is cloistered within the family and other institutions are free to disregard its demands.

The market assumes an unencumbered worker and is structured accordingly, punishing those who cannot conform. The state assumes self-sufficiency on the part of the family, punishing those units who do not conform. Society mandates the traditional, role-defined, marital family form. Even with the best of egalitarian intentions, marriages tend to slip into traditional and gendered patterns. Even the best single mother is viewed as inadequate. Within society, caretakers are required, but

---

[84] There is no societal consensus that derivative dependents have a legitimate claim to societal resources. In the context of "welfare reform," our society has rejected the notion that caretaking supplies a claim for social subsidy. See Martha Albertson Fineman, Legal Stories, Change, and Incentives—Reinforcing the Law of the Father, 37 N.Y.L. Sch. L. Rev. 227, 244-47 (1992).

[85] Supra note 52, at 411.

caretakers need resources, including time, money, energy, and accommodation from the workplace. The roles of head of household and dependent wife-caretaker provided both nurturing and economic resources. They did so, however, through the unpaid appropriation of the wife's labor—initially and most directly through the imposition of caretaking obligations to her husband and children. Fulfillment of these obligations not only benefits those family members who received them, however. Caretaking ultimately benefits the larger society, providing the workers, the voters, the students, and all of the other citizens that populate and contribute to its institutions.

Taking seriously the need for the resources supplied by both paternalism and maternalism in addressing dependency in today's society with its emerging norm of single-parent households will force us to look beyond the horizons of the institution of marriage and the relationship between husbands and wives. In fact, it may result in a radical reconfiguration of how we think about the family, a reconfiguration assessing the implications of both changed family form and essential family function.

Some of us already have begun to construct that reconfigured vision. Mine leaves behind the obsession with the marital tie and is built around the caretaker and dependent relationship.[86] It is this relationship that should be subsidized and protected. Recognizing both the inevitability of dependency and the society preserving work that caretakers do in meeting the demands of that dependency, I argue for the restructuring of our workplaces to accommodate a "dually responsible" worker, and the reinvigoration of our state so that caretaking and market work (maternalism and paternalism) are compatible, accomplishable tasks.[87] Only when this is accomplished will we have a society in which dependency is fairly and justly managed.

---

[86] See The Neutered Mother, supra note 1, at 230-35.

[87] See Cracking Foundational Myths, supra note 26, at 20; see also Fineman, supra note 58.

[19]

Marriage is for heterosexuals – may the rest of us be saved from it

Kenneth McK Norrie, Professor of Law, University of Strathclyde

INTRODUCTION

In the great movement towards gay and lesbian equality the major battles of the past few decades[1] – be it decriminalisation,[2] equality in ages of consent,[3] protection from discrimination[4] or access to military service[5] – have all concerned matters upon which there is a broad and fairly obvious consensus amongst gay men and lesbians. They have all, as well, involved individual rights. However, a new generation of disputes is emerging which concerns relationships rather than individuals,[6] and, excitingly, there is no clear consensus amongst gay activists and queer theorists as to the end result that is being sought.

More and more jurisdictions are granting recognition to same-sex relationships, some on an ad hoc basis, others more comprehensively. Denmark, in 1989, innovatively introduced a whole new domestic institution for same-sex couples, known as 'registered partnerships',[7] and that lead has been followed by a handful of European countries[8] and by the state of Vermont in the US (where the institution is known as 'civil unions'). The Dutch Parliament has voted in favour of opening up marriage itself to same-sex couples.[9] Many people would consider this a step too far. While welcoming any development that advances the cause of gay and lesbian equality, or that helps to change social attitudes towards a more tolerant and inclusive direction, I nevertheless consider the Dutch innovation a step in the wrong direction. Some activists and queer theorists take the view that opening up marriage to same-sex couples will be the ultimate recognition of both social and legal acceptability of homosexuality;[10] many feminists see marriage as a patriarchal oppressive institution which should be avoided by all, gay and non-gay alike;[11] others yet see it as an assimilationist threat to gay and lesbian

---

1 Not all of which, of course, have yet been won in all jurisdictions.

2 See *Dudgeon v UK* (1981) 4 EHRR 149; *Norris v Ireland* (1988) 13 EHRR 186; *Modinos v Cyprus* (1993) 16 EHRR 485.

3 *Sutherland v UK* (1998) EHRLR 117.

4 *Salgueiro da Silva Mouta v Portugal* (Case No 33290/96) 21 December 1999.

5 *Smith and Grady v UK* (2000) 29 EHRLR 493; *Lustig-Prean and Beckett v UK* (2000) 29 EHRR 548.

6 Disputes concerning the legal recognition of relationships have arisen in a number of jurisdictions. See *Fitzpatrick v Sterling Housing Association* [2000] 1 FLR 271 (England); *M v H* (1999) 171 DLR (4th) 577 (Canada); *National Coalition for Lesbian and Gay Equality v Minister for Home Affairs* (1999) (3) BCLR 280 (South Africa); *Baker v Vermont* 744 A2d 864 (1999). For a discussion of these cases see K. McK Norrie, 'Constitutional Challenges to Sexual Orientation Discrimination' (2000) 49 ICLQ 755.

7 See M. P. Broberg, 'The registered partnership for same-sex couples in Denmark' [1996] CFLQ 149.

8 See I. Lund-Andersen, 'Cohabitation and Registered Partnerships in Scandinavia', in J. Eekelaar and T. Nhlapo (eds), *The Changing Family: International perspectives on the family and family law* (Hart Publishing, 1998); W. Schrama, 'Registered Partnerships in the Netherlands' (1999) 13 Int J Law Pol & Fam 315.

9 An unofficial translation of the Bill accepted by the Dutch lower house of parliament in September 2000 can be found at http://ruljis.leiden.nl/user.cwaaldij/NHR/transl-marr.html

10 See D. Chambers, 'What If? The Legal Consequences of Marriage and the Legal Needs of Lesbian and Gay Male Couples' (1996) 95 Mich LR 447.

11 See, for example, N. Polikoff, 'We Will Get What We Ask For: Why Legalising Gay and Lesbian Marriage Will Not Dismantle the Legal Structure of Gender in Every Marriage' (1993) 79 Virg LR 1535.

lifestyles and to be avoided for that reason.[12] I want, in this article, to explain why I take the last of these approaches. I want to put forward the argument that, if marriage does retain relevance in the modern world, it does so only in the context of opposite-sex relationships. I should emphasise, however, that it is certainly no part of my argument that same-sex couples should be denied the rights, or be exempted from the liabilities, that the law grants to opposite-sex domestic partnerships, however few or many these legal consequences are in any particular jurisdiction. Any legal system that denies equality to different relationships based purely on the sexual orientation of the parties (and that includes most of them) is an iniquitous legal system. The point is that arguing for same-sex marriage is not, in my view, the best way to achieve equality.

THE DEFINITION OF MARRIAGE

Non-gay opponents to same-sex marriage often argue that the very concept is a contradiction in terms: marriage is, by definition, an opposite-sex relationship. A moment's thought, however, will show how unsatisfactory this assertion is. Marriage, as an institution, is not a natural phenomenon but is rather a legal structure, and, as such, it is one that is defined artificially by the law. So the law has the choice of how to define marriage and how to limit access to it. Every society defines marriage in a way that makes sense for itself and for its own (economic) needs and different societies define it differently. Indeed, they change their definitions as time goes by, the better to reflect contemporaneous social values. For example, some countries define it as a life-long relationship, escape from which is simply not possible,[13] others accept the idea of divorce.[14] Some countries define marriage as a relationship between no more than two persons; others define it to include polygamous relationships; others continue to accept child-marriage. Some jurisdictions refused to recognise interracial marriage.[15] The point is that there is no one, universally accepted, natural definition of marriage. It is entirely circular to say that marriage by definition is heterosexual because that is how marriage is defined.

Opponents of gay and lesbian equality often argue that marriage needs to be defended from same-sex attack because, as an institution, it is the basic building block of a settled and stable society.[16] I have never really understood how this can be used as an argument against same-sex marriage. If social stability is a good thing, which it is, and if marriage does serve a stabilising function, which it does (although, in truth, it is the fact that exit from marriage is far harder than entry into it, that is the stabilising factor), then more, not fewer, people should be encouraged into the 'ties that bind'. Opponents of gay equality really want to encourage gay people into opposite-sex marriage because that is the only marriage they recognise,[17] which is merely the 'definition' point again. A slightly more sophisticated argument (although in fact this too resolves itself into a definition argument) is that once you remove the requirement for heterosexuality, there is no justification for maintaining the other limitations on entry to marriage. Marriage might, therefore, evolve to include any relationship, however unstable,

12 The marriage debate is argued more extensively in the US than elsewhere, possibly because the institution of marriage provides the means whereby individuals access many private employment-related benefits, like pensions and health care, that in other countries are provided by the state. Extensive contributions to this debate are to be found in A. Sullivan (ed), *Same-Sex Marriage: Pro and Con* (Vintage, 1997) and R. Baird and S. Rosenbaum (eds), *Same-Sex Marriage: The Moral and Legal Debate* (Prometheus Books, 1997).

13 Until recently the Constitution of the Republic of Ireland prohibited courts in that jurisdiction from granting divorce.

14 In Scotland divorce has been a judicial remedy since the Reformation (originally only on the ground of adultery and since 1573 on the ground of desertion also: see APS 1573, c 1). In England it has been available to the courts only since the Matrimonial Causes Act 1857.

15 This was the case in some states in the US until the Supreme Court decision of *Loving v Virginia* 388 US 1 (1967).

16 See, for example, 'Defending Marriage' in A. Sullivan (ed), op cit, n 12, at pp 204–209 and L. Wardle, 'Same-Sex Marriage and the Limits of Legal Pluralism' in J. Eekelaar and T. Nhlapo, op cit, n 8.

17 An aspect of this argument was put forward by the state in the South African case of *National Coalition for Gay and Lesbian Equality* (1999) 3 BCLR 280, when they suggested that gay people were not discriminated against because they were free to marry persons of the opposite sex. The Constitutional Court of South Africa was contemptuous in its dismissal of this departure from reality.

such as polygamous, short-term and incestuous relationships, so leading to a breakdown in social stability.[18] However, this argument is based on a false premise. Removing one limitation to marriage, the requirement that it be between an opposite-sex couple, does not mean that we have to remove all limitations. What it does, of course, mean is that it is legitimate to question every limitation in order to ensure that it continues to serve some justifiable purpose in today's society. But there is nothing unusual about that. The limitations that UK law had on a man marrying his deceased wife's mother were scrapped in 1986.[19] The limitations on interracial marriage were held to be no longer sustainable in the US in *Loving v Virginia*.[20] All limitations should, in other words, be kept under constant review and the removal of one limitation does not in itself justify removing another. Today it is perfectly rational to say that the exclusion of incestuous and polygamous relationships continues to serve important social functions; while no purpose is served by excluding same-sex couples from marriage other than, self-referentially, the maintenance of the current definition.

SO, WHAT IS MY PROBLEM WITH SAME-SEX MARRIAGE?

None of the above amounts to an argument against same-sex marriage. It simply states that same-sex marriage does not, in itself, challenge or attack marriage, as currently understood. My problem is not that I think marriage ought to be attacked (although I do), but that using marriage as the route to gay and lesbian equality is misconceived. It simply shifts the goalposts for relationships that are currently outside the law's ken. We can see the operation of this phenomenon in many jurisdictions' attempts to recognise same-sex relationships by founding upon their similarities with opposite-sex relationships. This is exemplified in England by the *Fitzpatrick* case[21] and in Scotland by the first ad hoc statutory recognition of same-sex relationships.[22] Similarly in Canada, with its much more comprehensive recognition,[23] same-sex couples are recognised if they are in a relationship equivalent in all respects (except sexual orientation) to that of the opposite-sex couple who are 'living together as husband and wife'. By this means, paradoxically, the married relationship becomes the standard against which all other relationships are judged. The only way a same-sex couple can access statutory benefits[24] is, therefore, to emulate as closely as possible the opposite-sex couple. The difficulty I have with this is that it requires the denial of some very real differences between same-sex and opposite-sex couples, and by requiring emulation, it denies equal respect to those couples who *will not* or *cannot* model their relationship on the heterosexist norm. Equality is granted, but only on heterosexual terms.[25] Real equality, on the other hand, would come about by the law recognising the legitimacy of a variety of forms of domestic relationship, including those that have different perceptions of commitment and fidelity from how these notions are perceived in marriage.[26]

---

18 A. Sullivan (ed), op cit, n 12, at pp 273–294.

19 Marriage (Prohibited Degrees of Relationship) Act 1986.

20 388 US 1 (1967).

21 *Fitzpatrick v Sterling Housing Association* [2000] 1 FLR 271.

22 See s 87(2) of the Adults with Incapacities (Scotland) Act 2000 (asp 4) which includes members of same-sex couples within the meaning of 'nearest relative' for the purposes of that Act.

23 See, as a representative example, the Definition of Spouse Amendment Act 1999 (British Columbia).

24 In the UK there are, in fact, few statutory rights and liabilities attaching to opposite-sex cohabiting couples, but there are some. In such cases, by and large, the exclusion of same-sex couples serves no rational purpose. Why, for example, should a heterosexual survivor of a cohabiting couple receive damages under the Fatal Accidents Act 1976 or the Damages (Scotland) Act 1976 when a homosexual survivor in identical circumstances would receive nothing? Why should an opposite-sex cohabiting couple suffer aggregation of income for the purposes of calculating entitlement to means-tested benefits (and legal aid) when a same-sex couple in identical circumstances are exempt from that economic disadvantage?

25 In J. Millbank's words, 'In legal discourse, all roads lead to a heteronuclear Rome': para 14 in 'Which Then Would be the "Husband" and Which the "Wife?": Some Introductory Thoughts on Contesting the "Family" in Court' (1996) 3(3) *Murdoch Electronic Journal of Law*, at www.murdoch.edu.au/elaw/

26 See S. Boyd, 'Expanding the "Family" in Family Law' (1994) 7 *Canadian Journal of Women and the Law* 545.

I will give two examples where the social and emotional structures of same-sex relationships often or usually do not follow those of opposite-sex relationships, although within these two examples one might well find all life contained – property and sex.

Property first. There is little doubt that marriage historically was first and foremost a property relationship, at least in legal terms. For most legal systems in the western world, the most significant practical effect of marriage at common law was that the woman's property was automatically transferred into the ownership of her husband. Furthermore, in many legal systems she herself fell under his guardianship or otherwise had her own legal personality subsumed into his.[27] Marriage, in other words, was a powerful means whereby property (and with property, power) was concentrated in the male domain, and it was therefore the most significant means by which the inequality of the sexes was both institutionalised and perpetuated. Of course, past iniquities do not in themselves justify denying the worth of marriage today – rather the reverse, for marriage has proved itself able to develop and change and to respond to altering social needs. Today no western legal system maintains these original property effects of marriage.[28] However, the most significant consequence of marriage, as a legal institution, remains proprietorial. During marriage, under most legal systems, the income of both spouses can be accessed by the other, whether there is a community of property system or a postponed system. Both systems allow property or maintenance claims to be made at the end of the marriage, whether on death or divorce.[29] These rules are designed, if somewhat clumsily, to harmonise the wealth of both parties in relationships which, by and large, are between individuals who in terms of wealth creation, tend to be unequal. In other words, the major *legal* purpose of marriage today is to respond to the social, indeed systemic, inequality between the sexes. As such, it is uniquely appropriate for opposite-sex couples, in the sense that it serves a social function for them which is misconceived for same-sex couples who do not, by definition, reveal a systemic inequality.[30] Research has long shown that same-sex couples: (1) tend to be economically closer to each other, in terms of both wealth and earning power than opposite-sex couples; and (2) tend to avoid the economic inter-dependency on each other that so often characterises opposite-sex couples.[31] There are fewer joint bank accounts, in other words. Yet when judges seeking to benefit same-sex couples look for 'commitment' between the couple, this social phenomenon amongst opposite-sex couples is seen as one of the most potent indicators with same-sex couples also.[32] It may be appropriate for one, but it is far less appropriate for the other.

The same can be said for sex. In opposite-sex relationships an extremely high premium is paid in most societies to sexual fidelity. The marriage laws of most legal systems are full of concepts designed to emphasise the importance of keeping sex within marriage: concepts such as adultery, child-illegitimacy, consummation, incest and impotency. And the reason is not hard to find. For the single most important difference between heterosexual activity and homosexual activity is that the former has the unique potential, and the latter has absolutely no

27 See the sixteenth century Scottish text *William Hay's Lectures on Marriage*, translated from the original Latin by J. C. Barry, *Stair Society* (1967) 24. This work is representative of the European tradition in marriage, based very firmly upon the Canon law.

28 Although customary law in, for example, South Africa, does. For a general discussion, see C. Himonga and C. Bosch, 'The Application of African Customary Law Under the Constitution of South Africa' (2000) 117 SALJ 306.

29 See, as representative examples, the Matrimonial Causes Act 1973 (England) and the Family Law (Scotland) Act 1985 (Scotland).

30 This, in essence, was the argument used by Gonthier J in his dissent in *M v H* (1999) 171 DLR (4th) 577. However, in that case the point was subverted since the legislation at issue, being gender-neutral, allowed claims for financial support based not on systemic inequality but on actual need and, as such, it was illogical to deny claims by members of same-sex couples who had actual need, while at the same time not suffering systemic inequality. The same criticism can, of course, be made in relation to the point being made here.

31 G. Dunne, 'Balancing Acts: Lesbian Experiences of Work and Family Life', *Report to the ESRC* (1998); G. Dunne, 'A Passion for "Sameness"? Sexuality and Gender Accountability', in E. Silva and C. Smart (eds), *The New Family?* (Sage Publications, 1999), at pp 66–82.

32 This can be seen in the judgments in each of the cases listed at n 6 (above).

potential, to create new human life.[33] Child creation is of the utmost importance to society. But it should be remembered that these rules were not designed to ensure that children have a stable family upbringing – that is a very late twentieth century notion. More important was the need for safe and secure property devolution. A man needs to know that the children who inherit his property are actually *his* children. A child needs to know that his or her father is not spreading his seed, and the child's inheritance, abroad. The very terminology of the law tells us this quite clearly if we care to look: adultery is the adulteration of the male blood line (so gay sex and oral sex never were – and cannot be – adultery). 'Illegitimacy' referred not to the child, since that would be grammatically inept, but rather to the child's claim to inheritance. In other words, heterosexual activity outwith the family relationship is economically very risky and property claims from outwith the family disrupt both the family and, thereby, society itself. Child creation therefore needs to be controlled for the stability of society. This is the reason why sexual fidelity is so important for heterosexuals – because their sort of sex, as both common experience and literary tradition show, can seriously disrupt family finances and lines of succession. And this explains why society, as a whole, sees heterosexual activity outwith marriage as so threatening and disruptive, and why the law sees it as destructive of the marital relationship. It is not the mean-spirited fear that one's partner is getting a modicum of physical pleasure outwith the relationship, for otherwise masturbation would be as much a ground for divorce as adultery, but the fear that one's partner may be creating children outwith the family.

None of these fears applies to same-sex relationships where, when there are children, both parties will nearly always be fully aware of where they came from – not through sex between the parties but often through hard-fought and traumatic legal and medical battles. This, I think, is the real reason why sexual fidelity plays a far less central role in same-sex than in opposite-sex relationships. It is not that gay men and lesbians are naturally more promiscuous than non-gay people, nor even that men are naturally more promiscuous than women. It is that gay sex has, in practical terms, far fewer social consequences. It is therefore far lower down in participants' scale of values than non-gay sex, which might involve not only physical pleasure but economic costs, which is, of course, high on anyone's scale of values. The end result of this is that fidelity for gay men and lesbians tends to be understood in a rather different way. It is more emotional and less physical in meaning than it is for non-gay people: but it is no less important for all that.

CONCLUSION

So where is all this going? The real objection, in my view, to same-sex marriage is that if marriage does expand to include same-sex couples, it will not develop to reflect the needs and aspirations of same-sex couples when these differ from opposite-sex couples. Sex discrimination law has long recognised that equality is not necessarily achieved by treating different people identically. So too, relationship equality is unlikely to be achieved by treating different types of relationship identically, for that runs the risk of imposing inappropriate rules on some relationships. A good example of this is provided by the Vermont legislation permitting same-sex civil unions with almost all the same legal consequences as marriage.[34] In order to achieve what was perceived as equality, all the rules of marriage, including those for entry into the institution, were imposed on civil unions. This means that the rules concerning the forbidden degrees of relationship apply to same-sex civil unions,[35] notwithstanding that one of the primary purposes of barring incestuous marriages, although admittedly not the only one, is to avoid congenital abnormalities. This consideration is entirely irrelevant for same-sex couples. Such an example shows that with marriage would inevitably come all the (hetero)sexual baggage of consummation, incest, impotency and adultery. It would involve all

[33] Even methods of assisted reproduction require male and female gametes, which cannot be obtained solely from a same-sex couple. The nearest example one can imagine of a same-sex couple both contributing to child creation is when one woman provides the ovum and her lesbian partner provides the womb, but even here (human cloning remaining in the realms of speculation) a male is required to provide sperm. Of course, I am talking here only of child *creation*; child *rearing* is quite different and may well be quite common amongst same-sex couples.

[34] An Act Relating to Civil Unions, No 91 of 2000, effective from 1 July 2000.

[35] The Dutch Marriage Bill, mentioned above at n 9, adopts exactly the same, fallacious, approach.

the property baggage of loss of control of personal finances and all the inhibiting baggage of requiring the state's permission to escape from the relationship. The social advantage of status that marriage would bring is not, in my view, sufficient compensation.

But it may be argued if I, as an individual, am unwilling to subject myself to the heterosexual baggage associated with marriage then I am free to avoid the institution. I ought not, however, deny the opportunity to those who are willing so to subject themselves, gay and non-gay alike. But the point is that no such opportunity exists at the moment for same-sex couples and so the question must be posed: how ought the law change to accommodate the legitimate claims and expectations of such couples? There is a choice of solutions, only one of which is the opening of marriage. In my view the preferable solution for those seeking equal respect from the law for same-sex relationships is one which avoids the dangers of assimilation and inappropriate application posed by marriage.

The ideal solution

Sir Henry Maine, in the middle of the nineteenth century, identified, in his *Ancient Law*[36] that the transition from ancient to modern law was essentially characterised by a movement from status to contract. The law of domestic relations has not yet made that transition. Marriage remains a status, although as such, it has long since outlived its usefulness. The time has come to move on to a more sophisticated conception of how the law can operate fairly for all citizens. The solution is to break marriage, as a legal concept, down into its constituent legal parts, with rights and liabilities being allocated, not according to marital status, but according to need, fairness and appropriateness in the individual case.[37] Succession rights should no longer be allocated according to status, for that gives rights, irrespective of the realities of the relationship. Domestic violence remedies (surely self-evidently?) should be available whenever there is domestic violence, rather than only when the applicant fits in to an approved domestic status.[38] Obligations of maintenance and property adjustment at the end of the relationship should depend on individualised factors, such as dependency, unjustified enrichment and voluntary assumption of mutual financial responsibility, rather than on the blunt instrument of status. This solution, in its fundaments, would require the termination of marriage as an institution with inherent legal consequences. This would leave it, rather like baptism, as a sacrament open to all of those who, for religious reasons, wish to have an aspect of their private life blessed by the religious organisation to whose teachings they adhere, but which has no legal consequence whatsoever. It is unlikely that the 'abolition' of marriage, as this solution would inevitably be characterised, would fall foul of Article 12 of the European Convention for the Protection of Human Rights and Fundamental Freedoms 1950. After all, that provision, unlike, say, Article 6 of the German Constitution, does not guarantee any special legal protection to marriage in the form of preferential legal treatment. It is, however, even more unlikely that any mainstream political party in the UK would give support to this solution. So instead of the ideal, we must, as is so often the case, be content with the practicable.

The practicable solution

As a minimum, those legal systems subject to the European Convention must comply with the requirements of Articles 8 and 14. Because discrimination in the respect given to private and family life on the basis of sexual orientation is 'intolerable'[39] they must extend those legal consequences of unmarried cohabitation which already exist to same-sex cohabiting couples. In

---

36 Everyman's Library Edition, 1972, at p 100.

37 This suggestion was made some time ago as a means of dealing with the conflict of laws problems associated with marriage – see W. Reese, 'Marriage in American Conflict of Laws' (1977) 26 ICLQ 952 – but it has more general merit.

38 The remedies contained in the Family Law Act 1996 are, it has to be admitted, consistent with this suggestion. In Scotland, disgracefully, the remedies for domestic violence contained in the Matrimonial Homes (Family Protection) (Scotland) Act 1981 can be accessed only by 'spouses' or 'cohabiting couples', both phrases being defined in exclusively heterosexual terms. See further, K. Norrie, 'We are Family (Sometimes): Legal Recognition of Same-Sex Relationships After *Fitzpatrick*' (2000) 4 Edin L R 256.

39 *Da Silva Mouta v Portugal* 21 December 1999, ECHR.

the UK, where the consequences are so few, this will not involve any great radical change. Other jurisdictions, where the consequences are greater, will end up with significantly enhanced recognition of same-sex relationships. Interestingly, it is France, a country which has for long given extensive legal consequences to cohabitation and now recognises these consequences as being almost the same as for marriage, which has opened these consequences to same-sex couples.[40] In doing so, that country points the way to a practical solution more palatable than opening up marriage to or creating a new, analogous, institution for same-sex couples.[41] Cohabitants' rights (and liabilities) are gradually being increased in the UK, and the consequences of marriage itself are gradually being reduced. Eventual coalescence, on the French model, is likely to happen later than the inevitable extension of cohabitants' rights (and liabilities) to same-sex couples. For that reason, the efforts of gay and lesbian activists would be better spent campaigning for that end result rather than for marriage or a marriage-like institution which will attract virulent opposition.[42] Not only would that make the goal of equality more likely of achievement, but it would avoid the seductive dangers of false equality.

40 See A. Barlow and R. Probert, 'Addressing the Legal Status of Cohabitation in Britain and France: Plus ca Change ...?' (1999) Web J of Current Legal Issues, http://webjcli.ncl.ac.uk/1999/issue3/barlow3.html; R. Probert and A. Barlow, 'Displacing marriage – diversification and harmonisation within Europe' [2000] CFLQ 153.

41 But see E. Steiner 'The spirit of the new French registered partnership law – promoting autonomy and pluralism or weakening marriage?' [2000] CFLQ 1, for a contrary view.

42 The 'Keep the Clause' campaign in Scotland in early 2000, set up to oppose the Scottish Parliament's plans to repeal the statutory prohibition on promoting the acceptability of same-sex relationships (Local Government Act 1986, s 2A), although ultimately unsuccessful, acts as a stark warning which requires, tactically, to be heeded.

[20]

WE WILL GET WHAT WE ASK FOR: WHY LEGALIZING GAY AND LESBIAN MARRIAGE WILL NOT "DISMANTLE THE LEGAL STRUCTURE OF GENDER IN EVERY MARRIAGE"*

Nancy D. Polikoff †

THE arguments for and against making marriage a priority for the lesbian and gay rights movement have been presented extensively. Attorney Tom Stoddard justifies aggressively pursuing same-sex marriage on three bases. First, Stoddard cites practical reasons, including the right to obtain direct economic benefits (e.g., social security benefits, health insurance), the advantages of tax and immigration laws, and protection of the relationship from outside interference.[1] Stoddard next addresses the political justifications, asserting that only by marrying will gay and lesbian couples validate the significance of their relationships. In Stoddard's estimation, "marriage is . . . the issue most likely to lead ultimately to a world free from discrimination against lesbians and gay men."[2] Finally, Stoddard articulates a number of philosophical arguments to convince skeptics that the desirability of the right to marry does not require that one approve of that institution's current state. Indeed, Stoddard suggests that legalizing same-sex unions might even transform marriage into a state divested of its sexist base.[3]

In contrast, Stoddard's colleague, Paula Ettelbrick, contends that "[m]arriage runs contrary to two of the primary goals of the lesbian and gay movement: the affirmation of gay identity and culture and the

---

* Nan D. Hunter, Marriage, Law and Gender: A Feminist Inquiry, 1 Law & Sexuality 9, 18-19 (1991). This phrase forms the core of Professor Hunter's argument urging lesbian and gay rights activists to make the legalization of same-sex marriage a priority for the lesbian and gay civil rights movement. See id.

† Professor of Law, Washington College of Law, The American University. I would like to thank Meg Ciszek for research assistance and Lauren Taylor for editorial assistance.

1 Thomas B. Stoddard, Why Gay People Should Seek the Right to Marry, *in* Lesbian and Gay Marriage 13, 14-16 (Suzanne Sherman ed., 1992).

2 Id. at 17.

3 Id. at 18-19.

validation of many forms of relationships."[4] She argues that justice for lesbians and gay men depends upon accepting our differences from mainstream culture and the many choices we make about our relationships. Lesbian and gay marriage would not alter the current system, she maintains, which values marriage above all other relationships, but would instead create a double standard for lesbian and gay sex—accepted if one is married, outlawed if one is not. In addition, Ettelbrick insists that the economic benefits lesbians and gay men would obtain by marrying, such as the ability to be covered by a spouse's health insurance plan, help primarily those who already enjoy relative economic security: in order for an employee's partner to claim a right to health benefits, the employee must be working at a job providing those benefits. We should instead focus our efforts, she argues, on obtaining economic security and adequate health care for everyone, regardless of marital status or sexual orientation.

Let me acknowledge my own position in this debate. I "came out" as a lesbian feminist in the early 1970s, and my lesbian identity was intertwined with a radical feminist perspective. At the time, many heterosexual feminists chose not to marry in order to make a statement against marriage, which they believed to be an oppressive, patriarchal institution. I believe that the desire to marry in the lesbian and gay community is an attempt to mimic the worst of mainstream society, an effort to fit into an inherently problematic institution that betrays the promise of both lesbian and gay liberation and radical feminism.

The only argument that has ever tempted me to support efforts to obtain lesbian and gay marriage is the contention that marriages between two men or two women would inherently transform the institution of marriage for all people. Tom Stoddard peripherally alludes to this possibility, as does Professor Eskridge,[5] but law professor and lesbian and gay rights attorney Nan Hunter, now deputy general counsel at the Department of Health and Human Services, has expanded upon it more fully, identifying it as the major reason she

---

[4] Paula L. Ettelbrick, Since When is Marriage a Path to Liberation?, *in* Lesbian and Gay Marriage, supra note 1, at 20, 21.

[5] See William N. Eskridge, Jr., A History of Same-Sex Marriage, 79 Va. L. Rev. 1419, 1487-88 (1993).

supports efforts to obtain the right to marry for lesbians and gay men. She states:

> What is most unsettling to the status quo about the legalization of lesbian and gay marriage is its potential to expose and denaturalize the historical construction of gender at the heart of marriage. . . . Certainly marriage is a powerful institution, and the inertial force of tradition should not be underestimated. But it is also a social construct. Powerful social forces have reshaped it before and will continue to do so. . . . [T]he impact [of lesbian and gay marriage] . . . will be to dismantle the legal structure of gender in every marriage.[6]

It is in the context of responding to the view that lesbian and gay marriage will transform the otherwise marred institution of marriage that I examine Professor Eskridge's research on the historical and cross-cultural evidence of socially and/or religiously approved same-sex marriages. Although his study is impressive, its implications for the lesbian and gay rights movement demand closer study. Will lesbian and gay marriage "dismantle the legal structure of gender in every marriage," or does this research instead suggest that the gendered nature of marriage, and indeed of all of society, will survive same-sex unions? After discussing the significance of Professor Eskridge's research, I will explain why I find Professor Hunter's analysis ultimately unpersuasive and remain opposed to making the right to marry a priority for the lesbian and gay rights movement.

Professor Eskridge's research does substantially contribute to the debate on lesbian and gay marriage. The first clue to the significance of his work lies in the context within which it was generated. Professor Eskridge represents two District of Columbia men who were denied a marriage license and are challenging the District's action under the D.C. marriage statute[7] and the D.C. antidiscrimination ordinance.[8] The superior court judge, after hearing argument on the claim, requested that both sides research the history of marriage. In meeting this challenge, Professor Eskridge extensively researched scores of historical and anthropological materials. Upon concluding his study, he asserted that marriage has not at all times and for all

6 Nan D. Hunter, Marriage, Law and Gender: A Feminist Inquiry, 1 Law & Sexuality, 9, 18-19 (1991).

7 D.C. Code Ann. §§ 30-101 to -121 (1981).

8 D.C. Code Ann. §§ 1-2501 to -2533 (1981).

peoples been a union of a man and a woman, and that same-sex unions have not always been condemned.

In the context of this litigation, the evidence that same-sex marriages have existed and been accepted in numerous communities has a distinctly conservative tone; most of the marriages Eskridge uncovered support rather than subvert hierarchy based upon gender.[9] His historical and anthropological evidence contradicts any assumption that "gender dissent" is inherent in marriage between two men or two women.[10] Rather, most of the unions reported were in fact gendered. Although both partners were biologically of the same sex, one partner tended to assume the characteristics and responsibilities of the opposite gender, with both partners then acting out their traditional gender roles. Thus, early observers of the Native American *berdache* noticed that some men "marry other men who . . . go around like women, perform their duties and are used as such and who cannot carry or use the bow,"[11] and that some women "give up all the duties of women and imitate men, and follow men's pursuits as if they were not women. . . . [E]ach has a woman to serve her, to whom she says she is married, and they treat each other and speak with each other as man and wife."[12] Contemporary scholarship on the *berdache*, such as Walter Williams' acclaimed study, *The Spirit and the Flesh: Sexual Diversity in American Indian Culture*, supports the conclusion that marriages between men and *berdache* followed the gendered division of labor observed in traditional Native American marriages, with the man taking on the role of husband and the *berdache* taking on the role of wife.[13] Similarly, female *berdache* hunted and headed the household, assuming traditional male responsibilities.[14] Eskridge

---

[9] Eskridge notes that his review of the literature includes some relationships that were culturally but not legally recognized and others that attained some form of legal recognition. He refers to only the latter as "marriages," and in an overwhelming number of these relationships one partner assumed the social role and sex-linked rights and responsibilities of the opposite gender. See Eskridge, supra note 5, at Part II.

[10] For a discussion of "gender dissent," see Hunter, supra note 6, at 29-30.

[11] Francisco López de Gómara, Historia General de las Indias (1552), translated in Francisco Guerra, The Pre-Columbian Mind 85 (1971), discussed in Eskridge supra note 5, at 1454.

[12] 2 Pero de Magalhães, The Histories of Brazil 88-89 (John B. Stetson, Jr. trans., Cortes Soc'y 1922) (1576), discussed in Eskridge, supra note 5, at 1454.

[13] Walter L. Williams, The Spirit and the Flesh: Sexual Diversity in American Indian Culture 112 (1986), discussed in Eskridge, supra note 5, at 1456-57.

[14] Eskridge, supra note 5, at 1457-58.

quotes from a scholar of female *berdache* that " 'the cross-gender female's partner . . . was always a traditional female; that is, two cross-gender [dominant] females did not marry,' "[15] demonstrating that these same-sex partners assumed the traditional gendered roles of different-sex couples.

Eskridge's compilation is filled with many similar examples of same-sex relationships whose structure reinforces traditional notions of marriage as gendered and hierarchical. For example, Greek same-sex relationships are described by historian Kenneth Dover as including a courtship by the dominant party, the "husband/man," towards the receptive party, the "wife/boy," in which the receptive party responds coyly.[16] "Boy wives" among the Azande (now in the Sudan) were similarly described as performing the services normally rendered by women.[17] Among Eskridge's examples of traditionally gendered same-sex unions from Asia is the Chuckchee, whose "soft men" married men. While the other men hunted and fished, the "soft men" took care of the house and performed other domestic tasks.[18] Indian *hijras*, emasculated men with female dress and demeanor, likewise married "traditional" men and assumed the historical female role.[19]

Female couples likewise assumed conventional gendered roles. For example, marriages between women in Southern China in the nineteenth century resulted in the designation of one partner as "husband" and the other as "wife."[20] Similarly, African "woman-marriage" is an institution in which a woman gives " 'bridewealth for, and marr[ies], a woman over whom and whose offspring she has full control.' "[21] Eskridge cites one scholar whose assessment of this prac-

---

[15] Id. (quoting Evelyn Blackwood, Sexuality and Gender in Certain Native American Tribes: The Case of Cross-Gender Females, 10 Signs 27, 35 (1984)).

[16] See K.J. Dover, Greek Homosexuality 81-91 (1978), discussed in Eskridge, supra note 5, at 1444.

[17] See E.E. Evans-Pritchard, Sexual Inversion Among the Azande, 72 Am. Anthropologist 1428, 1429-90 (1970), discussed in Eskridge, supra note 5, at 1458-59.

[18] Eskridge, supra note 5, at 1463 (quoting 7 Waldemar Bogoras, The Jessup North Pacific Expedition: The Chukchee 451 (reprint 1975) (Franz Boas ed., 1904-09).

[19] Id. at 1463-64 (discussing Serena Nanda, The Hijras of India: Cultural and Individual Dimensions of an Institutionalized Third Gender Role, J. Homosexuality, Summer 1985, at 35).

[20] Id. at 1465-66 (discussing Bret Hinsch, Passions of the Cut Sleeve: The Male Homosexual Tradition in China 177-78 (1990)).

[21] Id. at 1460-61 (quoting Eileen J. Krige, Woman-Marriage, with Special Reference to the Lovedu—Its Significance for the Definition of Marriage, 44 Afr. 11, 11 (1974)).

tice is that it allows powerful, wealthy women to assume the social roles of men and thus serve as leaders in a male-dominated society.[22]

The vision of same-sex marriage presented in the research Professor Eskridge proffers is a profoundly constricted one. In some instances, the relationships he describes do not seem to be same-sex unions at all, as the relevant culture appears to recognize a third gender, such as the *berdache* and the *hijras*. Marriage within each gender did not exist. Furthermore, hierarchy was a component of all such ostensibly same-sex marriages, with the partner embodying the most male characteristics accorded higher status and greater control.[23] Accordingly, an argument based on continuity between lesbian and gay marriage today and same-sex marriages of other eras and cultures is not one that makes deconstruction of gender the core reason to fight for the ability of lesbians and gay men to marry.[24]

Should public debates arise as to whether to legislate in favor of contemporary lesbian and gay marriage, this type of historical research would probably be used to advance the proposition that there is nothing new or truly unconventional about same-sex marriage. Indeed, that was the precise assertion made by Professor Eskridge in the litigation sparking his research.[25] Similarly, the political and public relations campaign to legalize same-sex marriage would likely contend that our relationships are no different from het-

---

[22] See id. at 1461-62 & n.155 (discussing Denise O'Brien, Female Husbands in Southern Bantu Societies, *in* Sexual Stratification: A Cross-Cultural View 109, 122 (Alice Schlegel ed., 1977)).

[23] I do not intend my criticism of the gendered nature of marriage portrayed in much of the historical and anthropological material to be taken as criticizing the eroticization of difference inherent in, for example, butch-femme lesbian relationships. See generally, Elizabeth L. Kennedy & Madeline D. Davis, Boots of Leather, Slippers of Gold (1993) (describing the history of butch-femme culture). In the unions discussed in Professor Eskridge's collection, the more masculine partner was accorded by the larger community the higher social and economic status associated with the male gender. In contrast, the lesbian butch, as described by Kennedy and Davis and others, see, e.g., Leslie Feinberg, Stone Butch Blues (1993), paid an enormous social and economic price for displaying her gender-inappropriate demeanor, facing ostracism and violence as a result.

[24] In fact, some Greek literature cited by Eskridge as indicative of the Greek view of male same-sex love contains an underlying theme of misogyny. See Eskridge, supra note 5, at 1441-44.

[25] The Plaintiffs' Memorandum to the Court states on its first page that "there is nothing new in human history about same-sex marriage." Plaintiff's Memorandum on the History of Same-Sex Marriage at 1, Dean v. District of Columbia, No. 90-13892 (D.C. Super. Ct., filed Sept. 4, 1991).

erosexual marriages. In other words, the pro-marriage position would accept, rather than challenge, the current institution of marriage. I believe this process would be profoundly destructive to the lesbian and gay community.

Professor Hunter acknowledged this danger in her article advocating same-sex marriage in the hope that it would deconstruct gender. She writes:

> The impact of law often lies as much in the body of discourse created in the process of its adoption as in the final legal rule itself. . . . The social meaning of the legalization of lesbian and gay marriage . . . would be enormously different if legalization resulted from political efforts framed as ending gendered roles between spouses rather than if it were the outcome of a campaign valorizing the institution of marriage, even if the ultimate "holding" is the same.[26]

Everything in our political history suggests that a concerted effort to achieve the legalization of lesbian and gay marriage will valorize the current institution of marriage. Just as Professor Eskridge was propelled towards a litigation strategy that accepted marriage—even grossly hierarchical, gendered marriage—as a good, any effort to legitimize lesbian and gay marriage would work to persuade the heterosexual mainstream that lesbians and gay men seek to emulate heterosexual marriage as currently constituted.[27]

Demands for social change often have begun with a movement at first articulating the rhetoric of radical transformation and then later discarding that rhetoric to make the demands more socially acceptable. The movement's rhetoric is modified or altered when those opposing reform explore the radical and transformative possibilities of that rhetoric, causing its advocates to issue reassurances promising that such transformation is not what the movement is about at all.

Within the arena of eliminating gender hierarchy, women's access to abortion provides one such example of a movement redefining its goals to make them more politically palatable. Early abortion activists spoke of women's liberation and women's entitlement to sexual fulfillment, viewing access to abortion as part of a larger struggle to end male dominance. As abortion became a major political issue,

---

26 Hunter, supra note 6, at 29.

27 See generally Eskridge, supra note 5, at 1488-91 (outlining the argument that the process of seeking legal recognition for same-sex marriage compromises gay radicalism).

however, and with the battle to win public opinion in full gear, the rhetoric changed, adopting its current pro-choice vocabulary. In the judicial arena, the prevailing arguments spoke of privacy. In fact, it became fashionable to say that while one was not in favor of abortion, one was nonetheless in favor of choice,[28] to imply—if not to state—that abortion was an evil but a necessary one. In the face of conservative voices decrying abortion as a facilitator of unchecked sexual freedom, "pro-choice" voices denied or downplayed the relationship between women's access to abortion and women's ability to enjoy guilt-free sexual pleasure.[29]

By shifting their strategy, abortion rights activists lost the transformative potential of women's ready access to abortion. Supporters of abortion rights no longer link it to ending male supremacy or to affirming sexual pleasure for women. Indeed, "abortion on demand" is no longer the call of abortion supporters but the specter brought forth by antiabortion voices.[30]

---

[28] For example, in his acceptance speech before the Democratic National Convention, Bill Clinton emphasized that he was pro-choice, not pro-abortion. See Bill Clinton, Speech Accepting the Democratic Presidential Nomination (July 16, 1992), *in* N.Y. Times, July 17, 1992, at A14, A15.

[29] This position is explored in several essays in From Abortion to Reproductive Freedom (Marlene G. Fried ed., 1990). Marlene Fried summarizes as follows:

> The abortion rights movement essentially folded after abortion became legal. While more radical segments of the movement mobilized in 1977 after the Hyde Amendment prohibited federal Medicaid funding of abortion, it was not until the threat of a constitutional amendment that would ban all U.S. abortions was posed in 1981 that a visible mainstream abortion rights movement re-emerged.
>
> The 1980s movement formed as a reaction to the backlash, and was shaped by the need to respond to an all-out anti-choice campaign, one with initiatives in legislatures, in the courts, and in the streets. In an effort to hold the line, the new abortion rights movement rarely dared talk about abortion or women's rights, preferring instead to focus on the intolerance and extremism of the other side. The pro-choice movement attempted to sanitize its own demands. Insisting on abortion rights as a necessary condition of all women's sexual freedom continues to be seen as too threatening, too risky, too selfish. Instead, the movement turned to the more innocuous and ambiguous language of "choice" and "personal freedom." The women's movement fought to bring women's reproductive lives out of the private sphere, arguing that our personal choices were political. How ironic that the pro-choice movement now argues that abortion is private and personal, not political.

Marlene G. Fried, Transforming the Reproductive Rights Movement: The Post-*Webster* Agenda, *in* From Abortion to Reproductive Freedom, supra, at 5-6.

[30] Thus, we see the concept of "good" and "bad" abortions: "A 'good' or acceptable abortion is the result of circumstances outside the pregnant woman's control: her health, rape, or incest. A 'bad' or unacceptable abortion is one which results from her trying to take control

A reform movement's choice to change rhetoric is not costless. Abortion activists' continuing decision to portray abortion as an agonizing personal decision affects both how women who have abortions experience their decision and how abortion advocates and counselors respond to those decisions once made. With the moral legitimacy of abortion questioned, women who have abortions often feel secretive, shameful, and stigmatized.[31] Those who work in clinics performing abortions assume clients must be feeling something negative about their decision to abort, believing that there must be something terribly wrong with a woman who does not express grief, guilt, or both.[32]

By critiquing the strategic change in rhetoric of mainstream abortion rights organizations, I do not imply that the fight for legal and safe abortion should be abandoned. I do suggest, however, that the most radical bases of this fight—ending gender hierarchy and the sexual double standard—have been lost precisely because they are no longer articulated. Thus, if we are successful in maintaining the availability of abortion, we will have achieved what we asked for—the ability of a woman to make a difficult, even morally ambiguous, personal choice to abort as a matter of last resort. If the only alternative to this accomplishment is a return to the days of illegal abortion, such an achievement is preferable, but it is not transformative.

Similar analyses apply to the lesbian and gay rights movement. Specifically, the current rhetoric voiced in the campaign to end the military's practice of excluding lesbians and gay men is useful in imagining how a campaign to end the exclusion of lesbians and gay men from marriage would be shaped. Those challenging the military exclusion neither critique the military as an institution nor acknowledge the transformative potential of allowing lesbians and gay men to serve openly. I believe those campaigning for lesbian and gay marriage would adopt a similar strategy, neither critiquing the institution of marriage nor acknowledging the transformative potential of allowing lesbians and gay men to enter into state-sanctioned unions.

---

of her life, expressing a preference." Sara Buttenweiser & Reva Levine, Breaking Silences: A Post-Abortion Support Model, *in* From Abortion to Reproductive Freedom, supra note 29, at 121, 122.

31 See Lynn S. Chauncer, Abortion Without Apology, *in* From Abortion to Reproductive Freedom, supra note 29, at 113, 115.

32 Id.

The vehemence of military and congressional opposition to President Clinton's proposal to lift the ban caught most of the lesbian and gay rights lobby by surprise. In response, an ad hoc organization was formed to work exclusively on this issue on behalf of the lesbian and gay community. The name adopted by the organization, the Campaign for Military Service, was not an arbitrary or random choice. At the meeting at which the name was selected, a public relations professional cautioned the group that the words "justice" and "equality" should be avoided. Interestingly enough, the words "lesbian," "gay," "homosexual," "discrimination," and "rights" were also omitted. Instead, the emphasis is on military service, the willingness to enter the revered institution that is charged with this country's defense. It is a campaign that meets and embraces the military on its own terms, the implicit message being that the military is accepted as it now exists. The name serves to assure military leaders and mainstream society that there will be nothing transformative about allowing lesbians and gay men to serve their country openly.

The strategy that lesbian and gay rights activists have pursued in their quest to eliminate the military exclusion is filled with rhetoric professing respect for the armed services. Although the decision to employ troops in connection with Operation Desert Storm divided the gay community,[33] those lesbian and gay service members who performed in the operation are publicly paraded as heroes by lesbian and gay rights organizations.[34] Indeed, the campaign to lift the military ban would experience tremendous difficulty without the stories of the many lesbian and gay veterans whose ranks, honors, awards, and statures belie the notion that their presence could harm the military in any way. Lesbian and gay rights advocates proclaim that these ser-

---

[33] See Lou Chibbarro, Jr., NGLTF's Stand on Gulf War Expected to Spark Debate, Wash. Blade, Jan. 11, 1991, at 3.

[34] On the weekend of April 24-25, 1993, during the March on Washington for Lesbian and Gay Rights, one of the "heroes" honored at an event sponsored by the National Gay and Lesbian Task Force was Sgt. Joe Zuniga, decorated as a result of his participation in the Gulf War and subsequently named the Sixth U.S. Army's soldier of the year. See John Gallagher, Dream On, Advoc., July 27, 1993, at 32, 33.

It was widely publicized during Operation Desert Storm that discharge proceedings against lesbian and gay service personnel were held up to allow them to serve in the Persian Gulf. See Nick Bartolomeo, Military Sends a Dozen Gays to the Gulf, Wash. Blade, February 1, 1991, at 1. Thus, such service members now epitomize military hypocrisy, their continued deployment demonstrating that when morale and unit cohesion must be at their highest, i.e., in times of battle, the services chose to retain, rather than discharge, lesbians and gay men.

vice members, including those decorated in Vietnam[35] and ranked at the top of their service academy classes,[36] could not possibly impair unit cohesion or military morale.

Although several individuals working with the Campaign for Military Service are themselves antimilitarist,[37] those sentiments are subjugated to the imperative of ending the military exclusion. There is no way to publicly critique the military and simultaneously ask to be let into it, as such criticism would undermine the credibility of the dominant message: that the presence of openly lesbian and gay service members would not harm military effectiveness and, by implication, the United States' position as the world's foremost military power.[38]

There is no room in this campaign for the community's internal debate about the military's proper role. Suppressing this discussion reflects a value judgment on the part of lesbian and gay leaders, a conscious ranking of issues. Gay journalist Tommi Avicolli Mecca, while acknowledging that allowing lesbians and gay men to serve openly may legitimate us and may help break down negative views held by heterosexual soldiers,[39] nevertheless concludes that the advantages of a campaign for military inclusion do not outweigh the disadvantages:

> Asking for admission into the military . . . aligns us with regressive forces, those that refuse to see [that] . . . the military is part of America's problem right now.
>
> . . . .
>
> Instead of wanting in on the military, we should be advocating for non-military jobs that promote peace and train people to overcome

---

35 Margarethe Cammermeyer, for example, was a decorated army nurse forced out of the military because of her lesbian identity. See David S. Jackson, "I Just Don't Want to Go," Time, July 6, 1992, at 62 (interview with Margarethe Cammermeyer).

36 See Jeffrey Schmalz, On the Front Lines with Joseph Steffan; From a by-the-Book Midshipman to Gay Advocate, N.Y. Times, Feb. 4, 1993, at C1 (noting that Steffan had ranked in the top ten of his class at the Naval Academy).

37 Telephone Interview with Chai Feldblum, Legal Director, Campaign for Military Service (Feb. 1993).

38 Literature produced by the Human Rights Campaign Fund (HRCF) as part of its "Operation Lift the Ban" asks readers to write to their representatives and senators in Congress. The first two points that HRCF suggests using in the letters are that "The Current Policy of Excluding Gay Men, Lesbians and Bisexuals from Service Hurts the Armed Forces" and "Ending the Discrimination Would Benefit the Military." Momentum, Special Edition, Spring 1993, at 4.

39 Tommi A. Mecca, Between Little Rock and a Hard Place 125-26 (1993).

> poverty and despair. Why not put people to work in this country helping to rebuild our cities and feed the hungry? Channel some of that defense budget into social welfare programs that can be staffed by the same young men [and women] who now pursue Uncle Sam for a job. This is where queers should align themselves.
>
> Instead, we're stuck arguing with the Neanderthals in the Department of Defense and the religious right that queers will make good soldiers. We look to the studies, done by the military itself, that prove how obedient and loyal we can be. Look, queers can kill, too; look, queers can defend oil interests. Look, queers can be fodder.[40]

By the same token, I believe that an effort to legalize lesbian and gay marriage would make a public critique of the institution of marriage impossible. Long-term, monogamous couples would almost certainly be the exemplars of the movement, sharing stories of adversity resulting from their unmarried status: a partner who lacked health care because he was not eligible for spousal employee benefits, or who was denied hospital visitation rights because she was not family, or who was unable to make burial arrangements after her partner's death. Marriage would be touted as the solution to these couples' problems; the limitations of marriage, and of a social system valuing one form of human relationship above all others, would be downplayed.

It is impossible to imagine arguing that lesbians and gay men should be permitted to serve in the military in order to transform that institution, either in the macro sense—its mission—or in the micro sense—its daily reinforcement of hierarchy, submission, and discipline. Indeed, the argument that the military's socialization process would shift to accommodate the presence of acknowledged lesbians and gay men is currently being made by those who *oppose* lifting the ban. Ironically, it is they who, by arguing that unit cohesion and morale will be affected by accepting openly gay men and women, employ persuasively the possibility of a transformative effect, one that they do not at all like.

The political leaders and lobbyists of the movement to allow gays to serve openly reject such arguments. They believe that conduct can and should be regulated, with parity between heterosexual and homosexual conduct, and that absent conduct there is no effect on unit

---

[40] Id. at 126-27.

cohesion or morale that cannot be overcome by antiprejudice training similar to that used to surmount white racism when the armed forces were integrated.

Yet the potential for transformation does exist if the ban is lifted. Frank Browning described it in his recent book, *The Culture of Desire: Paradox and Perversity in Gay Lives Today*,[41] and in a *Washington Post* opinion piece.[42] Rather than accept the dominant "nothing will change" line used to sway public opinion and win votes, Browning embraces the possibilities for change inherent in admitting openly lesbian and gay service members. He states:

> [T]he commander who comes out of the closet will challenge the society's most primal understanding of what it means to be an "authentic" male. If a real authentic hero is revealed not to be conventionally authentic, i.e., straight, what becomes of the hero's subordinates? Won't the young privates, sergeants and ensigns who serve under him question their own authenticity, their own ideas of what it means to be male? Such questions are a test of our most conventional notions of how men wield power in daily life . . . . What is threatened is the integrity of the heterosexual male's comprehension of himself. What is being revealed is how frail that self-comprehension really is.
>
> . . . Ending the gay ban will change men's lives in America—change our lives with each other and with women.
>
> As we enter this most hierarchically ordered institution of American life, where sublimation of desire is critical to the authority of command, we will most certainly disorder and reorder what the generals revere as "military culture."[43]

Thus, Browning says that the presence of openly gay men in the military will disrupt gender roles. The relationship between the military's exclusion of lesbians and gay men and the social construction of gender has been addressed before. Professor Kenneth Karst's brilliant article[44] identifies society's desire to maintain the ideology of masculinity as the principal reason behind perpetuating the military exclusion:

---

41 Frank Browning, The Culture of Desire: Paradox and Perversity in Gay Lives Today (1993).

42 Frank Browning, From 'Poof' to 'Predator,' Wash. Post, Mar. 28, 1993, at C4.

43 Id.

44 Kenneth L. Karst, The Pursuit of Manhood and the Desegregation of the Armed Forces, 38 UCLA L. Rev. 499 (1991).

> For those who want to keep the public's gaze fixed on "the manliness of war," the tensions of male bonding demand a clear expression of the services' rejection of homosexuality. This expression is not just a by-product of the policy that purports to exclude gay men and lesbians from the armed forces; it is the policy's main function. When a gay soldier comes to the Army's official attention, the real threat is not the hindrance of day-to-day operations, but rather the tarnishing of the Army's traditionally masculine image.[45]

Michelle Benecke, who worked for the Campaign for Military Service, and Kirsten Dodge have described how the military exclusion facilitates lesbian-baiting, a practice that allows traditional constructions of gender to flourish in the services:

> The entry of women into nontraditional job fields makes it difficult for men to maintain masculinity in traditional terms. . . . [C]alling servicewomen "lesbians" is one way for servicemen to maintain their sense of masculinity when traditional gender distinctions based on job field begin to break down.
>
> . . . .
>
> [One way] to avoid demasculinization when a woman does a "man's job" is to make her *not* a woman. Women who perform "men's jobs" are "classed as deviants," "man-women," and lesbians.[46]

Francisco Valdes' study of sexual orientation and gender concludes that "the exclusion of sexual minorities from service in the armed forces, ostensibly a 'sexual orientation' issue, in fact implicates 'gender' issues as well."[47]

Although they are undoubtedly aware of the potential for transforming gender within the military by ending the military exclusion of lesbians and gay men, the Campaign for Military Service and other groups actively working to end the ban never make this argument. Rather, the implicit, if not explicit, message offered to sway public and political opinion is that everything will remain the same, that mil-

---

[45] Id. at 545-46.

[46] Michelle Benecke & Kirstin Dodge, Military Women in Nontraditional Job Fields: Casualties of the Armed Forces' War on Homosexuals, 13 Harv. Women's L.J. 215, 234, 237 (1990) (footnotes omitted).

[47] Francisco Valdes, Queers, Sissies, Dykes, and Tomboys: Deconstructing the Conflation of "Sex," "Gender," and "Sexual Orientation" in Euro-American Law and Society 122 (unpublished manuscript, on file with the Virginia Law Review Association).

itary culture will be unaffected; open lesbians and gay men will blend in, not transform, the institution. Neither is the argument being made, as part of the political process, that the military exclusion should end because the presence of lesbians and gay men would transform social attitudes towards homosexuality as a result of the close contact between heterosexual and homosexual service personnel. Rather, the implication is that attaining societal approval of homosexuality and permitting military service by lesbians and gay men are two completely different things.[48]

Just as transforming gender roles and achieving increased acceptance of lesbians and gay men are not politically viable reasons to advocate ending the military ban, so are they unlikely grounds around which to build support for legalizing lesbian and gay marriage. The danger in both instances is that the underlying critique of the institution, be it the military or marriage, becomes not only secondary but marginalized, even silenced.

If my hypothesis about the process of change is correct, then we must measure the value of the work it will take to legalize lesbian and gay marriage by how closely the arguments we make in advocating this change match what we really believe about and want for our relationships and our community. For those who support lesbian and gay marriage because it would allow us access to the package of benefits now associated with heterosexual marriage, or because it would demonstrate that our relationships are as valuable as their heterosexual counterparts, advocating lesbian and gay marriage is an obvious choice. I do not share that vision. Advocating lesbian and gay marriage will detract from, even contradict, efforts to unhook economic benefits from marriage and make basic health care and other necessities available to all. It will also require a rhetorical strategy that emphasizes similarities between our relationships and heterosexual marriages, values long-term monogamous coupling above all other relationships, and denies the potential of lesbian and gay marriage to transform the gendered nature of marriage for all people. I fear that the very process of employing that rhetorical strategy for the years it

48 The Secretary of Veterans Affairs, Jesse Brown, captured this distinction in his characterization of President Clinton's position as follows: "What the president is basically saying is this: 'I'm not trying to legitimize behavior, I'm trying to give people who want an opportunity to serve their country an opportunity to do so.'" Bill McAllister, VA's Brown Sidesteps Endorsing Gays Plan, Wash. Post, May 14, 1993, at A29.

will take to achieve its objective will lead our movement's public representatives, and the countless lesbians and gay men who hear us, to believe exactly what we say.

[21]

Law, Women and the Family: the Question of Polygyny in a new South Africa

FELICITY KAGANAS*
Brunel, University of West London
CHRISTINA MURRAY**
University of Cape Town

Political and legal change in South Africa seems imminent and, in contemplating this prospect, South Africans anticipate radical changes to the country's constitutional and administrative structures. But law reformers, faced with the enormous challenges presented by political restructuring on a grand scale, have tended to treat the reform of family law as unimportant. Relatively little attention has been paid to the impact on families and family law of colonialism and, more recently, of apartheid. And comparatively little thought has been given to refashioning family law to better reflect the needs of a democratic and non-racial society.

South African family law is founded on the Western model of companionable marriage and the nuclear family, and is characterized by a commitment to monogamous unions and to the principle of voluntary consent. Operating in the shadow of the civil law governing families in South Africa is the customary law system. It covers the marriages of African people by custom and it is tolerated but not really approved. The dominant feature of customary-law marriage in its traditional form,[1] that is its collective or non-individual nature,[2] makes it very different from civil marriage. This system does not require monogamy and the consent of the spouses is not necessarily central to the arrangements. Instead the interests of the particular wife or husband are incidental to family interests which are secured by institutions such as bridewealth. Other potentially polygynous marriages, such as those concluded by Muslim rites, are altogether outside the law and receive no protection from the state.

South African family law thus privileges one type of family and reluctantly gives second class status (or no status at all) to others. The dividing lines correspond to racial and ethnic divisions and, with the

*BA LLB (Wits) LLM (London), Department of Law, Brunel University.
**BA LLB (Stellenbosch) LLM (Michigan), Associate Professor, Department of Public Law, University of Cape Town. The author was assisted in the research for this paper by funding from the Institute for Research Development of the HSRC.

[1] Any discussion of customary law must obviously be informed by Martin Chanock's important arguments about the nature of what we term customary law and the impact colonial systems have had on it. See M Chanock *Law, Custom and Social Order: The Colonial Experience in Malawi and Zambia* (1985).

[2] This is discussed in R T Nhlapo *Family Law and Traditional Values* (unpublished DPhil thesis, Oxford 1990).

demise of apartheid, the system is in urgent need of re-evaluation. In undertaking this, we will have to consider whether the current law is merely a reflection of ethnocentric prejudice or whether there are indeed justifications for denying legal recognition to certain family forms.

The reform of South African family law raises difficult problems, and matters are made even more complex both by the demands of a democratic society which may challenge the legitimacy of certain cultural practices and by the fact that customary law has failed to respond to changes that have occurred in African family structures.[3] For instance, practices such as the levirate, arranged marriages and the designation of the man as head of the family may conflict with a commitment to equal rights for men and women within the family and thus be incompatible with a democratic order in which the dignity of all people is respected. Similarly, the failure of African customary law in its current institutionalized form to adapt to modern conditions means that some major changes will be necessary if it is to be retained.

Those most disadvantaged by customary law rules are women and, for many years, they have called for a thorough re-examination of the whole system.[4] However, their demands have been overshadowed by the issue of racial oppression. The liberation movement has tended to subsume women's interests under the broader political struggle.[5] Women are seen in terms of their strategic importance for achieving liberation goals and women's issues are treated as peripheral to the main objective, the elimination of apartheid. Indeed, feminism is frequently regarded as a potentially divisive force and so discouraged.[6] Beall, Hassim & Todes caution that this standpoint relegates women's concerns to the status of 'a bit on the side'[7] in the debate about social and political transformation. They point out that the gains to women arising out of their mobilization in liberation struggles are generally lost once the new political order is in place. This, they say, results from a failure to analyse political struggles in terms of gender relations and they urge South Africans to take cognizance of the insights of feminism. But feminist analysis of the

[3] T W Bennett *A Sourcebook of African Customary Law for Southern Africa* (1991) 145–6.

[4] See the Women's Charter of 1953 in C Walker *Women and Resistance in South Africa* (1982) 279 and, for more recent examples, the papers presented at the 1989 Malibongwe Conference (including 'What Do We Mean by the Emancipation of Women?' and 'Sexual Abuse and Aggression Against Women'), which are on file at the African Studies Library at the University of Cape Town.

[5] J Beall et al ' "A Bit on the Side"?: Gender struggles in the politics of transformation in South Africa' (1989) 33 *Feminist Review* 32. The draft constitution of the ANC Women's League of 1990 illustrates the point. The first of its 'aims and objectives' is '[t]o mobilise and organise South African women into participation in the struggle for the liberation of all oppressed groups', a commitment to popularize ANC policy and programmes is second, and only then appear aims related to the oppression of women. For a discussion of the growing conservatism regarding women's rights in Zimbabwe, see W Ncube 'Dealing with inequalities in customary law: action, reaction and social change in Zimbabwe' (1991) 5 *International J of Law & the Family* 58.

[6] Beall et al (n 5) 32. See also A Sachs *Protecting Human Rights in a New South Africa* (1990) 56–7.

[7] Note 5 above 33.

position of black women in South Africa is rendered problematic not only because it is treated as strategically unhelpful; feminism is branded as a bourgeois Western phenomenon and is dismissed as irrelevant.[8]

This criticism is not unique to South Africa; it is levelled at feminism by black women worldwide.[9] They assert that their concerns are very different from those of their white, Western counterparts. Challenging the notion that there exists an internally homogeneous category 'woman', they argue that it is impossible to generalize about women's experiences since those experiences vary with culture, race and class. The way in which a woman's identity is constituted is historically and culturally contingent and Western feminists cannot claim to speak for all women.

Feminism has responded to this charge, and a re-evaluation of theory and practice is taking place. For instance, an awareness of heterogeneity informs the work of recent feminist anthropology which cautions against judging all cultures according to Western norms.[10]

No longer able to assert with any confidence a single female viewpoint, many feminists acknowledge cultural specificity and the differences between women. Rather than undermining it, this position promises feminism a sound theoretical basis and does not necessarily imply a commitment to ethical relativism. Feminists can now abandon the quest for some essential 'womanness' and pay attention instead to the concept 'women' and how it is used both in overt politics and in the habits of ordinary practice. They can focus on the way some human beings are positioned oppressively, and in ways that may cause great suffering, through the designation 'woman'.[11] The move to acknowledging heterogeneity in no way prejudices the '"*ideal*" unity of feminism' which lies in its global commitment to abolishing the sex-class system.[12] Indeed, this project cannot proceed while denying any authoritative political or theoretical framework. In this context Lovibond has asked:

> '[I]f there can be no systematic political approach to questions of wealth, power and labour, how can there be any effective challenge to a social order which distributes its benefits and burdens in a systematically unequal way between the sexes?'[13]

Thus while feminists should be sensitive to cultural differences, the feminist enterprise is to eliminate 'patterns of disadvantage and

[8] Beall et al (n 5) 32–3.

[9] See, for just one of many exchanges on this subject, M Barrett & M McIntosh 'Ethnocentrism and Socialist-Feminist Theory' (1985) 20 *Feminist Review* 23 and 'Feedback: Feminism and Racism' (1986) 22 *Feminist Review* 82 with contributions by C Ramazanoglu, H Kazi, S Lees and H Safia Mirza.

[10] H L Moore *Feminism and Anthropology* (1988) 2 and 7–8.

[11] D Riley *'Am I That Name?' Feminism and the Category of 'Women' in History* (1988) provides a persuasive exposition of this position, one which informs this section of the paper.

[12] S Lovibond 'Feminism and Postmodernism' (1989) 138 *New Left Review* 28.

[13] Lovibond (n 12) 22.

dominance' wherever they are found.[14] The difficulty lies in determining whether particular, culturally-local institutions do lead to disadvantage and dominance.

This paper is concerned with one specific institution in African customary law, polygyny.[15] For a number of reasons polygyny provides a challenging starting point for an examination of the type of family structures feminists might argue for in South Africa. First, it is widely held to be fundamentally incompatible with a democratic social order and, more specifically, inevitably to be oppressive of women.[16] Secondly, traditional African family structures are often seen to be inextricably linked to polygyny. Finally, through examining polygyny we might also be drawn to reflect on more dominant Westernized family structures and to reconsider the extent to which the values they assert determine our assessment of other family forms.

I POLYGYNY AND SOUTH AFRICAN FAMILY LAW

In the earliest reported decisions in South Africa it was taken as self-evident that the Christian form of marriage was the only one that could be recognized in law and that polygyny, like bridewealth, was incompatible with this. In line with the dogmas of church and state, the judiciary regarded polygamy, as it was called, as a heathen practice, confined to the unenlightened.

The strong views of the church in this matter are typified by the evidence of missionaries put before the 1872 Commission on the Laws and Customs of the Basotho set up by the Cape Government:

> 'Cattle-marriages mean polygamy, they mean systematic sensualism and immorality. Take them away, and the whole fabric is broken in pieces,—the native heathen customs become meaningless,—polygamy becomes impossible,—woman is emancipated,—virtue, truth and honour cease to be empty names. . . . If we wish to reconstitute the family on the Christian mode . . . there must be no compromise with this embodiment of evil, this traffic in souls, this chain of bondage. . . .'[17]

Some years later, polygyny was described by missionaries as 'one of the gross evils of heathen society which, like habitual murder or slavery, must at all costs be ended'.[18] These sentiments are also evident in the

[14] Rhode in D L Rhode (ed) *Theoretical Perspectives on Sexual Difference* (1990) 7.

[15] Lawyers tend to use the term 'polygamy' to refer to the practice of a man having more than one wife, but polygamy simply means a plurality of husbands or wives. In anthropology 'polygyny' refers to the practice of a husband having more than one wife and 'polyandry' refers to the practice of a wife having more than one husband. Americans use the term 'plural marriage' for both institutions.

[16] For instance, like many other writers, Sachs (n 6) 72 (and see 55 and 76) lists some practices which he suggests should probably be disallowed whether a plural or unitary approach to family law is adopted in South Africa. One of these is polygyny. Arranged marriages and child marriages are others: *Protecting Human Rights* (n 6) 72; see also at 76 and 55.

[17] Cited by S M Poulter *Family Law and Litigation in Basotho Society* (1976) 65.

[18] Report of the World Missionary Conference held at Edinburgh in 1910, 'The Church in the Mission Field' 65–6, cited by A Hastings *Christian Marriage in Africa* (1973) 15. On

pronouncements of secular leaders; Governor Pine reported that, '[t]he wives of a man are practically his slaves'.[19]

The assumption that values like 'virtue, truth and honour' were to be measured by the standards of the colonizers also permeates early case law. In *Bronn v Frits Bronn's Executors*, Hodges CJ described marriage as a 'condition Divine in its institution' and said that

> 'it is only by the development of Christianity that the sacred and mysterious union has been revealed to mankind and has enjoined a strict observance of its requirements, and one of the first of these requirements is, amongst all Christian nations, that polygamy is unlawful. . . .'[20]

He looked forward to a time when marriage would

> 'be brought by some well-devised law within the reach of the people of this Colony who have not yet embraced the greater blessings which they would obtain by Christian marriage, by which I mean of course marriage to one wife, which, among the heathen ought to be sanctioned and encouraged by law'.[21]

Polygyny was held to fall within the scope of a Transvaal statute which debarred from recognition African customs that were inconsistent with the general principles of civilization adhered to in the civilized world.[22] Even foreign marriages were denied validity because international comity did not require recognition of an institution repugnant to domestic morality:

> 'Polygamy . . . is reprobated by the majority of civilized peoples, on the ground of morality and religion, and the Courts of a country which forbids it are not justified in recognizing a polygamous union as a valid marriage.'[23]

The consequences of non-recognition can be invidious for members of the family; left largely unprotected by the law, they are accorded few of the rights enjoyed by members of legally constituted families. Neither spouse has any right to claim support from the other;[24] their children are illegitimate;[25] there are no rights of succession between spouses on

the views of the Anglican Church, see Hastings *ibid* 13 and E Hillman *Polygamy Reconsidered; African Plural Marriage and the Christian Churches* (1975) 31–3. See, for the approach of the Catholic Church in Africa, Hillman *ibid* 27–30; Poulter op cit 68. See generally on the Church and polygyny: Harries in A Phillips (ed) *Survey of African Marriage and Family Life* (1953) 335ff.

[19] British Parliamentary Papers, Natal, 1853, 22–3, cited by H J Simons *African Women; Their Legal Status in South Africa* (1968) 21.

[20] (1860) 3 Searle 313 at 318.

[21] At 321.

[22] Law 4 of 1885 excluded from recognition customs that did not conform to the general principles accepted in the civilized world: *Kaba v Ntela* 1910 TS 964 and *Nalana v Rex* 1907 TS 407. See C R M Dlamini 'Should we legalise or abolish polygamy?' (1989) 22 *CILSA* 330 for criticism of the moral and religious arguments against polygyny.

[23] *Seedat's Executors v The Master (Natal)* 1917 AD 302 at 307–8. Cf *Estate Mehta v Acting Master, High Court* 1958 (4) SA 252 (FC) and *Kader v Kader* 1972 (3) SA 203 (RA).

[24] *Ismail v Ismail* 1983 (1) SA 1006 (A).

[25] *Kaba v Ntela* 1910 TS 964; *Bronn v Frits Bronn's Executors* (1860) 3 Searle 313; *Docrat v Bhayat* 1932 TPD 125. The children will be treated as legitimate if the marriage qualifies as a putative marriage (*Ex Parte Soobiah: In re Estate Pillay* 1948 (1) SA 873 (N)) or, where the marriage was celebrated outside South Africa, if the children are legitimate according to the law of the domicile of origin (*Seedat's Executors v The Master (Natal)* 1917 AD 302).

intestacy; and the spouses are competent and compellable witnesses against each other.[26]

Like other polygynous marriages, African customary marriages are invalid at common law, but, as we indicate above, they differ in that they are not left totally unregulated. In terms of the Black Administration Act 38 of 1927, they fall to be governed by customary law.

This legal dualism stems from the policies of the colonial administrations which feared a hostile response should any attempt be made to supplant completely custom by colonial laws.[27] In any event, drastic measures were thought to be unnecessary since it was widely believed that, as part of a natural evolutionary process, the African population would embrace the nuclear family.[28] The report of the Cape Native Laws and Customs Commission of 1883 stresses the advisability of restraint. While expressing the view that some aspects of customary marriage, in particular its polygynous nature, degraded women, it recommended reform rather than abolition. The aim should be 'to mould native law into some shape that would conform more closely to civilized law and to secure the sanctity of marriage and the rightful place of women'.[29]

However, these early aspirations, limited in themselves by the patriarchal ideology of the colonists,[30] have never culminated in systematic reform to transform customary family relationships.[31] Although customary law has been modified in some respects to eliminate what were perceived to be obvious inequities,[32] the translation of dynamic customary practices into the body of rules implemented by the colonial authorities was marked by the influence of African men seeking to secure their dominant position.[33] Thus, for example, legislation placing customary wives under the guardianship of their husbands has entrenched their subordinate legal status.[34] Customary law, designed to meet the needs of a rural, pre-industrial and patriarchal society is ill-equipped to deal with the reality of contemporary women's lives. And the refusal to recognize customary marriages means that, denied the

[26] See, eg, *Nalana v Rex* 1907 TS 407 and, most recently, *S v Johardien* 1990 (1) SA 1026 (C).

[27] Simons (n 19) 32. Simons (at 51 and 64) also points out that legal dualism was later embraced by separationists as consistent with their aims.

[28] Bennett (n 3) 145. See also Simons (n 19) 51.

[29] Simons (n 19) 32, quoting from Cape Native Laws and Customs Commission *Report* (1883) G.4, paras 28, 72, 73, 82.

[30] Walker in C Walker (ed) *Women and Gender in Southern Africa to 1945* (1990) 10.

[31] Bennett (n 3) 145.

[32] The consent of both parties to customary marriages is now required whereas under original customary law, the woman's consent was probably not necessary. See: Bennett (n 3) 145 and 175; J C Bekker *Seymour's Customary Law in Southern Africa* 5 ed (1989) 106–7; SA Law Commission *Marriages and Customary Unions of Black Persons* (1985) Working Paper 10 para 4.3.3 and authorities cited there. In addition, in determining custody disputes, the courts give pre-eminence to the welfare of the child, thus undermining the husband's absolute rights over the child at customary law (see below).

[33] See, for instance, Chanock in M J Hay & M Wright (eds) *African Women and the Law: Historical Perspectives* (1982) 53.

[34] Section 11(3) of the Black Administration Act 38 of 1927.

status of wives in South African civil law, customary wives fall, in principle, outside the ambit of measures devised by legislators and the courts to protect the interests of married women. Acknowledging this as a problem, Parliament has been prompted to intervene occasionally, on an ad hoc basis, to enact specific remedial provisions.

One of the most damaging effects of non-recognition was that a customary marriage was automatically dissolved if the husband entered into a subsequent civil marriage with a woman other than his customary wife. As a result, the discarded spouse would be deprived of any rights that she had at customary law and legislative intervention was necessary to safeguard these. Section 22 of the Black Administration Act prevented the consequences of community of property from attaching to the husband's civil marriage,[35] secured the customary wife's 'material rights',[36] and preserved her limited interests in the husband's estate on his death.[37] However, the protection afforded by this provision proved to be illusory[38] and in 1988 the statute was amended to preclude a man who is a partner in a subsisting customary union from entering into a civil marriage with another woman.[39]

Legislation was also needed to counter the effect of non-recognition on the law relating to dependants' actions for damages arising from the death of a breadwinner. Although an action instituted by a customary wife might succeed against a black defendant on the basis of the customary law duty of support,[40] civil law denied her relief. The Appellate Division held that since the plaintiff's marriage was invalid at common law, she could not prove that her deceased husband owed her a duty of support.[41] So, as the defendant happened to be a white person and therefore exempt from the application of customary law principles, the widow was bound to fail. In order to remove this anomaly and to provide her with a remedy, s 31 of the Black Laws Amendment Act had to be enacted.[42]

In the sphere of maintenance too, statute had to come to the aid of customary wives. Although a husband has a duty at customary law to

[35] Section 22(6). This was apparently intended to prevent the customary wife from losing all her interests in property acquired during the marriage: N S Peart 'Civil or Christian marriage and customary unions: the legal position of the discarded spouse and children' (1983) 16 *CILSA* 55.

[36] Section 22(7). This phrase referred to her right to support from house property or from the general family property: SA Law Commission (n 32) para 6.3.2. See also Peart (n 35) 54–9.

[37] Section 22(7).

[38] Peart (n 35).

[39] Section 22(2) of the Black Administration Act 38 of 1927, as amended by Act 3 of 1988.

[40] See Bennett (n 3) 173.

[41] *Santam v Fondo* 1960 (2) SA 467 (A).

[42] 76 of 1963. See Bennett (n 3) 173–4 for criticism of the technical requirements of the provision. To avoid analogous problems in relation to workmen's compensation, s 4(3) of the Workmen's Compensation Act 30 of 1941 includes in its definition of 'widow' a woman party to a customary union.

support his wife,[43] it appears that she herself has no actionable right against him.[44] Should he fail to maintain her, she will normally have to return to her former guardian who is obliged to support her by virtue of the bridewealth agreement.[45] Statute has, however, extended to customary wives the right to claim maintenance from their husbands[46] in most circumstances.[47]

The customary law of succession was also found wanting. The principle of primogeniture denies a wife the right to inherit from her husband. Movable house property cannot be disposed of under a will but devolves in accordance with customary law[48] and the widow has to look to the male heir for support from the estate. The Minister was, accordingly, given the power,[49] where it would otherwise be inequitable, to direct that property be distributed in terms of the common law of intestate succession, which entitles wives to a share.

None of these changes involved a reassessment of the traditional objections to polygyny and the decisions of the latter half of the nineteenth century which rejected polygyny as contra bonos mores were followed without serious reconsideration until 1983. Then, following an examination of the institution in Muslim law and speaking for a full bench of the Appellate Division, Trengove JA declined to deviate from the established precedents.[50] Although he did not adopt the strident moral tone of earlier judgments, he nevertheless suggested that recognition of polygyny would 'undoubtedly, tend to prejudice or undermine the status of marriage as we know it'. A further difficulty, Trengove JA said, was that, as South African marriage and family laws are all founded on the idea of a monogamous union, recognition of polygyny would give rise to practical problems.[51] Finally, he added what is perhaps best described as an ethical reason, but it is couched in very different terms from the moral arguments used in earlier judgments which proclaimed the 'unchristian' nature of polygyny:

[43] See Simons (n 19) 211; I Schapera *A Handbook of Tswana Law and Custom* (1938) 150–1 and 152–3; Kuper in A R Radcliffe-Brown & D Forde (eds) *African Systems of Kinship and Marriage* (1950) 92.

[44] Peart (n 35) 51; Simons (n 19) 211; SA Law Commission (n 32) para 4.4.10; Bekker (n 32) 140.

[45] Peart (n 35) 51.

[46] Section 5(6) of the Maintenance Act 23 of 1963; s10*bis* of the Black Administration Act 38 of 1927. See SA Law Commission (n 32) para 11.2.6.6; J D van der Vyver & D Joubert *Persone- en Familiereg* 2 ed (1985) 454; H R Hahlo *The South African Law of Husband and Wife* 5 ed (1985) 35; Peart (n 35) 51. Compare *Kabe v Inganga* 1954 NAC 220 (C) at 223 and *Gcumisa v Gcumisa* 1981 AC 1 (NE).

[47] But no provision is made for the customary wife whose marriage has been terminated.

[48] Section 23(1) of the Black Administration Act 38 of 1927. Immovable property in the form of land held in individual tenure under quitrent conditions devolves in accordance with tables contained in regulations: see s 23(2) and (10) of the Black Administration Act. All other property is capable of being devised by will (s 23(3)).

[49] Regulation 2(*d*) GN 1664 of 1929, as amended by GN 939 of 1947, repealed and replaced by reg 2 of GN R34 of 1966.

[50] *Ismail v Ismail* (n 24).

[51] At 1024E.

'Furthermore, in view of the growing trend in favour of the recognition of complete equality between marriage partners, the recognition of polygamous unions solemnized under the tenets of the Muslim faith may even be regarded as a retrograde step; . . . a Muslim wife does not participate in the marriage ceremony; and while her husband has the right to terminate the marriage unilaterally by simply issuing three "talaaqi", without having to show good cause, the wife can obtain an annulment of the marriage only if she can satisfy the Moulana that her husband has been guilty of misconduct.'[52]

Polygynous unions, specifically those solemnized in Muslim law, are, in Trengove JA's view, contrary to public policy because they run counter to a notion of equality that dominates and, it is implied, should dominate, our family law. While the examples of inequality that are given are specific to Muslim marriages it seems clear from the tenor of the judgment that the very basis of polygynous marriages, which is that a man is entitled to many wives, would also infringe Trengove JA's ideal of equality.

On the face of it then, *Ismail v Ismail* is a decision that feminists might welcome for its commitment to equality between women and men in marriage. But the outcome of the case suggests that one should be wary of a glib application of the notion of equality. For the case arose out of a claim for maintenance by a woman married by Muslim law, a claim which Judge Trengove refused.

Mr and Mrs Ismail were married by Muslim rites in 1976. According to Muslim custom a husband is 'obliged to maintain his wife on a reasonable scale, commensurate with his means, during the subsistence of the marriage as well as for the period of Iddat which consists of three full menstrual cycles if the wife is not pregnant at the time of the termination of the marriage'. A husband is also obliged to provide a dowry which is agreed upon between his and his prospective wife's families on behalf of the spouses and to 'donate to his wife two sets of gold jewellery, one at the time of the engagement and the other at the time of the marriage ceremony'.[53]

In April 1980, Mr Ismail terminated the marriage by three irrevocable 'talaaqi'. He had failed to maintain his wife for almost three years of the marriage and during the subsequent period of Iddat. Mrs Ismail accordingly claimed arrear maintenance from him as well as delivery of the dowry (which had been deferred) and the jewellery which she had returned to Mr Ismail for safekeeping. The Moulana, after hearing the case, ruled in her favour. When her husband failed to comply with the decision, Mrs Ismail sought to enforce her claims in the civil courts.

Trengove JA was unable to come to the plaintiff's aid as he found that the union was contra bonos mores and that it therefore could not give rise to a civil action. He described polygyny as

[52] At 1024H.
[53] At 1081B–D.

'contrary to the accepted customs and usages which are regarded as morally binding upon all members of our society or, as Innes CJ said in *Seedat's* case[54] . . ., "fundamentally opposed to our principles and institutions"'.[55]

In Trengove JA's account, equality for women is one of the principles that is offended by polygynous unions. However, his use of the equality argument is problematic for at least two reasons. First, at no point does the judgment attempt to explain how the concept of equality applies to family relations or what, exactly, is unequal in polygynous unions. Secondly, Trengove J disregarded the fact that his use of the principle of equality led to an outcome that is prejudicial to women. He appears to have been oblivious to the fact that while deploring the position of women in Muslim marriages, his decision added to their disadvantages. That women in Mrs Ismail's situation are denied any redress appears even more harsh in the light of the fact that many have no real choice in the system under which they marry; pressure to comply with cultural practices may be irresistible. By refusing her claim, the court compounded the inequities that it identified in Mrs Ismail's marriage. Mr Ismail was home and dry, able to avoid maintenance obligations *because* the union that he entered into treated his wife less favourably than himself. Mrs Ismail was left with the dubious comfort of legal rhetoric proclaiming the rights of women.

The purpose of invoking an argument based on equality is undermined if that argument is used without ensuring that the remedy one chooses is sensitive to the real conditions within which those who are discriminated against find themselves. Equality, one fears, may have been invoked in this case merely to provide a new rationalization for old prejudices. Instead of providing an example of the way in which conflicting cultural practices could be approached and of how values such as the equality of men and women can address oppression in diverse cultural contexts, the case caps one injustice (inequality within the marriage) with another (the release of Mr Ismail from his maintenance obligations). Rather than redressing inequality, the case recalls the tensions between different cultural traditions in South Africa. Women are caught in the cross-fire.

II EQUALITY, POLYGYNY AND FAMILY LAW

The ethnocentrism of white colonizers in their approach to African family law is now easily recognized and we should be alert to the dangers of generalizing from our culturally specific notions of 'virtue, truth and honour'.[56] But this insight need not inevitably lead to an ethical quicksand of cultural relativism and does not absolve us from a responsibility to respond to oppression and suffering in different cultures. Instead, as we suggest above, it reminds us of the dangers of uninformed value judgments and requires us to reach an understanding

[54] *Seedat's Executors v The Master (Natal)* 1917 AD 302.

[55] At 1026B–C.

[56] See text to n 17 above.

of different cultures before we condemn practices as denying human dignity, for instance.[57]

The international code of human rights which has developed this century incorporates various values, such as equality and freedom from discrimination, that deserve universal application and provide a useful starting point for the evaluation of social practices in different cultures.[58] However, in spite of their popular currency, these values can be extraordinarily difficult to apply.

Judging polygyny against the standard of equality between women and men may initially seem unproblematic. This is the approach adopted by CEDAW,[59] the United Nations committee entrusted with the implementation of the 1979 Convention on the Elimination of All Forms of Discrimination Against Women,[60] which has interpreted the article dealing with equality for men and women within families as implying that polygyny is unacceptable.[61] Yet on closer analysis it is not easy to justify this conclusion. Setting aside for the purposes of this article the question of whether women should continue pressing for equality or whether some notion of difference is a more appropriate claim for

[57] The position that we adopt here is sometimes referred to as 'weak cultural relativism' as we hold that culture is not the only determinant of the validity of a moral position, but that moral judgments about behaviour must be informed by an understanding of the cultural context in which that behaviour occurs. For a similar view see: J Donnelly 'Cultural relativism and universal human rights' (1984) 6 *Human Rights Quarterly* 400. We prefer to avoid the term 'relativism' altogether as we would argue that this position is not relativist but merely recognizes that no social practice has meaning outside its social context. We are aware that the position that we espouse here runs against a dominant trend in current philosophical thought. However, there is not the space in this article to explain our reservations about cultural relativism.

[58] This 'human rights regime' has not gone unchallenged and third world writers particularly have pointed to its individualist basis which, they argue, is incompatible with their non-Western ethical systems. Although we would not argue that the international code is valid merely because of its wide acceptance, the code incorporates values that we consider demand universal application. (For a fascinating challenge to the notion that the international order of nation states can secure human rights, see: P Allott *Eunomia* (1991).) We are simply not persuaded by arguments that reject these values on account of their Western origins. See, for a similar attitude, J Donnelly 'Human rights and human dignity: an analytical critique of non-Western conceptions of human rights' (1982) 76 *American Political Science Review* 303ff particularly 313–15.

[59] Committee on the Elimination of Discrimination Against Women, established in terms of art 17 of the Convention on the Elimination of All Forms of Discrimination against Women. CEDAW consists of 23 experts, elected by states parties to the convention from their nationals, who serve in a personal capacity. According to art 18(1) of the Convention, the experts should be elected from different geographical areas and should represent different forms of civilization as well as the principal legal systems. In practice, the composition of the committee has so far satisfied these requirements. For the membership of the committee in 1990, see E A Grannes *CEDAW No 9: A Report on the Ninth Session of the Committee on the Elimination of Discrimination Against Women* (1990) International Women's Rights Action Watch.

[60] GA Res 34/180, 34 UN GAOR Supp (No 46), UN Doc A/34/46 (1979).

[61] This emerges from the reports of CEDAW. See, for some of many indications: CEDAW/C/SR113 25 February 1988; CEDAW/C/SR117 29 February 1988; CEDAW/C/SR120 2 March 1988; CEDAW/C/SR157 1 February 1990; CEDAW/C/SR161 12 February 1990.

feminism, one might commence by considering in what ways women are unequal to men in polygynous unions. Examples spring to mind easily: women bear (and bear responsibility for) their children but have no rights over them—these are vested in men; women in polygynous unions carry the burden of labour both within and outside the home so that their husbands may prosper materially and enhance their status;[62] a polygynous man may, unilaterally, introduce new wives to the family and has many opportunities to marry while each wife may have only one, shared husband. But most examples simply point to a variety of oppressive, patriarchal features of the institution of customary marriage. Only the last of those given here relates to polygyny itself and it is difficult to subject it to a formal equality analysis.

The concept of equality implies a comparison, and an assertion that equality is denied suggests that one category of people enjoys advantages that another category does not. But one can hardly suggest seriously that feminist objections to polygyny would be addressed if women were given the same opportunities as men to accumulate spouses. The notion of a woman acting as wife to more than one man suggests greater oppression, not liberation.[63] However, underlying the argument that polygyny is unacceptable because of the opportunity it gives a man to have more than one wife may be the belief that it is only in a one-to-one relationship that structural inequality can be addressed. Alternatively, it might be that we object to the man having the authority to introduce a new family member without consulting his wife.

The first concern, that there is something inherently unequal in a family structure which comprises one man and many women, is dubious. It is not self-evident that the apparently symmetrical relationship of one woman to one man provides the *only* formula for equality within marriage.[64] A variation of the argument might be that the relationship is unequal and degrading for women because, while each woman in a polygynous marriage is committed to a single man, she has to compete with a number of other women for his attention and a share of the family's material resources. This also fails to withstand scrutiny. It is possible, outside the very specific and historically quite recent notions of romantic love and companionable marriage, that each wife's attentions are also divided among her husband, other members of her family and the community in which she is living. This point is well made in a study on polygyny in Nigeria by Ware when she notes that '[w]hether one considers that women who have to share a husband are underprivileged

[62] K Mann *Marrying Well: Marriage, Status and Social Change among the Educated Elite in Colonial Lagos* (1985) 58.

[63] J Goody *The Oriental, the Ancient and the Primitive: Systems of Marriage and the Family in the Pre-industrial Societies of Eurasia* (1990) 140.

[64] See, for instance, R Clignet *Many Wives, Many Powers: Authority and Power in Polygynous Families* (1970) whose research suggests that the balance of power between husbands and wives depends more on community attitudes to women than on the form of the marriage.

depends on the value placed upon husbands'.[65] Furthermore, while it is true that wives are dependent on their husbands for access to resources, they are not necessarily prejudiced by the introduction of new wives; in many polygynous societies, additional wives increase the wealth of the group rather than deplete it.

The power that polygyny may give husbands to introduce new wives and thus to determine the composition of the family raises different issues. On the face of it, the equality objection here is easily dealt with by making the introduction of new wives a matter to be decided jointly by the husband and any existing wives. Indeed, this is already the case in Indonesia.[66] However, a formal requirement of consent may be worth very little and we are likely to mistrust a wife's consent when it is exacted in a society in which men dominate. But this means that the problem lies in the society in which polygyny is practised rather than in the institution itself.[67]

An air of unreality surrounds all these arguments. But the preceding discussion does draw attention to other possible problems. What concerns us is not so much a lack of formal equality within polygynous relationships but, instead, the nature of the communities within which polygyny is found. Our suspicion that requiring the consent of existing wives may not be an effective constraint on unilateral action by the husband is an indication of this. The frequent suggestion that polygyny allows women to be dominated, treated as property and forced into stereotyped roles, is another.

The treatment of women as property, sexual stereotyping and domination are not limited to polygyny, nor are they practices that can be shown to be inevitable in polygyny. Nevertheless, it is extremely difficult to disassociate these practices from polygyny or to envisage a polygynous household in which the husband does not dominate. It is arguable that polygyny enables a man to acquire wives as same-sex substitutes, which facilitates stereotyping and the objectification of women to a greater degree than monogamy does. Polygyny in South Africa, for instance, has been described as a feature of societies based on 'the accumulation of fertile and productive women'.[68] In any event, is it

[65] H Ware 'Polygyny: women's views in a transitional society, Nigeria 1975' (1979) 41 *Journal of Marriage & the Family* 194.

[66] CEDAW/C/SR113 25 February 1988. In Indonesia law treats monogamy as the preferred form of marriage. Courts permit polygyny only if the first wife has consented and the husband is able to support all parties fairly. Pakistan also introduced a requirement of consent; see: Shah in N M Shah (ed) *Pakistani Women: A Socioeconomic and Demographic Profile* (1986) 13.

[67] We are, of course, aware that polygyny is not practised in a social vacuum. Here, however, we simply want to suggest that it is not the mere configuration of one man-many wives that lies at the root of the problem. As we argue below, polygyny is problematic because it is combined with social practices that involve male domination of women. As Phillips (n 18) xiv says, polygyny 'is normally associated with a social system in which there is unchallenged male dominance'.

[68] Jeff Guy 'Gender Oppression in Southern Africa's Pre-capitalist Societies' in Walker (n 30) 33 at 43.

not possible that symbolically polygyny has become so closely associated with the oppression of women that it could be seen as incompatible with a social order in which the liberation of women is a recognized goal? By contrast, although monogamous marriage incorporated, until not much more than a century ago, many of the oppressive elements of present-day customary unions (and has a long way to go before it can be regarded as an egalitarian institution), it might now offer possibilities that seem remote in the customary context. Women might press for monogamy because patriarchal practices are so pervasive in polygynous relationships that there appears to be virtually no potential for change.

III POLYGYNY AND THE CUSTOMARY LAW OF MARRIAGE

Under the version of customary law evolved by South African courts, women are seriously disadvantaged.[69] Always subordinated to the authority of a patriarch,[70] they are in the position of perpetual minors, passing from the guardianship of their fathers to that of their husbands.[71] Their contractual capacity and locus standi are therefore limited; the male head of the household represents the family in all its dealings with the outside world.[72] Within the home, his powers are extensive. He controls the wealth of the household in respect of which, although traditionally custom knows no concept of ownership, he acts as nominal owner. The wife has very few rights over property.[73] In the polygynous household, simple or complex, control of virtually all property vests in the head of the household. The wife's only right is a right to restrain him from diverting property from the house without good reason.[74] It is far more difficult for women than men to obtain a divorce. Provided a man is prepared to forfeit the bridewealth, he may unilaterally repudiate his

[69] See C R M Dlamini 'The transformation of a customary marriage in Zulu law' (1983) 16 *CILSA* 388.

[70] See Bekker (n 32) 71.

[71] See Julyan in A Rycroft (ed) *Race and the Law in South Africa* (1987) 140; Bennett (n 3) 167 and 228; Dlamini (n 69) 388; SA Law Commission (n 32) paras 4.4.11 and 4.1.3 and authorities cited there. Civil law, however, provides that all people attain the age of majority at 21: s 1 Age of Majority Act 51 of 1972. Under s 11(3) of the Black Administration Act 38 of 1927, for the purposes of contractual capacity and locus standi, Africans have full legal status at common law if common law is applicable to the issue in question.

[72] Olmesdahl in Rycroft op cit 94; Simons (n 19) 187.

[73] While it is true that a wife might keep a large part of her farming produce for her own use (Guy in Walker (n 30) 46), she owns only gifts she has received from her husband, items of a personal nature such as clothing and household utensils and, in some groups, a beast given to her as mother of a bride (SA Law Commission (n 32) para 4.4.6 and authorities cited there. See also, for variations among different groups, Bekker (n 32) 141ff and Simons (n 19) 194ff. All other property and earnings acquired by her are administered by her husband.

[74] *Sijila v Masumba* 1940 NAC (C&O) 42. The court pointed out that the notion of personal ownership vesting in the kraalhead (ie head of the family) stems from the imposition of the European concept of individualism on an institution founded on communitarian ideals.

wife. Alternatively, he may recover the bridewealth if he can show that she failed, without good cause, to fulfil her obligations. Women, on the other hand, may not resort to unilateral repudiation, and where grounds for divorce exist, they cannot themselves initiate the process. Instead, a wife must enlist the help of the bridewealth holder,[75] who may well be reluctant to co-operate for fear of having to return at least part of the bridewealth.[76] Once bridewealth has been paid, the husband's family group has absolute rights to any children borne by the wife. Although on divorce she may be permitted to take the children with her, particularly if they are very young, they still 'belong' to the husband or his heir.[77]

Polygyny is an integral part of this oppressive system and interacts with other aspects of customary law to secure access to resources for men. Among the politically more powerful, links can be forged between groups through the exchange of women and cattle. Since marriage is regarded as an alliance between families, it facilitates the creation of relationships of clientship.[78] In addition, polygyny serves the purpose among chiefs and commoners alike of increasing a man's labour force for the expansion of his agricultural holding, so adding to his wealth and enhancing his prestige. It is also thought to maximize the possibility of numerous offspring, another important source of labour, and to make it more likely that there will be a male heir to perpetuate his father's spirit.[79]

Yet, within this male-centred family structure, it might be argued that polygyny at least provides women with informal opportunities to attain some measure of autonomy. Indeed, there are ethnographic accounts of societies in which polygyny, it is said, provides benefits for women.[80] It enables co-wives to share the burden of domestic and farm work and, in some social contexts, this has the added advantage of freeing wives to engage in economic activities[81] and to join self-help groups.[82] Ware points out that, '[i]n some cases, wives in polygynous marriages may have greater autonomy because they have less invested in the marriage and because, in losing part of their husbands' economic and moral support, they also gain independence'.[83] Polygyny is seen as advantageous also because it: provides women with companionship, often in the

[75] See generally, SA Law Commission (n 32) para 4.5.1ff; Simons (n 19) 128ff.

[76] See Burman in Walker (n 30) 59 and 63.

[77] See, generally, Simons (n 19) 211–13. This rule has been modified by the courts, which will award custody to the mother when it is in the best interests of the child to do so and when the father is not a fit and proper person. See, eg, *Mbuli v Mehlomakulu* 1961 NAC 68 (S). See also Peart (n 35) 47–8.

[78] A Kuper *South Africa and the Anthropologist* (1987) 136.

[79] Poulter (n 17) 64.

[80] Howard in C E Welch & R I Meltzer (eds) *Human Rights and Development in Africa* (1984) 60; M Wilson *For Men and Elders* (1977) 122.

[81] Ware (n 65) 189.

[82] L Lamphere in D Raphael (ed) *Being Female; Reproduction, Power and Change* (1975) 126–7.

[83] Note 65 above 194.

form of a sister; reduces the sexual demands made on each wife;[84] and enables women to space their children.[85] Seen in this light, polygyny is not intrinsically detrimental to women but, on the contrary, it may actually alleviate the hardship they suffer in patriarchal societies.

However, whether or not polygyny offers benefits to women, a significant proportion of women in South Africa appear to favour its abolition. In surveys undertaken in the preparation of the Law Commission's report on customary law one of the findings was that more women than men support abolition.[86] But even among men, polygyny appears to have fallen out of favour; only two per cent of all the respondents indicated that they were partners in a polygynous union. In addition, an average of 82,2 per cent of all those replying supported the abolition of polygyny.[87] Although they voiced concern about unfairness and jealousy between wives, the main argument advanced by the abolitionists was that it is financially and emotionally impossible to support more than one wife.[88] When women used to work the fields for their husbands, each house was self-sufficient. This is no longer the case for many and, it was pointed out, a housing shortage made polygyny especially impractical.

These comments reflect the fact that changes in social and economic conditions have diminished the utility and attractiveness of polygyny, particularly in urban areas. Certainly, the account given here of customary law and polygyny is necessarily brief and simplified but it is readily apparent that it is a system that does not reflect contemporary life. The permeation of Western values such as individualism and the importance attached to the notion of personal property; education; urbanization; the dislocation of the family as a result of migrant labour; the reduction, with the prevalence of waged work, in the significance of the family as the site of economic relationships; the desegregation of conjugal roles; the involvement of women in the political struggle; and the attenuation of kinship ties have all contributed to a transformation.[89]

Rural wives, in the absence of their menfolk, take on additional responsibilities in the management of households.[90] Adultery is widespread as are desertion and marriage breakdown. Women have entered the exchange economy in large numbers. In particular, deserted wives, dissatisfied wives, divorced women, widows, women with illegitimate children and women in conflict with their kin often move out

[84] Ware (n 65) 189.

[85] Howard in Welch & Meltzer (n 80) 46.

[86] SA Law Commission (n 32) paras 10.5.11 and 10.6.11. Wilson (n 80) 122 found a similar difference in the views of men and women among the Nyakyuse-Ngonde.

[87] Paragraph 10.8.4.

[88] Paragraph 10.2.10. The results of the South African survey mirror the findings of research conducted among the urban elite in Ghana: J C Caldwell *Population Growth and Family Change in Africa (The New Urban Elite in Ghana)* (1977) 54ff.

[89] See Poulter (n 17) 27 and 35–6; Chanock (n 1) 228; B A Pauw *The Second Generation: A Study of the Family among Urbanized Bantu in East London* 2 ed 1973 194–6; Olmesdahl in Rycroft (n 71) 94; Beall et al (n 5) 43.

[90] Poulter (n 17) 27.

of rural areas in search of work and set up female-headed households.[91] This trend suggests that traditional marriage and the kinship network no longer provide security for these women and indeed, many women, motivated by the wish to avoid the burdens of marriage, choose not to marry at all.[92]

Changes in social and economic conditions have, inevitably, been accompanied by changing values, including, for many people, a changed perception of the nature and function of the family. This has meant that couples married by customary law may no longer view marriage primarily as an alliance between family groups. Thus, research by Urdang suggests that women in Mozambique conceive of marriage in terms of emotional attachment and companionship.[93] Wives spoke of their love for their husbands and indicated that, subjected to polygyny, they experienced feelings of rejection and abandonment. Moreover, as Urdang shows, the traditional demarcation of conjugal roles is no longer unquestioningly accepted. She describes a public meeting at which a man sought to justify polygyny on the grounds that it ensures that there will be someone to carry out domestic tasks if a wife falls ill. A woman in the group countered this by asserting that '[t]he question is not whether one woman cooks when the other is ill. I am the only wife of my husband. When I am ill, he cooks the food.'[94]

Despite these changes, allegiance to tradition is still strong in South Africa and customary marriages are common.[95] However, the incidence of polygyny is declining.[96] But, empirical evidence that the institution is losing favour does not dictate the attitude that the legal system should adopt and this is the issue that we address, briefly, in the last section of the paper.

IV LAW AND POLYGYNY IN THE FUTURE

The absence of persuasive evidence that polygyny inevitably entails the oppression of women does not avoid the difficult question of whether polygynous marriages should be sanctioned by law. But it does shift the premises. What it means is that the question cannot be answered by asserting the moral superiority of one marriage form over another. Instead, polygyny must be assessed in its social and historical context.

No comprehensive study exists of polygyny as it is practised in South Africa. However, if polygyny were found to be inextricably linked to

[91] See Krige in E J Krige & J L Comaroff (eds) *Essays on African Marriage in Southern Africa* (1981) 155; Kuper (n 78) 146; Moore (n 10) 96 and 97.

[92] Beall et al (n 5) 46.

[93] S Urdang *And Still They Dance* (1989) 210ff.

[94] At 215.

[95] See SA Law Commission (n 32) ch 10. Replies from Africans to a questionnaire distributed by the Commission revealed that many couples marry according to both customary and civil law. The main reasons given for entering into a civil marriage were to ensure recognition of their marital status, to achieve a degree of legal certainty, to create rights of succession and to facilitate the acquisition of housing.

[96] See, eg, Kuper (n 78) 138; Poulter (n 17) 69–71.

social practices that are oppressive of women, there are a number of ways in which law might respond. For instance, polygyny could be directly outlawed or the present system of denying recognition to polygynous marriages but accommodating some of them in limited ways could be maintained. Alternatively, polygynous marriages could be fully recognized by law and extra-legal strategies used to discourage them.

First, outlawing polygyny should be recognized as a drastic step. It is too optimistic to assume, for example, that where polygyny is but one aspect of a system of family law based on religion, a community will alter its customs to conform with systems that are asserted to be more democratic or less oppressive of women.[97] Accordingly, a legal prohibition of polygyny will, inevitably, leave some marriages unregulated. Evidence that the vast majority of Muslim marriages, for example, are in fact monogamous (although potentially polygynous) does not obviate the problem.[98] For while the legal system might choose to treat marriages that are de facto monogamous as monogamous for legal purposes, it would have no method of dealing with those few that are polygynous. Women are likely to bear the burden of this legal isolation and cases such as that of Mrs Ismail will recur.

Secondly, the present method of giving partial legal recognition to African customary marriages has proved unsatisfactory. As the outline of the law above shows, it has created uncertainty and hardship.

It follows that even if the case against polygyny is shown to be overwhelming, law does not provide a suitable strategy for challenging it.[99] A legal system can never prevent people from establishing family relations outside its ambit and women who are positioned in oppressive structures are often the least able to resist the demands of tradition. To say that a woman who has grown up in a patriarchal cultural setting and who has no obvious alternatives should defy the community and resist polygyny because this is required by law is unrealistic.

The South African Law Commission has recommended a similar approach. Rejecting the unification of family law in South Africa, the Report on the Marriage and Customary Unions of Black Persons states that the imposition of an imported legal system would be 'not only inequitable but unrealistic'.[100] Successful law reform, it says, requires popular consensus. However, the Commission recognized that the position of customary wives is, in many respects, untenable, and (with some concessions to patriarchal interests) recommended the reform of customary law. In other words, the solution preferred by the

[97] As Sachs (n 6) 74 appears to do.

[98] *Ismail v Ismail* 1983 (1) SA 1006 (A) at 1018A.

[99] This does not mean that we think that the law can never be useful in achieving feminist goals but only that its use must be carefully considered in each instance. One obvious danger involved in the use of law is that the system is insensitive to gender issues and, as in *Ismail's* case, may pursue a public policy approach that simply disregards the interests of women.

[100] Note 32 above para 11.2.1.2.

Commission is not to outlaw polygyny but to confer greater rights on women within such marriages.

It seems that polygyny is not at the root of the problem, but that patriarchy or what Lovibond terms the sex/class system is. To challenge patriarchy women must be empowered: they need education to widen their options,[101] greater economic independence, political organization and the support of community structures. In appropriate contexts, law may empower women too and it is clear that there is a pressing need to reform customary law. But law reform is unhelpful where it threatens to exclude or disadvantage women who do not conform to a prescribed norm. Feminism is threatened by many divisions and to introduce yet another category of 'outsider' is unlikely to be productive.

V CONCLUSION

Insofar as this paper appears to accept the practice of polygyny it may be controversial but it does not intend to take issue with those who point to the severe oppression of women in many polygynous marriages. Instead, it suggests that we should re-examine the basis of objections to polygyny and choose our responses carefully. Most importantly, perhaps, we believe that, until a great deal more attention has been paid to the real conditions of women in polygynous relationships and options for addressing them, we should be extremely cautious in identifying polygyny as the cause of oppression.

[101] The SA Law Commission survey (n 33) para 10.5.11 shows that the greatest rejection of polygyny occurs among those with post-school qualifications, while those with standard one or lower object the least. Research in other countries reaches the similar conclusions: see, eg, Ware (n 65) and Mann (n 62).

Part V
Law and Civil Registration

[22]

THE PACS AND MARRIAGE AND COHABITATION IN FRANCE

CLAUDE MARTIN* AND IRÈNE THÉRY**

ABSTRACT

Change in marriage and cohabitation began in France thirty years ago. 2.5 million cohabiting couples and more than 40 per cent of births outside marriage reveals not only a new acceptability of cohabitation and family formation out of wedlock, but a new social signification of marriage itself. In this paper, we analyse what appears to have been a 'soft' revolution, widely accepted, and a paradoxical mutation. While the abandonment of a strictly matrimonial conception of the family is generally accepted in France, attitudes are much more contradictory with respect to legal rights of unmarried couples. The long, complex and controversial story of the evolution of the Pacs (*Parte Civil de Solidarité*), shows, behind the issue of homosexuality, how difficult it is for French culture to conceive a legal status for non-married couples. The Pacs, as a new possibility for heterosexual as well homosexual cohabitees, is not easy to define from a legal point of view. This intermediate status, neither a union nor a contract, neither private nor public, expresses the ambiguity of the *French way* of responding to increasing cohabitation. Analysing the Pacs as a *transitory law*, we suggest that a complex jurisprudential story is now beginning in France. This paper ends with a broader perspective on the interpretation of family change: no consensus exists in academic and political circles. The new forms of social inequalities will certainly represent one of the main issues in the public, academic and political debate in the future.

1. A DEEP SOCIAL CHANGE IN BEHAVIOUR AND VALUES: THE NORMALIZATION OF HETEROSEXUAL COHABITATION IN FRANCE

Roussel (1978) and Gokalp (1981) were among the first to identify a serious change in the way partnerships between couples were being constituted in France. They spoke at that time of 'juvenile cohabitation' or 'marriage on a trial basis' (*mariage à l'essai*), to signify the fact that, after the social movements of 1968, the new generations wanted to delay entering marriage and having children. The emancipation process consisted in sexuality outside marriage and experiencing a love relationship before institutionalizing it. Pregnancy was nevertheless

* chargé de recherche CNRS et Professeur à l'Institut d'études politiques de Rennes.
** Directrice d'études à l'EHESS, Paris.

usually considered to be an imperative reason to marry before the birth of a child. It took almost ten years to realize that this phenomenon was not merely a simple postponement of entering marriage and institutionalizing a family, but was for a growing number of couples a new way of life. In the 1980s and 1990s, cohabitation became progressively a commonplace, which was connected to the decline of marriage. Thus, increasing numbers of couples decided to begin their shared life without marriage, and even to have a first or subsequent children out of wedlock. Unmarried cohabitation is nowadays the normal way to begin a partnership. In the 1960s, only 16 per cent of cohabiting unions began outside marriage. In the 1990s the figure was 87 per cent.

The number of marriages in France has steadily decreased since the end of the 1960s. In 1969 the annual number of marriages was 380,000.[1] This dropped to 253,000 in 1994, the lowest point since the Second World War, with a marriage rate of 4.4 (per 1000). Then there was a slight increase, particularly in 1996 (10 per cent increase), with 280,000 marriages (marriage rate: 4.8) as a direct result of a fiscal reform for non-married parents.[2] This increase was mainly the consequence of parents marrying in order to legitimize one or several children (37 per cent more than in 1995). Then there was a stable period with only a slight increase in 1997 (1.7 per cent); 282,100 in 1998 and 285,400 in 1999, with a marriage rate of 4.8. This slow but constant recovery of marriage may be seen as a significant tendency in the sense that over the past two years the number of marriages of couples without children, which had decreased constantly from 1972 to 1995, has slightly increased, which may mean that the legitimation of children is less important for the new generations of couples and that marriage is again an attractive institution (Prioux, 2000). Another aspect of this change concerns the proportion of marriages taking place in church. This decreased from 75 per cent at the beginning of the 1970s to 50 per cent at the beginning of the 1990s. But the most significant feature is probably the delay in age at first marriage. In 1998, women marry on average two years later than in 1990 and five years later than at the end of the 1970s (29.7 years old for men, and 27.7 for women in 1998).[3]

However, these transformations of marriage do not mean there has been a rejection of family life or of children. So cohabitation is growing constantly, compensating for the decrease in marriage. There were 2.4 million cohabiting couples in 1998, compared to 1.5 million in 1990, which means almost one couple in six in 1998, compared to one in ten in 1990 (Beaumel *et al,* 1999). In 1998 almost half of all cohabitants (1.1 million couples) were living with at least one child (see Table 1).

Cohabitants are young people: almost 30 per cent of people aged between twenty-five and thirty are living in cohabitation. More women under twenty-six and men under twenty-eight are living in cohabitation than in marriage. Nevertheless, cohabitation is no longer specific to the

Table 1: Married and cohabiting couples according to number of children

	1990 1000's	Per cent	1998 1000's	Per cent
Cohabiting	1,516	10.7	2,429	16.4
Without child	973	6.8	1,353	9.1
One child	332	2.4	587	4.0
Two or more children	210	1.5	490	3.3
Married	12,714	89.3	12,386	83.6
Without child	6,850	48.2	7,211	48.7
One child	2,439	17.4	2,126	14.4
Two or more children	3,425	24.0	3,049	20.5
Total	14,229	100.0	14,815	100.0

Source: INSEE, employment inquiry 1990 and 1998.

younger generations. A growing proportion of cohabiting couples are found among the elderly. As L. Toulemon (1996) observed, 'cohabitation has become established'.

The birth of a child is no longer a sufficient reason to get married. So we are also facing a strong increase of the number of children born out of wedlock: from around 6 per cent between 1945 and 1965; 6.8 per cent in 1970; 11.4 per cent in 1980 to 30 per cent in 1990, 39 per cent in 1996 and 40 per cent at the end of the 1990s. In France, more than 50 per cent of first children are now born out of wedlock. This increase means that France is now third after Sweden and Denmark in terms of percentage of live births outside marriage.

But this increase is in a very different context from earlier times. During the '*20 Glorieuses*' (1945–65), illegitimate children, as we called them at that time, were strongly stigmatized. They were considered to be prone to social maladjustment and delinquency because they had been abandoned by their father. Nowadays, most of the children are recognized by their father. In the 1970s one in five were so recognized at the time of their birth, one in two in 1980, and three in four in 1996. eighty-five per cent of children are now recognized by both parents after a year. Only 6 per cent of children are never recognized by their father and this proportion remains stable. Very often, cohabitation occurs between adults who already have children from an earlier relationship. Of the total number of unions between 1989 and 1993, with or without marriage, 16 per cent of men or women already had one child (Beaumel *et al*, 1999).

If the decline of marriage and the increase of cohabitation are the main tendencies of recent decades, we could add also the postponement in the first formation of partnerships. After 1990, the proportion of young people living in cohabiting couples decreased at every age, because they form their first partnership later, and even sometimes in their parents' home. In 1999, only 30 per cent of twenty-five-year-old men and 50 per cent women of the same age were living in couples, compared to more than 40 per cent of the men and 60 per cent of the women in 1990. This delay in the setting up partnerships may be a major transformation, linked to the social and economic conditions of young people, including a tendency to extend the time for studies, delay in access to a first job, the prevalence of unemployment in the younger generations and new intergenerational links between them and their parents.

In sociological terms, probably the main distinction is no longer best made as being between juvenile and adult cohabitation but between two forms of cohabitation (Théry, 1998):

—'provisional cohabitation' (*cohabitation au présent*) is a way of life associated with a new tolerance for sexual and affective relationship but without a long-term project of common life and/or family : this kind of cohabitation is widespread among young adults, but also among adults after a divorce or separation, or even after widowhood. Socially, this kind of cohabitation is not associated with a long term project, separation is not a very dramatic issue, and property is not considered common.

—'long-term cohabitation' is a way of living together associated with a long-term project, with or without children. In this type of cohabitation, the behaviour and values are no different from those in contemporary marriage: the partner is considered as an informal spouse, and cohabitation as a sort of 'marriage without papers' (*mariage sans papiers*). The similarity between cohabitation and marriage is particularly evident as far as parenting is concerned: the rights and duties of parents and children are considered to be exactly the same. The modern distinction is no longer between 'legitimate' and 'illegitimate' children, but between children with two parents and the 6 per cent of children born to a real 'lone mother'.

Of course, in spite of the fact that these different social significations are important, it is extremely difficult to distinguish between 'provisional cohabitation' and 'long-term cohabitation' in quantitative data (except when there are children). And, in fact, many of the long-term unions (married or not) begin as 'provisional cohabitation'. Sociologists underline that the new phenomenon is the tendency towards very 'soft' and informal transitions in the life cycle (Roussel, 1989; Kaufman, 1996). Another problem is that it is difficult to know whether people in long-term cohabitation consider that marriage is definitely excluded for the future or not. One study reveals that in 1986 only 6 per cent of cohabitants categorically rejected the institution of marriage (Léridon and Gokalp, 1994). This could be one of the reasons for the recent increase in the number of late marriages.

The problem of *separation* is linked to this ambiguity in the social significance of cohabitation. As in other countries, unmarried cohabitation in France is much more at risk of ending in separation than is marriage. But the significance of the separation differs according to whether the cohabitation is or is not provisional. Separation among young adults who have been cohabiting without children, for example, is not considered a dramatic phenomenon. Nevertheless, if we compare marriage with cohabitation with children, cohabitation is at far greater risk of breakup than marriage (Toulemon, 1996).

These developments show that cohabitation is now quite integrated in French society as a normal first stage in the establishment of a partnership, and even as a normal situation for millions of children. The situation of these children is very different from that of illegitimate children in past times, as almost three in four are recognized by their father when they were born, compared to the 6 per cent of illegitimate children at the end of the 1960s, who were also confronted with strong stigmatization and disapproval. This normalization process is leading to the total legal assimilation of legitimate and illegitimate children, and even the suppression of this old legal distinction, as has been suggested in two recent reports to the minister of Justice by Théry (1998) and Dekeuwer-Desfossez (1999). In that sense, cohabitation was not a major issue of public debate in France, not even in the field of family policy reforms, before the Pacs project was initiated. So, the nature of this project provided a means to avoid speaking exclusively about homosexual couples, and to bring together the interests of homosexual and heterosexual 'modernist' couples.

A. Homosexual cohabitation: towards social recognition

The distinction we suggested between provisional and long-term cohabitation may also be partially pertinent for homosexual relationships. Tolerance towards homosexual relationships has emerged roughly over the last decade. For example, in 1994, 75 per cent of a general population survey considered that 'homosexuals are normal people' (*les homosexuels sont des gens comme les autres*) (69 per cent expressed that opinion in 1992). Nevertheless, a significant proportion of the population still sees homosexual relationships in terms solely of sexuality, refusing to acknowledge the long-term projects of these couples. Public opinion seems to find it difficult to accept that homosexuality may take the form of stabilized couples. The stigmatization still operates. Thus, a majority of young homosexuals (60 per cent of those between sixteen and twenty years old) and a large minority of mature men (42 per cent of those between thirty-six and forty-five) still conceal their homosexuality from their parents, mainly their father (Schiltz, 1997). Anonymity of the big conurbations is still important in the acceptance and revelation of homosexuality.

The main recent sources for assessing the number of homosexuals in France are linked to the AIDS epidemic. The major survey (on a sample of 20,000 people from eighteen to sixty-nine years old) is the ACSF (*Analyse des comportements sexuels en France*) financed by the ANRS (*Agence nationale de recherche sur le Sida*) in 1990 (Spira *et al*, 1993). This inquiry reveals that 4.1 per cent of men and 2.6 per cent of women who had a sexual experience, had at least one same-sex partner. These largely occur in urban areas: 5.9 per cent of men and 4.1 per cent of women living in the Paris conurbation declared such a practice compared to only 1.6 per cent of men and 1.2 per cent of women living in the countryside. The maximum proportion was found among fifty to fifty-four-year-old men in the Paris conurbation (more than 11 per cent). Almost 50 per cent of these people mentioned that they had also had sexual relationships with people of the other sex, which means that homosexuality is often bisexuality, which poses a major problem for the prevention of AIDS. These data, which concern only sexual behaviours, could have indirectly reinforced the perception that homosexuality is mainly a sexual orientation, without concern for a long-term future as couples. Nevertheless, an inquiry undertaken each year from 1985 through the homosexual press shows other aspects of homosexuality (Schiltz, 1997). Ninety per cent of the 2,600 men who in 1995 answered a questionnaire distributed in ten homosexual magazines defined themselves as homosexuals, and even as exclusive homosexuals. Six in ten declared that they were living in a stable relationship, which does not necessarily mean an exclusive sexual relationship, nor even a cohabitation. Nevertheless, the effects of the AIDS epidemic led these people to be more sexually exclusive. But it is important to underline that 32 per cent of the respondents were cohabitants in an exclusive sexual and emotional relationship. Around 25 per cent were having apart-together relationships. Most co-residence was by people in their thirties. The increase of co-residency, which in a way makes homosexual couples nearer to heterosexuals, and the relative decline of multi-partnership, should not obscure the specificity of homosexual couples, which is still very close to a single way of life. For a homosexual, to be engaged in a stable relationship does not necessarily mean co-residence or fidelity. But despite these specificities, homosexuals increasingly demanded social recognition of their partnerships and legal protection. The debate about the Pacs was a result of that mobilization. The debate was clearly initiated by homosexual movements in order to obtain recognition of homosexual couples in the context of the AIDS epidemic. In particular, the associations close to the socialist party (*Les gais pour les libertés, Homosexualité et socialisme*, for example) succeeded in setting this issue on the political agenda. Initially, the Pacs emerged as a proposition to respond to the dramatic situation of homosexuals who were evicted from their homes after the death of a partner, or deprived of the fruits of a common enterprise, because of the total absence of legal protection.

This mobilization has in a way helped to construct an artificial 'homosexual community', or a sort of model of identity, around the common difficulties of homosexuals. Nevertheless, this debate triggered off a deep questioning on the frontiers of the family. To recognize the right of homosexuals to live in partnerships and to obtain legal advantages equivalent to those of 'legitimate' couples, and to break with discriminatory attitudes and homophobia leads ineluctably to the acceptance of homosexuality as a legitimate way of life and even as a form of family life.

The chronology of the events around the Pacs shows the importance of lobbying and the progressive setting of homosexual issues on the political agenda (Commaille and Martin, 2000). This lobbying began to appear more clearly when a very few socialist politicians publicly announced their homosexuality (coming-out).[4] The homosexual movement was increasingly structured and visible, from the grassroots level, with important resources of mobilization (such as the enormous success of the Lesbian and Gay pride, particularly in 1996), to the top levels of influence with experts, politicians, journalists, etc. In this process, family associations—the traditional, legitimized and official partners of the State and Parliament on family issues—were marginalized.[5]

The debate vacillated between many issues: recognition of homosexuality, which is not necessarily connected with family matters; recognition of homosexual couples' rights (frequently in terms of comparison with married and non-married heterosexual couples); recognition of households where children are living with one of their parents and a same-sex partner as a family ('homoparentality'); and, finally, recognition of the possibility for a homosexual couple to adopt or even to have a child with assisted reproduction. Some issues mainly concern recognition of the individual, while others concern the recognition of couples; and others concern issues of filiation. On these various issues, family associations defended a traditional position, mainly in its Catholic form (Commaille and Martin, 1999).

We suggest that we might speak of a change in 'citizenship regime' (Jenson, 1997), in the sense that the legitimized actors who define social norms and rules, and categories which might give rise to rights, are changing. In a way, the debate on the Pacs contributed to a visible and explicit decline of the legitimacy of the family associations as representatives of the family interests. Their positions appear to be too traditional and conservative to be acceptable to public opinion. With the debate on the Pacs, a new and increasingly recognized interest group appeared, the 'homosexual community', albeit that that hypothetical community is much more fragmented than it is generally represented to be (in terms of gender, generations and social stratification, with important consequences in terms of lifestyle and mobilization).

2. MARRIAGE AND COHABITATION: THE LEGAL CONTEXT BEFORE THE PACS

The growth of cohabitation in France has been, sociologically, a soft revolution. Nevertheless, this quiet change does not signify that in

France people unequivocally accept the historical phenomenon of 'démariage' (Théry, 1993). Ambiguity appears on any occasion *when legal issues or policy issues are concerned.* It appears difficult for French culture to think of marriage and cohabitation together: the one is constantly contrasted with the other. A certain social anxiety appears in this incoherence of social expression. French legislation is far from giving cohabiting couples the same social and fiscal rights as the married. The complexity of cohabitation's social signification must be remembered when considering legal evolution before the Pacs. French legal attitudes to cohabitation are very mixed.

A. *Cohabitants as a couple: persistence of the Napoleonic attitude*

Except in very particular circumstances, in civil law cohabitants are considered as independent persons, and not as a couple. In a way, the old Napoleonic attitude of 1804 is maintained: 'They don't want law, law pays no regard to them'. Consequently the civil law makes no provision in case of their separation or death. Cohabitants are treated as if they were strangers to each other. In case of illness, a cohabiting partner has no right to be consulted over medical decisions. In case of death, the partner has no right to make decisions about the funeral. And, of course, there are no inheritance rights. Nor can a cohabiting couple adopt a child together. In the recent past, jurists had a long debate over creating a 'status' for cohabitants, but this failed (Rubellin-Devichi, 1986; Meulders, 1999). So, 'in the shadow of the law', the courts have developed a jurisprudence based on '*société de fait*' or '*enrichissement sans cause*' where separation causes damage, a very indirect and limited way of solving problems (Hauser et Huet-Weiller, 1989; Carbonnier, 1999).

The attitude of the Civil Code towards cohabitation is followed in fiscal law. Cohabitants are not considered as a couple for the purposes of the annual income tax; only married couples can declare their income jointly, which is in most cases advantageous for them (this difference between the married and non-married was accentuated in 1995 when cohabiting parents lost the fiscal advantage they had previously enjoyed, as lone parents, regarding children). As far as succession rights are concerned, the free voluntary legacy which might be made to the cohabiting partner is severely limited by the '*reserve*' for children and ascendants. The taxation applicable to these so called 'strangers' is 60 per cent for amounts above 10,000 francs. On the other hand, social law is based on concrete situations, and tends to recognize 'concubinage', but mostly in a negative way. Holding '*de facto* solidarity' between the partners to be an advantage compared to living alone, social law increasingly refuses to treat all 'non married' persons equally. So, entering cohabitation will lead to the loss of some allowances which are targeted at lone persons, especially lone parents: the allowance for lone parents (API), the allowance for family support (ASF), and the allowance for widowhood (*pension de reversion*). It will reduce others, like minimum income benefit (RMI) or housing allowances. Compared to benefits conferred on cohabitants by many insurance companies, and by public and private transport companies (SNCF, Air France), French social law is very parsimonious. The only social rights derived from cohabitation are to remain in the common rented home after a separation or death, and to be considered as a social security beneficiary of the partner where there is no income. But this last advantage disappeared in 1998 with a new law on '*Couverture maladie universelle*' which gives to *everybody* a right to 'social security'. So, for civil and fiscal law, only a *married* couple is considered to be a real *couple*, while for social law, cohabitation is recognized, but usually in order to remove or diminish allowances for single people.

This legal situation arises from almost contradictory factors. On the one hand, there is a strong traditional 'marital preference' in French culture holding that people who are not legally linked together should not benefit from the State in the same way as people who have proved their mutual commitment. This attitude is widespread among the traditionalist part of the population who see the growth of 'individualism' as a threat to society (Sullerot, 1984). On the other hand, the new lifestyles have a strong influence. We can notice that until recently, most of long-term cohabitants seemed to accept the lack of legal protection as a consequence of the individual freedom of their relationships. For example, there is no claim between separating cohabitants for some '*prestation compensatoire*' which, in a divorce, can be paid to the spouse whose financial situation is damaged by the ending of the marriage in spite of the fact that, among cohabiting couples, the traditional gendered division of tasks continues. Similarly, it seemed accepted that if you want to make provision for the survivor after death of a partner, there were new private solutions: contracts, life insurance and so on. This is now beginning to change, since a significant proportion of French cohabitants are now in their fifties. The homosexual movement also illuminated the legal problems many heterosexual people faced in private life.

B. Cohabitation and parenthood: a soft revolution

The position of heterosexual cohabitants who are *parents* is entirely different. There is almost complete assimilation of rights and duties for children, independently of the legal situation of their parents.

(i) The great reforms of the 1970s

In 1972, the reform of filiation introduced a very important legal change. It allowed the natural child to inherit. This was considered as the legal acknowledgment of another form of family, alongside the family based on marriage: the 'natural family'. More than that, the principle of equality between legitimate and non legitimate filiation was guaranteed by a new article in the civil code (art 334 cc).This was, after centuries where the 'family' was based exclusively on marriage, *a revolution in the civil law* (Carbonnier, 1979). Traditional jurists and conservative politicians considered this to be a decisive attack on marriage. In fact, this reform was a legal compromise. Marriage as an institution had to be protected. So, children born from adultery only received half of the inheritance they would have had if they were legitimate.[6] During the same period, two important reforms indicated that marriage was considered the 'normal' way of family living:

—in case of non-marriage, no distinction is drawn in establishing filiation between cohabiting and non-cohabiting parents: the parents, especially the father, must recognize the child. But the reform on parental authority (1970) established that the exercise of parental authority (*exercice de l'autorité parentale*) will be attributed only *to the mother* since this was considered to be 'social reality'. If the father wanted to exercise parental authority, he needed to resort to a judicial procedure.

—in case of divorce, the reform of 1975 (introducing divorce by mutual consent) removed the link between fault and the attribution of custody. In all cases, custody had to be attributed to 'one *or* the other parent' according to the best interests of the child. This indicates that outside of marriage, namely outside a legal couple, French law considered that the child cannot have two parents with equal rights, exercising day-to-day responsibilities.

To summarize the legal situation at the end of the 1970s, apart from the important reform of filiation, marriage remained pre-eminent. We must remember that, at that time, nobody anticipated the rise of non-married parenthood nor the increase in divorce. The Minister of Justice (Jean Lecanuet) explained in Parliament in 1975 that 'marriage has never been as healthy as it is now', and that 'modernization of divorce will strongly reinforce marriage' (Théry, 1993). Legal change was not seen as a revolution. For society, it was no more than a way of being 'human' towards the rare situations of children born outside marriage, and a part of the modernization of the country engaged by the liberal right wing government (The Presidents were successively G. Pompidou, V. Giscard d'Estaing).

(ii) The growing equality of parenthood

But family change rapidly proved to be very important, and in the 1970s and 1980s the recent reform of civil code became an unexpected factor of social cohesion. When increasing numbers of non-married couples decided to have children, they knew that these children would not be social and legal outcasts. This is certainly one of the major reasons why the French 'revolution of marriage and cohabitation' was a soft one.

Nevertheless, two problems emerged in the social and political agenda: that of fathers' rights and their involvement in non-married and in broken families. These questions must also be seen as being as much a problem for women (who had most of the personal and financial burden of educating the children in a lone parent family, when the father did not assume his responsibilities), as a problem for men, when they protest against their 'eviction' by the mother after a separation or a divorce.

During the 1980s and 1990s claims for equal rights and responsibilities for fathers and mothers, and for all the parents whatever their situation increased. The same socio-cultural movement occurred as in other countries, the emergence of a strong response to 'démariage' in the affirmation of the double filiation as a family link founded on the principle of indissolubility of parenthood (Théry, 1998). The International Convention on Children's Rights (1989) expresses this principle in Article 7.1 which states the rights of children 'to know and be cared for by his or her parents'. But, in France, this principle turned out to be much more complex than it seems, and is not yet achieved. The main legal reform was the introduction in 1987 in the civil code of the possibility of acquiring joint parental authority, and in 1993 the affirmation of joint parental authority as the principle for all parents (Carbonnier, 1999). But these reforms also revealed the traditional French ambiguity. On the one hand, the law proclaimed equality (between married and unmarried parents, between fathers and mothers) but on the other hand expressed a real reluctance to give up the traditional preference for marriage, for (1) although after 1993 the unmarried father is entitled to exercise parental authority, this is only if the parents can prove they were living together at the moment of the legal recognition. (We can see here how difficult it is for French people to think of 'two parents' without seeing them as a couple); and (2) although divorced or separated parents have joint parental authority as a matter of principle, in 1987 and 1993, joint *physical* custody was strongly opposed on the ground of the child's psychological well-being (The very influential psychoanalyst, Françoise Dolto, played a great role in that debate, condemning parents who 'share their children as objects'). The legal obligation of designating the children's 'principal home' reintroduced the perception that, without the family unit, or the household unit, or the unity of a couple, it is impossible for children to have two 'real' parents.

One of the consequences of this debate is that many judges are reluctant to award joint physical custody, although parents increasingly choose this solution. Many divorced parents who share physical custody declare they are obliged to conceal this from the judge (Neyrand, 1996). Another consequence is that judges are extremely reluctant to order joint physical custody if one parent disagrees. However, the attitude of the courts is changing; growing numbers of divorced fathers see their children weekly (20 per cent in 1994), and for a longer period (often from Friday evening to Monday morning). Nevertheless, changes in parents' attitudes must not be overestimated: in 1994, 25 per cent of divorced fathers had lost contact with their children (Villeneuve-Gokalp, 1999). Fathers' involvement in the children's lives is significantly lower among the less educated part of the population (Martin, 1997; Villeneuve-Gokalp, 1999).

To summarize, the legal situation just before the Pacs debate began in France was highly complex: unmarried *parenthood* was almost assimilated to married parenthood, in spite of some 'residual' differences, specially for children born in adultery. As far as parenthood is concerned, the main issues were no longer between marriage or cohabitation, but over the problem of separated or divorced parents. At the same time there was a growing movement towards a dual responsibility, and the use of new criterion (*résidence principale*) accentuating the need to choose between mother and father. The legal situation of cohabitants as *couples* remained unchanged as far as civil law was concerned: they were considered as 'strangers'. Social and fiscal law was very problematic and contradictory.

3. THE PACS: THE COMPLEXITY OF THE LEGAL 'FRENCH WAY'

On 15 November 1999, the Pacs was promulgated (*loi sur le concubinage et le pacte civil de solidarité*), after a passionate debate in the National Assembly and the media. In contrast with a growing discussion about homosexuality, one can observe that the most important legal changes in the project from its first presentation (June 1998) to the final vote (October 1999) occurred without debate or even the opportunity for anyone but a handful of specialists to understand it. As a young student said, in February 1999, during a seminar devoted to the project : 'Everybody is for or against the Pacs, but nobody knows what it is'. To understand the 'French way' of giving rights to same-sex couples, and finally the main characteristics of the Pacs itself, it is necessary to revert to the beginning of the legal story.

A. *Before the Pacs: 1989–97*

As we said above, during the 1980s, in the context of AIDS, homosexual couples experienced many legal problems. The *Cour de Cassation* refused in 1989 to consider same-sex couples as cohabitants (*concubins*), and decided that cohabitation must be strictly defined as 'marital life', that is, heterosexual (this was confirmed by another decision in December 1997). Even the limited social rights of heterosexual cohabitants were therefore denied to homosexuals. A small group in the homosexual movement then initiated a long campaign for the 'legal recognition of the same sex couple'.

On the basis of proposals by some homosexual activists, four projects were successively put forward by the leftist parties:

—partenariat civil (Senate, 1990)

—contrat d'union civile (National Assembly, 1992)

—contrat d'union sociale (National Assembly, 1997)

—contrat d'union civile et sociale (National Assembly, 1997).

A legal analysis of these successive projects reveals a real diversity of conceptions among the homosexual activists and among the left wing (for a detailed analysis of the projects and the debate, see Théry 1997). The first project—*partenariat civil*—is the 'lightest': a contract between two persons, registered by the mayor, but ending without any formality should one partner decide to break his commitment (a registered letter would be sufficient to end the contract). In contrast to this 'light' commitment, the various marital property regimes would apply and the partner would inherit like a spouse, with the same taxes. The three other projects were much more elaborate. Their main common characteristic was a strong similarity to marriage, but with two important differences:

—divorce would not be necessary to break the contract. Separation would be an administrative act, instituted by only one party. In case of conflict the judge would only deal with property.

—the contracts would have no consequences for filiation and give no rights for adoption or artificial insemination.

Nevertheless, as far as couple-relationship is concerned, the projects can be defined as 'quasi-marriage' (Théry 1997): exclusivity of all other unions (marriage or another civil contract), registration by the mayor, change in civil status (implying support and assistance), the same regimes for property as in marriage, guarantee to the surviving partner of a right to inherit like a spouse, and also all the social and fiscal rights married people have. But the successive projects differ on one point: the people to whom they would be available. This has all along been the major point of divergence between the activists promoting a new legal status. Some consider that the contract must be open to every kind of 'pair' (couples, friends, brothers and sisters etc). This is the case in *partenariat civil, the contrat d'union civile* and *the contrat d'union civile et sociale*, which came from the same part of the movement. On the other hand, some activists consider that the major issue is to achieve legal recognition of same-sex couples as legal couples: the *contrat d'union sociale*, as in the Dutch legislation, would have been open only to couples, heterosexual or homosexual. In this project, incest is clearly excluded: prohibitions are the same as in marriage. But we must notice that the major part of the homosexual movement seems not to have distinguished between these two legal perspectives; during the 1990s, the claim for a *'contrat d'union sociale'* grew, but this was a general goal. Legal discussion was confined to a very small circle of activists.

(i) 1997–98: the moment of decision

In 1997, the leftist parties were successful in the legislative elections. The programme of the socialist party included the commitment to legislate for the *'contrat d'union sociale'*. Pressure from the homosexual movement was strong and the project was considered a priority. But ambiguity grew: was the contract intended to legalize solidarity between two persons or to create a new legal union for couples? Was it a 'light' contract or a quasi-marriage? The politicians gave no answer, other than to insist that the project was not confined only to homosexuals. But legal choices could not be avoided. In fact, the previous projects were abandoned and two MPs (J.-P. Michel and P. Bloche) were charged by the *Commission des Lois* of the National Assembly with elaborating a new one. The reason was that a 'quasi marriage' for all persons (even brothers and sisters) seemed absurd, but a project obviously devoted to homosexual couples could be divisive. Most leftist MPs feared they would not be re-elected if they supported homosexuality.

Three projects appeared in succession, the first two in official government reports. In February 1998, the *'pacte d'intérêt commun (PIC)'* was presented by Professor J. Hauser. It is only a private contract dealing with property, concluded in a solicitor's office, available to everyone, even married people. The PIC nevertheless confers substantial income tax benefits and social rights. The media saw this as the new solution. At the beginning of May 1998, Irène Théry delivered to the government a report on family change and the civil law, *Couple, filiation et parenté aujourd'hui* (Théry, 1998). In a section devoted to cohabitation (*concubinage*), it proposed that a specific article should be added to the civil code, treating 'concubinage' as cohabitation by a couple of the same sex or of different sexes. Cohabitation lasting at least two years would be afforded the same social and fiscal rights as in marriage.[7] At the end of May 1998, the Pacs was presented to the media by P. Bloche, J.-P. Michel and C. Tasca, the President of the Assembly Commission for Law. The new project was a 'quasi marriage', available to heterosexual or homosexual couples. As in the previous projects, filiation and adoption were not included, and divorce was not necessary in case of separation. Property was to be organized in the same way as the *'régime primaire'* in marriage (*'communauté réduite aux acquêts'*) and the partner was to be considered as legal heir. We must also notice that, even though no-one tried to amend the legal project accordingly, during

1997–98 some sections of the homosexual movement began to advance a new claim: the right to *marry* and *adopt* children. This was considered by its advocates as bringing about 'perfect equality' between homosexuals and heterosexuals (Borillo, 1998).

What choices did the French government make? The first choice was not to be directly implicated: the project would be the exclusive responsibility of Parliament. The second was to opt for the Pacs but, at the same time, to transform it radically. The Prime Minister, Lionel Jospin, did not wish the Pacs to be another form of marriage. It must not even be compared to marriage. During the summer 1998, important modifications of the project were imposed:

1. The Pacs would not be concluded before the mayor, but in the '*tribunal d'instance*', a place of much less symbolical significance; the property regime was changed to one of co-ownership; the partner of a Pacs was no longer to be treated as legal heir; the obligation of 'support and assistance' was removed; taxation in case of succession was to be much more onerous than for a spouse; the right to joint taxation would arise only after three years.
2. In spite of prohibition for close relatives, it was not clear if the Pacs was to be for couples only or for any kind of pairs of non-relatives (friends, colleagues, churchmen etc).
3. It was not clear if the Pacs would be a union or a simple contract for property: the only obligation would be for '*solidarité mutuelle et matérielle*'.

A strong indication of the ambiguity of the 'new' Pacs, transformed by a summer of negotiations, was that Théry's proposal of an article in the civil code about 'concubinage' was turned down. To introduce the expression 'same-sex couple' into the French Civil Code was considered 'shocking' for public opinion. This assumed that the jurisprudence of the *Cour de Cassation* would be maintained. This legal ambiguity showed the political anxiety of the socialist party about same-sex partnerships. In fact, at the beginning of the autumn, most socialist MPs were hesitating, and some were not convinced at all by the project itself. The consequence was that when the project was presented for the first time at the National Assembly on 9 October 1999, most socialist MPs were not present, and the project was rejected.

B. The three paradoxes of the Pacs

After this unexpected political defeat, a very heated debate took place in the National Assembly and in the media. The left decided to present immediately another Pacs, which the media dubbed 'Pacs II'. The main consequence of the first defeat was a radicalization. The left perceived that the political benefits were greater than the risks, and finally took up the defence of homosexual couples. On the right, the more conservative MPs defended 'family values' against the 'social decline' they considered symbolized by the Pacs. But paradoxically there were many divisions and debates in each camp, although they remained hidden. This appears more clearly if we look at legal issues.

Pacs II was to be open to brothers and sisters, so as to avoid a clear legal recognition of same-sex couples. During the autumn, leftist MPs became increasingly divided over same-sex cohabitation. Some were convinced that it was necessary to introduce a specific article into the law, but others (for example Elisabeth Guigou, Minister of Justice) refused this categorically. The argument was that legal recognition of same sex-couples would 'open the door to homosexual filiation' (Gélard, 1999, 298). The other growing division was about brothers and sisters: some wanted to exclude them and assumed the Pacs was a new form of legal union for couples, and others rejected this. The right was no less divided. Many did not agree with the so-called traditional family 'fundamentalists', such as the MP Christine Boutin, the leader of the 'Pacs out' campaign. The Senate rejected the project and in March 1999 the *Commission des Lois* of the Senate produced an alternative. Its purpose was to extend some fiscal advantages to cohabitants (but inferior to those enjoyed by married people), but the project declined to add an article on 'concubinage' in the civil code which would refer explicitly to same-sex couples (Gélard, 1999).

Finally, this legal battle, incomprehensible to almost all the French people, ended with a vote by the National Assembly in November 1999. The final text integrated some amendments. Pacs for brothers and sisters was rejected, and the article on 'concubinage' naming same-sex couples was introduced into the civil code, changing the title of the law (which becomes: 'Law on concubinage and Pacs'). In spite of these clarifications, the complex legal story explains why the law voted by the National Assembly on 15 November 1999 remains largely uncertain. The Pacs is neither a legal union nor a simple property contract. It is neither public nor private. It is neither for couples nor for pairs of friends. It is neither a legal recognition of same-sex couples nor is it non-recognition (Murat, 2000). The choice seems to have been a kind of 'neither-nor' politics.

In summary, the Pacs is available only to two persons of the same or the opposite sex, but excluding persons who are related to each other, or who are in an existing marriage or Pacs; it is entered by registration of the contract at a *tribunal d'instance*, but the tribunal does not scrutinize its contents. The Pacs is immediately terminated if either party marries, but otherwise may be terminated immediately by agreement, or three months after unilateral repudiation communicated to an official. Property relations will be determined by the contract, but in default co-ownership will apply. The parties are treated as partners for social security purposes. There are no succession rights except to tenancies, though after two years there is some tax advantage for gifts made on death, and after three years their income is taxed as if they were married. Distribution of property after termination is fixed by the parties, or, in default, by a court.

Three paradoxes of the law can be underlined (Théry, 1999):

1. The Pacs was not, in spite of the discourses and the heated debates, legal recognition for homosexuals as legal couples. This was only obtained by the article on 'concubinage' which was finally added to the law. It was only *after the final vote* that Constitutional council (*Conseil constitutionnel*) gave an official interpretation of the law and decided that only two persons *cohabiting as a couple* can conclude a Pacs.
2. The second paradox of the Pacs is the unexpected rejection of the 'free union' ('*union libre*') and of cohabitation that it implies. During the parliamentary debate, it was repeatedly declared that those who have no commitment to one another should not expect the State to give them social or fiscal rights ('No rights for those who have no duties'). In a way, whereas the law was proclaimed as resolving the problems of people 'who don't want to marry or cannot marry', as far as social and fiscal law is concerned, the Pacs seems to be a return to Napoleonic attitude on cohabitation. There are now in France three types of couples: the married, the 'pacsed', and cohabitants, with a hierarchy of taxation in fiscal law. People who live together for twenty years can still remain 'strangers' for the purposes of income or inheritance tax.
3. The third paradox is that the right of same-sex couples to conclude a real *legal union* (by a registered partnership or marriage) was not discussed in the Assembly. The principle of 'republican equality', which was proclaimed as the specific French way to avoid '*communautarist*' legislation for same-sex couples, has led to a much more unequal law than in other countries. Homosexuals who want to conclude a legal union will not have in France the equal rights and dignity they have, through registered partnerships, in other European countries like Denmark or Sweden. Marriage, now possible for same-sex couples in the Netherlands, has not been considered a serious legal issue by French politicians, in spite of the efforts of some very active leaders of the homosexual movement.

In conclusion, the Pacs seems to be a *transitory legislation*. There were 6,200 Pacs concluded by the end of December 1999, over a period of one month and a half. It is interesting to notice that sociological *statistics* have been forbidden by the '*decrets d'application*' of the new law. Age, profession, even the sex of the partners must not be communicated by the '*tribunal d'instance*'. Many sociologists and demographers protested, and this will certainly change in the near future, but it is a sign of the anxiety and uncertainty of the socialist party about this legislation. In spite of the lack of sociological research, some journalistic enquiries give an idea of the first Pacs concluded.[8] The 'neither-nor' politics, that we have described throughout the legal project, seems to have created a 'neither-nor' social and legal statute. By signing a Pacs, one party can consider himself or herself as 'almost married' and the other as 'almost in a free union'. For some couples, specifically among homosexuals, to conclude a Pacs is often an occasion for a ceremony and a feast very like a marriage, despite the fact that the '*tribunal d'instance*' is very different from the Town Council in French republican symbolism, and in spite of the very few rights and obligations contained in the law. One can see, here, a hope and an expectation for some institution which is much more official, symbolically and legally much more important, than a simple Pacs. For other couples, on the other hand, Pacs is concluded very briefly, without any ceremony, as a bureaucratic obligation to obtain advantages in employment or income tax. One can see, here, an expectation for a real recognition of the free union, and equal social and fiscal rights for '*concubins*' living together for some years.

But most of the problems, from a legal point of view, are just beginning to appear. French jurists and lawyers are now examining the legal consequences of the Pacs. Most of them agree that the breaking of a Pacs will create many problems regarding division of property because of the 'co-owner regime' (Murat, 2000). Nobody knows what will happen to property if the partners decide to marry one another. Another problematic issue is that the Pacs conventions are private, which means that they are *not verified* by any authority, not even a lawyer. Many conventions will turn out to be illegal. For example, many people believe that a Pacs is a means for bequeathing money or property to the other, but it is not. They might then illegally include some dispositions for inheritance in their convention, causing serious problems for the future survivor. All these examples show the uncertainty of the Pacs law. There will certainly be some legal change in the next few years. The history of the French Pacs is only beginning.

4. CONCLUSION: FROM MARRIAGE AND COHABITATION TO SOCIOLOGICAL INTERPRETATIONS OF THE FAMILY CHANGES

The contrast between the importance of social change in behaviours and values and the uncertainty of the legal provisions we have analysed in relation to the contemporary French perception of 'couples' is an indicator of a larger question. There is not yet in France a consensus about the changes in family and private life in general. A look to the academic debate is important, insofar as public debate is increasingly affected by the arguments and ideas of the experts, whose advice is frequently sought by politicians, in particular through the production of official reports. This phenomenon is so important that many analysts consider France as a 'Republic of reports'.

Two topics have dominated most of the French academic debates about family change during the past twenty years more than marriage and cohabitation: divorce and fertility. Fertility is a typically French political problem, originating in the long history of wars since the nineteenth century and accentuated specially by the First World War. We must emphasize that most of French family policy has been natalist for many years. There has sometimes been a very strong debate among demographers, between those who consider the fertility rate as the major indicator of a 'civilization crisis' and those who contest the use of this indicator, compared to the achieved birth rate (Le Bras, 1991). This theme reveals a real 'struggle over the meaning of statistics'. But recently, this debate seemed to be radically reoriented, when it began to be recognized that fertility is highly connected with women's access to the labour market. The long-standing link between the demographical preoccupation and a very traditional view of the family (woman as an housekeeper, three or more children) has been disrupted. Certainly this field of research and debate will be largely reorganized in the future, with growing attention being paid to the birth of the first baby, the life cycle, and a gendered approach to the relationship between family and work.

Divorce has been another important topic of debate among researchers. In a way, all the French debate about marriage was expressed, until recently, through divorce. During the 1980s, the focus on custody as a problem of inequality between fathers and mothers and the fact that a large number of groups for divorced fathers were established, explain why the issue of the lack of the exercise of responsibility by fathers (especially in the poorest sections of the population) has been largely underestimated. This debate has been associated with a largely psychological approach of 'how to avoid conflicts' (Théry, 1993; Bastard *et al,* 1996). Very little social research looked at social inequality in divorce or separation. Even if there are in France recurrent attacks from traditionalists in the conservative parties against 'one parent families', lone motherhood is not a political and academic issue in France as it is in Great Britain and the USA (Martin, 1998).

From the mid-1960s to the beginning of the 1980s, public opinion usually saw the transformation of the family as a crisis and a threat. This consisted in a caricature which contrasted the '20 *Glorieuses*' (1945–65) or the Golden Age of the family with the ensuing '30 *piteuses*', thirty pitiful years for the family. Indeed, if we want to understand the current transformation by a comparison with the traditional family of an hypothetical golden age corresponding to the 1945–65 period, the diagnosis seems simple: it compares the stable nuclear family (founded on marriage and institutions, very fecund, with strong ties and obligations, etc) to a fragile family, with weak links and solidarities (Sullerot, 1997). That nostalgic position ignores that this strength of the traditional family was founded on a strict and unequal division of the gender roles and on the dependence of the female within the marriage contract. It ignores also that this period was exceptional in the long-term history of French family. So, many aspects of recent family changes appear to have been extraordinarily dramatized and even falsified by a myopic approach, concentrated on the second part of the twentieth century (Théry, 1998).[9]

In the long term, French debate has been mainly organized through the opposition between *family* and *individual*. This is probably a consequence of a very long history, beginning with the French Revolution. The creation of civil marriage in 1792 was the symbol of a secularized society and equality of citizens before the law. Civil marriage was at the same time the symbol of the link between republican political ideals and the private sphere. From 1789 to 1793, a short but historically very important period, all the problems regarding the family were reconstructed as a problem of individual liberty and equality. The family was seen as a private sphere and revolutionary laws were introduced (the divorce introduced in 1792 was more liberal than French divorce today).

But rapidly after the period of 'Terror', another interpretation of 'family' emerged. Family was considered as a condition for assuring social order and as the natural bedrock of society. The Napoleonic code of 1804 promoted one unique model of family as 'the' family for more than a century and a half. Marital and paternal power organized the family as a very hierarchical unit. Only the married family was considered to be a family. Liberal revolutionary divorce was limited, and finally suspended in 1816 for almost one century (when divorce was reintroduced in 1884 it was only a fault-divorce, until the reform of 1975).

This history explains the long lasting opposition between conservative parties, strongly influenced by Catholicism, and progressive or socialist parties, contesting this family model in reference to individual liberty, secularism, and equality. This opposition is so strong in French culture and public debate, that the word 'family' seemed, until very recently to belong to the right wing. Until the 1990s, it was most unusual for the left wing to refer to the family as a value at all (Commaille and Martin, 1998).

This dichotomy led to the identification of the 'family' with the traditional family. So it is not surprising that the recent change in family behaviour and values was interpreted among academic commentators as 'the passage from family to individual' and a movement towards 'privatization' of norms. Demography and family sociology has expanded a great deal since the 1970s, but most of the researches were devoted to specific aspects, telling very little about family change in general. The reason is that a sort of explanation was largely accepted: we faced 'new behaviours', 'new values', 'pluralization' of the family forms. Depending of each political choice, this was seen as a symptom of decline, decadence, individualism, egotism (among jurists and some demographers), or, on the other hand, a cultural emancipation, more freedom and social tolerance (among sociologists). But the main expression was 'from family to families' (see *Revue française des affaires sociales*, 1983).

The 1990s changed the issues and the hypothesis of a 'passage from family to individual' was contested. This aspect became more important after 1995, when social problems and specifically teenage delinquency were attributed to a lack in family education, generating a strong political debate. So, beyond the ideological position which understands the present tendencies of transformation of the family as a destruction, a threat, a peril, and which considers that the best solution to be to go backwards, 'back to basics', we can identify different more theoretical positions which show the difficulty in understanding the present and the future.

The meaning of these transformations of the family may be synthesized in four main positions, often interconnected (see Déchaux, 1995; Commaille and Martin, 1998 and Théry, 2000):

—first, we could group together the positions of researchers who consider that the main transformation of family life corresponds to a process of emancipation from tradition (Beck, 1992), a progressive recognition of the individual within the family, and mainly a process of emancipation of women. This interpretation considers that this is mainly positive and gives the family a new structure, more horizontal and more equal, more contractual (*famille élective*), more centred on the production of identities than around transmission of goods (de Singly, 1993 and 1995). By analogy, it could also correspond to a new public order, not the vertical conception of social order founded on a structure of delegation of power from the top (God) to the bottom (the father), but a democratic order founded on mutual recognition (Giddens, 1992).

—But, this first position is immediately counterbalanced by the reminder of the limits of the individualization process in terms of the threat of 'de-institutionalization' (Roussel, 1989). How can we preserve the common good, the collective foundations of a society, without symbolic signs and collective norms? How may we even form a society if the only links we recognize are defined on the basis of the interaction between individuals? Such a position may insist on the role of law, as a symbolic link which gives meaning and consistency to the social relations inside family: horizontal (couple) or vertical (filiation). These limits to the 'de-institutionalization' of the family are very close to those identified by Alexis de Tocqueville in the nineteenth century or Durkheim at the beginning of the twentieth century in terms of the risk of individualism.

—A third position in these debates considers that a second risk and brake to this positive progress of individualization is constituted by inequalities: inequalities between social groups and classes and inequalities between genders. The process of emancipation is not equally accessible and the main proof of this inequality is, for example, the unequal consequences of separation and divorce, depending on the social and economic conditions of the families (Martin, 1997 and 1999, Commaille 1999). On the other hand, traditional norms still represent a reference for many social groups. Individuals in these configurations do not recognize themselves in the new gender or intergenerational roles. In these cases, separations, divorces, births outside marriage, etc, are still considered as pathologies and sources of social problems. In this perspective, the process of individualization has to be completed by a regulation of the social inequalities and problems linked to these transformations of family.

—Another position rejects the sociological hypothesis of individualism (as well positive or negative) and introduces a gender and age approach of family change (Théry, 2000). This hypothesis argues that growing equality between men and women is the most important factor of change, and has been largely underestimated in France for years. The general thesis is that the 'matrimonial model' of the family, presuming a gender share of public and private in fact implodes in the 1970s. It is an anthropological revolution we are just beginning to be conscious of, and is largely incomplete. Fertility, nuptiality, and divorce must be reconsidered in this perspective. The other major factor is the change in ages and inter-generational relationships in a context of a rising life expectancy (Attias-Donfut and Segalen, 1998). The entire life cycle is reconstructed. In this perspective, family change is a structural mutation, generating new forms of social inequalities and requiring the elaboration of new institutions, and a complete change in family policy defining a 'new gender contract' and a new 'generational pact'.

These different positions represent a very simplified scheme in which it is possible to place the arguments about family change and family reforms. We can easily consider that the arguments, the ideas, the social references are swinging in the political debate between these different interpretations of changes, according to circumstances and mobilization.

NOTES

[1] The marriage rate was 7.6 compared to 8.2 in 1949.

[2] Cohabitants can no longer claim for the supplementary fiscal relief for the first child. In that sense, they are encouraged to marry, and even more so if they are high earners, have many children and there is a big difference between the salaries of the partners.

[3] More precisely, the average age at the first marriage was 28.5 years for men born in 1965 (compared to 24.5 years for men born in 1948) and 26.6 for women born in 1965 (compared to 22.6 for women born in 1950).

[4] Coming out has been quite important in the battle for the city council of Paris, where most homosexuals live.

[5] The institutionalization of the family associations as official partners for the authorities was

established in 1942 (during the *'régime de Vichy'*) and confirmed in 1945. From this period, the federation of these movements, the 'Union nationale des associations familiales' has been represented in all the boards of the 'Caisses d'allocations familiales' (the administration of the family 'branch' of our social security system), but also in many other institutions, like the 'Conseil économique et social' or the commission that controls the quality of television programmes.

[6] France has been condemned over this law in January 2000 by the European Court of Human Rights: *Mazurek v France*.

[7] Six months earlier, Théry had suggested another solution which she considers more complete and satisfying: 'concubinage' for all cohabiting couples *plus* registered partnership for same-sex couples as in the northern European countries (Théry, 1997). This was rejected by the homosexual movement as *'communautarism'*, so she did not maintain it in the official report.

[8] For example, Joël Métreau, in a paper of the homosexual journal 'Têtu' in October 2000 presenting the results of a national survey about public opinion on homosexuality suggests that 19,054 pacs were registered by the end of June 2000, but these data are not official. See also Martel (2000).

[9] One of the fields where this anxious and even dramatic approach has been mainly developed as a so called 'decline' or 'crisis' of family is the field of civil law (Malaurie, Cornu). This traditional characteristic of jurists has been more or less hidden during the 1980s because of the influence of the French civilist, Jean Carbonnier. But recently he began himself to be more and more critical about social change and especially legal change (Carbonnier, 1999)

REFERENCES

Attias-Donfut, C., Segalen, M. (1998) *Grands-parents. La famille à travers les générations*, Paris: Odile Jacob.

Bajos, N., Bozon, M., Ferrand, A., Giami, A., Spira, A. (1998) *La sexualité au temps du Sida*, Paris: PUF.

Bastard, B., Cardia-Vonèche, L., Eme, B., Neyrand, G. (1996) *Reconstruire les liens familiaux. Nouvelles pratiques sociales*, Paris: Syros.

Beaumel, C., Kerjosse, R., Toulemon, L., 'Des mariages, des couples et des enfants', *Insee Premières*, no 24, janvier.

Beck, U. (1992) *Risk Society. Towards a New Modernity*, London: Sage.

Borillo, D. (1998) 'Le mariage, un droit fondamental', *Ex-Aequo*, février, 40.

Carbonnier, J. (1979) *Essais sur les lois*, Paris: Répertoire du notariat Defresnois.

Carbonnier, J. (1999) *Droit civil, II. La famille*, Paris: Presses Universitaires de France, coll *Thémis*.

Commaille, J. (ed, 1999) *Famille et chômage*, Rapport pour le Haut conseil de la population et de la famille, Ministère de l'emploi et de la solidarité.

Commaille, J. and Martin, C. (1998) *Les enjeux politiques de la famille*, Paris: Bayard.

Commaille, J. and Martin, C. (1999) 'Les conditions d'une démocratisation de la vie privée' in D. Borrillo, E. Fassin and M. Iacub (eds) *Au-delà du PACS. L'expertise familiale à l'épreuve de l'homosexualité*, Paris: PUF.

Commaille, J. and Martin, C. (2000) 'Pacs: la repolitisation du privé' in R. Mouriaux (ed) *L'année sociale*, Paris: édition Syllepse.

Déchaux, J.-H. (1995) 'Orientations théoriques en sociologie de la famille: autour de cinq ouvrages récents', *Revue française de sociologie*, XXXVI, 525–50.

Dekeuwer-Défossez, F. (1999) *Rénover le droit de la famille. Propositions pour un droit adapté aux réalités et aux aspirations de notre temps*. Rapport au Garde des Sceaux, Paris: La Documentation Française.

Festy, P. (2000) 'Les débuts du Pacs', *Population et sociétés*, no 355, mars.

Gélard, P. (1999) 'Rapport sur le Pacte civil de solidarité au nom de la commission des Lois du Sénat', *Rapports du Sénat* no 258.

Giddens, A. (1992) *The Transformation of Intimacy. Sexuality, Love and Eroticism in Modern Societies*, Cambridge: Polity Press.

Gokalp, C. (1981) *Quand vient l'âge des choix. Enquête auprès des jeunes de 18 à 25 ans: emploi, résidence, mariage*, Paris: PUF, INED *Travaux et documents*, cahier no 95.

Hauser, J. and Huet Weiller, D. (1989) *Traité de droit civil*, Paris: LGDJ.

Jenson, J. (1997) 'Fated to live in interesting times: Canada's changing citizenship regimes', 30 *Canadian Journal of Political Science* 4, 627–44.

Kaufmann, J.-C. (1993) *Sociologie du couple*, Paris: PUF, Que sais-je?

Le Bras, H. (1991) *Marianne et les lapins. L'obsession démographique*, Paris: Olivier Orban.

Léridon, H. and Villeneuve-Gokalp, C. (1994) *Constance et inconstances de la famille. Biographies familiales des couples et des enfants*, Paris: INED, collection *Travaux et documents*, cahier no 134.

Martel, F. (2000) 'Le Pacs, un an après', *Le Monde des débats*, no 17, septembre.

Martin, C. (1997) *L'après-divorce. Lien familial et vulnérabilité*, Rennes: Presses universitaires de Rennes.

Martin, C. (1998), 'Politiques sociales et monoparentalité. Evolution de l'action publique en France et au Royaume-Uni', *Solidarité, santé, Etudes statistiques*, Paris: Ministère des affaires sociales, no 2–3, 125–38.

Martin, C. (1999) 'Les situations monoparentales: des familles vulnérables', *Après-demain*, no 12, mars.

Meulders-Klein, M. T. (1999) *La personne, la famille et le droit*, Brussels, Paris: Bruylant/LGDJ.

Murat, P. (2000) *Le pacs, analyse juridique*, in Actes du colloque 'Pacs; mode d'emploi', École Nationale de la Magistrature/Barreau de Grenoble (roneo).

Neyrand, G. (1994) 'La résidence alternée de l'enfant: un hiatus entre les parents et la justice', *Recherches et prévisions* 35 1–18.

Prioux, F. (2000): 'L'évolution démographique récente en France', *Population* 3 441–76.

Rabin, B. (1992) 'De plus en plus de naissances hors mariage', 251 *Economie et statistiques* 3–13.

Revue française des affaires sociales (1983) no spécial 'Recherches et familles', no 4.

Rubellin-Devichi, J. (1986) *Les concubinages*, Lyon: Ed du CNRS.

Roussel, L. (1978) 'La cohabitation juvénile en France', *Population* 1 15–42.

Roussel, L (1989): *La famille incertaine*, Paris: Odile Jacob.

Schiltz, M.-A. (1997) 'Parcours de jeunes homosexuels dans le contexte du VIH/ la conquête d'un mode de vie', *Population* 6 1485–538.

Singly, F., de (1993) *Sociologie de la famille contemporaine*, Paris: Nathan, collection 128.

Singly, F., de (1996) *Le soi, le couple et la famille*, Paris: Nathan, coll *Essais et recherches*.

Spira, A., Bajos, N. and groupe ACSF (1993) *Les comportementss sexuels en France*, Rapport au ministre de la Recherche et de l'Espace, Paris: La Documentation Française.

Sullerot, E. (1984), *Pour le meilleur et sans le pire*, Paris: Fayard.

Sullerot, E. (1997) *Le grand remue-ménage. La crise de la famille*, Paris: Fayard.

Théry, I. (1993) *Le démariage. Justice et vie privée*, Paris: Odile Jacob.

Théry, I. (1997) 'Le contrat d'union sociale en question', *Esprit*, octobre.

Théry, I. (ed, 1998) *Couple, filiation et parenté aujourd'hui*, Paris: Odile Jacob et La Documentation Française.

Théry, I. (1999) 'Pacs, sexualité et différence des sexes', *Esprit*, octobre.

Théry, I. (2000) 'La mixité, figure nouvelle de l'égalité', 8 *La revue de la Confédération française démocratique du travail* 9–18.

Toulemon, L. (1996) 'La cohabitation hors mariage s'installe dans la durée', *Population* 6 675–716.

Villeneuve-Gokalp, C. (1997) 'Vivre en couple chacun chez soi', *Population* 5 1059–82.

Villeneuve-Gokalp, C. (1999) 'La double famille des enfants de parents séparés', *Population* 1 9–36.

[23]

COUPLINGS: CIVIL PARTNERSHIP IN THE UNITED KINGDOM

*Carl F. Stychin**

INTRODUCTION

In her wide-ranging scholarship, which responds to an often uncritical advocacy of the legal recognition of same-sex relationships through the institution of marriage, Professor Ruthann Robson has become an articulate and impassioned voice for those skeptical of (both) law and marriage. Writing specifically about lesbian relationships in her landmark book *Sappho Goes to Law School*,[1] Robson convincingly articulates the disciplinary way in which marriage would operate in a lesbian context and, one might argue, in other contexts. She describes the "codification of lesbian relationships as mimetic of traditional heterosexual ones,"[2] as conveyed by the "normative aspiration" of life-long monogamy[3] and the imposition of the legal form of divorce as a means of discipline.[4] Robson has also written of the way in which marriage can divide and rule a community, by the "award of benefits to those who comply [with the norm] and a concomitant disadvantage to those who do not comply."[5] Moreover, she has written of the extension of marriage as a form of economic privatization, which "seeks to encourage family responsibility while allowing the government to escape from its obligations" of care.[6] Finally, the differential class implications of the benefits and detriments of marriage have been underscored by Robson, who describes being "troubled by the rift between class and sexuality."[7]

In this article, I attempt to apply all of these insights in order to demonstrate that they are of wide-ranging analytical usefulness.

---

* Professor of Law and Social Theory and Pro Vice Chancellor at the University of Reading, United Kingdom.

I thank the many people who have generously commented on this work in draft in its different versions. Special thanks to Anneke Smit for superb assistance. Finally, I want to express my gratitude to Ruthann Robson for her intellectual, political, and personal presence.

1 RUTHANN ROBSON, SAPPHO GOES TO LAW SCHOOL (1998).

2 *Id.* at 116.

3 *Id.* at 119.

4 *Id.* at 116.

5 *Id.* at 127.

6 *Id.* at 150-51.

7 *Id.* at 209.

They provide the inspiration for my consideration of the United Kingdom's Civil Partnership Act 2004, which became law on November 18, 2004 (with the first civil registrations taking place on December 21, 2005). It is fitting, in my view, to analyze the British "solution" to same-sex relationships in a symposium for Ruthann Robson and her scholarship. Throughout her work, she displays sensitivity to national variations in the way in which sexualities are regulated, and her scholarship is informed by her knowledge of many legal regimes. Furthermore, the British approach to partnership should be of interest to an American audience because it is explicitly designed as a "new" legal institution for same-sex couples. Formally, it is not marriage, and this raises the interesting issue of the applicability of Ruthann Robson's concerns about *marriage* to regimes of legal regulation of relationship more broadly.

In this article, my theoretical grounding can be located within "queer legal theory."[8] It may appear counterintuitive to argue that the Civil Partnership Act is a text conducive to an analysis grounded in queer theory. After all, it is now a virtual cliché that the term "queer" is associated with a politics of radical sexualities, transgression of heterosexual norms, and a challenging of sexual binaries and traditional notions of family and kinship. Queer theory, in support of these politics, has paid much attention to subjecting texts—literary, legal, political—to a deconstructive analysis, seeking to uncover the incoherence of the hetero/homo binary at the heart of the construction of those texts specifically, and of sexual identities more generally. Of course, other theoretical and political movements have engaged in similar strategies both before and after the advent of queer politics and theory. However, I would argue that queer theory provided a fresh articulation at a particular historical moment, the impact of which should not be minimized.

It is also important that queer theory emerged in response to the right wing, homophobic politics of the 1980s, when homosexuality was readily associated with discourses of disease, degeneration,

8 *See, e.g.*, LESLIE J. MORAN, THE HOMOSEXUAL(ITY) OF LAW (1996); Lisa J. Bower, *Queer Problems/Straight Solutions: The Limits of a Politics of "Official Recognition," in* PLAYING WITH FIRE: QUEER POLITICS, QUEER THEORIES 267 (Shane Phelan ed., 1997); Paisley Currah, *Politics, Practices, Publics: Identity and Queer Rights, in* PLAYING WITH FIRE: QUEER POLITICS, QUEER THEORIES, *supra*, at 231; Pierre de Vos, *The Constitution Made Us Queer: The Sexual Orientation Clause in the South African Constitution and the Emergence of Gay and Lesbian Identity, in* LAW AND SEXUALITY: THE GLOBAL ARENA 194 (Carl Stychin & Didi Herman eds., 2001); Wayne Morgan, *Queering International Human Rights Law, in* LAW AND SEXUALITY: THE GLOBAL ARENA, *supra*, at 208; CARL F. STYCHIN, LAW'S DESIRE: SEXUALITY AND THE LIMITS OF JUSTICE 140-56 (1995).

and death.[9] In that context, the importance of theorization of *what was happening out there* was a particularly pressing political task. In 21st century Britain, many would argue that there is still a right-wing hegemony, but it is one in which the politics of sexuality has experienced a decided shift from the 1980s. In this respect, the British political experience of recent years is very different from the neoconservative revival in the United States. We see in the U.K. today a central government that understands lesbian and gay politics through the language of equality, rights, dignity, multiculturalism, and citizenship, rather than one that pathologizes the individual.[10] In addition, the language of active citizenship has become important as a discourse connected to the goal of the equal provision of government services to all communities within the population, including the lesbian and gay *community*.[11]

As well as the rhetoric, it would be churlish not to recognize the changed legal and political reality for lesbians and gay men in the U.K. It can be argued that satisfying a gay political agenda is attractive for the Labour government because it can be grounded primarily in a (low economic cost) politics of recognition, rather than the politics of redistribution. Nonetheless, this signifies a new political climate. The website of the government's Women and Equality Unit is self-congratulatory on the range of advances for which the government claims responsibility: the Adoption and Children Act 2002, as a result of which same-sex couples can apply to adopt a child jointly; paternity leave and flexible working practices available to same-sex partners; a right to register a death extended to same-sex partners; anti-discrimination legislation that tackles discrimination in employment and training on the grounds of sexual orientation and religion (a legal requirement for member states of the European Union); sexual offenses legislation that removes discrimination as between men and women, and as between those of different sexual orientations; the repeal of section 28 of the Local Government Act, which prohibited the "promotion

---

9 *See generally* CINDY PATTON, SEX AND GERMS: THE POLITICS OF AIDS (1985); CINDY PATTON, INVENTING AIDS (1990); THOMAS E. YINGLING, AIDS AND THE NATIONAL BODY (1997); SIMON WATNEY, IMAGINE HOPE: AIDS AND GAY IDENTITY (2000).

10 *See* Jean Carabine & Surya Monro, *Lesbian and Gay Politics and Participation in New Labour's Britain*, 11 SOC. POL. 312 (2004); CARL F. STYCHIN, GOVERNING SEXUALITY: THE CHANGING POLITICS OF CITIZENSHIP AND LAW REFORM 25 (2003) [hereinafter GOVERNING SEXUALITY]; DAVID BELL & JON BINNIE, THE SEXUAL CITIZEN: QUEER POLITICS AND BEYOND 38-43 (2000); Derek McGhee, *Joined-up Government, "Community Safety" and Lesbian, Gay, Bisexual and Transgender "Active Citizens,"* 23 CRITICAL SOC. POL'Y 345 (2003).

11 Carabine & Monro, *supra* note 10, at 317; BELL & BINNIE, *supra* note 10.

of homosexuality" by local government authorities;[12] the lowering of the age of consent to sixteen for gay men; the inclusion of same-sex partners in the Criminal Injuries Compensation Scheme; and the amendment of the immigration rules to improve the situation for same-sex partners.[13] Although many of these changes are less than ideal (and while many may continue to feel alienated from the omnipresence of a discourse of marriage and family emanating from the government), the reforms are significant.

As a consequence, does there remain a role for the deconstructive method of queer theory in this new, liberal-minded political environment? Recall that one of the productive tasks of queer theory of the 1980s and 1990s was to deconstruct the discourses that surrounded right wing policy initiatives, thereby underscoring the incoherence of the categorizations and constructions of sexuality that underpinned them.[14] In the context of liberal law reform—supported by many within the lesbian and gay communities—what place is there for the critical power of queer theory? In this article, I will attempt to demonstrate that there is still a useful role for this methodological toolbox. However, the focus of the deconstructive glare shifts, in my approach, away from the construction of sexual *identities* and practices per se, towards the ongoing and intense social construction of *relationships* within law and politics. In one sense, my approach might be seen to support the claim of Jeffrey Weeks that lesbian and gay politics has moved in its emphasis from identity to relationships.[15] However, where I may differ from Weeks is that I argue that a critical analysis of the way in which particular relationship forms are constructed, disciplined, and normalized, remains much needed.

The Civil Partnership Act, and the Parliamentary debates that occurred in 2004, provide rich material with which to engage in this analysis. By way of brief background, the government introduced the Civil Partnership Bill into the House of Lords on March 30, 2004. It emerged from the Women and Equality Unit of the Department of Trade and Industry. The proposed legislation, it

---

12 *See* GOVERNING SEXUALITY, *supra* note 10, at 25.

13 DEP'T OF TRADE & INDUSTRY, WOMEN & EQUALITY UNIT, *Sexual Orientation*, http://www.womenandequalityunit.gov.uk/lgbt/orientation.htm (Nov. 2004); DEP'T OF TRADE & INDUS., WOMEN & EQUAL. UNIT, *Sexual Orientation: What Has the Government Done So Far?*, http://www.womenandequalityunit.gov.uk/lgbt/what_done.htm (Mar. 2004).

14 *See, e.g.*, ANNA MARIE SMITH, NEW RIGHT DISCOURSE ON RACE AND SEXUALITY: BRITAIN, 1968-1990 (1994).

15 JEFFREY WEEKS, MAKING SEXUAL HISTORY 213 (2000).

was claimed, would create a new legal status that would allow adult same-sex couples to gain formal recognition of their relationship and grant same-sex couples who enter a civil partnership access to a wide range of rights and responsibilities.[16]

These rights and responsibilities were to include the duty to provide reasonable maintenance for a civil partner; the duty to provide reasonable maintenance for children of the family; assessment in the same way as spouses for child support purposes; equitable treatment for the purposes of life insurance; employment and pension benefits; recognition under intestacy rules; access to fatal accidents compensation; protection from domestic violence; and recognition for immigration and nationality purposes.[17] Couples would enter (opt into) a civil partnership through a statutory, civil registration procedure. A dissolution process—a formal process in the courts—would be created which mirrors divorce proceedings (rather than the simple ending of a contract unilaterally or bilaterally). There would be no requirement of cohabitation, nor any analogue drawn to the requirement of consummation. Nor would adultery be an explicit ground for dissolution. The marriage bans, however, were included.

The Bill was introduced in the House of Lords, receiving its third reading on July 1, 2004. In that process, however, it was amended by the Lords to extend its coverage to family members and carers who might wish to register and opt into the bundle of rights and responsibilities. The Bill then moved to the House of Commons, and that amendment (as well as other similar attempts to amend the legislation in order to expand its scope) was defeated. The Bill received its third reading in the House of Commons on November 9, 2004, receiving widespread parliamentary support (including from many members of the opposition Conservative party). The Commons amendments were approved by the House of Lords on November 17, 2004, and the Bill received Royal Assent the following day, making it law: the Civil Partnership Act 2004.

To repeat, my method in engaging with the Act, and the debates, is to return to queer theory's original focus on the deconstruction of binary categories. Whereas those binaries originally were centered on the foundational hetero/homo, act/identity cou-

16 Dep't of Trade & Indus., Women & Equal. Unit, *Sexual Orientation: Civil Partnership*, http://www.womenandequalityunit.gov.uk/lgbt/partnership.htm (June 2005).

17 *Id.*

plings, in the current political climate of relationship recognition, my choice of binaries shifts. I interrogate the Act and the debates through six closely related dichotomies that usefully underscore a fundamental incoherence in the government's approach to civil partnership. I characterize these binaries as: marriage/not marriage; sex/no sex; status/contract; conjugality/care; love/money; responsibilities/rights. In each case, it is possible to argue that the Civil Partnership Act is located on both sides of the binary, underscoring the social construction (and ideological character) of the idea (and ideal) of "partnership" itself. My ultimate claim is that it is only by unpacking and emptying out the concept that we might then begin to devise a more radical political response to civil partnership specifically, and relationship discourse more broadly.

Marriage/Not Marriage

> It would be odd indeed if those who espouse and defend traditional values of commitment and faithfulness opposed giving gay couples the choice to live their lives according to those values.[18]

The marriage/not marriage binary is an obvious starting point. Arguably, the ingeniousness of the Civil Partnership Act is the fact that it can produce a legal status of "civil partner" that does not depend upon marriage, but which displays virtually all of the characteristics of a civil marriage. This is undoubtedly a strategy on the part of the government to avoid what it perceives as the likelihood of a backlash to same-sex marriage in the U.K. At the same time, it can fulfill its promise of equality by granting legal status to committed same-sex couples. Throughout its term of office, the government has strongly supported the institution of marriage for opposite-sex couples—as helping to foster stable relationships and as the best means to raise children[19]—and civil partnership provides an alternative, politically saleable route for same-sex couples. The social benefits that marriage offers can be furthered through civil partnership, while avoiding the criticism that same-sex unions undermine the institution of marriage. As Labour Baroness Scotland made clear during the debate:

> This Bill does not undermine or weaken the importance of marriage and we do not propose to open civil partnership to opposite-sex couples. Civil partnership is aimed at same-sex couples

18 425 Parl. Deb., H.C. (6th ser.) (2004) 186 (Alan Duncan, an openly gay Conservative MP, supporting the legislation).

19 *See* Home Office, Supporting Families: A Consultation Document (1998).

> who cannot marry . . . [W]e continue to support marriage and recognise that it is the surest foundation for opposite-sex couples raising children.[20]

The stable couple form, it is argued, is good for the individual, for the couple, and for society (and the economy) as a whole. Long term, stable, legally recognized relationships thus become the socially preferred option. Marriage is the ideal, but civil partnership—for those unable to marry—becomes an alternative which can further the same social policy goals. As Government Minister Jacqui Smith explained in the House of Commons:

> [W]e seek to create a parallel but different legal relationship that mirrors as fully as possible the rights and responsibilities enjoyed by those who can marry, and that uses civil marriage as a template for the processes, rights and responsibilities that go with civil partnership. We are doing this for reasons of equality and social justice.[21]

Opponents of civil partnership, not surprisingly, draw on this point in arguing that the Act creates "a parody of marriage for homosexual couples,"[22] and there is certainly evidence for this claim, and not only in the fact that civil partnership will extend most of the privileges granted to the married couple. Although civil partnerships cannot be formalized in religious buildings, partners are encouraged by the government to arrange ceremonies of celebration that, it is pointed out, will benefit the hospitality industry in Britain.[23] Whether such ceremonies should be interpreted as parodies of wedding receptions remains to be seen. Alternatively, the encouragement to celebrate might be interpreted as a demand that same-sex partners become "true believers," demonstrating their "indoctrination" to this new(ish) institution.[24] But the prohibition on any religious element to civil partnership is an attempt to ensure the absence of any religious connotations similar to the marriage ceremony.

However, the Church of England representatives in the House of Lords were critical of the Act for its failure to more fully mimic the institution of marriage. First, they argued in favor of the auton-

20 660 PARL. DEB., H.L. (5th ser.) (2004) 388.

21 426 PARL. DEB., H.C. (6th ser.) (2004) 776.

22 660 PARL. DEB., H.L. (5th ser.) (2004) 405 (Baroness O'Cathain).

23 DEP'T OF TRADE & INDUS., WOMEN & EQUAL. UNIT, FINAL REGULATORY IMPACT ASSESSMENT (RIA): CIVIL PARTNERSHIP 22, *available at* http://www.dti.gov.uk/access/ria/pdf/final_ria_for_cp_bill.pdf [hereinafter FINAL REGULATORY IMPACT ASSESSMENT].

24 ROBSON, *supra* note 1, at 166.

omy of the churches in determining what is celebrated in a place of worship.[25] Second, the argument was made, in support of civil partnerships, that set words should be drafted (vows) to provide substance to the commitment of the partners. As it stands, the argument runs, partnership is a rather empty vessel that needs to be filled with appropriate state-sanctioned words of commitment. Thus, for example, the Lord Bishop of Oxford argued that the Act "could strengthen rather than undermine the Christian understanding of marriage,"[26] but urged that the commitment be made explicit as "a commitment of two people to one another to the exclusion of all others, through all the ups and downs of human existence, for life."[27] Of course, this might well be read as a not very subtle urging in favor of the practice of monogamy, in the absence of any mention of adultery as grounds for dissolution. Paradoxically, then, the government is criticized by the Church of England for *insufficiently* replicating the institution of marriage (although the absence of the verbal vow is one of the few means by which supporters of the legislation can claim that partnership is distinguishable from civil marriage).

Thus, we find a culturally unique "solution" to the issue of same-sex relationships. An alternative recognition route is created that parallels, but does not intersect with, the institution of marriage, with a bundle of rights and responsibilities that cannot be split up and which must be consciously accepted. This bundle is withheld from unmarried heterosexual couples and unregistered same-sex couples, both of which lack evidence of stability and commitment justifying the privileges of the status. The social good of committed long-term relationships justifies the benefits (but alongside the responsibilities) that accrue to married/registered couples.[28]

From a comparative perspective, this is distinctive. Unlike the United States, the desire for marriage does not overwhelm the political arena. In this regard, Barry Adam has described an "American exceptionalism" in which politics displays a "high-stakes, all-or-nothing symbolic contention over marriage," which has become the "central symbolic axis around which the inclusion and partici-

25 660 PARL. DEB., H.L. (5th ser.) (2004) 399 (Lord Bishop of Oxford).

26 *Id.*

27 *Id.* at 400.

28 The lack of judicial or legislative recognition of "common law couples" differentiates the U.K. from a number of other jurisdictions, and is a key explanation for the way in which the legislation has developed.

pation of lesbians and gay men turns."[29] Similarly, Paula Ettelbrick has critically described "stepping stone strategies toward the real prize of marriage" for activists.[30] In the U.K., however, the major pressure group Stonewall strongly supports the Civil Partnership Act:

> [It] will come without undermining, in any way, the institution of marriage. Civil partnership is a separate legal structure, designed for same-sex couples. There is no overlap in any way with marriage. Indeed, civil partnership arguably strengthens marriage, by recognising and valuing the importance of committed relationships to society generally.[31]

By contrast, the understandable aversion to any "parallel but different" status that could be described as "separate but equal"[32] likely would make the Civil Partnership Act instinctively unpalatable to many lesbian and gay Americans.

At the other end of the spectrum, the Act is very different in its ideological underpinnings from the French "solution" of the PACS (Du Pacte Civil de Solidarité et du Concubinage).[33] The PACS allows two people—whether living in a conjugal relationship or not—to register a contract in a municipality, which reduces to writing their commitment to each other, and which must include the obligation to provide mutual assistance and support. The parties are able to contract over most of the terms of their relationship and the PACS can be ended unilaterally, on notice.[34] The PACS can be located firmly within the French ideology of republicanism and universality. It is justified as a universally available contract to which all are equally entitled to participate on the basis of being members of the Republic.[35] By contrast, the Civil Partnership Act is explicitly and specifically designed for one group with no expec-

---

29 Barry D. Adam, *The Defense of Marriage Act and American Exceptionalism: The "Gay Marriage" Panic in the United States*, 12 J. HIST. SEXUALITY 259, 273-75 (2003).

30 Paula L. Ettelbrick, *Domestic Partnership, Civil Unions, or Marriage: One Size Does Not Fit All*, 64 ALB. L. REV. 905, 912 (2001).

31 *Civil Partnership Bill: Parliamentary Briefing Before the House of Lords* 2 (April 22, 2004) (briefing by Stonewall), *available at* http://www.stonewall.org.uk/docs/Lords_Second_Reading_Apr_2004.doc [hereinafter *Stonewall April*].

32 Plessy v. Ferguson, 163 U.S. 537 (1896).

33 *See, e.g.*, Anne Barlow & Rebecca Probert, *Reforming the Rights of Cohabitants: Lessons from Across the Channel*, 29 FAM. L. 477 (1999); Murray Pratt, *Post-Queer and Beyond the PACS: Contextualizing French Responses to the Civil Solidarity Pact*, *in* IN A QUEER PLACE: SEXUALITY AND BELONGING IN BRITISH AND EUROPEAN CONTEXTS 177-206 (Kate Chedgzoy *et al.* eds., 2002); Eva Steiner, *The Spirit of the New French Registered Partnership Law: Promoting Autonomy and Pluralism or Weakening Marriage?*, 12 CHILD & FAM. L.Q. 1 (2000); GOVERNING SEXUALITY, *supra* note 10, at 49.

34 *See* GOVERNING SEXUALITY, *supra* note 10, at 50-53.

35 *Id.* at 56.

tation that the needs of other constituencies can be satisfied by this legislation.

Moreover, unlike the PACS, which was intended to recognize a social reality with its emphasis upon easy exit from the relationship by either party, the Civil Partnership Act extends the perceived social policy benefits of marriage to a group, and attempts to discipline that group into a marriage-like institution with divorce-like dissolution procedures. Paralleling the abandonment by the government of no-fault divorce reform, the ending of a partnership through formal procedures signifies the importance of commitment, and empowers the courts with the same ability as in divorce to vary pre-existing contractual arrangements between the parties as they see fit.[36] As the Conservative Baroness Wilcox notes, civil partnerships "contain rights and responsibilities. They are serious and constitute a legally binding agreement. Getting out of such an agreement will be expensive and painful. We encourage the government to urge caution when promoting the Bill. Las Vegas is not where we are and not where we want to be."[37]

A paradox is apparent. While long-term commitment is advocated for its benefits to individuals and to society, the seriousness of this commitment is such that it should not be entered into lightly, because of the potential consequences upon exit. Like marriage, the bundle of rights and responsibilities includes a responsibility to stay the course, and longevity is assumed to be good in itself.

Thus, civil partnerships sit uneasily on the marriage/not-marriage binary, and this appears to be justified only by the government's fear of backlash from "middle England" against same-sex marriage. Yet Rosemary Auchmuty has argued that:

> [M]ost British people could not care less whether gays and lesbians have the right to marry or not. They would certainly not object to any such extension. For them, marriage has been stripped of so much of its religious, legal or social status as to be immaterial—a mere lifestyle choice.[38]

If that is the case—and this again may differentiate the U.K. from the U.S.A.—then what justification can there be for this awkward category that both is and is not marriage?

An answer can be found within the literature emanating from

---

36 Rosemary Auchmuty, *Same-Sex Marriage Revived: Feminist Critique and Legal Strategy*, 14 FEMINISM & PSYCHOL. 101, 115 (2004) [hereinafter *Same-Sex Marriage Revived*].

37 660 PARL. DEB., H.L. (5th ser.) (2004) 395.

38 *Same-Sex Marriage Revived*, *supra* note 36, at 115-16.

the law and economics movement, particularly in the work of Robert Rowthorn.[39] For him, the law has a legitimate interest in keeping couples together and marriage is the best predictor of the long-term duration of a relationship. Moreover, Rowthorn echoes the government position that marriage is a "marker" for numerous outcomes including mental, physical and sexual health, as well as healthy children, in large part because of the role that marriage plays in domesticating men.[40] From a social policy perspective, it might be asked why same-sex couples should not be encouraged to enter into such a socially beneficial institution. Rowthorn provides an answer in advocating precisely the parallel lines of marriage and civil partnership that comprise the government's approach. The justification is the "signaling function of marriage," which might be undermined if same-sex couples were allowed entry:

> Western society places a high premium on marriage as a life-long, sexually exclusive union and the opponents of same-sex marriage believe that homosexual couples would not subscribe to, or abide by, these rules. They would reject the ideal of life-long monogamy. They would divorce and remarry even more frequently than heterosexuals do at present and they would be highly promiscuous while married. Such attitudes and behavior, it is claimed, would bring the institution of marriage as a whole into disrepute and undermine its value for heterosexual couples and society in general.[41]

Recognizing that promiscuous gays might be less attracted to marriage than monogamous ones (a debatable proposition), Rowthorn identifies the difficulty of ensuring that "marriage was reserved for homosexuals who were suitably committed."[42] Rowthorn advocates "having distinct legal institutions for the two types of couples," because it is impossible to create such a screening device (although divorce proceedings may partially provide a mechanism).[43] The marriage/not-marriage dichotomy thus becomes explained, as lesbians and gays are channeled into an institution which will domesticate, but which does not have expectations they may be unable to meet.

---

39 Robert Rowthorn, *Marriage as a Signal, in* THE LAW AND ECONOMICS OF MARRIAGE AND DIVORCE 132 (Antony W. Dnes & Robert Rowthorn, eds., 2002).

40 *Id.* at 146-47.

41 *Id.* at 150.

42 *Id.* at 152.

43 *Id.* at 153.

SEX/NO SEX

This leads to the second binary that frames the Civil Partnership Act, namely, the sex/no sex dichotomy. In this respect, again, we find a culturally unique articulation of the basis of civil partnership. Throughout the explanatory material surrounding the Act, and in the debates themselves, there is an assumption—sometimes explicitly made—that civil partnerships are sexual relationships, and that they will be entered into by people who define themselves as lesbian or gay (and lesbians do not form civil partnerships with gay men).[44] This is an important point because it is necessary to essentialize the category of "partnership" in order to contain it, and prevent its extension to other categories that emerge in the debates, such as "carers," "siblings," "spinsters," "bachelors," and "friends." The government makes clear that the Act "is not a cure-all for the financial problems of those outside marriage,"[45] but that in privileging this category of relationship (in a way analogous to married couples), the sexual dimension is a fundamental means by which to justify why the stronger analogy is to a married couple rather than to other competing categories. As one Minister explained in the House of Commons, "there is a particular significance to a partnership between two people who have chosen to share their home and their life, to love each other and to care for each other."[46] It is only through the strength of that analogy that frequent claims to unfairness in treatment of—and *discrimination* against—other types of partnership, can be answered.

An interesting parallel can be drawn to other jurisdictions on this point. Susan Boyd and Claire Young describe a backlash to same-sex spousal rights in Canadian jurisdictions, in which the discourse focuses on the extension of domestic partnership benefits to any two people in a situation of "economic interdependence."[47] In this way, the significance of gay spousal rights is diminished by its extension that "may well de-sex the way we allocate rights and responsibilities,"[48] and perhaps problematically, may erase the specificity of lesbian and gay partnerships (of a certain form). The U.K. government, however, as we have seen, seeks to resist such an extension, claiming that the Civil Partnership Act is an inappropri-

44 Moreover, bisexuality as an identity is never mentioned in the debates.

45 660 PARL. DEB., H.L. (5th ser.) (2004) 389 (Baroness Scotland).

46 425 PARL. DEB., H.C. (6th ser.) (2004) 175 (Jacqui Smith).

47 Susan B. Boyd & Claire F.L. Young, *"From Same-Sex to No Sex?": Trends Towards Recognition of (Same-Sex) Relationships in Canada*, 1 SEATTLE J. SOC. JUST. 757, 768-70 (2003).

48 *Id.* at 784.

ate vehicle to deal with economic dependence more generally, and therefore must "sex" (rather than "de-sex") the partnership to contain the category. Surprisingly, then, we find that implicitly lesbian and gay sex (provided it is contained and disciplined within this relationship form) is one of the prime justifications for the privileging of the relationship. Sex has its privileges.

This also radically distinguishes the Civil Partnership Act from the PACS. In France, the formulation of the PACS was explicitly designed to avoid the question of sex in relationships.[49] Sex is a private matter that should not be relevant to the social recognition of a relational contract. In the French context, the privileging of relationships on the basis of a sexual partnership (other than marriage, of course) is seen as inappropriate, focusing as it does on the particularity of a relationship, rather than on the universal availability of the PACS as an aspect of republican citizenship.[50] As a consequence, the difference between the French and U.K. approaches lies in part in the distinction between a model of universal republican citizenship and a multicultural ideology increasingly focused on remedying the problems of specific, targeted communities.[51]

Curiously, although there is an assumption that civil partnerships are sexual relationships, the question of what constitutes lesbian and gay sex remains shrouded in mystery. Moreover, the norms of sex within lesbian and gay relationships remain equally mysterious within the material surrounding the Civil Partnership Act. Returning to the marriage/not-marriage dichotomy, there are interesting passages within the government commentary wherein the state recognizes explicitly that somehow (in an unexplained way) gay relationships are different from marriage, and this on the basis of sex. First, and perhaps most obviously, there is no provision for voidability on the grounds of non-consummation:

> Consummation has a specific meaning within the context of heterosexual relationships and it would not be possible nor desirable to read this across to same-sex civil partnerships. The absence of any sexual activity within a relationship might be evidence of unreasonable behaviour leading to the irretrievable

---

49 GOVERNING SEXUALITY, *supra* note 10, at 57.

50 *Id.*

51 *See generally* ADRIAN FAVELL, PHILOSOPHIES OF INTEGRATION: IMMIGRATION AND THE IDEA OF CITIZENSHIP IN FRANCE AND BRITAIN (2d ed. 2001); Jeremy Jennings, *Citizenship, Republicanism and Multiculturalism in Contemporary France*, 30 BRIT. J. OF POL. SCI. 575 (2000); Cécile Laborde, *The Culture(s) of the Republic: Nationalism and Multiculturalism in French Republican Thought*, 29 POL. THEORY 716 (2001).

> breakdown of a civil partnership, if brought about by the conduct of one of the parties. However, that would be a matter for individual dissolution proceedings.[52]

In this moment, there is recognition that same-sex relationships might involve "no sex," and the question of what constitutes "sexual activity," or its absence, remains unexplained.

Relatedly, the government has considered the issue, not of "no sex," but of too much sex, but too much sex outside of the partnership, namely, adultery. There is no provision in the Civil Partnership Act for automatic dissolution on the basis of adultery. As the government explains in its background material:

> Adultery has a specific meaning within the context of heterosexual relations and it would not be possible nor desirable to read this across to same-sex civil partnerships. The conduct of a civil partner who is sexually unfaithful is as much a form of behaviour as any other. Whether it amounted to unreasonable behaviour on which dissolution proceedings could be grounded would be a matter for individual dissolution proceedings.[53]

The adultery non-provision is reminiscent of the law and economics concern that lesbians and gay men might not "sign up" to monogamy were they to be given access to same-sex marriage, and therefore would not submit to its disciplinary, domesticating function. But the consummation non-provision suggests that it is only through heterosexual penetration that there can be a clear test of what constitutes sexual behavior, making the determination of same-sex adultery problematic. Consequently, in the context of lesbian and gay civil partnerships, we are very much in a "grey area" in determining when the parties are in a sexual relationship (with each other), and when they have committed adultery, and what the significance of adultery is for the partnership.

While the adultery problem concerns the potential "untameability" of gays, the non-consummation problem concerns the indefinability of gays as a category, and this is a point that connects very closely to the concerns of queer theory, which is aimed at fostering category crises as a way to de-naturalize the hetero/homo binary. The platonic gay *relationship*—like the celibate gay as an

[52] DEP'T OF TRADE AND INDUS., WOMEN AND EQUAL. UNIT, RESPONSES TO CIVIL PARTNERSHIP: A FRAMEWORK FOR THE LEGAL RECOGNITION OF SAME-SEX COUPLES 36 (2003), *available at* http://www.dti.gov.uk/access/ria/pdf/final_ria_for_cp_bill.pdf [hereinafter RESPONSES TO CIVIL PARTNERSHIP].

[53] *Id.* at 35.

identity[54]—troubles the civil partnership scheme. As one member of Parliament pondered, the legislation "refers simply to 'same-sex couples,' so I am left wondering whether platonic same-sex couples are excluded."[55] In this regard, there are some very queer moments in the House of Lords debate, particularly in the speech of Lord Higgins, who incisively underscored the issues involved:

> The trouble is that the Bill implies, to some extent, that these civil partners will have a sexual relationship. However, other speeches have suggested the opposite; namely, that the Bill does not do so. . . . [I]t is not at all clear why a same-sex couple in a sexual relationship entering into a civil partnership should enjoy the tax and other benefits which a same-sex couple entering into a civil partnership which does not have a sexual relationship would not have. This brings me immediately to the point . . . of people who are living together, but not necessarily in a sexual relationship. Should they be entitled to enter into a civil partnership and enjoy the benefits which result from that?[56]

This conundrum is neatly summed up by Lord Higgins' phrase, the "spinster problem": "why should it be the case that two spinsters who have lived together for many years should not enter into a civil partnership and, as a result, enjoy the various benefits that would accrue to a same-sex couple with a sexual relationship?"[57]

What Lord Higgins touched upon is the social construction of sexual identities, and the use of the term spinster is particularly apt in this regard. A brief turn to lesbian *her*story discloses the attempt to reclaim the identity of the spinster, reconstructing it as lesbian.[58] In other words, when is the elderly spinster couple also a couple of lesbians? The presumption of heterosexuality starts to become displaced, as the question of what amounts to an "authentic" couple (or a fraudulent one) surfaces. It seems unfair, so opponents argue, that the spinster couple cannot be civil partners–except, of course, that they can be, provided that they register and accept both the benefits and burdens of partnership. However, if they are spinster *sisters*, then they cannot register under this Act. The issue of when a couple is a "real" couple troubles the whole question of

54 *See* Carl F. Stychin, *To Take Him "At His Word": Theorizing Law, Sexuality and the U.S. Military Exclusion Policy*, 5 Soc. & Legal Stud. 179 (1996).

55 425 Parl. Deb., H.C. (6th ser.) (2004) 241 (Angela Watkinson).

56 660 Parl. Deb., H.L. (5th ser.) (2004) 428-29.

57 *Id.* at 429.

58 *See generally* Martha Vicinus, Independent Women: Work and Community for Single Women, 1850-1920 (1985); Sheila Jeffreys, The Spinster and Her Enemies: Feminism and Sexuality 1880-1930 (1985); Rosemary Auchmuty, A World of Women: Growing Up in the Girls' School Story 92-98 (1999).

coupling in that it de-essentializes the notion of a "stable relationship." Unwittingly, perhaps, the Lord Bishop of Chelmsford hit upon this very point when he stated, "perhaps I may say to some noble Lords opposite that this is not just about gay and lesbian couples; it is about same-sex partnership."[59]

The sex/no sex binary is further complicated by the fact that cohabitation is not a prerequisite for partnership. Therefore, there is nothing to stop the registration of a civil partnership of two people who neither have sex nor live together, but who wish to take advantage of the benefits, and agree to the responsibilities of the Civil Partnership Act. Consequently, civil partnership is available to two same-sex people who neither live together nor have sex, yet it is not available to two opposite-sex people who live together and have lots of sex with each other (for whom marriage remains the only option). Moreover, the state retains the ability, for the purposes of the determination of eligibility for public benefits, to deem an opposite-sex couple as married and, under the Civil Partnership Act, to treat an unregistered same-sex couple as civil partners. This underscores the extent to which civil partnerships can impact differentially depending upon social class, a point to which I return. With no functional test, the determination of what amounts to partnership raises difficult questions, and undermines the claim that this is a voluntary "opt in" process. The relationship of sex to partnership must be a fundamental question in any such determination. However, that, in turn, raises the issue of the relationship of physical intimacy to emotional interdependence, and the definition of gay sex. What about the roommate with whom you occasionally have sex (and hold a joint bank account), when you also have a valid civil partnership with someone else with whom you may (or may not) have sex, and with whom you do not live, and from whom you might have complete financial independence?

The role of conjugal activity in the determination of authentic (or fraudulent) relationships is fraught with difficulties, in part because of what Sasha Roseneil refers to as "the postmodernization of the regime of sexuality,"[60] in which the links between sex, cohabitation, and emotional and financial dependence and friendship may all be loosened, and capable of being continually reworked in an

59 662 PARL. DEB., H.L. (5th ser.) (2004) 1440.

60 *See* Sasha Roseneil, *The Heterosexual/Homosexual Binary: Past, Present and Future, in* HANDBOOK OF LESBIAN AND GAY STUDIES 27, 32 (Diane Richardson & Steven Seidman, eds., 2002).

infinite variety of ways. In this context, the creation of a new legal status that is so closely aligned to marriage seems problematic and unrealistic, particularly in the way in which it depends upon an ambiguous (but definite) connection to sex. This in turn provides evidence for Davina Cooper's analysis of "the desiring state,"[61] and what she describes as the "uncomfortable" relationship of the liberal state to desire. The sex/no sex binary, I would argue, demonstrates this unease, as well as the ongoing need to essentialize the category of same-sex partnership in order that it can be regulated intensely through law. As Ruthann Robson argues, it strengthens the primacy of the "dyadic couple" and, as a consequence, "'lesser' relationships, such as 'mere' roommates or 'mere' friends, are not really relationships, and are not deserving of legal respect."[62]

STATUS/CONTRACT

The sex/no sex binary is intimately bound up with another dichotomy: status and contract. In order to bolster arguments in favor of the extension of civil partnerships to carers, friends, spinsters, and spinster sisters, opponents of the Act, as it was introduced by the government, argued that the basis of the legislation should be explicitly contractual. Partnership, they argued, should focus on recognizing and supporting agreements between people to live intertwined, interdependent lives, and the state should provide its support to all such agreements. On this point, an amendment was made in the House of Lords to replace the term "relationship" with "contract," as part of the wider strategy of amendment to include carers, siblings, and other dependent relationships. This move is closely related to the sex/no sex binary, in that it removes any assumption about sexual relationships, changing the focus to agreements to share lives. In this way, opponents hoped that the limitation within the Act to same-sex assumed sexual relationships would be rendered more difficult to sustain. The contractual point mirrors the PACS, which is justified as the legal recognition of a contract. Thus, if civil partnership is not marriage, then what can it be except a domestic contract? And if a contract, then surely anyone can contract, including spinster sisters (or, for that matter, more than two people).

Conservative Baroness Wilcox makes this precise point, when

61 Davina Cooper, *Imagining the Place of the State: Where Governance and Social Power Meet*, *in* HANDBOOK OF LESBIAN AND GAY STUDIES, *supra* note 60, 231, 245-46.

62 ROBSON, *supra* note 1, at 116.

she argues for the extension of civil partnerships, and does so through repeated reference to contract:

> These civil contracts will, I hope, be extended or adapted to bring mutual security and comfort to spinsters, bachelors, carers and other partnerships who are also disadvantaged by not being able to marry. To these groups, such contracts would bring financial security and peace of mind, particularly in old age. Too many of us live alone. . . . Society will benefit greatly if more long-term partnerships are encouraged.[63]

Of course, there is nothing to stop the parties in any of these relationships from forming contracts as between themselves to structure their relationships. It is the state benefits that flow (or not) to the relationships that are of relevance, and the claim is made that the Civil Partnership Act discriminates against them. As one Conservative opponent observed in the House of Commons: "[W]hat is proposed . . . would restrict to one group only the rectification of the unkindnesses and injustices."[64]

These arguments were troubling for defenders of the Civil Partnership Act because they forced them to fall back on arguments that underscore the incoherence of the Act in terms of the marriage/not marriage binary. In particular, the government must point to the divorce-like proceedings, as well as the incest taboo, as justifications for limiting the scope. If you entered into a civil partnership with your grandmother, would you then be required to "divorce" your own grandmother in order to marry someone? Would you want to be your own grandfather? These arguments demonstrate that what is created is a status that is civil marriage in all but name.

But the more interesting arguments raised by both the government and the pressure group Stonewall focus on contract itself, and its apparent inapplicability to an understanding of same-sex relationships. Focusing on a relationship as a contract sullies and demeans the same-sex relationship, underscoring the sharpness of the distinction drawn between contract and (marital and marital-like) status. As Baroness Scotland explained:

> [W]e still believe that "relationship" is of real importance and signifies a difference from a mere "contract." We are dealing with intimate connections between people and we do not think that "contract" accurately expresses what we are seeking to uphold. . . . [W]e are talking about the tender relationships that

63 660 Parl. Deb., H.L. (5th ser.) (2004) 395.

64 425 Parl. Deb., H.C. (6th ser.) (2004) 203 (Ann Widdicombe).

> can happen within families, relationships of support. They are relationships. They are not contracts and we think that it would be inappropriate to describe them as such. It demeans the quality of the relationships that we hope that people in these partnerships will be able to enjoy.[65]

It is noteworthy in this passage that Baroness Scotland implies, in the final sentence, that quality of life will be enhanced by the legislation. Registration will improve the partnership because it provides legal recognition through the granting of a status. Moreover, her understanding of contracting is important. To view the relationship as grounded in contract seems to lessen its transcendental quality. Contracts are entered into by rational, self-interested actors, for mercenary reasons. Relationships, by contrast, simply "happen" because of, presumably, romantic and sexual love, which must not be tarnished by contract, with its implicit overtones of money and, therefore, prostitution and marrying for financial and other convenience. I will return to the binary of love and money, but this also suggests that prenuptial agreements, and the financial structuring of a relationship in advance through contract, are denigrated. So too is marriage (or civil partnership) entered into for purely pragmatic reasons. Clearly, the aim is to justify the limitation of a marital-like status to those who experience the mysteries of this transcendental, special relationship, which rises above the banalities of contract, namely, the status of same-sex partners. The presumption is that other kinds of relationships of care–which can be reduced to contract–lack these qualities.[66]

The pressure group Stonewall made a similar point in response to the proposed amendment:

> [R]eferring to the loving and committed long-term relationships of homosexual couples as "contracts" is demeaning, and downgrades the nature of [their] commitment . . . [A] civil partnership is more than just a contract, the very concept of which does not fit with family law which has traditionally been based on relationships . . . A civil partnership, like any family structure, is not a negotiable contract with optional components. This is why the contractual analogy is unsuitable.[67]

This passage is telling about the social conservatism of Stonewall.

---

65 663 PARL. DEB., H.L. (5th ser.) (2004) 395.

66 Of course, marriage itself is often referred to as a "relational contract"—a point that Baroness Scotland seems unaware of.

67 *Civil Partnership Bill: Parliamentary Briefing Before the House of Lords* 4 (June 24, 2004) (briefing by Stonewall), *available at* http://www.stonewall.org.uk/docs/Lords_Report_June_04.doc.

First, we find an uncritical acceptance of the language of "family" and its traditional underpinnings. Second, and more significant, is a failure to recognize the historical importance of private ordering and the structuring of same-sex relationships outside of the limitations of family law. The freedom to "unpack" the bundle of sticks that has constituted marriage and family, and to "pick and mix" them, may have helped facilitate the evolution of relationships in ways that are now increasingly imitated by many heterosexual couples. In fact, as Rosemary Auchmuty has argued, the dissolution proceedings provide a means for judges to undermine the contractual arrangements that may have been agreed to by the parties in advance.[68]

This yearning for traditional family status with no optional components sits very uneasily with what Judith Stacey and Elizabeth Davenport describe as "the postmodern family" characterized by "diversity, choice, flux and contest."[69] Contract represents the ideals of fulfilling the reasonable expectations of parties, rather than imposing the requirements of a status that imitates marriage. The rejection of the language of "options" in favor of "rights and responsibilities" and "tradition" thus may be a limiting and misplaced strategy. Contract (even as a metaphor) may be better positioned to respond to these postmodern relationship forms.

But the rejection of contract leaves us with a status that remains hollow (or, perhaps a more positive term is "flexible"). After all, there is no prescribed set of vows for entering a civil partnership, so it is not clear what the partners are promising to each other. So too, the absence of adultery as a per se ground for dissolution demonstrates that this aspect of marriage is not necessarily part of the partnership bundle. Moreover, a religious basis for partnership is precluded by the Act. All that the government offers is encouragement to the parties to hold a celebration to mark the occasion. Thus, while this is a status, its hollowness may allow it to be filled with the reasonable expectations of the parties.

CONJUGALITY/CARE

Another, closely related, way of understanding the dilemma of the Civil Partnership Act is through the binary of conjugality and care. As I have already argued, proponents of the Act must argue that same-sex relationships are fundamentally conjugal, or at least

68 *Same-Sex Marriage Revived*, *supra* note 36, at 115.

69 Judith Stacey & Elizabeth Davenport, *Queer Families Quack Back*, *in* HANDBOOK OF LESBIAN AND GAY STUDIES, *supra* note 60, at 355, 356.

have the potential to be so. If, by contrast, the *essence* of civil partnership is economic dependence, then the limitation to same-sex couples becomes difficult to sustain. We are left in a situation, then, of competing analogies: to married couples or to caregivers. By focusing on care rather than conjugality, skeptics of the Civil Partnership Act argued that it is inherently unfair, particularly given that, according to the Baroness O'Caithain, "fewer than 80,000 people live as part of a same-sex couple, whereas 4.6 million people live together in non-sexual co-dependent relationships . . . ."[70]

Sustaining such a distinction in benefits must be on the basis of conjugality. The difficulty, though, is that advocates of the Civil Partnership Act always argue on the basis of care rather than sex. As a strategic matter, this is hardly surprising, but it opens the door to opponents' arguments in favor of caregivers. Heart-wrenching stories of long-term same-sex dependence and care, which inevitably end in tragedy, were the discursive weapons of the proponents of the Act. But the difficulty is that those narratives are indistinguishable from, for example, the stories of the tragic spinster sisters. Because lesbian and gay conjugal relations are both present (by necessity) but absent (by strategy), a discourse of care predominated. But it also bears remembering that neither dependence nor cohabitation (nor conjugal relations for that matter) are prerequisites to registration as partners.

There is another dimension to the care and dependency discourse. Increasingly within government initiatives and debates, there is recognition that lesbians and gay people—both as individuals but mostly as couples—are involved in the care of "their" children. Legal changes under the Labour government have allowed the taking of parental responsibility by a lesbian or gay partner, and this is one of the justifications for registration. This is, however, a politically mixed message. On the one hand, it is gratifying to see lesbian and gay parenting brought into public discourse in a way that is not pathologized, and this demonstrates the changed political climate since the 1980s. On the other, the consistent message from the government is that children's best chance of success is within a married or, failing that, civilly partnered household because of the assumption (grounded in empiricism) that the two-parent married family is the most stable and healthy. Marriage is thereby assumed to be the best basis for the raising of children. It thus remains the case that a traditional model of family is privi-

[70] 660 Parl. Deb., H.L. (5th ser.) (2004) 407.

leged as an idealized locus of child-raising.[71]

The focus on care is also a significant part of the debates. All sides paid homage to the caregiver who sacrifices for others and therefore warrants special consideration by the state either through an amended Civil Partnership Act, or through separate legislation. The debates thereby usefully brought care into Parliamentary discourse and highlighted the relative paucity of benefits and privileges accorded to caregivers as well as the arguable unfairness of privileging sexual relationships (be they marital or otherwise) over other forms of privatized care. Ironically, opponents of civil partnership appear to advance the agenda advocated by feminists such as Martha Fineman who argues that "it is important to point out that focusing on the caretaker's position ultimately illuminates something general about the organization of society . . . ."[72] The debates give space for the articulation of the value of care, and the justice of treating caregivers equally and fairly through assistance from the state. This may represent some recognition of forms of citizenship that transcend paid employment and that center on human relationships, which is a significant change from the citizenship models that have dominated U.K. public discourse.[73]

However, this emphasis on caregiving, like child-raising, sends out a mixed message. While the exaltation of the caregiver as an ideal citizen (as opposed to wage earner or entrepreneur) may be welcomed, it can also be argued that the Civil Partnership Act remains ideologically grounded in a privatized notion of care, wherein the state facilitates the taking on of private responsibility rather than expanding its own public, active role. Moreover, for both opponents and proponents of the Act alike, the center of care is the long-term, stable partnership presumptively located in a "family home." As Boyd and Young argue in the Canadian context, partnership recognition is "grounded in an acceptance of marriage and family as a central organizing feature of citizenship."[74] This privatization of responsibility led proponents of the Civil Partner-

---

71 *See* HOME OFFICE, *supra* note 19.

72 MARTHA ALBERTSON FINEMAN, THE AUTONOMY MYTH: A THEORY OF DEPENDENCY 289 (2004).

73 *See generally* RUTH LEVITAS, THE INCLUSIVE SOCIETY?: SOCIAL EXCLUSION AND NEW LABOUR (1998); Martin Powell, *New Labour and the Third Way in the British Welfare State: A New and Distinctive Approach?*, 20 CRITICAL SOC. POL'Y 39 (2000).

74 Boyd & Young, *supra* note 47, at 781. *See also* ELIZABETH FREEMAN, THE WEDDING COMPLEX: FORMS OF BELONGING IN MODERN AMERICAN CULTURE vii (2002); ROBSON, *supra* note 1, at 150.

ship Act to argue that it is a cost-saving device for the state. Stonewall was explicit in its briefing paper, asserting that "[t]he taxpayer would actually save money in the area of benefit payments. Same-sex partners currently claim benefits as two individuals, meaning that they will receive more money than if their needs had been assessed as a couple."[75]

The assumption is that the outward appearance of partnership (however that might be defined) demands the assumption of responsibility for care, to the advantage of the state. Thus, the state presumes that it can determine what it defines as partnerships, roommates, and friends—all categories that a queer critique is intended to trouble.[76]

The Civil Partnership Act encourages this privatization of care; indeed, forcing it on those who appear to fall into the category of same-sex partner. In this way, the Act becomes another "essential component of the strategy of dismantling the welfare state."[77] After all, "the registration of a civil partnership involves both legal obligations as well as legal protections."[78] As a consequence, as the *Financial Regulatory Impact Assessment* of the government makes clear, "[i]t is expected that civil partners will share their resources and support each other financially, reducing demand for support from the State and, overall, consuming fewer resources."[79] Care thus becomes explicitly privatized on to the couple, making the differential impact of privatization depending upon social class transparent, and "the old principle of the main provider and dependent partner is still maintained."[80]

But the focus on care and its privatization in the same-sex couple is also a partial and incomplete analysis of the dynamics of caregiving today. Sasha Roseneil and Shelley Budgeon argue, based on empirical data, that care increasingly takes place beyond the cohabiting couple and in extra-familial contexts. They point to three dynamics now at work which impact upon intimacy and care: (i) "a decentring of sexual/love relationships within individuals'

---

75 *Stonewall April*, *supra* note 31, at 5.

76 FREEMAN, *supra* note 74, at xv. *See also* Sasha Roseneil, *Why We Should Care About Friends: An Argument for Queering the Care Imaginary in Social Policy*, 3 SOC. POL'Y & SOC'Y 409 (2004) [hereinafter *Queering the Care Imaginary*].

77 Alison Diduck, *A Family by Any Other Name . . . or Starbucks Comes to England*, 28 J. L. & SOC'Y 290, 307 (2001).

78 RESPONSES TO CIVIL PARTNERSHIP, *supra* note 52, at 38.

79 FINAL REGULATORY IMPACT ASSESSMENT, *supra* note 23, at 16.

80 Fiona Williams & Sasha Roseneil, *Public Values of Parenting and Partnering: Voluntary Organizations and Welfare Politics in New Labour's Britain*, 11 SOC. POL. 181, 187 (2004).

life narratives"; (ii) "an increased importance placed on friendship in people's affective lives"; and (iii) "a diversification in the forms of sexual/love relationships."[81] A focus on family fails to capture the increased provision of care through "networks and flows of intimacy,"[82] which do not center on the couple as partners in care. If friendship is replacing partnership as a central organizing principle of intimacy in many people's lives, then the maintenance of privileged categories—whether spouse or same-sex partner or even spinster sister—becomes difficult to sustain. Care may take place in the private sphere, but it is not within a set model of relationship form, and to the extent that the state may wish to privilege certain relationship forms on the basis of dependency and care, it does so in an exclusionary way. Indeed, it forces us back into the recognition that same-sex partnership is not necessarily coterminous with care or conjugality, and demands that we think about care "beyond the conjugal imaginary."[83] As one Conservative opponent suggested in the House of Commons (mirroring the queer theory critique), the legislation will "be an insult to all those who happily share their lives with relatives or friends outside marriage, because their relationships will be given institutional inferiority to [registered] homosexual ones."[84]

Love/Money

> [A]lthough it is paraded as an extension of human rights, it is nothing to do with fundamental human rights. It is about financial implications for homosexuals.[85]

Love and money is another dichotomy around which the Civil Partnership Act spins uneasily. For proponents of the Act, the relationship between love and money is straightforward. Long-term coupling is based upon romantic love (certainly not on contract or financial benefit), and long-term relationships are proven to be beneficial to society. Therefore, there is a social interest in providing a set of benefits to committed couples, but also in enshrining a set of responsibilities, which presumably same-sex couples in love would fulfill anyway. The rationale is that the state has an interest

81 Sasha Roseneil & Shelley Budgeon, *Cultures of Intimacy and Care Beyond "the Family": Personal Life and Social Change in the Early 21st Century*, 52 Current Soc. 135, 142 (2004).

82 *Id.* at 153.

83 *Queering the Care Imaginary, supra* note 76, at 411.

84 425 Parl. Deb., H.C. (6th ser.) (2004) 213 (Christopher Chope).

85 663 Parl. Deb., H.L. (5th ser.) (2004) 403 (Lord Maginnis).

in protecting and supporting stable relationships, be they married couples or same-sex partners.

For skeptics of the Act, by contrast, the rationale for the state support of relationships was probed more deeply and, for the Lord Bishop of Peterborough at least, the jury remains out on the issue: "it will remain a matter of judgment whether the extension of *positive discrimination* by creating a largely undefined or, perhaps, self-defined relationship will be beneficial to society, as well as to the individuals concerned."[86]

In this passage, the Bishop recognized that the state historically has positively discriminated in favor of married couples, and this in turn raises the question whether relationships per se are necessarily social goods warranting special treatment that, as Lord Higgins articulated, amounts to "a discrimination here against the single person."[87] The debate thus at least begins to raise the question of whether relationships—marital or otherwise—provide a sensible basis for making distinctions, for example, in the provision of employment pension benefits. As Lord Higgins made clear, the provision of a "wife's pension," justified by the likelihood of a diminished opportunity for making independent contributions may seem dubious as applicable to many same-sex couples.[88] The door is therefore open to thinking about unfairness in the ways in which provisions are made for old age. But only one member of Parliament linked these concerns to systemic *gender* inequality:

> [S]urvivors have had no right to a partner's pension. That has been a significant issue for many lesbian couples. Two women living together may have child care responsibilities. One of them may not work throughout her economically active life and reach retirement age without having acquired any pensionable service of her own. Bearing in mind the fact that many women are paid considerably less than men, the issue of poverty and rectifying injustice is important.[89]

But just as the debates on the Civil Partnership Act uncovered a class perspective with respect to those same-sex couples in em-

---

86 660 PARL. DEB., H.L. (5th ser.) (2004) 423 (emphasis added).

87 *Id.* at 428.

88 *Id.* The pension questions raised by the Act are complex and not entirely resolved. In particular, the issue of pension provision for dependent surviving civil partners remains a contentious issue. The argument that the survivor partner's pension should be based upon *all* of the deceased's pension contributions, and not just those made since the coming into force of the Civil Partnership Act, has not been accepted by the government. Further announcements are promised from the government on the pension implications of partnership.

89 425 PARL. DEB., H.C. (6th ser.) (2004) 226 (Chris Bryant).

ployment (winners) and those dependent upon the state through the benefit system (losers), the debate also discloses another differential class impact, this with respect to the role of inheritance tax, still often referred to as "death duties." In the U.K., wealth is taxed upon death, but can be transferred upon death between spouses exempt from inheritance tax. Registered same-sex partners likewise will be able to transfer wealth between themselves upon death free of tax. Critics of the Civil Partnership Act seized upon inheritance tax, questioning why those in other types of relationships of care and companionship should not also be entitled to exemption. Why should they continue to be discriminated against? As the Baroness O'Cathain stated:

> If we are to extend all the rights of married couples to others, what should be the criteria? Should they be extended only to those in homosexual relationships? . . . The theoretical examples are known to everybody: people who move into a flat to care for a friend with a long-term illness; a daughter giving up a well-paid job to care for a sick mother; or two sisters who never marry, living together all their lives in the home inherited from their parents. All of these people, when it comes to the death of one or other of them, will face a swingeing inheritance tax bill, which will in most cases lead to increasing dependency on the state by those people. These sorts of cases are appalling and something has to be done about them. . . . Inheritance tax merely punishes families and other beneficiaries.[90]

The widespread hostility towards inheritance tax (particularly amongst Conservatives) is perhaps not surprising, given that it impacts the transfer of wealth between generations, and only protects spouses, presumably in order to ensure that widows have provision for their old age. Whether such a justification has become anachronistic, and whether it is compelling in the case of same-sex couples[91] is open to debate, as is the question of whether inheritance tax provides an equitable and just means for redistribution.

However, what also became clear for those focused on the financial implications of civil partnership (money rather than love) is that the presence of the ban on registration with a family member can be explained, not in terms of the analogy to marriage, but in terms of money and, specifically, tax avoidance. The Earl of Onslow was most explicit in recognizing that the formation of legally-sanctioned relationships may be about money rather than roman-

90 660 Parl. Deb., H.L. (5th ser.) (2004) 405-06.

91 *See Same-Sex Marriage Revived, supra* note 36, at 114.

tic love, at least for those seeking to shield wealth from the tax collector:

> For some reason, the Biblical prohibition on close relationships is included in the Bill. Why? I cannot understand why. But I think I do. I think it is because I cannot register my son as my catamite and then hand the whole of my property to him without death duties. When I first heard of the Bill, I thought "Yippee. That is a frightfully good idea." But one cannot do that.[92]

Thus, for those who advocate a wider extension of the Civil Partnership Act, the issue is not so much about the recognition of relationships of love, but more fundamentally, about the avoidance (or at least a delay) in the redistribution of wealth. While the government, and Stonewall, emphasized that the Civil Partnership Act is cost-neutral for the state (a debatable proposition) this is achieved through the privatization of the cost of care, which reduces the responsibility of the state through the benefit system. With respect to private wealth and spousal pension benefits—the concerns primarily of the upper and middle classes—the advantages of registration are clear (while the poor are disadvantaged by being deemed partners for the purposes of public support). The Act thus sits uneasily on the dichotomy of love and money, in that the government is keen that non-registration should not be financially advantageous (for those dependent upon state benefits). As well, the financial benefits that may accrue to some are limited to a clearly defined and essentialized class that is grounded in status rather than contract, in order to prevent at least the appearance of partnerships of financial convenience. Money must follow from love (status) rather than from tax planning (contract), in large measure because of the desire to control the potential cost to the state of this legislation.

Responsibilities/Rights

The final binary that warrants at least a mention has already been foreshadowed throughout this article: responsibilities and rights. For government supporters, the Civil Partnership Act is a carefully designed bundle of rights and responsibilities for same-sex couples, rather than special benefits or financial privileges. This is no *à la carte* of relationship options. Rather, in order to take advantage of the benefits, the responsibilities must be assumed, and this can only be done through the conscious act of registration with the state. In fact, the relationship between rights and respon-

92 660 Parl. Deb., H.L. (5th ser.) (2004) 416-17.

sibilities is characterized within the material surrounding the Act as a careful balance between "the responsibilities of caring for and maintaining a partner with a package of rights for example, in the area of inheritance."[93] Inheritance rights thus become the pay off for assuming the responsibilities of care. This is a very utilitarian notion of rights and responsibilities in which the two are quantifiable and measurable to achieve a perfect harmony.[94]

It is the careful tailoring of this bundle to same-sex couples that makes it inappropriate for other carers and home-sharers who, it is promised, in due course will receive their own legislation. For example, the dissolution proceedings, power of judges to make property orders, and requirements to provide support (potentially even after dissolution), make this a set of responsibilities, the government argues, that would be ill-suited to such couples as spinster sisters.

What also underpins this bundle of responsibilities and rights, though, is an underlying faith in the power of the granting of rights to shape behavior (including claims that it will lead to a reduction in homophobic violence) and to foster stable relationships. On the one hand, the government recognizes the existence of long-term stable relationships that, it is assumed, are beneficial to individuals and to society. But, on the other hand, the assumption is that law reform will strengthen those relationships, foster the forging of new long-term relationships, and improve the quality of life of those who enter into them. The power of rights thus is substantial in shaping our choices, perhaps even as powerful as love is in shaping relationships.

Conclusions

> Perhaps part of the responsibilities that come with the seductive invitation to become the citizen you know you want to (and can) be is adherence to a vanillized homonormativity to complement the heteronormativity of the contemporary 'familization of the social.'[95]

The Civil Partnership Act can be read on one level as a very "unqueer" text: deeply assimilationist, furthering a privatization of care agenda, mimicking a marriage model, and foregoing the per-

93 Responses to Civil Partnership, *supra* note 52, at 15.

94 Governing Sexuality, *supra* note 10, at 28 (arguing that this linking of the granting of rights to the assumption of responsibilities is fundamental to New Labour Party ideology).

95 McGhee, *supra* note 10, at 366-67.

fect opportunity to rethink in a radical way the institution of the family in law. With respect to the last point, the Act is a lost opportunity. In trying to be all things to all people—perhaps inevitable with respect to the U.K. government's thinking on the family—I have tried to show that the Act often slips into incoherence in the way in which it straddles numerous dichotomies.

I have also touched upon how the Civil Partnership Act emerges out of a culturally distinct set of circumstances, despite the essentialism that often underpins the rhetoric. The similarity to the institution of marriage, but the aversion to the concept of same-sex marriage, shapes this distinctiveness. Cultural uniqueness, in this instance, can be rephrased as parochialism. Although the Act does make provision for the recognition of foreign partnerships, there remain complex issues surrounding recognition in the U.K. of those partnerships (such as the PACS) which may involve a very different bundle of rights and responsibilities and which are not limited to same-sex couples.[96] While the government seeks to essentialize same-sex relationships, it cannot essentialize the patchwork of legal regimes of relationship recognition occurring within the European Union and beyond. As Baroness Scotland conceded, "there is no common concept of same-sex registered partnership in other countries across the world."[97] The dichotomy of marriage/not marriage rises again to the surface, and, as without such a universally recognized status as marriage, there is no automatic basis upon which to determine whether to recognize a foreign registered partnership.

This problem is brought into sharp relief by legal developments within the European Union, and in particular, Directive 2004/58/EC on free movement of citizens of the Union and their family members, issued in April 2004. In defining "family member," the Directive includes "spouse" as well as "the partner with whom the Union citizen has contracted a registered partnership, on the basis of the legislation of a Member State, if the legislation of the host Member State treats registered partnerships as equivalent to marriage."[98] In this directive to member states of the European Union, we witness the attempt to impose transnational

---

96 *See generally* Barry Crown, *Civil Partnerships in the U.K.—Some International Problems*, 48 N.Y.L. SCH. L. REV. 697 (2004); Rebecca Probert & Anne Barlow, *Displacing Marriage—Diversification and Harmonisation Within Europe*, 12 CHILD & FAM. L.Q. 153 (2000).

97 660 PARL. DEB., H.L. (7th ser.) (2004) 391.

98 Council Directive 2004/58/EC, art. 2(2), 2004 O.J. (L 229) 35, 38.

coherence upon the culturally diverse pattern of regimes of recognition emerging across the E.U.

This transnational point further underscores the many limitations of the Act, which are covered over by the claims to justice and equality. In the material surrounding the legislation, and in the debates, what is apparent is a lack of engagement with the many types of relationships which lesbians and gay men form, and how that diversity might be reflected through law. Nor is there any room for progressive and feminist analyses of the institution of marriage: of why and how marriage is valued and whether it has become anachronistic. There is no serious critical discussion (except, ironically, from some Conservatives) of why we privilege conjugal relations rather than relations of economic interdependence, and whether it would be possible to use the state and public benefit to help privatized care giving, and whether care can be made *less* private. Finally, the debate touches upon, but never considers, the question of what constitutes authenticity in relationships, what might amount to a fraud on civil partnership, and, for that matter, what constitutes benefit fraud by unregistered same-sex cohabitants.

As I have tried to demonstrate in this article, the basis of relationships seems to be any, or many, or all of, love, money, sex, friendship and care, but the infinite variety of ways in which they combine make law a cumbersome device for the regulation of intimacy. This is particularly true when the model of regulation is drawn from the institution of marriage and then imposed upon what are increasingly complex, postmodern and queer lives. But the underlying incoherence of the legal category of partnership may well provide, I have also suggested, room for subversion and resistance in the ways in which lesbians and gays (and, indeed, others) map on to the law's attempt at categorization. Whether and how that will occur will require empirical data after the Act comes into force. That analysis will entail looking at how queer lives intersect with what appears, on its surface, to be a very unqueer law through what may be the manipulation of the very incoherence on which it is founded.

Part VI
Law and Conjugal Cohabitation

[24]

Regulation of Cohabitation, Changing Family Policies and Social Attitudes: A Discussion of Britain Within Europe[1]

ANNE BARLOW

This article considers the differing legal and policy responses to the common trends of family restructuring away from marriage within Britain and Europe. Conceding that Europe is in the process of losing heterosexual marriage as a universal epicenter of family law at the very time when legal harmonization within Europe is being promoted, it goes on to explore the best way forward for regulating same- and different-sex cohabiting couples. It concludes that the legal response to these trends should be "de-moralized" but principled. A plurality of legal regulative structures to accommodate the now diverse family forms that are found within our less marriage-centric societies should be put in place providing at least some default protection for all families, yet allowing people to opt out and make their own arrangements.

I. INTRODUCTION

Having seen how family structuring away from marriage—what the French term "*démariage*"—is sweeping across Europe (Kiernan 2004), this article aims to look at the legal responses to these social trends. In examining the main legal models which govern cohabitation relationships in Europe and other Common Law jurisdictions , Britain, in general and England and Wales in particular, stands apart. The law here does not fall neatly into any of the main groupings. While toying with American-style pro-marriage policy, it has also been prepared to take on an inclusive and functional approach to cohabitants on an ad hoc basis reminiscent of the Canadian and Australian experience and is now actively proposing a European-style civil partnership register for same-sex cohabitants (Great Britain. Department of Trade and Industry [DTI], Women and Equality Unit 2003a; Queen's Speech 2003). Despite widespread social acceptance of different-sex cohabitation as a family form in Britain, the government is still seemingly undecided as to how

* Address correspondence to Anne Barlow, Law Department, University of Wales, Abersytwyth, Ceredigion SY23 3DY, UK. E-mail: aeb@aber.ac.uk

best to react as illustrated in its consultation document *Supporting Families* (Great Britain. Home Office 1998). On one level, it acknowledges "families do not want to be lectured about their behaviour or what kind of relationship they are in" (ibid.: para. 4.2). Yet at another level, it states that the government's preferred option is to promote marriage, at least as a parenting structure:

> [M]arriage does provide a strong foundation for stability for the care of children. It also sets out rights and responsibilities for all concerned. It remains the choice of the majority of people in Britain. For all these reasons, it makes sense for the Government to do what it can to strengthen marriage. (Ibid.: para. 4.8).

Thus while the government has now shown commitment to the ending of discrimination against same-sex couples who are unable to marry (DTI. Women and Equality Unit 2003a; Queen's Speech 2003), legal discrimination against different-sex cohabitants is to continue, with only a need to provide them with better information being acknowledged (DTI. Women and Equality Unit 2003b: paras. 3.5–3.6). Thus government family policy remains far more equivocal about the position of different-sex cohabitants who parent and partner in a functionally similar manner to their married counterparts. It is here, and no longer perhaps in the same-sex context, that the moral and political malaise about *démariage* is at its most visible, making it a good focus for this discussion.

II. BACKGROUND

The Napoleonic adage, "Cohabitants ignore the law, so the law ignores them" is a fair summary of the legal attitude toward unmarried cohabitation in Britain and Europe up until the last quarter of the twentieth century. While cohabitation was not unknown in late nineteenth and early twentieth century Europe (see Probert 2004 and Kiernan 2004), none of the European civil codes governing family and succession law in Europe looked beyond married partnerships until Sweden extended marriage-like rights for both different- and same-sex cohabitants in two Acts in 1987.[2] In England and Wales, while informal common-law marriage had historically been recognized in law as a valid marriage providing prescribed conditions were met, this was abolished 250 years ago by the Clandestine Marriages Act of 1753 (although the phrase "common-law marriage" lingers persistently and confusingly in our language to denote unmarried heterosexual cohabitation). Thus in Europe, Scotland alone retains recognition of a form of common-law marriage[3] and throughout at least the first seven decades of the twentieth century, formal monogamous marriage founded on Christian principles was the universal and undisputed legal, social and moral norm within British and European societies. The complete dominance of the ideology of the married family in the 1950s was also reflected in the provisions of the Treaty of Rome and the European Convention on Human Rights and consequently this remains a cornerstone of Europe's supranational legal architecture (see Commaille & De Singly 1997).

However, in recent times many of the pillars upon which the traditional marriage contract was built have begun to crumble, albeit at different rates in different parts of Europe. In particular, marriage is no longer necessarily a lifelong institution but has become a "companionate" and negotiable partnership, with most European jurisdictions permitting divorce by separation and consent (Hamilton & Perry 2002). This development and the simultaneous rise in unmarried heterosexual cohabitation reflect the changed political, economic and social position of women in Western society which has strongly challenged the appropriateness of the traditional patriarchal nature of marriage for life reflected in our laws (see, e.g., O'Donovan 1993). The attempts to modernize marriage have in fact arguably rendered marriage more like the individually negotiated unmarried cohabitation, yet it is the form rather than the function of such families that is still the basis for legal differentiation in most jurisdictions. These changes have also combined with increased secularization of society and a general decline in religious adherence among the European population (De Graaf & Need 2000) to remove for many heterosexual couples the religious imperative to marry or indeed to refrain from divorce. The social response to these developments can be seen in rising divorce rates, a marked increase in both partnering and parenting outside marriage and declining marriage rates across Britain and many parts of Europe (see Kiernan 2004). At the same time and as developed below, an increased acceptance of same-sex cohabitation and a human rights-driven nondiscrimination agenda has focused political attention on the implications of the inability of same-sex couples to marry in many European states.

The legal responses across Europe to these broadly common trends of family restructuring have been fragmented and diverse in ways which cannot be fully explained by the extent of the differences in the social trends themselves (Bradley 2001). Thus ironically at a time when Europe is seeking increased legal harmonization,[4] family law has lost marriage as its universal unit of currency. As will be discussed, in some jurisdictions and not always those with the highest rates of cohabitation, there has been broad acceptance of the new social trends and the arrival of a new legal order which no longer focuses on heterosexual marriage but reflects the plurality of couple relationship styles. This approach might be seen as an example of what Teubner (1993) has termed "reflexive law" which is offered as a solution to the law's inability under modern conditions to restore consensual, moral and political values (King & Piper 1995: 36). At the other extreme, some states have yet to respond to unmarried cohabitation of any sort in any way, despite changing trends. Here, there is still faith in the law's power to uphold (or at least stem decline in) traditional family values and structures through rationally established a priori principles. Elsewhere in Europe a compromise has been struck in the form of the introduction of Civil Partnership Registers which in some but not all cases are directed exclusively at same-sex couples and which involve cohabitants opting in to an agreed set of broadly marriage-like rights and responsibilities, without enhancing the rights of unregistered cohabitants. Here the overriding desire to preserve the rationale of maintaining a priori principles established through law has conceded, in the face of changing social norms, a partial abandonment of traditional family values to permit modernization of the legal framework while maintaining its integrity.

However, Britain arguably remains the most confused in its legal response to changing social norms which does not fit neatly into any of these categories. As might have been expected given its common law tradition, it has used case law and statute to address the legal situation of cohabitants on an ad hoc basis, leaving the law complex, confusing and often illogical. This is not surprising when British family policy in the 1990s has swung away from the more neutral functional approach to regulation begun in the 1970s (Glendon 1981), through Thatcherite attempts to reassert "traditional family values" American-style (Smart 1997), and on to New Labour's aim of "strengthening marriage" which has involved justifying the legal status quo while ignoring different-sex cohabitation presumably in the hope that it might go away (Great Britain. Home Office 1998: ch. 4; Barlow & Duncan 2000).

Thus unlike the position in other comparable common law jurisdictions such as Canada (see Bala & Bromwich 2002; Bailey 2004), Australia (Bailey-Harris 2000; Finlay, Bailey-Harris & Otlowski 1997) and New Zealand (Richardson 2002) where, using both case law and statutory reform, far greater consistency has been achieved in the treatment of cohabitants by extending to them the legal privileges of marriage using functional justifications, English law remains schizophrenic. In some situations it regards heterosexual cohabitants as if they were married, in others it regards them as a family form inferior to marriage and in yet others, it chooses to ignore the cohabitation relationship altogether, treating partners as strangers. Same-sex cohabitants who until very recently were always treated as unconnected individuals are now being drawn in to the same ad hoc piecemeal reform process.[5] This has left the law regulating families in a compromise of tiers with the hierarchical order within a tier generally (but not always) placing married couples at the top with the most rights and remedies, same-sex couples at the bottom not recognized as a legal family and different-sex cohabitants in a middle position. However, the order of this hierarchy may reconfigure itself differently in particular legal contexts and is currently prone to change with every new piece of family legislation or court decision. Perhaps the most surprising of these developments is the Adoption and Children Act 2002 which will permit both same- and different-sex cohabitants in what is termed "an enduring relationship" to adopt a child. This is despite the fact that the law provides far less financial security for such couples on death or relationship breakdown and despite the fact that adoption by unmarried (and particularly same-sex) couples has proved unpalatable in most other European jurisdictions.

Added very recently to this confused state of the law is a government promise of legislation to introduce a European-style Civil Partnership Register giving registered partners marriage-like legal rights but, unlike previously proposed models, limited to same-sex couples (DTI. Women and Equality Unit 2003a; Queen's Speech 2003).[6] Scotland, which has agreed to adopt the English same-sex civil partnership model (DTI. Women and Equality Unit 2003b),[7] has also promised reform on different sex cohabitants (Scottish Executive 2000). In contrast, the Law Commission for England and Wales, which had over a ten-year period been reviewing property law relating to home-sharers including cohabitants, while admitting that the common law was in a very unsatisfactory state, felt unable to make any recommendations for reform that would significantly improve the law (Law Commission 2002). Thus contrary to previous trends and the predictions of many (e.g., Bradley 2001: 43), the current agenda in England and Wales for law reform in this area seems ready to borrow from less familiar civil law initiatives rather than those more compatible with its own legal culture (but less in tune with its family policy) to be found elsewhere in the common law world.

Having examined the main models for legal reform that currently exist, this article will consider whether Europe should now embrace a functional approach to family regulation, rather than continue to ascribe rights only according to family form. In making such a decision, we need to ask ourselves what is the main function of family law? Is it to protect families and particularly children from the bad consequences of family rupture, in which case it is what families do rather than the form they take that becomes the issue? If, on the other hand, family law is accepted to be a wider instrument of social policy which holds the power to reassert more "desirable" family forms within society by promoting marriage and other registered stable relationships, then we need to monitor the effects to ensure that the ends justify the means.

III. EUROPEAN MODELS

A. FUNCTION PLUS FORM—SWEDEN

Within Europe, only Sweden has responded to family restructuring by taking a deliberately functional approach based on social needs to both same- and different-sex cohabitation (Ytterberg 2001: 430; Agell 2003: 126). As long ago as 1987, it recognized that both different and same-sex cohabitants were faced by the same problems as married couples when relationships broke down. The Cohabitees (Joint Homes) Act 1987 (combined with the Homosexual Cohabitees Act 1987 which extended major provisions regulating heterosexual cohabitants to same-sex cohabitants) gives rights to cohabitants in relationships "reminiscent of marriage" (ibid.: s. 1). This is judged in accordance with the length of time the couple have been together, whether there are children of the relationship and whether they have shared daily housekeeping expenses. Once satisfied, the value of property acquired for joint use (limited to the joint home and household goods) will, after deduction of debts due, be divided equally between the parties at the end of the relationship, although this can be overridden by a written agreement (ibid.: s. 5, 7–8). The home or goods will be allocated to the party who is deemed to need it most subject to deduction of its value from the remainder of their share (ibid.: s. 10). A cohabitant may be able to retain more of their property where equal division would not be fair in view of the length of the relationship or other relevant considerations (ibid.: s. 9). Even during the relationship, the Act restricts a cohabitant from dealing with jointly used property without the consent of the other partner. These rules thus reflect those which apply to married couples under the Swedish community of property regime, but are less extensive. Nonetheless they are imposed without the consent of the parties in recognition of the functional similarities of married and unmarried cohabiting families. However the rules are not based directly on need, applying instead a minimum protection for a partner on death or relationship breakdown which can be enhanced or reduced by written agreement or will. Such a scheme based principally on equality is of course appropriate where any inequalities suffered as a consequence of the cohabiting relationship are minimized and addressed by the welfare regime operated by the Swedish state, which encourages full participation by parents in the labor market and undertakes to provide housing and childcare for its citizens (see, e.g., Bradley 1996). Perhaps surprisingly and contrary to what many Swedish cohabitants believe, Swedish law does not impose any marriage-like support obligations between cohabitants, although they are recognized as their partner's next of kin (Ytterberg 2001: 432). However, in the context of children, Swedish law has not progressed fully along the functional route. While unmarried heterosexual cohabitants can have joint custody of a child (Parents and Children Code 1949: ch. 6, s. 10a), or access publicly funded infertility treatment (Act on Insemination 1984: s. 2; Act on In Vitro Fertilisation 1988: s. 2), both are denied to their same-sex counterparts. Neither same- nor different-sex cohabitants can adopt jointly as a couple, although adoption by an unmarried individual is permitted (Parents and Children Code 1949: ch. 4, s. 3–4). While heterosexual couples have the option of marriage, this was not open to same-sex couples wanting to adopt.

Thus the functional approach taken in Sweden does not place cohabitants on par with married couples. While this might be justified in the case of heterosexual couples who have marriage as an option, same-sex cohabitants could not avoid legal discrimination. Partly in response to this and partly to assimilate Swedish law with that of its Scandinavian neighbors, the Registered

Partnership Act 1994 was introduced to provide same-sex couples with a legal framework corresponding to marriage. Following the Danish model, registration is not open to different-sex couples. While in its original form the 1994 Act continued to discriminate against same-sex couples with regard to joint custody and adoption of children, amending legislation in 2002 (Partnership and Adoption Act 2002) now permits registered partners to adopt a child (including the child of a registered partner) and to become joint custodians of a child in certain situations, such as where a child has suffered parental neglect. Thus in all respects other than infertility treatment (which is still under review),[8] registered partners have been placed on the same footing as married couples in Sweden (Savolainen 2002).

However, the position of unregistered cohabitants remains unaffected which means in Sweden unregistered same-sex cohabitants have fewest rights but are still overall better recognized in family law than in any other European state. Regulation of relationships continues to be tiered according to form first and function second, but Sweden has created a legal framework where the tiering is transparent, relatively easy to identify and understand while at the same time providing adequate family law-style regulation for other functionally identified informal families in line with the protective aims of family law.

B. EXTENDED FORM APPROACH

1. *The Diverse Marriage Model—From Scandinavia to Spain via The Netherlands*

Another approach which is inclusive of new family structures but based on family form rather than function can be seen in the Netherlands. In 1998 it was the first state to introduce a registered partnership model for both same- and different-sex cohabitants[9] and remains the first and only European jurisdiction to permit, with effect from 2001, same-sex marriage (Act Opening Marriage to Same-Sex Couples, 2000). Rather than attempt to regulate informal families, the Dutch response has been instead to first make an alternative legally regulated form available and subsequently to move marriage beyond its traditional heterosexual confines. Thus in the Netherlands, cohabitants, whether same- or different-sex, may marry, enter into a registered partnership or live as unregistered cohabitants. However, the unregistered have very few legal rights despite numbering upwards of 1.4 million (see Boele-Woelki 2003: 41) leaving such couples who are fulfilling traditional family partnering and parenting functions without any family law-style protection as between the partners. What is more, the legal position of the seven million married couples (ibid.), of whom just over four thousand are same-sex (ibid.: 45), and the eighteen thousand registered partners (ibid.: 47) is virtually identical, which leads one to question the usefulness of retaining the two institutions. Virtually the same formalities and conditions of eligibility apply to entering a marriage or partnership and similar rights and obligations pertain to both relationship contexts (Boele-Woelki 2003: 45). There are, however, major differences between the rights of same- and different-sex partners with regard to children in both marriage and registered partnerships (ibid. 2003: 46). Partners are required to maintain one another and community of property rules apply unless the couple have made an alternative agreement. However, a partnership, unlike a marriage, may not be dissolved by joint application but may be dissolved on the application of one partner without the intervention of the court (ibid.: 46). On the introduction of same-sex marriage, the law was changed to permit registered partnerships to be converted to marriage and marriages to partnerships which merely involves the drawing up of an "act of transformation" by the civil status registrar.[10] While these developments can be seen to have been primarily aimed at conferring status on same-sex cohabitants rather than dealing with cohabitation issues generally (Probert & Barlow 2000: 161) interestingly, the number of same-sex couples registering partnerships has been matched and more recently dwarfed by different-sex registrations (constituting 90% of all registrations in 2002) since the Partnership Act's introduction (see http://www.cbs.nl and Boele-Woelki 2003: 51). While this can to some extent be explained by the introduction of same-sex marriage in 2001, the attractiveness of a marriage-model partnership register to cohabitants may seem something of a mystery. However, it seems these figures belie the perceived social need for an administrative divorce by mutual consent, currently denied to those divorcing by the Dutch Civil Code, but possible by means of converting a failed marriage into a registered partnership which permits registration of an agreed divorce settlement and which can then be easily dissolved on the agreed terms. This phenomenon termed by Boele-Woelke as the "lightning divorce" by registered partnership (Boele-Woelke 2003: 49) is an unexpected consequence of the heterosexual registered partnership and one which will be considered fully when the need for the continuation of registered partnerships after the introduction of same-sex marriage is reviewed by the Dutch Parliament in 2006.

The most common model to be found among those other European jurisdictions that have reacted at all, is the same-sex registered partnership model aimed at couples who are unable to attain family law status and protection through marriage. Thus Denmark led the way by introducing a Registered Partnership Act in 1989 which essentially extends the legal consequences of marriage to registered partners. This model was subsequently adopted (although complemented by other measures in Sweden and Norway) in Norway in 1993, Sweden in 1994, Iceland in 1996 and most recently Finland and Germany in 2001.[11] It is a model which mirrors marriage in terms of conditions for entry and the rights and obligations it bestows, although the terms for exit from the partnership involve a system of notice rather than any separation- or fault-based court procedure. Thus only one partnership can be registered at a time, the parties must both have attained their majority, not be within prohibited degrees of relationship, not be committed to another formal relationship, make a declaration before the competent authority and accept community of property or make an alternative declaration. In return nearly all the legal rights and obligations appertaining to marriage, including community of property, succession and social security/insurance and pension rights are bestowed, save in some jurisdictions rights relating to joint custody and adoption of children. It is this model which Britain is now to follow, having specifically rejected the idea that the reform should extend to same- and different-sex couples.

Because marriage is already available to different-sex cohabitants, it is surprising that the marriage-mirror model has been adopted where the intention is also to address different-sex cohabitation. In some cases, such as the autonomous and strongly Catholic Spanish communities of Catalonia, Aragon, Navarra and the Balearic Islands which have responsibility for family and succession law in their regions (and relatively low rates of cohabitation), it may have been more politically acceptable to address reform globally rather than focus exclusively on the position of same-sex discrimination. In addition, most of the Spanish models,[12] unlike that of the Netherlands, are not exclusively opt-in partnership registers. They also operate in the case of different-sex couples (and in some regions also same-sex couples) to confer rights automatically after a period of two or three years cohabitation or the birth of a child which can be proven "by any means of proof admitted in law" (cf. Balearic Islands Stable Couples Law 2001: art. 2.1). In some cases (such as Catelonia) this is not extended to same-sex couples who can only gain the legally recognized status by means of a public declaration of the relationship. While the benefits of registered partnerships for same-sex couples unable to marry are obvious, they do also provide different-sex couples with an enforceable and more flexible means of agreeing their property arrangements, which is not always possible in the married context.

2. *New-Style Couple Regulation—France and Belgium*

It is only in France and Belgium that a real attempt has been made through registered partnership legislation to move away from the marriage model (see Probert and Barlow 2000). The French *Pacte Civil de Solidarité* (PACS) Law (Law no. 90-944 of 15 November 1999 amending French Civil Code) introduces the concept of a civil union pact which a cohabiting couple, whether same- or different-sex may register to regulate their relationship. It, alone, defines cohabitation (for the purpose of this and other laws regulating it) without reference to marriage as "a de facto union characterised by a communal life which demonstrates stability and continuity, between two persons of the same or different sex, who live as a couple."[13] This and the Belgian Law Establishing Legal Cohabitation 1998 (Law Establishing Legal Cohabitation 1998) are attempting to provide a real alternative for heterosexual cohabiting couples as well as a mechanism for endowing same-sex couples with increased family law-style rights and obligations. From the point of view of the lesbian and gay lobby, this falls short of marriage itself or even of the equality with marriage gained from marriage-model registered partnerships. However, for those both same- and different-sex cohabitants who reject marriage as an institution or are unhappy with its terms but wish to express and agree to an alternative but legally recognized symbolic and financial commitment to their partner, this can only be achieved in this small corner of Europe. Essentially, in both jurisdictions only those uncommitted to other formal relationships and who have capacity to contract are eligible. In Belgium a declaration that the couple wish to live together must be made whereas in France it is the *pacte* containing the agreement of terms and arrangements which is registered. These are broadly left to the parties to agree, although default provisions impose a limited form of community of property in both jurisdictions and limited maintenance obligations in Belgium (article 1479 of the amended Belgian Civil Code). However, the provisions go beyond that of a cohabitation contract as they impose a limited framework of rights. A *pacté* couple are recognized as a unit for most tax and social security benefits in France and couples must provide each other with "mutual and material assistance" (seemingly a little lower than the duty owed in marriage). Even compared to the marriage-model registered partnership, there is very little control over exit from partnerships in either the French or Belgian Act and so, unlike the other models discussed, those opting in are able to choose to make a lesser commitment than marriage in return for fewer privileges and substantive obligations yet gain a legally recognized new-style family status.

C. OTHER EUROPEAN PERSPECTIVES

Before considering the British context, it is important to take note of the fact that many jurisdictions have yet to consider legislation on cohabitation. In Ireland where cohabitation is growing apace and must be included among the middle range of states with reasonably high levels of cohabitation (Kiernan 2004), neither case law nor statutes have yet ameliorated the legal position of cohabitants whether of same or different sex. In Spain (other than in the autonomous communities), Italy, Portugal and Greece where European cohabitation is increasing but still relatively low (ibid.) there is no legislation planned, although Portugal and the Federal Parliament of Spain have at least debated the issue in the recent past. Neither is there pressure at the current time from either the European Court of Human Rights in Strasbourg or the European Court of Justice in Luxembourg to abandon the traditional moral stance, allowing member states a margin of appreciation in moral matters. The former in its interpretation of article 8 of the European Convention on Human Rights protecting the right to private and family life has confirmed that what amounts to "family life" within the context of article 8 is a question of fact and is capable of including the unmarried cohabiting family (*X, Y and Z v United Kingdom* 1997). However, to date it has not been held to be discriminatory under articles 8 and 14 to provide different rules for cohabiting as opposed to married fathers for the purpose of acquiring legal parental responsibility and rights for their child (*B v United Kingdom* 2000). Neither have same-sex cohabiting relationships been regarded by the Strasbourg court as protected from discrimination by article 8, as again their different treatment was considered within a state's margin of appreciation. Thus same-sex couples do not have a protected right to family life within article 8 (*S v United Kingdom* 1985), although they are guaranteed its right to private life (*ADT v United Kingdom* 2000). Similarly, it is permissible not to treat cohabitants as spousal family members for the purposes of European Union Law (*Netherlands v Reed* 1986; *Grant v South West Trains* 1998).

IV. BRITISH PROBLEMS WITH COHABITATION LAW

Let us now turn to treatment of cohabitants in the British context. While the *démariage* process is clear for all to see in Britain, both policymakers and the legislatures have been slow to respond. In Scotland, although proposals for reform which will include giving different-sex cohabitants the right to claim financial provision from a deceased partner's estate and will permit a claim to compensate for "economic disadvantage" suffered as a consequence of the relationship, have now broadly been accepted by the Scottish Executive (Scottish Executive 2000), these were put forward by the Scottish Law Commission as long ago as 1991 (Scottish Law Commission 1992). However, this does at least mean that Scotland's law is relatively consistent in its approach to cohabitants even if the law may operate harshly toward the vast majority of cohabitants who do not fall within the strict requirements of a marriage by cohabitation and repute (see generally Barlow and Bissett-Johnson 2003). In England and Wales on the other hand, in the 1970s an ad hoc but broadly functional and inclusive approach began to be adopted by both the courts and the legislature. Yet to date there still has been no cohesive response to the cohabitation phenomenon. Let us consider what this means to cohabitants at different points in a cohabitation relationship in England and Wales.[14]

A. DURING THE RELATIONSHIP

Whereas spouses in marriage automatically acquire occupation rights in the family home owned or rented by their spouse (Family Law Act 1996: s. 30), no such occupation rights are extended to cohabitants. Under domestic violence legislation, an "occupation order" can be made for no more than twelve months in favor of a heterosexual cohabitant when the relationship is breaking down due to domestic violence (Family Law Act 1996: s. 36). Unlike a married father, a cohabiting father does not automatically acquire parental responsibility[15] for his child on birth, and thus these fathers cannot automatically make formal decisions relating to their children, such as consenting to medical procedures or even adoption (Children Act 1989: s. 2(2)(b)). Although it can be acquired with the mother's consent by means of a simple procedure in which a parental responsibility agreement (in prescribed form) is signed and witnessed (ibid.: s. 4), only 5 percent of a recent and nationally representative British Social Attitudes survey of cohabitant fathers in England and Wales had done so (Barlow et al. 2001), leaving the vast majority with legal duties and obligations but without any positive legal status in respect of their child.[16] While the Adoption and Children Act 2002 implemented on December 1, 2003 now gives parental responsibility to unmarried fathers who, with the mother, jointly register the birth of their child, this is not retrospective and does not affect fathers who, for whatever reasons, do not jointly register the birth. As noted above, other provisions of the 2002 Act not yet implemented will permit same- and different-sex cohabitants in an "enduring relationship" to adopt a child. Ironically, however, no changes have been made or are proposed to extend the financial security benefits of marriage to such couples.

Although cohabitants, in contrast to spouses, have no legal duty to maintain each other during the relationship, on the application for any means-tested benefit or tax credit for the benefit of children, a cohabiting couple will be regarded as if they were married. Thus their means are aggregated to assess eligibility. However, in contrast to the spousal context, if the partner in receipt of the benefit or tax credit fails to share this income with their partner, there is no legal redress (cf. Matrimonial Causes Act 1973: s. 27; Domestic Proceedings and Magistrates' Courts Act 1978: s. 1). Neither do cohabitants benefit from capital tax concessions made to spouses. Thus whereas transfers between spouses are not subject to capital gains tax or inheritance tax (see Taxation of Capital Gains Act 1992 and Inheritance Tax Act 1984, respectively), cohabitants are treated as strangers liable to pay tax at the full rate.

B. ON RELATIONSHIP BREAKDOWN

On relationship breakdown, there is certainly no "divorce-law equivalent" for cohabiting couples in any British jurisdiction. There is no duty to pay maintenance to a former cohabitant, nor to redistribute property between the partners according to family law principles when cohabiting partners separate. Instead, strict property law normally applies.

While in English property law (in contrast to Scotland where there is no such redress) resulting and constructive trusts and proprietary estoppel are all devices which have been used to protect cohabitants (both same- and different-sex) from the harsher consequences of strict property law in some cases (*Hammond v Mitchell* 1999; *Drake v Whip* 1996; *Wayling v Jones* 1995), this has been significantly more restrictive than in Canada and Australia (see, e.g., *Peter v Beblow* 1993 and *Baumgartner v Baumgartner* 1987, respectively). While the application of these doctrines in the English context is far from uniform, the courts have at least been clear that homemaking contributions or contributions to the welfare of the family by a cohabitant are not alone sufficient to establish an interest in the family home. Such domestic services cannot constitute evidence of the requisite common intention to share the property unless there has also be a direct financial contribution to the acquisition of the family home or an express or implied promise of a share in the home which has been relied upon detrimentally (*Lloyds Bank plc v Rossett* 1991; *Midland Bank v Cooke* 1995; *Drake v Whip* 1996; *Eves v Eves* 1975; *Hammond v Mitchell* 1999; *Le Foe v Le Foe and Woolwich plc* 2001).

This is the case even where one partner was totally financially dependent on the other during a long-term relationship and/or the other partner has gained advantage from the domestic and/or childcare services provided. However, unless an order is made against the family home for the benefit of a minor child of the relationship under provisions themselves likely to be less generous than those available to married parents (see Children Act 1989: s. 15 and sch. 1), the proceeds will be divided in accordance with strict property law.[17] Perhaps most harshly, this is also the case where the cohabitants' relationship ends when their children have reached adulthood leaving the primary caring partner, often female and of an age where it is more difficult to find employment or acquire new skills, without any legal remedy. This is well illustrated by the facts in the classic case of *Burns v Burns* (1984, ch. 317), a decision which is still good law. After nineteen years of unmarried cohabitation during which she raised two children, worked part-time and paid some of the household bills, Valerie Burns was unable to establish either an express or inferred "common intention" sufficient to found a constructive trust under which she and her partner shared ownership of their family home. She thus had no beneficial interest in the home purchased in her partner's name and had no other legal redress available to her. She therefore left the relationship with nothing. As was recognized by the Court of Appeal in that case, this is in sharp contrast to spouses, where family assets may be redistributed on divorce whether or not there are minor children, and largely regardless of the original ownership of assets.[18] Indeed, recent developments in case law governing financial provision on divorce have served to widen the gulf between married and cohabiting couples on relationship breakdown. On divorce, the division of assets between spouses must now be measured against a "yardstick of equality" where assets exceed needs and provided there is no "stellar" contribution by one party to the marriage, an equal division of the assets should be made (in effect imposing a deferred community of property; see *White v White*

2001; *Cowan v Cowan* 2001; *Lambert v Lambert* 2002). Where there is no such surplus of assets, the housing needs of the parties and especially those of the parent caring for any minor children (whose welfare must in all cases be the court's first consideration when deciding financial provision on divorce[19]) should be met first (*Cordle v Cordle* 2002). Thus a divorcing homemaker spouse where the major assets including the home are in the name of the other spouse will usually receive at least half of the assets, whereas an equivalent homemaker cohabitant in a similar position must prove an interest under a constructive trust (or perhaps proprietary estoppel) to retain any share of the home, which as Valerie Burns found to her cost, is often a difficult and always an unpredictable prospect for the economically weaker cohabitant partner.[20]

Some remedies (usually inferior to those for married couples) are now available to heterosexual cohabitants in respect of the rented family home. Schedule 7 to the Family Law Act 1996 does now allow a nontenant cohabitant to apply for a transfer of tenancy order on relationship breakdown.[21] However, the criteria applied are less childcentric than in the married context in that again the welfare of the child is not the court's first consideration. Thus other factors, such as who was the original tenant, may weigh more heavily into the equation than in the divorce context. In the case of applications by nontenant cohabitants, extra criteria have to be applied including the nature of the relationship and the lack of the commitment given in marriage, although the presence of children "for whom both parties have parental responsibility" and the length of time the parties have cohabited must also be taken into account (Family Law Act 1996: sch. 7, para. 5 and s. 41).

Whereas the child support legislation applies equally to separated married and unmarried parents, capital orders made routinely between divorcing spouses to share out the family assets are rarely made in the unmarried context, where the remedies that are available draw no distinctions between former cohabiting parents and parents whose child was born of a more casual relationship. In principle lump sums, settlements and transfer of property orders between unmarried parents for the benefit of any child of the relationship are available (Children Act 1989: sch. 1, para. 2). However, because a cohabitant parent has no claim for financial provision against their former partner in their own right, orders made for the benefit of the children of cohabitant parents are far less generous than the combined package awarded to the resident parent and children on divorce.[22] In *T v S* 1994 a so-called *Mesher* order was made whereby the father was ordered to purchase a home for the benefit of the five children of his cohabiting relationship, to be held on trust until the youngest child reached the age of 21. However, an order made at first instance that the home then be sold and the proceeds of sale divided between the children was overturned on appeal on the grounds that following decisions in the divorce context,[23] it was inappropriate for the children to benefit as adults and furthermore, such an order would provide the mother and former cohabitant with an inappropriate "indirect windfall." Instead, the whole of the home was ordered to revert to the father. Rather than expanding the remit of orders that can be made for the benefit of a child to compensate for the lack of adult claims, the provisions have been restrictively interpreted by the courts, widening the gulf between the married and unmarried family (see also *A v A* 1994; *J v C* 1999).

C. ON DEATH OF A COHABITANT

The law applicable in the event of the death of a cohabitant is confused and contradictory. In the context of tenancy succession certain styles of rented family home will automatically be transferred to a cohabitant on the death of the tenant partner regardless of how long the couple have cohabited, effectively treating the couple as if they were married from the outset.[24] The cohabitant of a secure (local authority) tenant on the other hand will only qualify if they have lived with the deceased tenant for at least twelve months prior to the death (see Housing Act 1985: s. 87).

Only a spouse will automatically inherit all or some of their spouse's estate where their husband or wife dies without making a will (Administration of Estates Act 1925: s. 46), although both a spouse and a heterosexual cohabitant of at least two years' standing do now have the right to make a claim for financial provision under a deceased partner's estate where no or inadequate provision has been made for them by will (see Inheritance [Provision for Family and Dependants] Act 1975: s. 1(1)(a) and (b)(A)). However, in the case of a cohabitant (unlike that of a spouse), the claim is limited to reasonable "*maintenance*" (see Inheritance (Provision for Family and Dependants) Act 1975: s. 2; emphasis added). A spouse, in contrast, can expect to receive a more generous award, comparable to that which would have been made on divorce. This "similar but inferior" approach has also been taken in a number of other contexts including compensation claims for wrongful death of a cohabitant partner.[25] Strikingly, where a cohabiting mother dies, the child's father (unless he is one of the 5 percent who have acquired parental responsibility or the mother has appointed him as testamentary guardian) will have to apply to the court for parental responsibility for and guardianship of his own child with whom he has always lived (Children Act 1989: s. 4–5).

In yet other situations on death of a partner, cohabitants will be treated as strangers. Thus a cohabitant is not entitled to register the death of their partner. As previously observed, there is no exemption or reduction in inheritance tax payable on a gift left by a deceased cohabitant to their partner, including the family home, which must often be sold to pay the inheritance tax bill even when the home is jointly owned by partners. Pension payments on retirement to one partner will not be increased to maintain a dependent cohabitant nor will they have any widow's pension or automatic entitlement out of their partner's estate on death (Administration of Estates Act 1925: s. 46). It is also interesting to note that whereas same-sex cohabitants, who until very recently were almost completely ignored by the law, could draw a small amount of comfort from the fact that they at least had the advantage of knowing where they stood, they too are now being drawn in to a process of ad hoc reform, aided by the wording of Schedule 1 of the Rent Act 1977 and the Human Rights Act 1998.[26]

D. A BRITISH WAY FORWARD?

Thus family law's protective role of the weaker economic spouse and children does not extend in any consistent way to functionally similar cohabitants, leaving the law complex and confusing. In the property law context, there has been near unanimity among commentators that this situation is unsatisfactory (see, e.g., Gardner 1993, Wong 1998 and Barlow & Lind 1999), a view now endorsed by the Law Commission:

> The current requirements for establishing the existence of an interest under a trust are not ideally suited to the typical informality of those sharing a home. We feel that to demand proof of an intention to share the beneficial interest in the home can be somewhat unrealistic, as people do not tend to think about their home in such legalistic terms. The emphasis on financial input towards the acquisition of the home fails to recognise the realities of most cohabiting relationships. Finally and importantly, the uncertainties in the present law can cause lengthy and costly litigation, wasting court time, public funding and the parties' own resources. (Law Commission 2002: para. 2.112)

Of even greater concern, are research findings that those affected may well be completely unaware of their disadvantaged position. The most recent study in this connection was conducted as part of the British Social Attitudes Survey 2000 (the "BSA survey") in which a module of questions specifically addressing attitudes toward marriage, cohabitation and the law was asked of a nationally representative sample of 3,101 people (Barlow et al. 2001). A follow-up in-depth study of seventy-two cohabitants and former cohabitants sought to further explore the issues raised by the BSA survey (Barlow & James 2004).[27] Results clearly demonstrate that cohabitation is widely accepted across British society as both a partnering and parenting structure with 67 percent of respondents agreeing that 'it is all right for a couple to live together without intending to get married' and only 27 percent believing that married parents make better parents than unmarried ones. Interestingly, while only a tiny minority (9 percent) agreed that "marriage was just a piece of paper," despite the redistribution of assets available on divorce and death in the married context, only 48 percent thought that marriage offered greater financial security than living together.

That people see cohabitation or marriage as personal lifestyle choices was underlined by their surprising lack of awareness about the different legal consequences of these relationships. Fifty-six percent of the BSA national survey believed that cohabiting for a period of time gave rise to a common-law marriage giving them the same legal rights as married couples. Among cohabitants, this false belief rose to 59 percent and the in-depth sample found that the source of this was most often family and friends although the media and official social security application forms had also informed a significant number of views. None of the interviewees had sought legal advice specifically in relation to their position as cohabitants. The idea came through strongly that you only go and see an attorney if things go wrong. When you add to this the finding by another research team, that 41 percent of their sample of 173 engaged couples (73 percent of whom were cohabiting) thought that marriage would not change the legal nature of their relationship (Hibbs, Barton & Beswick 2001), a disturbing picture of legal misperceptions emerges. What is more worrying still to policymakers, is that consciously at least, in most cases people's perceptions of the legal consequences had no impact on their decision to cohabit or marry. As Melanie, one respondent to the in-depth survey, explained, "I don't think that affects us—or my choice or what I'm doing in any way." Neither were they prompted to seek legal advice or make wills or cohabitation agreements, despite over a quarter of cohabitants living in an owner-occupied home bought in their partner's sole name. In the national survey, just 14 percent of current cohabitants had made a will and only 10 percent had a written agreement about ownership shares in the family home. Not believing in common-law marriage did not significantly increase a respondent's likelihood to make legal arrangements, although many had long-held good intentions to see an attorney "to sort things out" (Barlow et al. 2001; Barlow & James 2004: 163). The national survey found clear support, among both cohabitants and the wider population, for reform of the law to assimilate the rights of married and unmarried couples as they considered key aspects of the current law unjust. Thus 61 percent thought a cohabitant of ten year's standing should have the same financial provision on relationship breakdown as if she were married, 91 percent thought such a cohabitant should be able to remain in the family home after the death of her partner and a resounding 97 percent believed a cohabiting father should have the right to consent to his child's medical treatment. Among cohabitants, the support for reform rose even higher, with 70 percent of cohabitants supporting marriage-like financial provision on breakdown, 98 percent on death with 99 percent considering the inability of an unmarried father to consent to medical treatment because he has no parental responsibility to be unjust (Barlow et al. 2001). Thus the vast majority of cohabitants in Britain do not seem to be cohabiting in order to avoid the legal consequences of marriage as has been suggested (Deech 1980; Freeman 1984), but would welcome the extension of marriage like rights as other commentators have claimed (e.g., Bailey-Harris 1996). At the same time, there was also acceptance found by the study that marriage-like rights may not be appropriate for all. As Caroline, one of our respondents observed, "There's different things about different people though—what situation is good for one couple might not be for another couple."

The idea of a French-style partnership law open to same- and different-sex couples was also popular among current cohabitants in the in-depth study, although the low numbers of cohabitants who actually make wills or cohabitation contracts begs the question of whether this would in practice be used.

So how should the law in Britain respond? The Law Commission has confirmed the need for reform and has suggested a relationship-based (rather than a property-based) approach to the problem:

> [W]e have identified, in the course of this project, a wider need for the law to recognise and to respond to the increasing diversity of living arrangements in this country. We believe that further consideration should be given to the adoption—necessarily by legislation—of broader based approaches to personal relationships. (Law Commission 2002: iv)

To date, this idea has fallen on stony ground. However sensible this might seem when one looks at the need to strive for legal cohesion and ensure that legal and social norms coincide, this does not tie in with current family policy in Britain which has as its primary guiding force the political imperative of not being seen to undermine marriage.

As a matter of family policy, the British government aspires to the American approach of strengthening marriage (Barlow & Duncan 2000; Bowman 2004). Yet it does not quite have the courage of its convictions and claims not to want to coerce people into the married state, employing instead communitarian persuasion. This is well illustrated in its 1998 family policy consultation paper *Supporting Families* (Great Britain. Home Office 1998):

> This Government believes that marriage provides a strong foundation for stable relationships. This does not mean trying to make people marry, or criticising or penalising people who choose not to. We do not believe the government should interfere in people's lives in that way. But we do share the belief of the majority of people that marriage provides the most reliable framework for raising children. (Ibid.: para. 4.3)

It goes on:

> The truth is that families are, and always will be, mainly shaped by private choices well beyond the influence of government. That is how it should be. But that is no excuse for government not to do what it can [to strengthen marriage]. (Ibid.: para. 16)

This 1998 blueprint for British family policy virtually ignored different-sex cohabitants, stating only "it might be worthwhile to produce a guide for cohabitees, made available through Citizen's Advice Bureaux, libraries etc." (ibid.: para. 4.15) and did not even mention same-sex cohabitants, who clearly in 1998 were not considered to be a "family" in need of support. Marriage alone was to be strengthened and there was to be no return to a neutral, functional approach to family regulation by policymakers and legislators under New Labour as a response to the social trends.

However, aided by the Human Rights Act 1998 (which essentially incorporated the European Convention on Human Rights into British domestic law), this is an approach which has come into favor with the courts, at least in the context of the rented family home. In *Fitzpatrick v Sterling Housing Association Ltd* 1999 the House of Lords (prior to implementation of the 1998 Act) permitted a same-sex cohabitant of longstanding to succeed to an assured tenancy of the family home as a member of his deceased partner's family under paragraph 3(1), schedule 1 to the Rent Act 1977 based on the marriage-like nature of their relationship, but ruled that being of the same sex, he could not live as his "wife or husband" as demanded by the definition of cohabitant contained in the Act. On this analysis, it meant that a surviving same-sex partner would always be denied a more favorable statutory tenancy available only to spouses or to different-sex cohabitants under paragraph 2(2). However, despite endorsement by both Strasbourg[28] and the House of Lords (see *Fitzpatrick* which approved *Harrogate Borough Council v Simpson* 1986) of such discrimination, this approach was successfully challenged in *Ghaidan v Mendoza* 2002. Here the Court of Appeal found that the statutory inclusion of different-sex but not same-sex cohabitants as spousal tenancy successors was a discriminatory breach of the right to respect for one's home under articles 8 and 14 of the European Convention. Accordingly, to avoid the apparent incompatibility of schedule 1 of the Rent Act 1977 with the Human Rights Act 1998, it was declared that paragraph 2(2) of the schedule was to be given effect as reading the words "as his or her wife or husband" to mean "as if they were his or her wife or husband" (ibid. at paras. 35–36).

This decision may have far-reaching consequences in other contexts where a heterosexual definition of cohabitants has been enacted by statute. This might include the right to apply for occupation rights in the family home vested in a partner's name (Family Law Act 1996: s. 36), and the right to apply for financial provision out of the estate on death of a partner (Inheritance Act 1975: s. 1A; Probert 2003; Loveland 2003), although this is contingent upon the right to private and family life, one's home and correspondence guaranteed by article 8, extending to these legislative areas. Whether in time, this so-called "horizontal effect" of articles 8 and 14 could also be used by the courts to further reduce discrimination against same- and different-sex cohabitants as compared to married couples remains to be seen, although according to some commentators this is not beyond the realms of possibility (see, e.g., Wong 2003).

In terms of legislative initiatives in England and Wales, it is the ending of direct discrimination against same-sex cohabitants using a *form* approach which fits more easily with New Labour's communitarian marriage-promotion agenda. While arguments rage in the Westminster parliament and beyond as to whether marriage is better than heterosexual cohabitation for children (Morgan 1999) or whether to assert this is to muddle correlation with cause (Lewis 2001; Barlow & Duncan 2000), the easy way out is to focus on a form-based remedy for same-sex cohabitants which, providing it can be distinguished from lesbian and gay marriage, largely avoids debates about the undermining of marriage. Therein lies the attractiveness of the Same-Sex Civil Partnership Register to the British government. At the same time, private ordering is to be encouraged for unmarried and unregistered partners. While acknowledging the existence of the common-law marriage myth whereby people believe cohabitation gives couples rights equivalent to marriage (Barlow et al. 2001), current policy goes no further than accepting the need for better information to be provided to encourage cohabitants to make wills and cohabitation contracts concerning their property. In its response to the consultation exercise following its Civil Partnership proposals, it sets out its case: "Opposite-sex couples can already attain legal (and socially recognised) status for their relationships through marriage. . . . We recognise that not all opposite-sex couples may wish to marry, but that decision is theirs to make, and they have the option to do so if they wish . . ." The Department of Constitutional Affairs is leading a cross-government working group to explore how best to raise public awareness about the rights and responsibilities of different-sex cohabitants and to dispel the myths around common-law marriage (DTI. Women and Equality Unit 2003b paras. 3.5–3.6). The fact that, as the BSA survey has shown, this is not likely to significantly increase the numbers of cohabitants who have the foresight and resources to enter into such complex and expensive legal arrangements (Barlow et al. 2001; Barlow & James 2004) particularly when they (or at least the weaker economic partner) intended to get married or register their agreement, is unlikely to sway government thinking.

The Law Society of England and Wales, echoing the calls of the Law Commission, have put forward proposals which would introduce an Australian-style functional approach to cohabitation relationships alongside a European-style partnerships register for same-sex couples (Law Society 2002). Its proposals for unregistered cohabitants are limited to same- and diferrent-sex cohabitants living together in a shared household in a relationship analogous to husband and wife who have a "relevant child" or whose relationship has lasted for at least two years (ibid.: para. 14). Family law-style protection would be extended to cohabitants against economic disadvantage in all areas of law where it is provided in the married context. However, it would offer less protection than that appertaining to marriage, deliberately retaining a clear legal distinction between the married and cohabiting status (ibid.: para. 17). Yet this idea has not been taken up by those in power. In Scotland (where very few legal concessions have yet been made to cohabitants) on the other hand, similar proposals giving cohabitants the right to compensation from a partner where "economic disadvantage" has been suffered have been endorsed by the Scottish Executive (Scottish Executive 2000) and will be acted upon.

Thus the law in England and Wales seems set to continue down its haphazard path and may well continue to ignore the need for reform identified by research, preferring instead to preserve a Napoleonic stance in the almost certainly unrealistic hope that this will strengthen marriage.

V. THE WAY FORWARD IN EUROPE

As we have seen, the law relating to cohabitation in Europe is struggling to respond to the changes in family restructuring and this has resulted in a diversification of approaches to the legal protection of families and family life. Many jurisdictions now recognize that there is diversity but which aspects of this diversity attract legal rights and remedies is enormously variable. Perhaps at a time of rapid social change, this is unavoidable, particularly when the preservation of traditional family values as a response to moral panic is still being attempted in some jurisdictions. However, from the point of view of legal harmonization of family law within Europe it is unhelpful. In essence, it seems that in Britain as in most other European jurisdictions the purpose of family law needs to be reexamined and a Europe-wide policy developed which is capable of accommodating diversity and difference. If its purpose is merely to regulate state-approved formal relationships, then some harmonization of what is available is needed. At the very least, the current trends support the general availability of heterosexual marriage plus marriage-like same-sex registered partnerships which are then recognized in other European states. However, this will undoubtedly leave the majority of cohabitants unregulated. A purely form approach would allow for a PACS-style law which does not carry the patriarchal baggage of marriage and which imposes fewer obligations in return for fewer rights to co-exist alongside the marriage model. This would enable another tier of cohabiting couples to gain a legally recognized family status and make enforceable yet personalized and perhaps flexible agreements concerning their family property while choosing a lesser public obligation or commitment than that of marriage in return for fewer automatic substantive family law rights.

However, the form approach presupposes that people think about the legal consequences of marriage and cohabitation before they enter into couple relationships, which certainly in Britain does not seem to be the case. In all European jurisdictions, it seems the majority of those marrying accept the default matrimonial property regime (Barlow, Callus & Cooke 2003), which again may indicate that people everywhere do not focus on the legal consequences of marriage at the outset of the relationship. In addition the form approach assumes that the law, by imposing form-driven legal norms, can act to make people structure their families in ways of which policymakers approve. Yet where social norms shift away from legal norms, the power of the law to act in this way is seriously open to question and may well be subject to a "rationality mistake" (Barlow & Duncan 2000). Support for this hypothesis can be seen by considering the Scottish example. In Scotland, where in contrast to England and Wales, no marriage-like legal rights and remedies have to date been extended to heterosexual cohabitants, the proportion of people cohabiting and social attitudes toward cohabitation are on par with those found in England and Wales (Barlow 2002). Thus while the lack of legal rights operates harshly on those choosing to cohabit in Scotland on breakdown or death, it does not appear to have in any way stemmed the tide in those choosing to cohabit rather than marry.

This of course begs the question of why people choose to cohabit. Are they attempting to avoid legal regulation, in which case it is arguably not appropriate to impose marriage-like rights and responsibilities? Or are they unaware of their legal vulnerability or have competing priorities which have delayed their marriage or their visit to obtain legal advice? What about situations where one partner wishes to marry or register a partner but the other is less than candid in their reasons for not wanting to go down this path? Here perhaps a functional approach is called for to avoid exploitation.

It is clear that the way forward is not easy to agree on and what is right in one situation may not be appropriate in another. Yet it is also clear that the choices people are making in this private sphere may not be true choices at all as people, at least in Britain, are not aware of their legal position or do not even consider it when making decisions about family structuring. However, at the point of crisis, there is no route back and the harshness of the law is felt by the more vulnerable family members (including children, indirectly) whom family law aims to protect.

Perhaps the best way forward is to "de-moralize" the legal response to these trends, and provide a plurality of legal regulative structures to accommodate the now diverse family forms that are found and provide at least some protection for all families, particularly where there are children, yet allow people to opt out and make their own arrangements where there is agreement that the default position imposed by law is unwanted. Such plurality would aim to balance the need for family law protection or "maternalism" (Bailey-Harris 1996) in its recognition of the way in which family relationships distort the labor market position of the primary caring parent against the right to individual choice and autonomy in regulation of family affairs. The new aims for family law would be made clear and, if not universally agreed upon, then at least respected across Europe. In essence, perhaps in this sphere of regulation at least, Europe should not be afraid to choose Teubner's "reflexive law" approach, sacrificing a priori principles for a functional approach which will safeguard better the protective aims of family law.

In looking at the existing models, the opt-in approach of the Spanish autonomous communities which may also be extended to functionally similar families in appropriate cases may be the best way forward. It is a cohesive family law response which aims to protect families, respect autonomy in individual cases yet ensure that there is a remedy for those on whom the law would otherwise act harshly. This, alongside the Swedish model and the proposals for the Law Society of England and Wales (Law Society 2002), comes closest to balancing individual autonomy with social reality and social justice, providing a cohesive response which can be easily understood by those affected. It avoids the piecemeal accretion of rights in particular contexts which have rendered the law so complex and inconsistent in England

and Wales and avoids the complete abandonment of unmarried or unregistered cohabitants who are performing for society the same partnering and parenting functions traditionally ascribed to marriage. It also avoids the disincentive to marriage for those unwilling to share their wealth with their partner and ensures such a result can only be guaranteed if their partner has consented to this.

Another important issue would be the definition of qualifying relationships. This could be limited to cohabiting couples who have shared a communal life for a period of time or could even encompass the wider functional approach taken in some Australian States where financial commitment and domestic support of another adult regardless of any relationship become the trigger for family law-style regulation.[29]

The scale of the changing trends and attitudes toward marriage and cohabitation (Kiernan 2004) surely now indicate that it is time for Europe to eschew its Napoleonic legacy in the family law sphere and acknowledge that in the twentieth century, some new and principled ideas are called for to meet the needs of our less marriage-centric society.

ANNE BARLOW *is a Reader in Law at the University of Wales, Aberystwyth. She has a particular interest in Family Law and Policy, especially the law relating to cohabitants which is the main focus of her research. She recently directed a research project funded by the Nuffield Foundation on Family Restructuring, the Common Law Marriage Myth and the Need for Legal Realism, conducted with Simon Duncan (Professor of Comparative Social Policy, Bradford University) and Alison Park, (Research Director, National Centre for Social Research).*

NOTES

1. The European perspective of this article focuses on West European states and principally those who are current members of the European Union.
2. The Cohabitees (Joint Homes) Act 1987 originally applied only to different sex cohabiting couples, stating that their assets were to be divided equally (s. 8) unless alternative provision had been agreed in writing (s. 5) or unless equal division was unfair in the light of the duration of the relationship or other relevant circumstances (s. 9). The Homosexual Cohabitees Act 1987 provided that its provisions should apply equally to homosexual couples.
3. Providing a cohabiting couple hold themselves out as married (which is increasingly rare), the court may declare a couple to have a "marriage by cohabitation, habit and repute," where they have lived together as husband and wife and held themselves out as married. This is little used but once recognized by the court, it creates a valid marriage (see further Barton & Bissett-Johnson 1999).
4. At the European level, work is ongoing on a draft European Civil Code under the leadership of Professor Christian von Bar of Osnabrück University. Similarly, as reported to the Sixth European Conference on Family Law, Strasbourg 14–15 October 2002, both the European Commission and the Council of Europe are considering Europeanization of Succession Law—see www.coe.int/legalco-operation. In the family law context, see Clarkson 2002 and note the initiative

by Professor Katharina Boele-Woelki of the University of Utrecht and other academics to set up a Commission on European Family Law to "study the feasibility of and to initiate practical steps towards the harmoni[z]ation of family law in Europe" (see http://www.law.uu.nl/priv/cefl).

5. See *Fitzpatrick v Sterling Housing Association* (1999) and *Ghaidan v Mendoza* (2002) where the right to succeed to a private rented tenancy was extended to same-sex cohabitants firstly as a member of their partner's family and subsequently as a "spouse." Note also that the Immigration Rules 2000 (para. 295A–295O) and the Criminal Injuries Compensation Authority scheme 2001 (para. 38[a]) have both extended their remit to include same-sex cohabitants and the Law Commission has recommended they should be eligible to make claims for the wrongful death of a partner (see Law Commission 1999).
6. The intention to introduce legislation was announced in the Queen's Speech, 26 November 2003. See http://politics.guardian.co.uk/queensspeech2003/story/0,13994,1093558,00.html. It is likely to follow the model contained in the government position paper *Civil Partnership: A Framework for the Legal Recognition of Same-sex Couples* (DTI. Women and Equality Unit 2003a) which was put forward following the withdrawal of the Civil Partnerships Bill 2002 (a Private Members Bill) which would have extended the register to both same- and different-sex cohabitants.
7. See http://www.scotland.gov.uk/pages/news/2003/09/SEJD309.aspx
8. The Report in 2001 of the Commission considering "Children in Homosexual Families" which recommended the recent changes to adoption and custody law for registered partners also has recommended that infertility treatment should be available to registered partners (Savolainen 2001: 39).
9. Act on Registered Partnerships of 17th December 1997 which amended the Dutch Civil Code and came into force on January 1, 1998.
10. Article 1: 149 and 1: 77 Dutch Civil Code.
11. Norway has introduced a Joint Households Act which deals with cohabitants of two years or more standing or who have or are expecting a child together but is not restricted to sexual relationships. It does not provide for the sharing of the value of jointly used assets as in Sweden but merely governs the right to take over the home or household goods on death or at the end of the relationship (see Agell 2003: 127).
12. Aragon Unmarried Couples Law 1999 article 3 and Catalonia Stable Union of De Facto Couples Law 1998 article 2 Navarre Unmarried Stable Couples Law 2000 article 12. For full details of these schemes see Casals (2003).
13. Author's translation of article 3, inserting art 5615-8 into the French Civil Code.
14. The following summary of the legal position in England and Wales draws on a similar discussion in Barlow and James (2004: 147–51).
15. The Children Act 1989: s. 3(1) defines parental responsibility as "all the rights, duties, powers, responsibilities and authority which by law a parent of a child has in relation to the child and his property."
16. As detailed below, this question was explored as part of the British Social Attitudes Survey conducted in 2000 (see Barlow et al. 2001).
17. See Trusts of Land and Appointment of Trustees Act 1996: s. 14–15. Unless a resulting or constructive trust can be proved to have arisen, a nonlegal owner will have no beneficial interest in the home. Even where such an interest has arisen, it may be impossible to avoid the home being sold, although s. 15 does require the court to have regard to the purpose for which the property was held under trust and the welfare of any minor occupying or reasonably expected to occupy the property as their home.
18. See Matrimonial Causes Act 1973: s. 25 for the full list of criteria applied. This includes the standard of living during the marriage, the age of the parties and

duration of the marriage, the parties' respective current and future income and assets, needs and resources as well as financial and (critically) nonfinancial contributions made and likely to be made to the welfare of the family by each of the parties.

19. The Matrimonial Causes Act 1973: s. 25(1) states: "It shall be the duty of the court on deciding whether to exercise its powers under ss. 23, 24, or 24A above and if so, in what manner, to have regard to all the circumstances of the case, first consideration being given to the welfare while a minor to any child of the family who has not attained the age of 18 years."
20. For a discussion of the unsatisfactory nature of the current law in this area see Barlow and Lind 1999 and more recently the Law Commission 2002. Some recent developments in the case law governing constructive trusts have improved the position where the nonowner partner has made a small but direct contribution to the purchase of the home at which point the court is now able to "undertake a survey of whole course of dealings between the parties" in quantifying the respective beneficial interests (*Midland Bank v Cooke* 1995 and *Drake v Whip* 1996), but this is far from being a precise science. In *Le Foe v Le Foe* 2001, financial but indirect contributions inter alia to clear a mortgage debt on the home in a long marriage were considered sufficient to found a beneficial interest under a constructive trust. However, these developments have not affected the law in situations analogous to those in *Burns*.
21. The Matrimonial Causes Act 1973: s. 24 was and remains only available to married couples. The Children Act 1989: sch. 1 has always allowed transfer of property orders between the unmarried for the benefit of a minor child of the relationship, which was deemed in *K v K* 1992 to include rented secure tenancies.
22. For a recent study of the gulf between the contrasting settlements made on relationship breakdown in the married and cohabiting contexts, see Arthur, Lewis and Maclean 2002.
23. See *Chamberlain v Chamberlain* 1974 followed in the unmarried context in *Kiely v Kiely* 1988.
24. Rent Act 1977: sch. 1, para. 2 as amended and Housing Act 1988: s. 17 extend this to protected and assured tenancies respectively.
25. The Fatal Accidents Act 1976 permits claims by cohabitants but are excluded from the generous award of statutory bereavement damages which is limited to spouses.
26. See *Fitzpatrick v Sterling Housing Association* 1999 and *Mendoza v Ghaidan* 2002 which have respectively extended tenancy succession of the Rent Act protected family home to same-sex couples first as members of their deceased partner's family and then as spouses The *Mendoza* decision if approved will have further major ramifications for similarly worded statutes extending spousal rights to those "living as husband and wife."
27. Both aspects of this project were funded by the Nuffield Foundation.
28. *S v United Kingdom* 1985 where the Court of Appeal decision of *Harrogate Borough Council v Simpson* 1986 was not found to be in breach of the European Convention on Human Rights.
29. See, e.g., Australian Capital Territories Domestic Relationships Act 1994: s. 31 as amended which defines a "domestic relationship" as "a personal relationship (other than a legal marriage) between two adults in which one provides personal or financial commitment and support of a domestic nature for the material benefit of the other" and the New South Wales Property (Relationships) Legislation Amendment Act 1999. Here the definition of a domestic relationship is any "close personal relationship between two adult persons whether or nor related by family, who are living together one or each of whom provides the other with domestic support and personal care." Other definitions can be found

in Canada Ontario Family Law Act s. 29 where the term spouse is extended to cohabitants and New Zealand where Property Law (Amendment) Act 2001 s. 2D defines cohabitants according to a list of criteria, an approach suggested by the Law Society in their consultation paper (Law Society 2002).

REFERENCES

Agell, Anders (2003) "The Legal Status of Same-Sex Couples in Europe—A Critical Analysis." In *Legal Recognition of Same-Sex Couples in Europe*, edited by K. Boele-Woelki & A. Fuchs. Antwerp: Intersentia.

Arthur, Sue, Jane Lewis, and Mavis Maclean (2002) *Settling Up: Making Financial Arrangements After Divorce or Separation.* London: National Centre for Social Research.

Bailey, Martha (2004) "Regulation of Cohabitation and Marriage in Canada," *Law & Policy* 26: 153–75.

Bailey-Harris, Rebecca (1996) "Law and the Unmarried Couple—Oppression or Liberation?" *Child and Family Law Quarterly* 8(2): 137–47.

Bailey-Harris, Rebecca (2000) "Dividing the Assets of the Unmarried Family—Recent Lessons from Australia," *International Family Law* (September): 90–92.

Bala, Nicholas, and Rebecca Bromwich (2002) "Context and Inclusivity in Canada's Evolving Definition of the Family," *International Journal of Law, Policy and the Family* 16: 145–80.

Barlow, Anne (2002) "Cohabitation and Marriage in Scotland: Attitudes, Myths and the Law." In *New Scotland, New Society?*, edited by J. Curtice, D. McCrone, A. Park & L. Paterson. Edinburgh: Edinburgh Univ. Press.

Barlow, Anne, and Alastair Bissett-Johnson (2003) "Cohabitation and the Reform of Scots Law," *Juridical Review* 2: 105–28.

Barlow, Anne, Therèse Callus, and Elizabeth Cooke (2003) "Community of Property: A Study for England and Wales," *Family Law* 34: 47–52.

Barlow, Anne, and Simon Duncan (2000) "Family Law, Moral Rationalities and New Labour's Communitarianism: Part II," *Journal of Social Welfare and Family Law* 22: 129–43.

Barlow, Anne, Simon Duncan, Grace James, and Alison Park (2001) "Just a Piece of Paper? Marriage and Cohabitation in Britain." In *British Social Attitudes: The 18th Report—Public Policy and Social Ties*, edited by A. Park, J. Curtice, K. Thomson, L. Jarvis & C. Bromley. London: Sage.

Barlow, Anne, and Grace James (2004) "Regulating Marriage and Cohabitation in 21st Century Britain," *Modern Law Review* 67(2): 143–76.

Barlow, Anne, and Craig Lind (1999) "A Matter of Trust: the Allocation of Rights in the Family Home," *Legal Studies* 19(4): 468–88.

Barton, Christopher, and Alastair Bissett-Johnson (1999) "The Similarities and Differences in Scottish and English Family Law in Dealing with Changing Family Patterns," *Journal of Social Welfare and Family Law* 21(1): 1–21.

Boele-Woelki, Katharina (2003) "Registered Partnership and Same-Sex Marriage in the Netherlands." In *Legal Recognition of Same-Sex Couples in Europe*, edited by K. Boele-Woelki & A. Fuchs. Antwerp: Intersentia.

Bowman, Cynthia Grant (2004) "Legal Treatment of Cohabitation in the United States," *Law & Policy* 26: 119–52.

Bradley, David (1996) *Family Law and Political Culture.* London: Sweet and Maxwell.

Bradley, David (2001) "Regulation of Unmarried Cohabitation in West-European Jurisdictions–Determinants of Legal Policy" *International Journal of Law, Policy and the Family* 15: 22–50.

Casals, Miquel (2003) "Same-Sex Partnerships in the Legislation of the Spanish Autonomous Communities." In *Legal Recognition of Same-Sex Couples in Europe*, edited by K. Boele-Woelki & A. Fuchs. Antwerp: Intersentia.

Clarkson, Christopher (2002) "Brussels III—Matrimonial Property European Style," *Family Law* 32: 683–86.

Commaille, Jacques, and François De Singly (1997) *The European Family: The Family Question in the European Community*. Dortrecht: Kluwer.

Deech, Ruth (1980) "The Case against Legal Recognition of Cohabitation," *International Comparative Law Quarterly* 29: 480–97.

De Graaf, Nan Dirk, and Ariana Need (2000) "Losing Faith: is Britain Alone?" In *British Social Attitudes: Focusing on Diversity. The 17th Report*, edited by R. Jowell, A. Park, K. Thomson, C. Bromley & N. Stratford. Cambridge: Sage.

Finlay H.A., Rebecca Bailey-Harris, and Margaret Otlowski (1997) *Family Law in Australia*. 5th ed. Australia: Butterworths.

Freeman, Michael D. A. (1984) "Legal Ideologies, Patriarchal Precedents, and Domestic Violence." In *The State, the Law and the Family: Critical Perspectives*, edited by M. D. A. Freeman. London: Tavistock.

Gardner, Simon (1993) "Rethinking Family Property," *Law Quarterly Review* 109: 263–300.

Glendon, Mary Ann (1981) *The New Family and the New Property*. Toronto: Butterworths.

Great Britain. Department of Trade and Industry. (DTI) Women and Equality Unit (2003a) *Civil Partnership: A Framework for the Legal Recognition of Same-Sex Couples: June 2003*. London: Department of Trade and Industry. Available at http://www.womenandequalityunit.gov.uk/research/index.htm

Great Britain. Department of Trade and Industry. (DTI) Women and Equality Unit (2003b) *Responses to Civil Partnership: A Framework for the Legal Recognition of Same-Sex Couples: September 2003*. London: Department of Trade and Industry. Available at http://www.womenandequalityunit.gov.uk/research/index.htm

Great Britain. Home Office (1998) *Supporting Families: A Consultation Document*. London: Stationery Office.

Hamilton, Carolyn, and Alison Perry (2002) *Family Law in Europe*. London: Butterworths.

Hibbs, Mary, Christopher Barton, and J. Beswick (2001) "Why Marry? Perceptions of the Affianced," *Family Law* 31: 197–207.

Kiernan, Kathleen (2004) "Unmarried Cohabitation and Parenthood in Britain and Europe," *Law & Policy* 26: 33–56.

King, Michael, and Christine Piper (1995) *How the Law Thinks about Children*. Aldershot: Arena.

Law Commission for England and Wales (1999) *Claims for Wrongful Deaths Report no. 263*. London: HMSO.

Law Commission for England and Wales (2002) *Sharing Homes: A Discussion Paper*. London: Law Commission for England and Wales.

Law Society (2002) *Cohabitation: the Case for Clear Law. Proposals for Reform: July 2002*. London: Representation and Law Reform Directorate, Law Scoiety.

Lewis, Jane (2001) *The End of Marriage?* Cheltenham: Edward Elgar.

Loveland, Ian (2003) "Making It Up as They Go Along? The Court of Appeal on Same-Sex Spouses and Succession Rights to Tenancies," *Public Law* (Summer): 222–35.

Morgan, Patricia (1999) *Marriage-Lite: The Rise of Cohabitation and Its Consequences*. London: Institute for the Study of Civil Society.

O'Donovan, Katherine (1993) *Family Law Matters*. London: Pluto Press.

Probert, Rebecca (2003) "Tenancies and Same-Sex couples," *New Law Journal* 152(7058): 1801.

Probert, Rebecca (2004) "Cohabitation in Twentieth Century England and Wales: Law and Policy," *Law & Policy* 26: 13–32.
Probert, Rebecca, and Anne Barlow (2000) "Displacing Marriage—Diversification and Harmonisation within Europe," *Child and Family Law Quarterly* 12(2): 153–66.
Queen's Speech, 26 November 2003. Available at http://politics.guardian.co.uk/queensspeech2003/story/0,13994,1093558,00.html
Richardson, Nicky (2002) "The New Zealand Property (Relationships) Amendment Act 2001," *International Family Law* May: 86–89.
Savolainen, Matt (2003) "The Swedish and Finnish Partnership Acts: Similarities and Differences." In *Legal Recognition of Same-Sex Couples in Europe*, edited by K. Boele-Woelki & A. Fuchs. Antwerp: Intersentia.
Scottish Executive (2000) *Parents and Children*. Edinburgh: Scottish Executive.
Scottish Law Commission (1992) *Report on Family Law*. Edinburgh: Scottish Law Commission.
Smart, Carol (1997) "Wishful Thinking and Harmful Tinkering? Sociological Reflections on Family Policy," *Journal of Social Policy* 26(3): 301–22.
Teubner, Gunther (1993) "Substantive and Reflexive Elements in Modern Law," *Law & Society Review* 17(2): 239–85.
Wong, Simone (1998) "Constructive Trusts over the Family Home: Lessons to be Learned from Other Commonwealth Jurisdictions?" *Legal Studies* 18: 369–90.
Wong, Simone (2003) "Re-thinking *Rossett* from a Human Rights Perspective." In *New Perspectives on Property Law, Human Rights and the Home*, edited by A. Hudson. London: Cavendish.
Ytterberg, Hans (2001) "A Swedish Story of Love and Legislation." In *Legal Recognition of Same-Sex Partnerships*, edited by R. Wintermute & M. Andenaes. Oxford: Hart.

CASES CITED

Australia
Baumgartner v Baumgartner (1987) 164 CLR 137.

Canada
Peter v Beblow (1993) 44 RFL (3d) 329.

England and Wales
A v A (A minor) (Financial provision) (1994) 1 FLR 657.
ADT v United Kingdom (2000) 2 FLR 697.
B v United Kingdom (2000) 1 FLR 1.
Burns v Burns (1984) Ch 317.
Cordle v Cordle (2002) 1 WLR 1441.
Cowan v Cowan (2001) 2 FLR 192.
Drake v Whip (1996) 1 FLR 826.
Eves v Eves (1975) 3 All ER 768.
Fitzpatrick v Sterling Housing Association (1999) 4 All ER 705.
Ghaidan v Mendoza (2002) EWCA Civ 1533, (2002) All ER (D) 32 (Nov).
Grant v South West Trains (1998) 1 FLR 839.
Hammond v Mitchell (1999) 2 All ER 109.
Harrogate Borough Council v Simpson (1986) 2 FLR 91.
J v C (Child: financial provision) (1999) 1 FLR 152.

K v K (Minors: property transfer) (1992) 2 FLR 220.
Kiely v Kiely (1988) 1 FLR 248.
Lambert v Lambert (2002) All ER (D) 208 (Nov).
Le Foe v Le Foe and Woolwich plc (2001) 2 FLR 970.
Lloyds Bank plc v Rossett (1991) 1 AC 107.
Midland Bank v Cooke (1995) 4 All ER 562.
Netherlands v Reed (Case 59/85) (1986) ECR 1283.
S v United Kingdom Application (11716/85) 47 DR 275.
T v S (Financial provision for children) (1994) 2 FLR 883.
Wayling v Jones (1995) 2 FLR 1029.
White v White (2001) 1 AC 596.
X,Y and Z v United Kingdom (1997) 24 EHRR 143.

LAWS AND INTERNATLONAL INSTRUMENTS CITED

European Convention on Human Rights and Fundamental Freedoms, Rome, 4 November 1950.
Treaty Establishing the European Community, Rome, 25 March 1967.

Australia
Australian Capital Territories Domestic Relationships Act 1994.
New South Wales Property (Relationships) Legislation amendment Act 1999.

Canada
Ontario Family Law Act.

Belgium
Law Establishing Legal Cohabitation 1998.
Belgian Civil Code.

Denmark
Registered Partnership Act 1989.

England and Wales
Administration of Estates Act 1925.
Adoption and Children Act 2002.
Children Act 1989.
Clandestine Marriages Act 1753.
Domestic Proceedings and Magistrates' Courts Act 1978.
Family Law Act 1996.
Fatal Accidents Act 1976.
Housing Act 1985.
Housing Act 1988.
Inheritance Tax Act 1984.
Inheritance (Provision for Family and Dependants) Act 1975.
Matrimonial Causes Act 1973.
Rent Act 1977.
Taxation of Capital Gains Act 1992.
Trusts of Land and Appointment of Trustees Act 1996.

Finland
Registered Partnership Act 2001.

France
French Civil Code.
Law No. 99-944 of 15 November 1999.

Germany
Law to Terminate Discrimination against Same-Sex Communities: Life Partnerships 2001.

Iceland
Registered Partnership Act 1996.

The Netherlands
Act on Registered Partnerships of 17th December 1997.
Act Opening Marriage to Same-Sex Couples of 20 December 2000.
Dutch Civil Code.

New Zealand
Property Law (Amendment) Act 2001.

Norway
Joint Households Act 2002.
Registered Partnership Act 1993.

Spain
Aragon Unmarried Couples Law 1999.
Balearic Islands Stable Couples Law 2001.
Catalonia Stable Union of De Facto Couples Law 1998.
Navarre Unmarried Stable Couples Law 2000.

Sweden
Act on Insemination 1984.
Act on In Vitro Fertilisation 1988.
Cohabitees (Joint Homes) Act 1987.
Homosexual Cohabitees Act 1987.
Parents and Children Code 1949.
Partnership and Adoption Act 2002.
Registered Partnership Act 1994.

[25]

Legal Treatment of Cohabitation in the United States*

CYNTHIA GRANT BOWMAN

This article discusses the variety of ways state legal systems in the United States treat cohabitation, both by same-sex and heterosexual couples. The different approaches are described along a spectrum that ranges from one extreme, under which cohabitants have essentially no rights against one another or against third parties, to the other extreme, under which cohabitants are to be treated as though they were married under state law. Different areas of law are discussed, including the rights of cohabitants both against one another (remedies upon dissolution, inheritance) and against third parties, such as state benefits, tort claims, health-related benefits, and rights concerning children. The article concludes with speculations concerning why the remedies offered to cohabitants in the United States are so limited, as compared with other countries.

The legal treatment of cohabitation in the United States has been radically and rapidly transformed during the first few years of the twenty-first century. Two states (Vermont and Massachusetts) have now extended all of the benefits of marriage under state law to same-sex cohabitants, and another (California) is poised to do so in January 2005. Other states and localities offer variegated bundles of rights to cohabitants in domestic partnerships, typically but not always excluding opposite-sex partners. There are great regional variances—from Massachusetts, where marriage will become available to same-sex couples in May 2004, to Nebraska, where the state constitution was amended in 2000 to prohibit recognition not only of same-sex marriage but also of civil unions or domestic partnerships of any sort (Neb Const, Art I, § 29). Similar variety exists as to opposite-sex cohabitants. The state of Washington grants many of the benefits of marriage to all cohabitants, both same- and opposite-sex, while Illinois extends no recognition at all to cohabitants, for fear that to do so would somehow denigrate the institution of marriage.

The terms of the public debate have also changed quite dramatically. The Massachusetts Supreme Court's ruling in November 2003 (*Goodridge v*

* Address correspondence to Cynthia Grant Bowman, Northwestern University School of Law, 357 East Chicago Avenue, Chicago, IL 60611. E-mail: cgbowman@law.northwestern.edu

Department of Public Health) that marriage must be extended to same-sex couples produced a substantial backlash; and the discussion has become increasingly polarized, with most politicians rushing to proclaim their allegiance to protecting the sacred institution of marriage. What is astonishing, however, is that the central question discussed now is whether the states are free to grant all the privileges of marriage to same-sex couples, so long as they are denied the appellation "marriage." Leaving these matters to the states is consistent with the assignment of family law to the states under the U.S. federal system. The result is certain to be even greater regional variety than already exists in the laws governing cohabitants, and increasing differences between the treatment of same-sex and opposite-sex couples as well. Whether the extension of benefits to the former will ultimately hurt or help the latter remains a question. Indeed, whether extension of marriage-like benefits to gay and lesbian couples is a first step toward same-sex marriage or will function to keep them permanently in a second-class status is also an open question.

This article attempts to make some sense of a legal situation that is in vast flux. The discussion concerns an issue of considerable social importance. A major goal of family law—of the off-the-rack terms that states provide for the governance of marriage and divorce—is the protection of parties who have entered into long-term relationships of dependence and interdependence—both economic and noneconomic—and of their children. Moreover, official recognition of marital and family units serves to privatize many welfare functions that might otherwise fall upon the state, such as support of a dependent spouse at the end of a long marriage. Reflecting these interdependencies, vulnerabilities and functions, the law extends a variety of benefits to and imposes obligations upon couples in the officially sanctioned unions called marriage.

Increasing numbers of people now live in cohabiting relationships that result in similar dependencies. The 2000 Census showed that less than 25 percent of U.S. households were traditional nuclear families, while the number of households headed by unmarried partners had doubled during the decade from 1990 to 2000 (Fields & Casper 2001: 3 fig. 1). Unmarried partner households made up at least 5.2 percent of total households and included some 5.5 million people, 4.9 million in opposite-sex households (Simmons & O'Neill 2001: 7). Although unmarried-partner households had increased in all states, the largest number were in California, and the highest percentage in Alaska and Vermont (ibid.). Of those households, 41 percent included minor children (Fields & Casper 2001: 13).

The lives of individuals living in these unmarried-partner households become interdependent in ways that may render them extremely vulnerable if, for example, the relationship ends. Although the debate over these issues in the United States is often carried out in religious or moralistic language, this is what is at stake: Will the legal system extend some or all of the protections inherent in marriage to the many persons whose living arrangements are functionally similar to it?

There is already some indication that courts and state legislatures have begun to acknowledge the substantial role that unmarried couples play in addressing the welfare needs of their citizens and in privatizing support. Legislative findings set forth as a preamble to the New Jersey Domestic Partnership Act (2003) make this connection explicit:

> a. There are a significant number of individuals in this State who choose to live together in important personal, emotional and economic committed relationships with another individual;
> b. These familial relationships, which are known as domestic partnerships, assist the State by their establishment of a private network of support for the financial, physical and emotional health of their participants;
> c. Because of the material and other support that these familial relationships provide to their participants, the Legislature believes that these mutually supportive relationships should be formally recognized by statute, and that certain rights and benefits should be made available to individuals participating in them. (NJ Assembly Bill 3743, § 2 [2003])

This preamble succinctly summarizes the rationale behind extending the benefits and obligations of marriage to cohabitants who fall within the qualifying characteristics of mutual caring and economic responsibility for one another's welfare. It acknowledges both the existence of substantial numbers of cohabitants and the functions they perform for the state by privatizing support for the welfare of its citizens, reaching the conclusion that the state should therefore support these couples in their performance of these functions. It is significant that this conclusion was reached by a legislature, and not forced upon it by a court. Although the New Jersey statute does not follow through with all the benefits necessary to fulfill its promise and does not apply to most opposite-sex couples, the logic of extending state recognition and support applies equally to all who have entered into committed relationships of mutual support.

In the sections that follow I describe, first, the ways in which U.S. law sought to protect cohabiting couples in the past; some of these remedial strategies still exist. I then present the immense variety of modern legal approaches to cohabitants' rights in the United States, describing approaches that range from one extreme, where cohabitants have no rights against one another or third parties, to the other extreme, under which cohabitants are treated as though they were married for all purposes of state law. Finally, I offer some conclusions about the instability of the diverse systems that now exist, as well as speculations and recommendations for the future. In discussing the various legal approaches to cohabitation, the extent to which each approach addresses the family law functions described above will be a central concern. Particular attention will be paid to the interaction between the extension of rights to heterosexual and to same-sex cohabitants, and the theoretical bases for treating the two groups in similar or different ways.

I. PROTECTING COHABITANTS IN THE PAST

Prior to the development of modern doctrines protecting cohabitants, those who lived together without benefit of formal marriage were not totally bereft of remedy. Some were protected by the doctrine of common-law marriage, which provided a remedy for many long-term cohabitants in the event of death or divorce and in relation to the receipt of government benefits. The beneficiaries were primarily women, and especially poor women, African Americans, Mexican Americans and Native Americans (see Bowman 1996: 754–70).

Common-law marriage, continuing the ancient tradition of informal marriage, does not require solemnization or registration. Instead, heterosexual cohabitants who agree to live as husband and wife and do so, holding themselves out to the community as spouses, are treated as married for all purposes under both state and federal law (see Clark 1988: 48, 50). Some courts will infer the parties' agreement simply from cohabitation and "holding out" (see, e.g., *Metropolitan Life Insurance Company v Johnson* 1982 at 361). No particular period of time is required for the relationship to "ripen" into marriage, so long as the couple are generally known in their community as husband and wife.

Unlike countries in Europe, almost half of the states in the United States recognized common-law marriage well into the twentieth century, and eleven jurisdictions still do.[1] Moreover, the doctrine is influential beyond the borders of the states that recognize it. If a relationship fits the criteria and was entered into within a recognizing jurisdiction, the marriage will also be regarded as valid in states that do not recognize common-law marriage (Clark 1988: 47, 57–59). Thus, if a couple were living in a common-law marriage in Pennsylvania and then moved to New York, courts in New York State would recognize the relationship for purposes, for example, of inheritance or divorce.

Common-law marriage, in short, was a real marriage—just one entered into in a different way. As such, it does not formally belong in a discussion of the legal treatment of cohabitants. The doctrine functioned primarily to protect women at the end of long relationships of dependence; if they qualified, courts would grant them all the rights of a wife or widow. Thus common-law marriage responded to the same types of legal dilemmas typically faced by courts deciding cases about cohabitants' rights, providing a remedy for women who were, for example, abandoned by men for whom they had performed domestic services for long periods or who were left penniless upon the death of a long-term partner to whom they were never formally married. Interestingly, common-law marriage, like gay marriage today, was also controversial on the grounds that recognizing it would somehow denigrate the sanctity of marriage (Bowman 1996: 736–37, 743–44).

The common-law marriage doctrine appears to be nearing the end of its useful career. Only eleven jurisdictions still recognize it, and it is under attack in some of them (see, e.g., *PNC Bank v Workers' Compensation Appeal Bd* 2002). Moreover, fewer persons could take advantage of the doctrine today. The status is available only to heterosexuals. Moreover, with the increase in cohabitation, its increased visibility and acceptance, a couple who are not married no longer feel the need to introduce themselves as husband and wife and thus will not be able to establish the basic elements of common-law marriage even in the states where it is still recognized.

Faced with cases in which great hardship might result from failure to recognize a long-term relationship as a marriage, courts have applied a number of other remedial doctrines. The only one that approaches the protections of formal marriage, however, is the putative spouse doctrine. Under this doctrine, a party who in good faith believed herself (usually it was a female in this position) to be married but was in fact not married because of some irregularity affecting the validity of the marriage ceremony was treated as though married.

The case often used to illustrate this doctrine is that of Mr. Vargas, who had a wife and children in one location and then went through a marriage ceremony (invalid because of bigamy) with another woman, setting up a separate household with her in another town; children were also born to this marriage (*In re Estate of Vargas* 1974). Amazingly, neither woman suspected the deception until Vargas died, when two widows claimed his estate. The court deciding this matter held that the second Mrs. Vargas was a putative spouse and split the estate between the two women. In short, the second Mrs. Vargas was treated as Mr. Vargas' widow although he had never legally been her husband, a situation one cannot describe as a marriage of any sort. The putative spouse is instead a remedial doctrine employed by courts to address situations where innocent parties are harmed by their reliance upon a long-term cohabitant.

In addition to the doctrines described above, courts have employed a number of equitable doctrines to provide at least partial protection to vulnerable cohabitants, most notably equitable restitution, constructive trust, and quantum meruit (see, e.g., Ellman, Kurtz & Scott 1998: 959–60). The typical situation under which one of these doctrines would be applied was when one cohabitant—usually a woman—had invested a substantial amount in property accumulated by a couple during their life together, for example, by contributing funds to the down payment on a house or to a business which was titled in the other cohabitant's name. In these circumstances, courts may disgorge the amount that had "unjustly enriched" the other party and return it to its original owner. Of course, if the two had owned the real estate jointly or entered into a formal business partnership, traditional legal remedies, such as partition, would be available.

If the disputes leading to appellate litigation are any indication, however, one of the enduring characteristics of intimate cohabitation is a simple trust that typically does not insist upon joint tenancy or a partnership contract, even though the underlying facts may reflect such a relationship. Women, in particular, freely contribute money and labor to the accumulation of a couple's property—property that would be jointly owned if they were married—without insisting that their names be placed upon the deeds (see, e.g., *Hewitt v Hewitt* 1979; *Ayala v Fox* 1990; *Wilcox v Trautz* 1998). Equitable doctrines available to address these situations can still be used in cohabitant cases today. Unfortunately, the types of contributions and services that trigger application of these equitable remedies must look very much like business arrangements to be recognized—that is, the sorts of co-ownership or partnership two individuals might enter into even if they were not cohabitants, especially if they are men. The more typical sorts of contributions made by female cohabitants—contributing to household expenses, including the mortgage, or rendering services within the household or within the male partner's business—are almost invariably not compensated under these doctrines upon the ending of the relationship (see Estin 2001: 1395). A variety of theories are available to explain this, most of them derived from traditional, and highly gendered, notions of marriage—for example, that services by a spouse are offered gratuitously and that contributions to their common life benefit both parties to the relationship (ibid.: 1401–02; Weisberg & Appelton 2002: 439). Thus if a long-term cohabitant is abandoned after many years of service as a homemaker, the court is likely to see her services, somewhat contradictorily, as both altruistic *and* as having been compensated by the fact that she was also supported by and benefited from the relationship (see, e.g., *Marvin v Marvin* (*III*) 1981 at 558).

In short, prior to development of the modern law of cohabitants' rights, some protection for vulnerable parties was available; but it was inadequate to protect the dependencies arising from long-term cohabitation and, in particular, to compensate for the contributions typically made by female cohabitants. To address these situations, within the last three decades many states have adopted, either by case law or statute, a variety of protections for cohabitants. Most of these are based upon contractual theories, but some base the state's legal treatment simply upon the status of cohabitation. The immense variety of these provisions, and their continuing inadequacy to protect the interests of most cohabitants, will be discussed in the section that follows.

II. THE DEVELOPMENT OF THE MODERN LAW OF COHABITANTS' RIGHTS

Over the last few decades, the legal treatment of cohabitation in the United States has developed through several strands, some of which coexist uneasily with one another in the same state. This section discusses each of those strands, in the following order: (1) states in which cohabitants are given no rights; (2) states in which cohabitants' rights are based on contract; (3) states that extend rights based upon the status of cohabitation, either by imposing that status upon cohabitants at the termination of their relationships or by providing for entrance into civil unions or domestic partnerships; and (4) other rights extended to cohabitants vis-à-vis third parties on a variety of bases. The section concludes with a brief discussion of cohabitants' rights pertaining to children.

A. NO RIGHTS FOR COHABITANTS

Before the development of contractual and status-based remedies for cohabitants, the traditional position was that cohabitants simply had no rights vis-à-vis one another or third parties. Three states—Illinois, Georgia,[2] and Louisiana—continue to adhere to this position (see Gordon 1998: 253–54). *Hewitt v Hewitt* (1979), the case frequently used to illustrate the Illinois position, is a stark one. Victoria and Robert Hewitt began cohabiting as students at Grinnell College. Subsequently they moved to Illinois, where he established a lucrative medical practice and she served as homemaker and mother to their children, while assisting him in building his practice. After fifteen years, they separated. Apparently believing that they were married (perhaps by common law), Victoria Hewitt sued for divorce. The court not only dismissed the divorce action but also, when she amended to add causes of action in contract and for equitable remedies, held that Mrs. Hewitt was entitled to no remedy at all, neither property distribution nor alimony. To give her any rights, the court reasoned, would be to denigrate the institution of marriage and in effect bring back common-law marriage, which Illinois had abolished in 1905 (*Hewitt* 1979 at 1209–11). In short, Mrs. Hewitt, after a fifteen-year period of reliance upon and contribution to the relationship, was left without anything.

Although *Hewitt* was decided in 1979, it appears still to be alive and well in Illinois. It was followed and, indeed, extended in *Ayala v Fox* (1990).[3] Illinois courts have also consistently refused to give any legal protection to cohabitants in other contexts, turning down, for example, claims for loss of consortium by cohabitants (*Medley v Strong* 1990) and holding that cohabitation may constitute appropriate grounds to remove children from the custody of cohabiting parents (*Jarrett v Jarrett* 1980), all based on *Hewitt*.

The *Hewitt* court's reasoning that extension of recognition to cohabitants would somehow harm the institution of marriage is open to dispute. In *Hewitt*, protections for the female cohabitant were denied even though the relationship was virtually identical to the most traditional of marriages, as Mrs. Hewitt stayed home to raise their children and assist her partner in his career. To deny property and support rights to cohabitants in a case like that in fact creates an incentive to *avoid* marriage—Mr. Hewitt was able to extract the benefit of his partner's contributions and get away with all the couple's accumulated wealth.

In states like Illinois, it is risky for a cohabitant to make any investment in a nonmarital relationship. As the leading cases show, the cohabitants most likely to make such investments—either because they simply trust the men they love or because they do not have the bargaining power to insist either upon marriage or even joint title for property—are women. The law's refusal to protect their investments leaves these women extremely vulnerable at the termination of a cohabiting relationship. The men in these relationships clearly benefit from such a legal rule.

B. COHABITANTS' RIGHTS BASED ON CONTRACT

With the exception of Illinois, Georgia and Louisiana, almost every state will now recognize express contracts between cohabitants, especially if they are written. This state of affairs required the breakthrough of the *Marvin v Marvin* "palimony" case in 1976. Prior to that time, cohabitants' contracts were considered unenforceable because they rested upon "meretricious" consideration, that is, the exchange of sex. The *Marvin* court, however, held that cohabitants could enter into contracts with one another just as other individuals could and, indeed, that the courts would enforce both written and oral express contracts; in dicta the court also indicated that recovery might be based upon contracts implied from the conduct of the parties and a variety of equitable grounds as well (*Marvin I* 1976 at 122–23).

Michelle Triola alleged that the well-known actor Lee Marvin had entered into a contract to support her for the rest of her life, in return for her service as his homemaker, entertainer and companion, and that she had given up her own career to do so. When they separated after six years, Marvin argued that such a contract was unenforceable under California law. In *Marvin I*, the court ruled against him on these grounds, thus establishing the cause of action, and remanded, but in *Marvin II* found that no such contract existed. Thus the *Marvin* case, which was attended by a great deal of publicity, in fact resulted in no recovery at all for the plaintiff; it simply established the principle that cohabitants' rights in California could be based upon express or implied contracts and that the consideration for them could include homemaking services.

While many states have adopted the *Marvin* approach, other states reacted with alarm to the long and messy *Marvin* litigation, especially because it required the court to examine and weigh highly intimate details of the couple's relationship. The Illinois court in *Hewitt* declined to adopt similar contract-based rights; other states moved to accept *Marvin* but to limit its application. New York, for example, restricted *Marvin* rights to those based on express contracts (*Morone v Morone* 1980). Minnesota and Texas went further, passing Statutes of Frauds that require cohabitants' contracts to be in writing (see, e.g., Minn Stat §§ 513.075–513.076 [2002]).

Indeed, the application of the *Marvin* case has been quite limited, even in California. In a 1993 California appellate court decision that attracted a good deal of attention, the court denied relief to a disabled woman after a relationship of twenty-five years and two children (*Friedman v Friedman* 1993; see also Ellman 2001: 1370–72). Terri and Elliott Friedman began to live together in 1967, when they were in their twenties, bought a house to which they took title as husband and wife, signed joint tax returns, and lived as a fairly conventional family, with Terri staying home to care for their children and Elliott going to law school and prospering economically. By the time she sued in 1992, however, Terri was disabled and could hardly walk. The case seemed to be a good one for the application of *Marvin* remedies; compared to *Marvin*, the relationship was longer in term, more conventional, and included the birth of children. Nonetheless, Elliott argued that he had never made a commitment to support Terri if their relationship terminated, and the court found that the couple's course of conduct did not support an implied contract to that effect.

The outcome of the *Friedman* case leads one to question the efficacy of contract remedies in general, so long as one party denies the contract. (Of course, if that were not so, that party would simply pay up and there would be no litigation at all.) Oral contracts are notoriously difficult to prove. Moreover, in *Friedman* the proof of an implied contract was rejected because the conduct of the parties did not specifically indicate an agreement by Elliott to provide spousal support upon termination. From this outcome, one may infer that cohabitants are only slightly more likely to obtain "palimony" in California than in New York if the claim rests upon an implied contract; and at least the courts in New York are more candid about disallowing it. In fact, California courts are inconsistent in this respect, with the result depending upon the discretion, and perhaps the personal prejudices, of the judge.

This inconsistency has been especially notable in cases where gay or lesbian cohabitants have sued for remedies upon dissolution of their relationships; courts have been very reluctant to grant support rather than property distribution in such cases. Two cases illustrate this trend. In one, *Jones v Daly* (1981), the lover-housekeeper-companion-cook alleged an oral agreement by his deceased partner to support him for life. Because the promise explicitly included a sexual component, by referring to his services as (among other things) "lover," the court refused to enforce it. By contrast, in *Whorton v Dillingham* (1988), a gay lover sued for property acquired during a relationship that had ended, alleging an oral agreement, yet the court severed any allegations referring to his services as companion and lover (which are, of course, implicit in all cohabitation contracts) and enforced the contract based upon the plaintiff's services as chauffeur, bodyguard, secretary and business partner. As commentators have noted, neither court regarded homemaking services as consideration for the contract; the only consideration that counted was that which appeared to have monetary value (see, e.g., Bullock 1992: 1048). This may reflect the fact that courts find it difficult to envisage a male in the role of a homemaker (see Chambers 1996: 483–84) or a more general distaste for same-sex cohabitant cases; but it does not derive from *Marvin*, in which compensation for homemaking services was approved in gender-neutral terms. And again, as with the equitable remedies described above, the more like a "male" business deal, the more likely the service is to be compensated.

A much more profound problem with the use of contract principles to redress inequities that may arise on termination of a cohabiting relationship is that cohabiting couples—like married couples—typically do not make contracts; they simply proceed trusting that their relationship will endure and that each party will treat the other fairly. One empirical study of Minnesota residents who self-identified as being in a committed unmarried relationship found that only 21 percent had written agreements about property; of these, 52.1 percent had a provision for dividing property if the relationship were to end, but only 35.4 percent set up duties of support upon termination (Robbennolt & Johnson 1999: 435–36, 439, 441). Most cohabitants simply proceed under vague agreements to pool resources and make no provision for remedies upon termination (Blumberg 1981: 1164–65).

It is hard to know what to make of the absence of a contract, whether to infer a caring relationship that would have resulted in provisions for property and support upon dissolution if the parties had thought to do so or to infer that the parties (or at least one of them) intended not to undertake such responsibility to one another. Much may depend upon the group of cohabitants under consideration. Some couples, like the Friedmans, fall into a cohabiting relationship that then persists, leaving them in circumstances neither would have envisaged when their union commenced. Terri Friedman, for example, eventually gave up her goal of obtaining a college degree because of the sickness of one of their children (*Friedman* 1993 at 895). Others may explicitly desire to stay unmarried because of objections to involving state or church in their relationship but still intend a caring and mutually supportive relationship. Or—the case most observers worry about—one or both may specifically intend to avoid any monetary commitments to one another. The implications of cohabitation are likely to differ for each of these groups, thus affecting the expectations that accompanied their living together and the likelihood of an implied contract between them. In short, even though contracts between cohabitants are now enforceable in many states, both the probability that such a contract can be proved and the desirability of inferring one from the conduct of the parties may vary, with the result that few cohabitants will in fact find a remedy in contract for any vulnerability they experience upon the ending of their relationship.

In sum, a contractual approach to cohabitants' rights returns to them the rights and remedies they would have had as individuals to enter into contracts of various sorts with one another, in a sense commodifying their relationships. The more the arrangement looks to the court like a business deal, the more likely it is to be recognized and compensated. By contrast, women's traditional contributions to relationships continue to be underrecognized and uncompensated. Although postrelationship support is theoretically available under a contract doctrine, it needs to have been a quite explicit expectation of the parties. Thus contractual remedies may not protect the Victoria Hewitts and the Terri Friedmans of this world, whose partners either never intended a caring and supportive relationship or—more likely—no longer recall their earlier intentions at the acrimonious point when the relationship is ending.

Moreover, cohabitants' rights based upon contract theories are severely limited in scope, applying only to rights *inter se*. That is, they are limited to rights of the two parties vis-à-vis one another and cannot create any rights against third parties. Thus, for example, inheritance, tort claims based on injury to the relationship or government benefits cannot be derived from a theory of contract. For this, a status-based theory of cohabitants' rights is required, although some status-based laws may also not provide all of these benefits. Ironically, given the derivation in California of cohabitants' rights for gay and lesbian persons out of contract theories developed for the protection of heterosexuals, in 2005 same-sex cohabitants there will become eligible for a broad range of benefits, including not only property distribution and support but also inheritance, standing in tort and government benefits if they are registered as domestic partners—a status unavailable to most heterosexuals in that state. I turn now to discuss the current variety of status-based legal approaches to cohabitation.

C. COHABITANTS' RIGHTS BASED ON STATUS

Dissatisfied with many of the limitations of contract-based remedies, a number of states have instead conferred rights upon cohabitants based upon their status as such, an approach that was rejected by the *Marvin* court (*Marvin I* 1976 at 119–22). Some of these remedies are available to both opposite- and same-sex couples, although the more comprehensive approaches are primarily limited to gay and lesbian couples, presumably because marriage has not been an alternative for them. There are now four general types of status-based regimes in the United States: (1) meretricious relationships in Washington; (2) civil unions in Vermont and gay marriage in Massachusetts; and (3) domestic partnerships in Hawaii, New Jersey and California. An important distinction among them—one many think relevant to the amount of backlash they occasion—is whether they have been initiated by the judiciary or the legislature. In a sense, however, virtually all of these arrangements have had their initial push from litigation, as states have enacted domestic partnership laws in response to court decisions invalidating the restriction of marriage to heterosexuals.

1. *Meretricious Relationships in Washington*[4]

The Washington Supreme Court rejected a contract approach to the thorny legal issues presented upon dissolution of cohabitant relationships. Its approach instead confers rights generally upon couples in what it calls a "meretricious relationship," defined as "a stable, marital-like relationship where both parties cohabit with knowledge that a lawful marriage between them does not exist" (*Connell v Francisco* 1995 at 834; see also *In re Marriage of Lindsey* 1984 at 331). Upon dissolution or death, property of individuals in such relationships which would have been community property if they were married is to be divided between them in a just and equitable distribution. Thus all income and property acquired by either party during the relationship is presumed to be owned by both—a type of community property by analogy. This legal rule, which protects vulnerable parties at the end of a relationship if they have property to divide, has been extended to same-sex couples (*Vasquez v Hawthorne* 2001).

The inquiry under a status-based cohabitant regime of this type is not whether the couple had any kind of agreement for property or support at dissolution or death (although their intent is relevant to the inquiry) but rather whether their conduct fits them into the definition of cohabitants. The Washington court directed judges to consider the following factors, among others, in making this determination (*Connell* at 834, quoting *Lindsey* at 331):

- continuous cohabitation
- duration of the relationship
- purpose of the relationship
- pooling of resources and services for joint projects, and
- the intent of the parties.

Unlike a contract-based system, the Washington approach, rather than assuming (and encouraging) individual autonomy, presumes that a couple in such a relationship is in fact a joint economic unit, thus encouraging the type of sharing behavior typical of marriage. If a couple in a long-term unmarried relationship do not wish to pool their income and undertake economic responsibility for one another, they need to contract *out* of such obligations in the state of Washington, unlike in California and other states following *Marvin*, where such obligations are undertaken by contracting *in*. Because registration is not required, Washington residents who are not well-versed in the law may have an unpleasant surprise upon ending their relationships.

Evaluating the status-based approach taken in Washington from the touchstone of protection for vulnerable parties, it clearly improves upon contract schemes in this respect, imposing upon cohabitants who have become interdependent an obligation to share their property upon termination of the relationship without the necessity of proving a contract. Washington's approach is limited in several ways, however. First, it only applies to property distribution; so if the couple have not accumulated property, it is worthless. Second, it pertains only to rights against one another, thus excluding, for example, both standing for tort claims and the plethora of government benefits tied to marital status. Third, it is activated only upon termination of the relationship by dissolution or death; the pseudo-community property does not attach during the relationship.

The inclusion of property distribution upon death is nonetheless important. Except in New Hampshire, where long-term cohabitants may be given inheritance rights under a form of common-law marriage applicable only at death (NH Rev Stat Ann § 457: 39 [2001]), cohabitants have been excluded from inheritance under the law of every state. Thus, unless they make wills, which many do not,[5] cohabitants receive no property upon the death of their partners. Yet recent studies show that a majority of both heterosexual and same-sex cohabitants prefer that a substantial share, if not all, of their estates go to their surviving partners upon death (Fellows et al. 1998: 9). Thus inheritance can be an important issue for cohabitants. It can be especially problematic for gay and lesbian couples, who may be alienated from family members, who then contest a will leaving property to the cohabitant; such will contests often succeed (Sherman 1981: 246). The desire to ensure such rights has led some gay males to attempt to adopt one another in order to obtain inheritance by a different route, but this approach is not available in all states and the adoption may also be challenged by relatives (see, e.g., *In re Adoption of Swanson* 1993; contra *Matter of Adoption of Robert Paul P.* 1984). Theoretically, of course, if the adoption is successful, the two could risk prosecution for incest as well. If the two live in Washington, however, the surviving partner may receive 50 percent of the total property accumulated by the two during their relationship at his partner's death.

In short, the approach taken in Washington provides some important, though limited, protections to many individuals who have become economically interdependent in the course of a longstanding relationship. Although now applicable in only a relatively small part of the United States, this is the general approach recommended by the American Law Institute (ALI) for adoption in all states.[6] Under the ALI *Principles of the Law of Family Dissolution*, the same rules that apply upon divorce of married persons are to be applied to either same-sex or heterosexual cohabitants if they qualify as "domestic partners" within the statute; those rules presume equal division of property acquired during the relationship and also provide for compensatory payments—alimony or spousal maintenance—to dependent parties in long-term unions (ALI 2002: §§ 6.04–6.05, 4.09–4.10, 5.04). Individuals are presumed to qualify either if they have cohabited continuously for a state-defined period and act jointly with respect to household management or if they have a common child; if not, they are entitled to establish a domestic partnership by proof of a number of factors having to do with financial interdependence, intimacy and reputation as a couple (ibid.: § 6.03; see also Ertman 2001: 107–09). Although ALI formulations have been influential upon state law in the past, thus far no state has moved to adopt its most recent recommendations in this respect.

The Washington scheme for meretricious relationships does not go as far as the ALI suggests, because it is limited to property distribution and does not include provision for postrelationship support if there is no property to distribute. It does offer, however, the most far-reaching protection available thus far in the United States for heterosexual cohabitants. It is interesting that the system is not very well-known—interesting because it has been in place since 1984 (although not extended to gay and lesbian couples until 2001) yet apparently has not occasioned widespread public controversy. This has not been the case when courts have moved to extend the rights of marriage to couples of the same sex.

2. *Civil Unions Versus Gay Marriage: Vermont and Massachusetts*

Apart from the Washington approach described above, most status-based cohabitation regimes in the United States have been created in response to the pressure for same-sex marriage. Cases challenging the denial of marriage licenses to gays and lesbians have been brought since the 1970s (*Baker v Nelson* 1971; *Jones v Hallahan* 1973), but the first to succeed was that in Hawaii (*Baehr v Lewin* 1993). A variety of legal bases have been used for these constitutional challenges. Sex discrimination was the successful ground in Hawaii (either member of the couple could have obtained the license if they were of the other sex), but only because the state constitution, unlike the U.S. Constitution, included an Equal Rights Amendment. In Alaska, a Superior Court case held that a fundamental right to choose one's life partner was contained within the state constitution's clause guaranteeing the right to privacy (*Brause v Bureau of Vital Statistics* 1998). In both states, however, the decision finding the denial of marriage licenses to same-sex couples unconstitutional was quickly overturned by constitutional amendment (Hawaii Const, Art I § 23; Alaska Const, Art I § 25).

When gay and lesbian couples challenged their exclusion from marriage in Vermont, they met with a more favorable outcome, again linked to a unique provision of the state's constitution. In 1999, the Vermont Supreme Court held, under the state constitution's Equal Benefits Clause, that same-sex couples could not be excluded from all the benefits associated with marriage under state law (*Baker v State* 1999). In response, the Vermont legislature passed a statute recognizing an alternative status to marriage, styled "civil unions" (15 Vt Stat Ann §§ 1201–1207 [Supp 2000]). Couples who register under this law receive all the benefits and protections of marriage under state law, including, among other things, property rights, adoption, tax treatment, insurance benefits, spousal standing for tort and criminal law, hospital visitation, and intestacy. No rights under federal law are available, however; and heterosexual cohabitants are not eligible to enter into civil unions. Nonetheless, unlike the contractual and status-based remedies discussed thus far, the benefits of a civil union expand beyond those the parties have vis-à-vis one another and include rights against third parties and the state.

In 2003, a same-sex marriage case made it to the Supreme Judicial Court of Massachusetts (*Goodridge I*). All of the arguments raised in other states were raised here as well—sex discrimination under the state's equal rights clause, as in Hawaii; the fundamental right to choose one's partner, as in Alaska; and the unconstitutionality of excluding one group from the state's benefits, as in Vermont. The only thing that had changed since all of those opinions was that the Supreme Court had invalidated laws criminalizing sodomy (*Lawrence v Texas* 2003), so that states could no longer argue that they were being asked to approve potentially criminal conduct.

The astonishing thing about *Goodridge* is that it was decided on none of these grounds, but rather on the basis that there was simply no rational reason for the state to exclude same-sex couples from the benefits conferred by the status of marriage. The argument came down, as in Vermont and Hawaii, to the effects upon children; but the state's position here, as in Vermont, had been seriously compromised by its previous approval of adoption by gays and lesbians. Indeed, the *Goodridge* court emphasized the detriments to children already living in same-sex-parented families if these unions are *not* recognized. As one commentator has remarked, in the United States, unlike Western Europe, the courts had already recognized gay and lesbian families; now it was being asked to recognize the same-sex unions around which those families were structured (*Harvard Law Review* 2003: 2027).

In Massachusetts, as in Hawaii, Alaska and Vermont, the legislature met to consider what to do in the wake of its supreme court's decision. In Hawaii and Alaska, the cases were not sufficiently advanced at the point of decision to cut off the time necessary to pass a constitutional amendment defining marriage as a heterosexual institution, which both promptly did. In Vermont, the state supreme court gave the legislature the option of conferring all the benefits of marriage without the status, and it did so. The Massachusetts legislature asked for an Advisory Opinion from the court as to whether establishing civil unions would comply with the court's holding. On February 3, 2004, the court replied that nothing short of marriage would do (*Goodridge II*). Moreover, the state was given only until May 17, 2004 to begin issuing marriage licenses to same-sex couples, which does not allow time for the passage of a constitutional amendment to overrule the court (which is not possible to effect before 2006). Thus Massachusetts is the first state in the United States where same-sex marriage will be allowed.

One problem that has already become apparent from the Vermont experience, however, is that couples who enter into civil unions have trouble obtaining "divorce" remedies and inheritance if they actually reside in or move to other states that do not recognize the status (Bernstein 2003: 2). This reflects the more general conflict of law problems attendant upon the vastly differing treatment of cohabitants' rights in different states (see Reppy 2002: 303–11). For example, will a cohabitant couple moving from Washington to California receive status-based rights upon dissolution? If they move to Illinois? If recognition is against the state's public policy, an exception to the Full Faith and Credit referred to in the U.S. Constitution may excuse it from recognizing a status entered elsewhere (ibid.: 275). Many states (more than thirty-five) and the federal government have also passed either "Defense of Marriage" acts or constitutional amendments providing that only marriages between opposite-sex partners will be recognized (Developments 2003: 2006, 2014). The federal Defense of Marriage Act also includes a provision to the effect that states are not required to give Full Faith and Credit to same-sex marriages (28 USC § 1738C [2000]). In contrast, the domestic partnership statutes recently passed by California and New Jersey (discussed below) explicitly provide that civil unions or domestic partnerships entered into in other jurisdictions where they are valid *will* be recognized in those states (CA Assembly Bill 205, § 299.2 [2003]; NJ AB 3743, § 6(c)).

The problems posed by conflict among the laws of different states will be exacerbated by the availability of same-sex marriage in Massachusetts, when as will doubtless occur, Massachusetts residents joined in same-sex marriages move to other states and then seek to dissolve their relationships. The legal issues arising from the many conflicts posed will doubtless require lengthy litigation to decide. In the meantime, there is a growing movement to pass an amendment to the U.S. Constitution confining the status of marriage throughout the country to persons of the opposite sex. The amending process is a slow one, however; and before it can be completed, numerous same-sex couples will become legal spouses in Massachusetts, posing serious questions about whether they can be deprived of that status retroactively.

The law governing interstate recognition of marriages is quite complex and cannot be fully discussed here (see Developments 2003: 2028–51). Whatever happens, however, cohabitants of the same sex in Vermont and Massachusetts may now receive all the protections state law provides for married couples, both during and upon termination of their relationships, at least as long as they remain residents of the state.

3. *Domestic Partnership Laws: Hawaii, New Jersey and California*

The demand for equal benefits has also resulted in a plethora of domestic partnership schemes throughout the United States, often passed by municipal or county ordinances; many apply to heterosexuals as well as same-sex cohabitants. Many such programs provide merely a system of registration and dissolution, with no attendant benefits except for municipal or county employees, who may receive family leave, family medical insurance and the like (Bowman & Cornish 1992: 1192). In California, for example, San Francisco provided a partnership registry in 1989, granting cohabitants hospital visitation rights, paid bereavement leave for city employees and health insurance for the partners of city employees (Hein 2000: 35–37). In 1996 San Francisco also passed an ordinance requiring contractors doing business with the city to extend benefits to domestic partners of employees (ibid.).

By contrast, in other states—Georgia, for example—similar municipal ordinances have been overturned as *ultra vires*, that is, exceeding the authority given to municipalities by the state (Christensen 1998: 1739; see also, e.g., *City of Atlanta v McKinney* 1995 at 520–21). Nonetheless, domestic partnership ordinances have proliferated, driven in large part by a desire to obtain employee benefits. Eligibility to enter into such a status may be relatively stringent, requiring nonrelationship, indefinite commitment, common residence and an agreement to joint responsibility for basic living expenses (Bowman & Cornish 1992: 1192–95).

More recently, a number of statewide domestic partnership laws have originated as a direct response to the litigation campaign for gay marriage. The scenario in Hawaii is a good illustration. Although the Hawaii Supreme Court's decision in favor of same-sex marriage was overturned by constitutional amendment, the legislature passed the Reciprocal Beneficiaries Act in 1997, giving couples excluded from the protections of marriage a few of its benefits (Hawaii Rev Stat §§ 572C-1 to -7 [1998]). Under the Act, couples legally prohibited from marrying may register and then receive rights of inheritance, workers' compensation survivorship benefits, health-related benefits such as hospital visitation rights, family leave and the right to make health care decisions for a partner, the right to sue in tort for wrongful death and the right to become beneficiaries of one another's health and life insurance policies (see Habegger 2000: 1002). Thus, the Hawaii statute gives cohabitants certain rights against third parties, but not against one another in case they dissolve the relationship, which either party is free to do at will. While in California and Washington rights for same-sex couples were derived from those granted to opposite-sex couples, the motivation of the Hawaii statute was clearly to benefit gay and lesbian couples; but it includes benefits for a limited group of heterosexuals as well—any persons who are unable to marry, thus covering, for example, mothers and their adult sons (or grandsons) who share the same residence.

The relationship between the drive for gay marriage and domestic partnership laws has not been as direct in New Jersey and California as it was in Hawaii, but it is still there. In New Jersey, a case challenging the exclusion of same-sex couples from marriage has been wending its way up through the state courts (*Lewis v Harris* 2003). Without any State Supreme Court decision on that question, however, the New Jersey legislature—apparently influenced by the dilemmas of those who lost domestic partners on September 11, 2001—passed a Domestic Partnership Act in January 2004, unaccompanied by any declaration that marriage was to be restricted to persons of the opposite sex (NJ AB 3743). The Act, effective on passage, provides that same-sex couples and heterosexual couples age sixty-two or older (who might lose their full individual entitlement to Social Security benefits from a former spouse if they remarry) may fill out an affidavit of domestic partnership if neither is married or has been in another domestic partnership dissolved less than six months previously, the partners are not related to one another,

and they share a common residence in the state, are jointly responsible for each other's common welfare (evidenced, for example, by joint ownership of various assets), agree to be jointly responsible for each other's basic living expenses, and "have chosen to share each other's lives in a committed relationship of mutual caring" (ibid.: § 4(b)).

Partners filing such an affidavit in New Jersey receive exemption from inheritance taxes and a limited state income tax deduction, along with hospital visitation privileges, health care decision making, and employment benefits, such as health insurance coverage if they are state employees, and broad protection against discrimination in relation to employment, housing and credit. There are no other benefits against third parties or the state, and no provision for equitable property distribution or support on dissolution of the relationship.

In contrast to domestic partnerships in Western Europe, domestic partners in New Jersey are required to go through a judicial dissolution proceeding to terminate their relationships, on grounds virtually identical to those for divorce in that state (NJ Stat Ann 2A: 34-2 [2000]):

- sexual intercourse with a person not the partner
- desertion for twelve months
- extreme cruelty
- separation of eighteen months with no reasonable prospect of reconciliation
- addiction or habitual drunkenness
- institutionalization for mental illness
- imprisonment

In short, domestic partnerships in New Jersey have quite stringent requirements for both entry and exit and very few benefits (NJ AB 3743, § 10). It will be interesting to see how many people find the arrangement attractive.

The demand by gays and lesbians for marital status is very high in California, although a statute prohibiting same-sex marriage was passed by a public initiative (Proposition 22) in March 2000 (Defense of Marriage Act, Cal Fam Code § 308.5 [2002]; Sawyer 2003: 733). Reflecting this demand, when the mayor of San Francisco decided unilaterally to begin issuing marriage licenses to same-sex couples in February 2004, thousands of individuals lined up to be joined in marriage, provoking a lawsuit to enjoin the practice as invalid under state law (Marshall 2004).[7]

In response to demand for equal benefits, the California legislature passed its first domestic partnership law in 2001, under which both same-sex cohabitants and heterosexual cohabitants over the age of sixty-two may register (Domestic Partner Registration Act, Cal Family Code § 297 [2000]). One of the factors leading to its passage was the highly publicized death of Diane Whipple, who was mauled to death by a dog in the hallway of the apartment she shared with her lesbian partner in San Francisco, and the desire to allow persons in her partner's situation to sue for wrongful death and negligent infliction of emotional distress (Gorback 2002: 275–77).

Under the new partnership act, domestic partners received the right to sue for these torts, as well as to make health care decisions for one another, to receive sick leave and unemployment benefits for reasons related to a partner, to adopt a partner's child as though a stepparent, and to administer a partner's estate (Sawyer 2003: 742–43).

As in New Jersey, heterosexual couples are included in the California domestic partnership statute if one member of the couple is over the age of sixty-two. One commentator has described this as "marriage lite" for older straight couples, allowing them to receive some benefits of marriage without losing rights that a surviving or divorced spouse would lose upon remarriage (Oldham 2001: 1431). Because inheritance was not included in this initial partnership law in California, registration as domestic partners also did not interfere with older couples' typical desire to leave their assets to children of a previous relationship. However, inclusion of heterosexuals over sixty-two in the statute is difficult to explain from a theoretical standpoint. There is no reason to believe that older cohabiting couples are more interdependent than ones who are younger; indeed, they may be less so, given the absence of children in common. The probable reason for including this group of heterosexuals in a statute clearly intended to benefit gay and lesbian couples was simply to gain more widespread support for passage of the legislation by extending the group who would benefit from it (Callan 2003: 458). By the same token, however, the inclusion of some heterosexuals within the statute may provide a wedge by which other opposite-sex couples may challenge their exclusion in the future, perhaps with the support of the sixty-two-plus set.

In September 2003 California passed a second partnership act, the Domestic Partner Rights and Responsibilities Act, which is to go into effect in January 2005 (AB 205). In the meantime, currently registered domestic partners are being given notice that as of that date the rights and obligations they have toward one another will be radically changed if they do not opt out. The new act will give the most extensive rights to cohabitants outside of Vermont and Massachusetts; indeed, it will affect many more people, both because such a large proportion of cohabitants live in California and because it includes opposite-sex couples over the age of sixty-two.

The provisions of the new California act are simple:

> Registered domestic partners shall have the same rights, protection, and benefits, and shall be subject to the same responsibilities, obligations, and duties under law, whether they derive from statutes, administrative regulations, court rules, government policies, common law, or any other provisions or sources of law, as are granted to and imposed upon spouses [or former spouses, widows and widowers]. (Ibid.: §§ 297.5 (a)(b)(c)).

In short, a regime equivalent to marriage will become available to same-sex and certain opposite-sex couples in California for all purposes of state law, except joint filing status on tax returns. Unlike comparable regimes in Vermont and Massachusetts, however, the new system was the result of legislative action rather than stemming from a decision of the state's highest court.

As in New Jersey, the dissolution proceedings necessary to end such a union under the new California Act are equivalent to divorce, but divorce is available in California on pure no-fault grounds. As under California divorce law, a summary procedure is provided by which shorter-term (five years or less) relationships without children, real property or many assets may be terminated if both parties consent; but a formal judicial proceeding will be required to end most domestic partnerships, at which property issues will be decided under California's community property rules, support will be considered, and all issues concerning custody and support of children adjudicated (ibid.: § 299). This marks a substantial departure from the system that now exists, in which partnerships may be dissolved by notice, hence the warnings being mailed to all current partners that they must file a Notice of Termination before January 1, 2005 or their relationship will be transformed into one involving many more benefits but also substantially more obligations.

Finally, the California legislation requires couples entering domestic partnerships to agree to continuing jurisdiction by the California courts over dissolution of their relationship, even if one or both should move out of the state—an obvious attempt to avoid the conflict of laws problems described in the previous section (ibid.: § 298 (c)(3)).

In sum, the legal landscape for cohabitants has become much more complicated with the passage of new partnership statutes and other status-based regimes with varying provisions, some exclusive to same-sex couples and some not, varying benefits and a variety of interstate recognition schemes. Partners or spouses will apparently be free to move among Vermont, Massachusetts, California and New Jersey without losing protection (although the marital status of Massachusetts couples may not be recognized as such in other states). At the same time, many domestic partnership arrangements provide only a limited number of benefits, and many are available only to limited groups of cohabitants. In Hawaii, New Jersey and California, very few heterosexuals are eligible. Moreover, unlike Washington's meretricious relationships, domestic partner status must be deliberately chosen by going through the procedure for registration. Thus if one member of a couple desires to register and the other does not, no protection is available; and couples are left to whatever other protections may be offered by the state's law on cohabitants' rights.

In a state like California, the result is a "hybrid" legal regime for cohabitants.[8] For most heterosexuals (those sixty-two and younger), cohabitants' rights *inter se* rest upon and are limited by contract, although a number of rights against third parties may be available from a domestic partnership ordinance if one exists in the city or county in which they live and it applies to opposite-sex couples. Same-sex couples who do not register as domestic partners will also be limited to contract-based rights under *Marvin* when they dissolve their relationships. By contrast, all of the benefits of marriage will be conferred in January 2005 upon those who choose to register as domestic partners.

Under the U.S. federal system, the states are often touted as laboratories of democracy, allowing experimentation with new arrangements that may subsequently be adopted in other regions. The new California domestic partnership law will be an ideal experiment. While some have objected to conferring benefits upon couples unwilling to undertake the obligations of marriage, California is now putting people to the choice. Those who now receive benefits without obligations will need to opt out before January 2005 if they do not want to become economically responsible for one another's support or to subject their property to community property rules. It will be very instructive to see how popular the newly enacted scheme is, how many new registrants it attracts and how many drop out by New Year's Eve 2004. For those who do not secede, the new law will fulfill the purposes of protecting vulnerable parties to the extent the state's marriage and divorce law performs this function; and it will fulfill the state's interest in the privatization of support as well.

D. A MILANGE OF RIGHTS AGAINST THIRD PARTIES

In addition to those available to registered domestic partners and spouses in the few states that confer that status, a number of benefits against third parties are available to cohabitants in some areas—both to heterosexuals and to same-sex cohabitants who live in states without domestic partnership or civil union laws or who fail to register their partnerships. As commentators have noted, rights and benefits against third parties may well be of more importance to working-class and middle-class cohabitants who have not acquired substantial amounts of property than are rights to property and support upon conclusion of their relationship (Blumberg 1981: 1126–27). In some states, benefits against third parties may be conferred upon cohabitants by a mishmash of remedies derived from case law, statute or ordinance. In this section, I describe a few of these approaches, in three areas: (1) benefits from the state, such as workers' compensation and taxation; (2) tort claims against third parties, such as for negligent infliction of emotional distress; and (3) health-related benefits, such as insurance and health care decision-making power.

1. *Benefits from the State*

One way in which third-party benefits for cohabitants may be derived is by courts embracing a functional definition of the family, which has happened in some areas with respect to workers' compensation and unemployment insurance. Workers' compensation statutes are typically written to cover "dependents" who survive the individual worker. The statutory concern to provide for dependents who have lost the wage earner upon whom they depend would seem to dictate that a dependent cohabitant should qualify for benefits, but courts historically refused recovery by cohabitants on grounds of public policy (ibid.: 1141). This may be changing. In California, opposite-sex cohabitants have been recognized as eligible for workers' compensation survivors benefits since 1979 if they can show that they were dependent upon the worker at the time of his or her death, and this eligibility was extended to the same-sex partner of a deceased employee in 1982 (*State v Workers' Compensation Appeals Board* 1979 at 186; *Donovan v Workers' Compensation Appeals Board* 1982 at 873). Similarly, although California courts in the past denied unemployment insurance benefits to cohabitants who had to relocate for reasons related to their partner's needs (*Norman v Unemployment Insurance Appeals Board* 1983), subsequent case law supports an award of benefits in these circumstances as well (*MacGregor v Unemployment Insurance Appeals Board* 1984). Thus while the recent California domestic partnership legislation guarantees eligibility for unemployment compensation benefits to same-sex and older heterosexual couples who register, the case law extends these benefits to a more extensive group of cohabitants.

Many of the most significant government benefits are universally unavailable to cohabitants, however, because they derive from federal law. Social Security survivors' benefits are available only to those who qualify as spouses as defined by state law (Social Security Act 2003: § 416(h)). Common-law spouses are eligible under this provision, but Congress hastened to ensure that same-sex spouses would not qualify for any benefits by providing that under all federal laws and regulations "the word 'marriage' means only a legal union between one man and one woman as husband and wife, and the word 'spouse' refers only to a person of the opposite sex who is a husband or a wife" (Defense of Marriage Act, 1 USC § 7 [2000]). Cases challenging the denial of Social Security benefits to cohabitants have been unsuccessful, on the ground that the wage-earner was never legally required to support his or her surviving cohabitant (Blumberg 1981: 1144–45). This rationale would no longer apply to registered or married partners in California, New Jersey, Vermont and Massachusetts, all of whom do have a legal duty of support.

Cohabitants also cannot file joint federal income tax returns, claim one another as dependents, or take advantage of spousal exclusions from federal estate and gift taxation (see Chambers 1996: 472–75). State tax benefits are available now, however, to same-sex couples in Vermont and Massachusetts; and cohabitants in Arizona may claim one another as dependents on their state tax forms (Ariz Rev Stat Ann § 43-1001 [2002]). California and New Jersey have not followed suit, apparently in order to maintain the same filing status on both state and federal returns.

2. *Tort Claims Against Third Parties*

Standing to bring a variety of tort claims—for the wrongful death of a partner or negligent infliction of emotional distress, for example—has been conferred by statute upon domestic partners in Hawaii, New Jersey and California and is available to persons in civil unions in Vermont and same-sex marriages in Massachusetts. In other states, and for persons who do not qualify as officially recognized partners in those jurisdictions (most heterosexuals), these issues have been fought out in the case law, with different states reaching opposing conclusions. Tort claims for negligent infliction of emotional distress (NIED) provide a good example. NIED damage claims are available in both California and New Jersey to family members who are at the scene of an accident caused by the defendant's negligence and witness the death or serious injury of a close family member (*Dillon v Legg* 1968; *Portee v Jaffee* 1980). But when a heterosexual cohabitant in California brought such a claim after witnessing his partner's death in an auto accident, recovery was denied on the familiar grounds that granting cohabitants such rights would interfere with the state's interest in promoting marriage (*Elden v Sheldon* 1988 at 586–87).[9] The court was also determined to draw a "bright line rule" that would not require courts to inquire into the details of an intimate relationship and would prevent extension of NIED claims to vast numbers of people (ibid. at 587–88). Thus same-sex couples registered as domestic partners in California may bring these claims, while heterosexual cohabitants cannot.

By contrast, when a similar case arose in New Jersey, involving a woman who witnessed the death of her fiancé in an auto accident caused by the defendant's negligence, the court rejected a bright-line approach based upon marriage and allowed recovery for NIED by cohabitants who could show that they were in an intimate and familial relationship, tested by its duration, mutual dependence and the like (*Dunphy v Gregor* 1994). The New Jersey court expressed itself confident that courts could identify relationships that entitled the parties to such treatment and disagreed with the California court that extension of this right would in any way damage the state's interest in protecting marriage, pointing out that the prospect of tort recovery in such a disastrous case would be unlikely to figure into the decision whether or not to get married (*Dunphy* at 379, quoting dissenting judge in *Elden* 1988). The inquiry the court must undertake to determine whether the couple is in a marriage-like relationship is similar to that for identifying meretricious relationships in Washington. The Supreme Court of New Mexico has followed similar reasoning in extending a cause of action for loss of consortium to cohabitants in an intimate familial relationship (*Lozoya v Sanchez* 2003).

In sum, the right of cohabitants to sue third parties for injuries to their relationships is limited and depends upon the state in which they live. Given the New Jersey court's insistence upon limiting these claims to cohabitants whose relationship mirrors traditional, conventional models of marriage, it is ironic that the majority of couples who are now in fact protected under these circumstances are same-sex—a result, apparently, of publicizing and personalizing their plight after 9/11 and the Diane Whipple dog-mauling case.

3. *Health-Related Benefits*

The final area in which a number of benefits are available from a variety of noncontract, nonstatus sources is health care. Health insurance coverage of cohabitants, especially of same-sex partners, is increasingly offered not only by municipalities and counties to their employees but also by private companies throughout the United States, especially high-tech companies, those in the entertainment industry and academic institutions, particularly on the east and west coasts (see Hein 2000: 28–34). The cost of providing this benefit has been fairly low, given the low participation rate, either because fear of coming out prevents gay and lesbian couples from applying or because cohabitants are likely each to be employed and thus may have separate health insurance already (ibid.: 32). Moreover, the net economic cost of the insurance is greater to cohabitants than to married couples because the benefit is taxed as income to the unmarried (Chambers 1996: 475). Challenges to exclusion of cohabitants from family health coverage as discrimination based on either marital status or sexual orientation have generally failed, on the grounds that married and unmarried couples may be treated differently since the latter have no legal duty of mutual support (see, e.g., *Phillips v Wisconsin Personnel Commission* 1992; see also Christensen 1997: 1375–79). In one Alaska case, however, the court found that denial of coverage to the gay male partner of an employee constituted discrimination on the basis of marital status (*Tumeo v University of Alaska* 1995).

Health care decision making can also be an important issue for cohabitants. It is possible for cohabitants to execute Power of Attorney for Health Care documents to designate one another in advance as the person to make decisions, including life and death decisions, in the event of incapacity; but many fail to do so (Robbennolt & Johnson 1999: 455 and n. 144).[10] To address this common failure to make provision in advance, states have passed health care surrogate statutes that list, in order of priority, the family members entitled to make health care decisions, beginning with a spouse and extending to more distant relatives; but very few states include domestic partners in such a list and at least one prioritizes them lower than adult children (ibid.: 426 and n. 69).[11] True to its policy of denying rights and benefits to cohabitants, Illinois considered but then intentionally excluded domestic partners from the list in that state, for fear that the bill would be politically unacceptable to the legislature (Closen & Maloney 1995: 491).

Unprotected by statute, cohabitants are left to the courts if they desire to assert rights in this respect. One especially egregious case in Minnesota attracted a great deal of attention to this issue. In it, the lesbian partner of

Sharon Kowalski, who had been incapacitated in an accident, sought both hospital visitation and the right to be named her partner's guardian and to make health care decisions on her behalf (*In re Guardianship of Kowalski* 1991). However, Sharon's parents, to whom she had never come out as a lesbian, succeeded in cutting off her partner's visitation, being named as her guardians, and in making health care decisions that placed Sharon in nursing homes without appropriate rehabilitative services. It took eight years of litigation for her partner to obtain the right to care for Sharon, concluding only when the Minnesota appellate court finally accepted a functional definition of family and also recognized Sharon's own rights and preferences in this matter. In other states, cohabitants may face similar legal battles, particularly if their authority is not recognized by hostile family members. Of course, in each of these situations—exclusion of cohabitants from health care surrogate statutes and court battles like *Kowalski*—the underlying purpose of the substitute decision making is defeated, for the partner is the person most likely to be able to articulate what the incapacitated individual would have wanted if she were able. Those who register as partners or spouses in California, New Jersey, Vermont and Massachusetts are now protected. Indeed, in all three of the areas described in this section, same-sex couples are now much more likely to be protected than are heterosexual cohabitants.

E. COHABITANTS AND THEIR CHILDREN

Finally, significant legal consequences can attach to cohabitation with respect to children. Historically cohabitation was seen and in some states can still be seen as tantamount to *per se* unfitness and thus grounds to lose custody of a child after divorce (*Jarrett v Jarrett* 1980). However, the trend in most states, with respect to heterosexual sexual behavior at least, is to provide that a parent's sexual behavior is relevant only if his or her conduct has an adverse effect upon the child (see Ellman et al. 1998: 634–37). Gay and lesbian cohabitants may still face problems relating to both custody and visitation, though (ibid.; see also Weisberg & Appleton 2002: 856).

Different issues are raised when a cohabiting couple decides to have children of their own, especially if the couple is of the same sex. Because rights concerning children depend largely upon biology, no problem is posed for cohabiting heterosexuals who decide to have children; rights to custody and visitation will parallel those afforded to married parents unless one of the partners has abandoned his or her relationship to the child (cf. *Stanley v Illinois* 1972 with *Quilloin v Walcott* 1978 and *Lehr v Robertson* 1983). Serious problems may arise for gay and lesbian parents, however, because of their inability to have children who are biologically related to both members of the cohabiting couple. For example, a cohabitant in the position of stepparent to his or her partner's child from a previous relationship does not have the rights of a stepparent who is married to the child's natural parent and thus must struggle to obtain visitation rights upon dissolution of the relationship, although stepparents in married relationships are increasingly afforded this right (Chambers 1996: 463–65).

More severe problems arise when gay or lesbian couples decide to have a child of their own and accomplish this either by having a lesbian partner artificially inseminated or a gay partner enter into a surrogacy agreement with a third party. Each of these arrangements is fraught with shoals. In most states, the nonbiological mother of her lesbian partner's child will be regarded as a legal stranger to that child, even though she has raised it as her own and is known as mother to it; upon dissolution, she may be denied both custody and visitation (see, e.g., *Alison D. v Virginia M.* 1991; *Nancy S. v Michele G.* 1991). Although a few state courts have begun to recognize *de facto* or quasi-parental status in these circumstances (see, e.g., *E.N.O. v L.M.M.* 1999; *V.C. v M.J.B.* 2000; *In re Guardianship of Olivia J.* 2000; Dalton 2003: 316–19), most courts still refuse to recognize a functional, or *de facto*, definition of parenthood. Moreover, while the child of a married woman produced by artificial insemination with the consent of her husband will automatically be presumed to be that of her husband and listed as such on the birth certificate, artificial insemination may confer rights upon the biological father of a lesbian couple's child (Chambers 1996: 467–68). Sperm donors have asserted rights against lesbian mothers with some success (see, e.g., *Thomas S. v Robin Y.* 1994). Moreover, gay males seeking to have a child that is biologically related to at least one of them may face many problems enforcing surrogacy contracts and cutting off the rights of the surrogate mother to custody and visitation (see, e.g., *In the Matter of Baby M* 1988).

Many same-sex couples choose to adopt their children, and this route is now possible in most states. Only Florida has a longstanding statutory ban on adoption by homosexuals, although it permits them to serve as foster parents; this prohibition was recently upheld against an equal protection challenge in federal court (*Lofton v Kearney* 2004). Mississippi and Utah have recently added prohibitions against adoption by homosexuals to their law, while New Hampshire dropped a similar prohibition in 1999 (Miss Code § 93-17-3 [2003]; Utah Code Ann § 78-30-2 [2002]; NH Rev Stat § 170-B: 4 [1999]; see also Cooper 2004). However, co-parent adoption, which would protect the rights of both partners to their child, is unavailable in about half the states. A 2002 survey of state adoption laws showed that second-parent adoptions had been approved by courts in twenty-four states and the District of Columbia (although the right to do so is only really secure in the handful of states with affirmative supreme court rulings on the issue), while twenty-six states have explicitly disapproved the practice (Lambda Legal 2002). Moreover, second-parent adoption procedures are costly, intrusive and risky; and a successful outcome results in a family in which the co-parents are legal strangers to one another, while most family benefits depend upon spousal status (Dalton 2001: 211–15).

This brief summary simply points to some of the recurring problems that may threaten cohabitants' rights to their children, and here the main distinction is the sexual orientation of the cohabiting parents. Although recent developments—for example, the increased approval of co-parent adoption by gay and lesbian parents—have improved the situation to some extent, severe problems remain which may threaten the security of the parent-child relationship of gay and lesbian couples. Some but not all of these problems are relieved by entering into domestic partnerships or civil unions in states where they are available.

III. CONCLUSIONS

As is clear from this discussion, the law concerning cohabitants' rights in the United States varies immensely from state to state and by sexual orientation; it is also rapidly changing in many respects. There is now a substantial history of attempts by the courts to protect vulnerable parties in cohabiting relationships. The case law of common-law marriage and the equitable doctrines used to address injustices resulting from cohabitants' dependence upon one another show that many courts have been uneasy with those injustices and determined to remedy them for a long time. It was only during the late 1970s and 1980s, however, that this unease led to the development of cohabitants' rights cases. The first of these extended rights based upon contract, express or implied. This approach offered some help to vulnerable parties at the end of cohabiting relationships but has proved inadequate, as courts have insisted upon finding express contracts and have refused to imply contracts in the absence of direct evidence of agreement. The state of Washington's meretricious relationship doctrine is better in this respect, looking first for the characteristics of a relationship of interdependence and then imposing property distribution remedies upon cohabitants at the end of their relationships even if they are unwilling. Developed by the courts to protect heterosexual cohabitants, both California's contract approach and Washington's meretricious relationship scheme were then extended to same-sex couples in the case law. Neither approach, however, addresses rights against third parties, whether it be the state or an employer or a tortfeasor, which are often more valuable than rights *inter se*.

In the 1990s, the focus of cohabitants' rights shifted to gay and lesbian couples and their exclusion from marriage. This campaign has resulted in only one totally successful case thus far (Massachusetts) but has spawned many and varied domestic partnership schemes, ranging from the limited remedies contained in Hawaii's Reciprocal Beneficiaries Act, the early California domestic partnership law, and various local ordinances, on the one hand, to granting all the benefits and obligations of marriage in Vermont (and by 2005 in California), on the other. In Vermont, Massachusetts and California, same-sex couples are now well protected; and many assume, or hope, that New Jersey will follow California's example and expand the benefits available to domestic partners in that state.

The result of all this activity is a rather confusing legal situation, in which cohabitants' rights are based upon a mixture of remedies that not only vary from state to state but also result in intrastate legal regimes based on different legal theories and offering a patchwork of remedies from a variety of sources. An additional result is that same-sex couples are better protected in many areas than are heterosexual cohabitants.

The system as it now exists is clearly unstable. The various conflict of law problems described above import a built-in instability, as couples who have been granted either the status or incidents of marriage move from state to state. The exclusion of heterosexuals from benefits available to gays and lesbians is another source of instability. As gay cohabitants' rights originally developed out of those granted to heterosexuals, the reverse may also prove true. The inclusion of some heterosexuals within the protections granted by Hawaii, New Jersey and California now undermines the argument that "they can always get married" and may provide the basis for an equal protection challenge to the exclusion of heterosexuals in general.

Some argue that extension of rights to heterosexual cohabitants will provide incentives not to marry and thus do serious harm to the institution of marriage. It may be that more heterosexuals would cohabit instead of marrying if the status were given more benefits, but the number of cohabitants has been increasing rapidly over the last decades despite substantial financial disincentives. For whatever reasons, large numbers of people find the institution of marriage lacking, but they forge ties of reliance and interdependence outside its confines nonetheless. Census data reveal that at least 5.5 million individuals fall into this category, and 41 percent of them have children whose welfare is affected by failure to recognize their status.

A system of family law should acknowledge the families that actually exist, particularly in a country that ties so many of the welfare functions central to life and health to family or spousal status. There is now a growing acceptance of extending economic benefits to same-sex couples, even in the face of substantial resistance to allowing them entry into the religious and cultural tradition of marriage (*Harvard Law Review* 2003: 2001). Perhaps a similar acceptance of granting benefits to functional families headed by unmarried heterosexuals will develop as well. In short, the instability of the current legal situation opens the possibility of change in many respects.

The ideal situation may turn out to be something like that which obtains in the Netherlands, a multi-status system that allows both same- and opposite-sex couples either to marry or to register as domestic partners. Yet to satisfactorily perform the family law functions of protecting vulnerable dependent parties and privatizing the costs of welfare, it would still be necessary to impose certain obligations on unregistered long-term cohabitants, under a system similar to that suggested by the ALI, which mandates both property distribution and support upon dissolution of the relationship. If cohabitants are unwilling to undertake these responsibilities to one another, they will need to execute contracts to that effect. Although this situation would also be a "hybrid" in many respects, it would be less confusing than the one that now exists, where the law may provide, within the same state, a patchwork of inconsistent remedies to different groups.

CYNTHIA GRANT BOWMAN, *Columbia University, J.D. Northwestern University School of Law, is Professor of Law and of Gender Studies at Northwestern University in Chicago, Illinois. She has written widely on family law, domestic violence, sexual harassment and abuse and a variety of other topics having to do with law and women.*

NOTES

1. Six states abolished common-law marriage between 1875 and 1917, and an additional sixteen have done so since 1920, primarily out of fears of fraudulent claims and to protect the institution of marriage (see Bowman 1997: 715 n. 24). The District of Columbia and ten states—Alabama, Colorado, Iowa, Kansas, Montana, Pennsylvania, Rhode Island, South Carolina, Texas and Utah—currently recognize common-law marriage (ibid.).
2. Despite its position on this issue, Georgia did recognize a contract partitioning property between two lesbians in *Crooke v Gilden* (1992).
3. There is some inconsistency in the application of the Illinois rule, however (see, e.g., *Spafford v Coats* 1983).
4. Nevada follows a similar approach (see Estin 2001: 1383, citing *Western States Construction, Inc. v Michoff* 1992 at 1224–25 and n. 17).
5. One study found that only about one-third of heterosexual committed partners had wills, though 60 percent of same-sex couples did (Robbennolt & Johnson 1999: 441).
6. The American Law Institute is a group of lawyers, judges and law professors who study various subject areas of the law and recommend reforms, often in the form of a model statute; its model laws depend upon subsequent adoption by state legislatures for authority.
7. The San Francisco City Attorney has also filed suit, maintaining that denial of marriage licenses to same-sex couples violates the state constitution's equal protection clause (Murphy 2004).
8. For examples of other types of hybrid regimes, see Reppy (2002: 286–90), who describes states where courts have found, based on express or implied contract, rights, such as standing to sue in tort, which no contract could impose, as well as states in which statutes or ordinances confer rights not available under the state's contract-based law of cohabitants' rights. Blumberg (2001: 1294) also describes states that follow contract rubric but make awards that cannot be justified under contract law.
9. California courts have followed similar reasoning in denying standing to sue for the wrongful death of a cohabitant, noting that to extend the action beyond the decedent's heirs would be the equivalent of bringing back common-law marriage (*Welch v State of California* 2000 at 433).

10. In the Minnesota study, 26.7 percent of opposite-sex cohabitants and 71.1 percent of same-sex cohabitants designated their partners as surrogate health care decision makers (Robbennolt & Johnson 1999: 455 and n. 144).
11. Robbennolt & Johnson (426) describe a New Mexico statute that includes an "individual in a long-term relationship of indefinite duration . . . [who] has demonstrated an actual commitment to the patient similar to the commitment of a spouse and in which the individual and the patient consider themselves to be responsible for each other's well-being" and refer to Delaware and Maine statutes possibly allowing a cohabitant to serve as a surrogate but only if listed family members are unavailable. Arizona statute law prioritizes domestic partners below adult children of the patient (ibid.: 426 and n. 69).

REFERENCES

American Law Institute (ALI) (2002) *Principles of the Law of Family Dissolution: Analysis and Recommendations*. Philadelphia: ALI.

Bernstein, Fred A. (2003) "Gay Unions Were Only Half the Battle," *New York Times* 6 April: 9–2.

Blumberg, Grace Ganz (1981) "Cohabitation Without Marriage: A Different Perspective," *UCLA Law Review* 28: 1125–80.

Blumberg, Grace Ganz (2001) "The Regularization of Nonmarital Cohabitation: Rights and Responsibilities in the American Welfare State," *Notre Dame Law Review* 76: 1265–1310.

Bowman, Craig A., and Blake M. Cornish (1992) "Note, a More Perfect Union: A Legal and Social Analysis of Domestic Partnership Ordinances," *Columbia Law Review* 92: 1164–1211.

Bowman, Cynthia Grant (1996) "A Feminist Proposal to Bring Back Common Law Marriage," *Oregon Law Review* 75: 709–81.

Bullock, Kristin (1992) "Comment, Applying *Marvin v. Marvin* to Same-Sex Couples: A Proposal for a Sex-Preference Neutral Cohabitation Contract Statute," *U.C. Davis Law Review* 25: 1029–54.

Callan, Megan E. (2003) "The More, The Not Marry-er: In Search of a Policy Behind Eligibility for California Domestic Partnerships," *San Diego Law Review* 40: 427–59.

Chambers, David L. (1996) "What If? The Legal Consequences of Marriage and the Legal Needs of Lesbian and Gay Male Couples," *Michigan Law Review* 95: 447–91.

Christensen, Craig W. (1997) "Legal Ordering of Family Values: The Case of Gay and Lesbian Families,"*Cardozo Law Review* 18: 1299–1416.

Christensen, Craig W. (1998) "If Not Marriage? On Securing Gay and Lesbian Family Values by a 'Simulacrum of Marriage,'" *Fordham Law Review* 66: 1699–1784.

Clark, Homer H., Jr. (1988) *The Law of Domestic Relations in the United States*, 2d ed. St. Paul, Minn.: West.

Closen, Michael L., and Joan E. Maloney (1995) "The Health Care Surrogate Act in Illinois: Another Rejection of Domestic Partners' Rights," *Southern Illinois University Law Journal* 19: 479–522.

Cooper, Molly (2004) "What Makes a Family? Addressing the Issue of Gay and Lesbian Adoption," *Family Court Review* 42: 178–88.

Dalton, Susan E. (2001) "Protecting Our Parent-Child Relationships: Understanding the Strengths and Weaknesses of Second-Parent Adoption." In *Queer Families, Queer Politics: Challenging Culture and the State*, edited by M. Bernstein & R. Reimann. New York: Columbia Univ. Press.

Dalton, Susan E. (2003) "From Presumed Fathers to Lesbian Mothers: Sex Discrimination and the Legal Construction of Parenthood," *Michigan Journal of Gender & Law* 9: 261–326.

Ellman, Ira Mark (2001) "'Contract Thinking' Was *Marvin's* Fatal Flaw," *Notre Dame Law Review* 76: 1365–80.

Ellman, Ira Mark, Paul M. Kurtz, and Elizabeth S. Scott (1998) *Family Law* 3d ed. Charlottesville, Va.: Lexis Law Publishing.

Ertman, Martha M. (2001) "The ALI Principles' Approach to Domestic Partnership," *Duke Journal of Gender Law & Policy* 8: 107–17.

Estin, Ann Laquer (2001) "Ordinary Cohabitation," *Notre Dame Law Review* 76: 1381–1408.

Fellows, Mary Louise, Monica Kirkpatrick Johnson, Amy Chiericozzi, Ann Hale, Christopher Lee, Robin Preble and Michael Voran (1998) "Committed Partners and Inheritance: An Empirical Study," *Law & Inequality* 16: 1–94.

Fields, Jason, and Lynne M. Casper (2001) *America's Families and Living Arrangements: 2000*. Washington, D.C.: U.S. Dept of Commerce, Bureau of the Census.

Gorback, Michael Jay (2002) "Negligent Infliction of Emotional Distress: Has the Legislative Response to Diane Whipple's Death Rendered the Hard-Line Stance of *Elden* and *Thing* Obsolete?" *Hastings Law Journal* 54: 273–309.

Gordon, Katherine C. (1998–99) "Note, The Necessity and Enforcement of Cohabitation Agreements: When Strings Will Attach and How to Prevent Them—A State Survey," *Brandeis Law Journal* 37: 245–57.

Habegger, Dee Ann (2000) "Living in Sin and the Law: Benefits for Unmarried Couples Dependent Upon Sexual Orientation?" *Indiana Law Review* 33: 991–1014.

Harvard Law Review (2003) "Developments—The Law of Marriage and Family," *Harvard Law Review* 116: 1996–2122.

Hein, Jonathan Andrew (2000) "Caring for the Evolving American Family: Cohabiting Partners and Employer Sponsored Health Care," *New Mexico Law Review* 30: 19–41.

Lambda Legal (2002) "*Overview of State Adoption Laws*, 8/27/2002." Available at http://www.lambdalegal.org/cgi-bin/iowa/documents/record?record=399 (accessed Feb 10, 2004).

Marshall, Carolyn (2004) "Rushing to Say 'I Do' Before City Is Told 'You Can't'," *New York Times* 17 February: A-10.

Murphy, Dean E. (2004) "San Francisco Judge Rules Gay Marriages Can Continue," *New York Times* 21 February: A-8.

Oldham, J. Thomas (2001) "Lessons from *Jerry Hall v Mick Jagger* Regarding U.S. Regulation of Heterosexual Cohabitants or, Can't Get No Satisfaction," *Notre Dame Law Review* 76: 1409–34.

Reppy, William A., Jr. (2002) "Choice of Law Problems Arising When Unmarried Cohabitants Change Domicile," *Southern Methodist University Law Review* 55: 273–323.

Robbennolt, Jennifer K., and Monica Kirkpatrick Johnson (1999) "Legal Planning for Unmarried Committed Partners: Empirical Lessons for a Preventive and Therapeutic Approach," *Arizona Law Review* 41: 417–457.

Sawyer, Christopher D. (2003) "Practice What You Preach: California's Obligation to Give Full Faith and Credit to the Vermont Civil Union," *Hastings Law Journal* 54: 727–49.

Sherman, Jeffrey G. (1981) "Undue Influence and the Homosexual Testator," *University of Pittsburgh Law Review* 42: 225–67.

Simmons, Tavia, and Grace O'Neill (2001) *Households and Families: 2000*. Washington, D.C.: U.S. Dept of Commerce, Bureau of the Census.

Weisberg, D. Kelly, and Susan Frelich Appleton (2002) *Modern Family Law*. 2d ed. New York: Aspen Law & Business.

CASES CITED

Alison D. v Virginia M., 572 NE2d 27 (NY 1991).
Ayala v Fox, 564 NE2d 920 (Ill Ct App 1990).
Baehr v Lewin, 852 P2d 44 (Hawaii 1993).
Baker v Nelson, 191 NW2d 185 (Minn 1971).
Baker v State, 744 A2d 864 (Vt 1999).
Brause v Bureau of Vital Statistics, 1998 WL 88743 (Alaska Super Ct).
City of Atlanta v McKinney, 454 SE2d 517 (Ga 1995).
Connell v Francisco, 898 P2d 831 (Wash 1995).
Crooke v Gilden, 414 SE2d 645 (Ga 1992).
Dillon v Legg, 441 P2d 912 (Cal 1968).
Donovan v Workers' Compensation Appeals Bd, 187 Cal Rptr 869 (Cal Ct App 1982).
Dunphy v Gregor, 642 A2d 372 (NJ 1994).
Elden v Sheldon, 758 P2d 582 (Cal 1988).
E.N.O. v L.M.M., 711 NE2d 886 (Mass 1999).
Friedman v Friedman, 24 Cal Rptr 2d 892 (Cal Ct App 1993).
Goodridge v Dep't of Public Health, 798 NE2d 941 (Mass 2003) [Goodridge I].
Goodridge v Dep't of Public Health, 2004 Mass. LEXIS 35 [Goodridge II].
Hewitt v Hewitt, 394 NE2d 1204 (Ill 1979).
In re Adoption of Swanson, 623 A2d 1095 (Del 1993).
In re Estate of Vargas, 111 Cal Rptr 779 (1974).
In re Guardianship of Kowalski, 478 NW2d 790 (Minn Ct App 1991).
In re Guardianship of Olivia J., 101 Cal Rptr 2d 364 (Cal Ct App 2000).
In re Marriage of Lindsey, 678 P2d 328 (Wash 1984).
In the Matter of Baby M, 537 A2d 1227 (NJ 1988).
Jarrett v Jarrett, 400 NE2d 421 (Ill 1980).
Jones v Daly, 176 Cal Rptr 130 (Cal Ct App 1981).
Jones v Hallahan, 501 SW2d 588 (Ky 1973).
Lawrence v Texas, 539 US 558 (2003).
Lehr v Robertson, 463 US 248 (1983).
Lewis v Harris, No. MER-L-15-03 (N.J. Super. Ct. Nov. 5, 2003).
Lofton v Kearney, 2004 WL 161275 (11th Cir).
Lozoya v Sanchez, 66 P2d 948 (NM 2003).
MacGregor v Unemployment Insurance Appeals Bd, 689 P2d 453 (Cal 1984).
Marvin v Marvin I, 134 Cal Rptr 815 (CA 1976).
Marvin v Marvin II, 5 Fam L Rep 3079 (1979).
Marvin v Marvin III, 176 Cal Rptr 555 (Cal Ct App 1981).
Matter of Adoption of Robert Paul P., 471 NE2d 424 (NY 1984).
Medley v Strong, 558 NE2d 244 (Ill App Ct 1990).
Metropolitan Life Ins. Co. v Johnson, 645 P2d 356 (Idaho 1982).
Morone v Morone, 413 NE2d 1154 (NY 1980).
Nancy S. v Michele G., 279 Cal Rptr 212 (Cal Ct App 1991).
Norman v Unemployment Insurance Appeals Bd, 663 P2d 904 (Cal 1983).
Phillips v Wisconsin Personnel Commission, 482 NW2d 121 (Wis Ct App 1992).
PNC Bank v Workers' Compensation Bd, 831 A2d 1269 (Pa Commonwealth Ct 2002).
Portee v Jaffee, 417 A2d 521 (NJ 1980).
Quilloin v Walcott, 434 US 246 (1978).
Spafford v Coats, 455 NE2d 241 (Ill App Ct 1983).
Stanley v Illinois, 405 US 645 (1972).
State v Workers' Compensation Appeals Bd, 156 Cal Rptr 183 (Cal Ct App 1979).

Thomas S. v Robin Y., 618 NYS2d 356 (NY App Div 1994).
Tumeo v University of Alaska, 1995 WL 238359 (Alaska Super Ct).
Vasquez v Hawthorne, 33 P3d 735 (Wash 2001).
V.C. v M.J.B., 748 A2d 539 (NJ 2000).
Welch v State of California, 100 Cal Rptr 2d 430 (Cal App 2000).
Western States Construction, Inc. v Michoff, 840 P2d 1220 (Nev 1992).
Whorton v Dillingham 248 Cal Rptr 405 (Cal Ct App 1988).
Wilcox v Trautz, 693 NE2d 141 (Mass 1998).

LAWS CITED

Alaska Const, Art I § 25.
Ariz Rev Stat Ann § 43-1001 (2002).
California Domestic Partner Rights and Responsibilities Act, AB 205, 2003–2004 Reg Sess (CA 2003).
California Domestic Partner Registration Act, Cal Family Code § 297 (2000).
California Defense of Marriage Act, Cal Family Code § 308.5 (2002).
Civil Unions Act,15 Vt Stat Ann §§ 1201-1207 (Supp 2000).
Hawaii Const, Art I § 23.
Minn Stat § 513.075-513.076 (2002).
Miss Code § 93-17-3 (2003).
Neb Const, Art I § 29.
NH Rev Stat Ann § 170-B: 4 (1999).
NH Rev Stat Ann § 457: 39 (2001).
New Jersey Domestic Partnership Act, AB 3743, 210th Legis, 2d Reg Sess (NJ 2003).
NJ Stat Ann 2A: 34-2 (2000).
Reciprocal Beneficiaries Act, Hawaii Rev Stat §§ 572C-1-7 (1998).
Social Security Act, 42 USC § 416(h) (2003).
U.S. Defense of Marriage Act, 1 USC § 7 (2000).
U.S. Defense of Marriage Act, 28 USC § 1738C (2000).
Utah Code Ann § 78-30-2 (2002).

Part VII
Law and Non-conjugal Relationships

[26]

Why we should Care about Friends: An Argument for Queering the Care Imaginary in Social Policy

Sasha Roseneil

ESRC Research Group on Care, Values and the Future of Welfare (CAVA), School of Sociology and Social Policy, University of Leeds
E-mail: s.roseneil@leeds.ac.uk

This paper sets out an argument for the re-imagining of care in social policy on three interrelated grounds: epistemological–theoretical, substantive socio-historical, and normative political–philosophical. It takes up the epistemological challenge offered by queer theory to propose a different gaze be cast on care which recognizes the practices of care which take place outside normative heterosexual couples and families. Following on from this, it suggests that the care that has been the object of study in social policy has failed to keep up with transformations in the realm of sociability which characterize the contemporary world. It outlines findings of research which show the increasing importance of friendship to those at the cutting edge of processes of individualization. Finally, it points to the new and valuable lens that the study of caring practices of friends might cast on the ethics of care, and it ends with some pointers to what it might mean for social policy to take friendship seriously.

Friendship is a virtue . . . to say so much implies that friendship is a noble thing – i.e. that it is worthy to be pursued as an end in itself. Further, friendship is among the most indispensable requirements of life: it is, in fact, valuable not only as an end, but as a necessary means to life . . . It is an observed fact that men find friendship indispensable in good fortune, in bad fortune, and at all periods of their life. (*The Nicomachean Ethics*, By Aristotle)[1]

I'll Be There For You
By The Rembrants[2]

So no one told you life was gonna be this way
Your job's a joke, you're broke, your love life's D.O.A.
It's like you're always stuck in second gear
When it hasn't been your day, your week, your month, or even your year,
Chorus
I'll be there for you
(When the rain starts to pour)
I'll be there for you
(Like I've been there before)
I'll be there for you
('Cause you're there for me too)

Introduction

From the symposia of ancient Athens to the sofas of Central Perk, philosophers – professional and lay – have believed that in terms of *care, values and welfare* friends matter. What was recognized by Aristotle,[3] and is the central conceit of one of the world's most successful television series, has, however, largely failed to register in the social scientific literature on care, or within social policy more widely.[4] This paper proposes that for those of us who are interested in the social organization of care, the values that underpin its provision and practice, and the welfare systems which enable its flourishing,[5] friends should similarly matter. Drawing on queer and feminist theory, and on empirical research conducted under the auspices of the ESRC Research Group for the Study of Care, Values and the Future of Welfare (CAVA), I set forth an argument about why those of us concerned to develop a radical, generative understanding of welfare should begin to think differently about care – an argument about why we should care about friends. My case for the re-imagining of care rests on three interrelated grounds, which have fed into, or are derived from, my CAVA research: epistemological–theoretical, substantive socio-historical, and normative political–philosophical.

We should care about friends because...

We should think beyond the heteronormative (the epistemological–theoretical argument)

The first strand of my argument that friendship deserves a place in social policy is derived from the insights of queer theory.[6] This rather amorphous body of work shares a critique of the minoritizing epistemology which has underpinned most academic thinking about homosexuality, and stakes a claim for knowledge produced from queer theory and from the analysis of queer lives way beyond its immediate, and obvious, audience. In the words of Eve Sedgwick (1991: 1), rather than seeing the 'homo/heterosexual definition... as an issue of active importance primarily for a small, distinct, relatively fixed homosexual minority', queer theory suggests 'seeing it... as an issue of continuing determining importance in the lives of people across the spectrum of sexualities'. Thus one of queer theory's foundational propositions is that an understanding of heteronormativity – the 'institutions, structures of understanding, and practical orientations that make heterosexuality seem not only coherent – that is, organized as a sexuality – but also privileged' (Berlant and Warner, 2000: 312) – must be central to any analysis of modern western society. From this, I would suggest that social policy, like all social science and humanities disciplines, should reject the 'epistemology of the closet' which both silences sexual difference and regards those living outside normative heterosexual frameworks as marginal to our interests.

This means we should seek to frame research questions from non-heteronormative standpoints, making a conscious effort to think outside and beyond heterosexual familial relations, and allowing lesbians, gay men, bisexuals and all those whose lives transgress heteronormative assumptions a central place in our analyses. It means both being open to seeing differences between homosexual and heterosexual lives, and according analytical importance to these, but at the same time not treating the categories of 'homosexual' and 'heterosexual', and the individuals who carry these identities, as essentially different, as fixed and firmly constituted.

If we take this epistemological–theoretical argument to heart and look to the growing field of lesbian and gay studies as a resource for thinking about social policy, there is considerable evidence to suggest that friendship is of foundational and particular importance in the lives of lesbians and gay men.[7] Networks of friends, which often include ex-lovers, form the context within which lesbians and gay men tend to build their personal lives, offering emotional continuity, companionship, pleasure and practical assistance. Building and maintaining lives outside the framework of the heterosexual nuclear family, and sometimes rejected, problematized and marginalized by their families of origin, lesbians and gay men have tended to ground their emotional security and daily lives in their friendship groups. Many groups of lesbian and gay friends refer to themselves quite consciously as 'family' (Weston, 1991; Nardi, 1992, 1999; Preston with Lowenthal, 1996). For some lesbians and gay men the boundary between friends and lovers is not clear and shifts over time – friends become lovers, and lovers become friends – and many have multiple sexual partners of varying degrees of commitment (and none). These practices de-centre the primary significance that is commonly granted to sexual partnerships and the privileging of conjugal relationships, and suggests to us the importance of thinking beyond the conjugal imaginary.

A lesson of queer theory is that we should resist the tendency to trivialize, infantalize and subordinate relationships which are not clear parallels of the conventional, stable, long-term, cohabiting heterosexual couple. We should avoid a 'life-course mindset' which focuses on generational reproduction within the heterosexual family as *the* significant, productive activity and space, at which analytical attention should be directed. Queer theory can encourage social policy to focus on the non-normative, on those who, knowingly or not, challenge the expectations, assumptions and regulations of heteronormativity. Queer theory's attention to the constructed nature of the homosexual/heterosexual binary, to the fluidity which exists between homosexual and heterosexual identities and practices, suggests that we work from the knowledge which exists about the salience of friendship to lesbians and gay men, to explore its relevance in the lives of heterosexuals too.

Friendship is becoming more important (the socio-historical argument)

Historical, sociological and anthropological writings on friendship point to historical and cultural variability in the meanings and practices of friendship.[8] Drawing on the idea that friendship is socially constructed and changes over time, the second element of my argument that we should take friendship seriously suggests that we do so because friendship is a relationship of increasing social significance in the contemporary world. The particular version of modern friendship which emerged in the mid-twentieth century, which promoted the companionate intimate heterosexual couple as the primary arena of intimacy, and emphasized a new culture of mutual disclosure between husband and wife and the importance of joint leisure activities, has recently started to be unsettled. Shifts in gender and family relations, processes of individualization and the postmodernization of relations of sexuality are socially and culturally de-centring hetero-relations and destabilizing – or *queering* – the distinctions between heterosexual and homosexual ways of life.[9] As geographical mobility increases, as marriage rates drop and marriage takes place later, as divorce rates have soared over the past 30 years, as births outside marriage, and indeed outside any lasting heterosexual relationship, increase steeply, as the proportion of people living in single person households rises and the proportion of women not having children climbs, patterns of sociability – as well as the more widely discussed patterns of intimacy (Giddens, 1992; Beck and Beck Gernsheim, 1995) – are undergoing transformation. A smaller proportion of the population is living in the heterosexual nuclear family of idealized mid-twentieth century form, and fewer people are choosing or able to construct their relations of cathexis according to the symmetrical family, intimate couple model. In 2003 only 22 per cent of households in the UK comprised a heterosexual couple with dependent children (ONS, 2004). This increasingly means that ways of life that might previously have been regarded as distinctively 'homosexual' are becoming more widespread. As Jeffrey Weeks, Brian Heaphy and Catherine Donovan (2001: 85) have suggested, 'one of the most remarkable features of domestic change over recent years is . . . the emergence of common patterns in homosexual and heterosexual ways of life as a result of these long-term shifts in relationship patterns'.

The significance of these processes of individualization calls for attention to the relationship and caring practices of those living at the leading edge of social change. Evidence from the British Household Panel Study shows that men and women who are divorced are more likely to see a close friend during the week than those who are married. Moreover the British Social Attitudes report suggests that people are more likely to have seen their 'best friend' than any relative who does not live with them in the previous week, and whilst there has been a decline in the proportion of respondents seeing relatives or friends at least once a week between 1986 and 1995, the decline in contact with friends was considerably smaller (Pahl, 1998). Peter Willmott's (1987) research also suggests that friends were, by the mid 1980s, more important than relatives or neighbours in terms of providing practical help with everyday tasks. It seems highly unlikely that this will suddenly change and that there will be a reversion to the forms of familial and neighbourly assistance which were reported in the working class localities researched in the community studies of the 1950s (e.g. Hodges and Smith, 1954; Young and Wilmott, 1957).

Against this backdrop, the findings of the 'Care, Friendship and Non-Conventional Partnership' project[10] within CAVA add weight to the idea that friendship is an increasingly socially significant relationship. This research has investigated how the most 'individualized' in our society – people who do not live with a partner – construct their networks of intimacy, friendship, care and support. We wanted to find out who matters to people who are living outside conventional families, what they value about their personal relationships, how they care for those who matter to them, and how they care for themselves. We carried out in-depth interviews with 53 people aged between 25 and 60 in three locations – a former mining town that is relatively conventional in terms of gender and family relations; a small town in which alternative, middle-class, 'downshifted' lifestyles and sexual nonconformity are common; and a multi-ethnic inner-city area characterized by a range of gender and family practices, a higher-than-average proportion of women in the labour force and a large number of single-person and non-couple households. We talked to men and women with and without children, of a diversity of ages, ethnic origins, occupations and sexual orientations, and with varying relationship statuses and living arrangements. This gave us detailed insights into the texture of people's emotional lives.

We found that, across a range of lifestyles and sexualities, friendship occupied a central place in the personal lives of our interviewees. Whether they were in a heterosexual couple relationship or not, the people we interviewed were turning to friends for emotional support. Jools, a heterosexual woman of 28 from a former mining town, spoke for many people when she said: 'I think a friendship is for life, but I don't think a partner is... I'd marry my friends. They'd last longer'. There was a high degree of reliance on friends, as opposed to biological kin and sexual partners, particularly for the provision of care and support in everyday life, and friendship operated as key value and site of ethical practice for many. Far from being isolated, solitary individuals who flit from one unfulfilling relationship to another, most of the people we interviewed were enmeshed in complex networks of intimacy and care, and had strong commitments and connections to others. In contrast to the mythology of the singleton in desperate search for a marriage partner – exemplified by Bridget Jones – very few showed any yearning to be part of a conventional couple or family. A great many, both of those with partners and of those without, were consciously placing less emphasis on the importance of the couple relationship. Instead, they were centring their lives on their friends. Of those with partners, almost all had *chosen* not to live together. Very few saw cohabitation as the inevitable and desirable next stage of their relationship.

Many of the interviewees had experienced the ending of a marriage or a long-term cohabiting relationship, and the pain and disruption this had caused had made them question the wisdom of putting all of their emotional eggs in one basket. Only one of the interviewees saw her partner as the most important person in her life, to the exclusion of others. She was a recent migrant to Britain whose family lived overseas. For everyone else, the people who mattered were either friends or a combination of friends, partner, children and family. This was not a temporary phase and people did not return to conventional couple relationships as soon as an opportunity arose. Re-interviewing people 18 months later, we found a remarkably consistent prioritization of friendship.

Friends were an important part of everyday life in good times and bad. Most of the people we spoke to put considerable effort into building and maintaining friendships in the place where they lived. A good number had moved house, or had persuaded friends to move house, with the aim of creating local friendship networks that could offer reciprocal childcare and help in times of illness, as well as pleasurable sociability. It was friends far more than biological kin who offered support to those who suffered from emotional distress or mental health problems, and who were there to pick up the pieces when love relationships ended. Many of the people we interviewed were opening up their homes to people who were not part of their conventionally defined family. It was not just the twenty-somethings who spent much of their leisure time hanging out with friends at each other's homes or having people round to dinner, for parties and barbecues. Friends were invited to stay during periods of homelessness, when out of work or when they were depressed or lonely.

What this research suggests is that social researchers have often failed to see the extent to which, often as a matter of preference, people are substituting the ties of friendship for those of blood, particularly in terms of everyday care and emotional support.

Friendship offers us a new and valuable lens on the ethics of care (the political/ philosophical argument)

Central to our collective project in CAVA is the grounded, sociological development, and normative elucidation, of the concept of an ethics of care, which holds as axiomatic the fundamentally relational, interdependent nature of human existence. We regard an ethics of care as important in countering the overwhelming emphasis in current, individualistic political discourse which promotes the ethic of work above all else.[11] However, many feminists have expressed reservations about the wholehearted embracing of an ethics of care, regarding it as over-reliant on a model of care developed from thinking about the fundamentally gendered care practices of mothers for their children, and fearing that it brings with it a diminution of concern about the ethics of justice and social equality.[12] I fully appreciate such concerns, and wish to keep a critical eye on the model of self with which an ethics of care operates, on the types of relationship from which it is theorized, and on the implications of these for the *welfare* of the *care-giver*. We should be wary that advocating an ethics of care might involve endorsing a model of self which is so fundamentally relational that any sense of individuality, separateness, and capacity to act autonomously is negated. I concur with Marilyn Friedman (1993: 5) in her call 'for introducing into care ethics a cautiously individualistic strain of thought, one that is consistent with a care-ethical conception of persons as inherently social beings'. With consideration to issues of politics, I am concerned that an ethics of care does not always adequately take into account the unequal, highly constrained, and even oppressive conditions in which many practices of caring, particularly those carried out by women, occur. We need to think about issues of equality and reciprocity, and about the needs of the carer for care. As Peta Bowden puts it: 'The challenge directed to care theorists is that their ethics fails to confront the morality of gender inequality itself, and in fact, perpetuates the reign of the dominant by encouraging self-sacrifice and servility in the guise of care' (1997: 8). We need to think not just about 'gendering ethics', as an ethics of care does, but also about 'the ethics of gender'.[13]

Attention to friendship can facilitate a useful reconceptualization of our notion of an adequate ethics of care.[14] Friendship is a significantly different relationship from that of mothering, lacking controlling institutions and firm cultural expectations and conventions. It is 'a sphere of social activity that is both exhilaratingly free from regulation and profoundly fragile' (Bowden, 1997: 60). It is, as Aristotle stated, a relationship (at least ideally) between equals, based in mutuality and reciprocity, to which the partners come of their own free will, not out of need, and which requires a firm sense of the separateness of the parties. Or, as Andrew Sullivan puts it:

> Friendship is for those who do not want to be saved, for those whose appreciation of life is here and now and whose comfort in themselves is sufficient for them to want merely to share rather than to lose their identity. And they enter into friendship as an act of radical choice. Friendship, in this sense is the performance art of freedom. (Sullivan, 1998: 212)

If we take friendship seriously we will have to confront the question of how care may be given and received by equals, without violating individual autonomy, without self-sacrifice and subservience, and maintaining the affection which constitutes the relationship. Aristotle offers an ethical theory based on a conception of the self as situated, particular and enmeshed in relationships, but as also concerned with its own individual needs and development which sets limits on the obligation to care. And his identification of the detrimental effects of excessive humility – which he sees as robbing the individual of what he (sic) deserves, as causing others to think badly of him, as evidence of a lack of self-knowledge and as leading him to fail to perform the noble actions of which he is actually capable – offers, Ruth Groenhout argues 'a healthy alternative to the complete self-effacement sometimes portrayed as "good mothering" in the popular press' (1998: 181). Finally, Aristotle's notion of the virtuous practice of friendship (see the quotation at the start of the paper) also militates against subservience, because subservience by the carer produces selfishness in the cared for, and the virtuous friend cannot act in such a way as to prevent the development of moral excellence in the other.

Returning briefly to the Care, Friendship and Non-Conventional Partnership project, we found that the people we interviewed were consciously seeking to create a way of life that would meet their need for connection with others while preserving their autonomy and independence. They placed a high value on the way in which friends offer care and support, love and affection without infringing personal boundaries, and without the deep emotional risks of sexual/love relationships. Catriona Mackenzie and Natalie Stoljar's (2000) phrase 'autonomous relationality' captures well this moral ontology (Butler, 1999), which values both attachments to others and self-determination.

And if we did care about friendship...

Taking friendship seriously, for each of these three reasons, can offer those of us interested in a progressive agenda for a welfare society important discursive resources. Firstly, it provides an important counterpoint to the pessimistic tone which characterizes the work of sociologists such as Zygmunt Bauman (2001, 2003) and Robert Putnam (2000), whose ideas have been taken up in a widespread public discourse about a supposed crisis in personal relationships and community. Such ideas feed into, and implicitly express, a patriarchal, conservative hankering after a lost golden age of stable families and seemingly more secure structures of care. A recognition of the value that people place on extra-familial relationships, and the care and support that they offer, also offers a challenge to the familialism that runs through the policies of New Labour (notwithstanding its commitment to diversity) (Stychin, 2003). From this we can start to map a policy agenda which moves beyond the rhetoric of 'supporting families' (Home Office, 1998), to consider how we can support, and recognize the importance of, friendship.[15]

For instance, work-life balance policies are called for which are framed in terms of the range of important personal relationships and commitments within which people live their lives, rather than narrowly with reference to family responsibilities.[16] Employment benefits should be redefined to extend bereavement leave to apply to all the people about whom an employee cares or with whom he or she shares a special relationship. More radically, it is time to explore an extension of the proposed legislation on civil partnerships for lesbian and gay couples to recognize any significant relationship – sexual or otherwise – and to open up fiscal benefits, inheritance and other 'next of kin' rights to those whose intimate lives do not map on to a policy framework which focuses on conjugal couples and families.[17] Interestingly, it is the Conservative Party and the queer campaigning group, Outrage,[18] who are currently voicing the demand for the recognition of diverse forms of caring relationship, against New Labour's determination to offer relationship recognition only to lesbian and gay couples. It is a queer world indeed in which these two groups find themselves bedfellows – and a queer world, by its very nature, throws up strange alliances which disrupt old binaries. In such a queer world, a radical, generative social policy is one that seeks to enable all of those who care for others, whoever they are, to do so with maximum social support and recognition, whilst never forgetting those – the strangers – who exist outside the charmed circle of love and friendship.

Notes

1 Aristotle (1940: 1–2).

2 The theme song from the global hit television show 'Friends': http://www/geocities.com/TelevisionCity/4151/theme.html

3 For a discussion of Aristotle and later philosophers of friendship, see Roseneil (2000a).

4 There is a small literature on the role of friends in the provision of care and support, for instance on caring for people with AIDS (Kurdek and Schmitt, 1987; Hays, Chauncey and Tobey, 1990; Adam, 1992; Turner, Pearlin and Mullan, 1994, 1997, 1998), for the elderly (Allan, 1986; Jerrome, 1992) and the dying (Seale, 1990; Young, Seale and Bury, 1998). Willmott (1986, 1987) provides policy-oriented reviews of the research on friendship networks and social support. See also Wellman and Wortley (1990).

5 This is the agenda of the ESRC Research Group for the Study of Care, Values and the Future of Welfare (ESRC award M564281001), under whose auspices this paper was written. Earlier versions of the paper were presented at a CAVA Workshop, and at the Universities of Hull, Greenwich, Swansea, Adelaide University, King's College, London, Lancaster University, RMIT and at the Social Policy Association Conference (University of Teeside, 2003). I would like to thank participants in all of these occasions for their comments and questions.

6 Texts which have come to assume foundational status within queer theory include: Sedgwick (1991), Butler (1991), de Lauretis (1991), Fuss (1991) and Warner (1991). There is a small literature at the intersection of queer theory and social policy/socio-legal studies, notably: Stychin (2003), Moran, Monk and Beresford (1998), Bell and Binnie (2000).

7 For example, Altman (1982), Weston (1991), Nardi (1992, 1999), Weeks (1995), Preston with Lowenthal (1996).

8 See Roseneil (2000a) for an overview of these writings.

9 For a detailed exposition of my 'queering of the social' thesis see Roseneil (2000b, 2002). Also relevant is the work of Maffesoli (1996) which sees the contemporary period as 'the time of the tribes', an era of affinity groups, networks and affective bonding, and which is taken up by Heath (2004).

10 This project was led by Sasha Roseneil, with Shelley Budgeon and Jacqui Gabb as research fellows. For a more detailed discussion of the methodology and findings see Roseneil and Budgeon (2004). For other work on intimacy and care beyond the conventional family, see contributions to Budgeon and Roseneil (2004).

11 On an ethics of care, see Tronto (1993) and Sevenhuijsen (1998). In relation to CAVA, see Williams (2001, 2004).

12 For feminist critiques of an ethics of care see Ferguson (1984), Card (1995), Spelman (1991), Hoagland (1991), Friedman (1993), Groenhout (1998) and Bowden (1997). Sevenhuijsen (1998) offers a reworking of an ethics of care which incorporates an ethic of justice.

13 See Hogan and Roseneil (2001).

14 This point is made by Bowden (1997) whose work seeks to explore the implications of three relationships of care which have been largely ignored by care theorists: friendship, nursing and citizenship.

15 A Law Commission of Canada (2002) report sets out an agenda for the support of close personal relationships beyond conjugality.

16 On 23 April 2004 Tony Blair announced an intention to explore the extension of rights to flexible working to those caring for elderly parents and friends. http://money.guardian.co.uk/news_/story/0,1456,1201654,00.html

17 The opening up of relationship recognition to friends has occurred in France, with the introduction of the PACS, and in 2003, in Tasmania.

18 On Conservative proposals, see http://politics.guardian.co.uk/conservatives/story/0.9061,1160289, 00.html. For Outrage's position on this matter see http://outrage.nabumedia.com/pressrelease.asp

References

Adam, B. (1992), 'Sex and caring among men: impacts of AIDS on gay people', in K. Plummer (ed.), *Modern Homosexualities: Fragments of Lesbian and Gay Experience*, London: Routledge.

Allan, G. (1986), 'Friendship and Care for Elderly People', *Ageing and Society*, 6, 1–12.

Altman, D. (1982), *The Homosexualization of America*, New York: St. Martin's Press.

Aristotle (1940), *Aristotle on Friendship, Being an Expanded Translation of the Nicomachean Ethics Books VIII and IX by Geoffrey Percival*, Cambridge: Cambridge University Press.

Bauman, Z. (2001), *The Individualized Society*, Cambridge: Polity.

Bauman, Z. (2003), *Liquid Love*, Cambridge: Polity.

Beck, U. and Beck-Gernsheim, E. (1995), *The Normal Chaos of Love*, Cambridge: Polity.

Bell, D. and Binnie, J. (2000), *The Sexual Citizen: Queer Politics and Beyond*, Cambridge: Polity.

Berlant, L. and Warner, M. (2000), 'Sex in public', in L. Berlant (ed.), *Intimacy*, Chicago: Chicago University Press.

Bowden, P. (1997), *Caring: Gender-Sensitive Ethics*, London: Routledge.

Budgeon, S. and. Roseneil, S. (eds) (2004), 'Beyond the conventional family: intimacy, care and community in the 21st century', *Special Issue Current Sociology*, 52, 2.

Butler, J. (1991), *Gender Trouble: Feminism and the Subversion of Identity*, New York: Routledge.

Butler, J. (1999), *Subjects of Desire*, New York: Columbia University Press.

Card, C. (1995), 'Gender and moral luck', in V. Held (ed.), *Justice and Care: Essential Readings in Feminist Ethics*, Boulder, CO: Westview Press.

de Lauretis, T. (1991), 'Queer theory: lesbian and gay sexualities', *Journal of Feminist Cultural Studies*, 3, 2, iii–xviii.

Ferguson, K (1984), *The Feminist Case against Bureaucracy*, Philadelphia: Temple University Press.

Friedman, M. (ed.) (1993), *What Are Friends For? Feminist Perspective on Personal Relationships and Moral Theory*, Ithaca, NY: Cornell University Press.

Fuss, D. (1991), *Inside/Out: Lesbian Theories, Gay Theories* New York: Routledge.

Giddens, A. (1992), *The Transformation of Intimacy: Sexuality, Love and Eroticism in Modern Societies*, Cambridge: Polity.

Groenhout, R. (1998), 'The virtue of care: Aristotelian ethics and contemporary ethics of care', in C. Freeland (ed.), *Feminist Interpretations of Aristotle*, University Park, PA: Penn State Press.

Hays, R.B., Chauncey, S., and Tobey, L.A. (1990), 'The social support networks of gay men with AIDS', *Journal of Community Psychology*, 18, 743–755.

Heath, S. (2004), 'Peer-shared households, quasi-communes and neo-tribes', *Current Sociology*, 52, 2, March, 161–180.

Hoagland, S. (1991), 'Some thoughts about "caring"', in C. Card (ed.), *Feminist Ethics*, Kansas: University Press of Kansas.

Hodges, M.W. and Smith, C. (1954), 'The Sheffield estate', in T. Simey (ed.), *Neighbourhood and Community*, Liverpool: Liverpool University Press.

Jerrome, D. (1981), 'The significance of friendship for women in later life', *Ageing and Society*, 1, 2, 175–197.

Hogan, L. and Roseneil, S. (2001), 'Gendering ethics, the ethics of gender: an introduction', *Gendering Ethics, The Ethics of Gender, Feminist Theory*, 2, 2, August, 147–149.

Home Office (1998), *Supporting Families: A Consultation Document*, London: HMSO.

Jerrome, D. (1992), *Good Company: An Anthropological Study of Old People in Groups*, Edinburgh: Edinburgh University Press.

Kurdek, L. and Schmitt, J.P. (1987), 'Perceived emotional support from families and friends in members of homosexual, married and heterosexual cohabiting couples', *Journal of Homosexuality*, 14, 3/4, 57–68.

Law Commission of Canada (2002), *Beyond Conjugality*, http://www.cga.state.ct.us/2002/olrdata/jud/rpt/2002-R-0172.htm.

Mackenzie, C. and Stoljar, N. (2000), *Relational Autonomy: Feminist Perspectives on Autonomy, Agency, and the Social Self*, Oxford: Oxford University Press.

Maffesoli, M. (1996), *The Time of the Tribes: The Decline of Individualism in Mass Society*, London: Sage.

Moran, L.D., Monk, D., and Beresford, S. (eds) (1998), *Legal Queeries: Lesbian, Gay and Transgender Legal Studies*, London: Cassell.

Nardi, P. (1992), 'That's what friends are for: friends as family in the gay and lesbian community', in K. Plummer (ed.), *Modern Homosexualities: Fragments of Lesbian and Gay Experience*, London: Routledge.

Nardi, P. (1999), *Gay Men's Friendships: Invincible Communities*, Chicago: Chicago University Press.

ONS (Office for National Statistics) (2004), *Social Trends No. 34*, London: Office for National Statistics.

Pahl, R. (1998), 'Friendship: the social glue of contemporary society?', in J. Franklin (ed.), *The Politics of Risk Society*, Cambridge: Polity.

Putnam, R.D. (2000), *Bowling Alone: The Collapse and Revival of American Community*, New York: Simon & Schuster.

Preston, J. with Lowenthal, M. (eds) (1996), *Friends and Lovers: Gay Men Write about the Families They Create*, New York: Plume.

Roseneil, S. (2000a), 'Why we should care about friends: some thoughts (for CAVA) about the ethics and practice of friendship', CAVA Workshop Paper No. 22, June 2000: http://www.leeds.ac.uk/cava/research/strand1/paper22Sasha.htm

Roseneil, S. (2000b), 'Queer frameworks and queer tendencies: towards an understanding of postmodern transformations of sexuality', *Sociological Research Online*, 5, 3, 1–19. http://www.socresonline.org.uk/5/3/roseneil.html

Roseneil, S. (2002), 'The heterosexual/ homosexual binary: past, present and future', in D. Richardson and S. Seidman (eds), The *Lesbian and Gay Studies Handbook*, London: Sage, pp. 27–44.

Roseneil, S. and Budgeon, S. (2004), 'Cultures of intimacy and care beyond the family: personal life and social change in the early twenty-first century', *Current Sociology*, 52, 2, 135–159.

Seale, C. (1990), 'Caring for people who die: the experience of family and friends', *Ageing and Society*, 10: 413–428.

Sedgwick, E.K. (1991), *Epistemology of the Closet*, Hemel Hempstead: Harvester Wheatsheaf.

Sevenhuijsen, S. (1998), *Citizenship and the Ethics of Care: Feminist Considerations on Justice, Morality and Politics*, London: Routledge.

Spelman, E. (1991), 'The virtue of feeling and the feeling of virtue', in C. Card (ed.), *Feminist Ethics*, Kansas: University Press of Kansas.

Stychin, C. (2003), *Governing Sexuality: The Changing Politics of Citizenship and Law Reform*, Oxford and Portland: Hart Publishing.

Sullivan, A. (1998), *Love Undetectable: Reflections on Friendship, Sex and Survival*, London: Chatto & Windus.

Tronto, J. (1993), *Moral Boundaries*, New York: Routledge.

Turner, H.A. and Catania, J.A. (1997), 'Informal caregiving to persons with AIDS: caregiver characteristics, conditions, and burden among 18–49 year olds living in US central cities', *American Journal of Community Psychology*, 25, 1, 35–59.

Turner, H.A., Catania, J.A., and Gagnon, J. (1994), 'The prevalence of informal caregiving to persons with AIDS in the United States: caregiver characteristics and their implications', *Social Science and Medicine*, 38, 11, 1543–1552.

Turner, H.A., Pearlin, L.I., and Mullan, J.T. (1998), 'Sources and determinants of social support for caregivers of persons with AIDS', *Journal of Health and Social Behaviour*, 39, June, 137–151.

Warner, M. (1991), 'Fear of a queer planet' *Social Text* Vol.9, No.14:3–17.

Weeks, J. (1995), *Invented Moralities: Sexual Values in an Age of Uncertainty*, Cambridge: Polity.

Weeks, J., Heaphy, B., and Donovan, C. (2001), *Same Sex Intimacies: Families of Choice and Other Life Experiments*, London: Routledge.

Wellman, B. and Wortley, S. (1990), 'Different strokes from different folks: community ties and social support', *American Journal of Sociology*, 96, 558–588.

Weston, K. (1991), *Families We Choose: Lesbians, Gay Men and Kinship*, New York: Columbia University Press.

Williams, F. (2001), 'In and beyond New Labour: towards a new political ethics of care', in *Critical Social Policy*, 21, 4, 467–493.

Williams, F. (2004a), *Rethinking Families*, London: Calouste Gulbenkian Foundation.

Willmott, P. (1987), *Friendship Networks and Social Support*, London: Policy Studies Institute.

Willmott, P. (1986), *Social Networks, Informal Care and Public Policy*, London: Policy Studies Institute.

Young, M. and Willmott, P. (1957), *Family and Kinship in East* London, London: Routledge & Kegan Paul.

Young, E., Seale, C., and Bury, M. (1998),) '"It's not like family going, is it?": negotiating friendship towards the end of life', *Mortality*, 3, 1, 27–42.

[27]

'Displacing the 'conjugal family' in legal policy – a progressive move?

*Lisa Glennon**

Drawing upon the passage of the Civil Partnerships Act 2004 in the UK and examples from Canadian jurisprudence, this article discusses how attempts to displace the centrality of the 'conjugal family' in legal policy tend to emerge at crucial points in the evolution of the relational status of same-sex couples.

INTRODUCTION

Kees Waaldijk observes how the legal recognition of homosexuality evolves, albeit at different times and paces, as a 'standard sequence' of legislative steps in most countries.[1] Broadly speaking, this evolutionary process involves the transition from protecting individual rights to recognising the partnership status of same-sex relationships. Starting with the decriminalisation of homosexual acts and the subsequent equalisation of the age of consent for sexual activity between adults, the enactment of legislation which prohibits discrimination on the grounds of sexual orientation in employment and other contexts tends to precede partnership recognition via ascription,[2] registered partnership legislation and, in some jurisdictions, civil marriage.[3] While the Civil Partnerships Act 2004 ensures that British policy is firmly located within this normative continuum of legal developments,[4] the passage of the Act

---

* *School of Law, Queen's University Belfast.*

The author would like to thank Professor Mary Hayes and the anonymous referee for helpful comments on an earlier draft. Any errors or omissions are, of course, the author's responsibility.

1 K. Waaldijk, 'Standard sequences in the legal recognition of homosexuality – Europe's past, present and future' (1994) 4 *Australasian Gay and Lesbian Law Journal* 50. See also K. Waaldijk, 'Civil developments: patterns of reform in the legal position of same-sex partners in europe' (2000) 17 *Canadian Journal of Family Law* 62, at p 66.

2 Ascription refers to the process where rights and obligations are 'ascribed' to unformalised relationships by operation of law, usually on the basis of a period of cohabitation or the presence of a child of the relationship.

3 See K. Waaldijk, 'Taking same-sex partnerships seriously – European experiences as British perspectives?', Fifth Stonewall Lecture. The full text of this lecture can be found on the author's website: http://www.meijers.leidenuniv.nl/index.php3?m=10andc=129. An abridged version of the lecture appears in [2003] IFL 84. MacDougall similarly identifies three sites in the evolutionary development of rights discourse in the area of gay and lesbian reform in Canada – compassion, condonation and celebration, which respectively correspond to the nature of the rights fought for in Canada, from the enactment of non-discrimination protection and the conferral of benefits to the positive legal integration of the gay and lesbian community into the 'fabric of society' by same-sex marriage: B. MacDougall, 'The celebration of same-sex marriage' (2000) 32(2) *Ottawa Law Review* 235, at p 253.

4 Indeed, in the parliamentary debates during the passage of the Civil Partnerships Bill, the Deputy Minister for Women and Equality noted the evolutionary nature of the gay and lesbian reform agenda: '[w]e have equalised the age of consent, outlawed discrimination in the workplace on the grounds of sexual orientation, secured protection from homophobic hate crimes and supported the abolition of section 28'. The Civil Partnership Act, in '[representing an] historic step on what has been a long journey to respect and dignity for lesbians and gay men in Britain ... [creates] a new legal relationship

is revealing in other respects. Just as the evolutionary development of same-sex rights tends to follow a standard pattern, so do the tactics of opponents. The purpose of this article is to discuss the deployment of one particular strategy during the passage of the Civil Partnerships Act 2004 where emerging concern for the welfare of those in non-sexual care-giving relationships led to proposals to allow other categories of family member to register under the proposed civil registration scheme. The development of such arguments just at the point of same-sex partnership recognition is not a unique phenomenon. Thus, the second part of this article will discuss two recent initiatives in Canada where the use of 'conjugality' as a trigger for the conferment of legal rights and obligations has been called into question. It will be suggested that these initiatives share a common theme with those who sought to widen the remit of the Civil Partnerships Act, that is, to undermine and/or deflect attention from the legal recognition of same-sex partnerships.

THE CIVIL PARTNERSHIPS ACT 2004

The introduction of the Civil Partnerships Act 2004, which will establish a same-sex registered partnership system for the UK[5] and give registrants quasi-marital status,[6] should come as no surprise. It is in line with the trend in Europe to enact registered partnership schemes for same-sex couples[7] and, indeed, is not the first time that civil partnerships have been proposed in the UK. The 2004 Act was preceded by

---

for same-sex couples': *Hansard*, HC Deb, vol 425, col 174 (12 October 2004). The following is a summary of the developments referred to. The Sexual Offences (Amendment) Act 2000 equalised the age of consent for homosexual and heterosexual activity, which is 16 in England and Wales and 17 in Northern Ireland. The Employment Equality (Sexual Orientation) Regulations 2003 (SI 2003/1661), which implement Council Directive 2000/78/EC of 27 November 2000 establishing a general framework for equal treatment in employment and occupation (2000) OJ L 303/16, make it unlawful to discriminate on grounds of sexual orientation in employment and vocational training. The Criminal Justice Act 2003 imposes a statutory requirement on judges to treat as an aggravating factor when sentencing, assaults involving or motivated by hostility based on sexual orientation (or presumed sexual orientation). Section 122 of the Local Government Act 2003 repeals s 2A of the Local Government Act 1986 (known as s 28), which prohibited local authorities from intentionally promoting homosexuality or publishing material with the intention of doing so, or from promoting teaching in schools of the acceptability of homosexuality. In addition, the Adoption and Children Act 2002 allows unmarried couples, including same-sex couples, who are in an 'enduring family relationship' to apply jointly for the adoption of children.

5 The Northern Ireland Office of Law Reform (OLR) recommended that civil registration be introduced in Northern Ireland as part of a co-ordinated, UK-wide scheme: Northern Ireland Office of Law Reform, *Civil Partnership: A Legal Status for Committed Same-Sex Couples in Northern Ireland* (OLR, 2003). The Scottish Executive also recommended the inclusion of Scottish provisions in the Westminster Bill: Scottish Executive, *Civil Partnership Registration: A Legal Status for Committed Same-sex Couples in Scotland* (SE, 2003). The Civil Partnerships Act 2004 thus extends to Scotland and Northern Ireland.

6 The terms of registration include a duty to provide reasonable maintenance for civil partners and children of the family; assessment in the same way as spouses for child support; joint treatment for income-related benefits and state pensions; recognition for immigration purposes; arrangements for property division on dissolution of the partnership; right to register the death of a partner; treatment in the same way as spouses for all tax purposes, and inheritance, intestacy and compensation rights.

7 Registered partnership legislation was first introduced in Denmark in 1989 and was followed by Norway (1993), Sweden (1995), Iceland (1996), the Netherlands (1998), France (1999), Belgium (2000), Germany (2000), Switzerland (2001) and Finland (2002). Spain is a federal state with 19 regions, some of which have enacted partnership registration models for same-sex partners – Catalonia (1998), Aragon (1999), Navarra (2000), Valencia (2001), Balearic Islands (2002), Asturia (2002) and Madrid (2002).

Lord Lester's Civil Partnerships Bill in 2002,[8] which was withdrawn during its second reading in the House of Lords in order to give the government the opportunity to carry out research in the area and to clarify its position. In December 2002, the Minister for Social Exclusion and Equalities announced that there was a strong case in favour of a civil partnership scheme in the UK and that a consultation paper would be issued during the summer of 2003. The consultation paper[9] was duly published within the predicted timescales and the intention to legislate on civil partnerships was included in the Queen's Speech on 26 November 2003. This attracted relatively scant media scrutiny, perhaps due to the fact that it was caught in the middle of contentious debates on university admission fees and government policy on asylum-seekers. Indeed, in many ways, the most significant gay rights issues, such as the removal of section 28 from the Local Government Act 1986, the equalisation of the age of consent and gay adoption, have been successfully debated in England and Wales.[10] In light of these measures, civil partnership registration could be presented as a logical development and thus less contentious than other issues on the political agenda. The Civil Partnerships Bill[11] was introduced into the House of Lords in March 2004 and received Royal Assent eight months later.

The Lords' Amendment

The Civil Partnership Act 2004, in applying to same-sex couples only, can be criticised as an opportunity missed to address the legal position of opposite-sex cohabitants who do not marry.[12] Indeed, many accept that the lack of a comprehensive legal framework to govern the relationship of unmarried cohabitants, particularly on relationship breakdown, remains one of the most urgent policy questions.[13] Despite

---

8 HL Bill 41 of 2001/02. This Bill, which was drafted in collaboration with Stonewall, differed from the Civil Partnerships Act 2004 in two ways. First, while Lord Lester's Bill was open to both same- and opposite-sex couples, in order to allow 'unmarried couples living in a mutually supportive relationship to make provision for their joint protection within a coherent legal framework' (*Hansard*, Lords Debates, vol 630, col 1691 (25 January 2002)), the 2004 Act is limited to same-sex couples. Secondly, the terms of registration under the 2004 Act are modelled on marriage and thus it creates a parallel opt-in scheme for same-sex couples, as opposed to a substantive alternative to marriage. By contrast, Lord Lester's Bill was a more thoughtful attempt to create a regime which did not simply borrow from the content of marital regulation. As such, this Bill sought to maximise registrants' autonomy in the regulation of their internal affairs, particularly through the organisation of their respective property rights, although in limiting registration to two sexual partners, the new legal category of civil registration was structurally analogous to marriage. Lord Lester's Bill was the second Bill to be introduced on partnership registration. In October 2001, Jane Griffiths MP introduced the Relationships (Civil Registration) Bill (Bill 36 of 2001/02), which sought to establish a civil registration scheme for same-and opposite-sex cohabitants.

9 Department of Trade and Industry, Women and Equality Unit, *Civil Partnership: A Framework for the Legal Recognition of Same-sex Couples* (DTI, June 2003).

10 See n 4.

11 Hereafter the Bill.

12 For example, the Law Society, in responding to the consultation paper which preceded the Bill, said that 'while welcoming the proposals ... to offer all the rights and obligations of marriage to same-sex cohabitants ... [w]e are disappointed ... that the paper deals only with the implementation of a system of registration for same-sex couples, and does not deal with the wider issues of the rights of cohabitants who do not marry or register their relationship. We consider that this is an area in which law reform is urgently needed and we would like to see a commitment to legislation dealing with the financial position of unmarried/unregistered cohabitants, although not necessarily by amendment of this Bill': The Law Society, *Response to the Civil Partnerships Consultation Paper* (Law Society, 2003).

13 See J. Eekelaar and M. Maclean, 'Marriage and the moral bases of personal relationships' (2004) 31(4) *Journal of Law and Society* 510; A. Barlow, 'Regulation of cohabitation, changing family policies

this, it was another issue which emerged to dominate parliamentary debates during the passage of the Bill. A primary focus of concern became the exclusion of family members, particularly those in non-sexual relationships of care-giving, from the proposed registration scheme. Indeed, several attempts were made to extend the Bill to cover such persons, the most notable of which was an amendment to allow close relatives, both over the age of 30, who had lived together for 12 years, to register their relationship.[14] This was supported by a cross-party coalition of peers and bishops and was passed at Report Stage in the House of Lords by 148 votes to 130.[15] Inspired by the belief that establishing a registered partnership scheme for same-sex couples would 'give rise to greater injustice than it claims to address',[16] supporters of the amendment alleged that the Bill in its original format would lead to discrimination against the family. These arguments focused, in particular, on the financial consequences on the death of a person who had been cared for by a relative and thus while it was recognised that relations currently have rights in relation to hospital visiting and on intestacy, the crux of the 'injustice' was their lack of exemption from inheritance and capital gains tax.[17] It was the extension of these benefits to same-sex registered partners that was said to create new inequalities'[18] and which led critics to describe the Bill as 'cruel ... suffused with unfair discrimination'.[19]

While opponents of this amendment expressed sympathy with the needs of wider family members and accepted that the position of carers is a matter that requires government attention, they were firmly opposed to using the Civil Partnerships Bill as a vehicle with which to achieve this. Civil partnership registration is designed to mirror the marriage model of 'couple-based' regulation. Thus, registrants are deemed to be involved in an exclusive relationship of mutual care and support which can only be terminated by a court-based dissolution procedure, the terms of which are modelled on the divorce process.[20] While the proposal to give other family members access to

---

and social attitudes: a discussion of Britain within Europe' (2004) 26(1) *Law and Policy* 57; A. Barlow and G. James, 'Regulating marriage and cohabitation in 21st century Britain' (2004) 67(2) *Modern Law Review* 143; S. Wong, 'Constructive trusts over the family home: lessons to be learned from other Commonwealth jurisdictions?' (1998) 18 *Legal Studies* 369; S. Wong, 'Re-thinking Rossett from a human rights perspective' in A. Hudson (ed), *New Perspectives on Property Law, Human Rights and the Home* (Cavendish, 2003); A. Barlow and C. Lind, 'A matter of trust: the allocation of rights in the family home' (1999) 19(4) *Legal Studies* 468; R. Bailey-Harris, 'Law and the unmarried couple – oppression or liberation?' [1996] CFLQ 137; Law Commission for England and Wales, *Sharing Homes: A Discussion Paper*, Law Com No 278 (TSO, 2002); Law Society, *Cohabitation: the Case for Clear Law. Proposals for Reform* (Representation and Law Reform Directorate, 2002).

14 Under this amendment, which was tabled by Baroness O'Cathain in the House of Lords, those within the specified degrees of family relationship entitled to register were adoptive child, adoptive parent, child, former adoptive child, former adoptive parent, grandparent, grandchild, parent, parent's sibling (meaning brother, sister, half-brother or half-sister) and sibling's child: *Hansard*, Lords Debates, vol 662, col 1438–1439 (24 June 2004).

15 Ibid, col 1389.

16 Ibid, col 1363, per Baroness O'Cathain.

17 Ibid, col 1366. The pre-Budget Report 2004 made it clear that the tax consequences of the Civil Partnership Act 2004 will be dealt with in the first available Finance Bill. For tax purposes, registered same-sex couples will be treated in the same way as married couples: *Opportunity for all: The strength to take the long-term decisions for Britain, Pre-Budget Report*, Cm 6408 (TSO, 2004).

18 *Hansard*, Lords Debates, vol 662, col 1368 (24 June 2004).

19 Ibid, col 1367.

20 Under s 44 of the Civil Partnerships Act 2004, a dissolution order can only be granted if the civil partnership has broken down irretrievably, which must be proved by one or more of the following facts: that the respondent has behaved in such a way that the applicant cannot reasonably be expected to

this system was, *prima facie*, an attempt to improve their financial position by the extension of tax exemptions, it was quite correctly pointed out that civil partnership registration is a wholly inappropriate response to the needs of carers. Stating that the amendment was based upon a 'false comparison'[21] between same-sex partners and family members, opponents highlighted the consequential range of 'legal absurdities'.[22] For example, while a married person caring for a parent or relative should, on the theoretical premise of the amendment, be able to register this relationship with the person being cared for, the fact of his/her marriage would prohibit this. Similarly, what of a child caring for married parents,[23] or three elderly siblings living together where only two can register as civil partners?[24] In tabling the amendment, Baroness O'Cathain imagined a daughter who was caring for her father suffering from Alzheimer's disease and noted that, as a result of being able to register the relationship, the daughter would be able to save inheritance tax on the family home on her father's death. As observed by the Lesbian and Gay Lawyers Association (LAGLA), however, this overlooked the issue of the capacity of the father to provide valid consent to the registration of the civil partnership, and the question of the dissolution of the partnership should the daughter wish to marry.[25] As LAGLA stated, the hypothetical daughter:

> '... would have to prove to a court that the relationship with her father had broken down, by applying for a dissolution either on the basis of the father's unreasonable behaviour or on the basis of separation from the father for 2 or 5 years. If she (as is likely) wants to continue to care for her father and their relationship continues, she will never be able to get married. This is only one aspect of why the amendment is unworkable.'[26]

In addition, insufficient attention was paid to the financial disincentives of civil registration. The financial gains acquired by those in a position to benefit from inheritance and capital gains tax exemptions have to be measured against the financial disadvantages of those at the lower end of the financial spectrum who, as civil partners, would lose entitlement to benefit from social security provision as individuals.[27] For such reasons, the government was steadfast in its determination to

live with him/her; that the applicant and the respondent have lived apart for a continuous period of at least 2 years immediately preceding the making of the application and the respondent consents to a dissolution order being made; that the applicant and the respondent have lived apart for a continuous period of at least 5 years immediately preceding the making of the application; that the respondent has deserted the applicant for a continuous period of at least 2 years immediately preceding the making of the application. As indicated, these terms mirror the grounds for establishing the irretrievable breakdown of marriage for the purposes of divorce, the only exception being that the fact of adultery does not appear as a separate fact to prove the irretrievable breakdown of a civil partnership.

21 *Hansard*, Lords Debates, vol 666, col 1473 (17 November 2004), per Lord Lester of Herne Hill. Lord Lester said that: '[t]hose whom the Bill is designed to protect – same-sex couples who are willing to enter into a partnership with rights and responsibilities as if they were married – are not comparable to two sisters who have lived together for 12 years'.

22 *Hansard*, HC Deb, vol 425, col 177 (12 October 2004), per the Deputy Minister for Women and Equality.

23 *Hansard*, Lords Debates, vol 662, col 1374 (24 June 2004).

24 Ibid, at col 1386; *Hansard*, HC Standing Committee D, col 014 (19 October 2004).

25 http://www.lagla.org.uk/partnership.htm.

26 Ibid.

27 This is because the joint incomes of the registered partners will be used to calculate income-related social security entitlements.

return the Bill to its original format, stating that to conflate the issues pertaining to same-sex relationships and carers 'is to do justice neither to the same-sex couples whom the Bill seeks to serve nor to carers'.[28] This was reinforced by the organisational response to the amendment. The Solicitors' Family Law Association, who dubbed the amendment an 'absurdity' resulting in an 'unworkable mess', stated that:

> '[c]ivil partnership is not a suitable arrangement for relieving carers and adult children of the burden of paying inheritance tax.'[29]

According to Carers UK:

> '... there could be many pitfalls with the new amendments to the Bill ... that could harm the welfare of both the older person and the carer. The changes could have a devastating impact on the income of the carer and the person for whom they care ... There is a danger that, after some time, the carer and the older person may become locked in a caring situation ... equally the carer may become locked into the caring situation, unable to choose about whether or not to continue.'[30]

In a similar vein, the Law Society said that:

> 'it is inappropriate simply to include [family members] within the categories of those who can register a civil partnership. Registration will not solve their problems and may even worsen their position.'[31]

That the extension of the Bill would simultaneously have undermined its original purpose in relation to the gay and lesbian reform agenda, and created many absurdities in its operation, leads one to pose questions about the true motivation of at least some of its proponents. On a generous construction one could say that advocates were opportunistic in their genuine attempt to address the issue of care-giving in the absence of the political will to do so directly. However, on a more cynical interpretation, the inclusion of family members was a tactic to disturb the passage of the legislation or, failing that, to make it easier to digest by displacing its central objective of extending the legal incidents of marriage to same-sex couples and, instead, making it about the value of care-giving responsibilities. Indeed, the amendment has been referred to as a 'fig leaf to disguise ... opposition to the Bill in total',[32] and it has been alleged that the tactic of pointing to other disadvantaged groups was being used as a 'stalking horse for those who [were] basically opposed to the whole purpose of the Bill'.[33]

These allegations appear to have foundation. The articulated rationale of the amendment was to remedy the injustice to which family members are subjected by falling outside the terms of the Bill. This context means that the alleged injustice is more than a neutral assessment of the legal position of such persons. Rather, it results from the comparative assessment with same-sex couples, both in terms of the practical effect of registration and the symbolism associated with the clear legislative will to enable same-sex couples to formalise their relationships to the exclusion of

[28] *Hansard*, HC Deb, vol 425, col 175 (12 October 2004).

[29] Solicitors Family Law Association Briefing Note, *The Civil Partnerships Bill, House of Commons, Second Reading* (SFLA, September 2004).

[30] *Hansard*, HC Standing Committee D, col 012 (19 October 2004).

[31] Ibid.

[32] *Hansard*, Lords Debates, vol 662, col 1370 (24 June 2004), per Lord Alli.

[33] *Hansard*, Lords Debates, vol 662, col 1374 (24 June 2004), per Lord Goodhart.

other family members. Indeed, it is noteworthy that in tabling the amendment, Baroness O'Cathain said that:

> '[t]he Bill sends out the message that long-term caring family relationships do not matter as much as same-sex relationships, irrespective of their duration.'[34]

Thus, by giving same-sex couples in a civil partnership a 'higher status than family relationships',[35] the Bill was accused of 'causing another major injustice'[36] and 'creat[ing] new inequalities'[37] against 'family members who all their lives have shown sacrificial love and commitment'.[38] This terminology is revealing. The injustice is deemed to be 'created' by the Bill, in other words, it is inherently bound with and, in fact, contingent upon the perceived benefits accorded to same-sex civil partners. That the real motivation of some who supported this proposal was the perceived prioritisation of same-sex relationships can be seen in the remedial suggestion of Lord Tebbit who, in addressing the reluctance to include other categories of family member, said that:

> 'this Bill is essentially a Bill about money. If the Treasury is the problem – I suspect it is – why do ... the Government [not] back off and say that no civil partners of any kind will have the advantages of the avoidance of inheritance tax. That would make the situation much easier.'[39]

Thus, the 'injustice' which prompted the introduction of the amendment would be remedied, or at the very least diminished, if the perceived central financial benefit of the new registration scheme continued to be withheld from all civil partners, however defined. On this line of reasoning it appears to be more important to secure the inclusion of family members to prevent the prioritisation, in both symbolic and practical terms, of same-sex couples. The irony is that the suggested 'trade-off' to allow this (that is the withholding of tax exemptions from civil partners, which may help to negate the resource implications of allowing wider categories of relationships to register), reveals a zero-sum mindset and a willingness to compromise on the core rationale for seeking the amendment in the first place. This is done in order to ensure that same-sex couples do not achieve a 'higher status' than 'ordinary family members'.[40] Indeed, it appears that the true nature of concern for some was not the potential financial hardship of family members involved in caretaking duties *per se*, but the fact that same-sex couples in civil partnerships would trump 'ordinary family members' in the newly aligned hierarchy of family. As such, there is force in the argument that these amendments, for some, were 'wrecking amendments'[41] which 'render[ed] the Bill unworkable'.[42] However, the overwhelming support for the Bill as drafted by the

---

34 Ibid, col 1364.

35 Ibid, col 1366.

36 Ibid, col 1386.

37 Ibid, col 1368.

38 Ibid, col 1366.

39 Ibid, col 1414.

40 Ibid, col 1377, per Lord Kilclooney.

41 *Hansard*, HC Deb, vol 425, col 177 (12 October 2004).

42 Ibid.

government ensured that it was, quite correctly, returned to its original state, applying to same-sex couples only.[43]

To support the rejection of these amendments is not to suggest that the strategy of the Civil Partnerships Act 2004 is without criticism. Indeed, by reinforcing the prioritisation of 'couple-based' legal categories and extending the normative model of familial rights and responsibilities, the Act helps to maintain responsibility for financial support and caretaking within the private family.[44] The implications of this and the legal treatment of care-giving relationships within sexual and non-sexual familial contexts, does require examination. However, supporting these amendments is not the way forward. Any serious attempt to aid the position of care-giving relatives requires a discourse which goes further than looking at the financial implications on the death of a person being cared for and its ideal terms would not be likely to involve the introduction of an exclusive couple-based registration scheme, nor a formalistic and exhaustive definition of carer. Indeed, the government indicated that in its consultation with Carers UK, the organisation revealed that:

> '[t]hrough … extensive surveys, carers have made it clear that issues such as capital gains tax and fatal accident compensation are not among their priorities. Their prime concerns include breaks for carers, services for disabled people, better financial support for carers while they are caring, the option for flexible working and the direct payments system.'[45]

Thus, the framework of civil partnership registration is wholly insufficient. However, the proposed extension of the Bill to family members demonstrates that strategies which appear to unearth more challenging family law questions by moving beyond an exclusive focus on marriage and marriage-like relationships, can be used in a subversive way to undermine same-sex partnership recognition.[46] This is not a unique phenomenon. Waaldijk, in response to the argument that the recognition of close relatives is more urgent than the recognition of same-sex couples, states that:

> '[i]t is difficult to assess whether this is true, or to what degree this argument is only being used to side-track the debate. There certainly is not a vocal interest group representing the neglected interests of siblings living together, or of adult

---

43 At Third Reading in the House of Commons, MPs voted in favour of the Bill in its original state by 389 votes to 47: see *Hansard*, HC Deb, vol 426 (9 November 2004). Upon return to the House of Lords, Baroness O'Cathain tabled a more limited version of her earlier amendment to establish, before the Bill was implemented, a parallel scheme for family members (now more narrowly defined to include adoptive child, adoptive parent, child, former adoptive child, former adoptive parent, parent and sibling) for the purposes of inheritance tax, capital gains tax, housing and tenancies, and fatal accident claims, but not for pension or benefit entitlements, see *Hansard*, Lords Debates, vol 666, cols 1453–1458 (17 November 2004). This was defeated by 251 votes to 136. A further unsuccessful attempt was made in the House of Commons to include cohabiting siblings in the Bill (whose registration would be subject to a simplified, paper-based dissolution procedure). The new clause was introduced by Conservative backbench MP, Edward Leigh, but was defeated by 381 votes to 74.

44 See S. Boyd, 'Expanding the "family" in family law: recent Ontario proposals on same-sex relationships' (1994) 7(2) *Canadian Journal of Women and the Law* 545–563; S. Boyd, 'Best friends or spouses? Privatization and the recognition of lesbian relationships in *M v H*' (1996) 17 *Canadian Journal of Family Law* 321.

45 *Hansard*, Lords Debates, vol 666, col 1452 (17 November 2004).

46 Another strategy adopted by some Northern Ireland politicians was to attempt to prevent the extension of the Bill to Northern Ireland in the absence of the approval of the local assembly, which is currently in suspension. Several unsuccessful attempts were made by the Democratic Unionist Party (DUP) at various points during the passage of the Bill. These were unsurprising given the party's very strong objections to homosexuality.

children living with a parent. Yet, the argument surfaces again and again in response to demands for gay and lesbian partner rights. I don't see why the unresearched situation of close relatives should be used as an argument to slow down legislation recognising same-sex partnerships ...'[47]

The following section will discuss recent examples in Canada where similar arguments have emerged. At the outset it is worth pointing out that these arguments have been made against a very different backdrop. Unlike the position in the UK, Canadian legal discourse has a long pedigree in the 'relational equality'[48] agenda, that is, removing the legal differences between married and unmarried relationships, both opposite- and same-sex. Notwithstanding this, it was at a crucial point in the recognition of same-sex partnerships that a parallel discourse emerged to challenge the inherent idealisation of the 'sexual family' within this agenda.

THE ASSIMILATIONIST AGENDA IN CANADA – RECENT INFRINGEMENTS?

From the 1970s, even prior to the enactment of the Canadian Charter of Rights and Freedoms,[49] unmarried opposite-sex cohabitants began to acquire legal recognition in Canada. While this was done on an ad hoc basis,[50] the introduction of the Charter in 1982, in particular the section 15 equality guarantee,[51] was used to great effect in rolling out this policy.[52] Its impact was twofold. First, it ensured that the definition of 'spouse' in legal policy was amended to include unmarried opposite-sex cohabitants on a more comprehensive basis.[53] Secondly, it provided the legal ground upon which

[47] K. Waaldijk, op cit, n 3.

[48] B. Cossman and B. Ryder, 'What is marriage-like like?' (2001) 18(2) *Canadian Journal of Family Law* 267, at p 277.

[49] Hereafter the Charter.

[50] See W. Holland, 'Cohabitation and Marriage – A Meeting at the Crossroads?' (1990) 7 *Canadian Family Law Quarterly* 31; W. Holland, 'Intimate relationships in the new millennium: the assimilation of marriage and cohabitation?' 17(1) *Canadian Journal of Family Law* 114; N. Bala and R. Jaremko Bromwich, 'Context and inclusivity in Canada's evolving definition of the family' (2002) 16 *International Journal of Law, Policy and the Family* 145. The extension of the law was based upon the need to protect women from the opportunity costs arising from relationships based upon dependency, and to ensure that the pool of financial resources available to dependent partners was located within the family rather than imposed upon the state: Bala and Jaremko Bromwich, at p 156.

[51] Section 15(1) of the Charter states that '[e]very individual is equal before and under the law and has the right to the equal protection and equal benefit of the law without discrimination and, in particular, without discrimination based on race, national or ethnic origin, colour, religion, sex, age or mental or physical disability'.

[52] The nature of s 15 as interpreted by the courts, in particular its remedial purpose in 'overcoming prejudicial stereotypes in society' (*Law v Canada (Minister of Employment and Immigration)* [1999] 1 SCR 497, at para 65), made it an attractive vehicle for unmarried cohabitants, both same- and opposite-sex, to challenge the exclusionary nature of the law.

[53] In *Miron v Trudel* [1995] 2 SCR 418, the differential treatment of unmarried opposite-sex cohabitants relative to spouses in Ontario's Insurance Act was challenged under s 15. The Supreme Court of Canada held that the exclusion of opposite-sex cohabitants amounted to the denial of the equal benefit of the law on the basis of marital status, which was held to be an analogous ground of discrimination for the purposes of s 15. The impact of this decision was felt outside the province of Ontario. Up to this point, the province of Alberta gave little recognition to unmarried opposite-sex cohabitants. In *Taylor v Rossu* (1998) 39 RFL (4th) 242 (Alta CA), however, the Alberta Court of Appeal, relying on *Miron v Trudel*, held that the exclusion of opposite-sex cohabitants from the province's spousal support regime violated s 15. This prompted the Alberta legislature to extend, for a range of purposes, the definition of

gays and lesbians could challenge heterosexual constructions of 'spouse' in law.[54] This culminated in the 1999 decision of *M v H*,[55] where the Supreme Court of Canada ruled that the exclusion of same-sex couples from Ontario's spousal support scheme amounted to an unjustified violation of section 15. Of significance, the court engaged in a comparative assessment of opposite- and same-sex relationships and held them to be functionally synonymous. This led to the enactment of federal and provincial legislation to give comprehensive statutory recognition to same-sex couples in order to pre-empt comparable Charter challenges.[56] The rights-based framework under the Charter thus legitimised the comparative assessment of normative and excluded family forms and created a culture of assimilation. Indeed, while somewhat anomalously, married couples retain privileged rights in relation to the possession and ownership of the matrimonial home,[57] there has been a uniform strategy of 'conjugal relational equality',[58] that is, the legal assimilation of married and unmarried couples (both opposite- and same-sex).

Against this background, activists re-launched challenges against the prohibition of same-sex marriage, an issue which, according to the Ontario Court of Appeal, concerns the 'recognition and protection of human dignity and equality in the context of the social structures available to conjugal couples in Canada'.[59] While the validity of heterosexual-only marriage is a question that has been presented to the courts before,[60] it was not until the July 2002 decision of the Ontario Superior Court of Justice in *Halpern v The Attorney-General of Canada*[61] that a Canadian court held that the exclusion of same-sex couples from 'legal marriage' violates the Charter.[62] While the

spouse to include opposite-sex cohabitants who had lived in a 'marriage-like' relationship for three years or who had a child together (SA 1999, c 20, s 2).

54 The use of s 15 to claim that the exclusion of same-sex couples from the legal definition of spouse amounted to discrimination on the grounds of sexual orientation became a serious reform strategy when, in *Egan v Canada* [1995] 2 SCR 513, the Supreme Court of Canada held unanimously that sexual orientation is a deeply personal characteristic that is either unchangeable or changeable only at unacceptable personal costs, and so falls within the ambit of s 15 protection as being analogous to the enumerated grounds. In addition, the majority recognised that gays, lesbians and bisexuals, 'whether as individuals or couples, form an identifiable minority who have suffered and continue to suffer serious social, political and economic disadvantage' (at 602, per Cory J).

55 [1999] 2 SCR 3.

56 See D. G. Casswell, 'Moving toward same-sex marriage' (2001) 80 *Canadian Bar Review* 810. The typical response has been to extend ascribed spousal status to same-sex couples where rights and obligations are conferred on those who have lived in a conjugal relationship for a prescribed period, typically ranging from one to three years. Some provincial jurisdictions, such as Nova Scotia and Québec, have combined this with the introduction of a civil registration scheme whereby unmarried couples automatically acquire quasi-spousal status once they register their relationship.

57 *Nova Scotia (Attorney-General) v Walsh* [2002] SCJ No 84 (QL), 32 RFL (5th) 81. See M. Bailey, 'Regulation of Cohabitation and Marriage in Canada' (2004) 26(1) *Law and Policy* 153.

58 B. Cossman and B. Ryder, op cit, n 48.

59 *Halpern v Canada (Attorney-General)* [2003] 65 OR (3d) 161, at para 2.

60 See *Layland v Ontario (Minister of Consumer and Commercial Relations)* (1993) 14 OR (3d) 658 (Div Ct) and *Re North and Matheson* (1975) 52 DLR (3d) 280.

61 2002 Ont Sup CJ LEXIS 1417.

62 While the three justices disagreed over the appropriate remedy, all concluded that the equality provisions of s 15(1) of the Charter were violated by the common law rule that defines marriage as the 'lawful and voluntary union of one man and one woman to the exclusion of all others'. This common law definition derives from *Hyde v Hyde and Woodmansee* (1866) LR 1 PandD 130. Subsequently both the British Columbia Court of Appeal (*EGALE Canada Inc v Canada (Attorney-General)* [2003] BCJ No 994 (QL)) and the Superior Court of Québec (*Hendricks v Québec (Attorney-General)* [2002]

majority suspended the ruling for 24 months to enable Parliament to amend the law accordingly, on 10 June 2003 the Court of Appeal for Ontario expedited this process by upholding the earlier ruling and rendering the decision of immediate effect.[63] The federal government indicated that it would not appeal against these decisions and on 31 October 2003, the Attorney-General issued a factum to the Supreme Court of Canada for a declaration as to the constitutional validity of proposed legislation to legalise same-sex marriage.[64] The Supreme Court released its response to the reference in December 2004,[65] ruling that the proposed federal redefinition of civil marriage (that is, the lawful union of two persons to the exclusion of all others) is constitutional.[66] In response to this ruling, the federal government introduced a Bill to legalise same-sex marriage in February 2005.[67] The legislation, which requires the backing of at least 155 legislators in the 308-seat House of Commons, is likely to pass.[68] If the Bill fails, same-sex marriage will remain legal in the seven provinces and

---

JQ No 3816 (QL)) ruled that the legal prohibition against same-sex marriage violates the Charter. Both courts suspended the ruling to give the government time to 'review and revise the relevant legislation'.

63 *Halpern et al v The Attorney-General of Canada et al* 65 OR (3d) 161. On 8 July 2003, the British Columbia Court of Appeal, in a similar vein, lifted the suspension of the remedy passed down in their earlier decision, which meant that the declaratory relief and the reformulation of the common law definition of marriage as 'the lawful union of two persons to the exclusion of all others' took immediate effect (*EGALE Canada Inc v Canada (Attorney-General)* [2003] BCJ No 1582). On 19 March 2004, the Québec Court of Appeal followed suit. The prohibition of same-sex marriage has subsequently been declared unconstitutional in Manitoba, Saskatchewan, Nova Scotia, Newfoundland and Yukon.

64 The questions put to the Supreme Court were: first, whether the draft bill is within the exclusive legislative authority of the Parliament of Canada; secondly, whether the proposed act is compatible with the Charter of Rights and Freedoms; and thirdly, whether or not the freedom of religion guaranteed by the Charter protects religious officials from being compelled to perform a marriage between two persons of the same sex that is contrary to their religious beliefs. In January 2004, the Liberal government, under new Prime Minister Paul Martin, inserted an additional question to the Supreme Court reference asking whether, and to what extent, the opposite-sex definition of marriage violates the Charter.

65 *Reference re Same-Sex Marriage* [2004] SCC 79.

66 The court also ruled that while the solemnisation of marriage is a matter within provincial jurisdiction (s 92(12) of the Constitution Act 1867), the question of legal capacity for civil marriage falls within federal jurisdiction (s 91(26) of the Constitution Act 1867). In addition, the court ruled that the guarantee of religious freedom under s 2(a) of the Charter protects religious officials from being compelled by the state to perform civil or religious same-sex marriages that are contrary to their religious beliefs. However, believing that the issue should be resolved in Parliament and not wishing to adopt a political role, the court declined to answer the belatedly inserted fourth question on the constitutional validity of the opposite-sex definition of marriage. Recognising that couples had already taken advantage of provincial court decisions which permitted same-sex marriage, the Supreme Court noted that the government had 'clearly accepted the rulings of lower courts on this question and ... adopted their position as its own ... [g]iven the government's stated commitment to this course of action, an opinion on the constitutionality of an opposite-sex requirement for marriage serves no legal purpose': *Reference re Same-Sex Marriage* [2004] SCC 79, at para 65.

67 Bill C-38 (Law on Civil Marriage).

68 Early predictions are that with the backing of the 38 cabinet ministers and the support of most in the Bloc Québécois and the New Democratic Parties, which have 54 and 19 seats, it will pass by some 25 votes: Clark, 'PM rejects same-sex referendum' *The Globe and Mail*, 13 December 2004. Indeed, the Bill passed its Second Reading on 4 May 2005 by 164 votes to 137. However, since writing this paper, a political scandal has forced a vote on the Liberal government's budget, scheduled for 19 May 2005. The Prime Minister has indicated that if the government loses this vote, he will ask that Parliament be dissolved and an election called immediately (*The Globe and Mail*, 11 May 2005). If the minority Liberal government were to lose the election, the future of the Bill to legalise same-sex marriage would almost certainly be placed in jeopardy.

one territory where the provincial courts have struck down its opposite-sex definition[69] and one could expect further court challenges in the remaining provincial jurisdictions.

While same-sex marriage has been a central focus in the judicial and now political arena, at the level of policy-making a different variety of questions have been raised. The Law Commission of Canada published a report in 2001 which sought to challenge the centrality of the 'conjugal family' in legal policy.[70] The exclusive attention on 'marriage and marriage-like relationships' led the Commission to 'pursue a more comprehensive and principled approach to the legal recognition and support of the full range of close personal relationships among adults'. Even more significantly, the province of Alberta enacted the Adult Interdependent Relationships Act which recognised familial relationships outside of the conjugal paradigm. Looking at these developments in turn, it will be argued that neither made use of the potential offered by a discourse on caregiving to explore the substantive obligations of family members and the interaction between the family and the state. Instead, both, with various degrees of subtlety, share common motivations with proponents of the amendments to the Civil Partnerships Act in the UK.

Beyond conjugality: recognising and supporting close personal adult relationships

The starting point for the Law Commission of Canada in its 2001 report *Beyond Conjugality*, was the Supreme Court jurisprudence which:

> 'put in place a constitutional requirement that governments respect a principle of relational equality, calling into question the validity of all differences in the legal status of married and unmarried (either same-sex or opposite-sex) cohabitants.'[71]

According to the Commission, this exclusive focus on narrowing the gap between the legal status of married and unmarried relationships failed to address the differences in the legal treatment of conjugal and non-conjugal cohabitants.[72] Furthermore, it was deemed to be ideologically flawed on the basis that conjugality is not an 'accurate marker of the qualitative attributes' of legally relevant relationships.[73] Calling into question reliance on relationship status as a marker to determine familial rights and responsibilities, the Commission recommended that the law respond to the 'functional attributes' of particular relationships, rather than their form.[74] Thus, rather than proposing the mere extension of the law to include non-conjugal relationships, the Commission sought to embark on a more ambitious task of rethinking the way in

---

69 Op cit, n 63.

70 Law Commission of Canada, *Beyond Conjugality: Recognising and supporting close personal adult relationships* (LC, 2001). In *Molodowich v Penttinen* (1980) 17 RFL (2d) 376 (Ont Dist Ct) the Supreme Court of Canada outlined the generally accepted characteristics of a conjugal relationship as including shared shelter, sexual and personal behaviour, services, social activities, economic support and children, as well as the societal perception of the couple. Not all are necessary to establish a conjugal relationship and thus the concept is not necessarily contingent upon the presence of a sexual relationship in Canadian jurisprudence. However, the Law Commission's reference to conjugal relationships refers to marriage or marriage-like relationships and thus is concerned with the prioritisation of sexual-coupledom to the exclusion of other emotionally and economically interdependent adult relationships.

71 *Beyond Conjugality*, ibid, at p 14.

72 Ibid, at p 15.

73 Ibid.

74 Ibid, at p 35.

which governments regulate relationships, which involved re-assessing 'when and why relationships should matter'.[75] Indeed, the question was posed:

> '... can we imagine a legislative regime that accomplishes its goals more effectively by relying less on whether people are living in particular kinds of relationships?'[76]

As such, the report's ambitious objectives were to support the full range of close personal relationships amongst adults; to eliminate the distinctions between conjugal and non-conjugal relationships; to prioritise the function of relationships over their form and to diminish government reliance on relationship status as the proxy for the conferment of rights and obligations.

The report is in two parts. First, it considers the use of relational concepts, such as spouse and common law spouse, in legislation outside of the family law arena, for example, the laws of evidence, commercial law and immigration law.[77] In such contexts it proposes a new methodology for assessing any existing or future law which employs relational terms to accomplish its objectives. The first step is to re-evaluate the purpose(s) of the law and to consider whether relationships are in fact relevant to the fulfilment of the legislative objectives. If they are, the report recommends giving individuals the right of self-selection; that is, allowing them to 'select their chosen beneficiaries under a particular law'.[78] However, if relationships do matter and self-selection is not possible, a system of default ascription is proposed under which legislation would designate the relevant relationships. In this respect, it recommends the deployment of a *range* of relational definitions based upon the functional attributes of particular relationships, rather than their form, which are tailored to meet the needs of individual legislative objectives.[79]

The second part of the report considers relationships from a family law perspective and, in particular, the rights and obligations of family members *inter se*. The starting point is the recognition that the role of the state is to provide a framework for individuals to define the terms of their own relationships. The report makes two specific recommendations to achieve this. First, the introduction of a registration scheme, available to both conjugal and non-conjugal relationships, under which registrants acquire rights and responsibilities from which they may opt out.[80] Secondly,

---

75 Ibid, at p xxv.

76 Ibid, at p 29.

77 The Report considers the use of relational definitions in the following areas of federal jurisdiction: the family compensation provisions of the Marine Liability Act; the provisions dealing with leave from employment in the Canada Labour Code; the family sponsorship provisions of the Immigration Act; the spousal evidence rules in the Canada Evidence Act; the regulation of economic transactions between related persons in the Employment Insurance Act, the Bankruptcy and Insolvency Act and the Bank Act; the Income Tax Act; benefits provided to older persons pursuant to the Old Age Security Act; and the survivor's pensions available under the Canada Pension Plan (and laws dealing with veterans' and employees' pensions): ibid, at p 37.

78 Ibid, at p 32. For example, it recommends that the Canada Labour Code be amended to allow employees to designate the relationships most meaningful to them for the purposes of bereavement leave. The Commission notes that such an approach, which moves beyond using spousal or familial status as the basis for inclusion, will allow individuals to select relationships most meaningful to them, possibly beyond marriage, conjugal or blood ties, for particular purposes: at p 33.

79 While a uniform definition of relevant relationship, based upon emotional intimacy, economic interdependency and, on occasion, shared residence, would have the benefit of certainty, it was rejected for potentially leading to both over-inclusive and under-inclusive results: ibid, at p 35.

80 The Commission did not commit to any particular model of registration, noting that it could carry a pre-determined set of rights and responsibilities perhaps modelled on spousal regulation, or 'more

the legalisation of same-sex marriage in order to expand further the opportunities for parties to voluntarily assume responsibilities to each other. In situations where parties do not enter into a formal relationship status,[81] ascription retains a residual role, although its use and remit are largely undeveloped, except for the clear position that such presumptive-based regulation is inappropriate in the context of non-conjugal relationships.[82] These recommendations display a cautious approach to delineating the familial relationships which are subject to presumptive internal (re)organisation. The clear preference is to enhance the opportunities for parties to enter into a formal relationship status where rights and responsibilities are perceived by law to be voluntarily assumed. As such, the trigger for the assignment of private rights and responsibilities within relationships is premised on the status-based concepts of marriage and registration.

In light of the report's objectives, however, one could have anticipated the development of a more critical assessment of familial obligations and a move away from generalised assumptions based upon 'relationship status' towards a regulatory scheme based upon functionalism and fact/context-specific assessments. Let us recall that the proposed methodology for considering the use of relational terms in federal legislation outside of 'family law' involved an initial assessment of the purpose of the law in question which was then used to inform the delineation of relevant family relationship. This led to the proposed range of relational definitions within different legislative contexts.[83] There was much potential in transposing this methodology to the second part of the report when considering the assignment of rights and responsibilities *within* committed adult relationships. Indeed, it could have provided the framework for a thought-provoking exercise which assessed the *substance* of family obligations, as opposed to merely the *application* of existing norms. For example, as opposed to simply questioning the legitimacy of extending financial obligations to a wider number of family members, the debate would be prefaced by a critical assessment of the rationale of 'spousal' support laws. Contemporaneously, the continued use of relationship status as an indicator of intent and expectation would be called into question. However, the potential for a more inquiring discourse was lost. The retention of marriage as the proxy for the assignment of rights and responsibilities, alongside the recommendation of a registration scheme, preserves the reliance on form in legal policy, and the mere extension of registration to non-conjugal relationships does little more than nod to other forms of care-giving. Indeed, the blanket exclusion of non-conjugal relationships from the ascription scheme reveals a similar type of essentialism which the Commission accused the 'conjugal relational equality' agenda of peddling. Thus, without suggesting that obligations

---

flexible arrangements that may respond better to the variety of care-giving relationships that exist': ibid, at pp 120–121. It was noted that the terms of registration could include caring arrangements, consent to treatment dispositions, support and sharing in property: recommendation 31, at p 122.

81 It was accepted that the number of people who choose to register their relationship may not be significant: ibid, at p 122.

82 Noting that ascription is a limited policy instrument which treats 'all conjugal relationships alike, irrespective of the level of emotional or economic interdependency', the report recommended that it should only be used 'sparingly, where there is evidence of exploitation' (ibid, at p 116), and only for conjugal relationships. Indeed, the report concluded that 'ascription is not the best way to respond to the needs of non-conjugal relationships. It would be inappropriate to presume that all older parents living with their adult children have the same needs or that adults with disabilities have equally similar patterns of caring and support'.

83 See text preceding n 79.

should automatically be imposed in the context of non-conjugal relationships,[84] one can observe that the Commission's proposals do not sit squarely with their underlying objective, expressed in absolutist terms, to diminish government reliance on relationship status, nor one of the report's core principles that:

> '... conjugality, like marriage itself, is not an accurate marker of the qualitative attributes of personal adult relationships that are relevant to particular legislative objectives.'[85]

Thus, the Commission's commitment to de-centralise the 'conjugal family' wavered and distinctions continued to be made between conjugal and non-conjugal relationships in the absence of any serious critical appraisal concerning the actual content of the private rights and obligations under discussion.

The extent of the report's incoherence leads to questions about its agenda. One could ask whether its overall thrust, that is, the ostensible attempt to remove conjugality as the centrally defining concept in legal policy, was a strategic device to diffuse controversy surrounding the same-sex marriage question which, quite correctly, seemed inevitable post-*M v H*.[86] Indeed, Nicholas Bala notes in general terms how:

> 'the de-emphasis on conjugality may be seen as a way of subverting conservative opposition to legal recognition of partnerships outside marriage. But it is also a way of hiding same-sex relationships.'[87]

It is of note that this report emerged at a point when the idea of 'conjugal relational equality' had truly taken hold in Canadian jurisprudence and was being applied in a gender-neutral way to incorporate same-sex relationships. In taking a critical approach to these developments and in seeking to concentrate on other forms of emotionally and economically integrated relationships outside of the conjugal paradigm, the report's headlining remit gives the appearance of a shift in emphasis from conjugal partners to caregiving relationships. As such, same-sex relationships lose position as

---

84 The regularisation of non-conjugal relationships sparks an interesting debate. Indeed, Bala and Jaremko Bromwich take the view that while non-conjugal relationships could be incorporated within some legal and policy contexts, it would be inappropriate to lose conjugality as the centrally defining concept for the purposes of determining the private rights and responsibilities within personal relationships. Emphasising the divergent interdependencies and expectations in conjugal and non-conjugal relationships, they argue that to impose 'legal burdens' on those who adopt care-giving responsibilities in non-conjugal contexts would 'have a very significant adverse impact on how many dependent adults receive care from relatives and friends': Bala and Jaremko Bromwich, op cit, n 50, at pp 170–171. Cossman and Ryder dispute this on the grounds that the authors incorrectly presume that conjugal relationships embody certain functional attributes, while non-conjugal relationships do not: '[c]ommitted relationships that involve the raising of children or the assumption of other caregiving or domestic roles may give rise to expectations of continued support to which the law should respond. But conjugal relationships do not always embody these or other relevant qualitative attributes; nor are they always absent from non-conjugal relationships', B. Cossman and B. Ryder, op cit, n 58, at p 320. To take an example, they argue that it may not always be unfair to impose support obligations on an adult child living with an adult parent 'if the circumstances of the relationship gave rise to a reasonable expectation of continued support and one party's earning capacity was adversely affected by responsibilities undertaken over the course of the relationship', at p 321. They also discuss how property division and support laws could apply on the termination of any personal relationship (both conjugal and non-conjugal) if based upon a compensatory model to remedy any 'economic disadvantages attributable to the roles taken on during interdependent relationships', at pp 319–320.

85 Op cit, n 70, at p 15.

86 [1999] 2 SCR 3.

87 Bala and Jaremko Bromwich, op cit, n 50, at p 172.

the central focus of jurisprudential concern and become subject to legal regulation, not on the basis of the 'conjugal relational equality' agenda but, in areas outside of private family law, on the basis of the relationship's functional attributes and, in the context of family law, on the basis that the parties have voluntarily assumed private rights and responsibilities *inter se* as a result of marriage/registration or, in cases of probable exploitation, via presumptive-based legal regulation. Thus, while the report did not expressly attempt to derail same-sex partnership rights – indeed the legalisation of same-sex marriage is recommended – the attempt to displace, or be seen to displace, the centrality of conjugal partners in legal policy could be viewed as a subtle strategy to undermine the significance of same-sex partnership recognition.

Turning to a less subtle attempt to mask the express recognition of same-sex relationships, the following section will highlight recent legislation in Alberta, commonly cited as the most conservative Canadian province.[88]

The Alberta Adult Interdependent Relationships Act

Recognising that the decision in *M v H*[89] required provincial governments to take 'legislative action to ensure that individuals in same-sex relationships are afforded equal treatment under the law with others who are in marriage-like relationships',[90] Alberta enacted the Adult Interdependent Relationships Act.[91] While other provincial legislatures responded to *M v H* by creating a new legal category of same-sex partner[92] or by including same-sex couples within the definition of spouse or common law spouse,[93] Alberta reclaimed the traditional definition of spouse[94] and relied upon

---

88 An Ipsos-Reid/CFCN/*Globe and Mail* poll in 2003 found that nearly six in ten Albertans (57%) opposed same-sex marriage and that a similar proportion (58%) would support the provincial government's use of the notwithstanding clause to exempt Alberta from recognising same-sex marriages: http://www.ipsos-na.com/news/pressrelease.cfm?id=1867 (s 33(1) of the Charter (the notwithstanding clause) permits Parliament to enact legislation notwithstanding that it is in violation of certain Charter provisions – s 2 (containing such fundamental rights as freedom of expression, freedom of conscience, freedom of association and freedom of assembly) and ss 7–15 (the right to life, liberty and security of the person, freedom from unreasonable search and seizure, freedom from arbitrary arrest or detention, a number of other legal rights, and the right to equality)). Another poll found that while 37% of Canadians supported the extension of marriage to same-sex couples, the Prairie region, specifically Alberta, was found to be the least supportive: *Public Divided About Definition of Marriage*, NFO CF group Report, 5 September 2003: http://www.nfocfgroup.com/news/03.09.05-samesex-report.pdf.

89 [1999] 2 SCR 3. See text following n 55.

90 Alberta Law Reform Institute, *Recognition of Rights and Obligations in Same Sex Relationships Research Paper No 21* (Edmonton, January 2002), at para 5. This was made more acute by the successful challenges to Alberta legislation alleging discrimination on the basis of sexual orientation: see *Johnson v Sand* (2001) ABQB 253; *Re A (Adoption)* (1999) 181 DLR (4th) 300 (Alta QB); *Vriend v Alberta* (1998) 156 DLR (4th) 385 (SCC). The report continued: '[i]f no comprehensive reforms are made to ensure that all provincial legislation conforms with the equality guarantee in the Charter, the Alberta government will likely be formed to incur the legal costs of numerous court challenges in the future. It is likely that the majority of these challenges will be successful, and legislation which discriminates against same-sex couples will be declared to be of no force and effect, resulting in the need for reform in any event' (para 54).

91 SA 2002, c A-4.5. The Act came into force on 1 June 2003.

92 For example, the province of Ontario passed an Act to Amend Certain Statutes Because of the Supreme Court of Canada Decision in *M v H*, SO 1999, c 6.

93 In Saskatchewan, for example, the definition of spouse was rendered gender-neutral by the Miscellaneous Statutes (Domestic Relations) Amendment Act 2001, SS 2001, c 50 and the Miscellaneous Statutes (Domestic Relations) Amendment Act 2001 (No 2), SS 2001, c 51.

94 Section 1(1)(g) of the Adult Interdependent Relationships Act states that 'spouse' means the husband or wife of a married person. This reverses the legislative amendments introduced in the wake of *Taylor*

the theoretical premise of the Law Commission's report, *Beyond Conjugality*[95], to create the new category of 'adult interdependent partner'. Under the Act, one becomes an 'adult interdependent partner' by entering into a written agreement,[96] or by force of law after cohabiting in a relationship of interdependence for a continuous period of at least three years, or in a relationship of some permanence where there is a child by birth or adoption. A 'relationship of interdependence' is defined as a relationship outside marriage in which any two persons share one another's lives, are emotionally committed to one another, and function as an economic and domestic unit.[97] Thus the Act simultaneously affirms the importance of marriage,[98] limits the meaning of 'spouse' to married partners, and ascribes spousal rights and obligations to a range of 'interdependent partners', the definition of which covers both conjugal and platonic relationships.[99] While same-sex couples are subsumed within this broad asexual definition, they are not expressly mentioned once in the legislation. Thus, while this legislation was specifically enacted to ensure provincial compliance with the Charter regarding same-sex relational rights, it does so in an indirect way by absorbing same-sex couples within this new asexual legal category.[100] Under the Act, it is not the sexual partnership of same-sex relationships that warrants the imposition of rights and obligations, but their economic and emotional interdependency.[101] Once

---

v Rossu (1998) 39 RFL (4th) 242 (see op cit, n 53), which incorporated unmarried opposite-sex couples within the definition of 'spouse'. Such persons now fall under the concept of adult interdependent partner.

95 Op cit, n 70.

96 Adult Interdependent Relationships Act, s 3(1)(b).

97 Ibid, s 1(1)(f). Section 1(2) specifies that in determining whether two persons function as an economic and domestic unit for the purposes of the legislation, all the circumstances of the relationship must be taken into account, including whether or not the persons have a conjugal relationship; the degree of exclusivity of the relationship; the conduct and habits of the persons in respect of household activities and living arrangements; the degree to which the persons hold themselves out to others as an economic and domestic unit; the degree to which the persons formalise their legal obligations, intentions and responsibilities toward one another; the extent to which direct and indirect contributions have been made by either person to the other or to their mutual well-being; the degree of financial dependence or interdependence and any arrangements for financial support between the persons; the care and support of children, and the ownership, use and acquisition of property.

98 The Preamble to the Act states that: 'Whereas marriage is an institution that has traditional religious, social and cultural meaning for many Albertans; and whereas it is recognized in Alberta as a fundamental principle that marriage is a union between a man and a woman to the exclusion of all others; and whereas the Legislature of Alberta affirms that a spouse is a person who is married', there are those in interdependent relationships outside of marriage for which a legal framework is required. This terminology reveals a deliberate intent to create a hierarchy of family relationships by affirming the superiority of marriage.

99 This Act amends 68 Alberta statutes to give an 'adult interdependent partner' spousal rights and obligations, see N. Bala, 'Controversy over couples in Canada: the evolution of marriage and OTHER adult interdependent relationships' (2003) 29 *Queen's LJ* 41, at p 91.

100 When introducing the Bill, the Minister stated: '[i]n Alberta marriage is an institution that has traditional, religious, social, and cultural meaning for many Albertans, and it is recognized by Albertans as a fundamental principle that marriage is a union between a man and a woman to the exclusion of all others. The terms "marriage" and "spouse" have particular meaning for Albertans, and government policy has been that we will protect those terms even to the extent, if necessary, of using the notwithstanding clause', Alberta *Hansard*, Legislative Assembly of Alberta, col 1185 (7 May 2002).

101 The Minister of Justice and Attorney-General said that: '... [this law] isn't limited to people who have sex, has nothing to do with people who have sex. It has to do with the type of personal emotional relationship that people have, and by coming together and having that type of relationship and intermingling their property and being co-dependent on each other both emotionally and financially ... so it makes sense to include those people who are in a platonic relationship of that type of personal

this is established as the proxy for the conferment of relational status, there are no grounds upon which to limit the framework to conjugal relationships, indeed, it would have gone against the ostensible rationale of the Act to do so.

There was no constitutional need to recognise non-conjugal relationships, and apart from one or two scant references to the Law Commission's Report *Beyond Conjugality*,[102] no comprehensive empirical or other evidence was presented during the passage of the legislation to justify the extension of family obligations beyond the conjugal paradigm. Indeed, it was somewhat fortuitous that this report had just been published, as it at least gave the Albertan government a theoretical reference point for this new approach. The lack of sound theoretical basis was exposed, however, when policy-makers could provide no defence when faced with criticisms surrounding the extension of the law to platonic relationships. During the passage of the legislation, concerns were expressed that the statute, as originally drafted, would result in the imposition of rights and duties on individuals contrary to their expectations, and that it would be subject to abuse by non-conjugal co-residents, particularly between relatives.[103] Thus, whilst trying to maintain the tenor of the Act as addressing the needs of those in economically and emotionally interdependent relationships, an amendment was introduced at committee stage in an attempt to claw back on the extent to which non-conjugal partners would be deemed to be living in such a relationship. In particular, this was to avoid the situation where family members would become interdependent partners by operation of law due to the care provided by one to the other through 'normal' family responsibilities. As a result, section 3(2) now states that those who are related to each other by blood or adoption may only become adult interdependent partners of each other by entering into a written agreement. Thus it seems that while relatives will not be deemed to be living in an interdependent relationship in the absence of a written agreement, non-related cohabitants may be so classified by operation of law, the distinction being made on the basis that care-giving between family members is 'a normal family responsibility' performed on a gratuitous basis.[104] However, one is left asking further questions about which non-conjugal relationships are envisaged as falling within the Act and, more particularly, on what basis? Debates during the passage of the legislation cast some light on this. During the second reading, the Minister introducing the Bill said:

> '[i]t is not the intention of this legislation that any two people living together as roommates for more than three years would qualify as adult interdependent partners. It is not the intent of this proposed legislation that every parent and child or brother and sister living together would qualify as adult interdependent partners. However, there are special platonic relationships that could meet the definition of a relationship of interdependence. These would be platonic relationships where the partners have an intense personal commitment to each other and where they clearly consider themselves to be a couple, although the relationship is platonic.'[105]

---

commitment and intensity ...'. Alberta *Hansard*, Legislative Assembly of Alberta, col 1593 (27 November 2002).

102 Op cit, n 70.

103 In particular, the Canadian Bar Association felt that the original version of the Bill did not 'go far enough ... to provide the certainty ... with respect to matters of defining who is actually in a relationship', Alberta *Hansard*, Legislative Assembly of Alberta, col 1593 (27 November 2002).

104 It should be noted, however, that caregivers who provide care for a fee or other consideration are excluded: s 4(2).

105 Alberta *Hansard*, Legislative Assembly of Alberta, col 1371 (19 November 2002).

It seems, therefore, that the intention is to include:

> 'platonic couples that have a relationship that is analogous to other recognized relationships or common-law relationships.'[106]

Thus, while the 'adult interdependent partner' category is constructed around the 'interdependent relationships model', as opposed to the 'conjugal relationships model',[107] in reality, the definition is more likely to be satisfied by conjugal partners. Indeed, the functional indicators pointing to the presence of an 'economic and domestic unit' draw upon the assumed characteristics of conjugality and, in fact, were constructed with reference to the factors referred to by the courts when defining de facto relationships.[108] As such, it is likely that non-conjugal co-residents will, more often than not, fall outside the requirements of interdependency. As Bala notes:

> '[t]he references ... to such factors as "degree of [presumably sexual] exclusivity of the relationship" and holding themselves out as a "domestic unit," as well as to conjugality itself and the "intentions" of the parties, are clearly intended as a signal to courts that they should be very reluctant to impose this status on two individuals who have lived together in a non-sexual relationship, even if it involved a degree of economic interdependence and emotional support.'[109]

In short, the Act's remit to incorporate non-conjugal relationships is little more than disingenuous flannel unsubstantiated by a sound analytical base. Indeed, as with the Law Commission's report *Beyond Conjugality*, the objective to recognise relationships on the basis of their functional attributes sits uneasily with the Act's intention to entrench marriage. Any serious attempt to establish factual interdependencies as the marker for determining legally significant relationships would, at the very least, raise questions about the continued role of such status-based indicators. It is very clear,

---

106 Ibid.

107 In a previous consultation document, Alberta Justice noted that the province could respond to its Charter obligations in light of *M v H* in one of two ways. First, under the 'conjugal relationships model', the legal rights and responsibilities currently provided to married couples could be extended to unmarried persons in conjugal relationships (defined as relationships of a long-term, committed nature where two adults live together and sexual intimacy can be expected). Alternatively, under the 'interdependent relationships model', such benefits could be extended to unmarried persons in committed 'interdependent relationships', thus recognising that 'in addition to common law and same-sex persons, there are people in unmarried relationships that are platonic but involve economic and emotional interdependency. For example, an adult child living with an elderly parent or an adult brother or sister living together'. See *Alberta Family Law Reform Workbook*, October 2002, http://www.justice.gov.ab.ca/families/justice_process.aspx?id=2247.

108 During the passage of the Bill, the Minister of Justice and Attorney-General said that the factors used to determine the presence of an 'economic and domestic unit' (s 2(a)–(i)): 'are the factors which have come out of the case-law over the years with respect to the determinations that courts have made in finding common-law relationships. These aren't invented or pulled out of the air. This comes from the body of law which has developed over time as the courts have developed this issue that relationships exist outside of marriage which have to be taken into account': Alberta *Hansard*, Legislative Assembly of Alberta, col 1593 (27 November 2002). The reported cases thus far which consider the Adult Interdependent Relationships Act (AIRA) all deal with couples in 'conjugal' relationships. It is noteworthy that in *Medora v Kohn* [2003] ABQB 700, the Alberta Court of Queen's Bench held that when considering whether parties to an opposite-sex common law relationship functioned as an 'economic and domestic unit' for the purposes of the AIRA, the test for 'spousal status' used in the earlier case of *Spracklin v Kichton* (2000) 95 Alta LR (3d) 371 (QB) should be followed as the factors in the AIRA 'bear a strong resemblance to those cited by Watson J in *Spracklin* ...': [2003] ABQB 700, at para 20.

109 N. Bala, op cit, n 99, at p 93.

however, that this Act was intended to do just the opposite.[110] The primary intention was to Charter-proof Alberta legislation, whilst entrenching the traditional definition of marriage and its superiority.[111] An uneasy compromise made possible by setting up factual interdependency as the marker for recognising non-marital relationships.[112] Thus, although the Act was held out as progressive,[113] in reality it was introduced as a smokescreen to avoid the express recognition of same-sex couples.[114]

DE-CENTRALISING THE 'CONJUGAL FAMILY' – A SUBVERSIVE TACTIC

These examples show that while policy moves to look beyond the 'conjugal family' may appear to be more progressive than the assimilation of same-sex relationships within dominant cultural and legal norms, they can also be used in a less radical way to undermine, with various degrees of subtlety, the express legitimation of same-sex partnership rights.[115] Indeed, Susan Boyd and Claire Young note that some are concerned:

---

110 See S. Boyd and C. Young, '"From same-sex to no-sex"? Trends towards recognition of (same-sex) relationships in Canada' (2003) 1 *Seattle Journal for Social Justice* 757, at p 769.

111 In an attempt to protect the traditional definition of marriage, the province had earlier passed the Marriage Amendment Act (SA 2000, c 3) which defined marriage as 'between a man and a woman'. In addition, the notwithstanding clause was attached in an attempt to enshrine this, although this is likely to be ultra vires, see n 112, below.

112 It seems, however, that the legalisation of same-sex marriage will not be so easy to avoid. While the Albertan Premier, Ralph Klein, has repeatedly stated that his government would use whatever means at its disposal, such as invoking the notwithstanding clause, to prevent same-sex marriage in the province, there are few legal options. As the capacity to marry is within federal jurisdiction, provincial governments do not have the authority to invoke the constitutional override on this issue. The Albertan Minister of Justice and Attorney-General recognised this in a statement released shortly after the Supreme Court decision (op cit, n 65) (Government of Alberta News Release, 9 December 2004, http://www.gov.ab.ca/acn/200412/173566FF2E11D-6F76-40BA-88FBFDCA26CE3B9F.html). Despite this, Premier Klein remains committed to using all political avenues to prevent the legalisation of same-sex marriage and has called for a national referendum on the issue, as well as urging individuals to lobby their federal politicians to 'defend the traditional definition of marriage'. In addition, he has indicated that if the legislation is passed he will urge federal MPs to demand the use of the notwithstanding clause: K. Harding, *The Globe and Mail*, 16 December 2004.

113 The Minister of Justice and Attorney-General said that 'this is probably the first time in at least a Canadian jurisdiction that the law has actually preceded the court in terms of defining the relationship': Alberta *Hansard*, Legislative Assembly of Alberta, col 1593 (27 November 2002).

114 It is also telling is that the Albertan government did not consider non-conjugal interdependent relationships to require legislative acknowledgment after *Taylor v Rossu* (1998) 39 RFL (4th) 242 (see op cit, n 53) and, at this time, followed the response of other Canadian provinces by extending the definition of spouse to cover opposite-sex cohabitants (for certain purposes).

115 This tactic can also be seen in South Australia, a jurisdiction with a poor track record of extending relational status to same-sex couples, despite the fact that it was one of the first Australian jurisdictions to outlaw discrimination on the grounds of sexuality (Equal Opportunity Act 1985, s 5). The first South Australian legislation to recognise same-sex couples was the Superannuation Act 1988, as amended by the Statutes Amendment (Equal Superannuation Entitlements for Same Sex Couples) Act 2003 (No 13 of 2003), which included same-sex couples within the term 'putative spouse' for the purposes of state superannuation laws. As Loader notes, however, rather than '… opposing the bill on the basis of homophobic moralism, [opponents] suggested that state legislation ought also to include other forms of domestic relationships, such as carers … and that, by not doing so, the … Bill entrenched "discrimination" against other non-traditional relationships': Matthew Loader, 'Recognising same-sex relationships: ideas and an update from South Australia' *Word is Out*: http://www.arts.usyd.edu.au/publications/wordisout/front.htm

' ... how ironic it is that as soon as lesbians and gay men begin to acquire spousal status, the move is to erase sex from that status, and to eliminate marriage as a legal category.'[116]

The common argument is that the extension of partnership status to same-sex couples places too much emphasis on sexual relationships and discriminates against other non-conjugal forms of care-giving. Proposals thus concentrate on substituting the current reliance on conjugality with asexual functional indicators of emotional and economic interdependency. However, at this point in the evolution of gay and lesbian relational status, strategies that seek to fuse together the recognition of same-sex and non-sexual care-giving relationships should be rejected for a number of reasons.

First, as indicated, absorbing same-sex couples within a broad, functional asexual definition can be a dangerous strategy peddled by those who oppose the ostensible recognition of such relationships. While attempts to de-centralise the sexual family in favour of a policy that absorbs couple and non-couple based categories may appeal to those who are genuinely concerned about the continued exclusion of relationships outside the conjugal paradigm, and to those who want a politically expedient way to give legal recognition to gays and lesbians, it will also appeal to those who want to keep same-sex couples within an invisible category in legal policy. The corollary is that subsuming same-sex couples within an asexual legal category dilutes the symbolic significance of partnership recognition under a formal equality agenda and, according to Kathleen Lahey, 'actually trivialises the effort it has taken to gain recognition'.[117] This concern can be seen in the recommendations of the Gay and Lesbian Rights Lobby in New South Wales.[118] Notwithstanding the desire to recognise all relationships of mutual care and support,[119] it was felt that to fuse together same-sex and non-couple based relationship recognition would be an unwise strategic move from 'both a symbolic and practical viewpoint'.[120] As noted by Jenni Millbank and Kathy Sant:

'[t]he consultation process of *The Bride Wore Pink* revealed that while members of the lesbian and gay communities were anxious to avoid excluding various kinds of relationships, they did not wish to see their own partner relationships identified by law as "other" than partner relationships. Nor did they believe that other relationships should always or automatically receive recognition in all the same areas as de facto relationships.'[121]

Thus, the final recommendation was the simultaneous but operationally distinct recognition of same-sex partners and those in other types of interdependent relationships.

---

116 S. Boyd and C. Young, op cit, n 110, at p 785.

117 K. Lahey, 'Becoming "persons" in Canadian law: genuine equality or "separate but equal?"' in R. Wintemute and M. Andenæs (eds), *Legal Recognition of Same-Sex Partnerships: a Study of National, European and International Law* (Hart Publishing, 2001), at p 275.

118 *The Bride Wore Pink* (GLRL, 1st edn, 1993); *The Bride Wore Pink* (GLRL, 2nd edn, 1994).

119 Indeed, concern was expressed by members of the gay and lesbian community during the consultation process that law reform which focused exclusively on sexual couples may be too narrow.

120 J. Millbank and K. Sant, 'A bride in her every-day clothes: same sex relationship recognition' (2000) 22 *Sydney Law Review* 181, at p 197.

121 Ibid. See also J. Millbank and W. Morgan, 'Let them eat cake, and ice cream: wanting something "more" from the relationship recognition menu' in R. Wintemute and M. Andenæs (eds), op cit, n 117.

Secondly, questioning the privileged status of conjugal partners raises issues surrounding the 'structural position of the family'[122] and requires a contestation of the boundaries between putative family and state responsibilities. However, neither the Albertan legislation nor the proposed amendments to the Civil Partnerships Act, when a Bill in the UK, engaged with such questions and merely sought to subject wider categories of family members to undisturbed quasi-marital regulation. The report of the Law Commission of Canada had the potential to develop more disruptive theories of family obligations, but was undermined by the failure to subject 'family law' to the methodology proposed for assessing the use of relational concepts in other areas. Of course, the purpose of this report was not to prevent the express conferment of same-sex partnership rights, but its headlining rationale, to be seen to undermine the significance of the conjugal family, leads one to ask whether it was a subtle attempt to take the bite out of the potential legalisation of same-sex marriage which may have appeared unavoidable as the equality discourse gathered momentum. The point is, however, that when proposals to recognise non-conjugal relationships are being used to undermine or deflect attention from the visible recognition of same-sex couples, the terms of reference do not seek to go beyond existing norms; in fact, the very purpose is to entrench these norms. This is an insufficient discursive framework in which to address non-couple based relationship recognition and the distribution of responsibility arising from the performance of care-giving duties. By contrast, one can point to the work of Martha Fineman, whose theorising is a genuine example of a project which seeks to displace the sexual family in legal and social policy in order to achieve wholescale transformation, particularly in the distribution of societal resources.[123] Fineman proposes that relationships of care-taking should replace the sexual connection between adults as the 'core, legally privileged, family connection'.[124] Her chief concern is to centralise the caretaker–dependent relationship in legal and social policy and thus to disperse the economic responsibility for care-taking outside of the private realm of the family. The core of her thesis is that 'inevitable dependency' – the 'need for care-taking embodied in the young, many of the elderly and disabled, as well as the ill'[125] – is a social concern which should be subsidised by the state and which requires a more reflective marketplace in which the worker is not perceived as an 'unencumbered' individual. As part of this, she calls for the abolition of marriage as a legal category in order to dissipate the current hub which bears the burden of care-taking responsibility, usually on a gendered basis, thus making dependencies more visible and allowing them to 'become the object of generalised societal concern'.[126] Thus, Fineman questions the state's responsibility for the consequences of dependency and, as such, examines the social value of care-taking beyond its meaning in the private relationships in which it takes place. Without suggesting that this is the way forward, it is worth noting how very different this is to the policies and proposals highlighted in this paper.

---

122 M. A. Fineman, *The Neutered Mother, the Sexual Family and other Twentieth Century Tragedies* (Routledge, 1995), at p 160.

123 Ibid; M. A. Fineman, 'Cracking the foundational myths: independence, autonomy, and self-sufficiency' (2000) 8(1) *Journal of Gender, Social Policy and the Law* 13; M. A. Fineman, 'Why marriage?' (2001) 9 *Virginia Journal of Social Policy and the Law* 239; M. A. Fineman, *The Autonomy Myth: A Theory of Dependency* (The New Press, 2004).

124 N. Polikoff, 'Why lesbians and gay men should read Martha Fineman' (2000) 8 *Journal of Gender, Social Policy and the Law* 167, at p 172.

125 M. A. Fineman, op cit, n 122, at p 8.

126 Ibid, at p 231.

Thus, while rethinking the prioritisation of the 'conjugal family' can provide a discursive framework for a critical assessment of the use of relational concepts, both in the wider concept of the law and for the purpose of assigning rights and obligations between family members, this opportunity is lost if the debate is hijacked by those who wish to use it in a subversive way. To avoid this, the gay and lesbian reform agenda should not become the vehicle by which to de-centralise the conjugal family, as the input of disingenuous actors can produce distorted results. However, once visible same-sex partnership recognition has been achieved and this less than genuine motivation for looking beyond the conjugal family has been eradicated, the framework is in place for a more serious critical assessment of the use of relational concepts in law.

CONCLUSION

It seems that the best strategic advice for those who fear that the continued recognition of 'couple-based' relationships 'further eclips[es] other relationships of choice',[127] is to seek to improve, by express means, the legal position of same-sex couples. This appears to have the desired effect of initiating debate amongst political actors about the prejudicial impact of focusing on sexual relationships to the exclusion of other forms of caregiving and generating a newly awakened concern for those in such relationships to the extent that one could be forgiven for thinking that care-giving within families is a new phenomenon. Indeed, it is very telling that attempts to de-centralise conjugality only seem to emerge, outside of the academic context, during debates on same-sex partnerships rights, and that such claims never extend to question the continued reliance on the use of 'marriage' as a relationship indicator in legal policy. It seems, therefore, that reform attempts which appear to be more progressive than traditional assimilation politics can mask agendas that seek to undermine same-sex partnership recognition. As such, the distinct and express legal recognition of same-sex partnerships is a preferable reform option to the possible absorption of lesbian and gay relationships within de-sexualised legal categories, which can amount to little more than homophobic responses to the demands for legal development. Boyd and Young conclude that, in recognising relationships:

> '... a focus on sex may well be unnecessary, except to the extent that it is needed to ensure the visibility of lesbian and gay lives, and that they are not erased in the very process of receiving recognition.'[128]

This is an extremely important point. The tactic of using non-sexual forms of interdependent relationship to derail same-sex partnership recognition or nullify its significance should be blocked, most powerfully achieved by pursuing an assimilationist model of partnership recognition.

---

127 P. Ettlebrick, 'Since when is marriage a path to liberation?' in S. Sherman (ed), *Lesbian and Gay Marriage: Private Commitments, Public Ceremonies* (Temple University Press, 1992), at p 23.

128 S. Boyd and C. Young, op cit, n 110, at p 787.

Name Index